T0304330

PRESS FREEDOM AND REGULATION
IN A DIGITAL ERA

Press Freedom and Regulation in a Digital Era

A Comparative Study

IRINI KATSIREA

OXFORD
UNIVERSITY PRESS

OXFORD
UNIVERSITY PRESS

Great Clarendon Street, Oxford, OX2 6DP,
United Kingdom

Oxford University Press is a department of the University of Oxford.
It furthers the University's objective of excellence in research, scholarship,
and education by publishing worldwide. Oxford is a registered trade mark of
Oxford University Press in the UK and in certain other countries

Published in the United States of America by Oxford University Press
198 Madison Avenue, New York, NY 10016, United States of America

British Library Cataloguing in Publication Data
Data available

Library of Congress Control Number: 2023948525

ISBN 978-0-19-885860-7

DOI: 10.1093/oso/9780198858607.001.0001

Printed and bound by
CPI Group (UK) Ltd, Croydon, CR0 4YY

MIX
Paper | Supporting
responsible forestry
FSC
www.fsc.org
FSC® C013604

Acknowledgements

The ideas that culminated in this book have accompanied me for the best part of the last ten years across two institutions, from London to Sheffield, and across two disciplines, from law to journalism studies. A British Academy/Leverhulme small research grant supported some of the preliminary work towards this book. Part of the research was conducted during a research sabbatical, and I am grateful to the Department of Journalism Studies at the University of Sheffield for this precious period of reflection. I had the opportunity to present some of these ideas at Society of Legal Scholars conferences, at invited research seminars at the Universities of Athens and Salford, and at a conference and workshops I convened at Middlesex University in the early stages of my research. I am grateful to Seamus Simpson (University of Salford) who saw the thread of argument that ran through different aspects of my work. I would also like to thank Karen Donders (Flemish Public Broadcasting Company VRT) who motivated my research in this area, though it soon developed a life of its own. Special thanks go to the wonderful colleagues who read and commented on draft chapters: Thomas Gibbons, Jan Kalbhenn, Andrew Kenyon, Jan Oster, and Maria Grazia Porcedda, as well as to the anonymous reviewers of this book. I also very much appreciated helpful exchanges with Jong-Sun Choi, Maria Donde, Stephan Dreyer, David Erdos, Jackie Harrison, Uwe Hasebrink, Petros Iosifidis, Hannu Nieminen, Reeta Pöyhtäri, Joe Purshouse, Jacob Rowbottom, Graham Smith, Konstantinos Stylianou, and Panayotis Voyatzis. I am particularly indebted to the Institute for Information, Telecommunication and Media Law (University of Münster) and to its Director, Bernd Holznagel, for generously granting me access to the Institute's resources over the years. I would also like to acknowledge the encouragement and kindness of Eric Barendt whose work has always been an inspiration. Finally, my wholehearted thanks and gratitude go to my husband Stefan and to my daughters Katerina and Anna, without whose support and patience the completion of this work would not have been possible.

The law is stated as of 4 July 2023.

Contents

Table of Cases

THE NETHERLANDS

UNITED KINGDOM

UNITED STATES

EUROPEAN UNION (COURT OF JUSTICE OF THE EUROPEAN UNION)

EUROPEAN UNION (GENERAL COURT OF THE EUROPEAN UNION)

Table of Legislation

Miscellaneous

IRELAND

UNITED KINGDOM

Statutes

Statutory Instruments

List of Abbreviations

AI	artificial intelligence
ARCOM	Regulatory Authority for Audiovisual and Digital Communication (*Régulateur pour la Communication Audiovisuelle et Numérique*)
ARD	Association of Public Service Broadcasters in Germany (*Abeitsgemeinschaft der öffentlich-rechtlichen Rundfunkanstalten der Bundesrepublik Deutschland*)
ATVOD	Authority for Television on Demand
AVMS	audiovisual media services
AVMSD	Audiovisual Media Services Directive
BDZV	German Newspaper Publishers and Digital Publishers Association (*Bundesverband Digitalpublisher und Zeitungsverleger*)
BVerfG	Federal Constitutional Court (*Bundesverfassungsgericht*)
CSA	French Broadcasting Council (*Conseil Supérieur de l'Audiovisuel*)
DSA	Digital Services Act
ECD	E-Commerce Directive
ECHR	European Convention on Human Rights
ECtHR	European Court of Human Rights
EPG	electronic programme guide
FCC	Federal Communications Commission
GG	Constitution for the Federal Republic of Germany (*Grundgesetz*)
GIF	Graphic Interchange Format
GMH	German Ministry of Health
ICTs	Information and Communications Technologies
IMPRESS	Independent Monitor for the Press
IPSO	Independent Press Standards Organisation
ISP	internet service provider
LDRS	Local Democracy Reporting Service
NetzDG	Network Enforcement Act
NMA	News Media Association
NRAs	national regulatory authorities
ODPS	on-demand programme services
PPA	Professional Publishers' Association
PSB	public service broadcasting/broadcaster
VOD	video on demand
VSP	video-sharing platform
ZAK	German Commission on Licensing and Supervision (*Kommission für Zulassung und Aufsicht*)

1
Introduction

1.1 Introduction

Press freedom has been at the forefront of international attention in recent times. The 2023 Reporters Without Borders (RSF) World Press Freedom Index report estimates that the environment for journalism is 'bad' in seven out of ten countries and satisfactory in only three out of ten.[1] Particular concern is expressed about the increase in violence and hostility against journalists, not only in countries at the bottom of the Index, but also in Europe and the US. The report raises the alarm about the impact on quality journalism of disinformation and propaganda campaigns, orchestrated by political actors in two-thirds of the 180 countries included in the Index. On World Press Freedom Day, celebrated annually on 3 May, the United Nations (UN) Secretary-General shared this concern about the future of journalism. He stated that '[F]reedom of the press is the foundation of democracy and justice. It gives all of us the facts we need to shape opinions and speak truth to power. But in every corner of the world, freedom of the press is under attack.'[2] The UNESCO Secretary-General painted an even bleaker picture by characterizing 2022 as 'the deadliest year for journalists'.[3] She noted that this frontline assault on journalism was especially pernicious because of its timing. It coincided with the advent of the digital era which underlined the importance of journalists in a forever altered information ecosystem.

This book is concerned precisely with the changed environment in which the press operates and the concomitant regulatory challenges in the digital era. The concept of 'the press' is understood in a wide sense to encompass not only the printed press but also the professional and non-professional actors who are active online and who fulfil an important information and watchdog function. Digitalization brought about the transformation of press products from printed newspapers to the now ubiquitous digital editions. This has been a technological development with far-reaching ramifications. In 1994, the *Daily Telegraph* launched the *Electronic Telegraph*, the first UK newspaper website, a static page with articles posted once a day in a bid to explore the commercial possibilities of the new technology.[4] Also in the US, the first newspaper websites made their appearance in the mid-1990s. Before long, the number

---

[1] Reporters Without Borders, '2023 World Press Freedom Index—Journalism threatened by fake content industry' <https://rsf.org/en/2023-world-press-freedom-index-journalism-threatened-by-fake-content-industry> accessed 31 May 2023.

[2] United Nations, 'Freedom of the press under attack worldwide', 2 May 2023 <https://news.un.org/en/story/2023/05/1136272> accessed 31 May 2023.

[3] ibid.

[4] E Siapera and A Veglis, 'Introduction: The Evolution of Online Journalism' in E Siapera and A Veglis (eds), *The Handbook of Global Online Journalism* (John Wiley 2012) 1.

Press Freedom and Regulation in a Digital Era. Irini Katsirea, Oxford University Press. © Irini Katsirea 2024.
DOI: 10.1093/oso/9780198858607.003.0001

of newspaper websites worldwide, enhanced with interactive multimedia features, rocketed.[5] The explosion of citizen journalism and the widening of the debate to amateur commentators on mainstream media completed the transformation. This raises the question of whether the traditional print newspaper is the same product as its digital version or an altogether different product, an *aliud*. This question was at the heart of a recent legal dispute over the VAT exemption for online newspapers.

1.2 Zero Rating for Digital Editions

The question of whether the digital issues of newspaper websites are 'newspapers' is of significance as regards the VAT to which they are subject. In the UK, newspapers are zero-rated under the Value Added Tax Act 1994.[6] Should this also apply to their digital editions? The UK Supreme Court (UKSC) answered this question in the negative in a case in which NewsCorp claimed for recovery of over £35 million against the Commissioners for His Majesty's Revenue and Customs (HMRC).[7] It held that, while the buyer of a physical copy obtained complete access to the news in that copy, this was not the case with the digital edition which could only be accessed when 'owning or buying something else', namely an electronic device and connectivity.[8] Even though the content of digital newspapers was 'the same or very similar' to that of the print editions, and despite the fact that they fulfilled the same social policy objectives, in other respects they were very different.[9] The UKSC considered that this was especially the case in view of the possibilities for interactive communication the technological development has opened up, which are not available in the case of physical copies.[10] Lord Leggatt, in his concurring opinion, mused further on the importance of the format of a medium as well as its form. Drawing on Marshall McLuhan's cryptic mantra 'the medium is the message' and on Elizabeth Eisenstein's seminal work on the printing press as an agent of change, he considered that the format of communication is as important as its content and can have 'far-reaching social implications and effects'.[11] He concluded that e-newspapers might have affinities with other online information services which are 'as great as (or greater than)' their affinities with their print editions.[12]

The conclusion reached in *NewsCorp v HMRC* is informed by the granular budgetary and political considerations involved in taxation. This finding is applicable only to the period up to 1 May 2020 given that zero-rating was extended to digital

---

[5] See A Rusbridger, *Breaking News. The Remaking of Journalism and Why It Matters Now* (Canongate 2019) 24.

[6] Value Added Tax Act 1994, s 30.

[7] *NewsCorp UK & Ireland Ltd v Commissioners for his Majesty's Revenue and Customs* [2023] UKSC 7.

[8] ibid para 53.

[9] The view that the content of digital newspapers is 'the same or very similar' to that of their print editions is debatable. See Chapter 3, p 35.

[10] *NewsCorp UK & Ireland Ltd v Commissioners for his Majesty's Revenue and Customs* [2023] UKSC 7, para 57.

[11] ibid para 116; E McLuhan and F Zingrone, *Essential McLuhan* (Routledge 1997) 155 (hereafter McLuhan and Zingrone, *Essential McLuhan*); E Eisenstein, *The Printing Press as an Agent of Change: Communications and Cultural Transformations in Early Modern Europe*, vols I and II (CUP 1980).

[12] *NewsCorp UK & Ireland Ltd v Commissioners for his Majesty's Revenue and Customs* [2023] UKSC 7, para 117.

editions of newspapers henceforth pursuant to Directive 2018/1713 and the VAT Order 2020.[13] However, the issue at the heart of this case, whether digital media should be regulated after the paradigm or under the influence of older media, is of enduring importance. McLuhan observed that '[A] new medium is never an addition to an old one, nor does it leave the old one in peace. It never ceases to oppress the older media until it finds new shapes and positions for them.'[14] In this process of 'remediation', also known as convergence, traditional media endure alongside the new media forms.[15]

1.3 Convergence and Media Transformation

Convergence forces the old medium to reposition itself to adjust to the new reality. This process of adaptation is often brutal as in the case of the dramatic destruction of print newspapers' business model. Digital only news companies, such as HuffPost and Vice, have recently also come to their demise, largely due to social media companies' capacity to siphon off digital advertising revenue.[16] Some argue that the newspaper business, as we know it, is doomed.[17] Others are more optimistic.[18] Yet others contend, somewhat cynically, that the currently ongoing collapse of newspapers will rebalance the equilibrium between supply and demand and will allow quality news to regain its visibility and value.[19] We do not know if this Darwinian prediction will materialize. What is clear is that the press and the broader information environment are on the cusp of transition to a still uncertain future. This monograph examines key regulatory adjustments that are being made to respond to this transient, often chaotic state.

The process of convergence means that the new medium also needs to adapt as it gradually blends with the older media, whilst being influenced and occasionally dominated by them. McLuhan observed that '[T]he BBC was set up to some extent ... , under the pressure of newspapers, post office, and various political pressures which felt that this form would be altogether too radical or mutational if it got out of hand'.[20] More often than not, older media leave their imprint on new ones.[21] This

[13] Council Directive 2018/1713 of 6 November 2018 amending Directive 2006/112/EC as regards rates of value added tax applied to books, newspapers and periodicals [2018] OJ L286/20; VAT (Extension of Zero-Rating to Electronically Supplied Books etc) (Coronavirus) Order 2020, SI 2020/459.
[14] McLuhan and Zingrone, *Essential McLuhan* (n 11) 269.
[15] J D Bolter and R Grusin, *Remediation. Understanding New Media* (MIT Press 2000) 222.
[16] M Sullivan, 'Vice is going bankrupt, BuzzFeed News is dead. What does it mean?' (*The Guardian*, 16 May 2023) <https://www.theguardian.com/commentisfree/2023/may/16/vice-bankruptcy-buzzfeed-news-dead-digital-age-revenue> accessed 2 January 2024.
[17] C Shirky, 'Newspapers and thinking the unthinkable' (*Edge*, 30 May 2023) <https://www.edge.org/conversation/clay_shirky-newspapers-and-thinking-the-unthinkable> accessed 2 January 2024.
[18] Economic Insight, 'Press sector financial sustainability. A report for the Department of Culture, Media and Sport' (May 2021) <https://assets.publishing.service.gov.uk/government/uploads/system/uploads/attachment_data/file/1073198/DCMS_Economic_Insight_final_report.pdf> 5; M Edge, 'Are UK Newspapers Really Dying? A Financial Analysis of Newspaper Publishing Companies' (2019) 16(1) Journal of Media Business Studies 1; H Bagdikian, *The New Media Monopoly* (Beakon Press 2004) 103ff.
[19] C Shirky, 'Newspapers and thinking the unthinkable', response by N G Carr (*Edge*, 30 May 2023) <https://www.edge.org/conversation/clay_shirky-newspapers-and-thinking-the-unthinkable> accessed 2 January 2024 .
[20] McLuhan and Zingrone, *Essential McLuhan* (n 11) 269, relying on the writings of Harold Innis.
[21] J D Harvey, *Collisions in the Digital Paradigm. Law and Rule Making in the Digital Age* (Hart Publishing 2017) 1ff, 16; see Chapter 9, pp 233–46.

cross-fertilization between older and newer media gives rise to what has been termed the 'hybrid media system'.[22] Old and new media have their own ' "internal" reserved domains of practice' which actors seek to preserve.[23] However, their boundaries are permeable. The disruptions caused by the newest medium give rise to ripple effects which reach the institutions of the previously dominant legacy media and reconfigure the practices and norms making up the media environment.

In the case of the newest medium, the internet, regulators are still in search of the most apposite regulatory paradigm, the one that will best capture its nature and functionalities. From the Supreme Court's comparison of the internet to a 'vast library' in *Reno v ACLU* to its much-derided likening to 'a series of tubes' rather than 'a big truck' by Senator Ted Stevens, analogies have served as a vehicle to render arcane technologies more accessible, to capture the public imaginary, and to frame the debate.[24] Historical analogies must, however, be used with caution lest they 'do more to obscure than reveal the true stakes of disputes'.[25] Traditional media are often at the forefront of lobbying for a public interest regulation of the internet to remedy perceived regulatory asymmetries and the resultant loss of their advertising revenue. It is, however, still unclear after which of these traditional media, if any, public interest regulation of the internet should be moulded.

Historically, the extent to which a medium has been shielded from, or subjected to, government regulation has depended on its technological characteristics.[26] As a result, a trifurcated regulatory structure encompassing the press, broadcasting, and telecommunications has crystallized. Convergence propelled by digitalization has upended the rationale behind these regulatory silos. Nonetheless, media regulation is still wedded to the paradigms of a press largely free from government regulation and of a broadcasting sector tightly controlled to serve the public interest. The latest Reuters Institute Digital News Report observed that 'The UK media scene is characterised by a well-funded and regulated broadcasting sector and a lively and opinionated national press'.[27] This statement implies that the UK press is vigorous because it is free from government regulation, and that it would have been more constrained if it was regulated in a broadcast-like fashion. The broadcasting sector is characterized as 'well-funded', but the question of the financial sustainability of the press is eschewed. Also, the assumption that the absence of external regulation is the best guarantee for press freedom is by no means unanimously shared.

---

[22] A Chadwick, *The Hybrid Media System: Politics and Power* (2nd edn, OUP 2017) 26.

[23] ibid.

[24] *Reno v ACLU* 521 US 844 (1997); A Seitz, 'It's a Series of Tubes: Network Neutrality in the United States and How the Current Economic Environment Presents Unique Opportunity to Invest in the Future of the Internet' (2009) 29(2) Journal of the National Association of Administrative Law Judiciary 683, 708; see H Kalven, 'Broadcasting, Public Policy and the First Amendment' (1967) 10 Journal of Law and Economics 15, 38.

[25] E Goldman, '"Must Carry" Lawsuit Against Search Engines—Langdon v. Google' (*Technology & Marketing Law Blog*, 8 June 2006) <https://blog.ericgoldman.org/archives/2006/06/must_carry_laws.htm> accessed 5 June 2023.

[26] 'The Message in the Medium: The First Amendment on the Information Superhighway' (1994) 107 Harvard Law Review 1062, 1069.

[27] N Newman, 'United Kingdom' (*Reuters Institute Digital News Report 2022*) <https://reutersinstitute.politics.ox.ac.uk/digital-news-report/2022/united-kingdom> accessed 20 March 2023.

1.4 Press Freedom and Regulation

The extent to which regulation is antithetical to press freedom has been the subject of extensive academic and policy contention. Some argue that the *mutatis mutandis* application of the broadcast regulation model to the press would enable it to better serve the public interest.[28] Others emphasize that the press has no *legal* obligation to serve the public interest and argue for coercive press regulation only insofar as harm to personal rights, but not to broader societal concerns, is at stake.[29] Still others contend that the broadcast regulation model is only acceptable because an uninhibited press provides a counterweight,[30] or they question altogether the continuous justifiability of this model in conditions of digital abundance.[31]

In the UK, the fronts in the debate over press regulation have hardened post-Leveson. The arguments on both fronts have recently been rehearsed once more over the planned repeal of the long-stalled section 40 of the Crime and Courts Act 2013, a provision that would force publishers to subscribe to an 'approved regulator' by enjoining them to pay both sides' legal costs even if they won a case.[32] The unceasing debate over the desirability of press regulation eludes the question of how far press freedom is already compromised because news publishers are caught in a whirlwind of legislative and policy reforms to provide short-term fixes to the perceived failings of the internet. Such legislative furore, occasionally accompanied by jurisprudential overreach, risks taking place without much consideration for the internet's future shape, let alone for the impact of the adopted measures on the independence and sustainability of journalism and on the pluralism of the information environment. The extent to which press freedom is consequently jeopardized is under-researched in academic writing.

The two strands of analysis that are interweaved in this monograph—the concepts of press freedom and regulation and the phenomena of convergence and digitalization—have hitherto largely been examined in isolation. Media freedom, and press freedom in particular, have been woefully neglected in English-speaking human rights literature, best treated as synonymous with freedom of expression.[33] The few existing excellent legal works on freedom of speech and media freedom pay little attention to the question of press regulation in a converged media environment[34]

---

[28] See eg E Barendt, *Freedom of Speech* (2nd edn, OUP 2007) 450 (hereafter Barendt, *Freedom of Speech*); L Blom-Cooper, 'Press Freedom: Constitutional Right or Cultural Assumption?' [2008] Public Law 260, 274; T Gibbons, *Regulating the Media* (2nd edn, Sweet & Maxwell 1998) 65.

[29] P Wragg, *A Free and Regulated Press: Defending Coercive Independent Press Regulation* (Hart Publishing 2020) (hereafter Wragg, *A Free and Regulated Press*).

[30] L C Bollinger, *Images of a Free Press* (University of Chicago Press 1991) (hereafter Bollinger, *Images of a Free Press*).

[31] See eg House of Lords, *Media Convergence*, 2nd Report of session 2012–13, HL Paper 154, 27 March 2013, para 114; C M Davis, '*Die dienende' Rundfunkfreiheit im Zeitalter der sozialen Vernetzung* (Mohr Siebeck 2019); B Hartmann, 'Dienende Freiheit—notwendige Verstärkung oder widersprüchliche Beschränkung subjektiver Rechte?' (2016) 71 Juristenzeitung 18; S Korte, 'Die dienende Funktion der Rundfunkfreiheit in Zeiten medialer Konvergenz' (2014) 139(3) Archiv für Öffentliches Recht 384.

[32] Crime and Courts Act, s 40; Draft Media Bill, cl 43(2); J Woodhouse, 'Media Bill: Policy background' (*House of Commons Library*, 28 February 2023) 50.

[33] W Lamer, *Press Freedom as an International Human Right* (Palgrave Macmillan 2018).

[34] Barendt, *Freedom of Speech* (n 28); Wragg, *A Free and Regulated Press* (n 29); H Fenwick and G Phillipson, *Media Freedom under the Human Rights Act* (OUP 2006).

or place their emphasis on the Strasbourg and other international jurisprudence, as opposed to that of the domestic courts.[35] More recent studies examine the ambivalent position of citizen journalists in the current media environment.[36] The standards of press regulation in the UK became the focus of academic debate in the aftermath of the phone-hacking scandal and the Leveson Inquiry.[37] This strand of research offers valuable insights into the legitimacy and limitations of press self-regulation in the UK, but does not touch upon the challenges posed by convergence. While the impact of digitalization on the economic basis of journalism and on journalism practice has been explored in a rich body of scholarship, academic discussion of the contradictions and increasing anachronism of current models of media regulation remains scant.[38]

The paradox of the disparity between broadcast and press regulation is by no means a novel field of academic enquiry. Scholars have long grappled with the rationale for this divergent treatment and with the question of which model should prevail, but have been unable to provide a definitive answer.[39] More recently, scholars have argued in favour of a more unified media order modelled after the broadcasting paradigm,[40] or in favour of a press-type voluntary regulation for all 'private' content across media platforms.[41] These studies take a clear standpoint, but further exploration and articulation of the competing interests at stake in the case of the online press is needed. Early legal analyses of the impact of convergence on the regulation of the German online press have remained sparse, focusing on specific manifestations of this phenomenon, without exploring its transformative power and its implications for the future of press

[35] J Oster, *Media Freedom as a Fundamental Right* (CUP 2015).
[36] P Coe, *Media Freedom in the Age of Citizen Journalism* (Edward Elgar Publishing 2021; J Schroeder, *The Press Clause and Digital Technology's Fourth Wave. Media Law and the Symbiotic Web* (Routledge 2018).
[37] C Dagoula, I Katsirea, and J Harrison, 'The Independent Press Standards Organisation and Accuracy: A Comparative Study of Complaints Handling Procedures in Four UK Newspapers' (2023) Journal of Applied Journalism & Media Studies 1; E Barendt, 'Statutory Underpinning: A Threat to Press Freedom?' (2013) 5(2) Journal of Media Law 189; T Gibbons, 'Building Trust in Press Regulation: Obstacles and Opportunities' (2013) 5(2) Journal of Media Law 202; G Phillipson, 'Leveson, the Public Interest and Press Freedom' (2013) 5(2) Journal of Media Law 220; P Wragg, 'The Legitimacy of Press Regulation' (2015) Public Law 290; D Carney, 'Up to Standard? A Critique of IPSO's Editors' Code of Practice and IMPRESS's Standards Code: Part 1 and Part 2' (2017) 22(3) Communications Law 77 and 112.
[38] See eg J Tong, *Journalism, Economic Uncertainty and Political Irregularity in the Digital and Data Era* (Emerald Publishing 2023); B Franklin and S Eldridge II, *The Routledge Companion to Digital Journalism Studies* (Routledge 2017); R McChesney, *Digital Disconnect. How Capitalism Is Turning the Internet Against Democracy* (The New Press 2013); A Charles and G Stewart (eds), *The End of Journalism: News in the Twenty-First Century* (Peter Lang 2011).
[39] Bollinger, *Images of a Free Press* (n 30); D W Vick, 'Regulatory Convergence?' (2006) 26(1) Legal Studies 26.
[40] D Tambini, *Media Freedom* (Polity Press 2021) 126ff (hereafter Tambini, *Media Freedom*); H-J Papier and M Schroeder, '"Gebiet des Rundfunks". Gutachten von H.-J. Papier und M. Schroeder zu presseähnlichen Angeboten' (2010) 60 epd medien 16; F G Kerrsenbrock, *Die Legitimation der Medien nach dem Grundgesetz. Zur verfassungsrechtlichen Stellung von Rundfunk und Presse im Zeitalter von Social Media* (Peter Lang 2015).
[41] L Fielden, *Regulating for Trust in Journalism. Standards Regulation in the Age of Blended Media* (Reuters Institute for the Study of Journalism 2011); L Fielden, 'UK Press Regulation: Taking Account of Media Convergence' (2016) 22(5) Convergence 472; J Kahl, *Elektronische Presse und Bürgerjournalismus: Presserechtliche Rechte und Pflichten von Wortmedien im Internet* (Nomos 2013); T Krattenmaker and L A Powe, 'Converging First Amendment Principles for Converging Communications Media' (1994–95) 104 Yale Law Journal 1719, 172.

regulation.[42] A comparative methodology promises to provide fruitful insights into the drivers and mechanisms of press regulation in a digital environment.

1.5 Press Regulation through a Comparative Lens

This book aims to shed further light on the regulation of the press in the digital era and on the impact of the proliferating media laws, policies, and jurisprudence on press freedom by taking a comparative approach. Such an approach befits media law, a discipline that knows no borders. However, application of a comparative methodology is hitherto underrepresented in media law, especially as regards the study of press compared to broadcasting regulation.[43] The inter- and supranational legal systems at the heart of this book are those of the Council of Europe and of the European Union (EU), with a focus on the case law of the European Court of Human Rights (ECtHR) and of the Court of Justice of the European Union (CJEU). As far as the area of domestic law is concerned, the emphasis is on the UK and Germany, while the US serves as a useful counterpoint. In constitutional terms, the German and US legal systems have a rich constitutional jurisprudence and scholarship on freedom of expression and media freedom. The latter is often characterized as exceptionalist in view of its unique First Amendment approach and of its reservations to major international human rights conventions.[44] The comparison between the UK and German media systems is of great interest because of the role model function and advanced digitalization of the former, and the pioneering steps towards regulation of the online world in both jurisdictions.

Hallin and Mancini, in their landmark comparative communication study, categorized Germany as a democratic corporatist media system, marked by the coexistence of powerful commercial and politically affiliated media, a degree of state intervention, and a high level of journalistic professionalism.[45] They classified the UK, together with the US media system, as representatives of the North Atlantic or liberal model, characterized by a strong commercial media sector, limited state intervention, high journalistic professionalism, and weak political ties, with the exception of the British

---

[42] Z Rahvar, *Die Zukunft des deutschen Presserechts im Lichte konvergierender Medien* (Nomos 2011); F Bronsema, *Medienspezifischer Grundrechtsschutz der elektronischen Presse. Darstellung des Grundrechtsschutzes in der Europäischen Union und Entwicklung eines Lösungsansatzes für den Grundrechtsschutz aus Art. 5 Abs. 1 GG* (LIT 2010); H Rossen-Stadtfeld, *Audiovisuelle Bewegtbildangebote von Presseunternehmen im Internet: Presse oder Rundfunk?* (Nomos 2009).

[43] See Wragg, *A Free and Regulated Press* (n 29); L Fielden, 'Regulating the press. A comparative study of international press councils' (*Reuters Institute for the Study of Journalism* 2012) <https://reutersinstitute. politics.ox.ac.uk/sites/default/files/2017-11/Regulating%20the%20Press.pdf>; D C Hallin and P Mancini, *Comparing Media Systems Beyond the Western World* (CUP 2012); Barendt, *Freedom of Speech* (n 28); I Katsirea, *Public Broadcasting and European Law. A Comparative Examination of Public Service Obligations in Six Member States* (Kluwer 2008); B Holznagel, *Rundfunkrecht in Europa: Auf dem Weg zu einem Gemeinsamen europäischer Rundfunkordnungen*, Jus publicum, vol 18 (JCB Mohr 1996); P Humphreys, *Mass Media and Media Policy in Western Europe* (Manchester UP 1996); W Hoffmann-Riem, *Regulating Media: The Licensing and Supervision of Broadcasting in Six Countries* (Guilford 1996).

[44] See eg US reservation to Article 19 of ICCPR in Senate Committee on Foreign Relations, Report on the International Covenant on Civil and Political Rights, reprinted in 31 ILM 645, 646 (1992); Tambini, *Media Freedom* (n 40) 26; L Eko, *American Exceptionalism, the French Exception and Digital Media Law* (Lexington Books 2013).

[45] D C Hallin and others, *Comparing Media Systems: Three Models of Media and Politics* (CUP 2004) 140ff.

press.[46] More recent studies have since revisited Hallin and Mancini's influential typology, and have further refined their models.[47] Hallin and Mancini themselves, when reassessing their research ten years later, questioned the impact of new media on the variation of media systems. They envisaged three possible outcomes. First, new media might follow technology and platform logics different from traditional media logics, and might therefore be a force for homogenization across media systems. Second, new media might follow a logic of path dependence, and develop differently in different media systems, leading to a continuity of national differences. Third, new media might develop differently in different media systems, but in ways that diverge from existing patterns with a view to filling gaps not covered by existing institutions.[48] The present monograph, though rooted in a predominantly legal rather than an empirical research methodology, takes up the question whether the digital press develops in a path-dependent or a path-divergent manner, and in similar or different ways across the jurisdictions under examination. At the heart of this study are the regulatory challenges posed by the convergence between broadcast and print media and between press and non-press speakers.

This book is divided in two parts, which focus respectively on the theory and practice of press freedom, and regulation. Part I Chapter 2 locates the press within the spectrum of traditional models of mass media regulation, discusses the implications of convergence, and assesses the options for regulating the new media. Chapter 3 traces the transformation from the print to the digital-native press, examines the increasingly press-like role performed by intermediaries, and debates the extent to which the privileges and responsibilities of the traditional media should be extended to non-professional actors. Finally, Chapter 4 discusses the interpretation of press freedom and its delineation from freedom of expression in Europe and the US, questions the merits of the adoption of a unified media freedom, and asks whether regulation poses a threat to press freedom. Part II Chapter 5 begins with an examination of the ECtHR case law on the ethics of journalism and of the shifting standards of accuracy and objectivity in the digital era. Chapter 6 considers a growing challenge for the online press that comes from a different direction, namely from the areas of data protection and privacy law. It discusses whether the right to erasure/right to be forgotten, as interpreted by the ECtHR, the CJEU, and national courts, undermines press freedom. Chapter 7 focuses on the liability of online news portals for user-generated content, and estimates its implications for their ability to uphold a source of revenue that is key for their financial viability. Chapter 8 turns to the convergence between press and broadcasting as manifested by the video content available on newspaper websites and social media sites and by news publishers' live streams. Finally, Chapter 9 is devoted to the contested relationship between the press and public service broadcasting and the attempt by the press to safeguard its financial viability in the online domain by seeking

---

[46] ibid 198ff.

[47] eg the study by M Brüggemann and others, 'Hallin and Mancini Revisited: Four Empirical Types of Western Media Systems' (2014) 64(6) Journal of Communication 1037, 1056 classifies Germany in the same Central cluster as the UK on account of their strong public broadcasting systems, absence of press subsidies, and high degree of politically linked media.

[48] D C Hallin and P Mancini, 'Ten Years After Comparing Media Systems: What Have We Learned?' (2017) 34(2) Political Communication 155, 164.

to finely delineate its online activities from those of public service broadcasters. The concluding chapter captures the key implications of digitalization and convergence for freedom and regulation of the online press in the areas examined in the present volume. It assesses the extent to which the emergent regulatory model is shaped by analogies from the past. It identifies the regulatory ruptures that persist, and formulates preliminary recommendations for the evolving online news ecosystem.

PART I
THEORY OF PRESS FREEDOM AND REGULATION

2

Divergent Regulation, Convergent Media

2.1 Introduction

Historically, different media have been subject to diverse regulatory models on account of their technological characteristics. Over time, three prevailing regulatory models have crystallized, which will be explored further in this chapter. The first is the model of the free press, the second that of broadcasting, and the last that of telecommunications, the so-called common carrier model.[1] These three regulatory paradigms will be discussed in the following section, and the question will be broached as to what might be the likely direction of travel for the regulation of the newest medium, the internet.

2.2 Traditional Models of Mass Media Regulation

The free press model seeks to safeguard the editorial autonomy of the press and its freedom from government regulation. According to this model, the press does not need to comply with a particularly cumbersome regulatory framework but is only subject to the generally applicable laws. In the US, the freedom of the press from government interference was firmly defended by the Supreme Court in the case of *Miami Herald*.[2] This case concerned a section of the Florida Election Code, which required a publisher to print a free reply from a candidate for office if the paper had attacked their character or record. The case arose when the *Miami Herald* declined to publish a reply by Pat Tornillo, a union official and candidate for the state legislature, to editorials accusing him of having led an illegal teachers' strike. The Court held that a government-enforced right of access would dampen the vigour, and limit the variety, of public debate as editors would avoid controversial election coverage.[3] The free press model is a manifestation of the negative conception of media freedom as a negative freedom from state control.[4] It is informed by the notion that the press only needs to be protected from governmental restraint, while positive state interventions, for instance by way of subsidies, are viewed with suspicion.

It is perhaps surprising that the Court in *Miami Herald* failed to pay heed to the sharply contrasting decision in *Red Lion Broadcasting* where it had unanimously upheld the constitutionality of certain aspects of the Federal Communications

---

[1] D McQuail, *McQuail's Mass Communication Theory* (6th edn, Sage 2011) 235ff (hereafter McQuail, *Mass Communication*).
[2] *Miami Herald v Tornillo* 418 US 241 (1974).
[3] ibid para 23.
[4] See T M Scanlon, 'Content Regulation Reconsidered' in J Lichtenberg (ed), *Democracy and the Mass Media* (CUP 2012) 331, 347.

Press Freedom and Regulation in a Digital Era. Irini Katsirea, Oxford University Press. © Irini Katsirea 2024.
DOI: 10.1093/oso/9780198858607.003.0002

Commission's (FCC) 'fairness doctrine', stating that radio and television stations had to provide a free right of reply to personal attacks.[5] The Court justified the 'personal attack rule' on the basis of the scarcity of the electromagnetic spectrum, which prevented all citizens from having access to the airwaves, and which would need to be shared by incumbents with others holding competing views since it was 'the right of the viewers and listeners, not the right of the broadcasters, which is paramount'.[6] Anything less than a right of access to the airwaves would amount to 'unlimited private censorship operating in a medium not open to all'.[7] Without as much as an attempt to justify this statement, the Court asserted the role of broadcasting as a 'unique medium', and dismissed the broadcasters' arguments about the chilling effect of a right of reply as speculative.[8] The Court also remained unconvinced by the broadcasters' claims about the expansion of the available spectrum, and opined that '[s]carcity is not entirely a thing of the past'.[9] In a later decision, the District of Columbia Court of Appeals pronounced that:

> There may be ways to reconcile *Red Lion* and *Tornillo* but the 'scarcity' of broadcast frequencies does not appear capable of doing so. Perhaps the Supreme Court will one day revisit this area of the law and either eliminate the distinction between print and broadcast media, surely by pronouncing *Tornillo* applicable to both, or announce a constitutional distinction that is more usable than the present one.[10]

A more principled constitutional distinction is still forthcoming. As long as this is the case, the *Red Lion* decision captures the broadcasting model of regulation. Broadcasting is the medium that has, since its inception, been subject to heavy licensing and content obligations that would have been considered unconstitutional in the case of the print media. The comparison between press and broadcasting regulation was considered by the US Supreme Court in its seminal decision in *Turner Broadcasting*.[11] The Court held that the more relaxed First Amendment scrutiny that applies to broadcasting in line with *Red Lion* would be inapposite in the case of cable television. The latter did not suffer from the physical limitations of the electromagnetic spectrum, which characterize the broadcast medium.[12] On the other hand, the Court concluded that cable could not be treated in the same way as the printed media, and that heightened First Amendment scrutiny would be unwarranted in view of the 'bottleneck monopoly power' exercised by cable operators. Given that these operators

---

[5] *Red Lion Broadcasting v FCC* 395 US 367 (1969); L C Bollinger, 'Freedom of the Press and Public Access: Toward a Theory of Partial Regulation of the Mass Media' (1976) 75(1) Michigan Law Review 1, 4 (hereafter Bollinger, 'Freedom of the Press').

[6] *Red Lion Broadcasting v FCC* 395 US 367 (1969), para 390.

[7] ibid para 392.

[8] ibid para 393. However, this argument gained more traction over time, also with the help of newspaper publishers who had in the meantime begun buying broadcast stations, leading to the formal repeal by the FCC of the 'fairness doctrine' in 1987 and of the 'personal attack rule' in 2000. *Syracuse Peace Council v FCC*, 867 F 2d 654 (DC Cir 1989); *RTNDA v FCC*, 229 F 3d 269 (DC Cir 2000); H Bagdikian, *The New Media Monopoly* (Beakon Press 2004) 120.

[9] *Red Lion Broadcasting v FCC* 395 US 367 (1969), para 396.

[10] *Telecommunications Research Action v FCC*, 801 F 2d 501 (DC Cir 1986), para 509.

[11] *Turner Broadcasting System v FCC* 512 US 622 (1994).

[12] ibid 639.

could determine which programmes were available to viewers, they were in a uniquely powerful position if compared to press publishers who could not prevent readers from accessing other newspapers.[13] Therefore, their differential treatment by way of must-carry was found to be justified by the special characteristics of cable.

Further, in *Playboy Entm't Group*, the Supreme Court also distinguished cable television from broadcasting. It acknowledged that cable television, like broadcast media, presented unique problems because of its ability to enter our homes and expose our children to indecent programming.[14] Nonetheless, the Court applied strict scrutiny to the content-based regulations in question, which barred sexually explicit programmes at times when children were likely to watch. The Court found the regulations unconstitutional based on what it regarded as the key difference between cable and broadcasting, namely the ability of cable systems to block undesirable channels on a household-by-household basis. This targeted blocking was, in the Court's view, a less restrictive measure than an outright ban. This judgment can be contrasted with the earlier *Pacifica* case, in which the Court stressed that broadcasting had 'the most limited First Amendment protection' of all forms of communication.[15] In *Pacifica*, the Court upheld the constitutionality of an FCC sanction against an offensive radio broadcast on account of this medium's unique pervasiveness and accessibility to children. Indeed, these features of broadcasting are traditionally considered as the main rationale for the medium's special regulation. Imposing greater restrictions on a more powerful and effective medium of communication might provide a certain rationale for regulation.[16] However, it seems problematic from a free speech perspective.[17]

Similar reasons for the disparate treatment of broadcasting have been put forward also in Germany. In its *First Television* case, the German Federal Constitutional Court (*Bundesverfassungsgericht*, BVerfG) held that both broadcasting and the press were equally important factors of public opinion formation. However, it posited that broadcasting, as a medium and factor of public opinion formation, was in a special situation (*Sondersituation*). This special situation was premised on the scarcity of frequencies and on the high financial investment required for broadcasting programmes, resulting in a relatively small number of broadcasters compared to newspaper publishers. It justified the public service broadcasting monopoly and mandated that broadcasting companies were structured in a way that all relevant societal forces had a say.[18]

Technological developments, in particular the advent of cable and satellite television, meant that the scarcity rationale became hard to sustain, if not redundant. Nonetheless, in the *Third Television* case (*FRAG decision*), the German Constitutional Court held fast to the notion that broadcasting deserved special treatment even if the scarcity of frequencies ceased to apply in the light of modern developments. It modified the *Sondersituation* doctrine by arguing that a 'market of opinions', like that

[13] E Barendt, *Freedom of Speech* (2nd edn, OUP 2007) 446 (hereafter Barendt, *Freedom of Speech*).

[14] *US v Playboy Entm't Group* 529 US 803 (2000); see also *Home Box Office Inc v FCC*, 567 F 2d 9 (DC Cir 1977) on the 'important differences between cable and broadcast television'.

[15] *FCC v Pacifica Foundation* 438 US 726, 727 (1978).

[16] J Rowbottom, *Media Law* (Hart Publishing 2018) 286 (hereafter Rowbottom, *Media Law*).

[17] *Telecommunications Research Action v FCC*, 801 F 2d 501 (DC Cir 1986), para 508; Barendt, *Freedom of Speech* (n 13) 446; Bollinger, 'Freedom of the Press' (n 5) 15.

[18] BVerfGE 12, 205 (1961), paras 180ff, 279.

existing in the case of supra-regional newspapers, might not arise in private broad-casting. Moreover, it warned that leaving a medium as important as broadcasting to the free play of market forces might lead to an undue concentration of opinion power, which could only be subsequently remedied with considerable difficulty, if at all.[19] The Court explained that broadcasting freedom served the free formation of opinion (*dienende Freiheit*) and could not be safeguarded just by warding off state interference. The legislature would also need to shape a positive broadcasting order to ensure that the variety of existing opinions would be expressed as comprehensively as possible.[20] Such a broadcasting framework did not amount in the Court's view to a restriction of broadcasting freedom.[21] In later judgments, the Court further justified the signifi-cance of the broadcasting medium by linking it to its broad effect, its immediacy, and its suggestive power (*Breitenwirkung, Aktualität, Suggestivkraft*).[22] These unique fea-tures of broadcasting echo the Supreme Court's view in *Pacifica*. The aptness of these characteristics as the foundation for the special treatment of broadcasting has since been questioned in academic literature. If the vague notion of a certain medium's relevance for opinion formation is the litmus test for its regulatory treatment, should not popular tabloid newspapers be subjected to the same level of regulation as broad-casting?[23] This bridge has only been crossed in Germany as regards newspaper streaming services, not their print editions.[24] The critique has mostly gone in the op-posite direction, targeted at the overregulation of broadcasting and the unproven need for a positive broadcasting order, especially in its public service broadcasting mani-festation, in an era of ostensible information abundance.[25] The merits of some of these arguments will be discussed later.[26] It suffices to observe for now that the broadcasting model is a manifestation of the positive theory of media freedom. It reflects the notion that the state should empower the media to support democratic discourse by not only protecting their right to impart but also the audience's right to receive ideas.[27]

This onerous broadcasting regulation stands in sharp relief to the third model of regulation, the so-called common carrier model, which applies to universal services such as the mail, telegraph, and telephone. This model is characterized by the strict regulation of ownership and infrastructure, and only very limited regulation of con-tent, reflecting an emphasis on the management of natural monopolies in the public

---

[19]   BVerfGE 57, 295 (1981), paras 109ff.

[20]   ibid para 104.

[21]   cf J Kühling, 'Art 5 GG' in H Gersdorf and P Paal (eds), *Informations- und Medienrecht Kommentar* (Beck 2014) para 61 (hereafter Kühling, 'Art 5 GG').

[22]   BVerfGE 90, 60 (1994), para 144; BVerfGE 119, 181 (2007), para 116.

[23]   F Schoch, 'Konvergenz der Medien—Sollte das Recht der Medien harmonisiert werden?' (2002) 17 Juristenzeitung 798, 804.

[24]   See Chapter 8, pp 214–15.

[25]   A Ingold, 'Digitalisierung demokratischer Öffentlichkeiten' (2017) 56(4) Der Staat 491, 502; C Franzius, 'Das Internet und die Grundrechte' (2016) 71 Juristenzeitung 650, 651; Kühling, 'Art 5 GG' (n 21) para 83; see C Michael Davis, *'Die dienende' Rundfunkfreiheit im Zeitalter der sozialen Vernetzung* (Mohr Siebeck 2019) 40, 41.

[26]   See Chapter 9, pp 237–38.

[27]   A T Kenyon, 'The State of Affairs of Freedom: Implications of German Broadcasting Freedom' in A T Kenyon and A Scott (eds), *Positive Free Speech. Rationales, Methods and Implications* (Hart Publishing 2021) 83.

interest.[28] In a case concerning 'dial-a-porn' telephone lines, the Supreme Court justified their disparate treatment from broadcasting by pointing to the fact that television intrudes into the privacy of the home without prior warning whereas affirmative steps need to be taken to access a dial-it medium.[29] It has been questioned in academic literature whether the heavily regulated broadcast medium is all that different from 'dial-a-porn' telephone lines, or the internet for that matter, which both enjoy full First Amendment protection.[30]

This takes us to the last regulatory model, the one which is applicable to the internet, a model that has yet to crystallize. The internet, while still being the 'newest kid on the block', is no longer in its infancy. In its genesis, this new medium was conceived of, by some of its advocates at least, as a 'common carrier medium', free from government control.[31] John Perry Barlow, author of 'A Declaration of the Independence of Cyberspace', proclaimed in 1996 that national sovereignty should not extend to the realm of the internet. More than that, he argued that governments were unable to control the web as a result of its cross-border nature, and that, in any case, culture, ethics, and unwritten codes governed the web far more effectively than any kind of state regulation ever could.[32] A lot of water has flowed under the bridge since Barlow's romanticized vision of cyberspace as a 'lawless anarchic frontier, free of the deadening hand of the lawyer and the industry monopolist'.[33] Cyberspace, having been captured by behemoths like Google and Facebook, exhibits the same oligopolistic traits that beset the offline world.[34] For a long time, governments put faith in international and national self-regulatory bodies, such as the Internet Corporation for Assigned Names and Numbers (ICANN) or the Internet Watch Foundation (IWF) and the internet service providers (ISPs), to govern the internet's architecture and content.

Increasingly, however, states have begun to question the capacity of the internet to self-regulate and have sought ever new ways of asserting their jurisdiction online to secure public interest objectives. Still, as a result of its transnational, disembodied character, the internet remains notoriously difficult to govern.[35] The fact that the internet is a virtual space that transcends national borders, has led to the notion that

---

[28] McQuail, *Mass Communication* (n 1) 236; J van Cuilenburg and D McQuail, 'Media Policy Paradigm Shifts: Towards a New Communications Policy Paradigm' (2003) 18(2) European Journal of Communication 181, 190.

[29] *Sable Communications v FCC* 492 US 115 (1989).

[30] Barendt, *Freedom of Speech* (n 13) 446.

[31] McQuail, *Mass Communication* (n 1) 237; R Collins, 'Hierarchy to Homeostasis? Hierarchy, Markets and Networks in UK Media and Communications Governance' (2008) 30(3) Media, Culture & Society 295, 297 (hereafter Collins, 'Hierarchy').

[32] J P Barlow, 'A declaration of the independence of cyberspace', 8 February 1996, <https://www.eff.org/cyberspace-independence>.

[33] A Taubman, 'Introduction: International Governance and the Internet' in L Edwards and C Waelde (eds), *Law and the Internet* (3rd edn, Hart Publishing 2009) 4.

[34] J Goldsmith and T Wu, *Who Controls the Internet?: Illusions of a Borderless World* (OUP 2006); M Hindman, *The Internet Trap. How the Digital Economy Builds Monopolies and Undermines Democracy* (Princeton UP 2018) (hereafter Hindman, *The Internet Trap*). In the following, reference will be made to Facebook rather than to its parent company, Meta.

[35] M Cappello (ed), *Media Law Enforcement Without Frontiers*, IRIS Special (European Audiovisual Observatory 2018); House of Lords, *Media Convergence*, 2nd Report of session 2012–13, HL Paper 154, 27 March 2013, paras 31ff (hereafter House of Lords, *Media Convergence*).

the online domain is separate from the physical world, and altogether eschews regu-lation.[36] This notion has long been exposed as a 'cyberspace fallacy'.[37] Internet trans-actions are anchored in specific jurisdictions where the actors or the communications equipment involved are located.[38] A related argument, which also echoes Barlow's still resonant cyber libertarian vision, is that internet governance should be distinct from that which applies to legacy media.[39] This argument is equally misguided as it implies that the internet is an altogether separate medium, different from the press, radio, or television. However, the internet is not a single medium that can be subjected to a single regulatory regime. As aptly described by Collins, it should rather be viewed as 'a stage in a continuing process of transformation from established technologically distinct media of communication to an integrated digital topology of interconnecting networks'.[40]

This process of transition from separate types of media—such as broadcast, print, and online—to those that are merged and can be delivered by the same distribution methods is often referred to as 'convergence'. Convergence can be seen as a phase in the 'natural life cycle of new media evolution'. A six-phase model, developed by Lehman-Wilzig and Cohen-Avigdor, aims to capture this life cycle and to explain the transformations of a new medium from its birth onwards.[41] Convergence is one of three possibilities in the last phase of this journey. A medium in danger of extinction may either adapt by developing new functions or preserve its functions by merging with other media. If both these options fail, the medium will naturally decline and eventually disappear, much like living organisms become extinct if they fail to adapt to change. In the following chapter, we will discuss some of the transformations trad-itional newspapers have had to undergo and the challenges they face as they fight to survive in the digital environment.

In the European context, the concept of 'convergence' is commonly associated with the European Commission Green Paper on convergence.[42] However, the blurring of lines between hitherto distinct media brought about by the process of digitalization was already discussed by de Sola Pool in his seminal work *Technologies of Freedom*.[43] De Sola Pool described two manifestations of convergence in the following way: 'A single physical means—be it wires, cables, or airwaves—may carry services that in the

---

[36] D G Post and D R Johnson, 'Law and Borders—The Rise of Law in Cyberspace' (1996) 48 Stanford Law Review 1367, 1378.

[37] C Reed, *Internet Law: Text and Materials* (2nd edn, CUP 2004) 1–2, 218; J Goldsmith, 'Regulation of the Internet: Three Persistent Fallacies' (1998) 73(4) Chicago-Kent Law Review 1119; L Lessig, 'The Zones of Cyber-space' (1996) 48 Stanford Law Review 1403, 1406.

[38] See *Google Spain SL and Google Inc. v Agencia Española de Protección de Datos (AEPD) and Mario Costeja González* [2014] ECLI:EU:C:2014:317, paras 45ff where the CJEU rightly considered the existence of advertising subsidiaries in Ireland as an appropriate 'territorial hook'. See, however, Chapter 6, p 172 on attempts extraterritorially to impose global dereferencing orders.

[39] See R Collins, 'Internet Governance in the UK' (2006) 28(3) Media, Culture & Society 337.

[40] ibid 339.

[41] S Lehman-Wilzig and N Cohen-Avigdor, 'The Natural Life Cycle of New Media Evolution: Inter-Media Struggle for Survival in the Internet Age' (2004) 6 New Media & Society 707, 711.

[42] Commission, 'Green Paper on the convergence of the telecommunications, media and information technology sectors, and the implications for regulation. Towards an information society approach' COM (97)623 (hereafter Commission Green Paper).

[43] I de Sola Pool, *Technologies of Freedom* (Harvard UP 1983).

past were provided in separate ways. Conversely, a service that was provided in the past by anyone medium—be it broadcasting, the press, or telephony—can now be provided in several different physical ways.'[44] This second manifestation, which is also referred to as 'multiplatform', could be conceived of as the opposite of convergence, as a form of divergence, as a single medium branches off into terrains previously occupied by other media players.[45] This phenomenon was noted in the House of Lords report on media convergence, which observed that 'paradoxically, ... convergence is leading to diverging sources of content and media consumption: in the range of suppliers at one end, and the range of devices and means of accessing content at the other'.[46] This is the case when, for instance, newspapers, while remaining rooted in print, also migrate to the web and offer their services via a website, a mobile platform, or an app. At the same time, these newspapers enter a competitive symbiotic relationship with other online operators such as news aggregators or broadcasters, which occupied separate physical spaces in the past. The two manifestations of convergence are therefore very much two sides of the same coin, so that overemphasizing the semantic distinction between them seems futile.

The vertical and horizontal integration of previously separate communications sectors unleashed by digitalization affects the ways in which audiences access content as well as their expectations across media. However, the different sectors that have come together in this multiplatform environment remain subject to the widely divergent regulatory traditions that have been outlined above. The European Commission viewed such regulatory divergence as a potential barrier that might hinder the development of new services and the implementation of the Information Society. It alleged that such regulatory barriers could occur, *inter alia*, as a result of regulatory uncertainty, the disparate treatment of similar services on the basis of the platform over which they are delivered, and the overburdening of services that straddle more than one regulatory area.[47] The Commission acknowledged that the appropriate response to the regulatory dilemmas unleashed by the process of digitalization is contested. Some would argue that this process calls for a reconsideration of the underlying rationale behind the regulatory approaches that govern the industries affected by convergence. Others would contend that the specific characteristics of the different sectors in question reflect social, cultural, and ethical values within our society that are independent of the technology of distribution and that need to be respected in the public interest.[48] While the former would likely favour a greater reliance on market forces to achieve regulatory objectives and a greater role for competition rules, the latter would question the ability of the market to safeguard the public interest and would subscribe to the need for sector-specific regulation.[49]

---

[44] ibid 23.
[45] K Hyung Whan, 'Media Convergence: Concept, Discourse and Influence', unpublished doctoral thesis (City, University of London 2019) 71.
[46] House of Lords, *Media Convergence* (n 35) 7.
[47] Commission Green Paper (n 42) 16.
[48] ibid.
[49] For a middle position see C R Blackman, 'Convergence between Telecommunications and Other Media: How Should Regulation Adapt?' (1998) 22(3) Telecommunications Policy 163.

The choice of either of these models is not predetermined by the process of media convergence, but is a political choice.[50] The tension between these options, and between the free press and common carrier model as opposed to the broadcasting regulation model, has been convincingly explained by the divide between the political theories of market liberalism and social liberalism.[51] The market liberal model, which was on the ascent in the mid-nineteenth century when the press achieved its breakthrough as a mass medium, provided the theoretical backdrop for the relative emancipation of the press from the state and for its reliance on advertising.[52] The same libertarian ethos also pervaded the telecommunications sector, and originally the internet. In many respects, media convergence has concurred with neoliberal ideals rooted in the belief that the benefits of technological change would best be reaped in an environment of unfettered competition and unlimited consumer choice.[53] On the other hand, the theory of social liberalism, which was prevalent at the turn of the twentieth century, posited that unrestrained media markets could not deliver socially responsible outcomes, and inspired the public service broadcasting model and, to a lesser extent, the regulation of commercial television.[54] The perceived need for greater regulation of the then nascent electronic media was arguably rendered more socially acceptable due to their prevalent image as being more geared towards entertainment than the print media, and hence less deserving of free speech protection.[55]

The way in which these competing models might influence the regulation of the internet is still uncertain. Some argue that the print model is gravely deficient on account of the increasing power and concentration of the press, which leads to a downward spiral for the quality of news and information.[56] In their view, the application of the print model to new technologies would engender a free for all for everything bar obscenity. The broadcast model is seen as superior because it fosters a laudable journalistic ethos, while recognizing the need for press freedom to change with the times. Its extension to new technologies would offer greater latitude to influence programming decisions.[57]

However, in Germany, online media services, so-called 'telemedia', have been subjected to a press-like order which aims to guarantee minimum standards rather than to a heavy, broadcast-like regulatory framework.[58] Also in the US, in *Reno v ACLU*, the Supreme Court held that the internet should receive extensive First Amendment

---

[50] W Hoffmann-Riem, W Schulz, and T Held, *Konvergenz und Regulierung. Optionen für rechtliche Regelungen und Aufsichtsstrukturen im Bereich Information, Kommunikation und Medien* (Nomos 2000).

[51] D W Vick, 'Regulatory Convergence?' (2006) 26(1) Legal Studies 26, 35ff.

[52] See J Curran and J Seaton, *Power Without Responsibility: The Press and Broadcasting in Britain* (7th edn, Routledge 2009) 7ff.

[53] P Humphreys and S Simpson, *Regulation, Governance and Convergence in the Media* (Edward Elgar 2018) 4.

[54] Vick, 'Regulatory Convergence' (n 51) 45ff.

[55] Bollinger, 'Freedom of the Press' (n 5) 19.

[56] T Krattenmaker and L A Powe, 'Converging First Amendment Principles for Converging Communications Media' (1994–95) 104 Yale Law Journal 1719, 1721 fn 14 (hereafter Krattenmaker and Powe, 'Converging First Amendment Principles'); see J Charney, 'Free Press: Necessary Illusions' (2019) 15(3) Law, Culture and the Humanities 826, 840.

[57] Krattenmaker and Powe, 'Converging First Amendment Principles' (n 56) 1722.

[58] M Cornils, 'Vielfaltssicherung bei Telemedien' (2018) 5 Archiv für Presserecht 377, 379; T Vesting, *Die Tagesschau-App und die Notwendigkeit der Schaffung eines 'Intermedienkollisionsrechts'* (KIT 2013) 12, 8.

protection in the same way as the print media.[59] Given that indecent material was not proscribed in print, it could not be prohibited online. The Court argued that the internet was less invasive than broadcasting. It was unlikely that users would accidentally encounter indecent material, so the argument went, as the dial-up technology of the time required a number of affirmative steps to be taken to access a specific website.[60] Also, the scarcity of frequencies that historically justified the extensive regulation of broadcasting was not present in cyberspace, which the Court compared 'from the readers' viewpoint, to both a vast library including millions of readily available and indexed publications and a sprawling mall offering goods and services'.[61]

This is not the only instance in which historical analogies have been drawn to conventional models of regulation. The classification of search engines as passive conduits, newspapers, or broadcasters has also been controversial. Some take the view that search engines are only intermediaries, which help speakers reach their audiences, but do not express an opinion of their own. The ranking of search results is algorithm-driven and wholly automatic and does not entail an editorial judgement on the search engine's behalf.[62] Others argue that search engines perform a press-like editorial role when they sieve through the internet to find those websites that serve the users' interests best.[63]

It is well known that search engines such as Google personalize their search results, taking the users' location, past searches, and other factors into account.[64] Also, even though most of Google's selection and ranking decisions are automatic, the fact remains that Google reserves the right to take manual action to demote or even remove from search results such sites that use so-called 'spammy techniques'.[65] These are techniques that aim to artificially rank a site at the top of the results page. Pages that have thin content with little or no added value such as automatically generated content or content from other sources can also attract manual action.[66] Conversely, search engines can also prioritize certain information. In 2020, Google prominently displayed

---

[59] *Reno v ACLU* 521 US 844 (1997).

[60] ibid 867.

[61] ibid 845, 853.

[62] *Metropolitan International Schools Ltd. v Designtechnica Corp* [2009] EWHC 1765 (QB), para 50 (hereafter *Metropolitan International Schools v Designtechnica*); see Joined Cases C-236/08 to C-238/08, *Google France SARL v Louis Vuitton Malletier SA* [2010] ECLI: EU:C:2010:159, paras 112ff (hereafter *Google France v Louis Vuitton*) for a more qualified answer as regards Google AdWords; R Elixman, *Datenschutz und Suchmaschinen. Neue Impulse für einen Datenschuz im Internet* (Duncker & Humblot 2012) 81; O Bracha and F Pasquale, 'Federal Search Commission? Access, Fairness and Accountability in the Law of Search' (2008) 93(6) Cornell Law Review 1149, 1193ff.

[63] OLG Hamburg, 22 May 2007, 7 U 137/06, para 36; A Milstein and M Lippold, 'Suchmaschinenergebnisse im Lichte der Meinungsfreiheit der nationalen und europäischen Grund- und Menschenrechte (2013) 4 Neue Zeitschrift für Verwaltungsrecht 182; E Volokh and D Falk, 'Google First Amendment Protection for Search Engine Search Results' (2012) 8(4) Journal of Law, Economics and Policy 883; A Haynes Stuart, 'Google Search Results: Buried if Not Forgotten' (2013) 35(3) North Carolina Journal of Law and Technology 463, 488 (hereafter Haynes Stuart, 'Google Search Results').

[64] E Pariser, *The Filter Bubble: What the Internet Is Hiding from You* (Penguin Press 2012); *The dangers of the internet. Invisible sieve*, 30 June 2011 http://www.economist.com accessed 11 December 2019.

[65] J van Hoboken, *Search Engine Freedom. On the Implications of the Right to Freedom of Expression for the Legal Governance of Web Search Engines* (Kluwer Law International 2012) 206; see *Search King, Inc v Google Tech, Inc*, No. CIV-02-1457-M (WD Okla 27 May 2003).

[66] Google, 'Manual actions report' <https://support.google.com/webmasters/answer/2604824> accessed 11 December 2019.

info boxes on health-related topics, so called 'Health Knowledge Panels', based on its cooperation with the German Ministry of Health (GMH). Following an action by NetDoktor, the leading online health portal in the German-speaking countries, the antitrust chamber of the District Court of Munich passed a summary judgment against Google, banning this preferential display of information as anticompetitive.[67] It did not consider that the agreement merited an exemption on the ground of an enhancement of the search engine's performance.[68] Interestingly, the Court held that the integration of the info boxes presented less of an improvement of Google's functioning as a shift to a different market, namely that of a publisher or of a provider of not entirely neutral content.[69] By highlighting the GMH content as the most relevant source of information, Google undertook a non-algorithm-driven editorial decision that was apt to contribute to public opinion formation in a not entirely transparent manner. It thus went beyond the role of an intermediary by providing its own products rather than offering third parties' products and services to users and answering their search queries. The right of the GMH or Google to press freedom was not taken into account in this competition analysis. This judgment has nonetheless been hailed as a milestone for media plurality and a free press.[70] While it has likely restored the visibility and click-through-rate of NetDoktor, it has spelt the end of the Knowledge Panels and condemned the GMH information to obscurity. The observations made in this ruling about Google's role as publisher, and the extent of its right to claim press freedom, are likely to stay relevant as generative artificial intelligence (AI) technologies become more prevalent.

However, even when search engines go about their normal business, automatically ranking search results, they make information accessible for their end-users. The automaticity of search engines' crawling, indexing, and ranking processes cannot call into question the human factor involved. The computer programmes that steer these processes are based on innumerable editorial decisions. Google's algorithms rely on 'more than 200 unique signals or "clues"', which are frequently updated to improve the search process. When ranking and presenting search results in response to a user's search query, search engines express an opinion on the search results' relevance.[71] They sift through the 'information overload' available online to choose the most relevant websites for their users.[72] They make editorial choices about what material to display to satisfy their audience. These factors support the conclusion that search engines

---

[67] LG Munich, 10 February 2021 – 37 O 15720/20.

[68] Consolidated Version of the Treaty on the Functioning of the European Union [2008] OJ 115/88, art 101(3) (hereafter TFEU).

[69] LG Munich, 10 February 2021 – 37 O 15720/20, para 118.

[70] T Höppner, 'Unhealthy ranking conspiracy: The German NetDoktor judgments banning the favoring of a health portal within Google search' https://www.hausfeld.com/en-gb/what-we-think/competition-bulletin/unhealthy-ranking-conspiracy-the-german-netdoktor-judgments-banning-the-favoring-of-a-health-portal-within-google-search/ accessed 5 January 2024.

[71] J Grimmelmann, 'Speech Engines' (2014) Minnesota Law Review 868, 913; Haynes Stuart, 'Google Search Results' (n 63) 488.

[72] See on the concept of 'information overload' A Toffler, *Future Shock* (Random House 1970) quoted by F Guerrini, 'Storytellers: Content curation as a new form of journalism' (*Reuters Institute*, 2013) <https://reutersinstitute.politics.ox.ac.uk/our-research/newsroom-curators-and-independent-storytellers-content-curation-new-form-journalism> accessed 22 May 2020.

exercise a level of editorial selection like that practised by newspaper editors.[73] At the same time, even though a search engine has control over the selection criteria, it cannot predict the exact mix of search results a given query will produce as this depends on the underlying online sources.

The comparison of search engines to newspaper editors does not yet answer the question as to the regulatory model that should be applied to them. On the one hand, it has been contended that the press model is the most appropriate one in view of the Supreme Court's reluctance in *Reno v ACLU* to extend the specific broadcasting regulation rationale to the internet.[74] Also, in *Langdon v* Google, a US District Court declined to grant injunctive relief against a number of internet search engine providers who refused to run ads for the plaintiff's gripe websites.[75] The Court held that such a 'must carry' obligation would contravene the providers' free speech rights in the same way that a right of reply was deemed unconstitutional in the case of *Miami Herald.*[76] On the other hand, the valid objection has been raised that Miami Herald was only one of very many newspapers at the time of the decision, while the Google search engine enjoys a dominant position. Moreover, newspapers mostly run their own content and exhibit their own editorial voice, while search engines merely provide links to foreign content, thus resembling broadcasters or cable operators who choose what to include in their schedules.[77] The analogy to broadcasters or to common carriers has been favoured by some in view of the increasingly invasive and ubiquitous nature of the internet and of the scarcity of attention and diversity in a highly concentrated online environment.[78] The choice of analogy matters. Comparing online platforms to common carriers means tackling monopolistic or near-monopolistic power and ensuring neutrality in access.[79] Comparing them to broadcasters means subjecting them to substantive regulations in the public interest.[80]

However, search engines and other online platforms do not—yet—actively produce or commission content as is common in print and broadcast journalism, but mostly rely on content which is available on other sites or which is posted on their site and shared by their users respectively. But while online platforms currently act as hosts of foreign content, this might change in future as strong economic incentives exist to produce content where the largest share of the audience is already located.[81] The

---

[73] I Katsirea, 'Search Engines and Press Archives between Memory and Oblivion' (2018) 1 European Public Law 125, 129.

[74] E Goldman, '"Must Carry" Lawsuit Against Search Engines—Langdon v. Google' (*Technology & Marketing Law Blog*, 8 June 2006) <https://blog.ericgoldman.org/archives/2006/06/must_carry_laws.htm> accessed 5 June 2023.

[75] *Langdon v Google Inc.* 474 F Supp 2d 622 (D Del 2007).

[76] *Miami Herald v Tornillo* 418 US 241 (1974).

[77] F Pasquale, 'Platform Neutrality: Enhancing Freedom of Expression in Spheres of Private Power' (2016) 17 Theoretical Inquiries in Law 487, 502 (hereafter Pasquale, 'Platform Neutrality').

[78] K Klonick, 'The New Governors: The People, Rules, and Processes Governing Online Speech' (2018) 131(6) Harvard Law Review 1598, 1661 (hereafter Klonick, 'The New Governors').

[79] See K Sabeel Rahman, 'Regulating Informational Infrastructure: Internet Platforms as the New Public Utilities' (2018) 2 Georgetown Law Technology Review 234, 242ff.

[80] A C Desai, 'Regulating Social Media in the Free-Speech Ecosystem' (2022) 73(5) Hastings Law Journal 1481, 1506ff; see J M Balkin, 'Information Fiduciaries and the First Amendment' (2016) 49 UC Davis Law Review 1183.

[81] Hindman, *The Internet Trap* (n 34) 79.

examples of Netflix and Amazon which started off as providers of existing film and television content before extending their business model to content production is a case in point. And while these companies do not currently produce news programmes, this might change in future. A further difference between online platforms and traditional media is that the former do not—yet—systematically make editorial decisions as to the accuracy or fairness of content.[82] Yet, this too might change as discussed later in this work.[83] At the same time, as will be explored further later on, online platforms are not the neutral conduits that they often portray themselves to be.[84] It has been extensively documented in academic writing that content moderation is at the heart of their modus operandi, rendering them distinctly different from neutral common carriers.[85]

The above discussion shows that the die has not yet been cast as regards the regulatory model to be applied to the internet, and comparisons between the old and new media are prevalent. The usefulness of such comparative exercises is doubtful and might obscure rather than clarify the issues at stake.[86] Uncertainty also reigns as regards the question of whether it is still appropriate to distinguish between different media sectors or whether it would be preferable to conceptualize the media landscape as a whole and to devise of regulatory principles that could be applied across the board.[87] Historic traditions and constitutional understandings of the different media seem to militate in favour of the maintenance of a policy per medium approach. However, convergence has undeniably brought about regulatory ruptures that have shaken the very foundations of the current media system edifice.

The next section will look more closely at some of the paradigm shifts that have occurred as a result of convergence, in particular as regards the online press. The notion of the 'online press' will be elucidated in the next chapter. It suffices to say for now that, in this monograph, this term is not understood narrowly in the sense of the online presence of the institutional press only, but in the sense of all factual news disseminated by traditional publishers but also by online only operators.

2.3 Paradigm Shifts: The Quest for a Regulatory Rationale Continues

Tensions underlying the abovementioned regulatory models have long been accepted as inevitable in view of the traditional segmentation of media markets. Licensing and due impartiality obligations for broadcasting, but not for the press, have been justified by the distribution of the former via the scarce and valuable electromagnetic

---

[82] Klonick, 'The New Governors' (n 78) 1660.
[83] See Chapter 5, pp 135–36.
[84] See Chapter 3, 46.
[85] Klonick, 'The New Governors' (n 78) 1661; T Gillespie, 'Platforms Are Not Intermediaries' (2018) 2(2) Georgetown Law Technology Review 198, 202.
[86] Klonick, 'The New Governors' (n 78) 1661; Pasquale, 'Platform Neutrality' (n 77) 512.
[87] See M Puppis, 'Media Governance: A New Concept for the Analysis of Media Policy and Regulation' (2010) 3(2) Communication, Culture & Critique 134, 142; Scientific Council for Government Policy, *Media Policy for the Digital Age* (Amsterdam UP 2005) 71; Q van Enis, *La liberté de la presse à l'ère numérique* (Larcier 2015) 28.

spectrum. The coexistence of balanced broadcast news with an unbridled partisan press has been abided by, even celebrated, as the enabler of a 'valuable mixed economy'.[88] Broadcasting, but not the press, has been regulated to protect minors, but also adult members of the public from harm and offence. The distinction turned on the fact that television invaded our living rooms and was consumed passively, while a newspaper had to be actively purchased. The public financing of public service broadcasting, but not of the press, has been defended on the ground that commercial media display unique structural deficits due to their reliance on private sources of funding.[89] The convergence between types of media content and of their modes of delivery has exposed the limitations of these technologically deterministic arguments and has laid bare their path dependence. Newspapers are not just 'news' printed on 'paper' but are also available on websites carrying videos that are reminiscent of television. Broadcasters publish websites that include text-based offerings similar to those available in print.

Yet even as convergence progressed, old paradigms and modes of thinking persevered. The Audiovisual Media Services Directive (AVMSD) aimed to create a level playing field between television and similar content offered via digital platforms.[90] At the same time, it reneged from this promise by imposing a lighter regulatory framework on on-demand audiovisual media services (AVMS) on the basis that these were 'different from television broadcasting with regard to the choice and control the user can exercise, and with regard to the impact they have on society'.[91] The application of a different regime to the same audiovisual content depending on its mode of delivery has been criticized as artificial and incongruous with user experience.[92] It has been further argued that the demarcation should not be based on the technical characteristic of linearity but on the journalistic-editorial influence on public opinion formation.[93] The revised AVMSD tried to make good on the initial promise by aligning the level of protection of minors and the derogations from the country of origin principle for linear and on-demand services.[94] This alignment took place by levelling up the rules applicable to on-demand AVMS while lowering those applicable to broadcasting. On-demand AVMS providers now need to ensure that programmes which 'may impair the physical, mental or moral development of minors are only made available in

[88] House of Lords, *Media Convergence* (n 35) 15.

[89] See Chapter 9, p 242. T Prosser, *Limits of Competition Law: Markets and Public Services* (OUP 2005) 210; R Foster, J Egan, and J Simon, 'Measuring Public Service Broadcasting' in D Tambini and J Cowling (eds), *From Public Service Broadcasting to Public Service Communication* (IPPR 2004) 151–52.

[90] European Parliament and Council Directive 2010/13/EC of 10 March 2010 on the coordination of certain provisions laid down by law, regulation and administrative action in Member States concerning the provision of audiovisual media services [2010] OJ L95/1 (hereafter AVMSD 2010), rec 10.

[91] ibid rec 58.

[92] J Weinand, 'The Revised Audiovisual Media Services Directive 2018—Has the EU Learnt the Right Lessons from the Past?' (2018) 1 UFITA: Archiv für Urheber- und Medienrecht 260, 273; A Breitschaft, 'Evaluating the Linear/Non-Linear Divide—Are There Any Better Factors for the Future Regulation of Audiovisual Media Content?' (2009) 20(8) Entertainment Law Review 291, 291.

[93] C-M Leeb and F Seiter, 'Rundfunklizenzpflicht für Streamingangebote?' (2017) 61(7) Zeitschrift für Urheber- und Medienrecht 573, 575.

[94] European Parliament and Council Directive 2018/1808/EC of 18 November 2018 amending Directive 2010/13/EU on the coordination of certain provisions laid down by law, regulation and administrative action in Member States concerning the provision of audiovisual media services (Audiovisual Media Services Directive) in view of changing market realities [2018] OJ L303/69 (hereafter AVMSD 2018), arts 2, 6, 6a.

such a way as to ensure that minors will not normally hear or see them'.[95] Regrettably, at the same time, broadcasters are now able to air the most harmful content, such as gratuitous violence and pornography, albeit subject to the 'strictest measures'.[96] Notwithstanding this halfway solution of sorts, the differentiation between linear and non-linear services, and the special treatment of television broadcasting remain.[97] This has been a matter of controversy during the revision negotiations, with the UK government arguing that the distinction between linear and on-demand services was still 'relevant, effective and fair', while the German government maintained that it was outdated and incompatible with the principle of technological neutrality. The former view prevailed, thus entrenching a differentiated treatment that becomes more and more untenable as media services increasingly converge. In the meantime, the UK government has backtracked from its original position. In its draft Media Bill, it has proposed modernizing broadcasting legislation, *inter alia* by extending broadcasting-like regulation to on-demand services, including those provided by larger non-UK platforms such as Netflix and Amazon.[98]

Furthermore, the revised AVMSD has extended the regulatory net one notch further to video-sharing platforms (VSPs).[99] However, the scope of the revised Directive is still not entirely clear. While YouTube is the prime service to which the newly minted regulations will apply, it is uncertain whether they will also cover the increasing amount of video content available on other social media platforms like Facebook, which host videos alongside written posts and images.[100] The Directive states that social media services will also be covered as VSPs if the 'provision of programmes and user-generated videos constitutes an essential functionality of that service'.[101] This would not be the case if the audiovisual content was 'merely ancillary to', or constituted 'a minor part of the activities of that social media service'.[102] In its detailed Guidelines on the practical application of the 'essential functionality' criterion, the Commission has indicated a range of factors that need to be taken into account when determining whether a service meets the VSP definition.[103] Facebook argues that it is still uncertain

---

[95] AVMSD 2018, art 6a(1)1. There were no restrictions for content 'likely to impair minors' provided by non-linear AVMS under AVMSD 2010.

[96] AVMSD 2018, art 6a(1)4. Linear services were banned from including content which might seriously impair minors in their programmes under AVMSD 2010, art 27(1). Member States can still ban the most harmful content under the minimum harmonization approach of AVMSD 2018. In the UK, punishable material and such that would be refused classification by the BBFC is prohibited. See Ofcom, 'On demand programme services ("ODPS") guidance. Guidance for ODPS providers on measures to protect users from harmful material', 10 December 2021 <https://www.ofcom.org.uk/__data/assets/pdf_file/0030/229359/ODPS-harmful-material-guidance.pdf> accessed 29 September 2022.

[97] See AVMSD 2018, art 1(1)(a)(i) on the distinction between a 'television broadcast' and an 'on-demand audiovisual media service', and the special rules for television broadcasting in AVMSD 2018, arts 14ff.

[98] Draft Media Bill (2023, CP822), cl 31–34.

[99] AVMSD 2018, arts 6, 6a, 28 a, b.

[100] L Kuklis, 'AVMSD and video-sharing platforms regulation: toward a user-oriented solution?' (*LSE Blog*, 28 May 2019) <https://blogs.lse.ac.uk/medialse/2019/05/28/avmsd-and-video-sharing-platforms-regulation-toward-a-user-oriented-solution/> accessed 15 January 2020.

[101] AVMSD 2018, rec 5.

[102] ibid.

[103] Commission, 'Guidelines on the practical application of the essential functionality criterion of the definition of a 'video-sharing platform service' under the Audiovisual Media Services Directive', 7 July 2020 [2020] OJ C223/02.

whether and to what extent a multipurpose online platform might be considered a VSP.[104] In any case, even if the Directive's reach is extended to social media services, the plethora of textual user-generated material that competes for online audiences with professionally produced content will remain firmly outside its ambit.

The AVMSD approach has as its starting point the implicit recognition that broadcasting regulation is needed, and that such regulation must logically be extended to other digital services that are deemed to be similar in nature. As has been aptly remarked, this view needs to be commended 'in so far as it avoids sleepwalking into deregulation'.[105] However, remarkably, it shies away from tackling the thorny question as to why certain media formats are regulated more or are afforded greater institutional guarantees than others.[106]

The divide between print and broadcast media that runs through our current system of media regulation, and the difficulty of locating internet services on either side of it has been discussed in the previous section. This divide is so firmly anchored in media regulation that it has been allowed to leave its imprint on the nascent regulatory system for the digital age rather than being abandoned as an old relic from the past. This is curious in view of the paucity of the justifications hitherto advanced in favour of the existing regulatory ruptures. The historical difference between the broadcast and print media, linked to their genesis in different periods in time, elucidates—but by no means justifies—the continued sway of their disparate treatment.[107] This disparity, which is partially linked to the historical accident of the genesis of the two media formats, is perpetuated by continuing to link standards 'to an accident of delivery platform'.[108]

We have seen that the technological argument linked to spectrum scarcity became untenable with the advent of digitalization. This provided leverage for the Peacock Committee, entrusted with a review into the financing of the BBC, to argue that broadcasting could be freed from regulation and be subject only to the general law of the land similarly to the printed press.[109] However, the extent to which the case for broadcast regulation rested primarily on spectrum scarcity as opposed to the economic characteristics of the broadcast market, has been contentious. The Supreme Court, in *Turner*, shrugged off demands to extend the *Red Lion* paradigm to cable in view of the alleged structural dysfunction of the cable market. It held that 'the special physical characteristics of broadcast transmission, not the economic characteristics of the broadcast market, are what underlies our broadcast jurisprudence'.[110] On the other hand, the Peacock Committee recognized that the broadcast model of regulation was conditioned not only by spectrum scarcity but also by the lack of a mechanism for subscription at the time.[111]

---

[104] S Nikoltchev, *Mapping of National Rules Applicable to Video-Sharing Platforms: Illegal and Harmful Content Online* (European Audiovisual Observatory 2021) 58.
[105] Rowbottom, *Media Law* (n 16) 283.
[106] ibid.
[107] ibid 285.
[108] House of Lords, *Media Convergence* (n 35) 13.
[109] A Peacock, *Report of the Committee on the Financing of the BBC* (HMSO 1986) para 694 (hereafter Peacock, *Report*).
[110] *Turner Broadcasting System v FCC* 512 US 622 (1994), 640.
[111] Peacock, *Report* (n 109) paras 423ff.

Also, as has been posited in the 'standard defence' of public service broadcasting, market failure in broadcasting was due to special economic characteristics of the broadcast medium, those of non-excludability, non-rivalry, and non-transparency, which would be unaffected by technological change.[112] The first two of these 'public good' characteristics of broadcasting have had considerable impact on media policy. They signify that the consumption of a TV programme by a viewer does not stop others from watching it, and that the marginal cost of adding extra viewers within a given transmission area once a programme has been produced is zero. By contrast, non-transparency, the fact that a programme's features are not apparent before consumption, has been less influential as it is not unique to broadcasting but applies equally to other cultural goods such as books.[113]

The extent to which broadcasting continues to be a 'public good' in view of the possibilities for encryption offered by digitization is questionable.[114] Digitization arguably does not diminish, and possibly renders more powerful, the case for public service broadcasting as will be discussed later in this volume.[115] However, to the extent that broadcasting is still supplied as a 'public good', the 'standard defence' of public service broadcasting fails to offer a convincing rationale for the special nature of broadcasting and for the broadcasting regulation model. Print journalism is arguably equally non-rival and non-excludable, given that any non-technological constraints arise from copyright law rather than being intrinsic to the medium as such, while the benefits it generates extend beyond those who pay for it.[116]

The main rationale for broadcasting regulation, its unique pervasiveness and accessibility to children, if problematic before, has been rendered even more questionable as a result of convergence. In *Animal Defenders*, the applicant argued that the ban of paid political advertising only on broadcast media was unsustainable. The argument that broadcasting had a uniquely powerful nature was unproven, especially in view of the 'growing impact of other forms of pervasive media'.[117] In any case, if the broadcast media were particularly powerful, this should be a reason to broadcast political speech, not curtail it. The European Court of Human Rights (ECtHR), contrary to the applicant's submission, held fast to the notion of 'the immediate and powerful effect of the broadcast media, an impact reinforced by the continuing function of radio and television as familiar sources of entertainment in the intimacy of the home'.[118] This is a recurring argumentative refrain in the Court's jurisprudence, the unique impact of the broadcast media having variably been attributed to the power of images,[119] the

---

[112] N Garnham, 'The Broadcasting Market and the Future of the BBC' (1994) 65(1) Political Quarterly 11, 13; Collins, 'Hierarchy' (n 31) 308.

[113] Collins, 'Hierarchy' (n 31) 308.

[114] J von Hagen and P Seabright, 'Introduction: The Future of Economic Regulation in Broadcasting Markets' in P Seabright and J von Hagen (eds), *The Economic Regulation of Broadcasting Markets. Evolving Technology and Challenges for Policy* (CUP 2007) 3.

[115] See Chapter 9, p 237.

[116] Collins, 'Hierarchy' (n 31) 309; M R Battagion and A Vaglio, 'Newspapers and Public Grants: A Matter of Quality' (2018) 65(1) Scottish Journal of Political Economy 21, 29.

[117] *Animal Defenders International v United Kingdom*, App no 48876/08, 22 April 2013, para 82.

[118] ibid para 119.

[119] *Jersild v Denmark*, App no 15890/89, 23 September 1994, para 31.

use of different techniques and means,[120] the passivity of the recipients,[121] the accessibility of broadcasting in remote regions,[122] the ability of national television to attract a wider audience on account of its objectivity and pluralism,[123] or the sensitivity of the audiovisual sector.[124] In *Animal Defenders*, the Court further argued that the internet and social media require certain choices to be made by the user, and therefore lack the synchronicity and impact of broadcast information.[125] Somewhat incoherently, the Court added that the UK ban on paid political advertising was proportionate given that the applicant had other effective means at their disposal so as to put their message across. The internet and social media, even though they had not been shown to be 'more influential than the broadcast media in the respondent State', were 'powerful communication tools'.[126]

The ECtHR's reasoning echoes the differential treatment of linear television from non-linear audiovisual media services that still underpins the AVMSD approach. Technology has surely given viewers more control over what they consume in a non-linear environment.[127] The image, however, of the media-literate and empowered users that can choose the offer that best meets their needs and can dispense with regulatory protection is questionable. The ECtHR has brushed off the argument that obscene websites are rarely visited accidentally, and normally have to be looked up by the user, by pointing out their free availability to anyone surfing the internet, including young persons that deserve protection.[128] It is doubtful that users have the know-how and tools at their disposal, and that they are indeed in a position of strength vis-à-vis service providers so as to be able to shoulder the regulatory responsibility to shape a safe, balanced, and diverse media diet. Unfair contractual terms and technical lock-ins are often skewed against them.[129] Also, in recent times, awareness of the impenetrability of often algorithmically generated editorial decisions at platform and intermediary level, have led to a quest for regulatory solutions to secure socially desirable outcomes linked to the diversity and findability of valuable editorial content.[130]

---

[120] *Schweizerische Radio- und Fernsehgesellschaft SRG v Switzerland*, App no 34124/06, 21 June 2012, para 64.

[121] *Murphy v Ireland*, App no 44179/98, 10 July 2003, para 74.

[122] *Manole and Others v Moldova*, App no 13936/02, 17 September 2009, para 97.

[123] *Pedersen and Baadsgaard v Denmark*, App no 49017/99, 19 June 2003, para 81.

[124] *NIT SRL v The Republic of Moldova*, App no 28470/12, 5 April 2022, para 192.

[125] *Animal Defenders International v United Kingdom*, App no 48876/08, 22 April 2013, para 119.

[126] ibid para 124.

[127] M Cole, J Ukrow, and C Etteldorf, *Research for CULT Committee—Audiovisual Sector and Brexit: The Regulatory Environment* (European Parliament 2018) 11.

[128] See *Perrin v United Kingdom*, App no 5446/03, 18 October 2005.

[129] N Helberger, 'From Eyeball to Creator—Toying with Audience Empowerment in the Audiovisual Media Services Directive' (2008) 19(6) Entertainment Law Review 128, 135.

[130] See Chapter 9, pp 253–54; E M Mazzoli and D Tambini, 'Prioritisation uncovered. The discoverability of public interest content online' (Council of Europe, November 2020) <https://rm.coe.int/publicat ion-content-prioritisation-report/1680a07a57>; Ofcom, 'Review of prominence for public service broadcasting. Recommendations to government for a new framework to keep PSB TV prominent in an online world' (Ofcom, 4 July 2019) <https://www.ofcom.org.uk/__data/assets/pdf_file/0021/154461/recommen dations-for-new-legislative-framework-for-psb-prominence.pdf>; Medienstaatsvertrag (MStV) of 14./28. April 2020, last modified by the 3d Medienänderungsstaatsvertrag of 1 July 2023 (hereafter 'MStV'), §§81ff; O Gerber, 'Background document' (50th EPRA meeting, Plenary session 2—Artificial intelligence and machine learning, Athens, 23–-25 October 2019) <https://www.epra.org/attachments/athens-plenary-2-art ificial-intelligence-machine-learning-background-paper> accessed 23 January 2020.

In any case, to the extent that digitalization has afforded viewers increased possibilities to filter out unwanted content, this no longer applies to pull services only, but also to traditional television. This raises a question mark on the dogma that linear and non-linear services require differential treatment.

As regards the respective impact of new and broadcast media, the Court's observation in *Animal Defenders* that there has not been a sufficiently serious shift no longer holds true. As far as overall news consumption in the UK is concerned, more people access news online than on linear TV.[131] TV still remains UK adults' favourite platform for news, but TV usage is on the decline while social media usage for news is on the rise.[132] For the 16–24-year-olds, the internet is already their most popular platform for news.[133] The decline in TV news consumption has been driven by the migration of audiences from live broadcast channels, where they might have lingered on to watch the evening news after a popular drama, to catch-up streaming services.[134] Meanwhile, audiovisual content is not only available on broadcast media and their permutations online, but also on print publications' online offerings and on digital-only publications. Admittedly, in the UK, the combined news consumption via the printed press and via newspaper websites/apps is also on the decline. The combined audience share of printed newspapers and of news accessed via newspaper websites/apps amounts to 38 per cent of all UK adults, down from 51 per cent in 2018.[135] However, this does not account for the uptake of newspaper news via social media, search engines, or news aggregators, which has yet to translate into a viable funding model.[136] Overall, the argument that television has a uniquely powerful role needs to be reassessed in the light of the changing ways by which audiences access news in the digital information ecosystem.

Underlying the dual system of media regulation is the perception that moving images call for special treatment, not least due to the ease with which children can access them even from a very young age.[137] The printed press, on the other hand, is a written medium whose use requires certain literacy skills. The moving image continues to act as a regulatory lever also in the digital age. However, the medium format becomes a less certain point of reference to determine which services to regulate, the more moving images and written word merge online. The extension of the AVMSD's material scope to video content in the digital press and on video-sharing platforms shows that, whilst the moving image still yields a unique power, this power is not distinctive to broadcasting. Still, the temptation is there to uphold engrained regulatory divides by way

---

[131] N Newman, 'United Kingdom' (*Reuters Institute Digital News Report 2022*) <https://reutersinstitute.politics.ox.ac.uk/digital-news-report/2022/united-kingdom> accessed 20 March 2023.

[132] Ofcom, 'News consumption in the UK: 2022', 21 July 2022, 13 <https://www.ofcom.org.uk/__data/assets/pdf_file/0027/157914/uk-news-consumption-2019-report.pdf> accessed 20 March 2023 (hereafter Ofcom, News consumption 2022).

[133] ibid 16.

[134] J Waterson, 'Young people in the UK abandon TV news "almost entirely"' *The Guardian* (London, 24 July 2019) <https://www.theguardian.com/tv-and-radio/2019/jul/24/young-people-uk-abandon-tv-news-almost-entirely-ofcom> accessed 24 January 2020.

[135] Ofcom, News consumption 2022 (n 132) 12.

[136] See on news publishers' efforts to obtain licensing fees from online platforms, Chapter 3, p 62 and Chapter 4, p 106.

[137] *FCC v Pacifica Foundation* 438 US 726, 727 (1978).

of criteria such as those of 'dissociability' or 'essential functionality'.[138] Such criteria aim to uphold the possibility of differentiating between media according to their preponderant mode of reception.[139] It will be discussed later in this book whether these criteria are meaningful and are able to yield the required legal certainty.[140]

A more plausible explanation for the special regulation of broadcasting is the notion that the use of a publicly held resource, the broadcast spectrum, calls for the imposition of public interest obligations that are devised and enforced by the state.[141] This quid pro quo rationale has been entangled in legal scholarship and jurisprudence with the critique of the scarcity argument.[142] However, there is no compelling reason why these two rationales should be viewed in tandem. While the scarcity rationale has passed its sell-by date, the fact remains that broadcasters are granted exclusive rights to use the broadcast spectrum, a benefit that is not extended to other media. Press publishers do not enjoy access to a governmentally allocated resource that enables the communication of their speech. They obtain the means for establishing their business in competition with other market players without the benefit of a government subsidy. Given that they do not enjoy the preferential treatment received by broadcasters, they do not have to operate their business on the explicit condition that they will serve the public interest, so the argument goes.

A difficulty with the quid pro quo rationale is that it is underpinned by the abovementioned market failure argument. The logic of regulating broadcasting based on the use of a public resource does not in itself explain why the imposition of public service obligations is needed. The justification is provided by the market failure argument, the idea that the market may not always produce the most socially beneficial programmes if left to its own devices. However, such market failure arguably also exists in the press. The same market pressures that force broadcasters to prioritize audience share at the expense of quality also bedevil the press. Print journalism is equally constrained by forces which endanger the supply of content that empowers the electorate and promotes political dialogue.[143] This begs the question why broadcasters are chosen to be the fiduciaries of the public interest, while the press is largely left to act in its own interest. Is the absence of the transactional relationship entered into by broadcasters a sufficient justification for relinquishing the power to further public interest objectives in other media sectors, including the press?

This question is addressed to some extent by the 'complementarity argument'. This argument seeks to justify the persistence of the longstanding dichotomy between the free press and regulated broadcasting models based on the complementarity between the two regimes.[144] The press, unbound by impartiality requirements, is given free

---

[138] AVMSD 2018, recitals 2, 5, and 6.

[139] See J Kahl, *Elektronische Presse und Bürgerjournalismus : Presserechtliche Rechte und Pflichten von Wortmedien im Internet* (Nomos 2013) 109.

[140] See Chapter 8, pp 223, 224.

[141] See C W Logan, 'Getting Beyond Scarcity: A New Paradigm for Assessing the Constitutionality of Broadcast Regulation' (1997) 85(6) California Law Review 1687, 1730ff.

[142] See ibid 1691.

[143] O M Fiss, 'Why the State' (1987) 100(4) Harvard Law Review 781, 788.

[144] Bollinger, 'Freedom of the Press' (n 5) 36; L C Bollinger, *Images of a Free Press* (University of Chicago Press 1991) 115; T I Emerson, *The System of Freedom of Expression* (Vintage Books 1970), 668; Rowbottom, *Media Law* (n 16) 286.

rein to be politicized and partisan, and to tread where media constrained by statutory regulation might be reluctant to go. Broadcasting, on the other hand, offers a more balanced, sober perspective, and provides a forum where the competing views voiced in the press can be made sense of and put to the test. Impartiality is considered key to ensuring that 'the broadcast media provide a counter-weight to other, often partial, sources of news'.[145] The 'complementarity argument' has been criticized as being too speculative and inadequately grounded in empirical evidence. It has been argued that, without hard facts about the performance of the two sectors, it is difficult to assess if the laissez-faire approach or the regulation model are optimal.[146]

Asymmetrical regulation is by no means confined to the press–broadcasting relationship. It is also at the heart of the German Constitutional Court's *Grundversorgung* doctrine.[147] According to this doctrine, as long as public broadcasters discharge their responsibilities effectively, programme requirements imposed on private broadcasters to attain balanced pluralism can be relaxed somewhat. Evidently, both the envisaged balance between public and private broadcasting as well as that between broadcasting and the press are idealized. What is more, the need to balance out competing models in the media market does not foreshadow the way in which the pieces of the regulatory jigsaw might need to be fitted to serve democracy in an optimal way. While statutory regulation of the press might seem unthinkable at present, a different regulatory scheme is not inconceivable. An imposition of certain public service duties on the digital press, perhaps accompanied by a relaxation of regulations on broadcasters' digital presence, has been envisaged as a possible way to reimagine the relationship between the traditional regulatory models.[148] It would, however, be precipitate to form a view as to the appropriateness of such a reframing of the regulatory expectations without having examined more closely the ways in which the press has been transformed on account of processes typically associated with convergence. These processes will be discussed in the following chapter.

2.4 Concluding Remarks

The traditional models of media regulation stem from a time when press publishers produced newspapers printed on paper while broadcasters transmitted radio or TV signals by utilizing the finite resource of radio frequencies. The press has been conceived of as a watchdog, and in the words of the German Constitutional Court, as a 'permanent intermediary and control organ between the people and its elected representatives', as the medium that enables public opinion to articulate itself.[149] The predominant understanding of press freedom has been as a negative freedom, a freedom from interference by the state. Broadcasting freedom, on the other hand, has been

---

[145] Department for Trade and Industry and Department for Culture, Media and Sport, *A new future for communications* (White Paper Cm 5010), para 6.6.1 quoted in Ofcom, 'Various programmes: RT, 17 March to 4 May 2018', Issue 369 (*Broadcast and On Demand Bulletin*, 20 December 2018) 21 fn 36.
[146] C Sunstein, *Democracy and the Problem of Free Speech* (The Free Press 1995) 108.
[147] BVerfGE 73, 118 (1986).
[148] Barendt, *Freedom of Speech* (n 13) 450; Rowbottom, *Media Law* (n 16) 287.
[149] BVerfGE 20, 162 (1966), para 35.

conceptualized as serving the free formation of individual and public opinion and as aiming at the creation of a positive, pluralistic system.[150] In the US, the regulatory divide between press and broadcasting is captured in the contrasting outcomes in *Miami Herald* versus *Red Lion*. In both legal systems a coherent constitutional justification remains to be found. Nonetheless, these diverse conceptions of press and broadcasting freedom have left an indelible imprint on media regulation, which has always vacillated between self-regulation and state control. The arrival of the internet has fundamentally transformed the two media sectors and has bridged the conceptual divides between them while exposing the inconsistency of their disparate regulatory frameworks.

The following chapter will focus on the transformation of the press sector, whereby the 'press' is understood not only as the institutional press in its print and online presence but also as the 'digital-native press' which comprises a range of online-only journalistic actors. First, it will trace the transition from the 'printed press' to the 'digital-native press'. Secondly, it will proceed to review the role of online platforms, social media, and search engines, which mediate a big part of the communication that takes place online. These 'new' players often dispute their media credentials and insist on being pure tech companies, while at other times they portray themselves as being akin to traditional media companies and strive to partake in their privileges. Finally, it will examine the position of the so-called 'citizen journalists', the (more or less) non-professional actors who engage in journalistic practices and news-making. It will consider the extent to which they should also be entitled to the rights, and asked to share some of the obligations, borne by traditional media.

---

[150] BVerfGE 136, 9 (2014), para 34.

3

The Notion of the Press Now and Then

3.1 Introduction

The word 'press', derived from the Latin 'pressare', describes first and foremost the method of 'producing written (or illustrated) texts by applying ink to moveable type or embossed engravings and pressing those onto sheets of paper, initially using a hand-operated press'.[1] The same word is also widely used to refer to journalists or to any type of news organizations. While it was the mechanical reproduction via steam-driven presses that enabled mass production and revolutionized printing in the nineteenth century, the arrival of the internet brought about a similarly radical transformation of the press. Since the 1990s most major newspapers have been publishing online editions of their print products. Initially, these online news offerings more or less replicated the content of the print editions, a phenomenon that was derogatorily referred to as 'shovelware'.[2] E-papers which offer all the presentational characteristics and a reading experience close to that of the print edition still exist, and are mostly targeted at an overseas market.[3] Online newspapers, on the other hand, offer a host of additional content, tools, and services, which differentiate them from the print edition.[4]

In the following we will consider, first, the impact of the disintermediation and personalization of news and of its dissemination by online intermediaries.[5] Second, we will examine the increasingly press-like role performed by these intermediaries and certain salient regulatory attempts to reign in their power. Finally, we will discuss the dissemination of press-like content by non-professional content creators and the German experiment at extending journalistic due diligence obligations to these actors without bestowing on them such attendant rights as may be required by their status.

---

[1] D Chandler and R Munday, *A Dictionary of Media and Communication* (OUP 2016).

[2] L Küng, N Newman, and R G Picard, 'Online News' in J Bauer and M Latzer (eds), *Handbook on the Economics of the Internet* (Edward Elgar 2016) 445 (hereafter Küng, 'Online News'); P van Aelst and others, 'Political Communication in a High-Choice Media Environment: A Challenge for Democracy?' (2017) 41(1) Annals of the International Communication Association 3, 6 (hereafter van Aelst, 'Political Communication'); C. A Scolari, 'Media Evolution: Emergence, Dominance, Survival and Extinction in the New Media Ecology' (2013) 7 International Journal of Communication 1418, 1424.

[3] M Deegan and K Sutherland, *Transferred Illusions: Digital Technology and the Forms of Print* (Routledge 2009) 36.

[4] See M Deuze, 'The Web and Its Journalisms: Considering the Consequences of Different Types of Newsmedia Online' (2003) 5(2) New Media and Society 503.

[5] When referring to 'online intermediaries' in the chapter, the emphasis is on social media platforms and search engines. The terms 'intermediaries' and 'platforms' are used interchangeably.

Press Freedom and Regulation in a Digital Era. Irini Katsirea, Oxford University Press. © Irini Katsirea 2024.
DOI: 10.1093/oso/9780198858607.003.0003

3.2 From the 'Printed Press' to the 'Digital-Native Press'

One of the most disruptive aspects of the transformation from the printed to the digital press has been the disaggregation of the different components of a traditional newspaper. As a result of digitalization, internet users can find articles on specific topics with the help of news aggregators, search engines, and social media while by-passing the publishers' actual sites.[6] This disintermediation of news content poses a risk for editorial integrity. It is harder to maintain overall balance when the emphasis is on standalone stories.[7] What is more, when reading a printed newspaper, readers are exposed to a wide range of content, including both soft news, that is, news that comprises a mixture of information and entertainment, hard news relating to stories of social significance, and non-news sections such as reviews or entertainment features. Printed publications aiming to attract a mass audience commonly place hard news in proximity to soft- or non-news content.[8] Similarly, public service broadcasters tend to schedule news bulletins between more popular programmes in the hope that they might retain the viewers' attention, a practice known as 'hammocking'.[9] However, the 'unbundling' of news content online means that users can more easily select articles they wish to view, potentially sidestepping public interest content.

Online platforms have little incentive to prioritize public interest news given that sensationalist content, coupled with attention-grabbing headlines, often referred to as click-bait, is likely to drive news engagement.[10] Headlines are the most-read part of online articles, and are crucial to increase the click-through rate, the proportion of visitors to a website who click on a link to a news article.[11] Given that a rising number of news articles are accessed via social media, search engines, or news aggregators, the function of headlines has shifted. In the past, headlines gave readers skimming through a paper an indication of an article's topic and of its importance. In the digital environment, they are primarily meant to lure readers into clicking through and engaging with the article.[12] The fact that headlines are disaggregated from the body of the article and from the rest of the newspaper, and that readers always effectively arrive at a notional 'front page' if they decide to click through, means that it is much

---

[6] Küng, 'Online News' (n 2) 449.

[7] K Riordan, 'Accuracy, independence and impartiality: How legacy media and digital natives approach standards in the digital age' (*Reuters Institute for the Study of Journalism* 2014) <https://reutersinstitute.polit ics.ox.ac.uk/our-research/accuracy-independence-and-impartiality-how-legacy-media-and-digital-nati ves-approach> 44.

[8] See R Fletcher and R Kleis Nielsen, 'Are People Incidentally Exposed to News on Social Media? A Comparative Analysis' (2018) 20(7) New Media & Society 2450, 2452.

[9] M Armstrong and H Weeds, 'Public Service Broadcasting in the Digital World' in P Seabright and J von Hagen, *The Economic Regulation of Broadcasting Markets. Evolving Technology and Challenges for Policy* (CUP 2007) 110.

[10] F Cairncross, 'Cairncross Review: A sustainable future for journalism', 12 February 2019 <https:// assets.publishing.service.gov.uk/government/uploads/system/uploads/attachment_data/file/779882/021 919_DCMS_Cairncross_Review_.pdf> accessed 24 February 2020 (hereafter 'Cairncross Review') 31; A S Kümpel, 'The Issue Takes It All? Incidental News Exposure and News Engagement on Facebook' (2019) 7(2) Digital Journalism 165, 171; J Kuiken and others, 'Effective Headlines of Newspaper Articles in a Digital Environment' (2017) 5(10) Digital Journalism 1300 (hereafter Kuiken, 'Effective Headlines').

[11] M Hindman, *The Internet Trap. How the Digital Economy Builds Monopolies and Undermines Democracy* (Princeton UP 2018) 150 (hereafter Hindman, *The Internet Trap*).

[12] Kuiken, 'Effective Headlines' (n 10) 1300.

more difficult for them to gain a clear understanding of the source and the importance of a given article. Since readers pay overall more fleeting attention to online newspaper articles compared to those of the print editions, their risk of exposure to less reliable news is heightened.[13]

To the readers' lack of orientation adds the fact that news accessed via newsfeeds or search results are in competition with a wealth of other online content such as gossip, humour, memes, posts by family and friends, and also content from groups and communities of interest. This blurring between personal and public information is especially pronounced in the case of the Facebook Feed, the platform's constantly updated, computer-curated selection of posts the users encounter when visiting their home page. The Feed has often been paralleled with the 'Daily Me', Nicolas Negroponte's futuristic vision of a virtual, daily newspaper tailored to each reader's individual preferences. The 'Daily Me' was imagined as a mix of 'headline news with "less important" stories relating to acquaintances, people you will see tomorrow, and places you are about to go to or have just come from'.[14] This early notion of an individualized news offering is not far removed from the Feed's blend of posts by 'people, places and things that you care about' as well as of ads.[15] Facebook allows users to sort their Feed to see only recent posts or posts from Favourites. By default, Facebook prioritizes the most popular stories, albeit users can choose temporarily to view the most recent stories first.[16] Popularity is driven by user interaction, and the more users consume, comment, and share news, the more visible they become, firing up further engagement. This self-fulfilling, cyclical process does not unfold in a vacuum, but is closely shaped by Facebook's ever-changing design choices.[17]

The ranking of Feed posts is not only influenced by the activity of an individual and that of their connections on Facebook, that is, the number of comments, likes, and shares a post receives, but also by the type of post in question, such as photo, video, or status update, as well as by other, not fully transparent algorithmic rules.[18] Researchers have tried to second-guess these rules by examining publicly available documents that Facebook has created in relation to its Feed, such as blog posts, patent filings, and Security and Exchange Commission filings.[19] These studies have confirmed that the factors that appear to guide Facebook's proprietary Feed algorithm are mostly

---

[13] N Thurman and R Fletcher, 'Has Digital Distribution Rejuvenated Readership? Revisiting the Age Demographics of Newspaper Consumption' (2019) 20(4) Journalism Studies 542, 556. See, however, on the difficulties of equating time spent with engagement T G Kormelink and I C Meijer, 'A User Perspective on Time Spent: Temporal Experiences of Everyday News Use' (2020) 21(2) Journalism Studies 271.

[14] N Negroponte, Being Digital (Hodder and Stoughton 1995) 153.

[15] Facebook, 'How feed works' <https://www.facebook.com/help/1155510281178725> accessed 5 April 2023 (hereafter Facebook, 'How feed works'); F Xhue and L Zhu, 'Social Information in Facebook News Feed Ads: Effects of Personal Relevance and Brand Familiarity' (2018) 25(4) Journal of Promotion Management 570.

[16] Facebook, 'How feed works' (n 15).

[17] M Carlson, 'Facebook in the News' (2018) 6(1) Digital Journalism 4, 13.

[18] D Matthieu and T Pavlíčková, 'Cross-media Within the Facebook Newsfeed: The Role of the Reader in Cross-media Uses' (2017) 23(4) Convergence 425, 427.

[19] K Cotter, J Cho, and E Rader, 'Explaining the News Feed algorithm: An analysis of the "News Feed FYI" blog', Proceedings of the 2017 CHI Conference (Association for Computing Machinery 2017) 1557; M DeVito, 'From Editors to Algorithms: A Values-Based Approach to Understanding Story Selection in the Facebook News Feed' (2017) 5(6) Digital Journalism 753 (hereafter DeVito, 'From Editors to Algorithms').

related to users' relationships; their preferences as gleaned from status updates; their consumption patterns, their past interaction with posts, their likelihood of future engagement; and the age and other content characteristics of stories. Interestingly, but perhaps not altogether unexpectedly, friend relationships seem to be the most important consideration, while content quality is the least decisive one.[20]

Facebook is protective of its Feed algorithm and has given no prior warning about its transformations in the past.[21] In January 2018, in a move designed, at least in part, to dampen the furore surrounding the circulation of 'fake news' during the 2016 American presidential election, Facebook tweaked its algorithm, so as promote content shared by friends and family over professional posts from businesses and publishers. Facebook touted this change as a way of prioritizing posts that 'spark conversations and meaningful interactions between people'.[22] This unexpected overhaul of the Facebook Feed, at the time called the 'News Feed', led to a decline in referrals to news websites with negative implications for their revenue streams and unsettling effects on their business models.[23] It particularly impacted on publishers' capacity to monetize branded and sponsored videos, which accounted for the lion's share of their revenue on the platform.[24] An earlier algorithmic tweak in 2014, prioritizing native videos directly uploaded on the platform over other formats, such as text and photo-based posts, had enticed news organizations to invest in native video production so as to maintain reach. The levels of effort and investment needed to adjust to this change were unevenly distributed between, on the one hand, broadcasting organizations and digital natives—video production being integral to their business model—and on the other hand, print publishers, hitherto accustomed to producing news in text and still-image formats.[25] Fast forward to 2016, and both print and broadcast news organizations had learned to play by Facebook's rules, creating content for its new Live video service in exchange for direct payments.[26] This period of mutually beneficial exchange did not, however, last for long. By 2019, not least due to Facebook's abovementioned about-face a year earlier, only approximately 4 per cent of its News Feed consisted of news posted by news publishers.[27] In 2019, Facebook launched a renewed media charm offensive by way of its News tab, offering initially US only and later European news publishers a monetary compensation in exchange for their content. Unlike

---

[20] DeVito, 'From Editors to Algorithms' (n 19) 762.

[21] On more recent attempts to increase transparency, see Facebook, 'Inside Feed' <https://about.fb.com/news/category/inside-feed/> accessed 26 February 2020.

[22] Facebook, 'News Feed FYI: Bringing people closer together' (*Facebook Business*, 11 January 2018) <https://en-gb.facebook.com/business/news/news-feed-fyi-bringing-people-closer-together> accessed 26 February 2020.

[23] N Newman, 'Executive summary and key findings' (*Reuters Institute Digital News Report 2018*) <https://reutersinstitute.politics.ox.ac.uk/sites/default/files/digital-news-report-2018.pdf> accessed 25 February 2020, 12.

[24] S Patel, 'Facebook news-feed changes will cut into publishers' branded content revenue' (*Digiday*, 22 January 2018) <https://wp.me/p2AShf-18TT> accessed 25 February 2020.

[25] E Tandoc and J Maitra, 'News Organizations' Use of Native Videos on Facebook: Tweaking the Journalistic Field One Algorithmic Change at a Time' (2018) 20(5) New Media & Society 1679, 1692.

[26] J Jackson, 'Facebook Live video service sees company paying news publishers' (*The Guardian*, 6 April 2016) <https://www.theguardian.com/media/2016/apr/06/facebook-live-video-paying-news-publishers-buzzfeed> accessed 25 February 2020.

[27] Cairncross Review (n 10) 66.

the News Feed medley, the News tab consists of articles drawn from reputable news publishers, notably including local news outlets, in exchange for remuneration.[28] However, recently, in a repeat of previous changes of heart, Facebook announced its plan to withdraw investment from news and to end human curation of the News tab, replacing it with a fully automated product instead.[29] This renewed loss of interest in news is widely linked to a growing raft of laws worldwide forcing both Facebook and Google to pay for news content.[30]

Facebook is not the only platform that is protective of its algorithmic ranking of news. The Google search engine, an even more important source of traffic to news media sites in the UK, is also secretive about the way in which its algorithm positions news in its Top Stories carousel. Only rare glimpses have been gained into the mysterious workings of the Google algorithm in the course of recent inquiries. In the context of the Australian Competition and Consumer Commission (ACCC) Digital platforms inquiry, Google revealed that two factors determine the position of news within search results: the strength of the user intent for news and the quality of news results. In other words, the clearer it is that a search query seeks to target news, and the better the quality of certain results, the higher these will be displayed on the Top Stories page.[31] The introduction of an algorithm transparency obligation in the Australian News Media Bargaining Code was fiercely resisted by both Google and Facebook on the ground that it would violate their right to business secrecy and undermine their business models.[32] A watered-down version of an algorithmic notification requirement was eventually included in the final version of the Code.[33] In the UK, Google informed the Cairncross Review that it had changed its algorithm to prioritize fact-based breaking news as opposed to opinion-based ones.[34] Not long after, it announced that it would elevate 'significant original reporting' in its search results, while conceding that there is 'no absolute definition of original reporting'.[35] Notwithstanding these small concessions to transparency, media businesses—print and broadcast alike—are hostage to the impact of search engines' and social media platforms' frequent algorithmic tweaks on the ways in which users access specific news items and

[28] S Levy, 'Facebook could help journalism by making news easier to find. The social media giant gave $100 million to help local news during the pandemic, but it still makes you hunt for trusted sources' (*Wired*, 30 March 2002) <https://www.wired.com/story/facebook-journalism-local-news-coronavirus/> accessed 27 April 2020.

[29] W Turvill, 'Meta to replace Facebook News tab's human editors with AI' (*Press* Gazette, 21 November 2022) <https://pressgazette.co.uk/news/facebook-news-tab-uk-automated/> accessed 5 April 2023.

[30] ibid; see the UK Digital Markets, Competition and Consumers Bill 294, 25 April 2023.

[31] Australian Competition and Consumer Commission, *Digital Platform Inquiry. Final Report* (Australian Competition and Consumer Commission 2019) 210.

[32] D Bossio and others, 'Australia's News Media Bargaining Code and the Global Turn towards Platform Regulation' (2022) 14 Policy & Internet 136, 141 (hereafter Bossio and others, 'Australia's News Media Bargaining Code').

[33] Treasury Laws Amendment (News Media and Digital Platforms Mandatory Bargaining Code) Bill 2021, 19 March 2021, s 52S; K Lee and S Molitorisz, 'The Australian News Media Bargaining Code: Lessons for the UK, EU and Beyond' (2021) 13(1) Journal of Media Law 36, 47.

[34] Cairncross Review (n 10) 65.

[35] D Bohn and S Hollister, 'Google is changing its search algorithm to prioritize original news reporting. Humans will train it, as usual' (*The Verge*, 12 September 2019) <https://www.theverge.com/2019/9/12/20863305/google-change-search-algorithm-original-reporting-news-human-raters> accessed 12 January 2024.

gauge the significance thereof. The concern is that if a news media business fails to comply with the platforms' underlying operational logic, they risk condemning their stories to invisibility, no matter how relevant or newsworthy these might be.[36]

The extent to which the 'shareworthiness' of news stories is influenced by traditional criteria of newsworthiness—such as negativity, positivity, and human interest—or is shaped by different considerations, triggering a turn to a more sensationalist direction, is subject to debate.[37] Similarly, it is uncertain whether social media audiences are more interested in soft news as opposed to hard news, thus furthering a softening of news and a much feared decline in informed democratic participation.[38] The research findings are mixed so far, suggesting that social media users do not only care for trivial human interest stories, but also for more socially relevant ones.[39]

There is also differentiation depending on the platform in question. Facebook, despite its capricious algorithmic shifts, is still valued as a traffic driver to news organizations' websites. However, its opaque 'relevance' criteria mean that it is more likely to suppress public interest stories, as in the much-decried case of the Facebook news gap on the 2014 Ferguson riots. Facebook's News Feed algorithmically curbed news stories about protests sparked off by the killing of an African-American teenager by a police officer in Ferguson, Missouri in August 2014. By contrast, Twitter's not algorithmically defined, reverse chronological feed acted as a catalyst for the elevation of this local news story to the national and international stage.[40] The handling of this incident chimes with Twitter's reputation as a platform for breaking news and participation in elite interactions.[41] As a result, Twitter is seen as a real-time source for news, to which users turn when purposefully looking for news, while news consumption is a more secondary by-product of Facebook use.[42] As has aptly been remarked, 'we seek news on Twitter but bump into it on Facebook'.[43] Since Elon Musk's takeover of Twitter

---

[36] T Bucher, 'Want to Be on the Top? Algorithmic Power and the Threat of Invisibility on Facebook' (2012) 14(7) New Media & Society 1164.

[37] T Harcup and D O'Neill, 'What Is News? News Values Revisited (Again)' (2017) 18(12) Journalism Studies 1470 (hereafter Harcup and O'Neill, 'What Is News?'); D Trilling, P Tolochko, and B Burscher, 'From Newsworthiness to Shareworthiness: How to Predict News Sharing Based on Article Characteristics' (2017) 94(1) Journalism & Mass Communication Quarterly 38 (hereafter Trilling, 'Shareworthiness'); P Napoli, *Social Media and the Public Interest: Media Regulation in the Disinformation Age* (Columbia UP 2019) 56 (hereafter Napoli, *Social Media*).

[38] See P Boczkowski and L Peer, 'The Choice Gap: The Divergent Online News Preferences of Journalists and Consumers' (2011) 61(5) Journal of Communication 857, 867; Van Aelst, 'Political Communication' (n 2) 9.

[39] Harcup and O'Neill, 'What Is News?' (n 37) 148; Trilling, 'Shareworthiness' (n 37) 55; A Kalogeropoulos, 'Online News Video Consumption. A Comparison of Six Countries' (2018) 6(5) Digital Journalism 651, 654.

[40] For consistency of terminology the name Twitter rather than X is used throughout this study. Z Tufekci, 'Algorithm Harms Beyond Facebook and Google: Emergent Challenges of Computational Agency' (2015) 13(2) Colorado Technology Law Journal 203, 213.

[41] A Cornia and others, 'Private sector news, social media distribution, and algorithm change' (Digital News Project, September 2018) 15 <https://reutersinstitute.politics.ox.ac.uk/sites/default/files/2018-10/Cornia_Private_Sector_News_FINAL.pdf> accessed 3 March 2020.

[42] A Hermida, 'Social Media and the News' in T Witschge and others (eds), *The SAGE Handbook of Digital Journalism* (Sage 2016) 81, 84.

[43] N Newman, 'Executive summary and key findings' (*Reuters Institute Digital News Report 2015*) 14 <https://reutersinstitute.politics.ox.ac.uk/our-research/digital-news-report-2015-0> accessed 30 March 2020.

in 2022, the platform's standing as a go-to destination for news and as the 'digital town square' has been somewhat tarnished. Meanwhile, the allure of the rival open-source social network Mastodon has quickly faded while TikTok has been mired in controversy amidst security concerns over user data.[44] The search for an alternative news platform continues.

The differences between platforms also have an impact on the so-called incidental news exposure of social media users. There is some evidence to the effect that users of social media, aggregators, and search engines often enjoy a more diverse and balanced news diet than non-users, and that this effect is stronger on YouTube and Twitter than on Facebook.[45] This has been attributed to the fact that internet users tend to consult a variety of sources of information, not least by way of search, leading to results which display hitherto unknown topics and sources. Also, as mentioned above, social feeds and recommendations tend to contain news next to non-news content.[46] As a result, even members of the public who actively avoid the news, either because they find it too depressing or out of resignation or otherwise, are still confronted with and potentially influenced by the news circulating in this 'ambient' news environment.[47] This incidental news consumption has been hailed as a way of breaking so-called 'filter bubbles' or 'echo chambers', and of closing possible information gaps.[48] It does, however, present a dilemma for news organizations who are dependent on consumer behaviour as well as on the opaque workings of the algorithm as far as news sharing on social media is concerned. So as not to remain hostage to fortune, news organizations have also embarked on the news personalization bandwagon, and embraced algorithmic processes of news production, in an effort to simulate the practices of social media platforms and to remain relevant, as will be seen in the next section.[49]

3.3 News Personalization and other Algorithmic Tools

The pursuit of news personalization by legacy media organizations is motivated by different aims. These range from the more commercial ones, to maximize clicks and the time audiences spend on site so as to increase advertising revenue, to the more

[44] J Nicholas, 'Elon Musk drove many people to Mastodon—but many are not sticking around' (*The Guardian*, 7 January 2023) <https://www.theguardian.com/news/datablog/2023/jan/08/elon-musk-drove-more-than-a-million-people-to-mastodon-but-many-arent-sticking-around> accessed 5 April 2023; M Ingram, 'Journalists want to recreate Twitter on Mastodon. Mastodon is not into it' (*Columbia Journalism Review*, 15 November 2022) <https://www.cjr.org/analysis/journalists-want-to-recreate-twitter-on-mastodon-mastodon-is-not-into-it.php> accessed 5 April 2023.

[45] N Newman, 'Overview and findings of the 2017 Report' (*Reuters Institute Digital News Report 2017*) <http://www.digitalnewsreport.org/survey/2017/overview-key-findings-2017/> accessed 4 March 2020; R Fletcher and R K Nielsen, 'Are People Incidentally Exposed to News on Social Media? A Comparative Analysis' (2018) 20(7) New Media & Society 2450, 2461.

[46] Cairncross Review (n 10) 31.

[47] A Hermida, 'Twittering the News. The Emergence of Ambient Journalism' (2010) 4(3) Journalism Practice 297; N Newman, 'Executive summary and key findings' (*Reuters Institute Digital News Report 2019*) <https://reutersinstitute.politics.ox.ac.uk/sites/default/files/inline-files/DNR_2019_FINAL.pdf> accessed 1 June 2020, 10.

[48] A Bergström and M J Belfrage, News in Social Media. Incidental Consumption and the Role of Opinion Leaders' (2018) 6(5) Digital Journalism 583, 594.

[49] Napoli, *Social Media* (n 37) 71.

editorial ones, to provide trustworthy and diverse information, to serve niche audiences, and to provide context.[50] It has been suggested that news personalization, if properly orchestrated, could help re-aggregate disaggregated news and restore the missing context by providing successive recommendations that include diverse perspectives and give the audience the 'whole picture'.[51] This would arguably restore the serendipity and heterogeneity that have been lost as a result of personalization.[52]

There is some evidence to the effect that news organizations have moved from the more commercial to the more editorial aims of news personalization in recent times. In other words, they have been more inclined to personalize their news as a means of reaching out to their audience, and of cultivating their customer loyalty and satisfaction. To be sure, this aim is not devoid of commercial interest. By fostering long-term commitment, news organizations aspire to enhance their customers' willingness to pay for a subscription. This is a shift from the original deployment of news personalization as a means of increasing the news sites' 'stickiness' and of harvesting user data to improve ad profiling and targeting.[53]

The value of ads increases dramatically when they are matched to the audience they are most likely to influence. However, personalized recommendation systems are challenging, and news publishers are at a disadvantage compared to online platforms when it comes to both technical expertise and user data.[54] News personalization therefore has only limited traction as a means of offering advertisers more optimal targeting opportunities. Nonetheless, it appears to have potential as a means of tailoring content to meet individual customer needs. One such success story is that of 'James, your digital butler', the bespoke email newsletter sent to subscribers by *The Times*. Set up in 2018 with the support of the Google Digital News Innovation Fund and in cooperation with Twipe, a Belgian analytics and artificial intelligence (AI) company, it prides itself of having reduced subscription cancellations, so-called 'churn', by 49 per cent.[55] Editorial decisions still rest with the journalists and editors, as reflected in *The Times* head of digital's aphorism that their 'editorial coverage is data-informed rather than data-led'.[56] The AI-powered digital butler's task is to deliver

---

[50] M Z van Drunen, N Helberger, and M Bastian, 'Know Your Algorithm: What Media Organizations Need to Explain to Their Users about News Personalization' (2019) 9(4) International Data Privacy Law 1, 14 (hereafter Drunen, 'Know Your Algorithm').

[51] B Bodo, 'Means, not an end (of the world)—The customization of news personalization by European news media' (2018) Amsterdam Law School Legal Studies Research Paper 9/2018, 15 <https://papers.ssrn.com/sol3/papers.cfm?abstract_id=3141810> accessed 17 March 2020.

[52] E Pariser, *The Filter Bubble: What the Internet Is Hiding from You* (Penguin Press 2012) 15–17; C Sunstein, *Republic.com 2.0* (Princeton UP 2007) 191.

[53] B Bodo, 'Selling News to Audiences—A Qualitative Enquiry into the Emerging Logics of Algorithmic News Personalization in European Quality News Media' (2019) 7(8) Digital Journalism 1054, 1063 (hereafter Bodo, 'Selling News'); N Thurman and S Schifferes, 'The Future of Personalization at News Websites. Lessons from a Longitudinal Study' (2012) 13(5) Journalism Studies 775, 776; W Kluth and W Schulz, *Konvergenz und regulatorische Folgen: Gutachten im Rahmen der Rundfunkkommission der Länder* (Hans-Bredow 2014) 10, 19.

[54] Cairncross Review (n 10) 44, 45; Hindman, *The Internet Trap* (n 11) 148.

[55] 'James—Automated and personalised reading lists' <https://www.twipemobile.com/media-innovation/james-your-digital-butler/> accessed 6 April 2023.

[56] M Kunova, 'The Times employs an AI-powered "digital butler" JAMES to serve personalised news' (journalism.co.uk, 24 May 2019) <https://www.journalism.co.uk/news/the-times-employs-an-ai-powered-digital-butler-james-to-serve-personalised-news/s2/a739273/> accessed 28 March 2020.

more relevant content to the right people at the right time, thus cultivating readers' habit.[57]

News personalization shows promise to achieve the desired aim of enhancing user satisfaction and cultivating audience loyalty, an aim shared between news organizations with both print and broadcast legacies.[58] However, a principal concern attached to news personalization remains. It is the concern that personalizing media organizations will reduce the level of diversity of the news on offer to users by locking them inside a bubble, consisting exclusively of content appealing to their own preferences and political orientation.[59] This could further undermine the 'linking function of a shared news narrative', which has already been put to the test by the widespread news consumption via social media.[60] Social media platforms, by stimulating alternative views and by providing a fertile ground for campaigning, have the potential to facilitate or even to promote the spread of sensationalist and misleading content, and to polarize.[61] There is some evidence that news publishers also tend to prioritize sensational, breaking, and entertainment news on their mobile platforms when compared to their own print and online sites.[62] If the mainstream media also cease to foster social cohesion, irreparable rifts are likely to arise with detrimental consequences for democracy. This is the risk of the experiment on which the *New York Times* embarked in 2017, namely to even personalize the story selection for its homepage. While the most important stories are still selected by editors, certain sections below the fold are algorithmically tailored based on individuals' geographic location and past consumption.[63] The *Times of London*, on the contrary, seeks to avoid the trap of a wholly individualized offering by restricting personalization to its distributed content, while maintaining the unifying experience of its homepage.[64] This makes sense also from an economic point of view given that the personalized newsletter is not likely to cannibalize consumption of the homepage content, but to add to it.[65]

News personalization is but one of the ways in which information technologies have changed the landscape of news production and consumption. Web analytics that allow newsrooms to monitor user behaviour online based on audience metrics is another. Online traffic affects not only story selection and placement on the homepage, but also

---

[57] M Migliore, 'The Times and The Sunday Times, The UK: James, Your digital butler' in European Broadcasting Union, 'News Report 2019—The next newsroom: Unlocking the power of AI for public service journalism' 15 <https://www.ebu.ch/publications/strategic/login_only/report/news-report-2019> accessed 28 March 2020.

[58] Bodo, 'Selling News' (n 53) 1065.

[59] Drunen, 'Know Your Algorithm' (n 50) 229.

[60] E Elvestad and A Phillips, *Misunderstanding News Audiences: Seven Myths of the Social Media Era* (Routledge 2018) 29.

[61] Council of Europe Recommendation CM/Rec(2022)4 of the Committee of Ministers on promoting a favourable environment for quality journalism in the digital age', 17 March 2022 (hereafter Council of Europe, 'Quality Journalism').

[62] A D Santana, 'Mobile Devices Offer Little In-Depth News: Sensational, Breaking and Entertainment News Dominate Mobile News Sites' (2019) 13(9) Journalism Practice 1106.

[63] 'Answering your questions about our new home page' (*New York Times*, 1 October 2018) <https://www.nytimes.com/2018/10/01/reader-center/home-page-redesign.html> accessed 1 April 2020.

[64] J Davies, 'The Times of London turns to a "digital butler" named James to increase subscriptions' (*Digiday*, 15 March 2018) <https://digiday.com/media/times-london-turns-digital-butler-named-james-increase-subscriptions/> accessed 1 April 2020.

[65] Napoli, *Social Media* (n 37) 73.

the phrasing of headlines and the use of accompanying photos, videos, and graphics. Web analytics programmes make placement recommendations, accompanied by predictions of the estimated number of visitors that these would bring to the site. These recommendations go as far as to dictate the selection or de-selection of a specific story. As a result, trending stories are likely to be followed up, while underperforming ones might be deselected in as little as twenty minutes.[66] The responsiveness of journalists in the online newsroom to algorithmically captured audience reactions is a far remove from the traditional separation between news organizations' editorial and business department. The rationale for this Chinese wall has been the protection of journalistic autonomy. Consistently with this separation, journalists have traditionally been reluctant to incorporate audience metrics into their decision-making concerning news content but have preferred to be led by news values and editorial judgement.[67] The tightrope news organizations currently walk between providing the public with the information they need and appealing to audience preferences is a narrow one, with the balance risking to tip towards a more consumer-driven logic.

To be sure, the need to maximize audience revenue and to compete with rival news organizations has been a constant feature of journalism.[68] However, the fact that the entire newsroom operation dances to the tune of market research raises the question as to whether media institutions can still be regarded as gatekeepers. Gatekeeping, one of the oldest social science theories used for the study of news, is understood as 'the process of selecting, writing, editing, positioning, scheduling, repeating and otherwise massaging information to become news'.[69] The dynamics of determining the flow of news items in the new media environment has been conceptualized as a turn from gatekeeping to gate-watching. Previously it was the journalists who 'kept the gates' by selecting which stories to report. Now it is the public at large which watches the gates that an item of information needs to pass in order to become news. It determines which of the material published by news organizations deserves to be granted an extended shelf life by discussing, evaluating, or republishing it.[70] In other words, users perform what has been described as an act of 'secondary gatekeeping' by boosting the visibility of a news item or by condemning it to invisibility.[71] News organizations, in turn, watch the gate-watchers in an effort to emulate and even anticipate public sentiment, all the while relinquishing control over news coverage, and ultimately their journalistic autonomy.

It is imperative that news organizations use algorithmic tools in news production and distribution only insofar as this is compatible with their editorial mission. Such use must be carried out in as transparent a manner as possible, allowing the public to

---

[66] E Tandoc, 'Journalism is Twerking? How Web Analytics Is Changing the Process of Gatekeeping' (2014) 16(4) New Media & Society 559, 568.

[67] ibid 563; P Napoli, *Audience Evolution. New Technologies and the Transformation of Media Audiences* (Columbia UP 2010) 32.

[68] J Harrison, *The Civil Power of the News* (Palgrave 2019) 80.

[69] P J Shoemaker, T P Vos, and S D Reese, 'Journalists as Gatekeepers' in K Wahl-Jorgensen and T Hanizsch (eds), *Handbook of Journalism Studies* (Routledge 2008) 73.

[70] A Bruns, '"Random Acts of Journalism Redux". News and Social Media' in J L Jensen, M Mortensen, and J Ørmen (eds), *News Across Media. Production, Distribution and Consumption* (Routledge 2018) 37 (hereafter Bruns, 'Random Acts').

[71] P J Shoemaker and T P Vos, *Gatekeeping Theory* (Routledge 2009) 7; J Singer, 'User-Generated Visibility: Secondary Gatekeeping in a Shared Media Space' (2014) 16(1) New Media & Society 1461.

know which parts of a news site are personalized, and to assess the factors that influence the prioritization of media content and the shape of their individualized news feed. Diversity in the selection, ranking, and distribution of news needs to be maintained.[72] Safeguards need to be put in place to guarantee that particularly important items of information will not be personalized, and that they will be prioritized.[73] Such prioritization needs to be performed in a transparent manner to ensure that no discrimination ensues against sources of news or media content on political, commercial, or other grounds.[74] Evoking normative arguments is, however, unlikely to be sufficient. News organizations will be more inclined to regulate the use of AI in their codes of professional ethics, and to adhere to these norms in their everyday practice, if this improves user experience, and hence makes good business sense.[75]

These imperatives are likely to remain forceful as news media, especially newspapers, and to a lesser extent broadcasters, decline in importance as the primary pathway to news even as they remain the main producers of original news stories.[76] As traditional sources of revenue fall, news media face the stark choice of pursuing new digital business models or being driven out of business. The impetus for media companies to develop sustainable online strategies is so strong that they seek to reconceptualize themselves as tech companies. The *New York Times*, for example, describes itself in job adverts as 'a technology company committed to producing the world's most reliable and highest quality journalism'.[77] Some news publishers seek to renew their brand identity to appeal to younger audiences, while others are less prepared to do so. The *Guardian Australia* uses the phrase 'We are not a newspaper' as their TikTok profile header. The *Washington Post*, by comparison, stresses its press credentials by proclaiming 'We are a newspaper' in its header on the same platform.[78] At the same time, technology platforms tend to dispute their characterization as media companies to fend off responsibility for the content they host. As has pointedly been remarked, this 'raises the specter of traditional journalistic news values' [sic] essentially being orphaned'.[79] The question whether digital intermediaries could be conceived of as media companies is the focus of the next section.

---

[72] ACMA, 'Australian Communications and Media Authority response to the Australian Competition and Consumer Commission Digital Platforms Inquiry preliminary report', February 2019 <https://www.accc.gov.au/system/files/Australian%20Communications%20and%20Media%20Authority%20%28February%202019%29.PDF> accessed 8 April 2020.

[73] Drunen, 'Know Your Algorithm' (n 50) 13.

[74] Council of Europe, 'Quality Journalism' (n 61) 22.

[75] N Diakopoulos and M Koliska, 'Algorithmic Transparency in the News Media' (2017) 5(7) Digital Journalism 809, 823.

[76] Cairncross Review (n 10) 17; R K Nielsen, A Cornia, and A Kalogeropulos, 'Challenges and opportunities for news media and journalism in an increasingly digital, mobile, and social media environment' 4 (Council of Europe 2016) <http://www.coe.int/web/freedom-expression/reports> accessed 7 April 2020; Pew Research Centre, 'New Media, Old Media. How Blogs and Social Media Agendas Relate and Differ from Traditional Press', 23 May 2010 <https://www.journalism.org/2010/05/23/new-media-old-media/> accessed 8 April 2020.

[77] Napoli, *Social Media* (n 37) 74 referring to a job advert by the The New York Times, 'Data scientist (machine learning)' <https://www.linkedin.com/jobs/view/data-scientist-machine-learning-at-the-new-york-times-1073768014/> accessed 7 April 2020.

[78] J Vázquez-Herrero, M Negreira-Rey, and X López-García, 'Let's Dance the News! How the News Media Are Adapting to the Logic of TikTok' (2022) 23(8) Journalism 1717, 1723.

[79] Napoli, *Social Media* (n 37) 74.

3.4 Digital Intermediaries as 'the Press'?

Social media platforms, search engines, and news aggregators curate, rank, and disseminate content, thus performing a powerful intermediary role between journalism and citizens. The early fantasies of 'disintermediation', the emancipation from middlemen that would come about with the internet age, have not been entirely borne out.[80] The expectation that control would 'shift from intermediaries—publishers, bookstore and music store owners, and so on—to speakers and listeners themselves' has not materialized, or at least not to the expected extent.[81] Users act as 'secondary gatekeepers', but they only do so on the back of digital intermediaries, which organize the wealth of information available online, algorithmically direct attention in the information economy, and shape interpersonal connections.

As already mentioned, companies like Facebook, Twitter, and Google have been at pains to stress in the past that they are not media companies but technology companies, that they do not produce but only host and distribute content.[82] Their resistance to their characterization as media companies has been a regulatory avoidance strategy, allowing them to position themselves outside the ambit of both content and economic policy rules. For a long time they successfully warded off their subjection to traditional media regulation for accuracy, fairness, or harm and offence. A motivation for pursuing this strategy has been the fact that the 'tech company' label brings the potential for higher valuations in the stock exchange compared to the 'media company' one.[83] The increase in the combined market value of the so-called 'Faang' tech companies, an acronym used for Facebook, Amazon, Apple, Netflix, and Google, is evidence of this strategy's success.[84]

A further motivation for digital platforms' self-portrayal as tech companies stems from the fact that a media-oriented competition analysis would subject their mergers to a public interest review. This would expose them to the risk of their enterprises being dismantled on grounds of plurality. Mathias Döpfner, Axel Springer CEO, in a discussion with Mark Zuckerberg, expressed scepticism about Facebook's forays into news curation lest the social media giant be qualified as a media company and split up as too dominant. He argued that Facebook should comply with requests to remove illegal content, but resist becoming the arbiter of what is good and accurate journalism.[85] It

---

[80] See E Volokh, 'Cheap Sspeech and What It Will Do' (1995) 104 Yale Law Journal 1805; R Gellman, 'Disintermediation and the Internet' (1996) 13(1) Government Information Quarterly 1, 5.

[81] G Magarian, 'Forward into the Past: Speech Intermediaries in the Television and Internet Ages' (2018) 71(1) Oklahoma Law Review 237, 251; D Ardia, 'Free Speech Savior or Shield for Scoundrels: An Empirical Study of Intermediary Immunity under Section 230 of the Communications Decency Act' (2010) 43 Loyola of Los Angeles Law Review 373, 383.

[82] 'Facebook CEO says group will not become a media company' (Reuters, 29 August 2016) <https://www.reuters.com/article/facebook-zuckerberg-idCNL8N1BA2UW> accessed 27 April 2020.

[83] P Napoli and R Caplan, 'Why Media Companies Insist They're Not Media Companies, Why They're Wrong and Why It Matters' (2017) 22(5) First Monday <https://journals.uic.edu/ojs/index.php/fm/article/view/7051/6124#2a> accessed 27 April 2020.

[84] R Neate, '$1tn is just the start: why tech giants could double their market valuations' (The Guardian, 18 January 2020) <https://www.theguardian.com/technology/2020/jan/18/1-trillion-dollars-just-the-start-alphabet-google-tech-giants-double-market-valuation> accessed 12 January 2024.

[85] <https://www.facebook.com/4/posts/10107028379388161?sfns=mo> (Facebook, 1 April 2019) accessed 27 April 2020.

is perhaps because of these concerns that Facebook was conspicuously slow in rolling out its abovementioned News tab and has initially all but hidden it from view in its mobile app's list of services.

In a US Congress hearing in the context of the Cambridge Analytica scandal, Mark Zuckerberg, Facebook's CEO, took a more qualified stance, disputing that Facebook was a media company while at the same time conceding that it not only hosted but also produced content.[86] This was an unavoidable concession given that Facebook had only a month earlier reached a deal with Major League Baseball for exclusive rights to live stream twenty-five games in 2018, marking the first time a major US league had agreed to show games exclusively on this platform.[87] In addition, Facebook Watch, Facebook's video-on-demand service, features a mixture of user-generated and original professional content as well as live streamed sports events.[88] Twitter also started streaming Major League Baseball and Major League Soccer games in 2018, in an effort to stave off competition from rivals such as Facebook and Instagram and to boost its advertising revenue.[89] The fact that these platforms' main source of income is the monetization of content by way of advertising suggests that they find themselves in the same market as traditional media businesses. This raises the question whether they should be regulated as such.

More recently, the big platforms, under increasing pressure to curb the spread of disinformation, have gradually become more susceptible to the notion of some form of state regulation. Zuckerberg agreed that online content should be regulated but argued that the level of regulation—in areas such as election and political advertising, and privacy and data protection—should be somewhere between that applicable to traditional media and telecommunication companies.[90] He argued that Facebook should not be called to make fine balancing judgements on free speech without democratic oversight.[91] Such moderation of user speech is typically outsourced to an army of human content moderators scattered around the globe. Notwithstanding the generally low pay of these moderators, their task is by no means peripheral to the service offered by platforms.[92] It has been demonstrated that 'content moderation is the

---

[86] M Castillo, 'Zuckerberg tells Congress Facebook is not a media company: "I consider us to be a technology company"' (*CNBC*, 11 April 2018) <https://www.cnbc.com/2018/04/11/mark-zuckerberg-facebook-is-a-technology-company-not-media-company.html> accessed 21 April 2020.

[87] S Shoshnick, 'Facebook signs exclusive deal to stream 25 MLB games' (*Bloomberg*, 9 March 2018) <https://www.bloomberg.com/news/articles/2018-03-09/facebook-says-play-ball-in-exclusive-deal-to-stream-25-mlb-games> accessed 21 April 2020; M Park, 'Separating Fact from Fiction: The First Amendment Case for Addressing 'Fake News' on Social Media' (2018) 46(1) Hastings Constitutional Law Quarterly 1, 11.

[88] Facebook Watch <https://www.facebook.com/watch/> accessed 22 April 2020.

[89] 'Twitter earnings boosted by major sports broadcasts' (*BBC*, 25 October 2018) <https://www.bbc.co.uk/news/business-45977288> accessed 22 April 2020.

[90] D Riley, 'Mark Zuckerberg: Facebook should be treated differently from media companies' (*SiliconANGLE*, 16 February 2020) <https://siliconangle.com/2020/02/16/mark-zuckerberg-tells-conference-facebook-treated-differently-media-companies/> accessed 27 April 2020.

[91] P Wintour, 'Mark Zuckerberg: Facebook must accept some state regulation' (*The Observer*, 15 February 2020) <https://www.theguardian.com/technology/2020/feb/15/mark-zuckerberg-facebook-must-accept-some-state-regulation> accessed 13 May 2020.

[92] A Chen, 'Inside Facebook's outsourced anti-porn and gore brigade, where "camel toes" are more offensive than "crushed heads"' (*Gawker*, 16 February 2012) <https://gawker.com/5885714/inside-facebooks-outsourced-anti-porn-and-gore-brigade-where-camel-toes-are-more-offensive-than-crushed-heads> accessed 13 May 2020.

central service platforms offer', the added value that sets them apart from the open web.[93] The abovementioned pressures have induced platforms to increasingly moderate obscene or violent content out of a sense of corporate social responsibility but also on economic grounds, so as to remain an attractive environment for users and advertisers alike.[94]

On occasions platforms' eagerness to protect their community by creating a sanitized environment has backfired. When Facebook removed the iconic Vietnam war Pulitzer-prize winning image of the 'Napalm girl', its decision was met with fury and disbelief. In an act of defiance, the editor-in-chief of Norway's daily *Aftenposten* republished the photo on the newspaper's front page along with an open letter, challenging Mark Zuckerberg to live up to his role as 'the world's most powerful editor'.[95] The editorial-like judgements platforms make about users' speech are carried out with little transparency or accountability.[96] Users can access the platforms' terms of service, but these typically consist of broad guidelines, which provide inadequate insight into the exact types of content that fail to pass muster in the ongoing process of systematic policing.[97]

In 2018, Facebook released for the first time a detailed version of its Community Standards in an attempt to restore users' trust in the aftermath of the Cambridge Analytica scandal. By bringing its hitherto secret content moderation rules to light, it exposed the enormity of its power to shape public discourse in ways that dilute First Amendment protections.[98] The 'Napalm girl' fiasco shows that the proscription of nudity, gratuitous violence, and hate speech can have unintended consequences for works of art or for legitimate political expression.[99] The extent to which this is actually happening is uncertain. Even the more in depth iteration of Facebook's Community Standards fails to convey the intricacies of enforcing them with the help of endlessly evolving guidelines that are only available to its teams of moderators.[100] It remains to be seen whether the establishment of Facebook's Oversight Board will lend more transparency to its content moderation process, a process that is criticized both for cutting 'much, much deeper than the law requires' and for allowing too much inappropriate content to stay on the platform.[101] The academic verdict on the Board has

---

[93] T Gillespie, *Custodians of the Internet: Platforms, Content Moderation, and the Hidden Decisions that Shape Social Media* (Yale UP 2018) 20 (hereafter Gillespie, *Custodians*); T Gillespie, 'Platforms Are Not Intermediaries' (2018) 2(2) Georgetown Law Technology Review 198, 202 (hereafter Gillespie, 'Platforms').

[94] K Klonick, 'The New Governors: The People, Rules, and Processes Governing Online Speech' (2018) 131(6) Harvard Law Review 1598, 1625ff (hereafter Klonick, 'The New Governors').

[95] Gillespie, *Custodians* (n 93) 10.

[96] M Heims, 'The Brave New World of Social Media Censorship' (2017) 127 Harvard Law Review Forum 325, 326 (hereafter Heims, 'Brave New World'); M Ammori, 'The 'New' New York Times: Free Speech Lawyering in the Age of Google and Twitter' (2014) 127 Harvard Law Review 2259.

[97] L Kuklis, 'Video-Sharing Platforms in AVMSD—A New Kind of Content Regulation' in P L Parcu and E Brogi (eds), *Research Handbook on EU Media Law and Policy* (Elgar 2020) 303, 311 (hereafter Kuklis, 'Video-Sharing').

[98] Facebook, 'Community Standards' <https://www.facebook.com/communitystandards/introduct ion> accessed 19 May 2020.

[99] Heims, 'Brave New World' (n 96) 326.

[100] J C Wong and O Solon, 'Facebook releases content moderation guidelines—rules long kept secret' (*The Guardian*, 24 April 2018) <https://www.theguardian.com/technology/2018/apr/24/facebook-relea ses-content-moderation-guidelines-secret-rules> accessed 20 May 2020.

[101] Gillespie, 'Platforms' (n 93) 207; J Naughton, 'Facebook's "oversight board" is proof that it wants to be regulated—by itself' (*The Guardian*, 16 May 2020) <https://www.theguardian.com/commentisfree/

been mixed so far. Some consider it 'a promising new tool for ensuring free speech around the world' while others lament the futility of its individualized ex-post review philosophy.[102]

Content moderation is but one of the ways in which social media platforms enforce editorial guidelines in a similar way to editorial desks or press self-regulators.[103] The ranking of posts by way of the Feed algorithm, discussed earlier on, is another example of the many ways in which platforms shape users' communication. As has pointedly been observed 'the moment that social media platforms introduced profiles, the moment they added comment threads, … the moment they did anything other than list users' contributions in reverse chronological order, they moved from delivering content for the person posting it to constituting it for the person accessing it'.[104]

Platforms have, however, been reluctant to acknowledge the human factor in their content curation processes. When the Trending News controversy erupted in 2016, sparked by a report which claimed that Facebook routinely suppressed conservative news stories in its Trending News panel, the platform went as far as to dismiss the human curators who were tasked with overseeing this module.[105] In an attempt to shake off the allegations, it entrusted the task of surfacing the most newsworthy and popular stories to algorithms, only to see Trending News turn into a breeding ground for conspiracy theories and false information, before abolishing this feature altogether.[106]

The criticism that platforms are engaged in a concerted effort to silence conservative speech persists. Both Texas and Florida adopted 'anti-online censorship' laws to prevent platforms from engaging in viewpoint-based censorship of users' posts.[107] NetChoice, a trade association representing large social media platforms, challenged these laws. Remarkably, the platforms argued that their content curation is protected speech, and that they are publishers akin to newspapers. The challenges let to two contrasting judgments. The Court of Appeals for the Fifth Circuit likened platforms to common carriers, which are subject to non-discrimination requirements. It disputed that their content curation amounts to First Amendment-protected speech and upheld the constitutionality of the Texas law.[108] The Court of Appeals for the Eleventh

---

2020/may/16/facebooks-oversight-board-is-proof-that-it-wants-to-be-regulated-by-itself> accessed 12 January 2024.

[102] K Klonick, 'The Facebook Oversight Board: Creating an Independent Institution to Adjudicate Online Free Expression' (2020) 129(8) Yale Law Journal 2418, 2499; E Douek, 'Content Moderation as Systems Thinking' (2022) 136(2) Harvard Law Review 526, 568ff.

[103] See Klonick, 'The New Governors' (n 94) 1631, 1660 for a rejection of the former analogy in favour of the latter.

[104] Gillespie, 'Platforms' (n 93) 211.

[105] M Nunez, 'Former Facebook workers: We routinely suppressed conservative news' (*Gizmodo*, 9 May 2016) <https://gizmodo.com/former-facebook-workers-we-routinely-suppressed-conser-1775461006>; Napoli, *Social Media* (n 37) 11.

[106] L Matsakis, 'Facebook is killing trending topics. The social network announced it was getting rid of the feature, which was the source of numerous scandals' (*Wired*, 6 January 2018) <https://www.wired.com/story/facebook-killed-trending-topics/> accessed 12 January 2024.

[107] HB No 20 <https://perma.cc/9KF3-LEQX>; Senate Bill 7072 <http://laws.flrules.org/2021/32#page=9> accessed 18 April 2023

[108] *NetChoice, LLC v Ken Paxton* (5th Cir 2022).

Circuit, on the other hand, rejected platforms' characterization as common carriers. It argued that their content moderation decisions are First Amendment-protected editorial judgements and declared the Florida law unconstitutional.[109] The Supreme Court's position on these diametrically opposed judgments is pending.[110]

The platforms' position to their classification has been clearly ambivalent, vacillating between their initial reluctance to acknowledge that they are more than mere conduits, and to acquiesce to their regulation as media companies, to their recent increased pre-paredness to portray themselves as publishers when opportune. Notwithstanding this ambivalence, extensive forays have been made in this direction, both at national and at supranational level, presenting the beginnings of a more coordinated approach if compared to the more small-scale, fragmented US laws. Still, these ventures have so far left the foundation of platform dominance, the providers' immunity from liability, unscathed. The following section does not claim to be a comprehensive survey of all attempts at platform regulation on a European, let alone global scale. It focuses in-stead on certain pioneering examples of such regulation in Europe: the AVMSD rules on video-sharing platforms, the Digital Services Act, the proposed European Media Freedom Act, the UK Online Safety Bill, the German Network Enforcement Act, and the Interstate Media Treaty. First, the legal framework, which has served as the foun-dation for online platforms' business model, will be briefly sketched before reflecting on the gradual sea change regarding the need to regulate digital intermediaries.

3.5 Regulating Digital Intermediaries as 'the Press'?

The meteoric rise of online platforms in the last two decades did not happen by acci-dent. The E-Commerce Directive intermediary liability exemptions, in tandem with section 230 of the Communications Decency Act, acted as catalysts for the unpre-cedented expansion of third-party content-based services in the European Union (EU) and the US respectively.[111] The so-called Good Samaritan provision of section 230 shields intermediaries from liability for the speech of their users if they take no steps to police it, while also extending this protection if they decide to restrict access to material in good faith. By averting the legal jeopardy for platforms that choose to moderate material rather than turn a blind eye to it, section 230 has been rightly char-acterized as 'a veritable Magna Carta of corporate impunity', more generous in its to-tality than the E-Commerce Directive conditional liability framework.[112]

However, after years of relatively unbridled growth, the tech giants have become the target of intense scrutiny by policymakers, the media, and the public amidst

[109] *NetChoice, LLC v Att'y Gen* 34 F.4th 1196 (11th Cir 2022).

[110] *Moody v NetChoice, LLC*, 22–277 (11th Cir 2023); *NetChoice, LLC v Moody*, 22–393 (11th Cir 2023); *NetChoice, LLC v Paxton*, 22–555 (5th Cir 2023) <https://www.scotusblog.com/case-files/cases/moody-v-netchoice-llc/> accessed 12 January 2024.

[111] See Chapter 7, p 177; European Parliament and Council Directive 2000/31/EC of 8 June 2000 on cer-tain legal aspects of information society services, in particular electronic commerce in the internal market ('Directive on electronic commerce') [2000] OJ L178/1 (ECD), arts 13–15; 47 USC §230(c); 47 USC §230;

[112] F Pasquale, 'Platform Neutrality: Enhancing Freedom of Expression in Spheres of Private Power' (2016) 17 Theoretical Inquiries in Law 487ff, 494; see J Kosseff, *The Twenty-Six Words that Created the Internet* (Cornell UP 2019) 65ff; see Chapter 7, p 177.

accusations of data protection breaches, rampant mis- and disinformation, and anti-trust issues. In line with the dual aims traditionally pursued by media regulation, some of the attempts at dealing with digital platforms seek to protect individual rights and the public order, while others intend to guarantee the openness and integrity of the information process, and the possibility of access to a wide range of trustworthy sources of information. An example of the former aim is the extension of the AVMSD to video-sharing platforms (VSPs) 'in order to protect minors from harmful content and all citizens from incitement to hatred, violence and terrorism'.[113] A further example is the controversial EU Terrorist Content Regulation.[114] While the former only covers audiovisual material on VSPs, the latter extends to all 'hosting service providers', and also covers images and text. The relation between the two instruments is by no means clear, but both reflect the resolve to police the digital world and to hold online platforms responsible for the content posted on their networks. This change of mood, captured by the term 'techlash', has also prompted a reconsideration of the continuous validity of the liability exemptions, especially regarding potentially dangerous or illegal content. These sector-specific laws have been complemented in recent times by means of the much-anticipated Digital Services Act (DSA) package, which sets horizontal rules that apply to all services and types of illegal content.[115] In the following we will consider the DSA and the proposed European Media Freedom Act (EMFA) before turning to German and UK (draft) legislation. While these regulatory forays are informed to a certain extent by platform logics, they occasionally hark back to parochial concepts used in 'old media' regulation. Pervasive uncertainty about the means and ends of the regulatory toolkit mean that the proposed frameworks are prone to incoherence and side-effects for freedom of expression and press freedom.

3.5.1 European Union

3.5.1.1 The Digital Services Act (DSA)

The DSA was adopted with the aim of ensuring a 'safe, predictable and trustworthy online environment'.[116] It entered into force on 16 November 2022, and it will become fully applicable for all entities in its scope on 17 February 2024. Its rules were meant to build on the experience gathered by audiovisual regulators under the AVMSD rules for VSPs. They were intended to set 'global standards which could be promoted at

---

[113] AVMSD 2018, rec 4.
[114] European Parliament and Council Regulation 2021/784 of 29 April 2021 on addressing the dissemination of terrorist content online [2021] OJ L172/79; see G Guillemin, 'EU Terrorist Content Regulation rights sell out' (*Medium*, 6 April 2020) <https://medium.com/@gabrielleguillemin/eu-terrorist-content-regulation-rights-sell-out-f982561d670d>; 'EU online terrorist content legislation risks undermining press freedom' (Committee to Protect Journalists, 11 March 2020) <https://cpj.org/2020/03/eu-online-terrorist-content-legislation-press-freedom.php>accessed 12 January 2024.
[115] European Parliament and Council Regulation 2022/2065 of 19 October 2022 on a Single Market for Digital Services and amending Directive 2000/31/EC (Digital Services Act) [2022] OJ L277/1 (DSA); European Parliament and Council Regulation 2022/1925 of 14 September 2022 on contestable and fair markets in the digital sector and amending Directives (EU) 2019/1937 and (EU) 2020/1828 (Digital Markets Act) [2022] OJ L265/1.
[116] DSA, rec 3.

international level', underpinned by a 'duty of care' and backed by a 'European regulatory oversight structure'.[117] They reflect the perceived need to harmonize the existing unwieldy emerging 'patchwork of national rules', such as the German Network Enforcement Act or the French Avia Law, which was declared unconstitutional by the French Constitutional Council.[118] This would ease market entry for newcomers who do not have the resources of the digital giants to respond to local laws. The Explanatory Memorandum to the DSA states that the Act focuses on illegal content, and largely stays clear of the regulation of 'harmful' content.[119] At the same time, the DSA obliges Very Large Online Platforms (VLOPs) and Very Large Online Search Engines (VLOSEs), which it defines as those with more than 45 million active monthly users, to assess the systemic risks stemming from the design or functioning of their service and to put in place mitigation measures.[120] One such systemic risk for society and democracy is recognized as being disinformation amplified by way of coordinated operations.[121] Consequently, even though the DSA does not specifically define or regulate disinformation, its provisions are likely to apply to disinformation and to serve as the basis for enforcing self-regulatory measures such as the EU Code of Practice on Disinformation.[122]

One of the potentially most promising aspects of the DSA are its algorithmic transparency obligations. The Act recommends that platforms make available an easily accessible functionality to allow users to modify the relative order of information presented to them, including by choosing an option not based on profiling.[123] The aim to empower users to exercise control over recommender systems is informed by the influence of such metrics on the ability of users to interact with information and by their 'important role in the amplification of certain messages, the viral dissemination of information and the stimulation of online behaviour'.[124] The DSA algorithmic transparency obligations could become the Act's most powerful weapon against the amplification of unreliable information or other harmful content. This will depend on the way in which platforms transpose these obligations and on the Commission's wiliness to enforce them. Regrettably, several factors already limit the scope and effectiveness of these provisions. The obligation to provide non-profiling options only applies to

---

[117] European Commission, 'DGx proposed priorities' <https://www.politico.eu/wp-content/uploads/2019/08/clean_definite2.pdf> accessed 13 May 2020.

[118] Act to Improve Enforcement of the Law in Social Networks (Network Enforcement Act) (*Gesetz zur Verbesserung der Rechtsdurchsetzung in sozialen Netzwerken (Netzwerkdurchsetzungsgesetz – NetzDG)*) of 1 September 2017, BGBl I 2017, 3352 last amended by way of Art. 3 of Law of 21 July 2022, BGBl I 2022, 1182 <https://www.gesetze-im-internet.de/netzdg/BJNR335210017.html> (hereafter NetzDG); Draft law aiming to fight hate speech online (Avia law) (Proposition de loi visant à lutter contre les contenus haineux sur internet) of 22 January 2020 <http://www.assemblee-nationale.fr/dyn/15/textes/l15t0388_texte-ado pte-seance> accessed 13 May 2020; French Constitutional Council, Decision 2020-801 DC of 18 June 2020.

[119] Commission, 'Proposal for a Regulation of the European Parliament and of the Council on a Single Market for Digital Services (Digital Services Act) and amending Directive 2000/31/EC: Explanatory Memorandum' COM (2020) 825 final, section 3.

[120] DSA, arts 34, 35, rec 76.

[121] DSA, rec 104.

[122] Commission, 'The Strengthened Code of Practice on Disinformation 2022' <https://disinfocode.eu/introduction-to-the-code/> accessed 15 May 2023.

[123] DSA, arts 27, 38.

[124] DSA, rec 70.

VLOPs and VLOSEs.[125] Beyond this non-profiling obligation, the DSA does not oblige platforms to offer a choice between different metrics, but only states that users should have this choice 'where several options are available'.[126] If platforms opt to offer this choice, their obligation will be limited to the 'main parameters' of recommender systems.[127] It is unclear though what these 'main parameters' are. In any case, if such options are hidden away in platforms' terms and conditions, the gain will likely remain minimal.[128] The extent to which such alternative metrics might cater to public interest-oriented goals as opposed to the platforms' business interests is also uncertain.[129] All these caveats limit the scope and effectiveness of these provisions.[130]

Other than this punctual attempt at enhancing algorithmic transparency, the DSA remains wedded to the somewhat parochial and limiting notion of publication. However, with the exception of certain content production ventures discussed above, platforms do not ordinarily actively curate or publish content in the way editorial desks would.[131] Social media platforms rely on their users to post or share content, and search engines depend on websites to make themselves accessible to them.[132] Their editorial decision-making is mostly related to the curation and organization of content rather than its production.[133] The difference in the editorial responsibility exercised by platforms and professional media has notably been recognized by the Council of Europe in its Recommendation on a new notion of media.[134] At EU level, it is reflected in recital 48 AVMSD, which clarifies that '[I]n light of the nature of the providers' involvement with the content provided on video-sharing platform services, the appropriate measures to protect minors and the general public should relate to the organisation of the content and not to the content as such'.[135] The Directive highlights 'displaying, tagging and sequencing' as methods of organizing content by automated means or algorithms.[136] It thus draws a line between the technical organization of content and its editorial selection that is carried out by audiovisual media service (AVMS) providers. While platforms are only required to meet the aims under Article 28b(3) AVMSD by appropriately shaping content distribution, AVMS providers are

---

[125] DSA, art 38.

[126] DSA, art 27(3)1.

[127] DSA, art 27(1), (2), rec 94.

[128] European Data Protection Supervisor, 'Opinion 1/2021 on the Proposal for the Digital Services Act', 10 February 2021, para 75 <https://edps.europa.eu/system/files/2021-02/21-02-10-opinion_on_digital_services_act_en.pdf> accessed 7 April 2023.

[129] See N Helberger, 'Regulation of news recommenders in the Digital Services Act: empowering David against the very large online Goliath' (2021) *Internet Policy Review* <https://policyreview.info/articles/news/regulation-news-recommenders-digital-services-act-empowering-david-against-very-large> accessed 5 January 2023.

[130] I Buri and J van Hoboken, 'The Digital Services Act (DSA) proposal: A critical overview' (*IViR Discussion Paper*, 28 October 2021) 38, 39 <https://dsa-observatory.eu/wp-content/uploads/2021/11/Buri-Van-Hoboken-DSA-discussion-paper-Version-28_10_21.pdf> accessed 7 April 2023.

[131] Klonick, 'The New Governors' (n 94) 1660.

[132] BVerfGE 152, 152 (*Recht auf Vergessen I*) 9.

[133] Kuklis, 'Video-Sharing' (n 97) 308; M D Cole and C Etteldorf, *Research for CULT Committee—Implementation of the revised Audiovisual Media Services Directive* (European Parliament 2022) 24.

[134] *Recommendation CM/Rec(2011)7 of the Committee of Ministers to member states on a new notion of media*, 21 September 2011, Appendix, para 15.

[135] AVMSD 2018, rec 48 (emphasis added).

[136] AVMSD 2018, art 1(1)(b)(aa).

also responsible for the selection of each individual item of content that appears in their schedules or catalogues. It is conceivable, however, that the configuration and prioritization of content might in future become more important than its actual selection, leading to a blurring of the two categories.[137]

3.5.1.2 The proposed European Media Freedom Act (EMFA)

The increased blurring between organization and editorial selection of content has been acknowledged in the proposed European Media Freedom Act (EMFA).[138] The EMFA aims to tackle problems affecting media services in the internal market with a view to protecting media pluralism and editorial independence.[139] It seeks to safeguard against both external undue political influence as well as internal interference with editorial decisions, to guarantee transparency in the allocation of state advertising and of state resources, and to protect the independence and sustainability of public service media. It also aims to replace the European Regulators Group for Audiovisual Media Services (ERGA), established under the AVMSD, with a European Board for Media Services ('the Board'). The EMFA is one of the pillars of the European Democracy Action Plan, the European Commission's blueprint for empowering citizens and building more resilient democracies across the EU.[140] The EMFA seeks to cast its net wide. It notes that VSP providers or VLOPS do not generally exercise editorial control over the content that they make available. However, in the ever more convergent media environment, providers have started to exercise such responsibility over certain sections of their services. As a result, the EMFA considers that they could be characterized simultaneously as VSP providers or VLOPS and as media service providers.[141] Presumably, this would only apply to these specific activities and not to the totality of the service. The qualification of certain sections of online platforms as media services makes sense in view of the gradual incorporation in their repertoire of more editorial functions. However, the classification as a 'media service provider' should be carried out based on the AVMSD criteria and not be left to the providers' discretion.[142]

The EMFA proposal has proved very controversial. The criticisms have primarily focused on the lack of EU competence to adopt such an overarching media regulation. While journalistic associations have been broadly in favour of the Commission's intention to support media freedom and pluralism, they have expressed concerns about

---

[137] L Woods, 'Video-Sharing Platforms in the Revised Audiovisual Media Services Directive' (2018) 23(3) Communications Law 127, 129.

[138] Commission, 'Proposal for a Regulation of the European Parliament and of the Council establishing a common framework for media services in the internal market (European Media Freedom Act) and amending Directive 2010/13/EU' COM (2022) 457 final (hereafter 'EMFA Proposal').

[139] Commission, 'Communication from the Commission to the European Parliament, the Council, the European Economic and Social Committee and the Committee of the Regions on the European democracy action plan' COM (2020) 790 final.

[140] Commission, 'European Democracy Action Plan' <https://commission.europa.eu/strategy-and-pol icy/priorities-2019-2024/new-push-european-democracy/european-democracy-action-plan_en>   accessed 12 April 2023.

[141] EMFA Proposal (n 138) rec 8 in conjunction with art 2(2), (10), (11).

[142] AVMSD 2018, Art 1(1)(a)(i); ERGA, 'Position on the Proposal of the Commission for a European Media Freedom Act (EMFA)', November 2022 <https://erga-online.eu/wp-content/uploads/2022/11/ EMFA-ERGA-draft-position-adopted-2022.11.25.pdf> accessed 11 April 2023 (hereafter 'ERGA Position').

the risk of interference with national media markets.[143] They have argued that the future cooperation between the Commission and the insufficiently independent future Board might jeopardize the sovereignty of national media systems. What is more, the extension of the Board's competencies to all media, including the printed press, compared to only the audiovisual media under ERGA, has been viewed as the beginning of regulatory oversight of the media at EU level and the death knell for press freedom.[144] ERGA has been quick to assert that 'it is neither its vocation nor its intention to regulate the press sector' and that it would seek explicit clarification, at least in the recitals, that the EMFA would not introduce 'any regulation of the written press per se' by the future Board.[145] The use of 'per se' suggests that the situation may not be clear-cut. The progressive intermingling of print and audiovisual, old and new media may mean that upholding their regulatory silos will be increasingly counterintuitive.

3.5.2   Germany

3.5.2.1 The German Network Enforcement Act (Netzwerkdurchsetzungsgesetz, NetzDG)

The NetzDG seeks to complement platforms' self-regulatory standards by exerting pressure on them to comply with the law. It imposes drastic obligations on social media networks only as regards unlawful content breaching specific provisions of the Criminal Code. It obliges them to typically remove clearly illegal content within twenty-four hours and other, not obviously illegal content, within seven days under pain of draconian sanctions for systemic noncompliance.[146] The law only applies to social media platforms that have at least two million registered users in Germany.[147] The NetzDG has been controversial. It has been credited by some as a possible foundation for the reform of platform liability in the US whilst being condemned by others as a 'prototype for global online censorship'.[148] The criticism has focused on the risk of stifling freedom of expression due to the 'overblocking' of content.[149] It

---

[143] European Magazine Media Association and European Newspaper Publishers' Association, 'EMMA-ENPA comments on the European Media Freedom Act Proposal', 19 January 2023, 1ff https://ec.europa.eu/info/law/better-regulation/have-your-say/initiatives/13206-Safeguarding-media-freedom-in-the-EU-new-rules/F3375767_en accessed 11 April 2023.

[144] ibid 3.

[145] ERGA Position (n 142) 1.

[146] NetzDG, §3(2) No 2, 3.

[147] NetzDG, §1(2).

[148] P Zurth, 'The German NetzDG as Role Model or Cautionary Tale? Implications for the Debate on Social Media Liability' (2019) 31(4) Fordham Intellectual Property, Media and Entertainment Law Journal 1084; J Mchangama and J Fiss, *The Digital Berlin Wall: How Germany (Accidentally) Created a Prototype for Global Online Censorship* (Justitia 2019).

[149] Wissenschaftliche Dienste des Deutschen Bundestages, 'Entwurf eines Netzwerkdurchsetzungsgesetzes. Vereinbarkeit mit der Meinungsfreiheit', WD 10-3000-037/17, 12 June 2017 <https://www.bundestag.de/resource/blob/510514/eefb7cf92dee88ec74ce8e796e9bc25c/wd-10-037-17-pdf-data.pdf> accessed 12 January 2024; K H Ladeur and T Gostomzyk, 'Gutachten zur Verfassungsmäßigkeit des Entwurfs eines Gesetzes zur Verbesserung der Rechtsdurchsetzung in sozialen Netzwerken (Netzwerkdurchsetzungsgesetz – NetzDG) i.d.F. vom 16. Mai 2017 – BT-Drs. 18/12356. Erstattet auf Ansuchen des Bitkom', May 2017 <https://www.cr-online.de/NetzDG-Gutachten-Gostomzyk-Ladeur.pdf>; accessed 12 January 2024;

has been rightly argued that the Act penalized the under- but not the over-removal of content. The actual existence of 'overblocking' has, however, been contested. Some studies conclude that the NetzDG incentivizes platforms to quickly remove content that has been the subject of a complaint.[150] Others deny that there is evidence for 'overblocking'.[151] Indeed, such conclusive empirical evidence has been hard to find given the intransparency of platforms' moderation practice. Facebook has prioritized the complaint mechanism based on its own community standards, while hiding away the NetzDG complaint form.[152]

The NetzDG has been amended in an effort to plug these loopholes and to strengthen users' rights. The amended law includes a broad definition of 'complaints about illegal content'.[153] As a result, transparency reports arguably also need to encompass complaints and deletions based on alleged contraventions of community standards, not only of the law.[154] Moreover, the amended NetzDG obliges platforms to establish an appeals procedure against their decisions and paves the way for an out-of-court settlement of disputes.[155] These amendments have been taken to signify a move away from a wholly compliance-based approach to one stipulating design principles for social media platforms.[156] Users' rights have been further strengthened beyond the NetzDG by way of recent case law requiring the notification of users prior to moderation decisions and account takedowns.[157] Furthermore, the government has announced its intention to introduce judicial oversight mechanisms before such takedowns.[158] These jurisprudential and legislative measures will help reduce the possible risk of 'overblocking'. However, given that the DSA fully harmonizes intermediaries' obligations to protect users from unlawful content, it is

J Wimmers and B Heymann, 'Zum Referentenentwurf eines Netzwerkdurchsetzungsgesetzes (NetzDG) – Eine kritische Stellungnahme' (2017) 2 Archiv für Presserecht 93, 98ff.

[150] M Liesching and others, *Das NetzDG in der praktischen Anwendung. Eine Teilevaluation des Netzwerkdurchsetzungsgesetzes* (Carl Grossman Verlag 2021) 10 (hereafter Liesching, *Das NetzDG in der praktischen Anwendung*); E Hoven and H Gersdorf, '§1 NetzDG' in H Gersdorf and P Paal, *Informations- und Medienrecht Kommentar* (2nd edn, Beck 2021) para 24 (hereafter Hoven/Gersdorf, '§1 NetzDG').

[151] Bundesjustizministerium, 'Bericht der Bundesregierung zur Evaluierung des Gesetzes zur Verbesserung der Rechtsdurchsetzung in sozialen Netzwerken (Netzwerkdurchsetzungsgesetz – NetzDG))', 9 September 2020 <https://www.rosenburg.bmj.de/SharedDocs/Downloads/DE/News/PM/090920_Eva luierungsbericht_NetzDG.html> 21 accessed 12 January 2023.

[152] C Kalbhenn and M Hemmert-Halswick, 'Der Regierungentwurf zur Änderung des NetzDG. Vom Compliance-Ansatz zu Designvorgaben' (2020) Multimedia und Recht 518, 519 (hereafter Kalbhenn and Hemmert-Halswick, 'Der Regierungentwurf zur Änderung des NetzDG'). NetzDG, §1(4).

[153] NetzDG, §1(4).

[154] Kalbhenn and Hemmert-Halswick, 'Der Regierungentwurf zur Änderung des NetzDG' (n 152) 521; contra Liesching, *Das NetzDG in der praktischen Anwendung* (n 150) 167; cf L Knoke and H Krüger, '§2 NetzDG' in H Gersdorf and P Paal (eds), *Informations- und Medienrecht Kommentar* (2nd edn, Beck 2021) paras 17, 20.

[155] NetzDG, §§3b, c.

[156] Kalbhenn and Hemmert-Halswick, 'Der Regierungentwurf zur Änderung des NetzDG' (n 152) 520.

[157] BGH, 29 July 2021, III ZR 179/20; L F Müller, 'Grundrechtsschutz durch Verfahren im Social Media Recht – Maßgaben für die Moderation nicht-justiziabler Inhalte in sozialen Netzwerken' (2022) 2 Archiv für Presserecht 104.

[158] Koalitionsvertrag 2021-2025 zwischen SPD, Bündnis 90/Die Grünen und FDP, 'Mehr Fortschritt wagen' <https://www.bundesregierung.de/resource/blob/974430/1990812/1f422c60505b6a88f8f3b3b5b 8720bd4/2021-12-10-koav2021-data.pdf?download=1> accessed 12 January 2024, 18.

likely that the NetzDG will be superseded once the DSA becomes fully applicable in February 2024.[159]

3.5.2.2 The German Interstate Media Treaty (Medienstaatsvertrag, MStV)
A different approach to platform regulation is taken by the German Interstate Media Treaty, which entered into force after lengthy negotiations on 7 November 2020.[160] A focal point of the new Media Treaty is the organization of content by digital platforms. It signified the first EU Member State legislative attempt to regulate social media platforms' algorithms for diversity and transparency, and to oblige them to publicize algorithmic changes.[161] It aims to do so by extending the existing Interstate Broadcasting Treaty (*Rundfunkstaatsvertrag*, RStV),[162] the main regulatory framework for nationwide broadcasting and online services, so-called telemedia (*Telemedien*) in the German terminology.[163] A type of online services covered by the Media Treaty are media intermediaries. They are somewhat cryptically defined as 'any telemedia, which also aggregates, selects and presents third-party journalistic-editorial offerings without bundling them in a complete offering'.[164] An earlier Treaty draft named search engines, social networks, app portals, user-generated content portals, blogs, and news aggregators as indicative examples of services that are considered to be intermediaries. This list of digital offers has been removed from the final text but gives an idea of the services to be covered by the new Treaty. Exempt from the new rules are media intermediaries that reach less than one million users in Germany per month on average of six months; that are specialized in the aggregation, selection, and presentation of content related to products or services; or that serve exclusively private and family purposes.[165] Further, the Treaty also regulates media platforms, defined as any telemedia which bundle broadcasting, TV-like services or journalistic-editorial content in a complete offering determined by the provider, such as in the case of Netflix, as well

[159] M Rössel, 'Digital Services Act. Eingehende Analyse und Überprüfung der regulatorischen Neuerungen aus dem Trilog und potentieller Lücken' (2023) 2 Archiv für Presserecht 93, 94; A Grünwald and C Nüßing, 'Vom NetzDG zum DSA: Wachablösung baim Kampf gegen Hate Speech? Diskussionsstand zu beiden Gesetzesvorhaben und deren Vereinbarkeit' (2021) Multimedia und Recht 283, 286ff. The same applies to other Member State laws that have pre-empted EU legislation, such as the French Decree 2022-32 of 14 January 2022 applying art 42 of Law no 2021-1109 of 24 August 2021 safeguarding respect for the principles of the Republic and fixing a connection threshold above which online platform operators must help combat the public dissemination of illicit content (Décret confortant le respect des principes de la République et relatif à la fixation d'un seuil de connexions à partir duquel les opérateurs de plateformes en ligne concourent à la lutte contre la diffusion publique des contenus illicites), JO 0013 of 16 January 2022, which will only apply until 31 December 2023.
[160] Medienstaatsvertrag (MStV) of 14./28. April 2020, last modified by the 3d Medienänderungsstaatsvertrag of 1 July 2023 (hereafter 'MStV').
[161] ibid §93(3).
[162] Staatsvertrag für Rundfunk und Telemedien of 31 August 1991, last modified by the 22nd Rundfunkänderungsstaatsvetrag of 1 May 2019, §54 (2) (hereafter 'RStV').
[163] The telemedia are an amalgamation of two originally distinct services: the tele services, intended for individual communication and regulated at federal level, and the media services, intended for the general public, and regulated at state level. This artificial dichotomy came to an end with the Telemediengesetz (TMG) of 26 February 2007. See J Weinand, *Implementing the EU Audiovisual Media Services Directive: Selected Issues in the Regulation of AVMS by National Media Authorities of France, Germany and the UK* (Nomos 2018) 235ff.
[164] MStV, §2(2)16.
[165] MStV, §91(2).

as user interfaces, which provide an overview over content or services of media platforms, such as smart TV interfaces or interfaces of OTT platforms such as Netflix.[166]
User interfaces are closely linked with media platforms. Their exact delineation from
media intermediaries, however, still needs to be thrashed out given that it has regulatory implications, as will be seen in the following.

A guidance document and a decision of the Commission on Licensing and
Supervision of Media Authorities (*Kommission für Zulassung und Aufsicht der
Landesmedienanstalten*, ZAK), the central organ that deals with the licensing and
monitoring of nationwide private broadcasters, platform regulation, and digital
broadcasting developments, have contributed to greater clarity in that regard. The
ZAK held that the *Google News Showcase* service, a dedicated news service which
pays fees to participating news publishers to prominently showcase their content, is
a platform and a user interface, not a media intermediary.[167] Making the distinction
between a media intermediary and a media platform needs to be carried out on a case-
by-case basis with view to the design, content, user group, and technical features of
a service.[168] Defining characteristics of a media platform are the specific selection of
service users and of the content on offer. These criteria are met in the case of the *Google
News Showcase* service but not, for example, in the case of the Google search engine.
Google decides which publishers will be admitted to the *Showcase* service. The inclusion of specific articles in the service is based on a contract between Google and the
publisher which determines the framework for the selection of content and the update frequency. Search engines do not perform such precise user and content selection
given that they crawl and index, at least in theory, the entirety of the open internet.

First, platforms are subject to a prohibition of discrimination as well as to transparency obligations.[169] These requirements apply both to broadcast content, to that
of TV-like telemedia as well as to that of telemedia with journalistic-editorial offerings, which reproduce in full or in part the content of periodic prints. It has been observed that platforms would be unlikely to discriminate against specific material as
this would go against their business model, which consists in the provision of a wide
variety of content.[170] This argument overlooks the fact that platforms and their recommendation algorithms have their own logics and ideologies, which do not always
prioritize the provision of a pluralistic offering.[171] Still, the proof that, for instance, one
genre was unjustifiably favoured over another, would be hard to furnish.[172] Besides,

---

[166] MStV, §2(2)14, 15.

[167] State Media Authorities, 'ZAK qualifiziert Google News Showcase als Medienplattform und
Benutzeroberfläche', 25 November 2021 <Meldung - die medienanstalten (die-medienanstalten.de)> accessed 24 February 2023.

[168] State Media Authorities, 'Merkblatt: Abgrenzung und Medienplattformen', 10 November 2021
<https://www.die-medienanstalten.de/themen/plattformregulierung> accessed 12 January 2024.

[169] MStV, §§82(2), 85.

[170] M Cornils and K Liesem, 'Stellungnahme zum Diskussionsentwurf eines Medienstaatsvertrages der
Rundfunkkommission der Länder' (*Mainzer Medieninstitut*, NK) <https://www.mainzer-medieninstitut.
de/stellungnahme-des-mainzer-medieninstituts-zum-diskussionsentwurf-eines-medienstaatsvertrages/>
accessed 29 May 2020, 7.

[171] A Markham, S Stavrova, and M Schlüter, 'Netflix, Imagined Affordances and the Illusion of Control' in
A Buck and T Plothe (eds), *Netflix and the Nexus: Content, Practice, and Production in the Age of Streaming
Television* (P Lang 2019) 29.

[172] S Dreyer and W Schulz, 'Schriftliche Stellungnahme zum zweiten Diskussionsentwurf eines
Medienstaatsvertrags der Länder vom Juli 2019' (*Hans-Bredow-Institut*, 9 August 2019) <https://www.

non-discrimination becomes somewhat less relevant given that the Media Treaty asks user interfaces to allow users to sort or organize content simply and permanently in a personalized manner.[173] Second, both platforms and user interfaces are required to disclose in a transparent manner the criteria by which they sort, arrange, and present content; the ways by which users can personalize content; and the fundamental criteria by which recommendations occur.[174] Finally, user interfaces are subject to a requirement of findability.[175] This entails the non-discrimination of content as regards its organization and presentation in a way that does not unduly impact the possibility for it to be found.[176] The Treaty even highlights specific permissible criteria for the sorting of content, namely by alphabetical order, genres, or popularity, raising concerns of overregulation.[177]

At the same time, an element of positive discrimination is introduced as regards content of general interest. A privileged position as regards their findability is afforded public service broadcasters' linear and telemedia offerings as well as commercial offerings, which especially contribute to diversity of opinion and media pluralism in Germany.[178] By including commercial providers, the legislator, rather optimistically, aims to give them an additional incentive to provide public interest content.[179] The Media Treaty specifies seven criteria which must be considered when identifying especially valuable commercial offerings: the proportion of time spent reporting on political and historical events; the proportion of time spent reporting on regional and local information; the ratio between in-house productions and programme content produced by third parties; the quota of accessible offers; the ratio between trained employees and employees who still need to be trained, involved in creating the programme; the European works quota; and the quota of offers for young audience groups.[180] All these criteria are geared towards broadcast content.

The fourteen state media authorities (*Landesmedienanstalten*) have been entrusted with stipulating details of the procedure and evaluation criteria in a statute.[181] These authorities are responsible for commercial broadcasting and telemedia including

---

hans-bredow-institut.de/en/publications/schriftliche-stellungnahme-zum-zweiten-diskussionsentwurf-eines-medienstaatsvertrages-der-laender> accessed 30 May 2020 (hereafter Dreyer and Schulz, 'Schriftliche Stellungnahme') 12.

[173] MStV, §84(6).
[174] MStV, §85.
[175] MStV, §84.
[176] MStV, §84(2).
[177] M Cornils, 'Die Perspektive der Wissenschaft: AVMD-Richtlinie, der 22. Rundfunkänderungsstaatsvertrag und der "Medienstaatsvertrag" – Angemessene Instrumente für die Regulierungsherausforderungen?' (2019) 2 Zeitschrift für Urheber- und Medienrecht 89, 93 (hereafter Cornils, 'Perspektive').
[178] MStV, §84(3), (4).
[179] D Frey and H Magnus, 'Landesmedienanstalten veröffentlichen Public-Value-Liste. Bild TV ist jetzt "wertvoll"' (*Legal Tribune Online*, 5 October 2022) <Public-Value-Liste im MStV: Bild TV ist nun 'wertvoll' (lto.de)> accessed 19 January 2023.
[180] MStV, §84(5).
[181] State Media Authorities, 'Satzung zur Durchführung der Vorschriften gemäß § 84 Abs. 8 Medienstaatsvertrag zur leichten Auffindbarkeit von privaten Angeboten', 24 June 2021 <Public-Value-Satzung (die-medienanstalten.de)> accessed 11 October 2022.

media intermediaries, media platforms, and user interfaces.[182] They are based in nearly every German state, while Berlin/Brandenburg and Hamburg/Schleswig Holstein share a media authority. The state media authorities have published a list of those commercial offers, which are deemed to make the envisaged public value contribution.[183] This list was drawn up after a public tender with two calls for bids for audio and audiovisual content.[184] The list features TV services and TV-like apps and has a particular emphasis on local radio. Streaming services not affiliated to a traditional broadcaster, such as Amazon or Netflix, have not been included in the 'public value' list. There are rare examples of services from the print publishers' stable, such as the BILD News app and the BILD TV app, Spiegel Geschichte, the WELT TV channel and app, and the WELT News app. The choice of BILD TV and of the BILD News app are surprising in view of the considerable criticisms about their journalistic quality.[185] The inclusion of a greater range of public interest-oriented hybrid newspaper and magazine apps in the 'public value' list would be desirable in view of their potentially equally important contribution to democratic opinion formation.[186] Exceeding the requirements of the Media Treaty, the state media authorities proposed a ranking of the channels and services as a 'non-binding recommendation' for user interface providers. This ranking, though non-binding, will be taken into account when assessing providers' compliance with the postulate of findability.[187] This is especially problematic in view of the opacity of the criteria employed for this hierarchical ordering.

Turning to the regulation of media intermediaries, the new legislative framework focuses, as in the case of platforms and user interfaces, on the principles of transparency and non-discrimination. However, the regulation of media intermediaries is less detailed than that applicable to platforms. It does not include for instance a requirement of findability. This difference might be based on practical considerations linked to the personalized nature of search results and social media recommendations. It might also reflect a more fundamental uncertainty as to the contribution of intermediaries to opinion formation. However, the importance of search engines and social media as gateways for both broadcast and print news content might necessitate a reconsideration of their disparate treatment in future.

---

[182] State Media Authorities, 'Über uns' <https://www.die-medienanstalten.de/ueber-uns> accessed 11 October 2022.

[183] State Media Authorities, 'Gesamtliste der privaten Angebote gem. § 84 Abs. 5 Satz 1 MStV', 30 June 2023 <Public Value - die medienanstalten (die-medienanstalten.de)> accessed 8 September 2023.

[184] State Media Authorities, 'Ausschreibung: Public Value' <https://www.die-medienanstalten.de/aussch reibung-public-value> accessed 20 January 2023.

[185] See D Wirsching, 'ARD-Programmdirektorin Strobl attackiert "BILD TV": "Ausrichtung auf Spaltung der Gesellschaft"' (*Augsburger Allgemeine*, 3 October 2021) <https://www.augsburger-allgemeine.de/panor ama/Interview-ARD-Programmdirektorin-Strobl-attackiert-Bild-TV-Ausrichtung-auf-Spaltung-der-Gesellschaft-id60694831.html>; F Überall, 'Journalismus ist kein Schlachtfest' (*DJV Blog*, 7 December 2021) <https://www.djv.de/startseite/service/blogs-und-intranet/djv-blog/detail/news-bild-journalismus-ist-kein-schlachtfest> accessed 20 January 2023.

[186] See H Hartung, 'Der Schutz von Medienangeboten gegenüber Plattformen ist legitim' (*medienpolitik. net*, 9 August 2019) <https://www.medienpolitik.net/2019/08/der-schutz-von-medienangeboten-gegenue ber-plattformen-ist-legitim/> accessed 5 June 2020.

[187] State Media Authorities, 'Empfehlung für die Reihenfolgen-Listungen zur Umsetzung durch die Anbieter von Benutzeroberflächen für Bewegtbild-, Audio- und Telemedienangebote', 30 June 2023 <https://www.die-medienanstalten.de/public-value> accessed 12 January 2024.

The rules on transparency require the disclosure of, firstly, the criteria that determine the access of a piece of content to a media intermediary and its placement; and, secondly, the central criteria for the aggregation, selection, and presentation of contents, including information about the functioning of algorithms in accessible language. Modifications of these criteria have to be communicated without delay.[188] As explained in the explanatory memorandum to the Treaty, this does not apply to inconsequential modifications, but only to substantial ones, which appreciably change the access and location or the aggregation, selection, and presentation of contents and their relative weighting.[189] The new Treaty thus attempts to walk a narrow tightrope between ambition and simplification, requiring the disclosure of complex, ever-changing information in a way that is understandable and that captures the central tenets of algorithmic decision-making.[190] The extent to which these requirements will succeed in penetrating the opacity of algorithms, and in delivering information that is intelligible, yet detailed enough to be useful, remains to be seen.

If the effectiveness of the rules on transparency is in doubt, those on non-discrimination run against much weightier objections. The Treaty specifies that media intermediaries should not discriminate against journalistic-editorial offerings whose visibility they are in a position to particularly influence.[191] The restriction of the provision's scope to journalistic-editorial offerings is questionable in view of the fact that intermediaries are the gateways to a host of other content beyond the news and current affairs category, such as content of a private or a commercial nature.[192] More fundamentally, the application of the neutrality postulate to intermediaries is in itself questionable.[193] The differential treatment of various types of content might be justifiable on perfectly legitimate grounds. As already discussed, search engines perform innumerable selection decisions.[194] The favouring of certain search results over others to satisfy users and to uphold a competitive edge over rivals is inherent in their modus operandi.

An artificial neutrality obligation might not only run counter to a platform's business model but might also be counterproductive for the attainment of other regulatory objectives. By way of example, if a media intermediary intended to prioritize trustworthy over unreliable or malicious news as increasingly favoured by policymakers, it could find itself in breach of the non-discrimination requirement if such prioritization was not considered to be justified.[195] Following a summary antitrust judgment

---

[188] MStV, §93(1), (3).

[189] Begründung zum Staatsvertrag zur Modernisierung der Medienordnung in Deutschland, §§93, 50 <https://www.rlp.de/fileadmin/rlp-stk/pdf-Dateien/Medienpolitik/Medienstaatsvertrag_Begru__ndung.pdf> accessed 29 September 2020 (hereafter 'MStV Explanatory memorandum').

[190] Cornils, 'Perspektive' (n 177) 102.

[191] MStV, §94(1).

[192] Dreyer and Schulz, 'Schriftliche Stellungnahme' (n 172) 14.

[193] See Chapter 5, p 128.

[194] See Chapter 2, p 21.

[195] Council of Europe, Declaration by the Committee of Ministers on the financial sustainability of quality journalism in the digital age, 13 February 2019 <https://search.coe.int/cm/pages/result_details.aspx?objectid=090000168092dd4d>; EU Code of Practice on Disinformation (*European Commission*, 26 September 2018) <https://ec.europa.eu/digital-single-market/en/news/code-practice-disinformation> rec vii; N Helberger, P Leersen, and M Van Drunen, 'Germany proposes Europe's first diversity rules for social media platforms' <https://blogs.lse.ac.uk/medialse/2019/05/29/germany-proposes-europes-first-diversity-rules-for-social-media-platforms/> (*Media@LSE*, 29 May 2019) accessed 9 June 2020.

against Google by the District Court of Munich, the ZAK determined that the search engine had contravened its non-discrimination obligation by prioritizing the contents of the national health portal <http://www.gesund.bund.de> between 10 November 2020 and 20 February 2021 based on a cooperation agreement with the Federal Ministry of Health.[196] This agreement was found to have unfairly disadvantaged other journalistic-editorial services.[197]

A further controversy erupted in Germany over the right of media intermediaries to discriminate against journalistic-editorial offerings so as not to pay fees for their display in line with the ancillary copyright for press publishers.[198] The question of whether platforms could try to limit their liability by choosing not to reproduce press publishers' content except perhaps for very short extracts was the subject of heated debate.[199] Google had done so in the past, bringing about a drastic reduction in website traffic to publishers' websites.[200] Press publishers' complaints before the Federal Cartel Office and the courts were unsuccessful.[201] The entry into force of the German ancillary copyright in line with the EU Digital Single Market (DSM) Directive, has resolved this debate.[202] The use of snippets is excluded from the scope of the DSM Directive. However, the recitals clarify that this exclusion should 'be interpreted in such a way as not to affect the effectiveness of the rights provided for in this Directive.'[203] These examples demonstrate that the maxim of non-discrimination comes with its own pitfalls and needs to be carefully fine-tuned to ensure the coherence of the regulatory framework. It may be that a requirement of transparency as to the considerations behind the differential treatment of different items or categories of content is a more tenable proposition than a blanket prohibition of discrimination.

3.5.3 United Kingdom

At the heart of the UK draft Online Safety Bill are the systemic risks posed by user-to-user and search services.[204] However, differently from the DSA and the NetzDG, the draft Bill seeks to tackle both illegal and harmful content. The extent to which moderation should extend to content that does not meet the criminal standard, yet

---

[196] See Chapter 2, p 21; LG Munich, 10 February 2021 – 37 O 15720/20.
[197] State Media Authorities, 'Neue Vorschriften zur Diskriminerungsfreiheit: ZAK entscheidet die ersten Fälle', 16 June 2021 <Meldung - die medienanstalten (die-medienanstalten.de)> accessed 24 February 2023.
[198] Dreyer and Schulz, 'Schriftliche Stellungnahme' (n 172) 15; contra H R Döpkens, 'Am Scheideweg: Politik für eine freie Presse oder für Google und Facebook?' (*medienpolitik.net*, 27 March 2020) https://www.medienpolitik.net/2020/03/am-scheideweg-politik-fuer-eine-freie-presse-oder-fuer-google-und-facebook/ (accessed 19 July 2023).
[199] MStV Explanatory memorandum, §52.
[200] Cairncross Review (n 10) 70.
[201] BkartA, decision of 8 September 2015, B6-126/14, *VG Media v Google*; LG Berlin, judgment of 19 February 2016, 92 O 5/14 Kart; T Steinvorth, 'Durchsetzung des Leistungsschutzrechts für Presseverleger gegenüber marktbeherrschenden Plattformen' (2021) 1 Archiv für Presserecht 10, 16.
[202] Act on the Copyright Liability of Online Content Sharing Service Providers (*Urheberrechts – Diensteanbieter -Gesetz* – UrhDaG) of 31 May 2021, BGBl 2021 I, 1204, 1215 §§87ff; European Parliament and Council Directive 2019/790 of 17 April 2019 on copyright and related rights in the Digital Single Market and amending Directives 96/9/EC and 2001/29/EC [2019] OJ L130/92 (hereafter DSM Directive).
[203] DSM Directive, art 15(1)4, rec 58.
[204] On the communication offences that have been incorporated in the Bill, see Chapter 5, p 131.

poses risks, proved controversial, especially as concerns content harmful to adults. The criticism focused on regulatory overreach and the potential for unnecessarily curtailing freedom of expression.[205] The government sought to meet these objections by sharpening the concept of 'harmful' content, and by defining it as content that 'presents a material risk of significant harm to an appreciable number of children/adults'.[206] However, it later removed the requirement to protect adults from encountering harmful content altogether. This requirement has been replaced by user empowerment duties to equip adult users with tools that enable them to limit their exposure to certain types of content and to filter out non-verified users.[207] The protection from legal but harmful material has been maintained only in the case of minors. Service providers are required to ensure that children do not encounter 'primary priority content' harmful to them, while they have greater leeway as regards 'priority content' harmful to children, to be designated by the Secretary of State in secondary legislation.[208]

These duties apply to a varying extent to different categories of service providers, to be designated through regulations. Services are divided into three categories, with the greatest range of duties incumbent on Category 1 services. These high-risk, high-reach user-to-user services are subject to additional duties, such as duties pertaining to content harmful to adults and to the protection of journalistic content. Category 2A services are made up of all regulated search services, while Category 2B services are all remaining user-to-user services.[209] This differentiated typology of content and of service providers seeks to ensure that the duties imposed on them are commensurate with the risk they pose. Ofcom, the UK's communications regulator, is entrusted with the power to oversee and enforce this regulatory framework.

The Online Safety Bill is inspired by a 'duty of care' philosophy, which seeks to place the regulatory emphasis on the platforms' own conduct as opposed to the users' content.[210] It is based on the recognition that the internet is fundamentally different from traditional media in its scale, audience, and functionalities.[211] It therefore seeks primarily to regulate the processes providers have in place. At the same time, the 'duty of care' is not over-arching, but only encompasses specific duties to mitigate risks posed by specific types of content.[212] The nexus between the duty of care and content-related harms means that the Bill's approach is not merely focused on systems but takes individual items of content into account. This is perhaps inevitable to a certain extent as a completely content-agnostic safety-by-design framework would pose the risk of interfering with all types of content, benevolent and malevolent alike. However, the Bill's

[205] Digital, Culture, Media and Sport Committee, *The Draft Online Safety Bill and the legal but harmful debate* (HC 2021–22, 1039) paras 13ff (hereafter HC 2021–22, 1039); House of Lords Communications and Digital Committee, *Free for All? Freedom of Expression in the Digital Age* (HL 2021–22, 54) paras 151ff.

[206] Digital, Culture, Media and Sport Committee, *The Draft Online Safety Bill and the legal but harmful debate: Government Response to the Committee's Eighth Report* (HC 2021–22, 1221) para 30.

[207] Online Safety Bill 151, 22 June 2023, s 12.

[208] ibid ss 54–56.

[209] HC 2021–22, 1039 (n 205) para 4 fn 4.

[210] Department for Digital, Culture, Media and Sport, and the Home Office, *Online Harms White Paper* (2019, CP 57) paras 16ff.

[211] Ofcom, 'Addressing harmful online content. A perspective from broadcasting and on-demand standards regulation', 18 September 2018 https://www.ofcom.org.uk/__data/assets/pdf_file/0022/120991/Addressing-harmful-online-content.pdf accessed 12 January 2024.

[212] HC 2021–22, 1039 (n 205) para 4.

content-based underpinning means that service providers will still need to make complex judgements about specific instances of harmful activity. This may lead to over-removal and be impractical at scale.[213]

3.5.4 Interim Concluding Remarks

The discussion so far has exposed the complexities of regulating digital platforms. Regulation for online safety veers between the notion of 'platforms as media companies', which need to assume liability for publication, and 'platforms as technology companies', which need to be accountable as regards the organization of content. Strengthening the public interest regulation of digital platforms is often pushed by traditional media on grounds of regulatory parity.[214] The economic model of both broadcast and print media has been destabilized by the arrival of the internet. Still, the former have perhaps a more credible claim when demanding platform regulation for the public good than the latter with their more ambivalent position between market liberalism and social responsibility.[215] Paradoxically, efforts to level the playing field, understandable though they may be, risk entrenching big tech's oligopolistic position by raising the barriers to entry for newcomers.[216] Such efforts are bound to remain fragmented and imperfect so long as a coherent US vision for the internet remains unarticulated and the split between a EU interventionist and a US hands-off approach over internet regulation prevails.

This regulatory stalemate is underpinned by a fundamental uncertainty about the scope of internet regulation for the public good. Regulation that strives not only for safety but also for equality of opportunities, openness, and transparency of communication with the aim of securing pluralism and opinion diversity in the online environment, is challenging. Both the envisaged aims and the enlisted means are contentious. Transparency stumbles across the limitations of meaningful disclosure of source code.[217] Non-discrimination is fraught with difficulties as it presupposes the ideal of a flawless, perfectly even-handed selection, and the knowledge of what such selection would entail. The need for regulatory intervention to safeguard pluralism online has long been disputed on the ground that the endless possibilities for dissemination of information online already result in a pluralistic media landscape. The counterargument, recently forcefully put forward by the German Constitutional Court, is that the internet is equally prone to concentration and monopolization; that it is hostage

---

[213] L Woods, 'The Duty of Care in the Online Harms White Paper' (2019) 11(1) Journal of Media Law 6, 17.

[214] Bossio and others, 'Australia's News Media Bargaining Code' (n 32) 147; T Flew, F Martin, and N Suzor, 'Internet Regulation as Media Policy: Rethinking the Question of Digital Communication Platform Governance' (2019) 10(1) Journal of Digital Media & Policy 33, 45 (hereafter Flew, Martin, and Suzor, 'Internet Regulation as Media Policy').

[215] See Chapter 4, p 102.

[216] Flew, Martin, and Suzor, 'Internet Regulation as Media Policy' (n 214) 44.

[217] D A Desai and J A Kroll, 'Trust but Verify: A Guide to Algorithms and the Law' (2017) 31 Harvard Journal of Law and Technology 1; L Edwards and M Veale, 'Slave to the Algorithm? Why a "Right to Explanation" Is Probably Not the Remedy You Are Looking for' (2017) 16 Duke Law & Technology Review 18.

to commercial interests that care little for media diversity; and that, last but not least, it is agnostic to the values of responsible journalism, but indiscriminately gives access to 'non-journalistic providers that do not prepare and refine information in a journalistic manner'.[218] The last of these arguments raises the issue of the journalistic profession's boundaries, the role of citizen journalists, the responsibilities they should bear, and the privileges to which they should perhaps be entitled. These questions will be explored in the following section.

3.6 Citizen Journalists as 'the Press'?

Legislators and policymakers increasingly recognize that internet intermediaries perform a media function when organizing and disseminating information, and seek ways to regulate them. An equally thorny question they face is the extent to which the myriads of purveyors of news and 'occasional public commentators' who are active on these platforms without being affiliated to the traditional news media also need to be classified as 'the press', to be afforded the same privileges and burdened with the same obligations.[219] Some of these privileges relate to the protection of confidential sources and of journalists' material,[220] the safeguarding of the newsgathering process from surveillance,[221] and journalistic exemptions from data protection and copyright law.[222] Such journalistic privileges come with a certain societal cost. The protection of confidentiality of sources, for instance, deprives courts of testimonial evidence, rendering prosecutions and civil discovery costlier and more cumbersome.[223] Reforming the very restrictive right of access to family courts needs to be balanced with the risk for children's confidentiality.[224]

In the past, it was fairly straightforward to keep this societal cost at bay by conferring journalistic privileges on a neatly confined group of recipients, namely to 'those who were engaged professionally as proprietors, editors, broadcasters and journalists'.[225] Journalistic privileges were manageable as they were linked to expensive means of production. So long as it was necessary to have access to a costly printing press or broadcasting equipment to communicate with the public at large, and the ties between publishers, journalists, and the forms of production were close, it was possible

---

[218] BVerfGE 149, 222 (2018) para 79 translated into English at <https://www.bundesverfassungsgericht. de/SharedDocs/Entscheidungen/EN/2018/07/rs20180718_1bvr167516en.html> accessed 8 September 2023.

[219] See S R West, 'Press Exceptionalism' (2014) 127 Harvard Law Review 2434, 2437 (hereafter West, 'Press Exceptionalism').

[220] Contempt of Court Act 1981, s 10; Police and Criminal Evidence Act 1984, Sch 1, para 4.

[221] Investigatory Powers Act 2016, s 2(5).

[222] Data Protection Act 2018 (DPA), s 124; Copyright, Designs and Patents Act 1988, s 30(2).

[223] J Alonzo, 'Note: Restoring the Ideal Marketplace: How Recognizing Bloggers as Journalists Can Save the Press' (2005/6) 9 New York University Journal of Legislation & Public Policy 751, 775; J Oster, *Media Freedom as a Fundamental Right* (CUP 2015) 63 (hereafter Oster, *Media Freedom*).

[224] See Practice Direction 27A to Family Procedure Rules 2010. On recent attempts at reform see House of Commons Justice Committee, 'Open Justice: Court reporting in the digital age', 5th Report of session 2022–23, HC 339, 1 November 2022, paras 99ff.

[225] *Commissioner of Police of the Metropolis v Times Newspapers Ltd* [2011] EWHC 2705 (QB), para 130.

to clearly define the activity of journalism and those exercising it.[226] Journalistic privileges were counterbalanced by the imposition of obligations to comply with professional codes of conduct, and to be guided by the ethics of journalism when gathering, editing, and disseminating information.[227]

The arrival of the internet enabled anybody to address the general public at virtually no cost, thus putting an end to the scarcity of publishing and obscuring the boundaries of the journalistic profession. This fusion between the roles of producers and consumers of information, labelled as 'produsage', has raised the question of how to decide who should be entitled to the abovementioned benefits and be subject to the concomitant obligations.[228] On the one hand, extending the protections afforded to professional journalists to the public at large would render such privileges 'a loophole too large to be borne by society'.[229] On the other hand, extending the expectations of responsibility that are incumbent on journalists to all the 'people formerly known as the audience' who now perform press-like functions could risk stifling freedom of expression.[230]

Before proceeding to examine how to define those actors who perform journalistic functions and hence who should be regulated accordingly, it is necessary to look more closely at the concept of 'citizen journalism'.[231] This fluid term is a shorthand to describe the different ways in which ordinary users engage in journalistic practices such as 'current affairs-based blogging, photo and video sharing, and posting eyewitness commentary on current events'.[232] While our focus for the purposes of this examination is on web-based practices, the concept of 'citizen journalism' is wider, and can include the integration of user-generated content in offline news media, such as broadcast or print publications. However, this section is not concerned with those manifestations of 'citizen journalism' that involve a collaboration between professionals and amateurs to generate new perspectives on a given news story. Such instances of so-called 'networked journalism' have been expected to democratize news production.[233] These idealistic expectations were tempered by the realization that those who got a stake in shaping the public sphere in the early phases of citizen journalism often had journalistic training or developed affiliations with the mainstream news media.[234] It has also been observed that journalists rarely sourced citizens in

---

[226] C Shirky, *Here Comes Everybody: The Power of Organising Without Organisations* (Penguin 2008) 71 (hereafter Shirky, *Here Comes Everybody*).

[227] See T Harcup, *The Ethical Journalist* (Sage 2007); T Hanitzsch, 'Deconstructing Journalism Culture: Toward a Universal Theory' (2007) 17(4) Communication Theory 367, 378; P Mitchell, 'The Nature of Responsible Journalism' (2011) 3 Journal of Media Law 19.

[228] A Bruns, 'Reconciling Community and Commerce?: Collaboration between Produsage Communities and Commercial Operators' (2012) 15(6) Information, Communication & Society 815.

[229] Shirky, *Here Comes Everybody* (n 226) 71.

[230] T McGonagle, 'User-Generated Content and Audiovisual News: The Ups and Downs of an Uncertain Relationship' in European Audiovisual Observatory, *Open Journalism*, 2 *IRIS Plus* (European Audiovisual Observatory 2013) 7, 14.

[231] See ibid 10.

[232] L Goode, 'Social News, Citizen Journalism and Democracy' (2009) 11(8) New Media & Society 1287, 1288.

[233] D Gilmore, *We the Media. Grassroots Journalism by the People, for the People* (O'Reilly 2006).

[234] Bruns, 'Random Acts' (n 70) 35.

their news reports, and when they did so it was under observance of standard jour-nalistic conventions.[235]

However, the arrival of social media served to somewhat broaden participation in news making.[236] To be sure, the vast majority of the online audience does little more than share and disseminate news on social media.[237] Still, on not infrequent occa-sions, ordinary social media users cover breaking news events, even major political stories, occasionally outperforming their professional counterparts.[238] The emphasis of this section is precisely on such user-generated news content that is created on so-cial media networks outside of professional routines and practices. It is not concerned with secondary acts of commenting to news articles on the websites of newspapers or broadcasters. Such comments and the possible liability of publishers that arises thereof will be considered in the second part of this monograph.[239]

Having shed some light on the notion of 'citizen journalism', and on the type of ac-tivities that it involves, it is appropriate to consider whether such activities should merit the protection and be subject to the additional obligations that apply to trad-itional media. This question goes to the core of what are the media. There are two schools of thought on this question: the institutional and the functional one.[240] The former posits that the institutional media should enjoy special rights and privileges in recognition of their unique role in keeping government accountable. This is epitom-ized by the metaphor of the 'Fourth Estate', a term that was used by the Scottish satirist Thomas Carlyle to describe the press gallery in Parliament.[241] A possible objection against the recognition of such a privileged position for the press is that it is elitist and discriminatory given that it singles out the media for special treatment, while denying it to other regular contributors to matters of public interest.[242] This argument ignores the special communicative power that is held by traditional media.[243] Even though the press has to a certain extent relinquished its gatekeeping function in the digital en-vironment, it is still in a unique position to use its specialized knowledge, experience, and resources to reach a broad audience by reporting matters in the public interest.[244] Bottom-up production of user-generated news content stands a better chance of gaining traction when it is promoted by the institutionalized media. The special priv-ileges bestowed on the press are in recognition of the unique functions it performs in

---

[235] S Meraz and Z Papacharissi, 'Networked Framing and Gatekeeping' in T Witschge and others (eds), *The SAGE Handbook of Digital Journalism* (Sage 2016) 95, 98.

[236] Bruns, 'Random Acts' (n 70) 40.

[237] Harcup and O'Neill, 'What Is News?' (n 37) 1474.

[238] I Gaber, 'Three Cheers for Subjectivity: Or the Crumbling of the Seven Pillars of Traditional Journalistic Wisdom' in A Charles and G Stewart (eds), *The End of Journalism: News in the Twenty-First Century* (Peter Lang 2011) 31.

[239] See Chapter 7.

[240] The distinction between the institutional and functional approach to defining the media draws on J Rowbottom, *Media Law* (Hart Publishing 2018) 27 (hereafter Rowbottom, *Media Law*) and J Oster, 'Theory and Doctrine of "Media Freedom" as a Legal Concept' (2013) 5(1) Journal of Media Law 57 (hereafter Oster, 'Theory and Doctrine').

[241] M Hampton, 'The Fourth Estate Ideal in Journalism History' in A Stuart (ed), *The Routledge Companion to News and Journalism* (Routledge 2009) 3.

[242] E Barendt, *Freedom of Speech* (2nd edn, OUP 2007) 421; Oster, *Media Freedom* (n 223) 26.

[243] Rowbottom, *Media Law* (n 240) 13, 27; see D Erdos, *European Data Protection Regulation, Journalism and Traditional Publishers: Balancing on a Tightrope?* (OUP 2020) 276.

[244] West, 'Press Exceptionalism' (n 219) 2444.

a democratic society. Equally, the responsibilities that go hand in hand are designed to stem its ability to abuse this power.

The functional approach, on the other hand, maintains that while the press possesses unique qualities, it might not be opportune to limit the privileges conferred upon it to institutional actors only. It would be desirable, so the argument goes, to extend these privileges to all actors who perform 'legitimate and valuable information gathering and dissemination functions'.[245] Such a functional approach underlies Article 85(2) of the General Data Protection Regulation (GDPR), which exempts from data protection law processing carried out for journalistic purposes so as to reconcile the right to protection of personal data with the right to freedom of expression.[246] This provision as well as its predecessor, Article 9 of the Data Protection Directive 95/46, have been interpreted to apply not only to the traditional media but to all persons engaged in journalism.[247] The Council of Europe also advocates a broad notion of media which encompasses all actors involved in the production and dissemination of content to potentially large numbers of people.[248]

This functional approach emphasizes not the status of a speaker but the communicative functions they fulfil.[249] Naturally, it raises the equally intricate problem of how to define these functions. They consist, broadly speaking, in the regular contribution to 'matters of general interest with information and ideas that have been gathered and edited according to certain standards of diligent conduct'.[250] If one attempts to further drill down into the detail of journalistic activity, the temptation is there to tie it to the processes and professional ideology of traditional news organizations.[251] The professional and ethical standards expected of journalists have been typified in academic literature as public service ethos; objectivity and neutrality; independence; immediacy, actuality, and speed; a sense of ethics.[252] While these standards capture much of the essence of journalism, they elide the complexity and diversity of the journalistic field, and cannot necessarily be applied *in toto* to non-mainstream, amateur activities.[253] To name but one example, the much vaunted concepts of objectivity and neutrality,

---

[245] B P McDonald, 'The First Amendment and the Free Flow of Information' (2004) 65 Ohio State Law Journal 249, 257.

[246] European Parliament and Council Regulation (EU) 2016/679 of 27 April 2016 on the protection of natural persons with regard to the processing of personal data and on the free movement of such data, and repealing Directive 95/46/EC, OJ L 119/1 (hereafter 'GDPR').

[247] *Tietosuojavaltuutettu v Satakunnan Markkinapörssi Oy en Satamedia Oy* [2008] ECLI:EU:C:2008:727, paras 57ff; see Chapter 6, p 147.

[248] *Recommendation CM/Rec(2011)7 of the Committee of Ministers to member states on a new notion of media*, 21 September 2011, para 7.

[249] West, 'Press Exceptionalism' (n 219) 2443; Oster, 'Theory and Doctrine' (n 240) 78; E Ugland and J Henderson, 'Who Is a Journalist and Why Does It Matter? Disentangling the Legal and Ethical Arguments' (2007) 22(4) Journal of Mass Media Ethics 241, 255; P Coe, 'Redefining "Media" Using a "Media-as-a-Constitutional-Component-Concept": An Evaluation of the Need for the European Court of Human Rights to Alter Its Understanding of 'Media' Within a New Media Landscape' (2017) 37(1) Legal Studies 25.

[250] Oster, 'Theory and Doctrine' (n 240) 78.

[251] See J Rowbottom, 'In the Shadow of the Big Media: Freedom of Expression, Participation and the Production of Knowledge Online' (2014) 3(3) Public Law 491 in relation to the public interest defence in defamation law.

[252] M Deuze, 'What Is Journalism? Professional Identity and Ideology of Journalists Reconsidered' (2005) 6(4) Journalism 442, 447.

[253] See M Deuze, 'What Journalism Is (Not)' (2019) 4(1) Social Media + Society 1, 3.

aspirational at best in the realm of professional journalism, bear little relevance for the opinionated blogosphere.[254]

The way in which the draft UK Online Safety Bill seeks to accommodate journalism is a case in point as it attempts an uncomfortable split between the institutional and the functional approaches. First, the Bill seeks to exempt news publishers' websites, including below the line comments, from its online safety duties.[255] It achieves this by completely exempting broadcasters' and press publishers' websites and users' comments on that content from the scope of the legislation. Presumably, this exemption also includes 'comments on comments', even though this is not specifically mentioned.[256] Second, recognized news publishers' content posted on in-scope social media platforms is exempt from the new online safety duties. Platforms are therefore not obliged to take action in respect of such content, but they may still do so.[257] Should they decide to take action in relation to a recognized news publisher or its content, they need to give them advance notification, unless publication of that content amounts to a relevant offence under the Bill or the platform would incur criminal or civil liability by hosting it.[258] Third, the Bill imposes a duty on Category 1 services to protect all 'journalistic content', including 'news publisher content', shared on their platform.[259] These types of content on Category 1 services are in scope, but service providers need to take the importance of freedom of expression into account when making decisions about them. To illustrate the risks of platform moderation for journalism, the government invoked the temporary short-lived closure of Ofcom regulated TalkRadio by YouTube for allegedly breaching its policies on medical misinformation related to Covid.[260] YouTube reversed its ban of TalkRadio within twelve hours amidst criticism of its policies.[261]

'News publishers' content' is defined as content that is either generated by a 'recognised news publisher' or is a reposting of such content.[262] 'Recognised news publishers' are UK-licensed broadcasters and other news publishers which fulfil a range of administrative as well as substantive requirements.[263] The administrative conditions aim to ensure that the entity publishing the material has a UK business address, that it is legally responsible for this material, and that it publishes its identifying details as well as those of the person controlling it. The substantive conditions require that the entity in question has as its principal purpose the publication of news-related material;

---

[254] See Chapter 5, p 128.

[255] Online Safety Bill, Sch 1, Part 1, para 4.

[256] cf Online Safety Bill, s 49(6).

[257] Department for Culture, Media and Sport and Department for Science, Innovation & Technology, 'Guidance: Fact sheet on enhanced protections for journalism within the Online Safety Bill', 23 August 2022, para 6 <https://www.gov.uk/government/publications/fact-sheet-on-enhanced-protections-for-journalism-within-the-online-safety-bill/fact-sheet-on-enhanced-protections-for-journalism-within-the-online-safety-bill> accessed 12 January 2024.

[258] Online Safety Bill, s 14(2)–(4).

[259] ibid ss 14, 15.

[260] Department for Culture, Media and Sport, 'Up next—The government's vision for the broadcasting sector' (CP 671, 2022) para 4.5.

[261] L Kelion, 'YouTube reverses decision to ban channel' (BBC, 5 January 2021) <https://www.bbc.co.uk/news/technology-55544205> accessed 12 January 2024.

[262] Online Safety Bill, s 49(8)–(10).

[263] ibid s 50(2).

that such material is created by different persons, is subject to editorial control, and is published in the course of a business; and that the entity in question is subject to a standards code and has complaint handling procedures in place. The definition of a 'recognised news publisher' may thus apply not only to the legacy media but also to non-traditional news publishers who satisfy the abovementioned conditions.[264]

'Journalistic content' is defined as UK-linked content generated for the purposes of journalism, including but not being limited to news publishers' journalistic content. 'Regulated user-generated content' also falls under this definition.[265] The duty to protect journalistic content consists of procedural requirements, including systems and processes, a dedicated and expedited complaints procedure, a right to reinstatement, and a consistent application of clear and accessible terms of service.[266] The expedited routes of appeal are hence available to both citizen journalists and recognized news publishers. However, only the latter are entitled to advance notification when platforms contemplate taking action in relation to their content.[267] These extent to which platforms will be required to comply with these procedural requirements depends on their size and capacity.[268] This poses a certain risk that journalistic content might still fall prey to smaller platforms' moderation efforts.

Overall, the need for these unevenly distributed procedural safeguards makes clear that the intended exemption of news media from the scope of the Bill might not be watertight. Also, the duty of care for journalistic content at large is far more tentative than the clear-cut exemption reserved to news publishers' content. Having said that, the convoluted description of the latter is relatively low threshold. A standards code, for instance, may be published by an independent regulator or by the entity itself.[269] The concern has been raised that this might enable outlets specializing in hate speech and disinformation to easily pass the threshold by drafting a code on the 'back of an envelope'.[270] At the same time, the requirement for recognized news publishers to have a business address and a variety of contributors might exclude certain bona fide journalistic outlets.[271] To avert some of these risks, an amendment was proposed to the effect that a 'recognised news publisher' should be required to be a member of an approved regulator. This narrower definition could not be agreed upon. The 'philosophical' concern was voiced that such an amendment would amount to mandatory regulation of the press in contradiction with press freedom.[272]

To be sure, the suggested amendment would not compel press publishers to join a regulator, though it would certainly create an incentive to do so. The extent to which

[264] cf the hard to operationalize exclusion of bloggers ('micro-businesses') who are not members of an approved regulator under Sch 15, para 8 in connection with the Crime and Courts Act 2013, s 41(7).
[265] Online Safety Bill, s 15(10).
[266] ibid s 15(2)–(8).
[267] ibid s 14(3).
[268] ibid s 15(9).
[269] ibid s 50(6)(b).
[270] House of Commons Public Bill Committee, 'Online Safety Bill', 24 May 2022, session 2022–23, 1st sitting, 370 (hereafter House of Commons, 'Online Safety Bill'); Hacked Off, 'Written evidence' (September 2021) <https://committees.parliament.uk/writtenevidence/39134/html/#_ftnref1> accessed 12 January 2024, para 17.
[271] Hacked Off, 'Written evidence' (n 272) para 17.
[272] House of Commons, 'Online Safety Bill' (n 270) 372.

a model of incentivized press regulation is at odds with press freedom is debatable. Countries that rank highly on press freedom operate incentivized or, rarely, even mandatory models of press regulation.[273] Besides this fundamental question, determining who is a UK 'approved regulator' could be mired in controversy. The Independent Press Standards Organisation (IPSO), which regulates most major UK media outlets, has never been recognized by the Press Recognition Panel (PRP) nor aspired to such recognition, while the *Guardian, Observer,* and the *Financial Times* have resisted external regulation altogether.[274]

It is interesting to compare the attempts to ringfence journalism in the Online Safety Bill with the convoluted position under the German NetzDG. It is stated therein that 'Platforms offering journalistic or editorial content, the responsibility for which lies with the service provider itself, shall not constitute social networks within the meaning of this Act'.[275] This clarification is redundant given that such media platforms are not social networks since they are not 'designed to enable users to share any content with other users or to make such content available to the public (social networks)'.[276] The explanatory memorandum to the NetzDG further expresses the intention to exempt social networks from the scope of the law, including its reporting and complaint handling obligations, insofar as they host news outlets' official social media presence.[277] This intention is not, however, reflected in the wording nor in the statutory system of the NetzDG and is hence inconsequential.[278] Besides, such an exemption would give rise to considerable definitional difficulties and a potential contravention of the constitutional principles of legal certainty and equality.[279]

The porous boundaries of journalistic work in tandem with concerns over the impact of moderation delays on the fight with disinformation meant that a proposed media exemption did not make its way into the DSA.[280] The DSA potentially offers a level of protection for the media by obliging platforms to have 'due regard to ... the freedom of expression, freedom and pluralism of the media, and other fundamental rights and freedoms' in their moderation decisions, and to include negative effects for the exercise of these freedoms in their systemic risk assessment.[281] These due diligence obligations are, however, procedural, and do not give rise to a self-standing right.[282]

---

[273] Ireland incentivizes membership of the Irish Press Council by way of the Irish Defamation Act 2009, while Press Council membership is compulsory in Denmark. See L Fielden, 'A Royal Charter for the Press: Lessons from Overseas' (2013) 5(2) Journal of Media Law 172, 175f; see Reporters Without Borders, 'World Press Freedom Index' <https://rsf.org/en/index> accessed 12 January 2024.

[274] The PRP is the body which was set up under the Royal Charter on self-regulation of the press to judge whether press regulators meet the criteria recommended by Lord Justice Leveson for recognition under the Charter.

[275] NetzDG, §1(1)2.

[276] NetzDG, §1(1)1.

[277] Draft Network Enforcement Act of 16 May 2017, German Parliament document BT-Drs. 18/12356, 19 <https://dserver.bundestag.de/btd/18/127/1812727.pdf> accessed 2 March 2023.

[278] BVerfGE 11, 126, para 21.

[279] Hoven/Gersdorf, '§1 NetzDG' (n 150) para 24.

[280] L Bertuzzi, 'Media exemption ruled out in DSA negotiations, but could return' (*Euractiv*, 29 November 2021) <https://www.euractiv.com/section/digital-single-market/news/media-exception-ruled-out-in-dsa-negotiations-but-could-return/> accessed 25 April 2023.

[281] DSA, arts 14(4), 34(1)(b), (c), rec 47.

[282] J P Quintais, N Appelman, and R Ó Fathaigh, 'Using Terms and Conditions to Apply Fundamental Rights to Content Moderation' (2023) 24 German Law Journal 881, 905.

The proposed EMFA provides such subjective rights in the shape of advance notification and appeal rights for media service providers that are, first, editorially independent from Member States and third countries and, second, subject to regulatory,
co-regulatory, or self-regulatory mechanisms governing editorial standards that are
widely recognized and accepted.[283] These criteria are so sensitive and complex that
they will be impossible to implement in a legally certain way. They are also potentially
at odds with the Media Pluralism Monitor's finding that only eight of the thirty-two
EU and candidate countries had effective systems of journalistic self-regulation in
place in 2022.[284]

The NetzDG's half-hearted solution and the hard distinctions drawn in the Online
Safety Bill and the proposed EMFA between citizen and professional journalism bring
to the fore the difficulty of circumscribing the media terrain in the digital era. The more
the definition of what the media does is minted in the image of the news industry as it
has been traditionally organized, the less likely it is that citizen journalists will be able
to benefit. The need for legal certainty and for a benefit-maximizing distribution of
limited resources occasionally dictates that prerogatives be conferred to, and that the
regulatory burdens be imposed on, a closely defined group of recipients. In the UK,
only a segment of online journalism is subject to an organized system of self-regulation,
while there is a whole swath of unregulated and unreliable online news providers. Such
gaps in online regulation prompted the House of Lords to recommend the establishment of a Digital Authority to coordinate and oversee regulation in the digital world.[285]
This task has now been assigned to Ofcom under the Online Safety Bill insofar as the
regulation of online intermediaries is concerned. As discussed earlier, the extent to
which online news sources fall under its remit is uncertain. In other jurisdictions, it is
also increasingly recognized that a widening of the definition of the press is appropriate
to foster journalistic activity wherever it takes place as well as to uphold editorial standards in the digital age.[286] In Germany, an extension of the regulatory framework for the
press has taken place by way of the regulation of so-called 'journalistic-editorial offerings'. The regulatory and constitutional difficulties that come with the attempt to delineate the terrain of the online press in Germany will be discussed in the next section.

3.7 The German Regulatory Framework
for the Online Press

In Germany, online news is regulated under the heading of 'telemedia with
journalistic-editorial offerings'. This concept is not defined in the Media Treaty, but is
interpreted widely to include not only the 'electronic press', but also all online offerings

---

[283] EMFA Proposal (n 138) art 17(1).

[284] Centre for Media Pluralism and Media Freedom, Monitoring media pluralism in the digital era
(European University Institute 2022) 80 <https://cadmus.eui.eu/bitstream/handle/1814/74712/MPM2022-
EN-N.pdf?sequence=1&isAllowed=y> accessed 9 May 2023.

[285] House of Lords Communications and Digital Committee, 'Regulating in a digital world', 2nd Report
of Session 2017–19, HL Paper 299, 9 March 2019, paras 227ff.

[286] In Finland, eg, the Council for Mass Media, a self-regulatory body, is responsible for the press, radio,
and television as well as for online media. See <https://jsn.fi/en/what-is-the-cmm/> accessed 19 May 2023.

that display a certain element of editorial work, a selection or commenting function that goes beyond the mere mechanical transmission of data.[287] Already under the Interstate Broadcasting Treaty, these online services, and in particular those which, in part or in full, reproduced texts or images of periodical print media, had to comply with common journalistic standards, in particular with the obligation to check the content, source, and truthfulness of news with due diligence prior to publication.[288] This expectation of self-regulatory compliance with journalistic standards has now been incorporated into the new Media Treaty.[289]

The Treaty extends journalistic due diligence obligations to other professional journalistic-editorial services, which regularly contain news or political information, and which do not already fall within the regulatory framework.[290] Blogs are likely to fall under this definition provided they are not of an exclusively private nature but display journalistic intent. The non-official translation of this provision refers to 'other *commercial*, journalistic-editorial offers'. However, the translation of '*geschäftsmäßig angeboten*' as 'commercial' rather than 'professional' seems at odds with the explanatory memorandum to the Media Treaty, which clarifies that this characteristic does not require an economic activity or the intention to make a profit but seeks to signify that the publication in question has a certain duration.[291] Somewhat redundantly, it then goes on to explain that this requirement is fulfilled in the case of the commercial orientation of a press publication that aims directly at the distribution of goods or services, or that includes advertisements. On the contrary, it is lacking in the case of exclusively private offerings or of such that only are only aimed at family and friends. In any case, in view of the broad understanding of professionalism, this requirement is not expected to make a difference in practice.[292]

The extent to which the inclusion of other services under the Media Treaty actually expands the existing category of 'telemedia with journalistic-editorial offerings' is questionable in view of the already wide definition thereof.[293] The explanatory memorandum draws a distinction between the 'online press' and other services which 'on account of their nature or structure do not resemble publishers' traditional offering and hence are not captured by §54 (1) [sic] of the Interstate Broadcasting Treaty, but possess journalistic relevance'.[294] This appears, however, more like an afterthought that does not chime with the wording and conventional interpretation of §54(2) of the Interstate Broadcasting Treaty (RStV).[295] Both the RStV and the MStV state that

---

[287] See F Fechner, *Medienrecht* (20th edn, Mohr Siebeck 2019) 371 para 55; T Held, 'Journalistisch-redaktionell gestaltete Angebote' in R Binder and T Vesting (eds), *Beck'scher Kommentar zum Rundfunkrecht* (4th edn, Beck 2018) §54, paras 38ff (hereafter Held, 'Journalistisch-redaktionell').

[288] RStV, §54(2).

[289] MStV, §19(1)1 (non-official translation): 'Telemedia with journalistic-editorial offers, particularly in which the entire or partial content of periodical print materials are reproduced in text or image, must comply with recognized journalistic principles.'

[290] MStV, §19(1)2.

[291] MStV Explanatory memorandum, §19.

[292] W Lent, 'Paradigmenwechsel bei den publizistischen Sorgfaltspflichten im Online-Journalismus—Zur Neuregelung des §19 Medienstaatsvertrag' (2020) 8/9 Zeitschrift für Urheber- und Medienrecht 593, 598 (hereafter Lent, 'Paradigmenwechsel').

[293] See Held, 'Journalistisch-redaktionell' (n 287) paras 56ff.

[294] MStV Explanatory memorandum, §§19, 21.

[295] Lent, 'Paradigmenwechsel' (n 292) 598.

the journalistic due diligence obligations apply *in particular* to those services which reproduce in part or in full texts or images of periodical print media.[296] It follows that §19(1)1 MStV is not confined to online editions of print media. It includes both online spin-offs of print publications that do not reproduce any of the contents of the print edition, or do so only in part, as well as to digital-only news media such as investigative news blogs or regional news portals. A different interpretation would be inconsistent with the manifold convergent manifestations of online journalism.[297] It seems plausible, therefore, that the addition of §19(1)2 MStV simply serves to highlight the subjection of the 'electronic press' in a wide sense to a framework of regulatory obligations analogous to those applying to the printed press. Nonetheless, as will be seen in the following, curiously disparate obligations attach to services falling under the second, compared to the first, sentence of §19(1) MStV.

The exact delineation of the services to be subsumed under §19(1)2 MStV is to be determined by one of the following authorities: the German Press Council or a still to be established recognized self-regulatory body, if the provider in question has joined either of them; or otherwise the competent state media authority, which can also step in if a self-regulatory body has exceeded its discretion.[298] Therefore, the Damocles sword of state supervision hangs over those 'other' services that do not fall under §19(1)1 MStV nor are they subject to self-regulation by the German Press Council or by a recognized self-regulatory institution.[299] The Media Treaty empowers state media authorities to sanction non-compliance with journalistic obligations by way of banning or blocking the services in question or by way of the withdrawal or revocation of a broadcasting licence.[300]

This extension of the state media authorities' powers vis-à-vis journalistic-editorial telemedia aims to fill a regulatory lacuna which existed under the RStV given that compliance with journalistic standards was exempt from external supervision.[301] The assumption under the RStV was that the online press was subject to the Press Council's supervision. The proliferation of unregulated online news providers undermined this assumption. The fact that there was no clear allocation of competence posed problems regarding the perceived need to tackle online disinformation.[302] The number of services that might fall under the state media authorities' remit is likely to be considerable. It is not certain whether further recognized self-regulatory bodies will be established nor whether online providers would be inclined to join them in view of the financial burden likely to be associated therewith.[303]

[296]   RStV, §54(2)1; MStV, §19(1)1.

[297]   W Lent, '§19 MStV' in H Gersdorf and P Paal (eds), *Informations- und Medienrecht Kommentar* (2nd edn, Beck 2021) para 8 (hereafter Lent, '§19 MStV').

[298]   MStV, §19(3), (8).

[299]   MStV, §§19(3)–(8), 109(1)4.

[300]   MStV, §§108, 109(1).

[301]   RStV, §59(3).

[302]   State Media Authorities, 'Stellungnahme der Medienanstalten zum überarbeiteten Diskussionsentwurf der Rundfunkkommision der Länder für einen Medienstaatsvertrag' 10 (9 August 2019) <https://www.die-medienanstalten.de/fileadmin/user_upload/die_medienanstalten/Ueber_uns/Positionen/2019_08_09_Stellungnahme_der_Medienanstalten_zum_Medienstaatsvertrag.pdf> accessed 5 June 2020.

[303]   J Kalbhenn and B Holznagel, 'Journalistische Sorgfaltspflichten auf YouTube und Instagram—Neue Vorgaben im Medienstaatsvertrag' in L Specht-Riemenschneider and others (eds), *Festschrift für Jürgen Taeger* (R&W 2020) 589, 607 (hereafter Kalbhenn and Holznagel, 'Journalistische Sorgfaltspflichten'); M

Interestingly, the Media Treaty thus follows a dualistic path for the regulation of the digital press by imposing on it minimal substantive obligations similar to those of the printed press, while subjecting it to the backstop powers of the fourteen state media authorities, which are responsible for the licensing and supervision of private radio and TV broadcasting in Germany. The supervision of journalistic-editorial telemedia by the state media authorities goes against the grain of the historic claim of the press to greater freedom, and the traditional suspicion towards its subjection to state regulation.[304] Some argue that the chosen regulatory model constitutes an unacceptable interference with press freedom.[305] Similarly to the arguments raised in the context of the Online Safety Bill, they contend that membership of a press self-regulator would need to be voluntary, not based on coercion.[306] The rules about the self-regulatory bodies are also considered problematic due to the unequal treatment of these bodies compared to the Press Council.[307] While there are no requirements as regards the Press Council, the self-regulatory bodies need to be recognized and supervised by the state media authorities. This is especially noteworthy in view of the criticism of the Press Council as toothless.[308] It is argued that, in order to avoid the clash of the Media Treaty with the rights guaranteed in the German Constitution, the second sentence of §19(1) MStV would need to be omitted. Press-like telemedia would hence fall in their entirety under §19(1)1 MStV and would only be subject to a framework of voluntary self-regulation.[309]

Others argue that §19(1)2 MStV should be confined to TV-like journalistic-editorial telemedia only.[310] However, such a restriction of the scope of §19(1)2 MStV would not necessarily solve the constitutional conundrum. Prior to the entry into force of the Media Treaty, all journalistic-editorial telemedia were free from state supervision regardless of whether they distributed text and still images or also video and audio.[311] They all enjoyed the same entitlement to press freedom in the same way as the printed press. The disregard for an ethical obligation only triggered state enforcement measures if a specific law was violated.[312] In any case, if the constitutional conflict was to be solved by narrowing the scope of §19(1)2 MStV, this amendment would need to be legislated upon so as to preserve the primacy of the legislator in

---

Heins and S Lefeldt, 'Medianstaatsvertrag: Journalistische Sorgfaltspflichten für Influencer*innen. Macht im Netz VI: Zwischen Selbstregulierung und Aufsicht – Die Regelungen des RStV und MStV' (2021) Multimedia und Recht 126, 130.

[304] Chapter 2, p 13.
[305] C Fiedler, '§109 MStV' in H Gersdorf and P Paal (eds), *Informations- und Medienrecht Kommentar* (Beck 2021) paras 8ff (hereafter Fiedler, '§109 MStV'); Verband Deutscher Zeitschriftenverleger, 'VDZ und BDZV zum neuen Medienstaatsvertrag' (*VDZ*, 5 December 2019) <https://www.vdz.de/nachricht/artikel/vdz-und-bdzv-zum-neuen-medienstaatsvertrag/> accessed 3 July 2020.
[306] Lent, '§19 MStV' (n 297) para 3.
[307] ibid.
[308] F Ferreau, 'Desinformation als Herausforderung für die Medienregulierung' (2021) 3 Archiv für Presserecht 204, 206, 207 (hereafter Ferreau, 'Desinformation als Herausforderung').
[309] Lent, '§19 MStV' (n 297) para 12; Fiedler, '§109 MStV' (n 305) paras 8ff.
[310] Lent, '§19 MStV' (n 297) para 2.
[311] See RStV, §54(2).
[312] Fiedler, '§109 MStV' (n 305) para 9.

accordance with the constitutional essential-matters doctrine (*Wesentlichkeitsgrun dsatz*).[313]

Yet others maintain that entrusting new media with the selection between public and self-regulation is a proper exercise of legislative discretion.[314] The BVerfG has not yet declared the incentivization of joining a self-regulatory body by way of the threat of state supervision as unconstitutional.[315] In any case, so the argument goes, the state media authorities are at arm's length from the state in line with the constitutional principle of freedom of broadcasting from state control (*Staatsfreiheit*).[316] Nonetheless, the policing of due diligence obligations by independent state media authorities, if ending up being politically motivated, might raise questions of democratic legitimacy.[317] In any case, the Media Treaty creates a regulatory dichotomy between traditional media and online only journalistic-editorial telemedia. For the former, membership of the Press Council is entirely voluntary, while the latter are obliged to choose between subjection to a self-regulatory body or to the supervision by the state media authorities. This is problematic in view of the equal constitutional protection to which both may be entitled.[318] As will be discussed in the following chapter, the divergence of opinion as to the proper regulatory regime for new media reflects a more fundamental disagreement about their constitutional position in Germany.

The subjection of journalistic-editorial telemedia to the new Media Treaty's regulatory framework means that they need to comply with journalistic due diligence obligations.[319] Also, they need to provide the name and address of a person with editorial responsibility for the service (*Impressumspflicht*), especially if they reproduce the content of print publications. If several persons are named, it is necessary to identify those responsible for each part of the service. Those named need to be permanently resident in Germany, be fully legally competent, have the ability to exercise an official function, and be prosecutable without restrictions.[320] Moreover, telemedia, in particular those that replicate the content of print products, need to provide a right of reply to persons affected by news content.[321] While the *Impressumspflicht* and the right of reply are somewhat qualified by the reference to affiliated print publications, the journalistic due diligence obligations unmistakably apply to the totality of journalistic-editorial telemedia. One would expect that, as a *quid pro quo*, all journalistic-editorial telemedia would be entitled to certain privileges. However, the Media Treaty creates an oddly bifurcated regime by extending press privileges primarily to those services which are spin-offs of print titles, but not to the newly created category of blogs and other journalistic-editorial telemedia which have no links to print-based companies.

---

[313] ibid; see V Jouannaud, 'The Essential-Matters Doctrine (Wesentlichkeitsdoktrin) in Private Law: A Constitutional Limit to Judicial Development of the Law?' in P M Bender (ed), *The Law between Objectivity and Power* (Nomos 2022) 223.

[314] Kalbhenn and Holznagel, 'Journalistische Sorgfaltspflichten' (n 305) 605.

[315] BVerfGE 57, 295 (1981) (*FRAG/Third Broadcasting case*), para 130.

[316] Kalbhenn and Holznagel, 'Journalistische Sorgfaltspflichten' (n 305) 605; BVerfGE 12, 205 (1961); BVerfGE 73, 118 (1986).

[317] Fiedler, '§109 MStV' (n 305) para 11.

[318] Ferreau, 'Desinformation als Herausforderung' (n 308) 207.

[319] MStV, §19(1).

[320] MStV, §18(2).

[321] MStV, §20(1).

The former have a right to obtain information from the authorities free of charge.[322] The beneficiaries need to have as their main aim the fulfilment of a journalistic function. The Federal Administrative Court (*Bundesverwaltungsgericht*, BVerwG) found that this did not apply to a company which operated internet portals, as well as a print and online publication, with a view to providing customers from the construction industry with mostly fee-based information about procurement procedures. Even though this information was partly accompanied by comments, the BVerwG argued that it lacked in editorial selection and in a contribution to opinion formation that went beyond the satisfaction of the business interests of individual users.[323] In other words, journalistic intent must be the main motivation for the undertaking in question, and not merely a cover-up for predominantly commercial aims. The Court referred the applicant to the possibility of obtaining this information by exercising their right to freedom of information, albeit at a cost.[324]

This narrowing down of the right to press freedom is understandable in view of the need to circumscribe the societal cost associated with a right to gratis information. However, the differentiation between 'journalistic-editorial' telemedia and others that do not meet the requirements for this qualification puts the press between a rock and a hard place. On the one hand, a recourse to qualitative, value-laden criteria risks jeopardizing long held, hard fought for press privileges.[325] More than that, it is potentially impermissible from a constitutional point of view, as will be explained later.[326] On the other hand, an emphasis on a formal definition of the press, based solely on its presentation, distribution, and mass media character, risks opening the floodgates to 'crowd-powered demagoguery'.[327] The exact contours of a democracy-oriented interpretation of the right to press freedom that is fit for the digital era remain to be drawn.[328] Such an attempt at a modern understanding of this right will inevitably need to walk the tightrope between creating too close an image of traditional media and subsuming everything under the concept of the press.

The attempt to walk this tightrope has not been fully achieved in the Media Treaty. The yet indeterminate category of other providers of online press-like services are excluded from the enjoyment of the right to information. This has the potential to limit the possibilities for bloggers to engage in investigatory journalism. While they are expected to adhere to journalistic editorial standards, including the requirement of accuracy, they are cut off from the source of information. Rights and obligations

---

[322] MStV, §18(4) in conjunction with §5(1).

[323] BVerwGE 165, 82 (2019), paras 8, 39.

[324] ibid para 26; Landesinformationsfreiheitsgesetz of 17 December 2015, §10.

[325] K N Peifer, 'Presserecht im Internet—Drei Thesen und eine Frage zur Einordnung, Privilegierung und Haftung der elektronischen Presse' in J Gundel and others (eds), *Konvergenz der Medien—Konvergenz des Rechts?* (Jenaer Wissenschaftliche Verlagsgesellschaft 2009) 54.

[326] A Rumyantsev, 'Journalistisch-redaktionelle Gestaltung: Eine verfassungswidrige Forderung? "Wiedergeburt" des wertbezogenen Medienbegriffes' (2008) 1 Zeitschrift für Urheber- und Medienrecht 33, 36; see Chapter 4, p 84.

[327] F Filloux, 'The Oxymoronic Citizen Journalism' (*The Guardian*, 17 May 2010) <https://www.theguardian.com/media/pda/2010/may/17/citizen-journalism> accessed 12 January 2024.

[328] See A Hofmann, 'BVerwG: Kein presserechtlicher Auskunftsanspruch für ein Wirtschaftsunternehmen mit vornehmlich außerpublizistischem Geschäftszweck' (2019) 17 Neue Zeitschrift für Verwaltungsrecht 1283.

should be balanced.[329] The imposition of journalistic duties without bestowal of the concomitant rights seems the more inequitable given that bloggers potentially face the prospect of sanctions imposed by the state media authorities if they fail to comply with these newly crafted expectations, a prospect not shared by their counterparts who are members of the German Press Council.[330] On the other hand, this burden might be counterbalanced by the fact that these actors are possibly not obliged to name a person who is responsible for their offerings nor to provide a right of reply in contrast to press industry spin-offs.[331] To be sure, given that the dividing line between the two types of services is unclear, the described disparity in treatment might prove to be of academic relevance only.

3.8 Concluding Remarks

The concept of the press is in the process of transformation. Both the press product and the it can be disseminated have been fundamentally transformed. News vies for audiences' limited attention with a host of sensationalist, entertaining, and personal, non-news content. In the fierce battle for eyeballs, news organizations mimic social media platforms' methods of algorithmic tailoring without sufficient regard for the societal cost involved. Online intermediaries have vacillated between their self-portrayal as technology or as media companies. The rising momentum of regulating online platforms for the public good is marred by a profound uncertainty about both the employed means and the ends to be attained. Combined with the blurred boundaries between professional and amateur news providers and the contested nexus of the latter's rights versus responsibilities, all the ingredients for a perfect storm are in place. The allocation of costs and benefits to new media actors will be revisited in the next chapter, which is focused on the right to press freedom, its demarcation from the right to freedom of expression, and its uneasy bed fellowship with press regulation.

---

[329] Held, 'Journalistisch-redaktionell' (n 287) para 41; contra T Hoeren, 'Das Telemediengesetz' (2007) Neue Juristische Wochenschrift 801, 803.

[330] Kalbhenn and Holznagel, 'Journalistische Sorgfaltspflichten' (n 303) 606, 607.

[331] MStV, §§18(2)1, 20(1).

4

The Notion of Press Freedom Now and Then

4.1 Introduction

The previous chapter examined the concept of 'the press' and shed light on the multiplicity of actors who resist or at times strive to be subsumed under this concept, to benefit from its privileges, and if possible, to escape its obligations. What might at first sight seem like an inconsequential semantic distinction between freedom of expression and press freedom, gains in importance as a result of the ambiguous position of citizen journalists. The rights these actors are entitled to depend on the adoption of an institutional or functional understanding of the 'press'. This chapter will turn its attention to the protection of freedom of expression and of press freedom at international and national level. Special attention is paid to the case law of the European Court of Human Rights (ECtHR), and to relevant developments in England, Germany, and the US. The aim of the analysis is, first, to trace the ways in which the two rights are delineated, and second, to identify the fault lines between press and broadcasting, and the ways in which they are increasingly superimposed by an overarching notion of 'media freedom'. Finally, the question is raised whether press freedom, as both constitutional right and cultural assumption, is put at risk by intentional regulation or by regulatory creep.[1]

4.2 Freedom of Expression and Press Freedom

The relationship between freedom of expression and press freedom is often hard to discern from international and national constitutional documents. The European Convention on Human Rights (ECHR) specifically protects the rights to freedom of expression and information, while it only refers to broadcasting, television, and film in the context of the licensing requirement under Article 10(1)3 ECHR. Despite the fact that the press is not explicitly mentioned in Article 10 ECHR, the Court has emphasized its essential role as a 'public watchdog', and its obligation to impart information and ideas of public interest, whilst extending these principles also to the audiovisual media.[2] At the same time, the Court has recognized that the realization of the function of the press is not limited to the media and professional journalists, but is open to other actors who create forums for public debate such as non-governmental organizations

---

[1] See L Blom-Cooper, 'Press Freedom: Constitutional Right or Cultural Assumption?' [2008] Public Law 260; C Jones, 'Regulatory Creep: Myths and Misunderstandings' (2004) 8 Risk & Regulation <https://www.lse.ac.uk/accounting/assets/CARR/documents/R-R/2004-Winter.pdf> 6.

[2] *Observer & Guardian v UK*, App no 13585/88, 26 November 1991, para 59; *Kaperzyński v Poland*, App no 43206/07, 3 April 2012, para 55; *Jersild v Denmark*, App no 15890/89, 23 September 1994, para 31.

Press Freedom and Regulation in a Digital Era. Irini Katsirea, Oxford University Press. © Irini Katsirea 2024.
DOI: 10.1093/oso/9780198858607.003.0004

(NGOs).[3] In *Steel and Morris* it held that the obligation to act in good faith in accordance with the ethics of journalism does not only apply to journalists but also to 'others who engage in public debate'.[4] This was taken to the extreme by the Court when it extended verification requirements incumbent on the press to NGOs who made defamatory allegations about a public official to the state authorities by way of private correspondence before these were leaked to the media, unbeknownst to them.[5] NGOs have more limited possibilities to corroborate the information in question compared to the press or to the public authorities. Still, the Court perversely found that they had increased duties to do so in view of their position as representatives of particular segments of the population, and that they should even have given the public official in question the opportunity to defend herself.[6]

While this judgment emphasized the responsibilities of civil society actors, a concurring opinion in a case concerning an NGO's right of access to information also pronounced that 'the difference between journalists and other members of the public is rapidly disappearing' online.[7] The enhanced opportunities for audience input and scrutiny should not, however, blind us to the fact that the media still yield an unparalleled communicative power as discussed in the previous chapter.[8] Online platforms outperform traditional media companies in website traffic terms. YouTube and Facebook boast staggering numbers of over two point five and two point nine billion monthly active users respectively.[9] The platforms' extraordinary reach needs to be taken with caution, however, given that the numbers of visitors vary at different points in time.[10] By comparison, in March 2020, at the height of the first wave of Covid-19, the *New York Times* and the BBC reached just over half a billion and one point three billion website visitors respectively.[11] Still, these numbers represent a 27 per cent increase in the case of the BBC and an astounding 102 per cent increase in the case of the *New York Times* on March 2019. They exemplify the fact that users turn to traditional media when they wish to obtain comprehensive and authoritative news coverage, a need that is heightened at times of crisis.

In view of the special role performed by the media, the ECtHR has recognized that media expression needs to be afforded privileged protection. The media are granted greater latitude not only as regards the substance of information and ideas, but also the

---

[3] *TASZ v Hungary*, App no 37374/05, 14 April 2009, para 27; *Animal Defenders International v United Kingdom*, App no 48876/08, 22 April 2013, para 103.

[4] *Steel and Morris v United Kingdom*, App no 68416/01, 15 February 2005, para 89; see also *Braun v Poland*, App no 30162/10, 4 November 2014, para 47.

[5] *Medžlis Islamske Zajednice Brčko and Others v Bosnia and Herzegovina*, App no 17224/11, 27 June 2017, para 109.

[6] ibid; contra Judge Kūris, dissenting, para 6.

[7] *Youth Initiative for Human Rights v Serbia*, App no 48145/06, 25 June 2013 (Judges Sajó and Vučinić, concurring).

[8] See Chapter 3, p 67.

[9] 'Most popular social networks worldwide as of January 2023, ranked by number of monthly active users' <https://www.statista.com/statistics/272014/global-social-networks-ranked-by-number-of-users/> accessed 27 April 2023.

[10] See Pew Research Centre, 'Social media factsheet' (*Pew Research Centre*, 12 June 2019). <https://www.pewresearch.org/internet/fact-sheet/social-media/> accessed 19 November 2020.

[11] W Turvill, 'BBC, NY Times and Guardian among biggest winners as Covid-19 sends global news traffic soaring' (*Press Gazette*, 17 April 2020) <https://www.pressgazette.co.uk/bbc-ny-times-and-guardian-among-biggest-winners-as-covid-19-sends-global-news-traffic-soaring/> accessed 26 October 2020.

form in which these are conveyed. The Court is not meant to substitute its 'own views for those of the press as to what technique of reporting should be adopted by journalists', and allows for recourse to a measure of exaggeration or provocation and the use of polemic language.[12] The fact that a certain publication is attributable to the media as opposed to a private individual reduces national authorities' margin of appreciation and heightens their duty to prove the existence of a pressing social need.[13] Measures which are capable of discouraging the press from debating questions of public interest are subjected to the most careful scrutiny.[14]

Intricate questions arise in cases in which journalists use social media to make their personal views public. In a case in which it was not clear whether certain internet postings were placed by a professional journalist in his capacity as such or whether they simply expressed his personal opinions as an ordinary citizen in the course of an internet debate, the ECtHR held that the distinction was immaterial. What mattered was the fact that he disclosed his identity and that the postings were publicly disseminated on a 'freely accessible popular internet forum, a medium which in modern times has no less powerful an effect than the print media'.[15] The Court ruled, however, that on occasions when journalists clearly acted as private individuals the right to press freedom was not engaged.[16]

Initially, the ECtHR has been hesitant to extend the safeguards and privileges that are available to the media to other non-media actors beyond NGOs. Thus, in a case concerning the distribution of homophobic leaflets in schools, the ECtHR held that the criminal conviction of the perpetrators did not amount to a violation of Article 10 ECHR.[17] In his concurring opinion, Judge Zupančič remarked that the publication of exactly the same words in a newspaper such as *Svenska Dagbladet* would probably not have been considered a matter for criminal prosecution.[18] However, in a more recent case concerning an NGO's request to access information of public interest held by the public authorities, the Grand Chamber opined that such a right ought not to apply exclusively to NGOs and the press, and that 'the function of bloggers and popular users of the social media may be also assimilated to that of "public watchdogs" in so far as the protection afforded by Article 10 is concerned'.[19] This interpretation of Article 10(1) ECHR as including a right of access to information held by the state criticized by the intervening UK government and by the dissenting judges as a form of 'judicial legislation'.[20] The latter also heeded a word of warning about the extension of the right of access to official documents to categories of users whose reach would 'prove exceedingly difficult to circumscribe in any sensible manner'.[21]

---

[12] *Stoll v Switzerland*, App no 69698/01, 10 December 2007, para 146; *Thorgeir Thorgeirson v Iceland*, App no 13778/88, 25 June 1992, para 67; *Oberschlick v Austria (No 2)*, App no 20834/92, 1 July 1997, para 33.
[13] *Éditions Plon v France*, App no 58148/00, 18 May 2004, para 44; *Kaperzyński v Poland*, App no 43206/07, 3 April 2012, para 70.
[14] *Jersild v Denmark*, App no 15890/89, 23 June 1994, para 35.
[15] *Fattulayev v Azerbaijan*, App no 40984/07, 22 April 2010, para 95.
[16] *Janowski v Poland*, App no 25716/94, 21 January 1999, para 32.
[17] *Vejdeland v Sweden*, App no 1813/07, 9 February 2012.
[18] ibid (Judge Zupančič, concurring) para 12.
[19] *Magyar Helsinki Bizottság v Hungary*, App no 18030/11, 8 November 2016, para 168.
[20] ibid para 103.
[21] ibid, Judges Spano and Kjølbro dissenting, para 16.

Further, in a case concerning highly aggressive and insulting comments about police officers published on a weblog the ECtHR showed a high level of tolerance for the
use of offensive language.[22] It held that the use of offensive language can be a stylistic
medium to convey one's information and ideas which deserves as much protection
under Article 10 ECHR as the substance of these ideas, the more so when debate of
matters of public interest is at stake.[23] Notably, the ECtHR compared the possible risk
of harm posed by internet communications to that posed by the press. It concluded
that the instantaneous and global reach of the former posed a higher risk that was,
however, counterbalanced by the potentially small readership of a statement released
online. This worked to the advantage of the blogger in question given that he was not
in any way well-known or influential, and his statement had attracted very little attention.[24] It follows that the latitude afforded private online forums to express offensive views is more conditional than that granted to the press. While in the case of the
former, corrosive speech is condoned so long as it only reaches a small circle, the latter
enjoys the freedom to address the public at large, constrained only by the law and journalistic ethics.

This weighing up between the harms and benefits of online communication is
characteristic of the ECtHR's position. The ECtHR has recognized on numerous occasions the important role of the internet 'in enhancing the public's access to news
and facilitating the dissemination of information in general', and of user-generated
expressive activity online as 'an unprecedented platform for the exercise of freedom of
expression'.[25] At the same time, it has acknowledged the risk of defamatory allegations
and hate speech or other unlawful speech spreading like wildfire and leaving an indelible mark online.[26] Despite this heightened risk of harm, the Court opined that the
internet 'is not and potentially will never be subject to the same regulations and control' as the printed media.[27] While this is a debatable conclusion, it leaves the question
open as to what the appropriate level of regulation of online communications should
be. In the case at hand, a local newspaper published an anonymous letter found on a
website which contained allegations against senior officials. The Ukrainian Press Act
provided a civil liability exemption for the verbatim reproduction of public interest
material published in the printed press that was subject to state registration, but not
for such material available on a publicly accessible news website. At the same time,
while there was a system for the state registration of print outlets, no such system existed for internet-based media.[28] The ECtHR held that this disparate treatment of print
compared to online media amounted to an interference with press freedom.[29] The
Court did not have occasion to clarify in this case whether the civil liability exemption

---

[22] *Savva Terentyev v Russia*, App no 10692/09, 28 August 2018.

[23] ibid paras 62, 68.

[24] ibid paras 80, 81.

[25] *Cengiz and Others v Turkey*, App no 48226/10, 1 December 2015, para 52 (hereafter *Cengiz and Others
v Turkey*); *Ahmet Yildirim v Turkey*, 18 December 2012, App no 3111/10, para 48 (hereafter *Ahmet Yildirim
v Turkey*); *Times Newspapers Ltd v. the United Kingdom (nos. 1 and 2)*, App nos 3002/03 and 23676/03, 10
March 2009, para 27 (hereafter *Times Newspapers Ltd v the United Kingdom*).

[26] *Delfi AS v Estonia*, App no 64569/09, 16 June 2015, para 110 (hereafter *Delfi AS v Estonia*).

[27] *Editorial Board of Pravoye Delo and Shtekel v Ukraine*, App no 33014/05, 5 May 2011, para 63.

[28] ibid paras 61, 62.

[29] ibid para 66.

should only benefit mainstream news media reproducing public interest material or also, say, anonymous bloggers.

The heighted protection afforded to the press is not unconditional. The ECtHR has long held the view that press freedom—for traditional and online media alike—needs to be limited to the publication of matters that are capable of contributing to a debate of general interest to society. In *von Hannover v Germany*, it distinguished public interest publications from press products whose aim was to satisfy the curiosity of their readership about the private life of celebrities.[30] The ECtHR is thus less concerned with press freedom as an expression of individual autonomy and a means of self-fulfilment. It views press freedom strictly as a mechanism by which to ensure the free flow of information relevant to democratic opinion formation and legitimate public debate.[31] This contentious understanding of press freedom as a *quid pro quo* for the dissemination of information in the public interest was also at the heart of the *Satamedia* case.[32] Similarly to the ECtHR, Advocate General Kokott embraced a conditional understanding of press freedom.[33] However, the Court of Justice of the European Union (CJEU) gave short shrift to this view. It held that the journalism exemption from data protection law applied to any 'disclosure to the public of information, opinions or ideas' regardless of its contribution to the public interest.[34]

The ECtHR's instrumental account of media freedom has found considerable, though not unanimous, resonance in UK academic thinking and case law.[35] It has been embraced also by some US scholars.[36] It resonates with Lord Justice Leveson's conception of press freedom as 'as an instrumental good, to be valued, promoted and protected to the extent that ... it is thereby enabled to flourish commercially as a sector and to serve its important democratic functions'.[37] There is nothing inherently unorthodox about the notion that the press is supposed to serve the public interest, and that it is this essential function that justifies its claim to a special status. This functionalist view does, however, pose risks insofar as it opens the door to value judgements

---

[30] *Von Hannover v Germany*, App no 59320/00, 24 June 2004, para 65.

[31] H Fenwick and G Philipson, *Media Freedom under the Human Rights Act* (OUP 2006) 71 (hereafter Fenwick and Philipson, *Media Freedom*); in more qualified terms T Mast, 'Die Rolle der Massenmedien in Zeiten der Krise' (2020) 3 Archiv für Presserecht 191, 193: 'subjective-objective conception of media freedoms espoused by the ECtHR' (author's translation).

[32] Case C-73/07, *Satakunnan Markkinapörssi and Satamedia* [2008] ECLI:EU:C:2008:727.

[33] ibid, Opinion of AG Kokott, para 65.

[34] Case C-73/07, *Tietosuojavaltuutettu v Satakunnan Markkinapörssi Oy en Satamedia Oy* [2008] ECLI:EU:C:2008:727, paras 58, 62. See W Hins, '*Satakunnan Markkinapörssi and Satamedia*' (2010) 47 Common Market Law Review 215, 229. For a discussion of the journalism exemption see Chapter 6, p 147.

[35] J Rowbottom, *Media Law* (Hart Publishing 2018) 5; E Barendt, *Freedom of Speech* (2nd edn, OUP 2007); Fenwick and Philipson, *Media Freedom* (n 31); T Gibbons, 'Free Speech, Communication and the State' in M Amos, J Harrison, and L Woods (eds), *Freedom of Expression and the Media* (Martinus Nijhoff 2012) 22; J Lichtenberg, 'Foundations and Limits of Freedom of the Press' in J Lichtenberg (ed), *Democracy and the Mass Media* (CUP 1990) 102, 120 (hereafter Lichtenberg, 'Foundations and Limits'); *Miranda v Secretary of State for the Home Department*, para 46; contra P Wragg, 'The Legitimacy of Press Regulation' [2015] Public Law 290 (hereafter Wragg, 'Legitimacy').

[36] C E Baker, *Media, Markets and Democracy* (CUP 2001) 195; F Schauer, 'Towards and Institutional First Amendment' (2005) 80 Minnesota Law Review 1256, 1275.

[37] Lord Justice Leveson, *An Inquiry into the Culture, Practices and Ethics of the Ppress* (House of Commons 780 2012) 63 para 3.7 (hereafter Leveson, *An Inquiry*).

about the importance of particular information.[38] One could argue that determining the types of journalism that better further the public interest should be beyond the purview of the law. However, the reality is different. Judgements about the value of information often need to be made, not least in the areas of privacy and defamation law. The extent to which they are prone to stifle press freedom depends on the latitude afforded to the press.

A seemingly more unconditional approach to press freedom is taken by the German Constitutional Court. In *von Hannover v Germany*, the BVerfG argued that entertainment fulfilled important social functions, and that personalization was a legitimate journalistic means of attracting attention.[39] This line of reasoning is characteristic of the BVerfG's formal conception of the press, which does not allow for a differentiation according to the content and quality of a press product.[40] The German Federal Court of Justice (*Bundesgerichtshof*, BGH) also considers that determining which type of content is in the public interest is at the core of press freedom and freedom of expression. Entertainment programmes, for instance about the private and everyday life of celebrities, benefit from this protection irrespective of the characteristics or quality of the coverage.[41] After all, judging the quality of news has been described as an endeavour 'as murky as critical judgment of poetry, chamber music or architecture'.[42] The difficulty of this task is compounded by the fact that audience members evaluate news quality differently than journalists or media experts.[43]

In view of these uncertainties, the prevailing academic opinion in Germany subscribes to the view that the 'serious press' and the tabloids are equally entitled to the right to press freedom regardless of their quality.[44] The content of the publication in question is only to be taken into account when balancing press freedom with competing personality rights. In other words, the contribution of a publication to the democratic process is only to be considered at the justification stage, not already when determining the substantive scope of application (*Schutzbereich*) of the fundamental right.[45] German press law is hence not entirely devoid of value judgements either, but only passes them at a later stage in the assessment compared to the ECtHR. A certain rapprochement between the position of the two courts can be seen in the *Mosley* case. The ECtHR conceded 'the Article 10 right of members of the public to have access to a

---

[38] Fenwick and Philipson, *Media Freedom* (n 31) 71.
[39] *Von Hannover v Germany*, App no 59320/00, 24 June 2004, para 25; for a criticism of the devaluation of allegedly unpolitical speech in the Court's case law, see M Cornils, 'Art. 10 EMRK' in H Gersdorf and P Paal (eds), *Informations- und Medienrecht Kommentar* (2nd edn, Beck 2021) para 8 (hereafter Cornils, 'Art. 10 EMRK').
[40] BVerfG 34, 269 (1973), para 31.
[41] BGH, 2 August 2022, VI ZR 26/21 para 14; BGH, 2 May 2017, VI ZR 262/16 para 24.
[42] L Bogart, 'Reflections on Content Quality in Newspapers' (2004) 25(1) Newspaper Research Journal 40, 44.
[43] C Neuberger, 'The Journalistic Quality of Internet Formats and Services: Results of a User Survey' (2014) 2(3) Digital Journalism 419; Y Tsfati, O Meyers, and Y Peri, 'What Is Good Journalism? Comparing Israeli Public and Journalists' Perspectives' (2006) 7(2) Journalism 152.
[44] R Ricker and J Weberling, *Handbuch des Presserechts* (Beck 2012) 17 et seq (hereafter Ricker and Weberling, *Handbuch des Presserechts*); T Held, '§54 Allgemeine Bestimmungen' in R Binder and T Vesting (eds), *Beckscher Kommentar zum Rundfunkrecht* (4th edn, Beck 2018) paras 42, 43.
[45] See F Neunhoeffer, *Das Presseprivileg im Datenschutzrecht. Eine rechtsvergleichende Betrachtung des deutschen und des englischen Rechts* (Mohr Siebeck 2005) 111.

wide range of publications covering a variety of fields', but openly expressed its disregard for 'sensational and, at times, lurid news, intended to titillate and entertain' when
it came to balancing freedom of expression with privacy.[46]

The formal conception of press freedom adopted by the BVerfG is potentially at
odds with the concept of 'telemedia with journalistic-editorial offerings' used in both
the old Interstate Broadcasting Treaty and the new Media Treaty.[47] Whereas the online
press needs to prove that it carries out 'journalistic-editorial' work, the same does not
apply to the printed press. This leads to the paradoxical situation whereby a concept
derived from the traditional media forms the basis for the imposition of a requirement
on the online press that cannot be extended to these very media.[48] The motivation
for this differentiation is understandable: whereas a journalistic modus operandi can
generally be presumed in the case of the mainstream media, this is not always the case
as far as online content is concerned. Journalistic-editorial telemedia need to fulfil the
classic journalistic criteria of universality, timeliness, periodicity, and publicity, aptly
modified to suit the online environment.[49] Universality signifies offerings that have
a journalistic, factual orientation. Timeliness expresses the fact that the publications
in question have news value even though they can also concern questions of timeless
interest. The journalistic requirement of periodicity is commonly recast as actuality
to capture the reality of constantly updated online publishing.[50] Publicity is usually a
given in view of the openly accessible nature of online content. Furthermore, the editorial nature of 'journalistic-editorial' offerings requires an editorial selection process
and structuring, which is lacking in the case of a collection of raw, unprocessed data,
for instance.

As far as the printed press is concerned, the BVerfG's formal conception prevents the imposition of overly restrictive qualitative requirements. At the same time,
the BVerfG has made clear that press freedom does not protect every expression of
opinion simply because it is contained in printed matter. In the *Critical Shareholder*
decision, the Court held that a pamphlet critical of the Bayer concern was 'only' protected under freedom of expression, and not under press freedom, despite its press-
like production and dissemination method, given that it lacked the significance of the
press for the free individual and public formation of opinion.[51] The interpretation of
the 'press' in a broad way in the Court's case law aims to protect above all 'the institutional autonomy of the press all the way from the acquisition of information to the dissemination of news and opinion.'[52] This raises the question as to where the line should
be drawn in the case of the online press.

---

[46] *Mosley v United Kingdom*, App no 48009/08, 10 May 2011, para 114.

[47] Chapter 3, p 72.

[48] A Rumyantsev, 'Journalistisch-redaktionelle Gestaltung: Eine verfassungswidrige Forderung?
"Wiedergeburt" des wertbezogenen Medienbegriffes' (2008) 1 Zeitschrift für Urheber- und Medienrecht
33, 40 (hereafter Rumyantsev, 'Journalistisch-redaktionelle Gestaltung').

[49] W. Lent, '§17MStV' in H. Gersdorf, P. Paal, *Informations- und Medienrecht Kommentar* (2nd edn,
Beck 2021) para 14; T Held, 'Journalistisch-redaktionell gestaltete Angebote' in Binder and Vesting
(eds), *Beck'scher Kommentar zum Rundfunkrecht* (4th edn, Beck 2018) §54, para 48 (hereafter Held,
'Journalistisch-redaktionell').

[50] Lent (n 49) para 14.

[51] BVerfGE 85, 11 (1991), para 46.

[52] BVerfGE 10, 118 (1959), para 18.

There needs to be evidence of journalistic selection. The imposition of narrow content restrictions seems, however, unjustified. Some argue that offerings that are exclusively concerned with the self-representation of the service provider, such as online diaries, should not be classified as 'telemedia with journalistic-editorial offerings'.[53] This view is potentially too restrictive.[54] While a 'journalistic-editorial service' should aim at public information and opinion formation, this objective can conceivably also be met by way of self-referential representations as long as the abovementioned journalistic criteria are fulfilled. At the same time, the extension of journalistic due diligence obligations to other professional journalistic-editorial services is qualified in the new Media Treaty by the orientation of these services to the regular provision of news or political information ('*in denen regelmäßig Nachrichten oder politische Informationen enthalten sind*').[55] It has been argued that this criterion is not fulfilled in the case of influencer blogs, which only occasionally contain news.[56] However, the law does not specify the required weighting of news or political information compared to other content types. Also, it is not always possible to sharply delineate news content from education, entertainment, or culture.[57] An interpretation of these categories on a case-by-case basis seems warranted. It is necessary to weigh press freedom and the right to information versus other vulnerable rights that require protection. Stretching wide the category of 'journalistic-editorial telemedia' risks saddling types of casual, informal expression with unnecessary regulatory burdens. Casting this category two narrowly risks depriving non-professional journalists of much-needed protection. A broad interpretation of journalism was embraced by the District Court of Amsterdam, which, relying on the CJEU *Satamedia* case, held that a well-known Dutch influencer who specialized in celebrity gossip was entitled to protection of journalistic sources.[58]

In Germany, the search for a neat demarcation between freedom of expression and press freedom is driven by the need to fairly allocate costs and benefits to new media actors. Across the Atlantic, courts have also grappled with these very questions. As in Germany, where the Constitution specifically guarantees freedom of the press in tandem with the freedom of reporting by means of broadcasts and films, the First Amendment protects 'the freedom of speech, or of the press'.[59] However, in Germany, the separate mention of the press has served as the basis for the recognition of rights that go beyond those that are available to individual members of the public. In the US,

---

[53]   Held, 'Journalistisch-redaktionell' (n 49) §54, para 51.

[54]   W Seitz, 'Teil 8 Zivilrechtlicher Persönlichkeitsschutz gegenüber Äußerungen im Internet' in T Hoeren, U Sieber, and B Holznagel (eds), *Multimediarecht* (53th supplement, Beck 2020) para 106.

[55]   See Chapter 3.

[56]   J Kalbhenn and B Holznagel, 'Journalistische Sorgfaltspflichten auf YouTube und Instagram—Neue Vorgaben im Medienstaatsvertrag' in L Specht-Riemenschneider and others (eds), *Festschrift für Jürgen Taeger* (R&W 2020) 596 (hereafter Kalbhenn and Holznagel, 'Journalistische Sorgfaltspflichten').

[57]   W Lent, 'Paradigmenwechsel bei den publizistischen Sorgfaltspflichten im Online-Journalismus—Zur Neuregelung des §19 Medienstaatsvertrag' (2020) 8/9 Zeitschrift für Urheber- und Medienrecht 593, 599.

[58]   Rechtbank Amsterdam, ECLI:NL:RBAMS:2022:2347, 29 April 2022; see also the wide definition of journalism as 'a function shared by a wide range of actors, including professional full-time reporters and analysts, as well as bloggers and others who engage in forms of self-publication in print, on the internet or elsewhere' in the UN Human Rights Committee General Comment no 34, 12 September 2011, para 44.

[59]   Constitution for the Federal Republic of Germany of 23 May 1949, last modified on 28 June 2022, BGBl I, p 968 (*Grundgesetz* (GG)), art 5(1)2; US Constitution, amend I.

this view has not prevailed. Legal commentators have been divided in their interpretation of the press clause.

Justice Potter Stewart, who served on the Supreme Court during many press cases in the 1970s, famously claimed off the bench that the press clause offered structural protection to the publishing business, which he dubbed 'the only organized private business that is given explicit constitutional protection'.[60] He argued that the press clause would be a 'constitutional redundancy' if it was synonymous with freedom of expression. This view met with approval by some scholars.[61] However, Justice Stewart's view also generated dissent, most sharply articulated on the bench by Chief Justice Burger in *First National Bank v. Bellotti*.[62] While in Justice Stewart's view the historic example of licensing and press censorship in England lent a powerful argument for a special protection of the organized press, in Justice Burger's view it discredited it as too narrow and fraught with difficulty. He argued that drawing a line between the institutional press and others would be 'reminiscent of the abhorred licensing system of Tudor and Stuart England'.[63] But Justice Burger was rather evasive in his explanation of who these 'others' were, vaguely describing them as 'all who exercise its freedoms', meaning the First Amendment's freedoms. His view mirrors that expressed on the other side of the Atlantic by the House of Lords in *AG v Observer Ltd* in the following words:

> The media have greater powers of disseminating information widely than other people have, but it has not been suggested by any party to this appeal that the media have any special privileges in law in the matter of freedom of speech. They have the same rights of free speech as anyone else, subject to the same constraints.[64]

Justice Burger's position is characteristic of the Supreme Court's reluctance to give a more far-reaching meaning to the press clause than that accorded to the speech clause. The extensive guarantees that are already available to ordinary speakers might be a reason why the Supreme Court has been loath to embrace distinct press rights.[65] The more significant reason for the emasculation of the First Amendment's press clause is linked to the complexity of identifying who the press is. In a deeply divided majority opinion in *Branzburg v Hayes*, the Court argued that the recognition of a newsman's testimonial privilege

> would present practical and conceptual difficulties of a high order. Sooner or later, it would be necessary to define those categories of newsmen who qualified for the privilege, a questionable procedure in light of the traditional doctrine that liberty

---

[60] P Stewart, 'Or of the Press' (1999) 50(4) Hastings Law Journal 705, 709.

[61] M B Nimmer, 'Introduction: Is Freedom of the Press a Redundancy: What Does It Add to Freedom of Speech?' (1975) 26(3) Hastings Law Journal 639; F Abrams, 'The Press is Different: Reflections on Justice Stewart and the Autonomous Press' (1979) 7 Hofstra Law Review 563, 585.

[62] *First Nat'l Bank of Boston v Bellotti* 435 US 765, 801 (1978) (Burger, CJ, concurring)</IBT<.

[63] ibid.

[64] *Attorney General v Observer Ltd* (1990) 1 AC 109, 201.

[65] S R West, 'Press Exceptionalism' (2014) 127 Harvard Law Review 2434, 2442 (hereafter West, 'Press Exceptionalism'); S R West, 'Awakening the Press Clause' (2011) 58 UCLA Law Review 1025, 1057.

of the press is the right of the lonely pamphleteer ... just as much as of the large metropolitan publisher ... [66]

These anticipated difficulties were almost a premonition of things to come. They pale in comparison to the uncertainties posed by the multiplication of non-media actors whose activities may warrant protection similar to that afforded to the press. In *Citizens United v Federal Election Commission*, the Court once more 'rejected the proposition that the institutional press has any constitutional privilege beyond that of other speakers' by alluding to the fact that '[w]ith the advent of the Internet and the decline of print and broadcast media ... the line between the media and others who wish to comment on political and social issues becomes far more blurred'.[67]

The Supreme Court has so far refused to listen to recent calls that advocate a First Amendment privilege for the press, and for those who perform the press function.[68] Still, its judgment in *Branzburg* could be read as signalling some receptiveness to the argument that the floodgates should be left ajar for those non-traditional speakers who function as the press.[69] *Branzburg* has been interpreted by many in this more lenient way by relying on Justice Powell's concurrence, which favoured a case-by-case balancing act between freedom of the press and citizens' testimonial duty.[70] To be sure, the Supreme Court has not yet been confronted with cases involving non-journalistic actors.[71] It has foreclosed potential claims by holding fast to its position that journalists do not have any more rights than ordinary citizens. By conceptualizing the press 'as a technology' rather than 'as an industry', it has killed two birds with one stone, at the same time denying both ordinary citizens' and journalists' rights of access to sources, or the protection of the confidentiality of sources.[72]

Meanwhile, both federal and state laws have bestowed journalists with various privileges relating to, for example, access to information, defamation law, or intellectual property law, while numerous state shield laws provide at least a qualified protection

---

[66] *Branzburg v Hayes* 408 US 665 (1972).

[67] *Citizens United v Federal Election Commission* 558 US 36 (2010).

[68] R D Sack, 'Reflections on the Wrong Question: Special Constitutional Privilege for the Institutional Press' (1979) 7(3) Hofstra Law Review 629, 633; A Lewis, 'The Right to Scrutinize Government: Toward a First Amendment Theory of Accountability' (1980) 34 University of Miami Law Review 793, 801; West, 'Press Exceptionalism' (n 65); J Alonzo, 'Note: Restoring the Ideal Marketplace: How Recognizing Bloggers as Journalists Can Save the Press' (2005/6) 9 New York University Journal of Legislation & Public Policy 751; N N Wentworth, 'Hot off the Press: An Argument for a Federal Shield Law Affording a Qualified Evidentiary Privilege to Journalists in Light of Renewed Concerns about Freedom of the Press and National Security' (2020) 53(3) Loyola of Los Angeles Law Review 745.

[69] M Bloom, 'Subpoenaed Sources and the Internet: A Test for When Bloggers Should Reveal Who Misappropriated a Trade Secret' (2006) 24(2) Yale Law & Policy Review 471, 474.

[70] *Branzburg v Hayes* 408 US 665 (1972) (Powell, J, concurring), 710; S R West, 'Concurring in Part & (and) Concurring in the Confusion' (2006) 104(8) Michigan Law Review 1951, 1952; R A Smolla, 'Information as Contraband: The First Amendment and Liability for Trafficking in Speech' (2002) 96(3) Northwestern University Law Review 1099, 1115.

[71] J Schroeder, *The Press Clause and Digital Technology's Fourth Wave. Media Law and the Symbiotic Web* (Routledge 2018) 116ff (hereafter Schroeder, *The Press Clause*).

[72] E Volokh, 'Freedom of the Press as an Industry or for the Press as a Technology? From the Framing to Today' (2012) University of Pennsylvania Law Review 459; *Saxbe v Washington Post* 417 US 843 (1974); *Cohen v Cowles* 501 US 663 (1991); *Miller v US* 125 US 2977 (2005).

for journalists who are asked to reveal confidential sources.[73] While some of these shield laws are narrowly tailored to traditional journalists, others apply more broadly to persons connected with any medium of communication to the public.[74] Aided by these laws or by an expansive reading of *Branzburg*, lower courts across the US have grappled with, and occasionally conceded to the request to grant, special privileges to a range of actors performing press-like functions.

Some of these courts have taken a formal approach, focusing on the journalistic credentials of the disseminator or on the similarity of the newsgathering process and of the outputs in question to traditional forms of news distribution.[75] Others have focused less on who does the publishing as on why, how, and what is published. In *O'Grady*, a case concerning the online publication of illegally obtained confidential information about an unreleased Apple product, a California state appeals court declined to draw a distinction between 'legitimate' and 'illegitimate' news as any such attempt 'would imperil a fundamental purpose of the First Amendment'.[76] In the court's view, the practice of publishing unedited, verbatim copies of Apple's internal information was salutary given that it provided readers with 'source materials rather than subjecting them to the editors' own "spin" on a story'.[77] The publication of information of interest to the public on a news-oriented website was deemed sufficient by the court to qualify the petitioners for the reporter's privilege. In another case that concerned a Freedom of Information (FOI) request, it was held that the corporate character of a blog communicating product safety information to the public did not preclude it from the news media fee waiver.[78]

These judgments suggest a more flexible understanding of the type of publications that are entitled to press privileges, compared to that displayed by the German Administrative Court, as discussed in the previous chapter.[79] However, also in the US, an important consideration in the FOI cases has been whether the information requested would be used to benefit the public rather than being primarily in the commercial interest of the requester.[80] In a case concerned with electoral disclosure requirements, the court found that public interest had not been served by an anonymous website that was created with the sole purpose of advocating the defeat of a gubernatorial candidate. The court argued that the state law's requirements, which compelled disclosure of the sponsors of political messages, served the public interest better than the application of the press exemption to a single-issue, not regularly updated website.[81]

---

[73] Freedom of Information Act 5 USC §552(a)(4)A(ii)(II)(2016); Lanham Act 15 USC §1125(a)(3)B (1998); an example of a Shield Law is the District of Columbia Free Flow of Information Act, DC Code §16-4701–4704 (1992).

[74] Schroeder, *The Press Clause* (n 71) 109; for a more broadly worded law see Oregon Revised Statutes §44.520 (2020).

[75] *Service Employees International Union Local 5 v Professional Janitorial Services of Houston*, 415 SW3d 387 (Tex App 2013); *Too Much Media, LLC v Hale*, 206 NJ 209 (NJ 2011); *Kaufman v Islamic Society of Arlington*, 291 SW3d 130 (Tex App 2009).

[76] *O'Grady v Superior Court of Santa Clara County*, 139 Call App 4th 1423, 1457 (Cal Ct App 2006).

[77] ibid.

[78] *Liberman v US Dep't of Transp*, 227 F Supp 3d 1 (DDC 2016).

[79] BVerwGE 165, 82 (2019); see Chapter 3, p 77.

[80] *Cause of Action v F.T.C,* 799 F 3d 1108, 1121 (DC Cir 2015).

[81] *Bailey v Maine Commission on Governmental Ethics*, 900 F Supp 2d 75 (2012).

Placing the public interest at the heart of the definition of a 'journalist' would go some way towards solving the 'practical and conceptual difficulties of a high order' alluded to in *Branzburg*. However, the patchwork of federal and state laws, coupled with the paucity in the Supreme Court jurisprudence, is not conducive to legal certainty for those who, while not full-time journalists, serve a journalistic function well. This raises the risk of withholding 'protection from those who most need it—speakers most likely to lack funds and libel insurance'.[82] While the protection of journalist-like actors under the guarantee of press freedom or under the right to freedom of expression remains contested, the constitutional boundaries of press versus broadcast freedom are also uncertain. The following section will be devoted to this question, and to the increasing tendency towards the conceptualization of a unified right to media freedom.

4.3 From Press Freedom to Media Freedom

Historical contingencies have led to a considerably disparate development of broadcasting and the press, as was discussed earlier in this monograph.[83] At first sight, these differences have not, however, left a clear imprint on the guarantees for the protection of media freedom under the ECHR or the Charter of Fundamental Rights of the European Union (ChFR).[84] The conception of freedom of expression under the ECHR is a holistic one, protecting the dissemination of information and ideas and the right of the public to receive them regardless of the medium used, whether this is the press, broadcasting, film, or the internet.[85] The fundamental role of freedom of expression in a democratic society and its embeddedness in the principle of pluralism are equally valid for the press and for broadcasting.[86] The ECtHR has not had occasion to draw on the conceptual differences between broadcasting and other electronic media. The distinction is, however, of importance not least insofar as Article 10(1)3 ECHR authorizes the licensing of television, broadcasting, or cinema enterprises, while this does not apply to other audiovisual media services such as video on demand.[87]

The material scope of protection and the proportionality assessment in cases engaging freedom of broadcasting are similar to those applicable to the press.[88] However, in recent times, the Court has emphasized the importance of pluralism in audiovisual broadcasting in a way that goes beyond what applies to the press on the ground of the wide dissemination of the former.[89] The principle of pluralism implies a duty on

---

[82] *Service Employees International Union Local 5 v Professional Janitorial Services of Houston*, 415 SW3d 387 (Tex App 2013) (Willett, J, dissenting) 5.

[83] Chapter 2, 13.

[84] Charter of Fundamental Rights of the European Union of 14 December 2007, [2007] OJ C 303/01.

[85] See *inter alia Ekin Association v France*, App no 39288/98, 17 July 2001, para 42; *Animal Defenders International v United Kingdom*, App no 48876/08, 22 April 2013, para 100; *Times Newspapers Ltd v the United Kingdom (Nos 1 and 2)*, App nos 3002/03 and 23676/03, 11 October 2005, para 27.

[86] *Informationsverein Lentia and Others v Austria*, App nos 13914/88, 15041/89, 15717/89, 15779/89, and 17207/90, 24 November 1993, para 38.

[87] Cornils, 'Art. 10 EMRK' (n 39) para 27.

[88] *Animal Defenders International v United Kingdom*, App no 48876/08, 22 April 2013, para 100.

[89] *Informationsverein Lentia*, para 38.

the state to guarantee, 'first, that the public has access through television and radio to impartial and accurate information and a range of opinion and comment, ... and, secondly, that journalists and other professionals working in the audiovisual media are not prevented from imparting this information and comment'.[90] The Court recognizes the contribution of public service broadcasting (PSB) to the quality and balance of programmes, but has clarified that states are not obliged under Article 10 ECHR to establish such a service provided there are other measures in place to attain the same end.[91] However, when there is a PSB system, and the commercial stations are unable to offer a genuine alternative, the PSB's duty to offer impartial, independent, and balanced news is particularly accentuated.[92] The judgment in *Manole v Moldova* is testament to the Court's preoccupation with the functional, objective dimension of broadcasting freedom. Similarly, the role of the press as 'public watchdog' encapsulates the ECtHR's functional conception of press freedom, which creates both rights and responsibilities of the press to impart information on all matters of public interest, while respecting the limits of Article 10 ECHR even when matters of 'serious public concern' are at stake.[93]

Nonetheless, the Article 10 ECHR case law has been criticized for being oriented to the protection of individual freedoms rather than to the creation of a functional media order.[94] This has led to uncertainty as to the relationship between Article 10 ECHR and Article 11 ChFR. Article 52(3) ChFR states that 'In so far as this Charter contains rights which correspond to rights guaranteed by the [ECHR], the meaning and scope of those rights shall be the same as those laid down by the [ECHR]' but does 'not prevent Union law providing more extensive protection'. Some argue that the guarantee of freedom and pluralism of the media in Article 11(2) ChFR does not fall within the 'most favoured nation clause' of Article 52(3) ChFR in view of the lack of guarantees for the institutional dimension of media freedom in the ECtHR case law.[95] This would mean that the CJEU would apply Article 52(2) ChFR limitations as opposed to Article 10(2) ECHR.[96] Others contend that this could not be the case given that media freedom is not specifically included in the Treaties.[97] This objection pays insufficient attention to the fact that the freedom of reception and retransmission of audiovisual media services gives specific expression to the right to freedom of expression.[98]

In any case, the significance of this potential application of Article 52(2) ChFR should not be overrated given that the differences between the limiting clauses in

---

[90] *Manole and Others v Moldova*, App no 13936/02, 17 September 2009, para 100.
[91] ibid.
[92] ibid para 101.
[93] *Erla Hlynsdóttir v Iceland*, App no 43380/10, 21 October 2014, para 62.
[94] M Cornils, 'Art. 11 EU-GR Charta' in H Gersdof and P Paal (eds), *Informations- und Medienrecht Kommentar* (2nd edn, Beck 2021) paras 14, 15.
[95] ibid.
[96] Article 52(2) ChFR states that 'Rights recognised by this Charter for which provision is made in the Treaties shall be exercised under the conditions and within the limits defined by those Treaties'.
[97] W Berka and H Tretter, 'Public service media under Article 10 of the European Convention on Human Rights' (*European Broadcasting Union*, December 2013) <https://www.ebu.ch/files/live/sites/ebu/files/Publications/Art%2010%20Study_final.pdf> accessed 9 April 2021.
[98] Opinion of Advocate General Saugmansgaard Øe, *Baltic Media Alliance v Lietuvos radijo* [2019] ECLI:EU:C:2019:566, para 70.

the ECHR and the ChFR are less pronounced than it might appear at first sight.[99] Overblown expectations for an independent development of media freedom under Article 11(2) ChFR have so far largely remained unfulfilled in view of the CJEU's as yet underdeveloped media jurisprudence, the rather limited importance attached to the Charter, and the CJEU's reliance on ECHR case law.[100] Article 11 ChFR parallels Article 10 ECHR not only as regards their exception clauses, but also as far as their substantive scope of application is concerned.[101] The Explanatory Memorandum to the proposed European Media Freedom Act (EMFA) also states that Article 11 ChFR 'corresponds to' Article 10 ECHR.[102] Like Article 10 ECHR, Article 11 ChFR protects media freedom without distinguishing between different types of media.

The open-ended scope of Article 10 ECHR has enabled the Court to extend it to various manifestations of internet communication.[103] In the *Delfi* case, which concerned the liability of online news portals for user-generated content, the domestic court characterized such portals as 'publishers' on the ground of their economic interest in the publication of comments, an interest also shared by the printed media.[104] The ECtHR neither objected to this characterization nor did it unequivocally treat online news portals as equivalent to press publishers. It recognized that the duties and responsibilities of the former may differ from those of the latter in view of the 'particular nature of the internet'.[105] Given that the case did not concern a press privilege, such as the confidentiality of sources, the Court did not need to reach a definitive conclusion on the nature of the online press.[106]

The flexible scope of Article 10 ECHR contrasts with the more rigid delineation of distinct types of media freedom under Article 5 of the German Constitution. Article 5(1) GG constitutes the constitutional basis for the regulation of the German broadcasting system. It stipulates:

> Everyone shall have the right freely to express and disseminate his opinion by speech, writing, and pictures and freely to inform himself from generally accessible sources. Freedom of the press and freedom of reporting by means of broadcasts and films are guaranteed. There shall be no censorship.

---

[99] M Borowski, 'Limiting Clauses: On the Continental European Tradition of Special Limiting Clauses and the General Limiting Clause of Art. 52 (1) Charter of Fundamental Rights of the European Union' (2007) 1(2) Legisprudence 197, 239.

[100] See *Scarlet Extended* [2011] ECLI:EU:C:2011:771, para 50; *SABAM* [2012] ECLI:EU:C:2012:85, para 48; *Sky Österreich* [2013] ECLI:EU:C:2013:28, para 51; *Digital Rights Ireland* [2014] ECLI:EU:C:2014:238, para 28; *Buivids* [2019] ECLI:EU:C:2019:122, para 66 (hereafter *Buivids*).

[101] *Philip Morris Brands and Others* [2016] EU:C:2016:325, para 147; *Buivids*, para 65; M Cornils, '§1 LPG Freiheit der Presse' in M Löffler (ed), *Presserecht* (6th edn, Beck 2015) para 103.

[102] Explanatory Memorandum, EMFA Proposal, para 3.

[103] *Cengiz and Others v Turkey*, para 52; *Ahmet Yildirim v Turkey*, para 48; *Times Newspapers Ltd v the United Kingdom (Nos 1 and 2)*, para 27; *Delfi AS v Estonia*, para 110; *Magyar Tartalomszolgáltatók Egyesülete and Index.hu Zrt v Hungary*, App no 22947/13, 2 February 2016, para 56.

[104] *Delfi AS v Estonia*, paras 126, 127.

[105] ibid para 113.

[106] C Grabenwarter, 'Begriff der Presse im Sinnes des Art. 5 Abs. 1 S. 2 GG' in T Maunz and G Dürig (eds), *Grundgesetz-Kommentar* (86th supplement, Beck 2019) para 270 (hereafter Grabenwarter, 'Begriff der Presse').

Article 5(1) GG contains a number of guarantees encompassing: freedom of speech and dissemination; freedom of information; freedom of the press; freedom of reporting by means of broadcasts and films; and a prohibition of censorship. The text of the Constitution itself offers little guidance as to how these rights and freedoms should be interpreted. Their contours have been concretized further in a series of landmark judgments of the German Constitutional Court, some of which have been discussed earlier in this monograph.[107] The Court has referred to these freedoms collectively as 'communication freedoms'.[108] To a certain extent, there has been a level of cross-fertilization between these freedoms. For instance, the concept of 'institutional freedom' was first developed in the context of the press to denote that the Constitution guarantees not only press professionals' subjective right to be free from state coercion, but also the institution of the 'free press', before this concept was later transplanted to the area of broadcasting.[109] The Court has also recognized that all fundamental freedoms under Article 5(1) GG serve the formation of free individual and public opinion.[110] However, important differences remain. Press freedom is predominantly oriented towards the protection of subjective rights.[111] Its objective dimension is relatively underdeveloped.[112] While there is an obligation to prevent the formation of press monopolies and to safeguard pluralism, there is no requirement to set up, say, public service press providers. A public service press after the dual broadcasting model is unanimously rejected as being incompatible with press freedom.[113] The institutional dimension of press freedom primarily serves to bolster the subjective rights of press publishers such as the right to be partisan ('*Tendenzschutz*') or to conceal confidential sources.[114]

On the contrary, in the case of broadcasting, the objective dimension prevails. The notion of an instrumental freedom (*dienende Freiheit*), which assists the free formation of opinion, is especially pronounced in the BVerfG's conception of broadcasting. This conditions not only a subjective right of non-interference by the state (*Staatsfreiheit*), but also an objective guarantee obliging the lawmaker to create a

---

[107] Chapter 2, p 15; see, for the role of the press, BVerfGE 20, 162, 174–76 (1966); for the role of broadcasting, BVerfGE 12, 205 (1961) – *First Broadcasting* Case (*Deutschland-Fernsehen*); BVerfGE 31, 314 (1971) – *Second Broadcasting* Case (*Umsatzsteuer*); BVerfGE 57, 295 (1981) – *Third Broadcasting* Case (*FRAG*); BVerfGE 73, 118 (1986) – *Fourth Broadcasting* Case (*Niedersachsen-Urteil*); BVerfGE 74, 297 (1987) – *Fifth Broadcasting* Case (*Baden-Württemberg-Urteil*); BVerfGE 83, 238 (1991) – *Sixth Broadcasting* Case (*Nordrhein-Westfalen-Urteil*); BVerfGE 87, 181 (1992) – *Seventh Broadcasting* Case (*Rundfunkfinanzierung*); BVerfGE 90, 60 (1994) – *Eighth Broadcasting* Case (*Rundfunkgebühren*).

[108] BVerfGE 90, 60 (1994), para 147: 'The fundamental communication freedoms were originally aimed against the subjugation of communication media by the state ... ' ('*Gegen die Gängelung der Kommunikationsmedien durch den Staat haben sich die Kommunikationsgrundrechte ursprünglich gerichtet ...*').

[109] BVerfGE 20, 162 (1966), para 37; BVerfGE 25, 256 (1969), para 29; BVerfGE 73, 118 (1986), para 202; C Witteman, 'Constitutionalizing Communications: The German Constitutional Court's Jurisprudence of Communications Freedom' (2010) 33(1) Hastings International and Comparative Law Review 95, 126.

[110] BVerfGE 80, 124 (1989), para 31 (*Postzeitungsdienst*).

[111] C Franzius, 'Das Internet und die Grundrechte' (2016) 71(13) Juristenzeitung 650, 652 (hereafter Franzius, 'Das Internet und die Grundrechte').

[112] J Kühling, 'Art. 5 GG' in H Gersdorf and P Paal (eds), *Informations- und Medienrecht Kommentar* (2nd edn, Beck 2021) para 14 (hereafter Kühling, 'Art. 5 GG').

[113] Franzius, 'Das Internet und die Grundrechte' (n 111) 651.

[114] Kühling, 'Art. 5 GG' (n 112) para 14.

positive order, which ensures that the variety of existing opinion is expressed as widely and completely as possible, and that comprehensive information is offered.[115] Public service broadcasters, in particular, are entrusted with the mission of guaranteeing the essential basic provision for all (*Grundversorgung*). They are expected to inform, educate, and entertain, to offer a range of programmes for the whole population that are comprehensive in their content.[116] The objective dimension of broadcasting is far more pronounced in the BVerfG case law than in that of the ECtHR.[117]

As already discussed, the considerably disparate development of press and broadcasting has been justified by the BVerfG based on the latter's 'special situation' (*Sondersituation*).[118] This disparate development and the unparalleled attention paid to broadcasting by the BVerfG necessitate a clear delineation between the substantive scope of application of press and broadcasting freedom in the German constitutional law dogma. Broadcasting is generally understood as the organization and dissemination of offerings of any kind for an indefinite circle of recipients by way of electric waves.[119] Near video-on- demand, the transmission of multiple copies of a programme at staggered time intervals, falls within the scope of broadcasting freedom.[120] In the case of video-on-demand, that is, the delivery of video content to individual consumers for immediate consumption, this depends on the editorial selection of the content in question. The classification as broadcasting is answered in the affirmative in the case of Netflix which also produces some content of its own.[121] By contrast, the presentation of films without editorial selection on online platforms such as YouTube does not fall within the scope of broadcasting freedom.[122]

As regards the press, the traditional view in Germany has been that it involves the transmission of content on printed paper or other physical means of dissemination, so long as these do not fall under the scope of film or broadcasting freedom.[123] In other words, the mode of transmission has traditionally been the decisive criterion for the delineation between press and broadcasting freedom. According to this view, the physical transmission of content by way of printed publications or CDs falls within the scope of press freedom, while its online transmission comes within the remit of broadcasting freedom.[124] Along this line of reasoning, all other forms of online dissemination of mass media content also constitute 'broadcasting'. This view has been criticized for overstretching the concept of broadcasting, and for being at variance

---

[115] BVerfGE 57, 295 (1981).

[116] BVerfGE 73, 118 (1986).

[117] Kühling, 'Art. 5 GG' (n 112) para 20.

[118] BVerfGE 12, 205 (1961) para 180ff.

[119] H D Jarass, 'Art. 5 GG' in H D Jarass and B Pieroth (eds), *Grundgesetz für die Bundesrepublik Deutschland* (12th edn, Beck 2012) para 36.

[120] C Bernard, *Rundfunk als Rechtsbegriff: Bedeutung, Inhalt und Funktion des Rundfunkbegriffs unter besonderer Berücksichtigung der Multimediadienste* (Springer 2001) 189.

[121] Kühling, 'Art. 5 GG' (n 112) para 63.

[122] ibid.

[123] Grabenwarter, 'Begriff der Presse' (n 106) para 239.

[124] BVerfGE 95, 28 (1996), para 26; Kalbhenn and Holznagel, 'Journalistische Sorgfaltspflichten' (n 56) 603; H-J Papier and M Schroeder, '"Gebiet des Rundfunks". Gutachten von H.-J. Papier und M. Schroeder zu presseähnlichen Angeboten' (2010) 60 epd medien 16 (hereafter Papier and Schroeder, 'Gebiet des Rundfunks').

with the linear TV model under the AVMSD.[125] It may be added that it also leads to the reduction of press freedom to a residual, ever diminishing role. The concern underlying this criticism is that the internet might end up being overregulated under the broadcasting regime.[126]

The prevailing view in recent case law and in some of the academic literature is that the 'online press' should benefit from freedom of the press, similarly to its offline counterpart.[127] The BVerfG held that including reports in an online archive or otherwise making them available online does not suffice to classify them as 'broadcasting' in a constitutional sense.[128] The decisive criterion for the distinction between press and broadcasting is not the mode of transmission, but the typical look and feel and the mode of consumption of the medium in question. Content primarily consisting of moving images constitutes broadcasting. Content that is mainly reliant on the written word and static images belongs in the realm of the 'press'. An exception is made in the case of activities that constitute an annex function to the medium's main modus operandi.[129] Text content published on a broadcaster's website constitutes an auxiliary activity, and therefore falls within the scope of broadcasting freedom. The same applies to printed TV programmes published by broadcasters. In a mirror-inverted way, video content published on the website of an online press publication predominantly consisting of text performs a supplementary function. It should therefore exceptionally benefit from the guarantee of press freedom.

Certainly, this debate is far from over. A comprehensive explanation for the constitutional classification of new media is still outstanding. The issue of online publications' entitlement to the right to press or broadcasting freedom might seem arcane at first sight. However, it is not inconsequential as is evident in a recent summary judgment of the Administrative Court Berlin.[130] At stake in this case was an investigative online platform's right to obtain information from the Federal Chancellery about the appointments of Gerhard Schröder, the former Chancellor, with Russian energy companies. In accordance with the Federal Administrative Court's established jurisprudence, this right to information could have been derived from the constitutional right to press freedom.[131] In fact, this would likely have been the only possible legal basis given that provisions for a right to receive information in the press laws of the federal states (*Länder*) do not cover claims against federal authorities.[132] However, following a summary examination of the merits of the case, the Administrative Court Berlin

[125] B Holznagel, 'Internetdienstefreiheit und Netzneutralität' (2011) 6 Archiv für Presserecht 532, 534 (hereafter Holznagel, 'Internetdienstefreiheit').

[126] K-E Hain, 'Ist die Etablierung einer Internetdienstefreiheit sinnvoll?' (2012) 2 Kommunikation & Recht 98, 102 (hereafter Hain, 'Internetdienstefreiheit').

[127] BVerfGE, judgment of 11 January 2021, 1BvR 2681/20, para 26; BVerfGE 152, 152 (2019) (*RTBF I* case), para 95; BVerfGE 19, 278 (2011) (*Any DVD* case), para 31; BGH, 1 April 2004, I ZR 317/01 (*Schöner Wetten* case), para 28; BGH, 14 October 2010, (2011) *Archiv für Presserecht* 249 (*Any DVD* case), para 41; BGH, 21 January 2021, I ZR 120/19 (*Clickbaiting* case), paras 39–42; J Kahl, *Elektronische Presse und Bürgerjournalismus: Presserechtliche Rechte und Pflichten von Wortmedien im Internet* (Nomos 2013) 29f, 138 (hereafter Kahl, *Elektronische Presse*); Kühling, 'Art. 5 GG' (n 112) para 64.

[128] BVerfGE 152, 152 (2019) (*RTBF I*), para 95.

[129] Grabenwarter, 'Begriff der Presse' (n 106) para 268.

[130] VG Berlin, 21 June 2022, VG 27 L68/22.

[131] BVerwGE 151, 348 (2015), para 24.

[132] BVerwGE 167, 319 (2020), para 28.

concluded that the applicant was not entitled to the right to press freedom given that they did not publish a print publication but only the online portal fragdenstaat.de.[133] Complicating things further, the Administrative Court considered that the question whether the applicant had a right to information derived from broadcasting freedom could not be conclusively answered in summary proceedings.[134] By leaving this question for the principal proceedings, the Administrative Court effectively denied the portal's right to information on what was an explosive topic. Fragdenstaat.de, consigned to a constitutional no man's land, took the matter into its own hands. By publishing a 2,000-copy first print run of its blog, it was able to claim the right to press freedom.[135] This example goes against the trend of print edition closures and vividly exemplifies the anachronism in the traditional delineation between print and broadcasting freedom.

Meanwhile, others maintain that not only online newspapers, but also editorially structured blogs are entitled to the right to press freedom.[136] However, they draw a line between blogs and the posting of messages in chat rooms or on social media platforms which would 'only' qualify for the right to freedom of expression.[137] The classification of online intermediaries, such as Google, Twitter, and Facebook, is uncertain. One could argue that they should be entitled to the right to press freedom given that the organization and provision of these services resemble the operation of press publishers. Search engines and social media platforms exercise a gatekeeping function, as well as increasingly engaging in the autonomous production of news content.[138] The fact that Facebook and Twitter also show videos could be considered immaterial as these could arguably be viewed as mere annex functions to the primary task of disseminating text messages and still images.[139] In this sense, press freedom could be conceived of as the default media freedom applicable to all journalistic communication online.[140] Intermediaries would hence be subjected to the same constitutional requirements and benefit from the same freedoms as the press. This path-dependent interpretation of media freedoms in the digital age is plausible. It might, however, pay insufficient regard to the differences of intermediaries from traditional mass media. As already discussed in this monograph, intermediaries mainly organize and filter third-party content with the help of algorithms. They thus structure public communication in a way that transcends traditional media logics.[141]

A further strand of thought posits that Article 5(1)2 GG guarantees a unified and open-ended communication freedom that is by no means confined to press, broadcasting, and film, at least as far as the negative protection from the state is

---

[133] VG Berlin, 21 June 2022, VG 27 L68/22, para 16.
[134] ibid para 22.
[135] D Werdermann, 'Dieser Blogbeitrag ist nicht von der Pressefreiheit geschützt: Zur Reichweite presserechtlicher Auskunftsansprüche von Online-Medien' (*Verfassungsblog*, 21 July 2022) <https://verfassungsblog.de/dieser-blogbeitrag-ist-nicht-von-der-pressefreiheit-geschutzt/> accessed 15 March 2023.
[136] Kühling, 'Art. 5 GG' (n 112) para 88; Franzius, 'Das Internet und die Grundrechte' (n 111) 654, 655.
[137] Kühling, 'Art. 5 GG' (n 112) para 88.
[138] See Chapter 2, p 22; Chapter 3, p 47.
[139] Kühling, 'Art. 5 GG' (n 112) para 88.
[140] ibid.
[141] Kühling, 'Art. 5 GG' (n 112) para 99d. This presents Kühling's qualified view compared to the one espoused in Gersdorf and Paal's 2014 edition.

concerned.[142] The positive scope of protection would still allow for differentiation to accommodate the contradiction between the conception of press freedom as classical, liberal right and broadcasting freedom as a 'serving freedom' (*dienende Freiheit*). This would allow for a system of graduated regulation that would potentially encompass new media within the broadcasting regulatory framework in response to pluralism threatening concentration trends.[143] Yet others argue, in common with the traditional view, that press freedom only applies to hard copy publications. Broadcasting freedom is narrowly understood as being applicable only to linear broadcasting in line with the AVMSD. The synchronicity of viewing ensures this medium's particular impact. The remaining media activity that unfolds online is best captured, according to this view, by way of a novel internet services freedom (*Internetdienstefreiheit*).[144] This new media freedom is conceived of as an omnibus freedom, catching all residual online mass media content, such as the online press, video services like YouTube, as well as other services combining video and text.

The introduction of a new internet services freedom has been critiqued on the ground that the existing media freedoms sufficiently cover also the online domain.[145] A functional interpretation of press freedom and of the freedom of broadcasting and film would adequately protect the online press, and the various manifestations of online broadcasting, from streaming services to online video-sharing platforms.[146] Moreover, the differentiation according to the embodiment of media content and the exclusion of all non-linear audiovisual content from the scope of broadcasting freedom seem counterintuitive. It is argued that it is not the introduction of a novel freedom for online services that is needed, but a new interpretation of Article 5(1) GG as an all-encompassing communication right.[147] According to some, this holistic conception of media freedom would need to cover both individual and mass communication alike.[148] It would need to be accompanied by a relinquishment of the special situation (*Sondersituation*) of broadcasting, and by its transformation to a subjective organization right (*Veranstalterrecht*). Why this should be so, is not fully spelled out, other than by way of a general critique of the ill-justified long-held conception of broadcasting as a 'serving freedom' (*dienende Freiheit*).[149] According to this model, broadcasting freedom does not authorize rightsholders to make arbitrary use of it. As a 'serving

---

[142] A Koreng, *Zensur im Internet. Der verfassungsrechtliche Schutz der digitalen Massenkommunikation* (Beck 2010) 98ff, 101.

[143] ibid; T Brand, *Rundfunk im Sinne des Artikel 5 Abs. 1 Satz 2 GG* (Duncker & Humblot 2002) 69, 70.

[144] Holznagel, 'Internetdienstefreiheit' (n 125) 535; Enquete Kommission „Internet und digitale Gesellschaft", 'Dreizehnter Bericht der Enquete Kommission „Internet und digitale Gesellschaft": Kultur, Medien und Öffentlichkeit', BT-Drs 17/12542 (Deutscher Bundestag, 19 March 2013) 12; W Mecklenburg, 'Internetfreiheit' (1997) 7 Zeitschrift für Urheber- und Medienrecht 525, 531ff.

[145] Hain, 'Internetdienstefreiheit' (n 126) 98ff; F Jäkel, 'Internetfreiheit und Grundgesetz—Ist eine Internetfreiheit wirklich nötig?' (2012) 3 Archiv für Presserecht 224 (hereafter Jäkel, 'Internetfreiheit und Grundgesetz').

[146] Jäkel, 'Internetfreiheit und Grundgesetz' (n 145) 229ff.

[147] Hain, 'Internetdienstefreiheit' (n 126) 103; Rumyantsev, 'Journalistisch-redaktionelle Gestaltung' (n 48) 40; Kühling, 'Art. 5 GG' (n 112) paras 88, 99d; A Hofmann, 'BVerwG: Kein presserechtlicher Auskunftsanspruch für ein Wirtschaftsunternehmen mit vornehmlich außerpublizistischem Geschäftszweck' (2019) 17 Neue Zeitschrift für Verwaltungsrecht 1283 (case note).

[148] Hain, 'Internetdienstefreiheit' (n 126) 103.

[149] ibid.

freedom', broadcasting freedom is not guaranteed primarily on the broadcasters' be-half, but rather on behalf of the free individual and public opinion formation. The legislator is hence obliged to set up a legal framework that ensures fulfilment of this objective.[150] The critique of broadcasting as 'serving freedom' focuses on the lack of foundation for broadcasting's uniquely 'suggestive power' in media effects research and on the inconsistencies of the traditional media sector regulation. It questions the justification for public service broadcasting and for the requirements of impartiality and balanced pluralism (*gleichgewichtige Vielfalt*) in the digital age.[151] The unease with the BVerfG's conception of broadcasting freedom is more pronounced the more broadcasting freedom is interpreted in line with the traditional view as encompassing all online mass media. It is considered that the framing of broadcasting freedom as a 'serving freedom' rather than an individual right denies '80,6 million inhabitants of the Federal Republic of Germany a special fundamental right entitlement'.[152]

There is undeniably an appetite for a re-interpretation of Article 5(1) GG as a unified communication right after the model of Article 10 ECHR and Article 11 ChFR. At first sight, such a unified communication right—be that in the form of the internet services freedom or of an all-encompassing communication freedom—might be seen to have the potential to overcome the existing rigid classifications, and to mirror the reality of convergent media much more accurately.[153] However, this appears doubtful on closer inspection. The internet is not one medium but a platform for many. It encompasses both online press publications, which fulfil the same function as the printed press, as well as audiovisual content which is received in a way similar to broadcasting.[154] There are also hybrid services, such as news portals, which combine text and video. In their case, a correlation of each of these individual elements with the relevant media freedom, or a search for the preponderant type of media format, might be needed.[155]

Even though it might seem attractive to abandon divisions that have partly be-come anachronistic, this cannot happen with a single brushstroke. So long as the en-grained press and broadcasting paradigms persist, overlaying them with the veneer of an overarching media freedom will not prevent these differences from resurfacing. Differentiations, would then, still need to be carried out.[156] A functional interpret-ation might have the potential to reduce the regulatory tensions between different

[150] BVerfGE 83, 238 para 453; see Chapter 2, p 32.
[151] M Cornils, 'Die Perspektive der Wissenschaft: AVMD-Richtlinie, der 22. Rundfunkänderungsvertrag und der "Medienstaatsvertrag"—Angemessene Instrumente für die Reg ulierungsherausforderungen?' (2019) 2 Zeitschrift für Urheber- und Medienrecht 89, 96ff; see Chapter 5, 126 and Chapter 9, p 237.
[152] C M Davis, 'Die dienende' Rundfunkfreiheit im Zeitalter der sozialen Vernetzung (Mohr Siebeck 2019) 40.
[153] B Holznagel, 'Internet Freedom, the Public Sphere and Constitutional Guarantees: A European Perspective' in M E Price, S G Verhulst, and L Morgan (eds), *Routledge Handbook of Media Law* (Routledge 2013) 141, 144.
[154] Grabenwarter, 'Begriff der Presse' (n 106) para 267.
[155] Jäkel, 'Internetfreiheit und Grundgesetz' (n 145) 229.
[156] Kahl, *Elektronische Presse* (n 126) 163; C Fiedler, 'Zunehmende Einschränkungen der Pressefreiheit. Verbraucherschutz, Persönlichkeitsrecht, Datenschutz und Sicherheitsrecht, Datenschutz und unzulängliches Urheberrecht gefährden die Freiheit der Presse' (2010) 1 Zeitschrift für Urheber- und Medienrecht 18; F Fechner, Medienrecht (20th edn, Mohr Siebeck 2019) 47, para 101; Franzius, 'Das Internet und die Grundrechte' (n 111) 656.

media formats.[157] Under such a functional interpretation, offerings that are broadcast-like, that have an impact and pose risks like those posed by traditional broadcasting, would be regulated under the 'broadcast paradigm'. Others that are predominantly text-based would benefit from greater regulatory freedom in line with the 'press paradigm', and its orientation towards the protection of subjective constitutional rights. The risk of too piecemeal an approach that might artificially pull apart coherent subject matters, and thus hinder media development and innovation, would need to be countered. Regulation would need to be attuned to the inevitable cross-fertilization between media formats, and to the opportunities and risks that this presents. The need to preserve the status quo, in particular the liberal orientation of press freedom, might not need to be seen as an axiom. The possibility of a greater development of its objective dimension in the public service, without shackling it with the full broadcast regulatory armoury, would be conceivable and might need to be entertained.[158] The question of whether regulation in the public interest poses a threat to press freedom will be turned to in the last section of this chapter.

4.4 Risks to Press Freedom from Media Regulation

When writing about the future of media freedom nearly forty years ago, De Sola Pool expressed grave concern that the breaking down of boundaries between publishing, broadcasting, cable television, and the telephone network could lead to an extension of public interest regulation to the print media given that these increasingly use regulated electronic channels.[159] The warning bells that de Sola Pool sounded with great foresight still resound today. The Online Safety Bill is a case in point. The Society of Editors, a body committed to freedom for the UK news media, has been at pains to ward off any unintended consequences from the Online Safety Bill. The government confirmed early on that exemptions would apply to content published by news publishers on their own site as well as to users' comments on that content. Furthermore, it gave assurances that journalistic content would enjoy robust protection even when shared on social media services.[160] We discussed in the previous chapter how the government has attempted to make good on these assurances in the Online Safety Bill.[161] The extent to which legitimate editorial output will be insulated from the moderation processes performed by online platforms in practice is yet unclear. The potential is

---

[157] Jäkel, 'Internetfreiheit und Grundgesetz' (n 145) 229; Grabenwarter, 'Begriff der Presse' (n 106) para 267.

[158] See J Rowbottom, *Media Law* (Hart Publishing 2018) 295; J Rowbottom, 'Media Freedom and Political Debate in the Digital Era' (2006) 69 Modern Law Review 489, 494.

[159] I de Sola Pool, *Technologies of Freedom* (Harvard UP 1983) 8 (hereafter De Sola Pool, *Technologies of Freedom*).

[160] Department for Digital, Culture, Media & Sport and Home Office, 'Online Harms White Paper: Full government response to the consultation' (DCMS and Home Office, 15 December 2020) <https://www.gov.uk/government/consultations/online-harms-white-paper/outcome/online-harms-white-paper-full-government-response#part-1-who-will-the-new-regulatory-framework-apply-to> para 1.12, accessed 15 February 2021; Chapter 8, p 225.

[161] See Chapter 3, pp 69–70.

there that platforms will still act as 'collateral censors' of journalistic content emanating from sources less established than the legacy media.[162]

The government has been happy to concede that the mainstream media adhere to high editorial standards and are overseen by strong regulatory bodies, also with respect to their members' moderated comment sections.[163] This assumption is not further substantiated. The wish to avoid duplication of effort might be understandable, especially given that regulation by Ofcom, as by any other statutory regulatory body, would have been an anathema to the press.[164] On the other hand, the historic blanket opposition of the press to any form of statutory underpinning of regulation has been rightly characterized as 'neurotic, rather than "philosophical"'.[165] It capriciously ignores the fact that the press is already subject to a spate of statutory restrictions on what can lawfully be published. Self-regulation does not connote an absence of law. Even this mode of regulation takes place within the framework of general media laws.[166] Moreover, it is worth noting that, in other jurisdictions, press laws have existed for a long time without attracting the opprobrium of censorship. In Germany, for instance, all *Länder* have press laws which cover issues related to the right of reply, imprint, duty of care, data protection, the right to refuse to give evidence, and the seizure of documents for criminal investigation purposes.[167]

The government's eagerness to oblige by exempting the press from the proposed Bill's remit could be questioned in view of the sustained criticism of the current system of UK press self-regulation. The Independent Press Standards Organisation (IPSO), which regulates most national newspapers and many other media outlets, is perceived as being too tightly controlled by the industry to be truly independent and effective.[168] The criticism hinges *inter alia* on the fact that IPSO is financed by the

---

[162] See on the concept of 'collateral censorship' J M Balkin, 'Free Speech Is a Triangle' (2018) 118(7) Columbia Law Review 2011, 2016.

[163] J Wright, 'Letter to Ian Murray' (DCMS, 10 April 2019) <https://assets.publishing.service.gov.uk/government/uploads/system/uploads/attachment_data/file/794520/20190410_DCMS_SoS_to_Society_of_Editors.pdf>; see also Department for Culture, Media and Sport, 'Government response to the Leveson Inquiry and its implementation. Section 40 of the Crime and Courts Act 2013 and Part 2 of the Leveson Inquiry', 1 March 2018, 24 <https://assets.publishing.service.gov.uk/government/uploads/system/uploads/attachment_data/file/684678/GOVERNMENT_RESPONSE_TO_THE_CONSULTATION_ON_THE_LEVESON_INQUIRY_AND_ITS_IMPLEMENTATION_.pdf> accessed 11 October 2023.

[164] B Ogbebor, *British Media Coverage of the Press Reform Debate. Journalists Reporting Journalism* (Palgrave Macmillan 2020) 190 (hereafter Ogbebor, *British Media Coverage*).

[165] E Barendt, 'Statutory Underpinning: A Threat to Press Freedom?' (2013) 5(2) Journal of Media Law 189, 201.

[166] Leveson, *An Inquiry* (n 37) 67, para 5.13; T Dwyer, *Legal and Ethical Issues in the Media* (MacMillan 2015) 122 (hereafter Dwyer, *Legal and Ethical Issues*).

[167] See eg Baden-Württemberg Press Act (*Gesetz über die Presse (Landespressegesetz) Baden-Württemberg*) (LPressG BW) of 14 January 1964, last modified on 24 April 2018.

[168] N Fenton, 'Regulation Is Freedom: Phone Hacking, Press Regulation and the Leveson Inquiry—The Story So Far' (2018) 23(3) Communications Law 118, 121 (hereafter Fenton, 'Regulation Is Freedom'); Home Affairs Committee, 'Oral evidence: Hate crime and its violent consequences' HC 20 February 2018, vol 683 Q268; FC Reporting Watch, 'IPSO: 296 days to correct a factual inaccuracy, effective press regulation?' (*Inforrm*, 23 June 2020) <https://inforrm.org/2020/06/23/ipso-296-days-to-correct-a-factual-inaccuracy-effective-press-regulation-fcreportingwatch/>; see S Carne and J Jessop, 'Debate: Is self-regulation failing in the UK newspaper industry?' (*Institute of Economic Affairs*, 18 December 2018) <https://iea.org.uk/debate-is-self-regulation-failing-in-the-uk-newspaper-industry/>.

newspaper industry it regulates.[169] This line of attack seems somewhat unfair given that such financing is largely in the nature of self-regulation. It is not seen as compromising the independence of other self-regulatory bodies such as the highly respected Advertising Standards Authority. The key question on which the effectiveness of self-regulation rests is whether there is a 'coincidence of interest between industry goals and public purposes'.[170] The press may be less willing now to invest in good journalism in view of the diminishing levels of newspaper circulation in the digital era.[171] Such investment is, however, imperative if it is to gain credibility and to rise above the noise.

Examining the merits and demerits of the current system of UK press self-regulation is beyond the scope of this work. Our focus is on the spectre of further press regulation 'under the unfree tradition of law that has been applied so far to the electronic media'.[172] Is this spectre real? This question will be broached in the second part of this work. If the answer to this question is in the affirmative, would such further regulation be necessarily detrimental or axiomatically antithetical to the very essence of press freedom? Before beginning to trace some of the ways in which this 'shadow darkens' in the second part of this study, it is necessary to shed more light on the meaning of press freedom and on the red lines that further regulation might potentially cross.

Freedom of the press from government regulation is mostly considered as unquestionable, as a hard-won liberation from the many shackles the printing press was subjected to in the first two and a half centuries of its existence. The abolition of pre-publication censorship in 1694 has been described by Macaulay as 'a greater contribution to liberty and civilisation than either the Magna Carta or the Bill of Rights'.[173] This romanticized view of press freedom, formed against the backdrop of a repressive government, is enduring. It is reflected in statements of the ECtHR about the 'public watchdog' role of the press. It has lost some of its allure and requires further justification in an age where trust in the news is low.[174] This is the more so given that large segments of the population equipped with a smartphone see themselves as performing key journalistic functions in a democracy: investigating; informing; creating a public conversation; generating social empathy; and encouraging accountability.[175] The distinction between news and information eludes. The contribution of journalism in bringing meaning and context to the information is less valued, even viewed with suspicion. What is needed is a concept of press freedom that takes account of the current communicative environment. However, the identification of the actors who are

---

[169] Media Standards Trust, 'The Independent Press Standards Organisation (IPSO)—Five years on. A reassessment' (*Media Standards Trust*, October 2019) <http://mediastandardstrust.org/wp-content/uploads/2019/10/MST-IPSO-2019-Final-Version.pdf> 6.

[170] T Gibbons, '"Club Government" and Independence in Media Regulation' in M E Price, S G Verhulst, and L Morgan (eds), *Routledge Handbook of Media Law* (Routledge 2013) 47, 60.

[171] ibid.

[172] De Sola Pool, *Technologies of Freedom* (n 159) 7.

[173] A Peacock, *Report of the Committee on the Financing of the BBC* (HMSO 1986) para 478.

[174] See N Newman, 'Overview and key findings of the 2022 Digital News Report' (*Reuters Institute for the Study of Journalism*, 2022) <https://reutersinstitute.politics.ox.ac.uk/digital-news-report/2022/dnr-executive-summary> accessed 9 May 2023.

[175] See S Craft and C N Davis, *Principles of American Journalism: An Introduction* (2nd edn, Routledge 2016) 11.

best placed to develop an understanding of press freedom fit for the digital era is not straightforward.

On the one hand, the public distrust of the media is matched only by its distrust of political elites. This wider distrust in government power is echoed in Schauer's suspicion of government's ability to draw the lines between speech that might need to be regulated and such that needs to be tolerated.[176] If the state cannot be trusted to regulate speech, then it cannot be trusted to determine the optimum model of press freedom unless its choice reflects the democratic will.[177] The courts are regularly called to forge a particular understanding of press freedom in their case law. Whether the lines are drawn in a way that strikes an optimum balance between press freedom and other vulnerable rights at stake is, however, a subject of endless debate.[178]

On the other hand, the credibility of the press when articulating its own understanding of press freedom is tarnished in view of its high stake in the matter. This possibly explains why newspapers rely on intuitive, and often incoherent, conceptions of press freedom.[179] In the UK, the recommendations of the Leveson Inquiry for ensuring press accountability in the wake of the phone-hacking scandal were largely portrayed by the print media as a threat to press freedom. The terms of the coverage were highly emotional, invoking a revival of the 'state licensing of newspapers' and the introduction of the 'the first press statute since censorship laws were abolished in 1695'.[180] This apocalyptic rhetoric was in sharp contrast to the more measured tone of *The Guardian* newspaper, which argued that a statutory backed press regulation model would not necessarily amount to a loss of press freedom.[181] However, the fact that *The Guardian* ultimately failed to sign up to the Royal Charter raises a question mark over the sincerity of its position in the press reform debate.

The conflicting articulations of press freedom in the meta-journalistic discourse about UK press reform are arguably inspired by two opposing theories of the press: the libertarian versus the social responsibility theory. The libertarian theory posits that the press can only function as the 'public watchdog' if it is free from state control. It frames press freedom in negative terms, as freedom from government, and puts faith in the market to deliver press accountability and pluralism.[182] In its neoliberal guise, it grudgingly concedes a limited role for state intervention to avert market failure.[183] The social responsibility theory is epitomized by the 1947 Hutchins Commission on freedom of the press, which was set up in response to pronounced criticism of the American press. It argues that the press should maintain key journalistic standards by way of self-regulation but does not altogether rule out a role for the state. Its

---

[176] F Schauer, *Free Speech: A Philosophical Enquiry* (CUP 1982).

[177] See Wragg, 'Legitimacy' (n 35) 297.

[178] See Fenwick and Philipson, *Media Freedom* (n 31).

[179] ibid.

[180] 'Leveson report: Media reaction' (*BBC*, 5 December 2012) <https://www.bbc.co.uk/news/uk-20546397>.

[181] 'How should the press be regulated?' (*The Guardian*, 8 November 2012) <https://www.theguardian.com/media/2012/nov/08/pros-cons-statutory-regulation-press>.

[182] D McQuail, *McQuail's Mass Communication Theory* (6th edn, Sage 2011) 176 (hereafter McQuail, *Mass Communication*); Ogbebor, *British Media Coverage* (n 164) 57.

[183] D Harvey, *A Brief History of Neoliberalism* (OUP 2007) 67; Ogbebor, *British Media Coverage* (n 164) 61.

conception of press freedom is a more positive one, recognizing a role for the government in ensuring a socially responsible press.[184]

These conflicting visions of press freedom are rooted in a fundamental conflict: How can the press fulfil its 'public watchdog' function while being accountable at the same time? This oxymoron at the heart of press freedom has been aptly described in the following terms: 'We are thus ambivalent. We want both a powerful and independent press that is free to check the government, and we also want a responsible press that is subject to government regulation.'[185] The question as to who is best placed to watch the watchdog is fraught with difficulties. The role of the press in a democratic society is equally controversial. Expectations that the press fulfil a special constitutional function are a feature of many continental European press laws and regulatory codes.[186] The increased protection bestowed on the press under the ECHR is subject to the concomitant obligation that it acts in accordance with the 'tenets of responsible journalism'.[187] However, the extent to which the language of 'right' and 'duty' used in press codes and in the ECHR case law actually creates an identifiable obligation on the press to serve the public good is subject to debate.[188] The duties imposed on the press, and to some extent the privileges afforded to it, are not ring-fenced, but are extended to an open circle of public communication participants.[189] Furthermore, some of the obligations contained in press codes are ethical rather than legal, and hence less amenable to law enforcement. For instance, the public enjoys a certain protection against violations of personality rights, but there are limited avenues of redress in the case of a breach of the editorial standard of accuracy when no such private rights are at stake.[190]

The uncertainties about the constitutional function of the press and about the duties incumbent upon it exemplify the continuous sway of the libertarian vision of press freedom. Unfashionable though this vision may be, it lends credence to the institutional ideology of the British press, which has been described as 'quick to assert rights but largely resistant to notions of attendant responsibilities'.[191] Let us not be mistaken. Press freedom should not be equated with a policy vacuum. As has astutely been remarked, '[F]reedom is also a policy ... A policy of freedom aims at pluralism of expression rather than at dissemination of preferred ideas.'[192] The wisdom of this policy choice has been questioned against the backdrop of a heavily concentrated newspaper industry, restrained by commercial and political forces and proprietorial intervention in its ability to speak truth to power.[193] Press freedom has been suspected of being

---

[184] McQuail, *Mass Communication* (n 182) 170; Ogbebor, *British Media Coverage* (n 164) 58.

[185] L C Bollinger, *Uninhibited, Robust, and Wide-Open: A Free Press for a New Century* (OUP 2010) 62.

[186] See eg Hamburg Press Act (*Hamburgisches Pressegesetz* (HambPG)) of 29 January 1965, §3 (hereafter HambPG): 'public service of the press'; German Press Code (*Pressekodex*), Preamble: 'responsibility towards the public' and 'duty to uphold the prestige of the press'.

[187] *Bédat v Switzerland*, para 50; *Pentikäinen v Finland*, para 90.

[188] P Wragg, *A Free and Regulated Press: Defending Coercive Independent Press Regulation* (Hart Publishing 2020) 83ff (hereafter Wragg, *A Free and Regulated Press*).

[189] ibid 89.

[190] ibid 174.

[191] R J Thomas and T Finneman, 'Who Watches the Watchdogs?' (2014) 15(2) Journalism Studies 172.

[192] De Sola Pool, *Technologies of Freedom* (n 159) 8.

[193] E Herman and N Chomsky, *Manufacturing Consent: The Political Economy of the Mass Media* (Vintage Digital 2010); C E Baker, *Media Concentration and Democracy: Why Ownership Matters* (CUP 2007); J Charney, *The Illusion of the Free Press* (Hart Publishing 2018) 2ff; P Coe, *Media Freedom in the Age of Citizen*

merely a rhetorical device to give market dominance free reign and to gloss over un-ethical transgressions.[194] Time and again, the question has been raised whether a different, more effective regulatory model for the press might be required.

Some argue that a form of statutory regulation of the press would be conceivable, especially given that the broadcast model of regulation has not led to excessive government interference with editorial autonomy.[195] They suggest that broadcasting standards, including standards of impartiality and protection from harm and offence, would be equally desirable for the press.[196] They contend, however, that such standards could only be achieved by licensing the press.[197] Having a more relaxed regulatory environment for the press—even with the occasional excesses that come with it—is a price worth paying so as to allow the press to perform its functions. It is not just about press freedom, so the argument goes, but about the public's right to information, which is better served by fiercely independent print media.[198]

What has largely been ignored in this debate is the fact that the current model of press freedom might already be in a slow and imperceptible process of transformation as technological and socio-cultural changes force us to revisit many of our fundamental assumptions about the role of the press. Press freedom cannot imply an ossification of long held conceptions, and a complete barrier to change. At the same time, there are certain tenets of press freedom whose violation would arguably strike at the heart of the meaning of the press as we know it. Such a distinguishing feature of the press is the exercise of editorial judgement, and the right of newspapers to be partisan.[199] Press partisanship entails the freedom of newspapers to take sides when commenting on the material they publish, and to determine content, tone, and style.[200] Editorial discretion involves the right of the press to decide about the 'if' and 'how' of reporting, including the use of photographs.[201] It covers the selection of topics, their presentation, and their placement within the press product.[202]

Other aspects of press freedom are more controversial. We have seen that, according to German constitutional jurisprudence, it is not for the courts to scrutinize

---

Journalism (Edward Elgar Publishing 2021) 16ff; T Gibbons, 'Building Trust in Press Regulation: Obstacles and Opportunities' (2013) 5(2) Journal of Media Law 212, 214; T Gibbons, 'Freedom of the Press: Ownership and Editorial Values' [1992] Public Law 279.

[194] Fenton, 'Regulation Is Freedom' (n 168) 121; Dwyer, *Legal and Ethical Issues* (n 166) 124; Lichtenberg, 'Foundations and Limits' (n 35) 120.

[195] G P Magarian, 'Substantive Media Regulation in Three Dimensions' (2008) 76 George Washington Law Review 845, 893; see L C Bollinger, *Images of a Free Press* (University of Chicago Press 1991) 115.

[196] L Blom-Cooper, 'Press Freedom: Constitutional Right or Cultural Assumption?' [2008] Public Law 260, 274; see Wragg, *A Free and Regulated Press* (n 188) 63.

[197] H Geller, 'Where We Are and Where We Should Be Going' in J Lichtenberg (ed), *Democracy and the Mass Media* (CUP 1990) 290, 292; Sir Alan Moses at 'IPSO Roadshow Sheffield: Local news in changing times', 21 May 2019.

[198] Moses (n 197).

[199] D A Anderson, 'Freedom of the Press' (2002) 80 Texas Law Review 429, 451 (hereafter Anderson, 'Freedom of the Press'); Wragg, *A Free and Regulated Press* (n 188) 178; Leveson, *An Inquiry* (n 37) 78–79, para 3.1.

[200] Wragg, 'Legitimacy' (n 35) 305.

[201] BGH, 29 September 2020 – VI ZR 449/19.

[202] BVerfGE 101, 361 (1999), para 98; *Von Hannover v Germany*, App no 59320/00, 24 June 2004, para 65.

the quality of a press product, while the ECtHR has taken greater liberties in that respect.[203] A further example where there are marked national variations is the right of
reply. In the US, a right of reply is seen as incompatible with press freedom.[204] The UK
IPSO Code offers 'a fair *opportunity* to reply to significant inaccuracies … when reasonably called for', but shies away from granting a *right* of reply, whilst the IMPRESS
Code relegates this opportunity to its Guidance.[205] In Germany, the right of reply only
applies to statements of fact, not opinion.[206] The BVerfG views it as a considerable en-
croachment on press freedom because of its propensity to diminish the readers' trust
in the reliability of the press product.[207] Behind the argument that the right of reply
encroaches on press freedom, and potentially creates a chilling effect, lurks an unarticulated cost consideration. Every reply published limits the space available for articles and adverts.[208]

The economic power of the press is of course in itself an important source of press
freedom.[209] The close nexus between the commercial flourishing of the press sector
and its ability to serve its democratic functions is evident, but too often forgotten.
A legislative and policy framework that undermines the economic viability of the
press also puts press freedom at risk. As already discussed, press freedom not only
protects the creation of press products, but also the institution of the 'free press'.[210] The
BVerfG has clarified that the institutional dimension of press freedom also safeguards
the financial conditions for the existence of an independent press.[211] It does not gen
erate an individual right of press publishers for specific benefits.[212] If press subsidies
are granted, they need to avoid any influence on the content and appearance of individual press products as well as any distortions of journalistic competition.[213] Both
direct and indirect subsidies in Germany have raised constitutional objections in the
past.[214] Such constitutional concerns arise on account of the axiom of state freedom
of a privately organized press and of the prohibition of state involvement in public
opinion formation.[215] At the same time, the BVerfG has held that the state has a duty
to ward off threats that could arise for a free press from the formation of monopolies.[216] The courts have therefore accepted in principle the legitimacy of press subsidies provided they are granted on the basis of a law that clearly lays down the exact

---

[203] BVerfG, 9 December 2020 – 1BvR 704/18.
[204] *Miami Herald v Tornillo* 418 US 241 (1974).
[205] Editor's Code of Practice, cl 1(iii); Guidance on the IMPRESS Standards Code, cl 1.21 (emphasis added).
[206] See, eg, HambPG, §11(1)1.
[207] BVerfG, 9 December 2020 – 1BvR 704/18, para 16.
[208] D Carney, 'Up to Standard? A Critique of IPSO's Editors' Code of Practice and IMPRESS's Standards Code: Part 1' (2017) 22(3) Communications Law 77, 82.
[209] Anderson, 'Freedom of the Press' (n 199) 484.
[210] Ricker and Weberling, *Handbuch des Presserechts* (n 44) 62ff, 64.
[211] BVerfGE 21, 271 (1967) (*Südkurier*), para 30.
[212] BVerfGE 80, 124 (1989) (*Postzeitungsdienst*), para 27.
[213] ibid para 28.
[214] Deutscher Bundestag, 'Presseförderung in den EU-Mitgliedstaaten', 15 April 2009, 10 <https://www.bundestag.de/resource/blob/412690/a9620ecbbccf69b2c7cf017401fdb454/wd-10-019-09-pdf-data.pdf> accessed 15 January 2024.
[215] ibid; BVerfGE 20, 56 (1966) (*Parteienfinanzierung I*); BVerfGE 80, 124 (1989) (*Postzeitungsdienst*).
[216] BVerfGE 20, 162 (1966) (*Spiegel*), para 37.

parameters of the assistance measures so that there is no room for discretion on the part of the executive.[217] Still, subsidies have also floundered because of doubts about their compatibility with competition law. In 2021, an attempt to award 200 million Euros exclusively to legacy publishers to assist them with digital innovation projects was ironically struck down amidst concerns that online-only media would be left empty-handed.[218]

A further attempt to assist ailing news publishers has been by way of levelling the playing field with digital platforms based on the controversial EU Digital Single Market Directive (DSM Directive).[219] The DSM Directive recognizes the economic value of extracts of press publications and seeks to protect the copyright of publishers, authors, and other rightsholders. Its proponents argue that it contributes to the financial stability of the press sector, while its opponents retort that it puts freedom of information and the very functioning of the internet at risk.[220] The German iteration of the ancillary copyright for press publishers (*Leistungsschutzrecht für Presseverleger*) was initially declared unenforceable by the CJEU due to Germany's failure to notify the European Commission.[221] In June 2021, the German ancillary copyright finally came into effect, in implementation of the parallel right in the EU DSM Directive.[222] However, the enforcement of the new ancillary copyright in Germany has been slow. News publishers are dependent on platforms and hence in no position to withdraw the use of their contents. At the same time, big publishers have partly compensated for the regime's shortcomings by making profitable advertising backroom deals.[223] Select publishers have also received considerable licensing fees for the prominent showcasing of their content in the framework of the *Google News Showcase* service. This service was made available to them in spring 2021 in exchange for their refraining from asserting their ancillary copyright. The Federal Cartel Office (*Bundeskartellamt*), Germany's competition regulator, recently ended competition proceedings against *Google News Showcase* after extracting binding commitments from Google that it would not prevent publishers from asserting their general copyright and that it would enable additional publishers to take part in the scheme.[224] This newly heightened sensitivity of competition authorities for the inequities of digital markets might add arrows to the news publishers' quiver that are more far-reaching than copyright law.

---

[217] OVG Berlin, 25 April 1975, 2 B 86.74, para 9.

[218] P Behme, 'Intiative im Bundesrat: Ein neuer Versuch zur Presseförderung' (*Deutschlandfunk*, 11 July 2022) <https://www.deutschlandfunk.de/bundesrat-pressefoerderung-100.html>.

[219] European Parliament and Council Directive 2019/790 of 17 April 2019 on copyright and related rights in the Digital Single Market and amending Directives 96/9/EC and 2001/29/EC [2019] OJ L130/92 (hereafter DSM Directive).

[220] T Steinvorth, 'Durchsetzung des Leistungsschutzrechts' (2021) 1 Archiv für Presserecht 10, 11.

[221] Eighth Law amending the Law on Copyright (*Achtes Gesetz zur Änderung des Urheberrechtsgesetzes*) of 7 May 2013, BGBl 2013 I No 23, 1161; *VG Mediagesellschaft zur Verwertung der Urheber- und Leistungsschutzrechte von Medienunternehmen mbH v Google LLC* [2019] ECLI:EU:CI:2019:716.

[222] See Chapter 3, p 62; Act on the Copyright Liability of Online Content Sharing Service Providers (*Urheberrechts—Diensteanbieter -Gesetz*—UrhDaG) of 31 May 2021, BGBl 2021 I, 1204, 1215 §§87ff.

[223] I Dachwitz and A Fanta, 'Leistungsschutzrecht: Deutshe Verlage scheitern an Google' (*Netzpolitik*, 29 September 2022) <https://netzpolitik.org/2022/leistungsschutzrecht-deutsche-verlage-scheitern-an-google/> accessed 15 January 2024.

[224] Bundeskartellamt, 'Improvements for press publishers using Google News Showcase', 21 December 2022 <Bundeskartellamt - Homepage - Improvements for publishers using Google News Showcase>.

In the UK, a pending class action lawsuit against Google for abuse of its dominant position in the online advertising marketplace could also lead to recovery of substantial costs by news publishers and a significant increase of their advertising revenues in future.[225] As far as state aid is concerned, we have already seen that the UK press receives an indirect subsidy in form of a complete exemption from VAT.[226] Further, a requirement on local authorities to publish statutory notices in the local press effectively amounts to a direct subsidy even though its primary aim is to bring such notices to the attention of a wide public.[227] The Cairncross Review recognized that more needs to be done and that commercial efforts would be insufficient to guarantee the supply of public interest news, especially at local level. At the same time, both publishers and policymakers as well as the public are hostile to direct press subsidies on account of the unhealthy state dependency they might generate.[228] A different scheme that has been more favourably received is the Local Democracy Reporting Service (LDRS), which has been set up by the BBC in tandem with the News Media Association. The aim of the LDRS has been to counteract widespread local newspaper closures by creating local reporter positions across the UK, funded by the BBC licence fee. Still, the LRDS scheme poses a different set of challenges, as will be discussed later in this monograph.[229]

4.5 Concluding Remarks

The press and its hitherto unassailable right to press freedom are caught in a tumult of change. This change is conditioned, on the one hand, by the empowerment of a multitude of non-media actors who can now access the means of communication. The ECtHR as well as national courts in Europe and the US grapple with the extension of press privileges to ordinary speakers and with the questions of fair cost and benefit allocation that this entails. The ECtHR applies its instrumental account of media freedom to traditional and online media alike. On the contrary, the BVerfG's formal conception of press freedom bars a second-guessing of the quality of journalistic work. At the same time, German law opens the door to such value judgements regarding the online press. While this seems paradoxical at first sight, a more searching qualification of journalistic activity might be indispensable to ensure that new media actors perform communicative functions in the public interest. The contribution of these new actors to citizens' information diet forces the press to also prove its added value and to even reassert its *raison d'être*.

---

[225] B Maher, 'The US and UK Google ad-tech litigation which could win billions for publishers' (*Press Gazette*, 2 March 2023) <https://pressgazette.co.uk/media_law/ad-tech-lawsuits-google-us-uk-doj/> accessed 14 March 2023.

[226] HM Revenues & Customs, 'Guidance: VAT rates on different goods and services', 11 July 2022 <https://www.gov.uk/guidance/rates-of-vat-on-different-goods-and-services> accessed 15 January 2024; see Chapter 1 para 2.

[227] F Cairncross, 'Cairncross Review: A sustainable future for journalism', 12 February 2019 <https://assets.publishing.service.gov.uk/government/uploads/system/uploads/attachment_data/file/779882/021 919_DCMS_Cairncross_Review_.pdf> 85, accessed 24 February 2020.

[228] ibid 82.

[229] Chapter 9, pp 251–52.

The change is driven, on the other hand, by the search for a new communications policy paradigm at a time when boundaries between traditional media freedoms crumble in a converged media ecosystem. The open-ended scope of Article 10 ECHR contrasts with the more rigid delineation of distinct types of media freedom in the German Constitution. The divide between the subjective-libertarian conception of the press and the objective-institutional conception of broadcasting leads to paradoxical outcomes in the online realm. A functional, holistic interpretation that has the capacity to reduce regulatory inconsistencies is much needed but keeps being consigned to the future. For now, policymakers react to challenges in a piecemeal fashion, while traditional media actors defend their entrenched positions from notional or real encroachments.

The second part of this monograph will examine notable regulatory requirements to which the online press is subjected in a convergent media landscape, whilst drawing attention to the endurance of old media logics in the new media age. It will ask whether these requirements are conducive to enabling it to perform its much vaunted 'public watchdog' role, to minimizing regulatory inconsistencies and facilitating a forward-looking development of an increasingly convergent media landscape. It will examine whether the extension of the regulatory net is a threat to press freedom or a natural, if not inevitable, consequence of the digitalization of the press, and of its coexistence with other traditional and new media in the online domain. Finally, the second part of the monograph will examine some of the ways by which the press tries to circumscribe its online terrain from that of its perceived competitors and will consider solutions that are more attuned to the realities of the online media ecosystem.

PART II
PRESS FREEDOM AND
REGULATION IN PRACTICE

5

Regulating the Press for Accuracy and Objectivity

5.1 Introduction

Accuracy is a cardinal norm of journalistic practice. This is recognized in the codes of ethics of many press councils worldwide which place accuracy at the apex.[1] In the words of Lord Justice Leveson, accuracy is 'the foundation stone on which journalism depends'.[2] A study of core journalism principles in the US found that factualism, the accurate reporting of facts, was the value most widely embraced by participants.[3] However, developments around the phenomenon of 'fake news' in recent times have sparked off an intense debate about whether mainstream media can live up to the ideal of accuracy. News organizations, faced with shrinking budgets and a fierce competition for readers, are often presented with a stark choice between speed and accuracy. In an age of viral news, the temptation is there to publish first and verify later.[4] In the face of overall low levels of trust in professional media, many newsrooms have invested in hubs which fact-check user-generated content. At the same time, their own news reports are scrutinized—and occasionally suppressed—by online platforms and by external fact-checking sites, situated on the cusp between 'traditional journalism and digital network logics'.[5]

This chapter will, first, examine the way in which the ethics of journalism have been interpreted by the European Court of Human Rights (ECtHR). Next, it will focus on the obligation of accuracy that is incumbent on broadcasting and the press, as well as on print journalism's traditional norm of objectivity and the more rigorous obligation of impartiality to which broadcast journalists are subject. The emphasis will be on the UK, enriched by certain comparative observations from Germany and the US. Furthermore, it will discuss the recent phenomenon of 'fake news', the ambivalent

---

[1] See IPSO, 'Editors' Code of Practice' <https://www.ipso.co.uk/editors-code-of-practice/> (hereafter 'IPSO Code'), cl 1; IMPRESS, 'The IMPRESS Standards Code' <https://impress.press/standards/impress-standards-code.html>, cl 1 (hereafter 'IMPRESS Code'); German Press Code <https://www.presserat.de/en.html>, cl 1 (hereafter German Press Code); Society of Professional Journalists, 'Code of Ethics' <https://www.spj.org/ethicscode.asp> accessed 12 May 2023.

[2] Lord Justice Leveson, *An Inquiry into the Culture, Practices and Ethics of the Press* (House of Commons 780, 2012), Vol 2, ch 6, para 9.1 (hereafter Leveson report).

[3] Media Insight Project, 'A new way of looking at trust in media: Do Americans share journalism's core values?' (*American Press Institute*, 14 April 2021) <https://www.americanpressinstitute.org/publications/reports/survey-research/trust-journalism-values/> accessed 17 January 2024.

[4] C Porlezza, 'Accuracy in Journalism' in *Oxford Research Encyclopedia of Communication* (City Research Online 2019) <https://openaccess.city.ac.uk/id/eprint/22556/> (hereafter Porlezza, 'Accuracy in Journalism').

[5] W Lowrey, 'The Emergence and Development of News Fact-Checking Sites. Institutional Logics and Population Ecology' (2017) 18(3) Journalism Studies 376, 381.

Press Freedom and Regulation in a Digital Era. Irini Katsirea, Oxford University Press. © Irini Katsirea 2024.
DOI: 10.1093/oso/9780198858607.003.0005

use of this heavily politicized term, and the concomitant rise in scepticism about the accuracy and objectivity of news media, and in particular the press. Finally, it will ask whether there has been a shift in the editorial standards adhered to by news media and in their role and self-perception as guarantors of accuracy. The influence of online platforms and of fact-checking sites will be explored in this context.

5.2 The Case Law of the European Court of Human Rights on the Ethical Standards of Journalism

The ECtHR has accorded a central role for the furtherance of democracy to the free press. It is incumbent on the press to impart information and ideas 'concerning matters that come before the courts', 'on political issues just as on those in other areas of public interest', on 'deficiencies in the operation of Government services, including possible illegal activities'.[6] The press performs a vital role as a 'public watchdog'.[7] While freedom of expression constitutes one of the essential foundations of a democratic society, it is not unrestricted nor are journalists meant to operate in an ethical vacuum. The ECtHR has recognized that journalists who report on matters of public interest are subject to the proviso 'that they are acting in good faith in order to provide accurate and reliable information in accordance with the ethics of journalism'.[8] The requirement of accuracy and the obligation of verification are well established in the ECtHR case law.[9]

The ECtHR recognizes the 'essential nature of the veracity of the disseminated information' and its fundamental importance for the protection of the reputation of others.[10] However, it does not require journalists to guarantee the accuracy of their reporting. In *Bladet Tromsø*, the ECtHR held that the reliability of a confidential official report as the source for defamatory allegations about cruelty by seal hunters, a matter of legitimate public concern, had to be assessed on the basis of the knowledge available at the time, not with the benefit of hindsight.[11] Further, in *Thorgeir Thorgeirson*, the ECtHR held that it would have been 'an unreasonable, if not impossible task' to require the applicant to establish the truth of their allegations of police brutality committed by unspecified members of the Reykjavik police force.[12] These judgments stand in sharp relief to some of the ECtHR's more recent case law, which has tended to place the privileged position afforded to the press under close scrutiny.

In a series of controversial judgments, the ECtHR second-guessed media compliance with journalistic ethics, in contradiction with its mantra that it would not

---

[6] *Sunday Times v UK*, App no 6538/74, 26 April 1979, para 65; *Lingens v Austria*, App no 9815/82, 8 July 1986, para 41; *Observer and Guardian v UK*, App no 13585/88, 26 November 1991, para 75.
[7] *Observer and Guardian v UK*, App no 13585/88, 26 November 1991, para 59.
[8] *McVicar v UK* (2002), App no 46311/99, 7 May 2002.
[9] *Fressoz and Roire v France*, App no 29183/95, 21 January 1999, para 54; *Tønsberg Blad AS and Marit Haukom v Norway*, App no 510/04, 1 March 2007; *Bladet Tromsø and Stensaas v Norway*, App no 21980/93, 20 May 1999; *Selistö v Finland*, App no 56767/00, 10 Febraury 2004; *Fuchsmann v Germany*, App no 71233/13, 19 October 2017, para 45.
[10] *Couderc and Hachette Filipacchi Associés v France*, App no 40454/07, 10 November 2015, para 134.
[11] *Bladet Tromsø and Stensaas v Norway*, App no 21980/93, 20 May 1999, para 66.
[12] *Thorgeir Thorgeirson v Iceland*, App no 13778/88, 25 June 1992, para 65.

question the technique of reporting adopted by journalists.[13] In *Pedersen*, two TV journalists had been convicted for defaming a Police Superintendent by criticizing the police's handling of a murder investigation.[14] The ECtHR doubted that the applicants' research was adequate to substantiate the allegation that the police force had suppressed a vital fact in the murder case.[15] Interestingly, the ECtHR justified its finding not only on the basis of the 'nature and degree of the accusation', but also by reference to the fact that the programme in question 'was broadcast at peak viewing time on a national TV station devoted to objectivity and pluralism and, accordingly, was seen by a wide public'.[16] This reasoning was also applied in the Grand Chamber judgment.[17] Recourse to the mantra 'that the audio-visual media often have a much more immediate and powerful effect than the print media' was used to bolster the finding of no violation of Article 10 of the European Convention on Human Rights (ECHR).

The Court's questioning of journalists' compliance with the ethical standards of their trade is by no means limited to the audiovisual media. In *Flux v Moldova*, the Court held that the publication of anonymous allegations of bribery and corruption against a school principal without a basis in fact and without offering them the possibility to reply amounted to unprofessional behaviour of the applicant newspaper.[18] In *Stoll v Switzerland*, the Court held that the publication of a confidential diplomatic briefing document in a Sunday newspaper treated a serious matter in a trivial manner, aiming at sensationalism and ridicule rather than the fostering of public debate. The ECtHR criticized 'the truncated and reductive form of the articles in question, which was liable to mislead the reader' both about the personality of the Swiss ambassador to the US and about the timing of the events in question. The ECtHR concluded there had not been a violation of Article 10 ECHR.[19]

In the earlier case of *Prager and Oberschlick v Austria*, the Court also concluded that the applicant, a print journalist, could not invoke his good faith or compliance with the ethics of journalism given that the research he had undertaken into the functioning of the judicial system did not appear adequate. In particular, the defamed judge had never been offered the opportunity to comment on the criticism levelled against him.[20] This finding is at variance with the more lenient approach in *Krone Verlag v Austria (No 5)* where the ECtHR stated that the mere fact of not obtaining comments before publishing the impugned article was 'not sufficient to hold that the interference with the applicant company's right to freedom of expression was justified'.[21]

It follows that in some cases the Court is prepared to grant journalists protection under article 10 ECHR even though they have not complied with the norms of good

---

[13] *Flux v Moldova (No 6)*, App no 22824/04, 29 July 2008, paras 26ff; *Stoll v Switzerland*, App no 69698/01, 10 December 2007, para 146; *Thorgeir Thorgeirson v Iceland*, App no 13778/88, 25 June 1992, para 67; *Oberschlick v Austria (No 2)*, App no 20834/92, 1 July 1997, para 33.

[14] *Pedersen and Baadsgaard v Denmark*, App no 49017/99, 19 June 2003.

[15] ibid para 82.

[16] ibid para 81.

[17] *Pedersen and Baadsgaard v Denmark*, App no 49017/99, 17 December 2004, para 79.

[18] *Flux v Moldova (No 6)*, App no 22824/04, 29 July 2008, para 31.

[19] *Stoll v Switzerland*, App no 69698/01, 10 December 2007, paras 145ff.

[20] *Prager and Oberschlick v Austria*, App no 15974/90, 26 April 1995, para 37.

[21] *Krone Verlag & Co KG v Austria*, App no 9605/03, 14 November 2008, para 44.

journalistic practice.[22] This is in line with the conception of the public interest defence in UK defamation law.[23] The non-exhaustive factors listed in *Reynolds*, which continue to be relevant under the public interest defence, are not meant to 'be interpreted as a checklist or set of hurdles for defendants to overcome'.[24] The court is meant to handle them flexibly with due regard to 'all the circumstances of the case' and 'with such allowance for editorial judgement as it considers appropriate'.[25]

The fact that the tenets of responsible journalism are not imposed on all occasions when Article 10 ECHR is invoked, has been taken to imply that journalistic ethics do not amount to a legally enforceable 'duty' that can be relied upon to hold the press to account.[26] Indeed, in the UK context, the 'duty-interest test', in other words inquiry into the duty of the press to publish a statement and of the public's interest to receive it, is superseded by the balancing exercise between privacy and freedom of expression in privacy law, and by the notion of a publication in the public interest in defamation law.[27] Lord Bingham observed that, '[I]f the publication is in the public interest, the duty and interest are taken to exist', while Lord Hobhouse argued that '[N]o public interest is served by publishing or communicating misinformation'.[28] This is not, however, the same as saying that the requirement on the press to observe journalistic ethics is beyond the purview of the law. The 'ethics of journalism' are a shorthand for a legal standard that is applied both in UK and in ECtHR case law to enable reporting in the public interest even where there is a risk of error. The embedding of these standards in the public interest defence and in the ECtHR case law serves to both incentivize compliance with them and to give the press 'some slack and space to breathe' when performing its democratic functions.[29]

However, the breathing space for journalism has been narrowing. In more recent cases the ECtHR has emphasized that the obligation of journalists to act in accordance with the 'tenets of responsible journalism' does not only encompass 'the content of information which is collected and/or disseminated by journalistic means', but also, '*inter alia*, the lawfulness of the conduct of a journalist'.[30] To be sure, 'the fact that a journalist has breached the law is a relevant, albeit not decisive, consideration when determining whether he or she has acted responsibly'.[31] The focus of the

---

[22] D Voorhoof, 'Freedom of Journalistic News-Gathering, Access to Information and Protection of Whistle-blowers under Article 10 ECHR and the Standards of the Council of Europe' in O Andreotti and others, *Journalism at Risk: Threats, Challenges and Perspectives* (Council of Europe 2015) 105, 111.

[23] Defamation Act 2013, s 4.

[24] *Reynolds v Times Newspapers Ltd* [2001] 2 AC 127; *Serafin v Malkiewicz and others* [2020] UKSC 23, para 57.

[25] Defamation Act 2013, s 4 (2), (4).

[26] See P Wragg, *A Free and Regulated Press: Defending Coercive Independent Press Regulation* (Hart Publishing 2020) 91 (hereafter Wragg, *A Free and Regulated Press*).

[27] *Sir Cliff Richard v BBC* [2018] EWHC 1837, para 274; *Jameel v Wall Street Journal* [2006] UKHL 44, para 50.

[28] Lord Bingham of Cornhill in *Jameel v Wall Street Journal* [2006] UKHL 44, para 50; Lord Hobhouse in *Reynolds v Times Newspapers Ltd* [2001] 2 AC 127, also quoted by Lord Bingham of Cornhill in *Jameel v Wall Street Journal* [2006] UKHL 44, para 32.

[29] J Rowbottom, *Media Law* (Hart Publishing 2018) 89, 91.

[30] *Bédat v Switzerland*, App no 56925/08, 29 March 2016, para 50; *Pentikäinen v Finland*, App no 11882/10, 4 February 2014, para 90.

[31] *Bédat v Switzerland*, App no 56925/08, 29 March 2016, para 50.

proportionality assessment is instead on the public interest in the published information.[32] The illegality of a journalist's conduct per se will therefore not undermine their claim under Article 10 ECHR so long as the published information is in the public interest. In *Bédat*, the Court disputed the public interest in the impugned article not only on the ground of its alleged interference with the right to a fair trial, but also on account of its mocking and sensationalist tone.[33]

The Court's close scrutiny of the ethical parameters of journalistic work has been sharply criticized both by dissenting judges and in academic writing for introducing 'an element of censure regarding the form chosen by the journalist' and for leading the Court to step into the role of a private press regulator.[34] In *Pedersen*, the dissenting judges commented that this ruling weakened 'considerably . . . , the role that the press enjoys in a democratic society to exercise close and vigorous control over matters of public interest and concern'.[35] In *Flux v Moldova*, they sharply remarked that 'in the Court's view the social need to fight poor journalism is more pressing than that of fighting rich corruption', and that '[W]hen subservience to professional good practice becomes more overriding than the search for truth itself it is a sad day for freedom of expression'.[36] Its ruling in *Stoll* has also been found to be in clear contrast to the principle laid down in the 19 December 2006 Joint Declaration according to which 'journalists should not be held liable for publishing classified or confidential information where they have not themselves committed a wrong in obtaining it'.[37] The ECtHR's close second-guessing of journalistic standards with the benefit of hindsight risks inhibiting media freedom and undermining the editorial choices made by journalists in the context of rolling news coverage where there is little room for extensive deliberation.

The press has two arrows in its quiver when defending its editorial choices. The first is the distinction between facts and value judgements, and the second the protection of journalistic sources. These will be considered in turn. The duty of verification to which journalists are ordinarily subject does not apply to so-called value judgements. The distinction between factual allegations and value judgements is well established in the case law of the Court as well as in national jurisdictions.[38] It goes back to the

[32] D Kagiaros, 'Introductory note to Bédat v Switzerland (Eur. Ct. H.R.)' (2016) 25 International Legal Materials 1126.
[33] Bédat v Switzerland, para 60.
[34] ibid, Judges Zagrebelsky, Lorenzen, Fura-Sandström, Jaeger, and Popović dissenting; R Ó Fathaigh and D Voorhoof, 'The European Court of Human Rights, Media Freedom and Democracy' in M E Price, S Verhulst, and L Morgan (eds), Routledge Handbook of Media Law (Routledge 2013) 107, 115; T McGonagle, 'User-Generated Content and Audiovisual News: The Ups and Downs of an Uncertain Relationship' in European Audiovisual Observatory, Open Journalism, 2 IRIS Plus (European Audiovisual Observatory 2013) 7, 14.
[35] Pedersen and Baadsgaard v Denmark, App no 49017/99, 19 June 2003 , partly dissenting Opinion of Judge Rozakis, joined by Judge Kovler and Judge Steiner.
[36] Dissenting Opinion of Judge Bonello, joined by Judges Davíd Thór Björgvinsson and Šikuta in Flux v Moldova (No 6), App no 22824/04, 29 July 2008, para 18.
[37] D Vorhoof and others, Freedom of Expression, the Media and Journalists (6th edn, European Audiovisual Observatory 2021) <https://rm.coe.int/iris-themes-vol-iii-2020-edition-en-28-april-2021-/1680a24eee> accessed 8 June 2021; Joint Declaration (UN, OSCE, OAS and ACHPR, 19 December 2006), 'International mechanisms for promoting freedom of expression' <http://www.oas.org/en/iachr/expression/showarticle.asp?artID=746&lID=1> accessed 8 June 2021.
[38] Spiller v Joseph [2010] UKSC 53, para 114; BVerfGE 90, 241 (1994) ('Auschwitz Lie' case).

seminal *Lingens* case where the Court ruled that 'The existence of facts can be demonstrated, whereas the truth of value-judgements is not susceptible of proof ... as
regards the latter the requirement of proof is impossible of fulfilment and it infringes
freedom of opinion itself'.[39] The applicant was absolved of the obligation to prove
his comments about the behaviour of the Federal Chancellor as such a requirement
would have been impossible to fulfil, and would have infringed freedom of opinion
itself.[40] Nonetheless, even value judgements need to have some factual basis so as not
to be considered excessive.[41] In *Lingens*, the ECtHR found that the facts on which
the applicant rested his value judgements were undisputed, as was his good faith.[42]
Drawing the distinction between value judgements and allegations of fact falls primarily within the national authorities' margin of appreciation.[43] In some cases the
Court challenged the classification made by national authorities,[44] while in others it
was guided by it.[45] On occasion, the characterization opted for by the Court has been
controversial.[46]

The second arrow in the press's quiver is the protection of journalistic sources. The
ECtHR has emphasized that the right of journalists not to disclose their sources, as a
cornerstone of press freedom, 'cannot be considered a mere privilege to be granted
or taken away depending on the lawfulness or unlawfulness of their sources, but is
part and parcel of the right to information, to be treated with the utmost caution'.[47]
Disclosure orders potentially have a detrimental impact not only on the source itself,
but also on the publication targeted by the order, whose reputation may be tarnished
in the eyes of future sources, and also on members of the public who may be deprived
of information imparted by anonymous sources.[48] The Court considers the authority
and reliability of sources, as it presented itself to the newspaper at the material time,
to be a factor to be taken into consideration when determining the level of verification
that had to be undertaken.[49] At the same time, the ECtHR emphasized that 'the conduct of the source can never be decisive in determining whether a disclosure order
ought to be made'.[50] National courts need to be slow to assume that a source acted in
bad faith and disclosed intentionally fabricated information.[51] In *Financial Times*, the

---

[39] *Lingens v Austria*, App no 9815/82, 8 July 1986, para 46.
[40] ibid.
[41] *GRA Stiftung gegen Rassismus und Antisemitismus v Switzerland*, App no 18597/13, 9 January 2018,
para 68; *De Haes and Gijsels v Belgium*, App no 19983/92, 24 February 1997, para 47; *Prager and Oberschlick
v Austria*, App no 15974/90, 26 April 1995, para 37.
[42] *Lingens v Austria*, App no 9815/82, 8 July 1986, para 46.
[43] *Prager and Oberschlick v Austria*, App no 15974/90, 26 April 1995, para 36.
[44] *Unabhängige Initiative Informationsvielfalt v Austria*, App no 28525/95, 26 February 2002, para 46;
Scharsach and Newsverlagsgesellschaft v Austria, App no 39394/98, 13 November 2003, para 41.
[45] *Prager and Oberschlick v Austria*, App no 15974/90, 26 April 1995, para 36; *Pedersen and Baadsgaard v
Denmark*, App no 49017/99, 19 June 2003, para 71.
[46] Dissenting Opinion of Judge Martens, joined by Judges Pekkanen and Makarczyk in *Prager and
Oberschlick v Austria*, App no 15974/90, 26 April 1995, para 9; partly dissenting Opinion of Judge Rozakis,
joined by Judge Kovler and Judge Steiner in *Pedersen and Baadsgaard v Denmark*, App no 49017/99, 19
June 2003.
[47] *Tillack v Belgium*, App no 20477/05, 27 November 2007, para 65.
[48] *Financial Times and Others v United Kingdom*, App no 821/03, 15 December 2009, para 63.
[49] *Fuchsmann v Germany*, App no 71233/13, 19 October 2017, para 43.
[50] *Financial Times and Others v United Kingdom*, App no 821/03, 15 December 2009, para 63.
[51] ibid.

ECtHR held that the lack of authenticity of the leaked document had not been sufficiently established, and the disclosure violated the publication's right to freedom of expression.[52]

In the following, we will look more closely at the ways in which the media are regulated for accuracy and objectivity at the national level, and at the strategic rituals that underpin these requirements.

5.3 Media Regulation for Accuracy and Objectivity

This section will begin by considering the requirements of accuracy and impartiality to which broadcasting is subject in the UK before comparing the relevant press standards. A comparison will be made with relevant expectations in Germany and the US.

All programmes broadcast in the UK, including those of the BBC, are required to comply with obligations of due accuracy and due impartiality laid down in section 5.1 of the Ofcom Broadcasting Code.[53] The BBC Editorial Guidelines explain that accuracy 'is not simply a matter of getting facts right. If an issue is controversial, relevant opinions as well as facts may need to be considered. When necessary, all the relevant facts and information should also be weighed to get at the truth.'[54] Similarly, 'due impartiality' is not simply about balancing opposing viewpoints nor does it require absolute neutrality about every issue.[55] Seeking to achieve 'due weight' means that 'minority views should not necessarily be given similar prominence or weight to those with more support or to the prevailing consensus.'[56] Still, the BBC has been criticized time and again for getting the balance wrong, for example by giving undue weight to minority scientific viewpoints, such as on the MMR vaccine or on climate change.[57] It has even been argued that impartiality rules consign broadcasters to a 'mealy-mouthed neutrality giving the same prominence to a false as to a true statement'.[58] However, as explained in the BBC Editorial Guidelines, impartiality does not mean giving equal weight to all sides of a debate without weighing the evidence. At the same time, it is necessary to bear in mind that today's scientific heresy might become tomorrow's orthodoxy. An interpretation of impartiality that seeks to broaden

---

[52] ibid para 67.

[53] Ofcom, 'The Ofcom Broadcasting Code (with the Cross-Promotion Code and the On Demand Programme Service Rules)', 3 April 2017 <https://www.ofcom.org.uk/tv-radio-and-on-demand/broadcast-codes/broadcast-code>; *An Agreement Between Her Majesty's Secretary of State for Culture Media and Sport and the British Broadcasting Corporation* (Cm 9366), December 2016, Sch 3.3 <https://www.bbc.co.uk/corporate2/insidethebbc/managementstructure/bbccharterandagreement>.

[54] BBC Editorial Guidelines, s 3.3.1 <https://www.bbc.co.uk/editorialguidelines/guidelines>.

[55] ibid s 4.1.

[56] ibid s 4.3.2.

[57] K Marsh, 'Kevin Marsh, ex-Executive Director, BBC College of Journalism on Issues of Impartiality in News and Current Affairs' (2012) 1(1) Journal of Applied Journalism and Media Studies 69, 76; for a recent case of a breach of the obligation of due accuracy under the Ofcom Code, 5.1, see Ofcom's Broadcast and On Demand Bulletin, Issue 351 of 9 April 2018, 'BBC Radio 4, 10 August 2017, 6:00', 12.

[58] M Doherty, 'Should making false statements in a referendum campaign be an electoral offence?', 4 July 2016 <https://ukconstitutionallaw.org/2016/07/04/michael-doherty-should-making-false-statements-in-a-referendum-campaign-be-an-electoral-offence/> accessed 18 July 2023.

the range of voices to be heard rather than silence unpopular ones is much needed in our polarized world.[59]

As far as the press is concerned, both press self-regulatory bodies currently active in the UK, the Independent Press Standards Organisation (IPSO) and the Independent Monitor for the Press (IMPRESS), stipulate in the very first clause of their Press Code that their respective member publishers need to adhere to the obligation of accuracy.[60] It is important to note that journalistic truth does not require 'infallibility'.[61] It demands that care should be taken 'not to publish inaccurate, misleading or distorted information or images'.[62] The Code's understanding of the truth is hence a procedural as opposed to an objective one. The Code does not further explain what 'taking care' involves. Instead, it relies on the Codebook, the interpretive guide to the Code, to put flesh on the bones of this obligation by outlining verification steps, which if neglected can lead to inaccuracies. Significant inaccuracies 'must be corrected, promptly and with due prominence, and—where appropriate—an apology published'.[63]

Effective complaints handling is important, especially given that the majority of complaints made against the UK press concern the accuracy of reports.[64] In January 2016, the IPSO Code was supplemented by a new reference to the need for headlines to be supported by the text of the article beneath.[65] IPSO found that a story published by *The Sun* under the headline 'Queen backs Brexit' was significantly misleading given that it contained an unsupported allegation that the Queen had fundamentally breached her constitutional obligation to remain strictly neutral as regards political matters.[66] IPSO ordered the publication of its adjudication in full on page two. IPSO has the power to determine the nature, extent, and placement of corrections and adjudications.[67] In the 'Queen backs Brexit' case, the newspaper complied. However,

---

[59] R Sambrook, 'Delivering trust: Impartiality and objectivity in the digital age', July 2012 <https://reutersinstitute.politics.ox.ac.uk/our-research/delivering-trust-impartiality-and-objectivity-digital-age> (hereafter Sambrook, 'Delivering trust'); see, however, the BBC's position on climate change reporting in L Hickman, 'Exclusive: BBC issues internal guidance on how to report climate change', 7 September 2018 <https://www.carbonbrief.org/exclusive-bbc-issues-internal-guidance-on-how-to-report-climate-change>.

[60] After the Leveson Inquiry, a Press Recognition Panel (PRP) was established under the Royal Charter on self-regulation of the press to access whether press regulators meet the criteria recommended by the Leveson Inquiry for recognition under the Charter. By 2016 the UK had two new press regulatory bodies which succeeded the now defunct Press Complaints Commission (PCC): the Independent Press Standards Organisation (IPSO), which regulates most national newspapers and many other media outlets, and IMPRESS, which regulates a much smaller number of mostly local and online outlets. The latter is the only one recognized by the PRP. IPSO, 'Editors' Code of Practice' <https://www.ipso.co.uk/editors-code-of-practice/> (hereafter 'IPSO Code'), cl 1; IMPRESS Code, cl 1.

[61] Editors' Code of Practice Committee, *The Editors' Codebook. The Handbook to the Editors' Code of Practice* (The Regulatory Funding Company 2020) <https://www.editorscode.org.uk/downloads/codebook/Codebook-2020.pdf> (hereafter 'Editors' Codebook').

[62] IPSO Code, cl 1i).

[63] ibid cl 1ii).

[64] Editors' Codebook, 20; D Dagoula, I Katsirea, and J Harrison, 'The Independent Press Standards Organisation and Accuracy: A Comparative Study of Complaints Handling Procedures in Four UK Newspapers' (2023) 1(1) Journal of Applied Journalism & Media Studies 1, 2; J Petley, 'Lessons for Leveson' (2011) 40(4) Dispatches: Index on Censorship 14, 19.

[65] IPSO Code, cl 1i).

[66] IPSO, 01584-16 *Buckingham Palace v The Sun*, 20 April 2016 <https://www.ipso.co.uk/rulings-and-resolution-statements/ruling/?id=01584-16>.

[67] IPSO Regulations (*IPSO* 2013) <https://www.ipso.co.uk/media/1240/regulations.pdf>, No 30.

editors are accorded a certain amount of discretion as to the eventual placement of corrections.[68] IPSO's direction that a given correction should appear on page two of the newspaper might hence be overridden by the editor on the ground of the impending publication of an important news story, as happened in the case of a libellous story about a beautician published by the *Mail on Sunday*.[69] The risk that corrections might be hidden away cannot easily be discounted, therefore. This risk is compounded by the fact that 'due prominence' is not the same as 'equal prominence'. Both the elusiveness of the criterion of 'due prominence' and IPSO's reluctance to require that corrections should have equal prominence as the original article have attracted sustained criticism.[70]

These shortcomings in IPSO's remedial arsenal have led academic commentators to dispute the effectiveness of the accuracy standard, especially when it aims at the protection of public and private decision-making as opposed to personal rights.[71] Most accuracy complaints are made by 'third parties' to the story.[72] Such third-party complaints are, however, only taken forward by IPSO if the inaccuracy is deemed to be 'significant'.[73] It has been argued that the commitment to third-party accuracy is a purely ethical issue, and that more decisive policing would ignore the responsibility of readers who choose to believe misleading information in agreement with their worldview.[74] However, shifting the entire responsibility for placing faith in inaccurate information to the readers seems inequitable in view of the enormous communicative power held by the press. The ethical nature of the third-party accuracy standard should not detract from the need for effective sanctioning of transgressions by means of the available self-regulatory mechanisms, with due regard for the crucial distinction between facts and opinions. Conspiracy theories about the origin of Covid-19 were found to originate mostly from alternative rather than mainstream sources. Nonetheless, conspiracy theory posts from news media were shared four times more compared to those emanating from user-generated content.[75] It is in view of the asymmetrical power relation between individuals and the press that the Leveson Inquiry emphasized the need for the press to be bound by

---

[68] Editors' Codebook, 22.

[69] B Cathcart, 'IPSO: The toothless master rolls over its masters (again)' (*Inforrm*, 26 October 2018) <https://inforrm.org/2018/10/26/ipso-the-toothless-puppet-rolls-over-for-its-masters-again-brian-cathcart/> accessed 13 March 2021; IPSO, 20864-17 *Hindley v The Mail of Sunday*, 5 July 2018 <https://www.ipso.co.uk/rulings-and-resolution-statements/ruling/?id=20864-17> accessed 13 March 2021.

[70] House of Lords Select Committee on Communications, 'Press regulation: Where are we now?', 3d Report of Session 2014–15, HL 135 <https://publications.parliament.uk/pa/ld201415/ldselect/ldcomuni/135/135.pdf>; D Carney, 'Up to Standard? A Critique of IPSO's Editors' Code of Practice and IMPRESS's Standards Code: Part 1' (2017) 22(3) Communications Law 77; P Magrath, 'Press regulation: Why we are unimpressed by IPSO' (*Transparency Project*, 17 October 2016) <https://www.transparencyproject.org.uk/press-regulation-why-we-are-unimpressed-by-ipso/> accessed 28 May 2021.

[71] Wragg, *A Free and Regulated Press* (n 26) 191.

[72] K Bell, 'IPSO Blog: Third party complaints made under Clause 1 (Accuracy)' (*IPSO*, 16 October 2019) <https://www.ipso.co.uk/news-press-releases/blog/ipso-blog-third-party-complaints-made-under-clause-1-accuracy/> accessed 28 May 2021.

[73] IPSO, 'Complain' <https://www.ipso.co.uk/complain/#WhoCanComplain> accessed 28 May 2021.

[74] Wragg, *A Free and Regulated Press* (n 26) 173, 191.

[75] O Papakyriakopoulos, J S M Serrano, and S Hegelich, 'The Spread of Covid-19 Conspiracy Theories on Social Media and the Effect of Content Moderation' (2020) 1 Harvard Kennedy School Misinformation Review 1, 4.

higher standards than those that apply to ordinary individuals expressing their own views.[76]

The German Constitutional Court (BVerfG) also regards the duty of accuracy as primarily but, crucially, not exclusively required for the sake of protecting the honour of persons concerned.[77] It considers it to be 'at the same time rooted in the importance of public opinion-formation in the total organism of a free democracy. It is only where the reader is, within the limits of the possible, correctly informed that public opinion can form properly.'[78] In other words, the duty of accuracy is founded both in the protection of individual rights and in the protection of public opinion formation. The BVerfG argues that even though the duty of verification should not be exaggerated, carelessly passing on untrue information or, even worse, deliberately distorting the truth by concealing essential circumstances, violate this duty and are inadmissible.[79] Therefore retaining only a fig leaf of truth while twisting the events by leaving essential features out so that the presentation is at a far remove from reality does not comply with the duty of accuracy. The justiciable dimension of the accuracy obligation is mostly seen as based on and concomitant with the guarantee of press freedom under Article 5(1)1 of the German Constitution.[80] The commitment of the press to truthful reporting is also recognized in most *Länder* Press Codes.[81] However, it is mostly expressed therein as a duty of care as opposed to a justiciable obligation.[82]

A more fundamental critique of the third-party accuracy standard maintains that it is unattainable as it rests upon the assumption of complete objectivity.[83] In the UK, the print media are not subject to a strict duty of objectivity in the sense of impartiality in the same way that the broadcast media are. The press is allowed to be partisan as long as its reporting does not become inaccurate.[84] Under the terms of the IPSO Code, the press is free to editorialize and campaign so long as it distinguishes clearly between comment, conjecture, and fact.[85] It is hence objectivity in the sense of neutrality in the presentation of news, and the absence of value judgements, which features in the press's own perception of its standards of performance.[86] We have seen that, in the US, the Supreme Court upheld the print media's right to deny access, and considered only the broadcast media to be bound by the now defunct 'fairness doctrine'.[87] The Hutchins

---

[76] Leveson report, Vol 1, ch 4, paras 2.1ff, 3.1ff.

[77] T Mast, 'Die Rolle der Massenmedien in Zeiten der Krise' (2020) 3 Archiv für Presserecht 191, 193.

[78] 12 BVerfGE 113 (1961).

[79] ibid.

[80] ibid; M Dittmayer, *Wahrheitspflicht der Presse: Umfang und Gewährleistung* (Nomos 2013) 62 (hereafter Dittmayer, *Wahrheitspflicht der Presse*); W Thieme, 'Über die Wahrheitspflicht der Presse' (1980) 33 Die Öffentliche Verwaltung 149.

[81] See eg Nordrhein-Westfallen Press Act (*Landespressegesetz NRW*) of 24 May 1966, §6.

[82] Dittmayer, *Wahrheitspflicht der Presse* (n 80) 42.

[83] Wragg, *A Free and Regulated Press* (n 26) 177; D McQuail, *Media Performance: Mass Communication and the Public Interest* (Sage 1992) 187 (hereafter McQuail, *Media Performance*).

[84] IPSO, 00154-19 *Stirling v The Daily Telegraph*, 4 April 2019 <https://www.ipso.co.uk/rulings-and-resolution-statements/ruling/?id=00154-19> accessed 8 June 2021; V Julian, 'Reporting on Muslims and Islam' (*IPSO*, 9 November 2020) <https://www.ipso.co.uk/news-press-releases/press-releases/press-regulator-publishes-guidance-on-reporting-of-muslims-and-islam/> 9.

[85] IPSO Code, cl 1iv).

[86] See McQuail, *Media Performance* (n 83) 357.

[87] See Chapter 2, p 13; *Miami Herald v Tornillo* 418 US 241 (1974); *Red Lion Broadcasting v FCC* 395 US 367 (1969).

Commission on Freedom of the Press, the only general inquiry conducted into the state of the American press, referred to the separation of fact from comment and the presentation of both sides of disputed issues as aspects of the obligation to provide 'a truthful, comprehensive, and intelligent account of the day's events'.[88] Media scholars also recognize the fact/opinion separation as a key criterion of media credibility.[89]

In the Anglo-Saxon world, accuracy is hence interlinked with the notion of objectivity. This fundamental assumption has been put in the following terms:

> To accuse a journalist of being biased is to impugn his journalistic integrity in the deepest possible sense. For it is to claim that a journalist is, intentionally or otherwise, not adhering to the truth-respecting methods required for him to achieve the proper goal of journalism: arriving at the truth of the matter.[90]

The *New York Times* thus strives to cover the news impartially, 'without fear or favour'.[91] However, 24-hour news channels like *CNN* and *Fox* are more partisan than many printed newspapers. Having said that, even in the case of the printed press, the expectation that the press needs to be objective has, however, not always been there, and is by no means universal. It has arguably been brought about by the conscious economic decision of newspaper proprietors to expand their reach by abandoning overt political bias.[92] The fact that journalists traditionally had to satisfy large audiences they could not measure or control chimed with the requirement of objectivity.[93]

Still, this requirement has not been espoused everywhere. Partisan reporting has continued to exist, for example, in Scandinavia.[94] Also in Germany, there is no expectation of press neutrality nor of separation between fact and comment.[95] The state media authorities' assertion that the journalistic due diligence standards for print, broadcasting, and online media encompasses the need to avoid one-sided reporting is fanciful.[96] The German Press Code does not contain such a generalized obligation for the press. Only in the case of election campaign reporting does the Code stipulate

---

[88] R Hutchins, *A Free and Responsible Press: Commission on Freedom of the Press* (University of Chicago Press 1947) quoted in McQuail, *Media Performance* (n 83) 37.

[89] C Gaziano and K McGrath, 'Measuring the Concept of Credibility' (2012) 63(3) Journalism Quarterly 451, 455; M Koliska and others, 'Exploring Audience Perceptions of, and Preferences for, Online News Videos' (2021) 22(9) Journalism Studies 1161, 1164.

[90] M Kieran, 'Objectivity, Impartiality and Good Journalism' in M Kieran (ed), *Media Ethics* (Routledge 1998) 24.

[91] *New York Times*, 'Ethical journalism. A handbook of values and practices for the news and editorial departments' <https://www.nytimes.com/editorial-standards/ethical-journalism.html#>.

[92] W R McChesney, *Rich Media, Poor Democracy: Communication Politics in Dubious Times* (The New Press 2015) 49; S Forde, 'Public Opinion, Markets and Technology: Evaluating the Economic and Political Pressures on the Contemporary News Media' (2005) 19(1) Continuum 141, 144 (hereafter Forde, 'Public Opinion').

[93] M Ananny, *Networked Press Freedom: Creating Infrastructures for a Public Right to Hear* (MIT Press 2018) 100.

[94] Forde, 'Public Opinion' (n 92) 144.

[95] 'Begründung', §19; W Lent, 'Paradigmenwechsel bei den publizistischen Sorgfaltspflichten im Online-Journalismus—Zur Neuregelung des §19 Medienstaatsvertrag' (2020) 64(8/9) Zeitschrift für Urheber- und Medienrecht 593, 599.

[96] State Media Authorities, 'Programme Supervision' <https://www.die-medienanstalten.de/en/areas-of-interest/programme-supervision> accessed 22 May 2023.

that the duty of accuracy entails the press also reporting about opinion that it does not share.[97] Also, the Code exhorts journalists and publishers not to perform any tasks that could cast doubt on the credibility of the press.[98] By contrast, German broadcasters are required to strictly separate news from comments.[99] In the course of the latest reform of the public service broadcasting mission, it was decided that this separation would need to be more strictly enforced in future.[100] The latest amendment of the Media Treaty, which entered into force on 1 July 2023, emphasizes that public service broadcasters are particularly bound to observe journalistic standards, and to ensure independent, factual, truthful, and comprehensive information and reporting. Furthermore, they are required to respect the principles of objectivity and impartiality that correspond to a public service profile and to present as broad a range of topics and opinions as possible in a balanced manner.[101] The constitutional requirement of balanced plurality also applies to private broadcasting, albeit with a lesser intensity than applies in the case of public service broadcasting.[102]

All in all, even in the Anglo-Saxon world, objectivity is one of the most contested ideas in journalism in view of the futility of striving to attain it in full. Nonetheless, impossible though it may be to divest journalism entirely of subjective judgement, there is something to be said for objectivity in its simplest form. Stripped to its essentials, objectivity comprises factuality, the information quality of news, as well as verifiability, the ability to check facts against reliable sources, and the absence of sensationalism.[103] The presentation of supporting evidence that enables verification is one of the strategies employed by journalists to navigate the murky 'politics of reality', and to protect themselves from criticism and libel suits. The procedures followed by journalists to defend the objectivity of their work have been described by Tuchman as a 'strategic ritual'.[104] This description suggests that the procedures followed by journalists are meant to evidence an attempt to distinguish between their views and what they report, rather than to attain objectivity. This is in line with longstanding criticisms of the ways in which the press constructs or distorts reality, all the while preserving the illusion that it represents an independent view of the world.[105] It is also in line with the honest characterization of journalism as 'the best obtainable version of the truth'.[106]

In the following, we will consider how, in recent times, the role of the press as 'public watchdog' has been discredited, and its quasi-scientific journalistic rituals of

---

[97] German Press Code, cl 1.2.

[98] ibid cl 6.

[99] MStV, §6(1)4.

[100] C Tieschky, 'Politik macht Auflagen für Unterhaltung bei ARD und ZDF' (*Süddeutsche Zeitung*, 2 June 2022) <https://www.sueddeutsche.de/medien/oeffentlich-rechtlicher-auftrag-ministerpraesidenten-unter haltung-1.5596762> accessed 18 January 2024.

[101] MStV, §26 (2).

[102] BVerfGE 73, 118, paras 180ff, 183.

[103] McQuail, *Media Performance* (n 83) 205ff.

[104] G Tuchman, 'Objectivity as Strategic Ritual: An Examination of Newsmen's Notions of Objectivity' (1972) 77(4) American Journal of Sociology 660, 666.

[105] See J Charney, 'Free Press: Necessary Illusions' (2019) 15(3) Law, Culture and the Humanities 826, 842; T Gibbons, "'Fair Play to All Sides of the Truth': Controlling Media Distortions' (2009) 62(1) Current Legal Problems 286, 290ff.

[106] C Bernstein, quoted by A Rusbridger, *Breaking News: The Remaking of Journalism and Why It Matters Now* (Canongate 2018) 12.

truth-telling have been contested with renewed vigour, fuelled by a widespread rise of populism and science denialism. The question will be raised whether there could be any justification for the use of the trope of 'fake news' to castigate the mainstream media.

5.4 The Press as 'Fake News'?

The phenomenon of 'fake news' came to the fore in the aftermath of *Buzzfeed*'s revelations about the commercial exploitation of fabricated news stories on Facebook, and allegations of Russian interference in the US, French, and German elections by way of propaganda campaigns.[107] The term 'fake news' is notoriously vague and highly politicized. On the one hand, it has been used to describe foreign interference in elections and referendums, sparking fears over the threat posed to democracy. On the other hand, it has been employed by the former US President but also by nationalist, far-right parties such as the German party Alternative for Germany (*Alternative für Deutschland*, AfD) who tapped into pervasive feelings of political alienation and distrust of scientific epistemology for political advantage.[108] Former President Trump and nationalist parties who lambast the mainstream media in their tweets, election campaigns, and demonstrations join a long tradition of press victimization. In the First World War, the notion of 'Lügenpresse' was enlisted in the effort to discredit reporting by the enemy. Before the NS party's seizure of power, this concept was weaponized against the 'unpatriotic' press of the Weimar Republic, which failed to stand up to the demeaning Versailles Treaty; later it was used against foreign media, not least by the chief Nazi propagandist Joseph Goebbels.[109]

It is against this backdrop of historic and recent abuse of the term 'fake news' for political ends that the Department for Culture, Media and Sport (DCMS) recommended that the term 'fake news' be rejected, and that an agreed definition of the terms 'misinformation' and 'disinformation' be put forward.[110] In response to this recommendation, the government distinguished between disinformation as the 'deliberate creation and sharing of false and/or manipulated information that is intended to deceive and mislead audiences, either for the purposes of causing harm, or for political, personal or financial gain' and misinformation as the 'inadvertent sharing of false information'.[111] The distinction between these two types of information challenges draws on

---

[107] C Silvermann and D Alexander, 'How teens in the Balkans are duping Trump supporters with fake news' <https://www.buzzfeed.com/craigsilverman/how-macedonia-became-a-global-hub-for-pro-trump-misinfo?utm_term=.abwQX0Y5JL#.psmLE4WAZp> accessed 18 January 2024.

[108] L Monsees, 'Information Disorder, Fake News and the Future of Democracy' (2023) 20(1) Globalizations 1, 4; S Waisbord, 'Truth is What Happens to News. On Journalism, Fake News, and Post-Truth' (2018) 19(13) Journalism Studies 1866, 1875 (hereafter Waisbord, 'Truth is What Happens to News').

[109] R Blasius, 'Unwort des Jahres: Von der Journaille zur Lügenpresse' *Frankfurter Allgemeine Zeitung* (Frankfurt am Main, 13 January 2015) <http://www.faz.net/aktuell/gesellschaft/unwort-des-jahres-eine-kleine-geschichte-der-luegenpresse-13367848.html> accessed 18 January 2024; see T McGonagle, '"Fake News": False Fears or Real Concerns?' (2017) 35(4) Netherlands Quarterly of Human Rights 203, 205 et seq for historic examples of 'fake news'.

[110] House of Commons Digital, Culture, Media and Sport Committee, 'Disinformation and "Fake News": Interim Report', 5th Report of Session 2017–19, HC 363, 24 July 2018.

[111] House of Commons Digital, Culture, Media and Sport Committee, 'Disinformation and "Fake News": Final Report', 8th Report of Session 2017–19, HC 1791, 14 February 2019.

Wardle and Derakshan's typology of 'information disorder'.[112] It attempts to separate inaccurate content on the basis of the disseminating agent's motivation. Indeed, intent to deceive is key when attempting to draw a line between calculated falsehoods and legitimate forms of political expression such as 'news satire', which ordinarily aim to mock, not to deceive.[113]

Meanwhile, the European Commission and the High Level Group on Disinformation (HLG) have added further elements to the definition of 'disinformation'. The 2022 strengthened Code of Practice, which succeeded the 2018 Code of Practice on Disinformation, postulates that disinformation be spread 'with an intention to deceive or secure economic or political gain and which may cause public harm'.[114] The HLG definition aims to capture 'all forms of false, inaccurate, or misleading information designed, presented and promoted to intentionally cause public harm or for profit'.[115] Public harm is understood as 'threats to democratic political and policy-making processes as well as public goods such as the protection of EU citizens' health, the environment or security'.[116] Defining harm in the widest possible terms does not enhance definitional clarity.[117] The HLG's definition differs from the Commission's one on the question if harm needs to be a condition for disinformation. However, both agree that disinformation does not cover the online dissemination of illegal content that is already regulated under EU or national laws.[118] The EU's regulatory framework that is aimed at tackling disinformation is thus directed at 'merely' harmful as opposed to also illegal content.

The need for this added layer of regulation of legal but untruthful expression and its potential conflict with national and international freedom of expression standards have begun to be explored in academic writing.[119] This section focuses on the question of whether there is a grain of truth in the polemic characterization of mainstream media as 'fake news'. While the terms of 'misinformation' and 'disinformation' are less

---

[112] C Wardle and H Derakhshan, 'Information disorder: Toward an interdisciplinary framework for research and policymaking', DGI (2017) 09 (*Council of Europe*, 27 September 2017) <https://rm.coe.int/information-disorder-toward-an-interdisciplinary-framework-for-researc/168076277c> accessed 18 January 2024.

[113] I Katsirea, '"Fake News": Reconsidering the Value of Untruthful Expression in the Face of Regulatory Uncertainty' (2019) 11(1) Journal of Media Law 159, 164 (hereafter Katsirea, 'Fake News').

[114] Commission, 'The Strengthened Code of Practice on Disinformation 2022' 1 fn 8 <https://disinfocode.eu/introduction-to-the-code/> accessed 15 May 2023 (hereafter Commission, 'Strengthened Code of Practice'); Commission, 'EU Code of Practice on Disinformation' <https://digital-strategy.ec.europa.eu/en/library/2018-code-practice-disinformation> accessed 15 May 2023.

[115] Directorate-General for Communications Networks, Content and Technology, *A multi-dimensional approach to disinformation. Report of the independent High level Group on fake news and online disinformation* (European Commission 2018) 11 (hereafter 'HLG 2018').

[116] Commission, 'Tackling online disinformation: A European approach' COM (2018) 236 final, s 2.1 <EUR-Lex - 52018DC0236 - EN - EUR-Lex (europa.eu)> accessed 16 May 2023 (hereafter Commission, 'Tackling online disinformation').

[117] See Katsirea, 'Fake News' (n 113) 166–67.

[118] HLG 2018 (n 115) 11; Commission, 'Tackling online disinformation' (n 116) s 2.1.

[119] Katsirea, 'Fake News' (n 113); J Bayer and others, 'The Fight Against Disinformation and the Right to Freedom of Expression' (European Parliament LIBE Committee 2021) 18ff; A Kuczerawy, 'Fighting Online Disinformation: Did the EU Code of Practice Forget about Freedom of Expression?' in G Terzis and others (eds), *Disinformation and Digital Media as a Challenge for Democracy* (Intersentia 2020) 291, 297ff; R Ó Fathaigh, N Helberger, and N Appelman, 'The Perils of Legally Defining Disinformation' (2021) 10(4) Internet Policy Review 2, 7, 12ff.

politically loaded and more amenable to a definition than the term 'fake news', one needs to pay heed to the fact that the label 'fake news' is likely here to stay as 'part of the vernacular that helps people express their frustration with the media environment'.[120] One might even consider that this term could serve as a useful shorthand to distinguish between legitimate news outlets and unreliable ones, in other words to separate the wheat from the chaff.

There are numerous, well-documented instances in which the media have published outrageously inaccurate information to attract traffic or to pander to the prejudices of their readership.[121] However, not all mistakes in mainstream media are calculated. The never-ending news cycle with the digital-first or social-first pressures creates incentives to prioritize speed over accuracy.[122] It is important to draw a line between knowingly false content circulated by the media; such where the error has been due to carelessness; stories which contain mistakes, even though they have been researched with due care; and finally, stories that are not outright false but are exaggerated, biased, or tendentious. It is equally important to bear in mind that the mainstream media are subject to the previously described regulatory framework that is still largely absent in the case of social media and other online content, including digital-first news providers such as *Huff Post* or *Buzzfeed*.[123] If one was to tar all mainstream media with the brush of 'fake news', this would further lower public trust in them and would undermine their ability to act as 'public-watchdogs'.[124] More fundamentally, if one was to label mainstream media as 'fake news', this would beg the question as to what is the touchstone against which to measure media reliability, the antipode of 'fake news'.

The public's mistrust in the news media and their denigration as 'fake news', whilst drawing on a long historical tradition, has been fuelled in recent times by the rise of the digital ecosystem's disinformation industry.[125] Advances in artificial intelligence (AI), most recently embodied by ChatGPT, risk further blurring the line between truth and falsity and undermining public trust in journalism. In the following section, we will consider more closely some of the challenges to the standards of accuracy and objectivity in the current online media environment.

---

[120] R K Nielsen and L Graves, '"News you don't believe": Audience perspectives on fake news' (Oxford University, Reuters Institute for the Study of Journalism, Factsheet October 2017) <https://reutersinstitute.politics.ox.ac.uk/sites/default/files/2017-10/Nielsen%26Graves_factsheet_1710v3_FINAL_download.pdf> accessed 18 January 2024.

[121] J Ball, *Post-Truth: How Bullshit Conquered the World* (Biteback Publishing 2017); N Davies, *Flat Earth News: An Award-Winning Reporter Exposes Falsehood, Distortion and Propaganda in the Global Media* (Vintage Digital 2011).

[122] S C Shivek and S Bloyd-Peshkin, 'Where Do Facts Matter? The Digital Paradox in Magazines' Fact-Checking Processes' (2019) 13(8) Journalism Practice 998, 999.

[123] H Gibson and others, 'News Literacy Report: Lessons in building public confidence and trust' (IMPRESS, November 2022) 21 <https://www.impress.press/wp-content/uploads/2023/01/impress-news-literacy-report-2022.pdf> accessed 7 March 2023. However, see Chapter 3, 72 on the introduction of journalistic due diligence obligations for online news providers in the new German Media Treaty.

[124] UN and others, 'Joint Declaration on freedom of expression, "fake news", disinformation and propaganda' (3 March 2017) <https://www.osce.org/files/f/documents/6/8/302796.pdf>, rec 6; Campaign for press and broadcasting freedom, 'Trust in journalism at all-time low' <https://www.cpbf.org.uk/2016/12/12/trust-journalism-time-low/> accessed 18 January 2024.

[125] Reporters Without Borders, '2023 World Press Freedom Index'; House of Lords Communications and Digital Committee, 'Breaking news? The future of UK journalism', 1st Report of Session 2019–21, HL Paper 176, 27 November 2020, para 55.

5.5 Ethical Standards of Digital Journalism

The UK regulatory framework—whereby broadcasting is subject to obligations of due impartiality; the press is expected to separate fact from comment, and aspires to objectivity, but is free to editorialize; while both are committed to obligations of due accuracy—has been transported without much reflection, almost by default, to the digital era. The fact that these divides are challenged by convergence led policy-makers to argue that the requirement of due impartiality be lifted for all non-public service broadcast (non-PSB) news providers. In other words, that they should be treated in the same way as non-broadcast news providers.[126] Others have maintained that the adherence of broadcasting to standards of impartiality, and the freedom of the press to express opinion, even where it develops TV-like online content, should be protected. Even though the promotion of consistency in content standards was desirable, it should be limited to cross-platform, not cross-media consistency.[127] In other words, regulatory standards should be the same regardless of whether broadcast or printed news content was delivered respectively on air, in print, or online. Indeed, there is much to be said for the creation of an even playing field across platforms.

However, neither the cross-platform consistency nor the controversial lowering of non-PSB: broadcasters' impartiality commitments has materialized. In fact, the Draft Media Bill, intended to 'help public service broadcasters better compete with media giants', proposes to level the regulatory playing field between video-on-demand and traditional linear TV by extending certain impartiality requirements to designated Tier 1 Services.[128] The Secretary of State has not yet designated such services but they are likely to comprise Netflix, Amazon Prime Video and Disney+.[129] At the same time, the Ofcom Broadcasting Code does not apply to online content, raising concerns that PSBs such as ITV and Channel 4 might not maintain the same accuracy and impartiality standards online as on air. The concern is less pronounced in the case of the BBC's virtual presence which, despite not being subject to the Code, falls under Ofcom's overall purview.[130] This regulatory patchwork creates a real risk that audiences might be confused and that their expectations might be frustrated. The House of Lords proposed that a solution for this anomaly in current standards regulation could consist in applying the Ofcom Code to any service operating under the same channel name or brand as a licensed broadcast service.[131] This solution has yet to be adopted.

---

[126] House of Lords, *Media Convergence*, 2nd Report of session 2012–13, HL Paper 154, 27 March 2013, para 114.

[127] N Warner, 'Life after Leveson. The challenge to strengthen Britain's diverse and vibrant media' (IPPR 2012) <https://www.ippr.org/articles/life-after-leveson-the-challenge-to-strengthen-britains-diverse-and-vibrant-media> accessed 18 January 2024, 7.

[128] Draft Media Bill (2023, CP822), cl 368HF (2) (e), 368HG (hereafter Draft Media Bill).

[129] Department for Culture, Media and Sport, 'New laws to help bring great shows to British screens and airwaves', 28 March 2023 <https://www.gov.uk/government/news/new-laws-to-help-bring-more-great-shows-to-british-screens-and-airwaves> accessed 17 May 2023.

[130] Communications and Digital Committee, 'Breaking news? The future of UK journalism' (2019–21 HL 176) <https://publications.parliament.uk/pa/ld5801/ldselect/ldcomuni/176/17602.htm> accessed 18 January 2024, para 60.

[131] House of Lords, *Media Convergence* (n 126) para 51.

Against the background of this regulatory maze, a novel understanding of the standards of accuracy, objectivity, and impartiality in the online domain is emerging. Objectivity has always been a contested norm, and the dissonance between ideal and reality has become especially accentuated in the online environment. Hybrid journalism and the use of social media by journalists to voice their opinions under disclaimer in a 'private' capacity pose challenges for news organizations striving to be objective.[132] Legacy print outlets consider the segregation between fact and comment to be challenging in the era of live-blogging.[133] However, the move towards opinion-based journalism is more problematic in the area of broadcasting, especially given that the majority of the UK public still values impartiality in current affairs programmes.[134] Broadcasters, unregulated by the Ofcom Code online, relax strict impartiality in blog posts and in journalists' social media presence.[135] When Jon Snow broadcast an emotional video on children in Gaza on YouTube and on the Channel 4 website, Channel 4 was supportive of his decision. Had this video been aired on live TV, it might have fallen foul of Ofcom's due impartiality rules.[136]

Emotions run higher when BBC impartiality rules are ignored. When star pundit, Gary Lineker, tweeted that the government's new Illegal Immigration Bill was an 'immeasurably cruel policy' and that the language used resembled that 'used by Germany in the 30's', Ofcom's chief executive held that this episode went to the heart of BBC's reputation. At the same time, she considered that greater room for freedom of expression might be appropriate in the case of freelancers if compared to news presenters.[137] Indeed, in a previous instance of controversial political tweets, the BBC management supported Lineker.[138] The current BBC social media guidance is ambivalent.[139] On the one hand, it states that '[A]ctors, dramatists, comedians, musicians and pundits who work for the BBC are not subject to the requirements of impartiality on social media'. On the other hand, it states that the duty of compliance of a non-staff member, contributor, or presenter with the Editorial Guidelines depends on their contractual relationship whilst cautioning that high-profile individuals are expected to 'avoid

---

[132] See BBC, 'Guidance: Editorial use of social media' (*BBC Editorial Guidelines*, 29 October 2020) <https://www.bbc.co.uk/editorialguidelines/guidance/individual-use-of-social-media> accessed 18 January 2024.

[133] K Riordan, 'Accuracy, independence and impartiality: How legacy media and digital natives approach standards in the digital age' (*Reuters Institute for the Study of Journalism* 2014) 40 <https://reutersinstitute.politics.ox.ac.uk/our-research/accuracy-independence-and-impartiality-how-legacy-media-and-digital-natives-approach> accessed 18 January 2024 (hereafter Riordan, 'Accuracy, independence and impartiality').

[134] Ofcom, 'News consumption in the UK: 2020', 13 August 2020 <https://www.ofcom.org.uk/__data/assets/pdf_file/0013/201316/news-consumption-2020-report.pdf> accessed 18 January 2024, 94.

[135] Riordan, 'Accuracy, independence and impartiality' (n 133) 51.

[136] J Deans, 'Jon Snow Gaza video backed by Channel 4' (*The Guardian*, 31 July 2014) <https://www.theguardian.com/media/2014/jul/31/jon-snow-gaza-video-backed-channel-4> accessed 18 January 2024.

[137] J Gregory, 'Gary Lineker row goes to heart of BBC reputation—Ofcom boss' (*BBC*, 14 March 2023) <https://www.bbc.co.uk/news/uk-64953421> accessed 17 May 2023.

[138] M Bekerman, 'Garry Lineker tweet scandal shows how the BBC has struggled to adapt to the social media age' (*Inforrm*, 18 March 2023) <https://inforrm.org/2023/03/18/gary-lineker-tweet-scandal-shows-how-the-bbc-has-struggled-to-adapt-to-the-social-media-age-marek-bekerman/#more-54207> accessed 17 May 2023.

[139] BBC, 'Guidance Note: Individual use of social media', October 2020 <https://www.bbc.co.uk/editorialguidelines/guidance/individual-use-of-social-media> accessed 18 May 2023.

taking sides on party political issues or political controversies and to take care when addressing public policy matters'.

The Lineker affair has prompted the BBC to commence a review of its social media guidance for freelancers.[140] It is not clear why freelance journalists, especially those with large social media followings, should be treated differently from staff members. The BBC impartiality rules on social media are in flux, amidst profound uncertainty as to who is a 'journalist' in the digital era and how far their celebrity status should afford them greater rights to freedom of expression. The bigger question behind this debacle is the tension between BBC's public service ethos and its submission to celebrity culture.

Meanwhile, in the US, the argument for a fairness doctrine 2.0 for the digital environment has gained traction in recent times as a means of tackling the growing polarization in American society. There is no consensus though on whether this modern iteration of the fairness doctrine should rest on private governance initiatives or on governmental regulation. Nor on whether it should aim for greater accuracy and completeness of information or also for balance, the latter being potentially easily manipulated to create a false sense of equivalency.[141] We can thus observe two opposing trends taking place at the same time: while the legacy media loosen their adherence to ideals of objectivity and requirements of impartiality online, the argument gains ground that the digital space should be regulated for fairness.

This argument sparked controversy in Germany when it was voiced in 2019 by Angela Kramp-Karrenbauer, at the time Chancellor Merkel's aspiring successor as Christian Democratic Union (CDU) party leader. The bone of contention was a video by German YouTuber Rezo which went viral a few days before the 2019 European Parliament elections. Rezo's video openly attacked the CDU. It was followed by another short video published by over seventy other German vloggers, encouraging voters to boycott the ruling coalition parties.[142] CDU supporters castigated Rezo's video as 'fake news'. Kramp-Karrenbauer argued that had such an orchestrated appeal been mounted by seventy German newspapers before the elections, it would have been a clear case of political bias, and should hence also be treated as such when performed online. The comparison of one YouTube video with seventy German newspapers seems far-fetched at first sight. It does, however, exemplify influencers' considerable reach and gatekeeping power. Still, Kramp-Karrenbauer's argument is unconvincing given that the German press is free to be partial, and is not banned from making recommendations on election choices.[143] Having said that, the leading German newspapers would be unlikely to launch such an appeal.

---

[140] BBC, 'BBC launches review into social media guidance for freelancers' (*Media Centre*, 31 March 2023) <https://www.bbc.com/mediacentre/2023/bbc-launches-review-into-social-media-guidance-for-freelancers> accessed 18 January 2024.

[141] M P Vandenbergh, 'Social Checks and Balances: Private Fairness Doctrine' (2020) 73(3) Vanderbilt Law Review 811, 815; I Klein, 'Enemy of the People: The Ghost of the F.C.C. Fairness Doctrine in the Age of Alternative Facts' (2020) 42(1) Hastings Communications and Entertainment Law Journal 45 (hereafter Klein, 'Enemy of the People').

[142] J Delcker, 'YouTube tirade disrupts Merkel party's EU campaign' (*Politico*, 24 May 2019) <https://www.politico.eu/article/youtube-tirade-disrupts-merkel-partys-eu-campaign/> accessed 18 January 2024.

[143] BVerfGE 52, 283 (1979), para 30.

The imposition of journalistic duties on the vloggers in question would ultimately depend on the characterization of their videos as 'journalistic-editorial' in the sense of the Media Treaty.[144] Their main aim would need to be the contribution to opinion formation as opposed to the pursuance of commercial or other aims. This could likely be answered in the positive in Rezo's case in view of his reliance on numerous verifiable sources.[145] The video's flippant dismissal by CDU supporters as 'fake news' was ill-founded. Having said that, most influencers challenge their characterization as professionals. This is remarkable given that their reach often dwarfs that of traditional media. Moreover, influencers like Rezo are regularly backed by professional agencies.[146]

Rezo's case raises the broader question as to whether the internet could be regulated for neutrality even though no such obligation exists for the print media. In Germany, the free press model serves as the archetype for the regulation of the online press. Platforms aggregating journalistic-editorial offerings, which reproduce in full or in part the content of periodic prints are subject to a requirement of non-discrimination.[147] However, this requirement does not apply to specific offerings but to the overall organization and presentation of content. A more far-reaching interpretation of neutrality online to the effect that controversial subjects would need to be presented in a fair and objective manner would hardly be justifiable from a freedom of expression perspective.

In the US, leading print outlets strive for neutrality, but this is certainly not a regulatory obligation. The Supreme Court resolutely declined the extension of the right of reply to print media.[148] In *Reno v ACLU*, the Supreme Court held that the internet should receive extensive First Amendment protection in the same way as the print media.[149] Given that indecent material was not proscribed in print, it could not be prohibited online. The calls for the introduction of a fairness doctrine 2.0 for the digital environment go against the grain of this case law, and against the repeal of the fairness doctrine by the Federal Communications Commission (FCC) in 1987.[150] Even if the fairness doctrine was to be reinstated for the broadcast media, its extension to online news and social media would meet with considerable constitutional hurdles. The seemingly infinite nature of the internet would arguably be a barrier to the introduction of such restrictive regulation for online news. The argument that the introduction of a fairness doctrine 2.0 should rest on the public's right to be informed and on the scarcity of its attention is illusory.[151] Any attempt to monitor the countless editorial choices made online and to instil balance in all debates about controversial

---

[144] MStV, §109(1).

[145] L Dereje, 'Sorgfaltspflichten auch für Laien im Netz!' (*Verfassungsblog*, 5 June 2019) <https://verfassungsblog.de/sorgfaltspflichten-auch-fuer-laien-im-netz/> accessed 18 January 2024 (hereafter Dereje, 'Sorgfaltspflichten').

[146] ibid.

[147] MStV, §§82(2), 85; see Chapter 3 58.

[148] *Miami Herald v Tornillo* 418 US 241 (1974); see Chapter 2, p 23.

[149] *Reno v ACLU* 521 US 844 (1997); see Chapter 2, p 20.

[150] General Fairness Doctrine Obligations of Broadcast Licensees, 50 Fed Reg 35418, 30 August 1985; *Syracuse Peace Council v FCC*, 867 F.2d 654.

[151] See Klein, 'Enemy of the People' (n 141) 69.

public affairs issues would be, at best, a Sisyphean task. At worst, it would be an invitation for opaque and unfair interventions prone to chill free speech.[152]

If the requirement of objectivity is partly relaxed by legacy media in the online sphere, while making a tentative comeback in the guise of online news neutrality, the accuracy norm has also gone through a transformation. Online only news providers, and occasionally also traditional media, sacrifice accuracy on the altar of shareability.[153] The extent of sharing and engagement that a news story is capable of eliciting on social media is such a powerful driver of editorial decisions that it has been included in the canon of online news values.[154] News providers, especially those that prioritize virality and speed over the quest for the truth, tend to place the responsibility of verification on the audience.[155] This turn to crowd-sourced or 'collaborative verification' has been welcomed as a way to loosen the reliance on institutional voice. At the same time, relying on the public to supply and authenticate information signals a break with the journalistic norm of verification and harbours risks that false messages might slip through the net.[156]

These practices are dwarfed by the deluge of unregulated, unreliable news content online which, in 2020, prompted the World Health Organisation (WHO) to raise the alarm about the emergence of a so-called 'infodemic'.[157] The problem is exacerbated by the complexity of the regulatory landscape, and the widespread incapacity of the public to distinguish between news produced in line with ethical journalism norms and other forms of content creation.[158] Even social media posts or tweets may be viewed as 'news items' deserving media attention depending on their provenance.[159] The attack on the Capitol as a result of President Trump's unsubstantiated claims of widespread election fraud underscored the capacity of disinformation to undermine democratic processes. These developments have further prompted governments to adopt policy responses to stem the flood, either by holding social media platforms to account or by relying on the abovementioned traditional or more novel media law instruments.[160] While some of the attempts to tame the power of intermediaries were previously outlined, we will now focus on the communication offences in the Online

---

[152] W Jayne, 'Fairness Doctrine 2.0: The Ever-Expanding Definition of Neutrality under the First Amendment' (2018) 16(3) First Amendment Law Review 466.

[153] Riordan, 'Accuracy, independence and impartiality' (n 133) 50.

[154] T Harcup, *What's the Point of News? A Study in Ethical Journalism* (Palgrave Macmillan 2020) 26; on the role of algorithmic tools in news production, see Chapter 3, 41.

[155] Riordan, 'Accuracy, independence and impartiality' (n 133) 10; Sambrook, 'Delivering trust' (n 59) 6.

[156] A Hermida, 'Tweets and Truth: Journalism as a Discipline of Collaborative Verification' (2012) 6(5–6) Journalism Practice 659, 664; T Atamurto, 'Crowdsourcing as a Knowledge-Search Method in Digital Journalism: Ruptured Ideals and Blended Responsibility' (2016) 4(2) Digital Journalism 280, 290.

[157] World Health Organisation, 'Managing the Covid-19 infodemic: Promoting healthy behaviours and mitigating the harm from misinformation and disinformation', 23 September 2020 <https://www.who.int/news/item/23-09-2020-managing-the-covid-19-infodemic-promoting-healthy-behaviours-and-mitigating-the-harm-from-misinformation-and-disinformation> accessed 18 January 2024.

[158] See H Gibson, L Kirkonnell-Kawana, and E Procter, 'News literacy report: Lessons in building public confidence and trust' (IMPRESS, November 2022) <https://www.impress.press/events-research-and-resources/research-reports/news-literacy-report/> 19ff, accessed 19 May 2022.

[159] M Park, 'Separating Fact from Fiction: The First Amendment Case for Addressing "Fake News" on Social Media' (2018) 46(1) Hastings Constitutional Law Quarterly 1, 5.

[160] See Chapter 3, 50.

Safety Bill as well as on the supervision of online journalism under the German Media Treaty and the NetzDG's disingenuously proclaimed intent to combat disinformation.

In the UK, the Online Safety Bill attempts to strengthen the norm of accuracy in the online communication infosystem by entrusting Ofcom to establish an Advisory committee on disinformation and misinformation, and by introducing a false communications offence alongside a threatening communications offence.[161] These norms are meant to replace existing offences in the Malicious Communications Act 1988 and the Communications Act 2003.[162] A previous proposal for an offence against harmful communications, defined as such that would risk causing psychological harm amounting to at least serious distress to a likely audience, has been removed from the Bill amidst concerns over its implications for freedom of expression.[163] The false communications offence, as currently worded, criminalizes the sending of a message known to be false with the intent of causing non-trivial psychological or physical harm to a likely audience without reasonable excuse.[164] The Bill exempts recognized news publishers and UK-licensed broadcasters from the scope of this offence, thus questionably drawing a line from other news providers.[165]

Online platforms subject to considerable fines will be inclined to take down content perceived to be false without evidence of harm but on the mere basis that this content might cause harm to an indeterminable audience. The Bill does not define what amounts to 'non-trivial psychological or physical harm', raising the possibility of unduly stifling freedom of expression if the bar is set too low. In addition, it does not specify what would constitute a reasonable excuse. While in the case of the abolished harmful communications offence the contribution to a matter of public interest was a possible, though not necessarily absolving, excuse, the same does not necessarily apply to false communications.[166] A citizen journalist reporting on President Trump's suggestion that disinfectant could be used as a cure for Covid-19 might hence find themselves criminally liable. They might not have the intent to cause harm. However, if intent to harm is inferred from the communication act itself, as exemplified in a factsheet that tested the operation of the Bill by way of a series of case studies, then the door is opened for legitimate content to cross the threshold of criminal liability.[167]

In Germany the new Media Treaty seeks to add teeth to the bite of the accuracy standard enforcement by subjecting journalistic-telemedia to the backstop powers of state media authorities.[168] It creates a three-pronged supervisory framework for

---

[161] Online Safety Bill 151, 22 June 2023, s 141.

[162] Malicious Communications Act 1988, s 1; Communications Act 2003, s 127.

[163] Online Safety Bill 121, 11 May 2022, s 152; see House of Lords Communications and Digital Committee, 'Free for all? Freedom of expression in the digital age', 1st Report of Session 2021–22, HL Paper 54, 22 July 2021, paras 97ff.

[164] Online Safety Bill 151, 22 June 2023, s 162.

[165] ibid s 163; See Chapter 3, pp 69–70.

[166] Law Commission, 'Harmful Online Communications: The criminal offences. A consultation paper', 11 September 2020 <https://s3-eu-west-2.amazonaws.com/lawcom-prod-storage-11jsxou24uy7q/uplo ads/2020/09/Online-Communications-Consultation-Paper-FINAL-with-cover.pdf> 136, accessed 18 May 2023.

[167] Department for Culture, Media and Sport, 'Online Safety Bill: Communications offences factsheet', 19 April 2022 <https://www.gov.uk/government/publications/online-safety-bill-supporting-documents/onl ine-safety-bill-communications-offences-factsheet> accessed 18 May 2023.

[168] Chapter 3, pp 74–77.

journalistic-editorial telemedia.[169] The first level encompasses services that are subject to self-regulation by the German Press Council. Their position remains unchanged compared to the one that existed prior to the entry into force of the Media Treaty. The second level includes services that will come under the purview of still to be established recognized self-regulatory bodies.[170] The final level covers services which are not subject to self-regulation by the German Press Council nor by a recognized self-regulatory institution.[171] If these news providers decline to join the Press Council or another recognized self-regulatory body, once one has been established, state media authorities' backstop powers might come into play. These authorities would then be able to single-handedly initiate a challenge to the truthfulness of news reports instead of only reacting to complaints as the Press Council does.

The Media Treaty thus empowers the state media authorities to second-guess editorial choices made by digital news media, including based on their alleged inaccuracy. This is especially problematic given that the press cannot be obliged to report the truth, but only to strive for the truth, whilst being allowed to be tendentious.[172] The concern cannot easily be dismissed that such powers might be abused to purge unfavourable political opinions.[173] Differently from traditional journalism, the online press is thus committed to a state-sanctioned duty of accuracy. The Commission on Licensing and Supervision of Media Authorities (*Kommission für Zulassung und Aufsicht der Landesmedienanstalten*, ZAK) decided that a blog commenting on an Italian newspaper article about the use of Covid-19 detection dogs in South Tyrol schools breached the journalistic due diligence obligation to research.[174] This decision, which led to the blog being blocked and administrative costs being imposed, was nearly unanimous. Only one state media authority questioned the classification of the blog as a journalistic-editorial telemedium and rightly argued that the challenged passage voiced exaggerated comments rather than factual allegations.[175] Indeed, as explained earlier, the distinction between value judgements and factual allegations protects editorial choices and is a core tenet of the ECtHR's case law.

The NetzDG's explanatory memorandum also envisaged the aim of tackling 'fake news'.[176] This has been a shot in the dark from the outset. No case of illegal 'fake news' was known to the government prior to the adoption of this legislation.[177] Despite the

[169] Chapter 3, 65.

[170] MStV, §19(3)1.

[171] MStV, §§19(3)–(8), 109(1)4.

[172] F Ferreau, 'Desinformation als Herausforderung für die Medienregulierung' (2021) 3 Archiv für Presserecht 204, 207.

[173] C Fiedler, '§109 MStV' in H Gersdorf and P Paal (eds), *Informations- und Medienrecht Kommentar* (Beck 2021) para 11.

[174] German Press Code, cl 2.

[175] M Kompa, 'Staatliche Sperrverfügung gegen Blogger. Landesmedienanstalten praktizieren eine weite Auslegung von §§19, 109 MStV' (2022) Multimedia und Recht 273, 274.

[176] Draft Network Enforcement Act of 14 June 2017, German Parliament document BT-Drs. 18/12727, 1 <https://dserver.bundestag.de/btd/18/127/1812727.pdf> accessed 2 March 2023.

[177] F Greis, 'Hate-Speech-Gesetz: Regierung kennt keine einzige strafbare Falschnachricht', 19 April 2017 <www.golem.de/news/hate-speech-gesetz-regierung-kennt-keine-einzige-strafbare-falschnachricht-1704-127370.html> accessed 18 January 2024.

wording of the memorandum, the fight against 'fake news' is not an actual aim of the NetzDG nor is it mentioned in the wording of the law.[178] The NetzDG only seeks to target unlawful online content breaching specific provisions of the Criminal Code. However, the untruthfulness of a news report does not necessarily entail its unlawfulness. The criminal law provisions whose enforcement the law intends to strengthen, including Holocaust denial and defamation laws, are only suited to tackling the problem of 'fake news' to a limited extent.[179]

In the following, we will consider two possible alternatives to the regulation and criminalization of false expression as answers to the problem of online dis- and misinformation: fact-checking and the promotion of reliable media content.

5.6 Possible Solutions to the Problem of 'Fake News'

A carefree attitude to accuracy is prone to jeopardize a news outlet's credibility. An example is NowThisNews, a news outlet specializing in sharing video stories harvested on social media.[180] It strives for the 'closest version of the truth *at that time*, rather than waiting for the full facts to unfold' even if this means that its coverage is 'dirty and it's not always right, but it's instantaneous.'[181] As a result, NowThisNews has received rebukes from fact-checking sites for publishing inaccurate stories. In 2015, for example, PolitiFact gave it a 'Pants on Fire' rating for its unproven claim that CNN deleted an online poll, which showed Bernie Sanders as the winner of the first Democratic Presidential debate, so as to help Hillary Clinton.[182]

PolitiFact is but one of at least a hundred fact-checking initiatives that are active around the world.[183] Some of these initiatives emanate from the journalism ecosystem, both print and broadcast.[184] Others are linked to academia or civil society organizations or are independent outlets operating as charities.[185] The majority of fact-checkers target claims by politicians, while only few regularly fact-check the

---

[178] E Hoven and H Gersdorf, '§1 NetzDG' in H Gersdorf and P Paal (eds), *Informations- und Medienrecht Kommentar* (Beck 2021) para 4.
[179] P Zurth, 'The German NetzDG as Role Model or Cautionary Tale? Implications for the Debate on Social Media Liability' (2021) 31(4) Fordham Intellectual Property, Media and Entertainment Law Journal 1084, 1111; G Nolte, 'Hate-Speech, Fake News, das "Netzwerkdurchsetzungsgesetz" und Vielfaltsicherung durch Suchmaschinen' (2017) 61(7) Zeitschrift für Urheber-und Medienrecht 552, 555.
[180] <https://nowthisnews.com/> accessed 25 August 2021.
[181] Riordan, 'Accuracy, independence and impartiality' (n 133) 12 (emphasis added).
[182] K Sanders, 'No, Internet, CNN did not delete its poll showing Bernie Sanders won the Democratic debate' (*Politifact*, 19 October 2015) <https://www.politifact.com/factchecks/2015/oct/19/nowthis/no-internet-cnn-did-not-delete-its-poll-showing-be/> accessed 25 August 2021.
[183] A Mantzarlis, 'There's been an explosion of international fact-checkers, but they face big challenges' (*Poynter*, 7 June 2016) <https://www.poynter.org/fact-checking/2016/theres-been-an-explosion-of-international-fact-checkers-but-they-face-big-challenges/> accessed 7 September 2021.
[184] eg *The Washington Post*'s Fact Checker <https://www.washingtonpost.com/news/fact-checker/>; the BBC Reality Check <https://www.bbc.com/news/reality_check> accessed 7 September 2021.
[185] eg FactCheck.org <https://www.factcheck.org/>, a project of the Annenberg Policy Center of the University of Pennsylvania; PolitiFact <https://www.politifact.com/>, operated by the Poynter Institute, but originally a project of the *Tampa Bay Times* (then the *St Petersburg Times*); FullFact.org < https://fullfact.org/about/> accessed 7 September 2021.

news media.[186] Even though the present day fact-checking movement is very much digital, driven by the publication of fact-checks online, fact-checking is actually not a product of the digital era. It is another word for the editorial technique of verification that has been practised in newsrooms since time immemorial. In the 1920s, it was introduced as a job title by US magazines to designate a new group of staffers hired to check the accuracy of reporters' notes.[187] The main difference between traditional journalistic fact-checking and its modern-day incarnation is that the former is *ante hoc*, identifying errors before publication, while the latter is *post hoc*, checking something that has already been published.

This reversal of the ordinary verification process signifies a departure from the contested notion of objectivity. As a form of accountability journalism, fact-checking professes to expose and counter misinformation. It does this by selecting checkable facts, by aggregating relevant information to compare them against, and by ultimately providing readers with definitive verdicts about the truthfulness of these facts.[188] Most fact-checkers use rating systems to represent degrees of truth.[189] Their verdicts are often playful, even sensational, relying on well-known cultural tropes for mendacity such as 'Pinocchio' or 'Pants on Fire'.[190] They blatantly take sides, all the while dressing their judgements in a cloak of pseudo-scientific reproducibility. They purport to cut through the false balance of the 'on-the-one-hand, on-the-other-hand journalism', but risk eroding their legitimacy and being exposed to accusations of bias.[191] Openly embracing opinion-led journalism is more problematic for broadcasters than for the press, certainly as far as the UK and German media systems are concerned.

Advertent or inadvertent bias, especially as regards the selection of cases whose veracity is tested, is one of the common critiques levied against the fact-checking movement.[192] It is argued that by cherry-picking which cases to verify, and by passing summary judgement on them, fact-checkers shape reality and paint potentially misleading images of political actors.[193] Furthermore, a question mark hangs

---

[186] L Graves and F Cherubini, 'The rise of fact-checking sites in Europe' (Reuters Institute for the Study of Journalism 2016) <https://reutersinstitute.politics.ox.ac.uk/our-research/rise-fact-checking-sites-europe> accessed 18 January 2024 (hereafter Graves and Cherubini, 'The rise of fact-checking sites') 19.

[187] C Silverman, 'Verification and Fact Checking' <https://datajournalism.com/read/handbook/verificat ion-1/additional-materials/verification-and-fact-checking> accessed 7 September 2021.

[188] See L Graves, *Deciding What's True: The Rise of Political Fact-Checking in American Journalism* (Columbia UP 2016) 81ff.

[189] Only a minority of fact-checking organizations rejects the use of ratings as too reductive and confrontational. See Full Fact, 'Frequently asked questions: Why don't you have ratings?' <https://fullfact.org/about/frequently-asked-questions/#ratings> accessed 18 January 2024; Graves and Cherubini, 'The rise of fact-checking sites' (n 186) 19.

[190] The FactChecker awards Pinocchios and a Geppetto Checkmark, while PolitiFact's Truth-O-Meter is set aflame when its needle hits the 'Pants on Fire' rating.

[191] B Adair, 'Determining if a politician is telling the truth. "Through our 'Truth-O-Meter', we graphically show the relative truth of each claim"' (*Nieman Reports*, 15 June 2008) <https://niemanreports.org/articles/determining-if-a-politician-is-telling-the-truth/> accessed 7 September 2021; W Lowrey, 'The Emergence and Development of News Fact-Checking Sites' (2017) 18(3) Journalism Studies 376, 382.

[192] M Marietta, D Barker, and T Bowser, 'Fact-Checking Polarized Politics: Does the Fact-Check Industry Provide Consistent Guidance on Disputed Realities?' (2015) 13(4) The Forum 577, 587; E Ostermeier, 'Selection bias? PolitiFact rates Republican statements as false at 3 times the rate of Democrats' (*Smart Politics*, 10 February 2011) <https://smartpolitics.lib.umn.edu/2011/02/10/selection-bias-politifact-rate/> accessed 7 September 2021.

[193] J Uscinski and R Butler, 'The Epistemology of Fact-Checking' (2013) 25(2) Critical Review 162, 164ff (hereafter Uscinski and Butler, 'The Epistemology of Fact-Checking').

over fact-checkers' methodology, which occasionally extends to statements that do not qualify as facts, even to claims about the future, or vague claims.[194] Fact-checkers defend their modus operandi by taking pride in the transparency of their 'show your work' attitude. The fact-checking movement thus defies both of journalists' abovementioned defences: the distinction between facts and value judgements and the protection of journalistic sources. By blurring the boundary between facts and value judgements, it distances itself from a long tradition in freedom of expression law. By using only 'on the record' sources to check published material *post hoc*, it risks overlooking other anonymous information.

The fact-checking movement is a manifestation of the rise in the norm of transparency as a new journalistic norm.[195] Transparency in news organizations' news production processes has been embraced in American newsrooms as an antidote to the problem of 'fake news'. The *New York Times*'s longest-serving public editor, Margaret Sullivan, recently recommended 'radical transparency' about reporting techniques and primary information as an antidote to public distrust in mainstream media and as a media literacy tool.[196] However, this has not been a universal trend. German newsrooms, for instance, have been more reluctant to adopt this norm in their everyday practice. They have viewed it as a distraction from their actual work and have questioned the link between transparency and credibility.[197] Certainly, there is a potential tension between the rise in the norm of transparency and the ever-important right to protection of journalistic sources.[198] Being aware of this tension, Lord Justice Leveson recommended that the press be as transparent as possible in relation to information *in the public domain*, not as regards confidential sources.[199] More fundamentally, the very premise of fact-checkers' crusade to rid politics of falsehood is questionable. Politics is by definition a contested terrain with few black-and-white certainties. By suggesting that it is otherwise and by attempting to uncover the truth behind many statements, fact-checkers turn away from the procedural understanding of truth that underlies professional codes towards a more objective one, which often exceeds most fact-checkers' journalistic arsenal.[200]

The struggle between competing narratives injected into the political discourse by the fact-checking movement becomes even more complex when commercial, not only

---

[194] ibid 170ff, 174; S Nieminen and V Sankari, 'Checking PolitiFact's Fact-Checks' (2021) 22(3) Journalism Studies 358, 362.

[195] H T Vu and M Saldaña, 'Chillin' Effects of Fake News: Changes in Practices Related to Accountability and Transparency in American Newsrooms under the Influence of Misinformation and Accusations Against the News Media' (2021) 98(3) Journalism & Mass Communication Quarterly 769 (hereafter Vu and Saldaña, 'Chillin' Effects').

[196] M Weaver, '"Media must be more open to save democracy", says former standards editor' (*The Guardian*, 2 June 2023) <https://www.theguardian.com/education/2023/jun/02/media-must-be-more-open-to-save-democracy-says-former-standards-editor> accessed 12 June 2023.

[197] M Koliska and K Chadha, 'Transparency in German Newsrooms. Diffusion of a New Journalistic Norm?' (2018) 19(16) Journalism Studies 2400.

[198] Vu and Saldaña, 'Chillin' Effects' (n 195) 784.

[199] Lord Justice Leveson, *An Inquiry into the Culture, Practices and Ethics of the Press: Executive Summary* (House of Commons 780, 2012) 15, para 63.

[200] P Cavaliere, 'From Journalistic Ethics to Fact-Checking Practices: Defining the Standards of Content Governance in the Fight Against Disinformation' (2020) 12(2) Journal of Media Law 133, 163; Uscinski and Butler, 'The Epistemology of Fact-Checking' (n 193) 163.

political motivations, come into play. In a case decided by the Higher Administrative Court Karlsruhe (OLG Karlsruhe), a news magazine article on climate change was fact-checked on Facebook by a not-for-profit organization which also published journalistic-editorial material online.[201] The OLG Karlsruhe found the fact-checker's characterization of the article as 'partly false' to be misleading on two grounds: firstly, because the verdict actually concerned statements made by third parties in an 'open letter', which were referred to in the fact-checked article, but did not concern the article itself; and secondly, because the fact-checker criticized value judgements in the news magazine article about the scientific rigour of the third parties' claims, not statements of fact. The potential of the 'partly false' verdict to mislead was aggravated in the court's view by the fact that the title of a fact-checker gives rise to higher expectations of proficiency and neutrality. These expectations were thwarted in the present case by the fact-checker's involvement with a competitive news outlet. The court held that, by discrediting the plaintiff's publication on Facebook and by posting a link to a rival publication of its own, the fact-checker had acted in an anti-competitive way. This case throws into sharp relief the limitations of fact-checking as a quick fix, which is often embraced by online platforms to enhance their own credibility and to gain a foothold in the politics of truth. It also demonstrates how fact-checking pits news publishers against each other without necessarily helping citizens to navigate disputed realities in a divided political environment. The fact that citizens are often eager to be confirmed in their opinions and resistant to corrections raises further questions about the effectiveness of fact-checking as a bulwark against the spread of disinformation.[202]

Notwithstanding these weaknesses of fact-checking, online platforms have forged close ties with a network of certified third-party fact-checkers who are asked to flag or remove false claims and conspiracy theories.[203] Such cooperation with the fact-checking community is encouraged by the 2022 Code of Practice.[204] From a freedom of expression perspective, the flagging of clearly inaccurate information is a more proportionate response compared to its outright removal. However, the identification of false information with the help of independent fact-checkers bears risks. The characterization of a fact-checking service as 'independent' is not cast in stone and can become a matter of contention. Facebook has cooperated with partisan fact-checkers in the past, and other platforms might tread the same path.[205] Nor is it implausible to assume that erstwhile neutral fact-checkers could become subject to media capture. Even greater risks are posed by the reliance on automated content moderation as well as appeal and review processes. Such recourse to automation has been increasingly

[201] OLG Karlsruhe, 27 May 2020 – 6 U 36/20.

[202] Porlezza, 'Accuracy in Journalism' (n 202); Waisbord, 'Truth is What Happens to News' (n 108) 1872.

[203] I Katsirea, 'Covid-19, fake news and the future of platform regulation. Part 2' (*Sheffield Political Economy Research Institute*, 10 February 2021) <http://speri.dept.shef.ac.uk/authors/irini-katsirea/> accessed 17 September 2021.

[204] Commission, 'Strengthened Code of Practice' (n 114) 31ff.

[205] A Robertson, 'Facebook fact-checking is becoming a political cudgel' (*The Verge*, 3 March 2020) <https://www.theverge.com/2020/3/3/21163388/facebook-fact-checking-trump-coronavirus-hoax-comment-politico-daily-caller> accessed 17 September 2021.

resorted to in recent times to make up for depleted workforces as a result of the pandemic.[206]

If fact-checking is a contentious solution to the problem of 'fake news', another often-proposed answer is the promotion of quality media content. The promotion of accurate information has been the second prong of technology companies' two-pronged strategy to combat the influx of mis- and disinformation. Facebook, for example, has been providing free ad space at the top of result pages for educational pop-ups from the WHO and national health authorities in response to the pandemic. This is a potentially promising way of countering misinformation. However, as we discussed in Chapter 3, it may raise competition and discrimination concerns.[207] Also, it is one thing to promote accurate official information and another to prioritize trustworthy media content. Interventions to facilitate due prominence of certain types of content could strengthen media pluralism and contribute to a better informed citizenry, but they could also be seen as unwelcome interferences with media freedom.[208] The Journalism Trust Initiative (JTI), a Reporters Without Borders (RSF) project aiming to develop and implement indicators for trustworthiness of journalism, shies away from a definition of hierarchy of content. It considers that such a hierarchy could smack of censorship.[209] Instead, it recommends the adoption of technical standards that could inform journalism practice and content governance and that would need to be respected by news media outlets and internet intermediaries respectively.[210] The JTI standards aim to complement, not replace, existing standards operated by self-regulatory bodies, and to add a further independent and voluntary compliance level.[211]

Besides such standard-setting initiatives, there is one type of news content that is widely regarded as an embodiment of the values of accuracy and reliability, namely public service news.[212] Both in the UK and in Germany, public service broadcasters (PSB) are among the most trusted news brands, and regulatory initiatives seek to prioritize their content on smart TVs, within TV platform recommendations as well as on electronic programme guides (EPGs) and other user interfaces.[213] The promotion

---

[206] J Posetti and K Bontcheva, 'Disinfodemic: Deciphering Covid-19 disinformation' (Unesco 2020) <https://en.unesco.org/sites/default/files/disinfodemic_deciphering_covid19_disinformation.pdf> accessed 19 January 2024.

[207] See Chapter 3, p 61.

[208] E M Mazzoli and D Tambini, 'Prioritisation Uncovered: The Discoverability of Public Interest Content Online' (Council of Europe 2020) <https://www.coe.int/en/web/freedom-expression/-/discoverability-of-public-interest-content-online> accessed 19 January 2024 (hereafter Mazzoli and Tambini, 'Prioritisation Uncovered') 10; F Cairncross, 'Cairncross Review: A sustainable future for journalism', 12 February 2019 <https://assets.publishing.service.gov.uk/government/uploads/system/uploads/attachment_data/file/779882/021919_DCMS_Cairncross_Review_.pdf> 36, accessed 24 February 2020.

[209] Journalism Trust Initiative, 'Help desk: Is the JTI judging or ranking news content, and wouldn't that be a form of censorship?' <https://www.jti-app.com/helpdesk> (hereafter Journalism Trust Initiative, 'Help desk').

[210] ibid; Mazzoli and Tambini, 'Prioritisation Uncovered' (n 208) 16.

[211] Journalism Trust Initiative, 'Help desk' (n 209).

[212] Recommendation CM/Rec(2022)4 of the Committee of Ministers on promoting a favourable environment for quality journalism in the digital age', 17 March 2022, 11, 12.

[213] N Newman, 'United Kingdom' (Reuters Institute Digital News Report 2022) <https://reutersinstitute.politics.ox.ac.uk/digital-news-report/2022/united-kingdom>; (hereafter Newman, 'United Kingdom 2020')S Hölig and U Hasebrink, 'Germany' (Reuters Institute Digital News Report 2020) https://www.digitalnewsreport.org/survey/2020/germany-2020/ (hereafter Hölig and Hasebrink, 'Germany'); Ofcom, 'Review

of PSB is certainly laudable. However, the less favourable treatment of reliable press publishers in that regard might be inequitable.[214] A line of counterargument could point to the fact that the press is not subject to the same impartiality and pluralism requirements as PSB, and hence does not merit the same kind of prominence.[215] However, both in the UK and Germany, certain nationwide as well as local or regional newspapers enjoy high levels of brand trust.[216] If the 'complementarity argument', which goes some way towards explaining the regulatory disparity between the press and broadcast sectors, is to be given some credence, then reliable news sources from both sectors should be afforded equal prominence on online platforms and user interfaces so as to allow the strengths of both systems to play out in a digital environment. This is of paramount importance to ensure that the 'the best obtainable version of the truth' is allowed to prevail over the cacophony of falsehoods and trivia online.

5.7 Concluding Remarks

The ethical standards of accuracy and objectivity, interlinked in the Anglo-Saxon world, are in a process of flux in the digital era. The growth of the disinformation industry, aided by the rise of social media and by increasingly advanced forms of AI, has cast a long shadow on the credibility of news. The mainstream media are victimized for political advantage whilst they themselves provide ammunition for their critics. Pushed into survival mode in a highly competitive environment, they are forced to make stark choices between speed and accuracy. These pressures risk fuelling the ECtHR's eagerness to second-guess the ethical parameters of journalistic work. New forms of regulation of online journalism, such as that adopted in Germany's Media Treaty to combat disinformation, exemplify the hybrid nature of the internet between press and broadcasting and threaten to impose a state-sanctioned version of the truth. Furthermore, in the era of live-blogging, adherence to the norm of objectivity is relaxed, whilst a chimerical argument for a fairness doctrine 2.0 for the digital environment gains traction. The enforcement of such a fairness doctrine would distance online journalism further from the free press model and would be hard to justify from a freedom of expression perspective.

---

of prominence for public service broadcasting. Recommendations to government for a new framework to keep PSB TV prominent in an online world', 4 July 2019 <https://www.ofcom.org.uk/__data/assets/pdf_file/0021/154461/recommendations-for-new-legislative-framework-for-psb-prominence.pdf>; Ofcom, 'EPG prominence. A report on the discoverability of PSB and local TV services' <https://www.ofcom.org.uk/__data/assets/pdf_file/0026/116288/report-psb-local-tv-discoverability.pdf>; MStV, §84(3), (4); cf Government of Canada, *Canada's Communications Future: Time to Act*, January 2020 <https://publications.gc.ca/collections/collection_2020/isde-ised/Iu37-14-2020-eng.pdf> 158 all accessed 17 September 2021.

[214] Chapter 9, p 253.
[215] S Hartmann, B Holznagel, and J Kalbhenn, 'Stellungnahme zur schriftlichen Anhörung des Ausschusses für Kultur und Medien des Landtags Nordrhein-Westfalen', 12 June 2020 <https://www.landtag.nrw.de/portal/WWW/dokumentenarchiv/Dokument/MMST17-2795.pdf> accessed 19 January 2024, 12.
[216] Newman, 'United Kingdom 2020' (n 213); Hölig and Hasebrink, 'Germany' (n 213).

This chapter has examined how the fight against 'fake news' has provided the impetus for regulators and fact-checkers to interpret and police the accuracy norm in ways that are apt to stifle press freedom. The following chapter will discuss how wholly accurate information also risks becoming suppressed in a bid to redraw the boundary between public and private domains and to reverse the unfairness of 'being judged out of context' at the expense of press freedom.[217]

---

[217] See J Rosen, 'The Purposes of Privacy: A Response' (2000–2001) 89 Georgetown Law Journal 2117.

6

Search Engines, Online Archives, and the Right to Erasure ('Right to be Forgotten')

6.1 Introduction

In its 2014 landmark judgment in *Google Spain*, the Court of Justice of the European Union (CJEU), found in favour of a Spanish lawyer who requested Google to dereference information concerning the past seizure of his property due to social security debts, which appeared in a widely read Spanish daily's electronic edition.[1] The *Google Spain* judgment made headlines both in Europe and the US. Some characterized it as a 'victory for privacy'.[2] Others condemned it as 'one of the most significant mistakes the Court has ever made',[3] as 'misguided in principle and unworkable in practice'.[4] On the other side of the Atlantic, it was predicted that the 'right to be forgotten' (RTBF) would represent 'the biggest threat to free speech on the Internet in the coming decade' and that it could transform Google 'into a censor-in-chief for the European Union'.[5] Even though the majority of US adults would favour keeping certain personal information from being retrievable online, the prospect for a US-style RTBF is slim.[6] The strong protection for First Amendment freedoms and intermediary immunities, in tandem with the comparatively underdeveloped right to privacy, means that such a right would be unlikely to be recognized in the US.[7] An attempt to adopt a similar law in New York stalled,[8] while California's 'eraser button law', a law designed to give minors

---

[1] *Google Spain SL and Google Inc. v Agencia Española de Protección de Datos (AEPD) and Mario Costeja González* [2014] ECLI:EU:C:2014:317 (hereafter *Google Spain*).

[2] 'Europe:1, Google:0: EU Court ruling a victory for privacy' (*Spiegel International*, 20 May 2014) <http://www.spiegel.de/international/business/court-imposes-right-to-be-forgotten-on-google-search-results-a-970419.html> accessed 24 May 2023.

[3] J Polonetsky, *Future of Privacy Forum*, quoted in J Toobin, 'The solace of oblivion in Europe, the right to be forgotten trumps the internet' (*The New Yorker*, 29 September 2014) <http://www.newyorker.com/magazine/2014/09/29/solace-oblivion> accessed 24 May 2023.

[4] House of Lords European Union Committee, *EU Data Protection law: a 'right to be forgotten'?*, 2nd Report of session 2014–15 (TSO, 2014) <http://www.publications.parliament.uk/pa/ld201415/ldselect/ldeucom/40/40.pdf> accessed 24 May 2023, 16.

[5] J Rosen, 'Response: The Right to Be Forgotten' (2012) 64 Stanford Law Review <https://www.stanfordlawreview.org/online/privacy-paradox-the-right-to-be-forgotten/> accessed 24 May 2023.

[6] B Auxier, 'Most Americans support right to have some personal info removed from online searches' (*Pew Research Center*, 27 January 2020) <https://www.pewresearch.org/short-reads/2020/01/27/most-americans-support-right-to-have-some-personal-info-removed-from-online-searches/> accessed 24 May 2023.

[7] J Kosseff, *The Twenty-Six Words that Created the Internet* (Cornell UP 2019) 154ff, 158.

[8] D Bernstein, 'Why the "right to be forgotten" won't make it the United States' (*Michigan Technology Law Review*, NK) <https://mttlr.org/2020/02/why-the-right-to-be-forgotten-wont-make-it-to-the-united-states/> accessed 24 May 2023.

Press Freedom and Regulation in a Digital Era. Irini Katsirea, Oxford University Press. © Irini Katsirea 2024.
DOI: 10.1093/oso/9780198858607.003.0006

a second chance as regards their online activities, is very limited in scope.[9] Google recently granted US users a limited version of the RTBF as regards specific types of information such as personal details, non-consensual intimate images, or fake pornography.[10] However, this is merely a corporate policy expansion, not a legal remedy.[11]

In the European Union (EU), the right to request a search engine to dereference information so that it is not retrievable upon typing one's name has since been codified in the General Data Protection Regulation (GDPR) as the 'right to erasure (right to be forgotten)'.[12] The reference to the RTBF in brackets next to the 'right to erasure' (RTE) in the Article 17 GDPR heading could be interpreted in the sense that that the two rights are synonymous.[13] However, the RTE under Article 17 GDPR has a wider scope than the RTBF as it was conceived of in *Google Spain*. First, the RTE applies to all data controllers, including the webmasters of the source webpages, not just to search engine operators.[14] Second, the RTE can be invoked on a potentially wider range of grounds than the RTBF. The RTBF requires the dereferencing of data, in particular when these appear to be 'inadequate, irrelevant or no longer relevant, or excessive in relation to those purposes [of the processing] and in the light of the time that has elapsed'.[15] By comparison, the RTE can be relied upon in additional cases, for example when the original processing was unlawful, the erasure is required to comply with a legal obligation or when a minor's data were collected by an information society service. Third, Article 17 GDPR shifts the burden of proof from the data subject to the data controller. While under the Data Protection Directive (DPD) data subjects had to substantiate their claim to the RTBF based on the nature of the data or on 'compelling legitimate grounds' relating to their particular situation, Article 17 GDPR requires the data controller to prove 'compelling legitimate grounds ... which override the interests ... of the data subject'.[16] Finally, Article 17 GDPR allows the permanent removal of data, not only their mere dereferencing.[17]

---

[9] Cal Bus & Prof Code §22581 (2013); see E DiRoma, 'Kids Say the Darndest Things: Minors and the Internet' (2018) Cardozo Law Review 43, 55ff.

[10] V Dressler, 'Google quietly rolls out the right to be forgotten mechanism in the US' (*Intellectual Freedom Blog*, 14 June 2022) <Google Quietly Rolls Out the Right to be Forgotten mechanism in the U.S. - Intellectual Freedom Blog (ala.org)> accessed 18 August 2023.

[11] U Kohl, 'The Right to Be Forgotten in Data Protection Law and Two Western Cultures of Privacy' (2023) International and Comparative Law Quarterly 737, 757.

[12] Regulation (EU) 2016/679 of the European Parliament and of the Council of 27 April 2016 on the protection of natural persons with regard to the processing of personal data and on the free movement of such data, and repealing Directive 95/46/EC [2016] OJ L 119/1, art 17 (hereafter GDPR).

[13] H Yaish, 'Forget Me, Forget Me Not: Elements of Erasure to Determine the Sufficiency of a GDPR Article 17 Request' (2019) 10(1) Journal of Law, Technology and the Internet 1, 2.

[14] 'Guidelines 5/2019 on the criteria of the right to be forgotten in the search engine cases under the GDPR (Part 1)' (European Data Protection Board, 7 July 2020) <https://edpb.europa.eu/our-work-tools/our-documents/guidelines/guidelines-52019-criteria-right-be-forgotten-search-engines_en> para 6 (hereafter EDPB Guidelines). These Guidelines are not binding for the UK, but they may still provide 'helpful guidance'. See Information Commissioner's Office, 'How shall we draft our privacy information?'<https://tinyurl.com/2fstk3jm> accessed 10 October 2023.

[15] *Google Spain*, para 93.

[16] European Parliament and Council Directive (EC) 95/46 on the protection of individuals with regard to the processing of personal data and on the free movement of such data [1995] OJ L 281/31, arts 12(b), 14(a) (hereafter 'Directive' or 'DPD'); GDPR, art 17(1)(c) in combination with art 21(1)2.

[17] EDPB Guidelines, para 10; BGH, 13 December 2022, VI ZR 54/21, paras 16ff, 26ff.

The CJEU took the latter approach in *Google Spain* when 'merely' obliging search engines to remove links to webpages from the list of results displayed following a name-based search. This meant that the links would still be retrievable when searching under a different search term, and that the information would remain available on the source webpage.[18] The European Data Protection Board (EDPB), the independent European body that oversees the consistent application of data protection rules throughout the EU, confirmed that, also under the GDPR, dereferencing requests would not result in the data being completely erased from the source website. However, it warned that search engine providers would not be 'exempt in a general manner from the duty to fully erase'.[19] It is clear that the need to carry out actual and full erasure in their indexes or caches would be confined to exceptional cases.[20]

As will be shown in this chapter, not only search engines, but also source webpages are increasingly at the receiving end of requests to reduce the visibility of embarrassing information. In a speech given in the early days of the EU Data Protection Reform, Commissioner Viviane Reding, attempted to assuage fears about the impact of the forthcoming RTBF on freedom of expression and the right to information by stating that:

> The right to be forgotten is of course not an absolute right. There are cases where there is a legitimate and legally justified interest to keep data in a data base. The archives of a newspaper are a good example. It is clear that the right to be forgotten cannot amount to a right of the total erasure of history. Neither must the right to be forgotten take precedence over freedom of expression or freedom of the media.[21]

This chapter will examine whether the promise that the RTBF would not undermine freedom of expression or press freedom has been honoured. It will assess, first, the interpretation of the RTE/RTBF in the CJEU case law. It will briefly revisit central tenets of the *Google Spain* case before discussing more recent case law on the RTE/RTBF and its implications for freedom of expression and information. It will then turn its attention to the ECtHR case law and that of national courts in Germany and the UK. It will trace the trend of extending the RTBF from its original domain, the activity of search engine providers, to that of publishers of third-party websites, aided by the expansive scope of application of Article 17 GDPR. It will seek to identify the ways in which the courts at both European and national level strike the balance between data protection and freedom of expression, and the factors that swing the pendulum one way or another. This chapter will finally assess whether the growing entanglement of online news archives in the strictures of data protection law prevents them from fulfilling their function, and undermines the right of the public to be informed.

---

[18] See *Google Spain*, para 88.
[19] EDPB Guidelines, para 10.
[20] ibid.
[21] V Reding, 'The EU Data Protection Reform 2012: Making Europe the standard setter for modern data protection rules in the digital age', 22 January 2012 <https://ec.europa.eu/commission/presscorner/detail/en/SPEECH_12_26> accessed 24 May 2023.

6.2 The Case Law of the Court of Justice of the European Union

A defining characteristic of the RTBF is the fact that it can be triggered by the exist-ence of information online that was completely lawful at the time of its publication. Mr Costeja's attempt to clean his digital record is understandable in view of the incon-venience it posed for a practising lawyer who might have been perceived by his clients as imprudent with his finances, and by extension with theirs. Still, it did not change the fact that the publication of the announcements about the attachment proceed-ings in the press was not only legal but was in fact mandated by Spanish law so as to give maximum publicity to the auction. The CJEU reasoned in *Google Spain* that even accurate data that were initially lawfully processed could fall foul of the Directive's requirements over time if they appeared irrelevant or excessive in the light of the pur-poses for which they were collected or processed and in the light of the time that had elapsed.[22] It follows that the balance between freedom of expression and other vul-nerable interests changes with the passage of time. Accurate personal information of public interest that is distributed online may be most newsworthy close to its publica-tion, but may lose its relevance as time goes by. While the benefit to the public initially outweighs the loss to privacy, a point comes at which the balance is reversed. The loss to privacy is then deemed to be greater than the value of the wholly lawful information in question.[23] The decoupling between the legality of the underlying information from a privacy law perspective and of the processing of any personal data contained therein gave rise to considerable criticism against the *Google Spain* decision.[24]

A further contentious aspect of the *Google Spain* judgment are the principles guiding the balancing exercise between the fundamental rights at stake. The CJEU devoted only two paragraphs of the entire judgment to a weighing of the data subject's fundamental rights to privacy under Article 7 of the Charter of Fundamental Rights of the European Union (CFEU) and to data protection under Article 8 CFEU against 'merely the economic interest which the operator of such an engine has in that pro-cessing' and the 'legitimate interest of internet users potentially interested in having access to that information'.[25] It dismissed the notion out of hand that the consider-able interference with the fundamental rights of the data subject could be justified by the mere economic interests of the search engine operators. By narrowly focusing on the relationship between search engines and data subjects, the CJEU eclipsed the rights of website publishers which are also involved in this complex web of interests. It attached more weight to the interest of internet users to have access to the informa-tion in question only to immediately downgrade it by apodictically saying that it is overridden, as a general rule, by the data subject's rights. This represents a departure

---

[22] *Google Spain*, para 93.

[23] P Korenhof and others, 'Timing the Right to Be Forgotten: A Study into "Time" as a Factor in Deciding about Retention or Erasure of Data' in S Gutwirth, R Leenes, and P de Hert (eds), *Reforming European Data Protection Law* (Springer 2015) 171.

[24] J Wimmers, 'Der Intermediär als Ermittler, Moderator und Entscheider in äußerungsgerichtlichen Auseinandersetzungen?' (2015) 3 Archiv für Presserecht 203, 209 (hereafter Wimmers, 'Der Intermediär').

[25] *Google Spain*, paras 81 and 97; Charter of Fundamental Rights of the European Union of 14 December 2007, OJ C 303/01, 2007.

from Viviane Reding's abovementioned promise and from the European Court of Human Rights (ECtHR) approach, which holds that the rights under Articles 8 and 10 of the European Convention on Human Rights (ECHR) deserve equal respect.[26] It also lessens the importance of the *rights* to freedom of expression and information by demoting them to the status of mere *interests*.[27]

An exception could only be made in specific cases depending 'on the nature of the information in question and its sensitivity for the data subject's private life and on the interest of the public in having that information, an interest which may vary, in particular, according to the role played by the data subject in public life'.[28] The reference to the public role of the data subject is not exhaustive but only indicative of the counter-interests that may weigh against the RTE/RTBF request. Such factors need to be considered in a holistic manner as became apparent in the *Manni* case.[29] This case concerned the request by the former sole director of an insolvent building company to have information in the companies' register linking him to the liquidation erased, anonymized, or otherwise blocked. The CJEU held that this request required account to be taken 'of all the circumstances surrounding the data subject's particular situation'.[30] The companies' register aimed to guarantee legal certainty in third parties' dealings with companies, and to protect their interests for an indefinite time after a company's dissolution.[31] Only after the passage of a sufficiently long period of time may there be specific situations, to be established by national legislation and the courts, in which the overriding concerns of the data subject would justify an exceptional limitation of access to such data.[32] The CJEU departed on this point from the more uncompromising answer put forward by AG Bot who rejected such a right under any circumstances.[33]

The CJEU's balanced findings in *Manni* provide a welcome reminder that the RTBF/RTE does not represent a cure-all for all situations, contrary to what the *Google Spain* judgment and the misnomer 'right to be forgotten' has led many to assume.[34] However, there are important differences between *Manni* and *Google Spain*. The former concerned a public register performing important functions in the public interest, while the latter concerned Google's omnipresent search engine. Manni's plans to sell properties in a tourist complex only two years after his former company's liquidation were allegedly stalled because of targeted searches in the companies' register, not because of the flotsam and jetsam of information washed up on Google. It thus remains to be seen in how far the findings in *Manni* might influence the shape of the RTE/RTBF in future,

---

[26] *Węgrzynowski and Smolczewski v Poland*, App no 33846/07, 16 July 2013, para 56; *Delfi AS v Estonia*, App no 64569/09, 16 June 2015, para 110.

[27] M Arning, F Moos, and J Schefzig, 'Vergiss (,) Europa! Ein Kommentar zu EuGH, Urt. V. 13. 5. 2014 – Rs. C-131/12 – Google/Mario Costja Gonzalez, CR 2014, 460' (2014) 7 Computer und Recht 447, 449 (hereafter Arning, Moos, and Schefzig, 'Vergiss').

[28] *Google Spain*, para 81; see I Katsirea, 'Search Engines and Press Archives between Memory and Oblivion' (2018) 1 European Public Law 125, 132 for a discussion of the complex evaluations that underlie these factors (hereafter Katsirea, 'Search Engines').

[29] *Camera di Commercio v Manni* [2017] ECLI:EU:C:2017:197.

[30] ibid para 47.

[31] ibid paras 48ff.

[32] ibid para 60.

[33] ibid, Opinion of AG Bot, paras 98, 100.

[34] Katsirea, 'Search Engines' (n 28) 136.

and serve to tilt the balance more towards the rights to information and freedom of expression.

A first test case came along by way of *GC and Others*.[35] This case concerned a reference for a preliminary ruling by the French Council of State (*Conseil d'État*) after both Google and the French Data Protection Authority (DPA) (*Commission nationale de l'informatique et des libertés* (CNIL)) refused to accede to four applicants' independent requests to dereference third-party websites containing sensitive information about them which emerged following searches of their names on the search engine. The said information related to a satirical photomontage of a former politician placed pseudonymously on YouTube; an article in a daily newspaper naming a public relations officer of the Church of Scientology; articles that appeared mainly in the press concerning the judicial investigation of a politician who had since been discharged; and press reports about the sentencing of another individual for sexual assaults on minors.

The questions submitted to the CJEU sought to establish the applicability to search engines of the prohibition on processing special categories of personal data. The CJEU confirmed that the prohibition on processing such sensitive data also applies to the operator of a search engine in the context of his 'responsibilities, powers and capabilities'.[36] A general derogation for the activity of search engines would defeat the purpose of Articles 9 and 10 GDPR.[37] However, in view of the specific features of processing carried out by search engines, the said prohibition could not apply *ex ante*, but only *ex post*, under the supervision of competent national authorities, on the basis of a request by the data subject.[38] Even so, the CJEU held that search engine operators would need to accede in principle to requests for dereferencing of sensitive data unless if one of the exceptions under Article 9(2) GDPR was to make such processing lawful. In particular, they would need to ascertain whether the inclusion of the link to a webpage in the list of search results was *strictly necessary* for reasons of substantial public interest, namely so as to enable internet users to exercise their right to information.[39] The CJEU drew the balance between privacy/data protection and the right to information in the same way as in *Google Spain*. It repeated its dictum that 'the data subject's rights protected by Articles 7 and 8 of the Charter override, as a general rule, the freedom of information of internet users', subject to the same abovementioned factors.[40]

By qualifying the proportionality requirement by way of the use of the adverb 'strictly', the Court further emphasized the precedence afforded to the data subject's rights. The CJEU used the same adverb in *Satamedia* in relation to derogations to the right to data protection.[41] It does represent a departure from the wording in Article 85 GDPR which, in line with Article 52(1) CFEU, only requires that derogations be '*necessary* to reconcile the right to the protection of personal data with the freedom of

---

[35] Arning, Moos, and Schefzig, 'Vergiss' (n 27) 449; Case C-136/17, *GC and Others v CNIL* [2017] ECLI:EU:C:2019:773.
[36] *GC and Others v CNIL* [2019] ECLI:EU:C:2019:773, para 43.
[37] ibid para 44.
[38] ibid para 47.
[39] ibid paras 68, 69; GDPR, art 9(2)(g) in connection with CFEU, art 11.
[40] *GC and Others v CNIL* [2019] ECLI:EU:C:2019:773, para 66.
[41] *Satakunnan Markkinapörssi and Satamedia* [2008] ECLI:EU:C:2008:727, para 56; see also *Digital Rights Ireland* [2014] ECLI:EU:C:2014:238, para 52.

expression and information.'[42] The question arises of whether the CJEU would have accorded this a priori primacy to data protection, had it included publishers' right to freedom of expression in the equation. AG Szpunar remarked parenthetically that the Court should have expressly mentioned freedom of expression in *Google Spain* for the avoidance of any doubt that this right also needed to be taken into account.[43] However, the Court did not heed this advice in *GC and Others*, but again only acknowledged the freedom of information of internet users. Nor did it expressly refer to freedom of expression in the *Google v CNIL* case which was decided on the same day as *GC*.[44] This is a curious omission given that the CJEU accepts in principle the need to balance the rights to data protection and freedom of expression.[45]

In *GC and Others*, the Advocate General diverged from the CJEU also on the application of the journalism exemption to search engines.[46] The journalism exemption is laid down in Article 85 GDPR (ex Article 9 DPD) and seeks to relieve processing for journalistic purposes from the obligations arising from the GDPR. In *Google Spain*, the CJEU opined that processing carried out by a search engine 'did not appear' to fall within the scope of this exemption.[47] AG Szpunar recommended that the temptation to exempt the operator of a search engine should be resisted.[48] He based his view on the importance of the internet in 'enhancing the public's access to news and facilitating the sharing and dissemination of information', and on the fact that Article 10 ECHR applies 'not only to the content of information, but also to the means of transmission or reception'.[49] From this AG Szpunar concluded that both the information on the source webpages and the information provided by the search engines should come under the scope of Article 10 ECHR.

The proposition that the dissemination of information by search engines should attract the protection of the right to freedom of expression is controversial. As already discussed in Chapter 2, some argue that search engines are passive and neutral conduits, while others convincingly point to the active editorial judgements baked into their algorithms.[50] The German Constitutional Court (BVerfG) took an intermediate position in the *Right to be forgotten II* case, to be discussed in greater detail later on.[51] It recognized that search engines cannot be considered neutral in view of the considerable impact they exercise on the formation of users' opinions. At the same time, it held that these services were not in the business of disseminating specific opinions nor did they claim to do so. They would, therefore, not be able to invoke freedom of

---

[42] C Bagger Tranberg, 'Proportionality and Data Protection in the Case Law of the European Court of Justice' (2011) 1(4) International Data Privacy Law 239, 245 (emphasis added).
[43] *GC and Others v CNIL* [2019] ECLI:EU:C:2019:773, Opinion of AG Szpunar, para 68.
[44] *Google LLC v CNIL* [2019] ECLI:EU:C:2019:772.
[45] *Lindqvist* [2003] ECLI:EU:C:2003:596, para 90; *Satakunnan Markkinapörssi and Satamedia* [2008] ECLI:EU:C:2008:727, para 56.
[46] GDPR, art 85; DPD, art 9.
[47] *Google Spain*, para 85; see D Erdos, 'Special, Personal and Broad Expression: Exploring Freedom of Expression Norms under the General Data Protection Regulation' (2021) Yearbook of European Law 405 fn 58 (hereafter Erdos, 'Special, Personal and Broad') on the more definitive wording in the Spanish version.
[48] *GC and Others v CNIL* [2019] ECLI:EU:C:2019:773, Opinion of AG Szpunar, para 83.
[49] *Neij and Sunde v Sweden*, App No 40397/12, 19 February 2013, paras 9, 10.
[50] Chapter 2, p 21.
[51] BverfGE 152, 216, para 105 (hereafter BVerfG, *RTBF II*).

expression.[52] This is in line with the conception of Article 5(1) of the German Basic Law as a guarantee of the right to express one's opinions rather than to merely facilitate the dissemination of those held by others.[53] On the contrary, Article 10 ECHR and Article 11(1) CFEU protect not only the content of information but also the means of dissemination given that the right to receive and impart information is equally affected when these means are curtailed.[54]

In any case, the protection of search engines under the Convention and Charter rights to freedom of expression does not by itself explain why they should also come within the scope of the journalism exemption. The CJEU has clarified that the special regime applicable to processing carried out for journalistic purposes not only applies 'to media undertakings but also to every person engaged in journalism'.[55] Journalism has been interpreted broadly to cover all activities whose 'object is the disclosure to the public of information, opinions or ideas, irrespective of the medium which is used to transmit them'.[56] The need for a broad interpretation of the notion of 'journalism' so as to take account of the importance of the right to freedom of expression is also emphasized in the GDPR.[57] At the same time, the interpretation of what constitutes journalism falls primarily within the competence of the Member States. The EU only has a narrow competence in that regard, limited by the confines of the freedom to provide audiovisual services. The argument has been put forward that Member States could legitimately limit the media privilege to the press, broadcasting, and their electronic equivalents.[58] Breathing space for the new media could be provided by way of Article 85(1) GDPR, a provision that seeks to reconcile the right to data protection with the right to freedom of expression and information.[59]

The normative scope of Article 85(1) GDPR has been particularly contested. Some interpret it as a reconciliation mandate with purely programmatic character, while others see it as a proper opening clause in its own right.[60] In any case, Article 85(1) GDPR requires legislative action at national level, which is not forthcoming any time soon.[61] In the UK, Article 85(1) GDPR has not been incorporated into the relevant implementing legislation.[62] This provision would therefore be unlikely to provide sufficient protection for non-traditional journalistic work in the public interest. At the same time, the journalism exemption cannot be interpreted as covering the

---

[52] Contra J Kühling, 'Art. 5 GG' in H Gersdorf and P Paal (eds), *Informations- und Medienrecht Kommentar* (Beck 2021) para 99d.

[53] J Oster, 'Communication, Defamation and Liability of Intermediaries' (2015) 35(2) Legal Studies 348, 352.

[54] *Öztürk v Turkey*, App No 2247993/93, 28 September 1999, para 49; *Ahmet Yildirim v Turkey*, 18 December 2012, App No 3111/10, para 50; *Cengiz and Others v Turkey*, App Nos 48226/10 and 14027/11, 1 December 2015, para 56.

[55] Case C-73/07, *Satakunnan Markkinapörssi and Satamedia* [2008] ECLI:EU:C:2008:727, para 58; *Sergejs Buivids* [2019] ECLI:EU:C:2019:122, para 52.

[56] Case C-73/07, *Satakunnan Markkinapörssi and Satamedia* [2008] ECLI:EU:C:2008:727, para 61.

[57] GDPR, rec 153.

[58] N Peifer, 'Datenschutz und Medienrecht nach den BVerfG-Entscheidungen zum Recht auf Vergessenwerden' (2020) 6 Archiv für Presserecht 462, 466.

[59] ibid.

[60] M Cornils, 'Art. 85 DS-GVO' in H Gersdorf and P Paal (eds), *Informations- und Medienrecht Kommentar* (Beck 2021) para 20.

[61] Erdos, 'Special, Personal and Broad' (n 47) 28.

[62] Data Protection Act 2018, Sch 2 Part 5, art 26.

entire area of freedom of expression, and hence all information published online.[63] Such an overbroad interpretation would undermine the required narrow application of the derogations to the right to data protection. Moreover, it would amount to an acknowledgement of their editorial role, which would stand in conflict with their entitlement to the safe harbour exemptions under the E-Commerce Directive and the Digital Services Act.[64] To answer the question of whether the journalism exemption should apply to search engines, it is necessary to take these contradictory imperatives into account.

In *Satamedia*, the CJEU held that a text-messaging service, which enabled the public to receive publicly available information about the income and assets of individuals earning over a certain threshold, fell in principle within the scope of Article 9 DPD if its sole object was 'the disclosure to the public of information, opinions, or ideas'.[65] The CJEU left it to the national courts to decipher the meaning of what has been characterized as an 'enigmatic' phrase, and to determine the question of its applicability in the case at hand.[66] Given that the activities of a search engine arguably have as their object 'the disclosure to the public of information, opinions or ideas', it could be inferred from this judgment that they should benefit from the journalism exemption.[67] Support for this view could be drawn from the Article 29 Working Party's Opinion 1/2008, which suggested that, so as to strike a fair balance between privacy and freedom of expression, search engines should come within the scope of Article 9 DPD.[68] Google initially argued that it was not a content creator and hence not entitled to the exemption.[69] By the time of the *NT1 & NT2 v Google LLC* case, to be discussed in greater detail in the following, Google's self-perception had changed. It sought to rely on the journalism exemption, albeit unsuccessfully.[70] Justice Warby held that the concept of journalism is 'not so elastic that it can be stretched to embrace every activity that has to do with conveying information or opinions', and that doing so would 'elide the concept of journalism with that of communication'.[71] This accords with the

---

[63] See Chapter 4, p 83; Case C-73/07, *Satakunnan Markkinapörssi and Satamedia* [2008] ECLI:EU:C:2008:727, Opinion of AG Kokott, para 65; Case C-345/17, *Sergejs Buivids* [2019] ECLI:EU:C:2019:122, para 58.

[64] See Chapter 7, p 176; European Parliament and Council Directive (EC) 2000/31/EC of 8 June 2000 on certain legal aspects of information society services, in particular electronic commerce, in the Internal Market ('Directive on electronic commerce') [2000] OJ L 178/1, arts 12ff; Regulation 2022/2065 of the European Parliament and of the Council of 19 October 2022 on a single market for digital services and amending Directive 2000/31/EC (Digital Services Act) [2022] OJ L 277/1, arts 4ff.

[65] Case C-73/07, *Satakunnan Markkinapörssi and Satamedia* [2008] ECLI:EU:C:2008:727, para 62.

[66] P Oliver, 'The Protection of Privacy in the Economic Sphere before the European Court of Justice' (2009) 46 Common Market Law Review 1443, 1461. On the implementation of *Satamedia* by the Finnish Supreme Court see D Erdos, 'From the Scylla of Restriction to the Charybdis of Licence? Exploring the Scope of the 'Special Purposes' Freedom of Expression Shield in European Data Protection' (2015) 52 Common Market Law Review 119, 132 (hereafter Erdos, 'From Scylla to Charybdis').

[67] S Kulk and F Borgesius, 'Google Spain v. Gonzalez: Did the Court forget about freedom of expression?' (2014) 5(3) European Journal of Risk Regulation 389, 395.

[68] Article 29 Data Protection Working Party, 'Opinion 1/2008 on data protection issues related to search engines', 4 April 2008 <http://ec.europa.eu/justice/policies/privacy/docs/wpdocs/2008/wp148_en.pdf> accessed 19 January 2015, 13.

[69] E Schmidt, Google's Executive Chairman, Public meeting of the Advisory Council to Google on the right to be forgotten, London, 16 October 2014.

[70] *NT1 & NT2 v Google LLC* [2018] EWHC 799 (QB), para 25.

[71] *NT1 & NT2 v Google LLC* [2018] EWHC 799 (QB), para 99.

view of the German Constitutional Court and the German Federal Court of Justice (*Bundesgerichtshof*, BGH), which also held that data processing by search engines cannot be considered to fall within the scope of the journalism exemption.[72]

In *GC and Others*, AG Szpunar added a further twist to his argument in support of search engines' entitlement to the journalism exemption. He explained that Article 9 DPD might not apply directly to the activity of a search engine operator in view of the secondary nature of that activity to that of the original publisher. However, this should not prevent the search engine from relying on the journalism exemption when the source webpage fell within its scope.[73] This argument was interestingly also put forward in the *NT1 & NT2 v Google LLC* case, but was dismissed by Justice Warby. He accepted that the activity of an entity that facilitates publication of journalistic material by a third party could benefit of the journalism exemption. However, he subscribed to the view of the all-automatic nature of search engine operations. When Google included journalistic sources in its search results, 'this was purely accidental, and incidental to its larger purpose of providing automated access to third party content of whatever nature it may be'.[74] He added further that processing by Google is not undertaken 'solely' for journalistic purposes, an argument that is now redundant after the omission of this requirement under Article 85(2) GDPR.[75]

While one may doubt whether search engine operators are such neutral conduits as Justice Warby made them out to be, there is good reason why the extension of the journalism exemption to them would not be appropriate. Such a wide conceptualization of the journalism exemption would risk transforming it to a general 'freedom of expression' derogation. It could pave the way for a generalized exemption also of social media platforms from data protection law given that they do not only facilitate access to, but also the publication of, journalistic content, while increasingly also producing professional content.[76] Utmost caution is needed before treading this path, not least in view of the grave harm that can potentially be inflicted on individuals as a result of unchecked citizen journalists performing the role of a 'social bloodhound'.[77] Mapping services in Sweden showing the residence of ex-offenders for a fee are a case in point. In any case, search engines do not enable the publication of material aimed at the general public, but only facilitate information dissemination triggered by individualized requests. The provision of information with the aim of satisfying private interests as opposed to the public interest arguably falls outwith the scope of the exemption.[78]

What is more, the exemption of search engine processing from data protection law would deprive users of a procedural safeguard, of the assurance that 'right to erasure' requests would be dealt with the necessary regulatory oversight.[79] While it might seem

---

[72] BVerfG, *RTBF II*, para 36; BGH, 27 February 2018, VI ZR 489/16, para 44.

[73] Case C-136/17, *GC and Others v CNIL* [2019] ECLI:EU:C:2019:773, Opinion of AG Szpunar, para 86.

[74] *NT1 & NT2 v Google LLC* [2018] EWHC 799 (QB), para 100.

[75] ibid para 101.

[76] B Wong, 'The Journalism Exception in UK Data Protection Law' (2020) 12(2) Journal of Media Law 216, 225; see Chapter 3, p 68.

[77] *Reynolds v Times Newspapers* [2001] 2 AC 127, 205 (Lord Nicholls); see Erdos, 'Special, Personal and Broad' (n 47) 15.

[78] Erdos, 'From Scylla to Charybdis' (n 66) 130ff; Case C-73/07, *Satakunnan Markkinapörssi and Satamedia* [2008] ECLI:EU:C:2008:727, Opinion of AG Kokott, paras 69ff.

[79] *NT1 & NT2 v Google LLC* [2018] EWHC 799 (QB), para 101.

counterintuitive at first sight, the handling of the 'right to erasure' within the data protection framework offers certain safeguards for users' right to freedom of expression when compared to leaving it at the behest of search engine operators.[80] Search engines can still rely on Article 85(1) GDPR. As discussed earlier, the scope of protection offered by this provision is uncertain. Even if Member States were to adopt relevant laws, a contribution to public opinion formation would still be needed to substantiate the need for exemption from data protection law without completely eroding the information safeguards its protective framework offers.

A final noteworthy aspect of the *GC* judgment relates to the contextual integrity of search results.[81] One of the dereferencing requests in this case concerned contemporaneous reports into the funding of a political party which were subsequently closed by an order discharging the applicant, an outcome that was naturally not mentioned in the said reports. In an interesting *obiter dictum*, the CJEU subscribed to the view that search results needed to give an accurate picture of the current situation. The CJEU held that even if the dereferencing request was not granted, the search engine would be obliged 'to adjust the list of results in such a way that the overall picture it gives the internet user reflects the current legal position, which means that links to web pages containing information on that point must appear in first place on the list'.[82]

The notion that search results should as far as possible be up-to-date is hardly contentious. A 'reordering' of such results to reflect the current position might be more equitable than the dereferencing remedy established in *Google Spain*.[83] It does, however, potentially stand in conflict with the practice of ordering search results based on their perceived relevance for the user.[84] Also, situations are conceivable where chronological ordering is inimical to conveying an accurate picture, for instance when more recent results are erroneous in a different way. Determining what information best conveys the full picture, and choosing the arbiter who is competent to decide this point, are vexed issues. Further, the question could be raised whether this *obiter dictum* could also apply to other internal types of search results, including those provided by online news archives.[85] If so, online news archives might need to meet the onerous obligation of continuously updating their entries so as to reflect the most current legal position. As will be discussed in the following section, the added value of news archives in not primarily capturing a snapshot of the present, but in conveying information about the past, would need to be taken into account.

The need for search results to be kept up-to-date resurfaced in a recent CJEU Grand Chamber preliminary ruling following a reference by the BGH.[86] This is an important

---

[80] J Ausloos, *The Right to Erasure in EU Data Protection Law: From Individual Rights to Effective Protection* (OUP 2020) 359.

[81] See for a wider discussion of no longer accurate search results the study by J Bayer and others, 'The fight against disinformation and the right to freedom of expression' (European Parliament, July 2021) <https://www.europarl.europa.eu/thinktank/en/document/IPOL_STU(2021)695445> 22ff.

[82] Case C-136/17, *GC and Others v CNIL* [2019] ECLI:EU:C:2019:773, para 78.

[83] S de Mars and P O' Callaghan, 'Privacy and Search Engines: Forgetting or Contextualising?' (2016) 43(2) Journal of Law & Society 257, 280.

[84] Google, 'How search algorithms work' <https://www.google.com/intl/en_uk/search/howsearchworks/algorithms/> accessed 22 January 2024.

[85] J Globocnik, 'The Right to Be Forgotten Is Taking Shape: CJEU Judgments in *GC and Others* (C-136/17) and *Google v CNIL* (C-507/17)' (2020) 69(4) GRUR International 380, 385.

[86] BGH, 27 July 2020, VI ZR 476/18.

ruling as it clarifies for the first time the conditions for the exercise of the RTBF where information in the source website is potentially inaccurate. It also sheds further light on the complex relationship between primary publishers and search engines. The case concerned a dereferencing request by a couple who held senior positions in financial services companies and who had been accused in connection with the investment model of these companies in online articles published by a US news website with the self-described aim of fraud prevention. The news stories were accompanied by photos showing the plaintiffs' affluent lifestyle, which appeared as thumbnails upon a Google search based on the companies' names. The plaintiffs disputed the veracity of the published allegations, and claimed that the said news website specialized in publishing fraudulent reports to blackmail companies with the aim of extracting a protection fee. Google declined to dereference the links as it had no way of establishing the truthfulness of the claims in question. The BGH sought to establish, first, whether a decisive factor when deciding on the dereferencing requests should be the question of whether the plaintiffs could have reasonably obtained injunctive relief to provisionally clarify the truthfulness of the allegations. Secondly, it asked if the context of the original publication would need to be considered when ruling on a request to dereference a thumbnail even if the source website was linked but not specifically named and the resulting context was not revealed by the search engine.

As far as the first question is concerned, the CJEU held that it would be disproportionate to either require the person requesting dereferencing to obtain a judicial decision against the website publisher or to require the search engine operator to establish the accuracy of the referenced content.[87] The CJEU considered that a fair solution would be to require the data subject to provide 'relevant and sufficient evidence' to substantiate their request and to establish the 'manifest inaccuracy' of the information in question or, at the very least, of a part of it which was 'not minor in relation to the content as a whole'.[88] The search engine operator would then be required to accede to the dereferencing request. The CJEU further held that the search engine operator was required to provide users with relevant and up-to-date information about any judicial proceeding initiated concerning the alleged inaccuracy of the referenced content which were brought to their attention.[89] This is in line with its statement in *GC* that search results would need to reflect the current position.

The CJEU's finding that neither the data subject nor the search engine could be expected to conclusively prove the inaccuracy of the allegations makes sense. It is consistent with the CJEU's and the BGH's constant mantra that recourse against the search engine operator is not subsidiary to recourse against the content provider.[90] Having said that, in *RTBF II*, the BVerfG added the caveat that 'the reasonableness (*Zumutbarkeit*) of protective measures imposed on the search engine operator and the reasonableness of other possibilities open to affected persons' would need to be taken into account.[91] Indeed, affected persons might increasingly need to have recourse to

---

[87] *TU and RE v Google* [2022] ECLI:EU:C:2022:962, paras 68, 71.
[88] ibid para 72.
[89] ibid para 76.
[90] *Google Spain*, paras 83ff; *GC and Others v CNIL* [2019] ECLI:EU:C:2019:773, paras 36–37; BVerfG, *RTBF II*, para 112.
[91] BVerfG, *RTBF II*, para 119.

other avenues of redress following the *TU and RE* decision. The CJEU's expectation that data subjects would establish the 'manifest inaccuracy' of the information is a tall order, which many data subjects may be unable to meet. Nonetheless, it pays tribute to search engines' communicative function and serves to redress the imbalance between privacy/data protection and press freedom after *Google Spain*.[92]

As regards the second question, the CJEU held that the decision whether to dereference a thumbnail image displayed upon a name-based search would depend on the information value of the photographs in question in tandem with any accompanying text elements, but regardless of the context of their publication on the source webpage. The CJEU's assessment was guided by two considerations: first, that the protection of the right to privacy is of paramount importance where images are involved; and second, that the publication of images in a list of thumbnails, stripped of their context, constitutes autonomous processing, distinct from the original publication of the source page and from its referencing in the context of a web search. From these considerations the CJEU drew the following conclusion. If the dereferencing request regarding the source webpage was to be rejected because of its information value, this would be immaterial as regards the dereferencing of the thumbnails. If, on the contrary, the dereferencing request regarding the source webpage was to be granted, then the thumbnail images would also need to be removed. This outcome is paradoxical. It is unrealistic that users would consume thumbnail images without accessing the linked content in the source webpage.[93] By condemning the images to oblivion despite the attested contribution of the source webpage to public debate, this judgment risks undermining the accessibility and hence the information value of the source website of which they form part and parcel. This risk was acknowledged but lightly shrugged off by AG Pittruzella.[94] This is particularly problematic in cases where thumbnail images become obnoxious because of their connection with critical media reporting as in the present case.

Whilst the *TU and RE* case concerned the dereferencing of recent but potentially inaccurate information, the following section will consider ECtHR case law in which the passage of time had an impact on the Court's preparedness to protect the integrity of news archives containing accurate reports of past events.

6.3 The Case Law of the European Court of Human Rights

The first case in which the ECtHR had the opportunity to pass verdict on the importance of news archives is the case of *Times Newspapers Ltd. v The United Kingdom*.[95] This case concerned libel proceedings brought by a Russian businessman in respect of the publication of two articles in the print and online edition of *The Times* newspaper,

[92] A Ohly, 'Zwei gordische Knoten beim Anspruch gegen Suchmaschinenbetreiber auf Auslistung. Zugleich Bespreschung von EuGH "TU and RE/Google"' (2023) 125(3) Gewerblicher Rechtschutz und Urheberrecht 147, 148.

[93] ibid 149.

[94] Case C-460/20, *TU and RE v Google* [2022] ECLI:EU:C:2022:962, Opinion of Advocate General Pittruzella, para 58.

[95] *Times Newspapers Ltd v The United Kingdom*, App Nos 3002/03 and 23676/03, 10 March 2009.

alleging his involvement in large-scale money laundering. The applicants, Times Newspaper Ltd, argued that the internet publication rule in operation at the time in the UK had a chilling effect on its freedom of expression and on its willingness to maintain an internet archive. The internet publication rule meant that a new cause of action accrued in libel each time defamatory material was accessed online. The Court of Appeal accepted that archives have a 'social utility', but argued that they are 'a comparatively insignificant aspect of freedom of expression'. It pointedly quipped that '[A]rchive material is stale news and its publication cannot rank in importance with the dissemination of contemporary material'.[96]

The ECtHR disagreed with this view. It argued that internet archives 'constitute an important source for education and historical research, particularly as they are readily accessible to the public and are generally free'.[97] It recognized that the maintenance of internet archives is a valuable secondary role performed by the press, next to its primary function of acting as the 'public watchdog'. At same time, it clarified that the margin of appreciation granted to states was likely to be greater in the case of news archives of past events than in the case of reporting of current events. The Court explained that 'the duty of the press to act in accordance with the principles of responsible journalism by ensuring the accuracy of historical, rather than perishable, information published is likely to be more stringent in the absence of any urgency in publishing the material'.[98] In other words, newspapers would face a higher burden of ensuring the accuracy of archives, with the advantage of hindsight in their hands, compared to when publishing under time pressure. The Court found that, in the present case, the newspaper should have published a qualification to the online version of the articles, informing readers that a libel action had been initiated. The Court deemed this not to be a disproportionate interference with the newspaper's right to freedom of expression. It subscribed to the Court of Appeal's view that such a notice would 'normally remove any sting from the material'.[99] The Court of Appeal did not contemplate the complete removal of these articles from the internet archive, and the ECtHR sensibly implied that such a requirement would have been excessive.[100]

In the similar case of *Węgrzynowski and Smolczewski v Poland*, two lawyers who had won a libel case against the daily newspaper *Rzeczpospolita*, complained that the libellous article remained accessible on the newspaper's website. The ECtHR reiterated the importance of archives for education and historical research, especially given that they are readily accessible to the public and generally free.[101] The Court held that this function would be undermined if newspapers had to remove news articles from their archives. This would not only be the case if the information contained therein was embarrassing but truthful, but even if it was undoubtedly libellous. In its view, it is 'not the role of judicial authorities to engage in rewriting history by ordering the removal from the public domain of all traces of publications which have in the past been

---

[96] *Lutchansky v The Times Newspapers Limited* [2001] EWCA Civ 1805, para 74.
[97] *Times Newspapers Ltd v The United Kingdom*, App nos 3002/03 and 23676/03, 10 March 2009, para 45.
[98] ibid.
[99] ibid para 16.
[100] ibid para 47.
[101] *Węgrzynowski and Smolczewski v Poland*, App no 33846/07, 16 July 2013, para 59.

found, by final judicial decisions, to amount to unjustified attacks on individual reputations'.[102] The bar for limiting access to information which the public has the right to receive would need to be set very high.[103] As in *Times Newspapers Ltd v The United Kingdom*, the Court held that the publication of an appropriate qualification to the online version of an article, informing readers of the outcome of the libel proceedings, would have been a proportionate remedy.[104] However, during the first set of civil proceedings, the applicants failed to make any claims whatsoever concerning the online presence of the defamatory article. When they eventually brought a new action challenging the continuous presence of the article on the newspaper's website, they failed to request that it be supplemented by a reference to the earlier judgments in their favour.[105] Taking these circumstances into account, the ECtHR concluded that the national courts did not violate the applicants' private life and reputation by declining to order the removal of the libellous article from the website.

A third case, that of *M.L. and W.W. v Germany*, gave the ECtHR further opportunity to stress the importance of media archives, and to protect them from challenges on the ground of the rights to privacy and reputation. The targeted archives in this case were those of the radio station Deutschlandradio, the weekly magazine *Der Spiegel*, and the daily newspaper *Mannheimer Morgen*, thus spanning the spectrum of both broadcast and print media. These three outlets maintained on their online archives transcripts of reports concerning the applicants' conviction to life imprisonment for the murder of a famous actor. When the applicants were released on probation, but before their conviction became spent under German law, they brought proceedings before the German courts, requesting the anonymization of the reports. While the national courts initially granted their requests, the applicants were unsuccessful on appeal.[106]

The ECtHR recognized that 'after a certain period of time has elapsed and, in particular, as their release from prison approaches, persons who have been convicted have an interest in no longer being confronted with their acts, with a view to their reintegration in society'.[107] At the same time, it paid attention to the interest of the public in being able to conduct research into past events.[108] Also, while anonymizing a report is less intrusive than altogether deleting it, a chilling effect could arise as a result of the media being reluctant to include in their reports identifying elements that they would subsequently need to remove.[109] This would be particularly detrimental given that Article 10 ECHR guarantees journalists' freedom to determine the elements that would need to be included in a news story in order to safeguard its credibility, provided that the choices made complied with the ethical standards of their trade.[110]

---

[102] ibid para 65.
[103] ibid para 57.
[104] ibid paras 59, 66.
[105] ibid paras 66, 67.
[106] BGH, 9 February 2012, VI ZR 243/08 and VI ZR 244/08.
[107] *M.L. and W.W. v Germany*, App nos 60798/10 and 65599/10, 28 June 2018, para 100; see also *M. L. v Slovakia*, App no 34159/17, 14 October 2021, para 38; *Österreichischer Rundfunk v Austria*, App no 35841/02, 7 December 2006, para 68.
[108] *M.L. and W.W. v Germany*, App nos 60798/10 and 65599/10, 28 June 2018, para 101.
[109] ibid paras 103, 104.
[110] ibid para 105; see Chapter 4, p 104.

Furthermore, the ECtHR deemed the inclusion of individualized information to be particularly important in high profile criminal cases.

Further factors, derived from the ECtHR's earlier case law, such as the applicants' notoriety and the fact that they had courted the media to succeed in reopening the criminal proceedings against them, also militated against the anonymization request in the present case.[111] The style of reporting was objective, and even though it occasionally included intimate details about the applicants' lives, it did not intend to disparage them. The ECtHR also made some interesting observations regarding the division of responsibility between primary publishers and search engines. It held that the interference with the applicants' right to privacy primarily resulted from the news portals' decision to keep the compromising information available on their websites, while the search engines only amplified the scope of this interference. In line with the CJEU's reasoning in *Google Spain*, the ECtHR accepted that the responsibilities incumbent on the former might differ from those of the latter.[112] In the case at hand, the dissemination of the reports in question was limited, as a result of their being partly placed behind paywalls, or being accessible on a subscriber-only basis, or having been archived so that they were only findable by way of a targeted search. In any case, the applicants had not made any attempts to further limit the dissemination of information concerning them by contacting search engine operators.[113] All these carefully weighted considerations led the Court to conclude that there had not been a violation of Article 8 ECHR.

While these cases show the ECtHR's appreciation of the important role performed by news archives and its reluctance to compromise this role for the sake of the protection of private rights, the tide appears to have turned with two recent cases. The first case, *Hurbain v Belgium*, concerned the complaint by the editor of one of Belgium's leading French language newspapers, *Le Soir*, against an order to anonymize an article freely available on its website.[114] The article, which was originally published in 1994, concerned the dangers of road transport and referred *inter alia* to a fatal car accident, under mention of the name of the responsible driver, 'G', in full. G was convicted, served his sentence, and was rehabilitated in 2006. However, the article still appeared upon a search under G's name both on *Le Soir*'s internal search engine and on Google. G claimed that the easy retrieval of this piece of information about his past could damage his reputation as a doctor. The newspaper refused to anonymize the contested article, and asked Google to dereference it instead, albeit to no avail. G subsequently brought his case to the Belgian courts on the basis of his right to private life, which includes a 'right to be forgotten'. The courts held that G's continuous identification created a 'virtual criminal record', and ordered *Le Soir* to replace G's name with the letter 'X'. Mr Hurbain, *Le Soir*'s editor, complained that this order violated his right to freedom of expression under Article 10 ECHR.

The ECtHR emphasized once more the significance of digital news archives and the risks for their integrity that might ensue from an order to anonymize an article whose

---

[111] *M.L. and W.W. v Germany*, App nos 60798/10 and 65599/10, 28 June 2018, para 95.
[112] ibid para 97.
[113] ibid paras 112ff, 114.
[114] *Hurbain v Belgium*, App no 57292/16, 22 June 2021, para 102.

initial lawfulness was not in question.[115] However, the Court went on to explain that the right to maintain digital press archives for public use was not absolute. It needed to be balanced in line with the criteria developed in earlier case law, in particular in the *Axel Springer* case, bearing in mind that some of these criteria had to be modified in view of the passage of time.[116] It agreed with the Court of Appeal's view that the naming of G twenty years after the tragic events in question had no news value, and did not contribute to a debate of general interest.[117] Further, the Court paid attention to the fact that G did not exercise any official function, and that his involvement in the car accident did not receive any media attention except for the contested article. Differently from the case of *M.L. and W.W. v Germany*, G had never sought the spotlight. Turning to the content, form, and consequences of publication, the Court observed, on the one hand, that the article's original publication was undoubtedly lawful, and that its retrieval in the newspaper's archives would require an active search. On the other hand, the Court noted that the archives could be accessed free of charge, and that a simple search on Google, motivated by reasons unrelated to G's criminal record, would allow this story to resurface, causing indefinite and grave harm to his reputation.[118] The key question of the publication's potential relevance for the future was left unaddressed by the Court.

A particularly problematic aspect of the ECtHR's assessment concerned the proportionality of the anonymization order. The Court gave three possible alternatives short shrift before discarding them all: the addition of a qualification to the original article; the inclusion of a no-index tag by the newspaper; and the dereferencing by the search engine. The Court held that the two first alternatives would not have been adequate to protect G's privacy. It is conceded that the addition of a note to the original article to the effect that G had been rehabilitated would do little to alleviate his predicament. It is less clear why a no-index tag by *Le Soir* would not have been suitable to protect G's privacy. The addition of a robots.txt control file or meta tag in the page source code allows publishers to 'hide' certain webpages from search engines. The only difference is that publishers cannot specifically prevent the inclusion of their articles in the results list of a name search. While search engines have the capacity to block access to specific content upon a name-based search, this does not currently apply to the originators of this content who have no such way of selective filtering.[119] In other words, had *Le Soir* been instructed to include a no-index tag, the contested article would have vanished from the Google results list altogether. This would have effectively protected

---

[115] ibid para 102.

[116] ibid para 104; *Axel Springer v Germany*, App no 39954/08, 7 February 2012, paras 89–95.

[117] *Hurbain v Belgium*, App no 57292/16, 22 June 2021, para 106.

[118] ibid paras 121, 122.

[119] Deutsche Gesellschaft für Recht und Informatik, 'Stellungnahme in der Vergfassungsbeschwerde des Herrn T. AZ 1 BvR 16/13' 2, 4ff (*DGRI*, 28 April 2014) <https://www.dgri.de/68/pn/2/Stellungnahmen. htm> (hereafter DGRI Opinion); S Schweda, 'Hamburg Court of Appeal Obliges Press Archive Operator to Prevent Name Search in Archived Articles' (2015) 4 European Data Protection Law 299, 300; A Koreng, 'Das "Recht auf Vergessen" und die Haftung von Online-Archiven. Schlussfolgerungen für Pressearchive aus der EuGH-Entscheidung "Google Spain"' (2015) 46(6) Archiv für Presserecht 514, 516; J Siegel, 'Oberlandesgericht Hamburg: Ein Urteil gegen Online-Archive' (*iRights info*, 31 August 2015) <https://irig hts.info/artikel/oberlandesgericht-hamburg-ein-urteil-gegen-online-archive/25984>; see also Katsirea, 'Search Engines' (n 28) 141.

G's privacy, but would arguably have been an even more restrictive option than the anonymization of the article.

Turning to the third and final alternative, the dereferencing by the search engine, the ECtHR's reasoning is especially perplexing. The ECtHR declined to entertain this option 'in the abstract' given that G had never explicitly requested it.[120] However, G had asked for the no-index tagging by the newspaper as an alternative should the anonymization have proved technically impossible. He erroneously assumed that this option could be limited to name-based searches.[121] It follows that G would have been equally satisfied with the dereferencing by the search engine, which would have been best placed to bring about the desired outcome. In his dissenting Opinion, Judge Pavli rightly commented that this would have been a milder option compared to anonymization despite the significant restriction on freedom of expression and information as a result of dereferencing.[122] He compared the Court's reasoning to granting a plaintiff's claim for a neighbour's wall to be demolished to get rid of a graffiti without taking less intrusive solutions into account.[123] He intimated that the anonymization of the source webpage would have only been compatible with Article 10 ECHR if the information contained therein concerned particularly sensitive personal data or a particularly vulnerable data subject. None of these considerations seemed applicable to the case at hand.[124] Importantly, Judge Pavli also noted that the *von Hannover* criteria for balancing privacy and freedom of expression were not necessarily applicable to a case concerning an alleged assault on reputation by a publication whose initial legality was not in question.[125]

The case was referred to the Grand Chamber, which confirmed the outcome of the Chamber judgment with twelve votes to five. The Court agreed that the criteria traditionally used to resolve the conflict between Article 10 ECHR and Article 8 ECHR had to be modified in view of the fact that the present case concerned the lawfulness of the continuous availability of a news article, not of its original publication.[126] It therefore developed a new set of criteria to take account of: (1) the nature of the archived information; (2) the time that had elapsed since the events and since the initial and online publication; (3) the contemporary interest of the information; (4) whether the person claiming entitlement to be forgotten was well known and his or her conduct since the events; (5) the negative repercussions of the continued availability of the information online; (6) the degree of accessibility of the information in the digital archives; and (7) the impact of the measure on freedom of expression and more specifically on freedom of the press. This meticulous list of criteria was unfortunately applied to the case at hand in a manner that shows scant appreciation for the importance of preserving press archives as a key aspect of press freedom.

---

[120] *Hurbain v Belgium*, App no 57292/16, 22 June 2021, para 127.
[121] ibid para 11.
[122] ibid, Judge Pavli dissenting, para 19.
[123] ibid para 21.
[124] ibid para 20.
[125] ibid paras 15–17; *Von Hannover v Germany* (No 2), App nos 40660/08 and 60641/08, 7 February 2012, paras 108–113.
[126] *Hurbain v Belgium*, App no 57292/16, 4 July 2023, para 205.

The ECtHR held that there was no continuous public interest in being informed about a driver's identity in an article that 'merely made a statistical contribution to a public debate on road safety'.[127] By taking such a narrow view of the public interest in the preservation of the archived article, the Court easily concluded that its anonymization was not excessively onerous for the applicant. It was less detrimental than its unpublishing, and it left its content otherwise intact.[128] In any case, the original, non-anonymized version of the article was still available in print form.[129] The fact that this considerably hampered the findability of the said article, effectively opening this option only to researchers with a specific interest in the case, did not play a role in the Court's deliberations. Perhaps this was precisely the intended outcome.

However, both investigative journalism and historical as well as other scientific research are nowadays greatly reliant on the ready availability of online sources.[130] By anonymizing the source webpage to keep it away from prying eyes, the Court risked throwing the baby out with the bathwater. The Court of Appeal's intimation that the responsibility for the indexing of the article by the search engines rested squarely on the newspaper publisher was left unchallenged by the ECtHR.[131] The chilling effect of anonymization of a lawfully published article on press freedom was wryly dismissed with the argument that it fell within the '"duties and responsibilities" of the press and the limits which may be imposed on it'.[132] All in all, the one-sided perspective chosen by the majority in tandem with an unduly deferential approach to the domestic judgments has swung the pendulum far towards the protection of privacy. This comes at a cost for press freedom and for journalists' discretion to determine whether to preserve individualized information in a news story. This new willingness to tamper with the historic record sits uncomfortably with the heightened concern for accuracy, the orchestrated attempts to undermine the press, and the rising authoritarianism in the current geopolitical climate.[133]

If the *Hurbain* case concerned events that took place more than twenty years earlier, the *Biancardi* case came to test the notion of recency. This case concerned the editor of a small online newspaper which in 2008 published an article concerning a fight, followed by a stabbing between two brothers in a restaurant in Italy.[134] In 2010 one of the brothers, V.X., asked the applicant to remove the article from the internet. When his request was unsuccessful, he lodged proceedings in the domestic courts. In 2011, the applicant de-indexed the said article with a view to settling the case. The district court found that by maintaining the article online in the period up to 2011, the applicant had breached the claimant's reputation and his right to private life and awarded compensation. The Supreme Court upheld the first-instance decision in 2016. It clarified that the unlawfulness of the processing was not linked to the content of the article or to its

---

[127] ibid para 225.
[128] ibid para 249.
[129] ibid para 252.
[130] ibid, Judge Ranzoni joined by Judges Kūris, Grozev, Eicke, and Schembri Orland dissenting, para 8; *Hurbain v Belgium*, App no 57292/16, 22 June 2021, Judge Pavli dissenting, para 7.
[131] *Hurbain v Belgium*, App no 57292/16, 4 July 2023, para 248.
[132] ibid para 254.
[133] See ibid, Judge Ranzoni joint by Judges Kūris, Grozev, Eicke, and Schembri Orland dissenting, para 6.
[134] *Biancardi v Italy*, App no 77419/16, 25 November 2021.

online publication and dissemination nor to its conservation and digital archiving.[135] It arose from the easy accessibility of the article online even after V.X. served formal notice in 2010, asking for it to be removed. Notably, at the time of the Supreme Court's decision, the criminal proceedings against V.X. were still pending.

The ECtHR disagreed with the applicant's argument that he could not be held responsible for de-indexing the article in question, such a possibility only being open to the search engine. Indeed, this assertion was contradicted by the fact that the applicant did eventually de-index the article in 2011. The ECtHR emphasized that it was the failure to de-index the article in a timely manner that instituted the applicant's liability. To avoid any misunderstanding in this respect, neither the permanent removal of the article nor its anonymization was at issue before the domestic courts. The ECtHR deliberated on the criteria that would need to guide the balancing exercise between freedom of expression and the right to reputation without referring to the *Hurbain* case. It was, however, possibly influenced by Judge Pavli's dissenting Opinion insofar as it acknowledged that the strict application of the *Axel Springer* criteria would be inappropriate in the present case. While *Axel Springer* concerned the publication of contemporaneous reports about the arrest and conviction of a well-known television actor, the present case related to the maintenance online of an article concerning criminal proceedings against private individuals.[136]

The ECtHR determined that special attention needed to be paid to the period during which the article was kept online; the sensitive nature of the data at issue; and the gravity of the sanction imposed on the applicant. It rather cryptically noted that the information contained in the article had not been updated since its publication, without however clarifying how the article should have been updated, especially given that criminal proceedings were still pending at the time of the Supreme Court judgment. Nor did the ECtHR accept the applicant's submission that the case could have been resolved by requiring the publication of supplementary information or of a clarification.[137] The ECtHR further observed that the relevance of the applicant's right to freedom of expression decreased over the passage of time compared to V.X.'s right to the protection of his reputation.

This inverse proportion equation oversimplifies the issues as it eclipses the public interest value of the information in question. The ECtHR contrasted the case concerning the disclosure of confidential information about President Mitterrand's health, thus ostensibly suggesting that information about criminal proceedings was of less public interest value by comparison.[138] However, the Court did not substantiate this view nor did it explain from which point onwards the public's right to information about a crime was on a diminishing scale and whether there was a specific point in time when the balance tipped in favour of the right to reputation. At any rate, it is striking that only two years had passed by the time the complainants asked for the information about their crime to be removed.

---

[135] ibid para 14.
[136] ibid para 62.
[137] ibid para 35.
[138] ibid para 66; *Editions Plon v France*, App no 58148/00, 18 May 2004.

Finally, the ECtHR paid attention to the fact that the data in question were sensitive since they were related to criminal proceedings, as well as to the not excessive amount of compensation awarded. However, the gravity of the sanction should not only be measured in pecuniary terms, but also in terms of its chilling effect on press freedom. In particular, the severity of the compensation needs be seen in relation to the size of the publisher. In the case at hand, the 10,000 Euros in reputational damages forced the affected news site to stop operating.[139] Moreover, classifying all information about crimes as sensitive regardless of the public's right to retrieve it, and notwithstanding that it is already in the public domain, seems counterintuitive. Rather, the presumption should be that information of public interest value should remain available online, especially when it is included in a news report. This presumption should only be considered rebutted in the face of the particularly sensitive or defamatory character of the information in question or the special vulnerability of the data subject.[140]

The judgment in *Biancardi* shows extreme deference to the position of the Italian courts, declining to recognize 'strong reasons' that would be required to substitute its view for that of the domestic courts in line with its earlier case law.[141] At the same time, it departs in more than one respect from the CJEU's and the European Data Protection Board (EDPB)'s understanding of the RTBF.[142] In its Guidelines, the EDPB explained that a delisting request should not lead to the deletion of a link from the indexes of the search engine altogether. In other words, the information should remain retrievable by using other search terms.[143] However, the obligation to de-index imposed on *Le Soir* likely rendered the contested report completely inaccessible by way of the search engine. The only option available to interested parties would be to try to find it by visiting the publisher's digital archive. Moreover, the EDPB Guidelines state that data relating to a criminal offence would more likely be dereferenced if they concerned a minor offence that happened a long time ago and caused prejudice to the data subject.[144] It follows that a dereferencing request would be less likely to succeed in the case of a more serious crime that happened more recently.[145] This should apply *a fortiori* as regards the more invasive de-indexing of the said information. Consequently, the conditions stipulated in the EDPB Guidelines were not fulfilled in the present case given that it concerned a serious crime that had happened in the more recent past.

---

[139] Reporters Committee for Freedom of the Press, 'Application for leave to intervene in Biancardi v Italy' <https://www.rcfp.org/briefs-comments/biancardi-v-italy/>.

[140] See Third party intervention in *Biancardi v Italy*, App No 77419/16, 25 November 2021, para 39 (*Media Defence*, 22 February 2021) <https://www.mediadefence.org/wp-content/uploads/2021/02/20210217-Biancardi-Draft-FINAL.pdf>; third party intervention in *Biancardi v Italy*, App No 77419/16, 25 November 2021, para 4 (*Reporters Committee for Freedom of the Press*, 28 December 2020) <https://www.rcfp.org/wp-content/uploads/2021/01/Reporters-Committees-Third-Party-Intervention-App.-No.-77419-16.pdf>.

[141] *Palomo Sánchez and Others v Spain*, App Nos 28955/06, 28957/06, 28959/06, 28964/06, 12 September 2011, para 57; *MGN Limited v the United Kingdom*, App no 39401/04, 18 January 2011, paras 150, 155.

[142] The European Data Protection Board (EDPB) succeeded the Article 29 Data Protection Working Party, which dealt with issues of privacy and data protection until the entry into force of the GDPR on 25 May 2018.

[143] EDPB Guidelines, para 8.

[144] ibid para 32.

[145] See also 'Guidelines on the implementation of the Court of Justice of the European Union judgement on "*Google Spain SL and Google Inc v. Agencia Española de Protección de Datos (AEPD) and Mario Costeja González*"' (Article 29 Data Protection Working Party, 26 November 2014) 20 No 13 (hereafter Art 29 WP Guidelines).

All in all, the ECtHR has continued to pay lip service to the valuable role of internet archives in its recent case law. At the same time, it has undermined this role by according an even greater importance to the protection of reputation of private individuals from the ready availability of lawfully published information about their past, both recent and more remote. The ECtHR has incrementally bolstered reputation from a mere limitation to the right to freedom of expression under Article 10(2) ECHR to an aspect of the right to privacy under Article 8 ECHR in deviation of this right's legislative history.[146] Furthermore, the ECtHR has diverged from the CJEU's emphasis on the search engines' unique ability to provide universal access to information in such a manner that enables a near to complete profiling of the data subject.[147] Precisely this propensity is absent in the case of online news archives. By approving of the interference with the underlying content, the ECtHR has elided the difference between source webpages and search engines and has ignored the distinct functions they perform.[148] The imposition of no-index tagging obligations on newspapers means that information of public interest can be effectively hidden from public view. The following section of this chapter will consider the ways in which courts in Germany and the UK have struck the balance between press freedom and data protection. In particular, the question will be asked whether these courts have extended the RTBF beyond its original scope, casting an ever-broadening net over press archives.

6.4 Comparative Insights into the Right to Erasure ('Right to be Forgotten')

6.4.1 Germany

The German courts have played a decisive role in shaping the liability of search engine providers, and increasingly also of content providers, based on the RTE/RTBF and on the right of personality protected by Article 2(1) of the German Constitution (GG). They have developed an extensive body of case law on the question of whether the media can be obliged to remove publications about past convictions in the interests of the protection of personality rights and of the facilitation of rehabilitation. The German courts have repeatedly held that the public interest in crime reports in the news media generally outweighed other individual interests but could become unjustified over time.[149] However, personality rights did not entitle criminals to not be confronted with their deeds in public ever again.[150] Even a spent conviction did not confer an unconditional right 'to be left alone'.

---

[146] Article 12 of the Universal Declaration of Human Rights (UDHR) provides that 'No one shall be subject to attacks ... upon his honour and reputation'. The *travaux préparatoires* on Article 8 ECHR, which was modelled on Article 12 UDHR, reveal that a conscious decision was made to omit these words. See Katsirea, 'Search Engines' (n 28) 130.

[147] *Google Spain*, para 37.

[148] See ibid para 23.

[149] BGH, 22 February 2011, VI ZR 114/09, paras 22, 23; cf BVerfGE 35, 202 (1973) (*Lebach I*).

[150] BVerfG, 25 November 1999, 1 BvR 348/98 and 1 BvR 755/98 (*Lebach II*).

In the case of online archives, the Federal Court of Justice (*Bundesgerichtshof*, BGH) time and again denied a removal request, often quashing privacy-friendly decisions handed down by the Hamburg judiciary.[151] The truthfulness and non-stigmatizing nature of the report and the lack of broad public impact of the medium in question weighed in favour of publication.[152] Given that a targeted search in the online archive was needed to find the relevant information, a right to deletion of all pages which would enable the identification of a rehabilitated person, would amount to an unwarranted rewriting of history and to full immunity for the perpetrator.[153] The Higher Regional Court of Berlin also shared the Federal Court's reluctance to condemn online archives to remove or anonymize identifiable information, echoing its view of online archives as a 'pull service'. It argued that the newspapers' archival function was covered by the right to freedom of expression under Article 5(1) GG, and was mandated by federal and state laws on the submission of deposit copies to libraries.[154]

However, the recognition of the RTE/RTBF has tilted the balance between press freedom and personality rights in a way that may lead to the gradual erosion of the integrity of press archives. The BVerfG, in its landmark decision *Right to be forgotten I*, reversed the BGH's *Apollonia* decision.[155] The complainant, who was convicted of a double murder on board a yacht forty years earlier, claimed a violation of his general right of personality because of the continuous availability of articles in the *Spiegel* online press archive, which covered his conviction and identified him by name. The BVerfG held that the correct standard of review in this case were the fundamental rights of the Basic Law, and in particular the complainant's right of personality, given that the case concerned an area of EU law which was not fully harmonized. This followed from the fact that EU Member States have discretion when reconciling fundamental rights under the journalism privilege.[156]

The BVerfG emphasized that the right of personality did not vest the individual with the power to determine unilaterally what information about them was to be remembered in line with the self-perceived image of themselves, but would need to be balanced against competing fundamental rights to freedom of expression and press freedom.[157] An essential aspect of this freedom was the right of media outlets to publish individualized reports and to maintain press archives in which such reports were archived unaltered in their entirety. This was especially important since print versions could neither satisfy the public's right to information nor could they financially sustain news publishers.[158] The BVerfG stressed further that the press did not have a proactive review obligation but was entitled to assume that a lawfully published article could be

---

[151] See eg OLG Hamburg, 17 November 2009, 7 U 78/09; BGH, 22 February 2011, VI ZR 346/09; OLG Hamburg, 29 July 2008, 7 U 20/08; BGH, 9 February 2010, VI ZR 243/08; BVerfG, 6 July 2010, 1 BvR 923/10.

[152] BGH, 15 December 2009, VI ZR 227/08.

[153] BGH, 1 February 2022, VI ZR 345/09 (*Sedlmayr*); BGH, 22 February 2011, VI ZR 114/09; BGH, 13 November 2012, VI ZR 330/11 (*Apollonia*).

[154] Kammergericht Berlin, 19 October 2001, 9 W 132/01.

[155] BVerfGE 152, 152 (hereafter BVerfG, *RTBF I*); BGH, 13 November 2012, VI ZR 330/11 (*Apollonia*).

[156] BVerfG, *RTBF I*, para 51.

[157] The BVerfG only remarked in passing that freedom of broadcasting is not relevant in the case of online press reports simply because they are disseminated 'by means of electronic information or communications systems'. See BVerfG, *RTBF I*, para 95 and Chapter 4, p 95.

[158] BVerfG, *RTBF I*, para 112.

made available to the public in an online archive unless its continued publication was challenged by affected persons.[159] The balancing of the conflicting fundamental rights involved would need to take into account the following factors: the subject matter of the article and the effect of its continuous dissemination on the private life of affected persons; the renewed relevance of the events covered in the article as a result of subsequent occurrences; the extent to which the affected persons have sought to stay in the limelight; the type of publication in question and its search engine ranking. These factors constitute a reasonable adjustment of the *Axel Springer* criteria for cases arising from the storage of information about past convictions in online news archives.[160] Understandably, the criterion about the method of obtaining the information and its veracity does not feature in this checklist given that it concerns the lawfulness of the original publication rather than the question of its continuous availability.

The BVerfG further hinted at technical possibilities which might sufficiently take the conflicting interests into account while being less incisive than the permanent deletion of the names of the persons involved. It explained that the de-indexing of a document would lead to the entire 'locked' text not being picked up by search engines, and could thus not be limited to concealing names. A possible combined solution could consist in referring the crawler to a duplicate site in which the article would be searchable but on which the names in question would not be found.[161] The BVerfG could not make a conclusive determination on the technical feasibility of such layering of two different versions of an article. It did however point out, first, that such measures should not be considered unsuitable simply because they did not guarantee comprehensive protection, provided they at least reduced the burden on the affected persons. Secondly, the BVerfG recognized that the ordered measures would need to be reasonable for the media outlets concerned without this meaning that they 'may not at all entail technical efforts or costs'.[162] Indeed, the German Society for Law and Information Science, in its Opinion advising the BVerfG on the *Apollonia* case, had pointed out that the cost of selective de-indexing could be considerable depending on the available software mechanisms.[163] Nonetheless, the BVerfG highlighted that media outlets may not seek to divest their responsibility for the risks to personality rights arising from the online publication of their articles to search engines. Given that increased dissemination was a desired effect of posting articles online, media outlets would need to assume responsibility in this regard. The BVerfG noted that measures protecting affected persons against old articles would generally be reasonable if these persons had 'a special need for protection'.[164]

Taking all these considerations into account, the BVerfG concluded that the BGH did not sufficiently consider the impact of the continued dissemination of the articles in question for the complainant and for the possibility of his reintegration into society. It took special issue with the fact that the complainant's unobtrusive conduct since

---

[159] ibid paras 118–19.
[160] *Axel Springer v Germany*, App no 39954/08, 7 February 2012, paras 90ff.
[161] BVerfG, *RTBF I*, paras 134ff.
[162] ibid para 138.
[163] DGRI Opinion (n 119) 17.
[164] BVerfG, *RTBF I*, para 139.

his release from prison had not been accorded due weight. The BVerfG did not, however, particularly substantiate the complainant's 'special need for protection' in a way that would differentiate him from other cases of reporting about spent convictions committed decades ago which are picked up by search engines. After all, the complainant had been out of prison for seven years before he found out that the said articles were available online. The potentially wide-ranging implications of this judgment for media outlets are not yet clear. The BVerfG observed that ongoing technical developments entail uncertainty about the extent to which content providers can act on the dissemination of their articles online. It therefore referred the task of shaping effective and reasonable protective measures, including the identification of a potential need to develop new technical solutions, to the ordinary courts.[165] However, the extent to which the ordinary courts will be able to offer a satisfactory response depends on their ability to engage with the fast-changing technologies of search.[166]

The case was subsequently referred to the BGH which held that the contested judgment of the Higher Regional Court Hamburg did not withstand scrutiny.[167] The Appeal Court's finding that the continued availability of the articles online was illegal was not accompanied by an indication of effective and reasonable measures that would allow their suppression or restriction. The BGH concluded that a conclusive balancing of the conflicting interests in question was not possible unless these technical questions were resolved. The judgment was thus set aside and remanded to the Court of Appeal. The BGH's verdict is pragmatic and suggests that the success of the applicant's claim in the *Apollonia* case will ultimately hinge on the publisher's capacity to put equitable technical measures in place that further his rehabilitation without unduly restricting press freedom.

A second judgment handed down by the BVerfG on the same day in the *Right to be forgotten II* case provides an interesting counterpoint.[168] This case concerned a broadcast on the *Panorama* show of the Norddeutscher Rundfunk (NDR) broadcasting corporation, which accused the CEO of a company, the complainant, of unfairly dismissing an employee after he had tried to establish a works council in the company. The transcript of the broadcast had been uploaded on the NDR website, and the link to this content surfaced among the top search results when searching under the complainant's name on Google. The search engine rejected the complainant's request to dereference the link, and their action before the Higher Regional Court Celle was unsuccessful. The BVerfG held that this case concerned a fully harmonized area of data protection law. The applicable standard of review was therefore that of the EU Charter of Fundamental Rights, applied in a quasi-horizontal manner.[169] The GDPR journalism exemption was not applicable to the circumstances at hand given that it concerned a dispute with a search engine.[170]

---

[165] ibid para 142.
[166] cf M G Porcedda, 'Sentencing Data-Driven Cybercrime. How Cybercrime with Cascading Effects Is Tackled by UK Courts' (2023) 48 Computer Law & Security Review 1, 4 on the UK courts' approach to the evolving environment of cybercrime.
[167] BGH, 22 September 2020, VI ZR 476/19.
[168] BVerfG, 6 November 2019, 1 BvR 276/17 (hereafter BVerfG, *RTBF II*).
[169] ibid paras 97, 105.
[170] ibid para 41.

The BVerfG concluded that the Higher Regional Court had struck a satisfactory balance between the fundamental rights at stake, namely on the one hand the complainant's right to privacy and data protection under Articles 7 and 8 CFEU, and on the other hand the search engine's right to conduct a business under Article 16 CFEU. The fundamental rights of third parties impacted by the dispute, namely the internet users' right to receive information and the broadcaster's right to disseminate it had also been sufficiently accommodated. Interestingly, the BVerfG emphasized that a dereferencing obligation on the search engine operator directly impacted on the source website. It was not a mere side-effect given that it specifically targeted the dissemination of the contents in question.[171] Further, the BVerfG noted that, in line with the CJEU's case law, the lawfulness of the dissemination by the search engine operator had to be distinguished from the lawfulness of the initial publication by the content provider. It therefore required a separate balancing exercise, even though these questions were interlinked.[172]

The BVerfG accorded less weight to the search engine's economic interests than to the public *interest* in obtaining information and to the content provider's *right* to freedom of expression. The use of the term 'interest' might be interpreted in the sense of a demotion of the right to information. However, the BVerfG stressed that the conflicting fundamental rights involved in this multipolar relationship had to be balanced on an equal footing, and that the right to personality did not take precedence.[173] It sought to explain an ostensible divergence from the CJEU case law by arguing that the *Google Spain* and *GC* cases were singular in that the former concerned an announcement issued by a public authority, while the latter concerned special categories of data.[174] This is hardly a convincing explanation, but seems more like an attempt to gloss over differences and to signpost the way ahead. In substance, the BVerfG paid attention to the following factors: there was continuous public interest in the complainant's professional conduct, especially given that she still held the position of a managing director; the complainant had agreed to the interview featured in the programme; the broadcast was not defamatory; and the period of seven years since the interview was not overly long.[175]

The *Right to be forgotten I* and *II* decisions highlight the conundrum between publication by a content provider and dissemination by a search engine. The BVerfG argues that the lawfulness of the initial publication does not guarantee the lawfulness of the online dissemination of this publication *in perpetuum*. A separate balancing of interests is required when assessing the lawfulness of the initial publication and that of its referencing by a search engine in view of the potentially different interests involved. This difference is reflected in the disparate obligations imposed on content providers and search engines. The former have to examine the legality of publications *ab initio*, while the latter only have to dereference on a 'notice and takedown' basis.[176] At the same time, the BVerfG argues, rather bewilderingly, that the decision on the legality

---

[171] ibid para 109.
[172] ibid paras 112ff, 118.
[173] ibid paras 121, 141.
[174] ibid para 141.
[175] ibid paras 128ff, 134.
[176] ibid para 113.

of online publication by the content provider must generally also inform the decision concerning the dissemination by the search engine.[177]

How is the seeming contradiction between these two statements to be explained? The BVerfG clarifies that the lawfulness of online publication cannot be assessed once and for all, but needs to take account of the realities of internet dissemination, including the possibility of retrieval by search engines and the passage of time.[178] In other words, the right of media outlets to publish individualized reports and to maintain them in archives unaltered in their entirety is inextricably linked with, and conditioned by, the effects of web search technology. The desire to harness search engines' comprehensive digital memory increasingly impacts on integral aspects of press freedom, in ways extending beyond the original conception of the RTBF in *Google Spain*. Publishers face an impossible dilemma: to sever their links with search engines or to compromise the integrity of their archives. The former option is unthinkable. Media outlets depend on search engine optimization, so that their titles are easily retrievable, thus generating more clicks and greater advertising income.[179] The latter option is unpalatable. It represents an erosion of their press freedom which is the more problematic the less clarity exists about the technical solutions at hand.

A recent judgment of the BGH partly followed the guidelines of the BVerfG, but also raised new questions. In a case concerning a request against Google to dereference seven-year-old news articles in the regional press about the million Euro financial deficit of a charitable organization and the poor health of its managing director based on Article 17(1) GDPR, the BGH found in favour of the search engine, and upheld the decision of the Higher Regional Court Frankfurt am Main.[180] There was no dispute about the truthfulness of the facts described in these news reports. The BGH agreed with key tenets of the BVerfG's case law. It took the view that a separate balancing exercise was in order when assessing the lawfulness of the dissemination by the search engine, while paying heed to the fact that the legality of the dissemination by the content provider was generally decisive.[181] It emphasized the equal standing of the fundamental rights involved and the fact that no precedence could be accorded to the personality rights of the plaintiff.[182] Further, the BGH reiterated insights from its earlier case law about search engines' pivotal role for the use of the internet.[183] At the same time, it drew a somewhat surprising conclusion from the equal ranking of the conflicting fundamental rights at play. It departed from the BVerfG's position and from its pre-GDPR case law on search engines' liability. While traditionally search engines were only required to only act on a notice-and-takedown basis, the BGH implied that they might also face pre-monitoring obligations in future, without however

[177] ibid para 118.
[178] ibid.
[179] D Giomelakis and A Veglis, 'Investigating Search Engine Optimization Factors in Media Websites. The Case of Greece' (2016) 4(3) Digital Journalism 379; Wimmers, 'Der Intermediär' (n 24) 514; Arning, Moos, and Schefzig, 'Vergiss' (n 27) 453.
[180] BGH, 27 July 2020, VI ZR 405/18.
[181] ibid paras 37, 38.
[182] ibid para 61.
[183] ibid para 40.

clearly spelling this out.[184] It remains to be seen how courts will implement this stricter liability standard without destroying search engines' business model.

In substance, the BGH found against the plaintiff on account of the continuous high public interest in the reported events, which led to long-lasting financial issues. It took account of the fact that the reports were only retrievable by way of a combined name-place search and were to be found among numerous other, partly higher-ranking links.[185] The BGH further held that the passage of seven years since the reported events was not yet long enough to justify the interest in keeping the reports in question out of sight. At the same time, it observed that the criterion of the passage of time is not amenable to a schematic approach that would allow for a clear description of the point in time from which an open-ended weighing of the interests involved would turn into a relationship of rule and exception.[186] This judgment serves as an interesting contrast to the *Biancardi* case where the ECtHR deemed only two years since the original publication to be a sufficiently lengthy period to justify its de-indexing.

6.4.2 United Kingdom

The most comprehensive examination of the RTBF/RTE in the UK to date has been in the case of *NT1 & NT2 v Google*.[187] The two joined cases concerned two businessmen who had been convicted of criminal offences in the context of their businesses. Their convictions had become spent under the Rehabilitation Act 1974, and they both unsuccessfully asked Google to dereference links to news reports and other material about their offending and convictions from the list of search results being returned on a name-based search.[188] They brought claims under the Data Protection Act 1998 and the law of misuse of private information, seeking injunctions and financial compensation.[189] The two cases were quite separate, but they were tried on the same day by the same judge given that they involved similar issues of principle. Both these cases involved claims against the search engine, as opposed to the source publications, but are of interest as to their implications for press freedom.

Despite the similarities between the two cases, Warby J found that there were significant differences in the details. The time after which a conviction can become spent under the 1974 Act depends on the length of the sentence. NT1's conviction was for criminal conspiracy to defraud consumers and attracted a prison sentence of four years. Were it not for a change in the law in 2014, his conviction would never have become spent. NT2's conviction was one of six months' imprisonment for phone tapping to identify the perpetrators of unlawful acts against his company, which were carried out in protest against its controversial environmental practices. This sentence was always capable of becoming spent regardless of the change in the law. Warby J also paid particular attention to the attitude of the two claimants to their conviction and to their

---

[184] ibid para 41; cf BGH, 27 February 2018, VI ZR 489/16 para 33ff.
[185] BGH, 27 July 2020, VI ZR 405/18 para 60.
[186] ibid para 62.
[187] *NT1 & NT2 v Google* [2018] EWHC 799 (QB) (hereafter High Court, *NT1 & NT2*).
[188] Rehabilitation of Offenders Act 1974 (ROA 1974).
[189] Data Protection Act 1998 (DPA 1998).

conduct since leaving prison. He found that NT1 did not admit to his guilt, nor did he show remorse for his actions. The information about NT1's past was still relevant for the protection of the public as he remained in business. He reasoned that, by contrast, NT2 acknowledged his guilt and showed sincere remorse. The information about his past was of little relevance. His present business activity was unrelated to his past one, and there was no evidence of a risk of reoffending.

Still, a certain similarity in the conduct of the two claimants arguably consists in the fact that they both engaged with the media on advice in order to limit the impact of other unfavourable publicity. NT1 enlisted the services of a reputation management company so as to demote the negative posts and to present himself in a deceitfully favourable light. NT2 gave two press interviews about his conviction and his business plans, and he published a personal website and a blog in which he sought to portray himself as a successful businessman. Warby J, however, disapproved only of NT1's efforts, while he showed understanding for those of NT2.

Taking all these factors into account, Warby J decided to grant NT2's dereferencing claim, but to reject NT1's one. NT1 lodged an appeal, which is currently pending. Warby J acknowledged that these cases brought up 'novel questions, which have never yet been considered in this Court'.[190] He also intimated that his decision, reached on the cusp of the transition from the DPD to the GDPR regime, would unlikely have an impact on other cases.[191] His judgment is indeed fact-sensitive, inevitably so as it is conditioned by the balancing exercise between the rights to data protection/privacy and the rights to freedom of expression/access to information. Still, several principles have been identified by Warby J, which are worth commenting on.[192] The starting point of this judgment is, first, that information about historic criminal convictions disclosed in open court does not initially attract privacy protection, but may do so at a later point in time. Secondly, Warby J held that the right to rehabilitation as an integral aspect of the right to privacy is not absolute, but needs to be reconciled with the rights to freedom of expression and information. The fact that a conviction is spent is a weighty but not conclusive factor against the further disclosure of information as it needs to be balanced against these competing rights. None of these rights prevails in this balancing exercise, but all carry equal weight.[193] This starting point aligns with the position of the ECtHR and of the BVerfG, while it justifiably departs from the CJEU's acceptance of a preponderance of privacy.

In carrying out this balancing exercise, Warby J attached significant weight to the length of the sentence and to the nature of the offence. Both NT1 and NT2 were rehabilitated offenders, but only the latter was deemed worthy of online redemption, not least because of the less severe nature of his offence. This suggests that a serious offence that could never have become spent, as in the *RTBF I* case, would not deserve to be 'forgotten' in the UK. Such an automatic alignment of the RTE/RTBF scheme with the law of rehabilitation would be antithetical to a fine-grained balancing exercise. It would

---

[190]   High Court, *NT1 & NT2* para 10.
[191]   ibid para 105.
[192]   These principles were also taken into account in *Hayden v Dickenson* [2020] EWHC 3291 (QB), para 49.
[193]   High Court, *NT1 & NT2*, para 166.

also exacerbate the differential application of the RTE/RTBF with its concomitant implications for press freedom across the EU in view of the diversity of approaches to the consignment of conviction information to history.[194] A further decisive consideration in Warby J's ruling was the continuous relevance of the historic conviction information and the societal benefits to be gained from its disclosure. This consideration is in line with *Google Spain* and with the BVerfG's position in *RTBF II*. However, the objective examination of the public interest in disclosure is somewhat obscured by a very subjective assessment of the claimants' character and of their reliability as witnesses. The use of the criteria of 'honesty' and 'remorse' to determine if claimants deserve online rehabilitation departs from the 1974 Act, which is meant to 'rain upon the just and the unjust', and adds a further layer of complication to the already unpredictable RTE/RTBF scheme.[195]

The assessment of the claimants' attempts to clean up their digital record also raises questions. Warby J acknowledged that past offenders should not be criticized for using self-help methods to remove unlawful information about their offending history from the public domain.[196] He did not, however, pursue this line of thought further. As mentioned earlier, he delved into the claimants' exculpation efforts, and found them to differ even though they were motivated by the same rehabilitation desire. What is most striking about this reasoning is that it departs both from the ECtHR's and the BVerfG's case law in that it sees no contradiction between past attempts to stay in the limelight and subsequent claims to be 'forgotten'. Having said that, the ECtHR has cautioned that an individual should not be deprived of all protection against a publication merely on the basis of having cooperated with the press on previous occasions.[197] Finally, Warby J assessed the nature and extent of the actual or prospective harm for the claimants, and found it more credible in the case of NT2 than in that of NT1. This is a notable but perhaps understandable departure from the CJEU's dictum in *Google Spain* according to which it is not necessary to prove prejudice to the data subject to substantiate a dereferencing request.[198] Having said that, while courts are well placed to assess such proof of harm, search engines would probably be overstretched if they had to include this consideration in their decision process.

Finally, a conspicuous gap in the *NT1 & NT2* judgment is the absence of consideration for the implications of dereferencing for the source websites. Warby J accepted that the source publications were lawfully published as a foreseeable consequence of NT2's offending with the exception of one newspaper article that he found to be inaccurate.[199] However, once he was satisfied that the information about NT2's transgression was of little relevance to protect investors, customers, or the general public, he had no difficulty in reaching the conclusion that the retrievability of the news items was not in the public interest so that they could safely be dereferenced. He did not contemplate the impact of such dereferencing on the integrity and availability of historical

---

[194] ibid para 162; see Katsirea, 'Search Engines' (n 28) 138.
[195] See R Costello, 'The Right to Be Forgotten in Cases Involving Criminal Convictions' (2018) 3 European Human Rights Law Review 268, 277.
[196] High Court, *NT1 & NT2*, para 130.
[197] *Axel Springer v Germany*, App No 39954/08, 7 February 2012, para 92.
[198] *Google Spain*, para 96.
[199] High Court, *NT1 & NT2*, paras 212, 219ff.

records. Nor was he prepared to accept Google's argument that the dereferencing of the implicated URLs would also inhibit the findability of further potentially relevant information about the claimant contained in the source publications.[200] The resultant devaluation of news archives is especially problematic in the UK context in view of the absence of comprehensive public judicial reports. The court's reasoning reflects a certain disregard for the inherent value of freedom of expression, and a rather narrow view of its instrumental value, which mirrors the overall weakening of this right in the RTE/RTBF scheme.[201]

6.5 Concluding Remarks

The RTE/RTBF has been expansively interpreted in recent years from a tool to counteract search engines' indelible digital memory to an instrument to reshape the ways in which the past is reflected in online press archives. At first sight, this might seem like a welcome development given that it is the news publishers who made the information public in the first place, and are hence in a better position to assess its continuous newsworthiness and the lawfulness of its dissemination, and to balance the fundamental rights at stake.[202] This view disregards, however, the premise on which the *Google Spain* ruling was based, namely that search engines might need to dereference information even if its publication on the source webpage was entirely lawful. The CJEU justified this principle based on the search engines' unique ability to provide universal access to information in such a manner that enables a near to complete profiling of the data subject.[203] However, it is precisely this ability that is absent in the case of online news archives. Google's dominance in search has thus come to taint wholly legitimate media functions, across the divide of press and broadcast media. Having said that, a snapshot of Google's Transparency Report shows that, in the UK, two newspaper websites, those of the *Daily Mail* and *The Mirror*, but no broadcaster websites, feature in the list of sites most impacted by RTBF/RTE requests.[204] This likely reflects the comparatively harder online access to broadcast compared to print archival records.[205]

The Article 29 Data Protection Working Party argued that '[T]he impact of the exercise of individuals' rights on the freedom of expression of original publishers and users will generally be very limited'.[206] It is doubtful whether this original prediction will hold true. Certainly, not all judgments surveyed in this chapter were based on the RTE/RTBF as such. However, those that were not reflect an interpretation of personality rights that is very much influenced by *Google Spain* and its statutory enactment

---

[200] ibid para 202.
[201] See ibid para 166.
[202] See *Google Spain*, para 63.
[203] ibid para 37.
[204] Google, 'Requests to delist content under European privacy law', 24 May 2023 <https://transparencyreport.google.com/eu-privacy/overview?hl=en_GB&impacted_sites=country:GB&lu=impacted_sites>.
[205] The *Daily Mail* allows free access to its archive <https://www.dailymail.co.uk/home/sitemaparchive/day_20191201.html>, while access to the BBC Archive Services is restricted to programme makers <https://archiveservices.tools.bbc.co.uk/signup/>.
[206] Article 29 WP Guidelines, 6.

in the GDPR. Utmost caution is in order before undiscerningly extending the obligations imposed on search engines to the source webpages and thus condemning whole swaths of lawful information to oblivion.

The diversity of solutions chosen by international and national courts reveals their uncertainty as to how to draw the boundaries between memory and forgetting, freedom of information and privacy online. Some of these solutions are impracticable while others risk throwing the baby out with the bathwater. The indispensable role performed by search engines in the internet ecosystem means that obliging news publishers to completely block the indexing of their webpages undermines the public interest to be informed.[207] The more far-reaching solution of retrospective anonymization of the source webpage is even more problematic. It risks draining a pool of information that could potentially become vital if past events gained new significance or needed to be revisited for purposes of historical research.[208] These quick fixes also raise the spectre of a 'chilling effect' that might stifle critical reporting in the first place to prevent later modification. It is of concern that the migration of the RTE/RTBF from search engines to press archives takes place in the face of profound regulatory uncertainty about the technological answers at hand. The BGH rightly recognized that clarity about the arsenal of technological solutions at news publishers' disposal is essential to fairly balance the conflicting interests involved.[209] It is also imperative that press codes provide guidance about exceptional circumstances in which retrospective anonymization or no-index tagging requests might need to be honoured.

The perils of the RTE/RTBF were recognized by AG Szpunar when he referred in *Google v CNIL* to 'a genuine risk of a race to the bottom, to the detriment of freedom of expression, on a European and worldwide scale'.[210] These risks were implicitly acknowledged by the CJEU when it put a tentative halt to global dereferencing, especially in view of the fact that the US does not recognize such a right.[211] Based on the CJEU's judgment, the French Council of State (*Conseil d'État*) limited the scope of the French DPA's dereferencing order to the EU.[212] The spectre of a 'race to the bottom' acknowledged in *Google v CNIL* is linked to a geographic expansion of the RTE/RTBF beyond Europe, but equally grave risks loom from its substantive expansion to source websites. A presumption in favour of the findability of newsworthy information online, with the exception of rare cases of grave harm, would allow for more balanced solutions between individual privacy and the public interest in a free and vigorous press.

---

[207] See J van Hoboken, *Search Engine Freedom. On the Implications of the Right to Freedom of Expression for the Legal Governance of Web Search Engines* (Kluwer Law International 2012) 620.

[208] The exemption under art 17(3)(d) GDPR applies when the search engine providers themselves, not only their users, pursue research purposes. See EDPB Guidelines, para 80. In the UK, the DPA 2018, Part 2, Ch 2, s 19 requires that processing for historical research purposes will not cause *substantial* damage or *substantial* distress to the data subject.

[209] BGH, 22 September 2020, VI ZR 476/19.

[210] Case C-507/17, [2019] *Google v CNIL* ECLI:EU:C:2019:15, Opinion of AG Szpunar, para 61.

[211] ibid paras 59, 60; see *Garcia v Google Inc.* 786 F 3d 733 (9th Cir 2015); for the argument that there is an incremental development of a RTBF/RTE of sorts in the US by judicial means see A Gajda, 'Privacy, Press, and the Right to Be Forgotten in the United States' (2018) 93(1) Washington Law Review 201.

[212] Conseil d'État, Decision 399922 of 27 March 2020 ECLI:FR:CECHR:2020:399922.20200327. Compare the controversial global de-indexing in a case concerning intellectual property infringements ordered by the Canadian Supreme Court in its judgment of 6 December 2016, *Google Inc v Equustek Solutions Inc.*, 2017 SCC 34.

Such a presumption would also need to be reflected in press ethics codes and news-room guidance.[213] Currently, there is a certain paucity of concrete policies helping journalists navigate the troubled waters of reputation management.[214] The German Press Code, for instance, provides extensive guidance about the protection of personality rights and the appropriateness of identification in criminal reporting.[215] However, there is no advice about the extent to which retrospective anonymization requests should be granted. The IPSO Code and Codebook do not include guidance regarding such requests either. The recently revamped IMPRESS Code offers the non-committal recommendation that journalists 'give reasonable consideration' to anonymization requests.[216] The IMPRESS Guidance highlights that such 'reasonable consideration' is particularly merited in the case of data subjects who were minors when the identifying news report was published.[217]

While this chapter discussed the growing entanglement of the digital press in the strictures of data protection law, the following chapter will consider a different source of liability for online publishers, namely that triggered by users' comments posted 'below the line'. Both the RTE/RTBF and the liability for users' comments pitch press freedom against personality rights and bring to the fore the limitations of online intermediaries when asked to step in as moderators. The balancing exercises that form part and parcel of such a role are closer to journalistic processes of editorial decision-making and accountability than to platforms' conduit function. Still, while publishers are arguably institutionally better equipped than platforms to negotiate the vulnerable rights at stake, the ubiquity and vastness of online communication coupled with the ever-evolving technical and societal expectations makes for a minefield that risks putting the essence of press freedom at risk.

---

[213] See J E McNealy and L B Alexander, 'A Framework for Unpublishing Decisions' (2018) 6(3) Digital Journalism 389.

[214] See, with regard to American newsrooms, D L Dwyer and C Painter, 'Erasing the Past: Untangling the Conflicting Journalistic Loyalties and Paradigmatic Pressures of Unpublishing' (2020) 35(4) Journal of Media Ethics 214, 216.

[215] German Press Code, cl 8.

[216] IMPRESS Code, cl 7.3.

[217] IMPRESS, Guidance on the Standards Code, cl 7.3 <https://www.impressorg.com/wp-content/uplo ads/2023/02/Impress-Standards-Code.pdf#page=26> accessed 26 June 2023. cf the more boldly worded recommendations by the Canadian Association of Journalists, 'The ethics of unpublishing', 27 October 2010 <https://caj.ca/the-ethics-of-unpublishing/#:~:text=Unpublish%20by%20consensus%3A%20No%20 one,journalistic%20reasons%20to%20resist%20unpublishing>.

7

Holding Online News Websites Liable for User Comments

7.1 Introduction

Readers' letters have been the main means by which newspapers have traditionally engaged with their audience and which have compensated for the lack of a universal right of access to the media.[1] While newspapers are responsible for offensive or defamatory readers' letters, especially if they have not distanced themselves from them, they are not expected to verify all facts contained in these letters prior to publication.[2] In recent times, the capacity of readers to access the press has increased exponentially by means of the commenting forums that are available in online newspapers. User comments have become a prevalent feature of journalism in the digital era as a way by which to increase democratic participation while boosting website traffic, making online news sites stickier, and enhancing brand loyalty.[3] These benefits have been perceived as particularly lucrative for the online press at a time of fierce competition with digital platforms.[4] At the same time, the realization soon took hold that vitriolic comments and ad hominem responses written on the spur of the moment could become toxic to online news websites' brand identity, and could risk alienating the very audience these were trying to appeal to. To tackle the problem of online incivility, news organizations have resorted to several strategies, ranging from the moderation of user comments and the ban on anonymity to the migration of public discussion to the outlets' social media presence or, ultimately, the closure of online forums.[5] The *Christian Science Monitor* is but one of many news outlets that disabled comment spaces so as to enable staff to make more productive use of their time.[6]

---

[1] See for a defence of a right to access to mass media J A Barron, *Freedom of the Press for Whom? The Right of Access to Mass Media* (Indiana UP 1973).
[2] BVerfG, 25 June 2009, 1BvR 134/03, para 67; IPSO, Decision 01071-18 *Mander v Maidenhead Advertiser*, 23 March 2018 <https://www.ipso.co.uk/rulings-and-resolution-statements/ruling/?id=01071-18>; R Ricker and J Weberling, *Handbuch des Presserechts* (Beck 2012) 330, para 17a; J Oster, *Kommunikationsdeliktsrecht: Eine transnationale Untersuchung am Beispiel des Ehrschutzes* (Mohr Siebeck 2019) 364.
[3] I Manosevitch and O Tenenboim, 'The Multi-Faceted Role of User-Generated Content in News Websites. An Analytical Framework' (2017) 5(6) Digital Journalism 731, 735 (hereafter Manosevitch, 'User-generated content'); M Hindman, *The Internet Trap. How the Digital Economy Builds Monopolies and Undermines Democracy* (Princeton UP 2018) 18.
[4] L Brunner, 'The Liability of an Online Intermediary for Third Party Content' (2016) 16(1) Human Rights Law Review 163, 172 (hereafter Brunner, 'Liability').
[5] M Nelson, T Kziazek, and N Springer, 'Killing the Comments: Why Do News Organizations Remove User Commentary Functions?' (2021) 2(4) Journalism and Media 572, 573.
[6] Manosevitch, 'User-Generated Content' (n 3) 735.

Press Freedom and Regulation in a Digital Era. Irini Katsirea, Oxford University Press. © Irini Katsirea 2024.
DOI: 10.1093/oso/9780198858607.003.0007

Online news portals' choice of preferred strategy has been influenced in recent times by the spectre of liability for hate speech and defamatory user comments. The extent to which online news portals should assume editorial responsibility and should be liable for user comments has been shaped by national law, by the E-Commerce Directive framework for intermediary liability, and by the extensive and not entirely consistent body of case law developed by the European Court of Human Rights (ECtHR) in this area. First, this chapter will outline the E-Commerce Directive and the Digital Services Act exemptions from intermediary liability, taking the Directive's implementation in Germany and the UK into account. Second, it will discuss the liability of online news portals for user comments from an EU and comparative perspective. Third, it will examine the criteria crafted by the ECtHR by which to determine website operators' liability for third-party comments. Finally, it will conclude by considering the impact of online news platforms' enhanced responsibility for user-generated content on press freedom.

7.2 EU and Comparative Perspectives on Immunities from Intermediary Liability

The liability of website operators for third-party content is limited by the so-called 'safe harbour' provisions of the E-Commerce Directive (ECD).[7] These exemptions have now been incorporated in the Digital Services Act (DSA).[8] They shield online intermediaries from all kinds of liability for content which violates laws on defamation, but also laws on copyright, protection of minors, etc.[9] They distinguish between different types of activities rather than between different types of online operators. The three types of activities covered by the safe harbours are mere conduit, caching, and hosting. Mere conduit concerns the transmission of or access to information, while caching concerns the temporary storage of information. The type of activity which is typical in the case of publication of third-party content on online portals, hosting, consists in the permanent storage of information. The immunity for hosting providers under Article 14 ECD, now incorporated in Article 6 DSA, is subject to the following two conditions: first, that the provider does not have actual knowledge of illegal activity or information and, as regards claims for damages, is not aware of facts or circumstances from which the illegal activity or information is apparent, and second, that the provider, upon obtaining such knowledge or awareness, acts expeditiously to remove or to disable access to the information. In other words, knowledge of the existence of illegal content forfeits a claim to immunity.

---

[7] European Parliament and Council Directive (EC) 2000/31/EC of 8 June 2000 on certain legal aspects of information society services, in particular electronic commerce, in the Internal Market ('Directive on electronic commerce') [2000] OJ L 178/1, arts 12ff (hereafter 'ECD').

[8] Regulation 2022/2065 of the European Parliament and of the Council of 19 October 2022 on a single market for digital services and amending Directive 2000/31/EC (Digital Services Act) [2022] OJ L 277/1, arts 4ff, 89(2) (hereafter 'DSA').

[9] But see the exemption from the application of art 14 ECD for situations falling under European Parliament and Council Directive 2019/790 of 17 April 2019 on copyright and related rights in the Digital Single Market and amending Directive 96/9/EC and 2001/29/EC [2019] OJ L 130, art 17(3) (hereafter 'EU Copyright Directive'). See also DSA, rec 11 to the same effect.

This provision has given rise to more complexities than meets the eye, *inter alia* as regards the role required of intermediaries to qualify for immunity, and the level of knowledge that would divest them of this protection. These two issues will be considered in turn. Before doing so, it is worth briefly casting our eyes to the ways in which some of these issues are dealt with on the other side of the Atlantic. In the US, intermediaries are afforded a safe harbour by way of § 230 of the Communications Decency Act (CDA).[10] Ironically, the original purpose of the Act was to criminalize online pornography. While this aspect of the Act was deemed unconstitutional by the US Supreme Court,[11] a bipartisan amendment intended to shield online intermediaries from liability survived.[12] Section 230 CDA provides a twofold protection for all interactive computer services, including internet service providers (ISPs), search engines, social media platforms, and websites.[13] First, it immunizes them from liability by stating that they are not to be treated as 'publishers' of their users' content.[14] As a result, intermediaries, much like common carriers, are under no obligation to police such content. Second, even if intermediaries choose to moderate objectionable material, they do not lose their safe harbour protection. In other words, they are not obliged to police all content on their sites because they opted to intervene on occasion.[15] This second prong of section 230 CDA, the so-called 'Good Samaritan' clause, was crafted with the aim of allowing intermediaries to act as 'good citizens' without facing liability for any offensive content that slips through.[16] The robust protection afforded online intermediaries in the US—even when they knowingly choose to do nothing—has been credited with the flourishing of innovation and freedom of expression online, even with the creation itself of the internet as we know it.[17] However, in recent times, accusations of anti-conservative bias and the proliferation of mis- and disinformation and hate speech online have led to a quest on all sides of the political spectrum for ways to reform the 'internet exceptionalism', which was paved by section 230 CDA, without stifling its virtues.[18]

The sweeping protection afforded intermediaries under section 230 CDA so far stands out in sharp relief against the more cautious European approach. In the US, intermediaries are shielded from liability even when they have taken an active role in disseminating illegal content. Notwithstanding this broad intermediary protection, the notion of the 'active hosting provider' recently served to justify a narrow interpretation of intermediary immunity by the California First District Court of Appeal. In a case concerning the sale of skin-lightening creams on Amazon without warning

[10] 47 USC §230.
[11] *Reno v ACLU* 521 US 844 (1997); see Chapter 2, p 20.
[12] 47 USC §230.
[13] T Gillespie, 'Platforms Are Not Intermediaries' (2018) 2(2) Georgetown Law Technology Review 198, 204.
[14] 47 USC §230(c)(1).
[15] 47 USC §230(c)(2). However, a notice and takedown liability framework applies to copyright claims in the US on the basis of the Digital Millennium Copyright Act 17 USC §512.
[16] D Citron, *Hate Crimes in Cyberspace* (Harvard UP 2014) 171.
[17] J Kosseff, *The Twenty-Six Words that Created the Internet* (Cornell UP 2019).
[18] ibid 78; A Shahbaz, 'US initiatives to counter harmful speech and disinformation on social media' (*Transantlantic Working Group*, 11 June 2019) <https://www.ivir.nl/twg/research-brief-u-s-initiatives-to-counter-harmful-speech-and-disinformation-on-social-media/> accessed 23 January 2024.

the public that they contained ingredients which can cause cancer or reproductive damage, Judge J Anthony Kline held that Amazon was not simply a passive forum for retailers. In exchange for the service provided, Amazon charged a fee, and took charge of most communication with customers who had no way of contacting third-party sellers except via the platform.[19] It enabled businesses who might not be able to place their products in traditional retail stores 'to reach a vast audience of potential customers'.[20] Given that these hazardous products were likely to have been manufactured outside of the US, Amazon was the only company who could easily be compelled to provide a warning. The Supreme Court, however, halted attempts at an over-expansionist interpretation of the legal fiction of the 'active hosting provider' in two cases concerning the algorithmic amplification of content. In the case of *Twitter v Taamneh*, the Court held that the tech giants were not liable for actively aiding and abetting terrorism only because they provided the infrastructure, including the recommendation algorithms, that matched ISIS content with certain users.[21] On the same day, the Supreme Court remanded a further case, *Gonzalez v Google*, in which a similar claim was made, to the lower court to reconsider in the light of its ruling in *Twitter v Taamneh*.[22] As noted in Justice Jackson's concurring opinion, this is a narrow judgment, conditioned by the facts of this case.[23] Another case with a more plausible claim of platform culpability might lead to a different outcome.

Also in the European Union (EU), one way by which the 'safe harbour' exemptions of the E-Commerce Directive have been limited has been the fiction of the 'active hosting provider'. Controversy exists around the question whether intermediaries need to take a passive stance towards the content users generate so as to fall within the scope of the 'safe harbour' exemptions. Recital 42 ECD provides that the activity of information service providers needs to be 'of a mere technical, automatic and passive nature', which implies that they have 'neither knowledge of nor control over the information which is transmitted or stored'. In *L'Oréal*, Advocate General Jääskinen objected that recital 42 did not apply to hosting, but only to mere conduit and caching, while recital 46 explicitly referred to the storage of information and was hence applicable to hosting.[24] He argued that if the requirement of passivity, which was set out for search engines in *Google France and Google*, was also to apply to electronic marketplaces, this would seriously hamper their development.[25] However, the Court of Justice of the European Union (CJEU) held fast to the condition of passivity, which it considered to be satisfied where the service provider did not play 'an active role of

---

[19] *Lary Lee v Amazon*, 291 Cal.Rptr.3d 332, 76 Cal.App.5th 200 (2022) 15; see *Fair Housing Council of San Fernando Valley v Roommates.com LLC*, 489 F 3d 921 (9th Cir 2007) for an earlier case in which an online roommate matching website was found to lose its immunity under §230 by eliciting information on race, gender, and sexual orientation and by using it to algorithmically show profiles to users; cf DSA, art 5(3) which links liability to the potential for consumers to be misled that the information, product, or service is provided by the platform itself or by its agent.

[20] *Lary Lee v Amazon*, 291 Cal.Rptr.3d 332, 76 Cal.App.5th 200 (2022) 78.

[21] *Twitter v Taamneh* 598 US_(2023) 29ff.

[22] *Gonzalez v Google* 598 US_(2023).

[23] *Twitter v Taamneh* 598 US_(2023), Justice Jackson, concurring.

[24] *L'Oréal SA v eBay International AG* [2010] ECLI: EU:C:2010:757, Opinion of AG Jääskinen, paras 139ff (hereafter *L'Oréal v eBay*).

[25] ibid para 142; *Google France SARL and Google Inc v Louis Vuitton Malletier SA* [2010] ECLI: EU:C:2010:159, paras 112ff (hereafter *Google France v Louis Vuitton*).

such a kind as to give it knowledge of, or control over' the data provided by its customers.[26] This would not be the case simply because 'the operator of an online marketplace stores offers for sale on its server, sets the terms of its service, is remunerated for that service and provides general information to its customers'.[27] The entitlement for immunity may, however, be forfeited where the operator 'has provided assistance which entails, in particular, optimising the presentation of the offers for sale in question or promoting those offers'.[28]

A warning bell has been sounded that a broad construction of passivity by the CJEU as 'technical noninteractivity' would be at a remove from the business model of most hosting providers and could stifle innovation.[29] In the case of communication intermediaries, it has aptly been remarked that the notion of their 'mere passiveness' was flawed given that the facilitation of postings online entailed an active role by definition.[30] Moreover, their advertising-driven business models force them to become 'co-creators of the digital sphere'.[31] By moderating, ranking, personalizing, or otherwise influencing the information individual users should receive, not least so as to maximize the time these individuals spend on these platforms, online providers take on an inevitably active role. At the same time, the 'active hosting provider' role is only forfeited by the knowledge of specific illegal acts committed by platform users.[32] This means that risk-prone platforms whose business model is geared towards, or hazards, law infringements can still hide under the cloak of passivity.

Despite the conceptual inconsistencies in the CJEU case law, the DSA upholds the passive/active distinction as the lynchpin for the exemption from liability.[33] The Commission DSA proposal emphasized the importance of not equating automatic, algorithmic ordering, displaying, and tagging or indexing of stored content with an active role. This would be incompatible with the critical role of these activities for making content findable online.[34] The Commission also noted that national courts have interpreted the CJEU case law in contradictory ways, thus endangering legal certainty.[35] Indeed, national courts have sought to limit the immunity of online intermediaries by resorting to various interpretations of the requirement of passivity. In Germany, courts have argued that third-party content could be attributed to an

---

[26] *L'Oréal SA v eBay*, para 113; *Google France v Louis Vuitton*, para 114.

[27] *L'Oréal SA v eBay*, para 115.

[28] ibid para 116.

[29] M Husovec, *Injunctions against Intermediaries in the EU: Accountable but Not Liable?* (Cambridge UP 2017) 55 (hereafter Husovec, *Injunctions*).

[30] J Oster, 'Communication, Defamation and Liability of Intermediaries' (2015) 35(2) Legal Studies 348, 356 (hereafter Oster, 'Communication').

[31] M C Buiten, 'The Digital Services Act: From Intermediary liability to Platform Regulation' (2022) 12 Journal of Information Technology, Intellectual Property and E-Commerce Law 361 para 1.

[32] *YouTube and Cyando* ECLI:EU:C:2021:503, para 103.

[33] Regulation 2022/2065 of the European Parliament and of the Council of 19 October 2022 on a single market for digital services and amending Directive 2000/31/EC (Digital Services Act), recs 18ff (hereafter 'DSA').

[34] Commission, 'Commission Staff Working Document—Impact assessment accompanying the document Proposal for a Regulation 2022/2065 of the European Parliament and of the Council of 19 October 2022 on a single market for digital services (Digital Services Act) and amending Directive 2000/31/EC', 15 December 2020, SWD(2020) 348 Final Part 1/2, para 112 (hereafter Commission, DSA Impact assessment).

[35] ibid.

intermediary and be treated as their own.[36] This is the case when they identified themselves with it and incorporated it into their own chain of thought so that it appeared as their own.[37] The conditions for such allocation of responsibility would have to be carefully examined with due regard for freedom of expression and press freedom.[38] In recent case law, the attribution of third-party content has been pegged to the active role of the intermediary. The BGH held that by exercising editorial control over user-generated reviews and by single-handedly deciding whether to keep, alter, or delete them, without letting the affected person know, the intermediary abandoned its position as a neutral conduit and assumed an active role.[39]

In the UK, there was uncertainty in the past about the question of whether a website operator publishing material posted by others could be classified as a publisher. While earlier case law suggested that this would be the case, albeit defences might have been available, later judgments concluded that this was impossible without control over the publication in question.[40] This interpretation is reflected in section 5(2) of the Defamation Act 2013, which provides a defence for website operators if they can show that the material posted on the website was not their own. Section 5(12) states that the defence is not defeated only because the website operator moderated the statements posted by others. However, the Act does not specify when the threshold from non-actionable moderation to actionable editing is crossed.[41] The purpose of the 'notice and notice' system under section 5 is to allow the claimant to act against the poster of the material within a specified timeframe.[42] If this proves impossible, the defence may be defeated under section 5(3) of the Defamation Act 2013.

Further protection from damage claims is available under Regulation 19 of the E-Commerce Regulations, which implemented the E-Commerce Directive into UK law.[43] For hosting services to be protected under the 'notice and takedown' system of Regulation 19, they need to act 'expeditiously to remove or to disable access to the information' upon receiving knowledge or awareness of its existence. The Regulation 19 protection extends to hybrid websites, which combine user-generated content with other content for which the website provider has editorial responsibility.[44] Exclusion from liability applies to the part of the service which only serves to store information.[45]

In *Kaschke v Gray*, the High Court held that even limited interventions consisting of checking for spelling and grammar and making corrections before promoting a post on the homepage of a website by placing it in a more prominent position could

---

[36] BGH, 12 November 2009, I ZR 166/07 (marions-kochbuch.de), paras 27ff.

[37] BGH, 27 March 2012, VI ZR 144/11 (*RSS-Feeds*), para 16.

[38] ibid.

[39] BGH, 4 April 2017, VI ZR 123/16 (*Klinikbwertung*).

[40] *Godfrey v Demon Internet Ltd* [1999] EWHC 449 (QB); *Bunt v Tilley* [2006] EWHC 407 (QB); *Metropolitan International Schools v Designtechnica* [2009] EWHC 1765 (QB); *Davison v Habib* [2011] EWHC 3031 (QB).

[41] J Price and F McMahon, *Blackstone's Guide to the Defamation Act 2013* (OUP 2013) 99, para 6.55.

[42] Defamation (Operators of Websites) Regulations 2013 (SI 2013/3028), Sch, para 2 (hereafter Defamation Regulations 2013).

[43] The Electronic Commerce (EC Directive) Regulations 2002 (SI 2002/31).

[44] *Karim v Newsquest Media Group* [2009] EWHC 3205 (QB) (hereafter *Karim v Newsquest*); *Kaschke v Gray* [2010] EWHC 690 (QB), para 68 (hereafter *Kaschke v Gray*).

[45] *Kaschke v Gray*, para 75.

expose a provider to liability for defamatory content.[46] Even though the checking for grammar and spelling might have been marginal otherwise, in this case it was viewed as part and parcel of the more far-reaching ranking of content. The promotion of interesting material and the removal of offensive material are typical examples of editorial control. The High Court's potentially strict position on active intervention was, however, tempered by a narrow view of the relevant service for the purposes of the Regulation 19 defence. The High Court held that the relevant service was not the website as a whole or the homepage or even the general storage of blog posts on webpages made available on the website but the specific blog posted by the defendant.[47] This broad interpretation of the Regulation 19 immunities begs the intractable problem of how to distinguish between staying passive and consciously deciding that there is no need to amend certain items.[48]

As regards the level of knowledge that would divest an intermediary of protection, there is no harmonized standard under the E-Commerce Directive, so that divergent solutions exist across the EU.[49] The Directive distinguishes between actual knowledge of illegal activity for criminal liability and awareness of facts or circumstances from which the illegality is apparent for damages.[50] It does not, however, specify the requirements for actual and constructive knowledge nor does it clearly delineate the two types of knowledge.[51] The Digital Services Act goes somewhat further in requiring that notices be 'sufficiently precise and adequately substantiated', and in listing the elements to be contained in the notice.[52] Notices can also be submitted by 'trusted flaggers', entities with particular expertise and competence that will be appointed by the Digital Services Coordinators, the national authorities in charge of enforcing the DSA. However, if such trusted partners submit 'a significant number of insufficiently precise, inaccurate or inadequately substantiated notices', their status might be revoked.[53] Notification is not the only way by which an operator can acquire knowledge. The CJEU explained in L'Oréal that knowledge can arise both as a result of own investigations by the operator as well as following a notification about the existence of illegal activity or information.[54] In any case, national courts need to examine whether

---

[46] ibid para 81.

[47] ibid para 88.

[48] V McEvedy, 'Defamation and Intermediaries: ISP Defences' (2013) 19(4) Computer and Telecommunications Law Review 108, 111 fn 46.

[49] Husovec, *Injunctions* (n 29) 53; A Kuczerawy, 'Intermediary Liability and Freedom of Expression: Recent Developments in the EU Notice & Action Initiative' (2015) 31 Computer Law & Security Review 46, 51; cf the elements of notification under the Digital Millennium Copyright Act, 17 US Code, §512(c)(3).

[50] ECD, art 14(1)(a); cf EU Copyright Directive, art 17(4)(c): 'upon receiving a sufficiently substantiated notice from the rightholders', interpreted by the CJEU in *YouTube and Cyando* ECLI:EU:C:2021:503, para 116 as notification containing 'sufficient information to enable the operator of that platform to satisfy itself, without a detailed legal examination, that that communication is illegal and that removing that content is compatible with freedom of expression'.

[51] European Commission, 'Impact Assessment Report accompanying the document Proposal for a Regulation of the European Parliament and of the Council on a Single Market for Digital Services (Digital Services Act) and amending Directive 2000/31/EC' (Staff Working Document) SWD (2020) 348 final, Part 2/2, 161 (hereafter Impact Assessment Part 2).

[52] DSA, art 16(2).

[53] DSA, art 22 (6), (7).

[54] DSA, rec 22.

the online provider 'was actually aware of facts or circumstances on the basis of which a diligent economic operator should have identified the illegality'.[55]

The DSA also states that providers can obtain actual knowledge or awareness through their own-initiative investigations or through notices submitted by users or by 'trusted flaggers'.[56] As far as the first avenue is concerned, the DSA seeks to shield intermediaries from liability when they, 'in good faith and in a diligent manner', take steps to detect and remove illegal content.[57] This provision resembles the section 230 'Good Samaritan' clause, but it is narrower in scope. The exemption is only granted when platforms seek to restrict illegal, not other forms of inappropriate content. Also, it is arguably limited to cases where platforms 'solely' carry out such own-initiative investigations, while they may still incur liability when they otherwise encounter illegal content. This may be the case, for example, following a notice which is not properly substantiated.[58]

As far as the second avenue is concerned, only notices that are 'sufficiently precise and adequately substantiated' are deemed to equip the diligent provider with actual knowledge or awareness of illegality, and to enable them 'to reasonably identify, assess and, where appropriate, act against the allegedly illegal content' in a way that complies with freedom of expression and information.[59] Notices need to contain certain elements to meet these requirements. The DSA requires 'a sufficiently substantiated explanation of the reasons' behind the allegation of illegality.[60] As under the E-Commerce Directive, it is not entirely clear when the requisite threshold of obvious illegality will be reached. The E-Commerce Directive is, however, even vaguer as regards the notice and action mechanisms that had to be put in place. It states that Member States are allowed to establish 'specific requirements which must be fulfilled expeditiously prior to the removal or disabling of information'.[61] However, most Member States have not introduced formal notification procedures, but have left it to the courts to develop more specific criteria.[62]

In Germany, courts interpret knowledge as 'positive knowledge of each specific content' so that mere presumed knowledge or negligent ignorance do not suffice.[63] It is controversial whether the operator's knowledge needs to extend to the illegality of the information or merely to its existence.[64] Article 14 ECD refers to the provider's lack of 'actual knowledge of illegal activity or information'. This suggests that the adjective 'illegal' not only applies to the activity, but also to the information in question.

---

[55] *L'Oréal SA v eBay*, para 122.

[56] DSA, rec 22.

[57] DSA, art 7.

[58] M Cappello (ed.), *Unravelling the Digital Services Act Package*, IRIS Special (European Audiovisual Observatory 2021) 16.

[59] DSA, recs 22, 53.

[60] DSA, art 16(2)(a).

[61] ECD, rec 46.

[62] P Van Eecke and M Truyens, 'EU Study on the Legal analysis of a Single Market for the Information Society, New rules for a new age?' (*European Commission*, November 2009) <https://op.europa.eu/en/publication-detail/-/publication/a856513e-ddd9-45e2-b3f1-6c9a0ea6c722> accessed 23 January 2024, Ch 6, para 4.5.

[63] BGH, 23 September 2003, VI ZR 335/02 (*Rassistische Hetze*).

[64] B Paal and M Hennemann, '§10 TMG' in H Gersdorf and P Paal (eds), *Informations- und Medienrecht Kommentar* (2nd edn, Beck 2021) paras 27ff.

Consequently, awareness of the lack of defences is needed for the provider to be exculpated. This interpretation accords with the BGH case law, which requires the notice to be so specific that it would enable the platform operator to establish the illegality of the objected content without need for a detailed legal and factual check.[65] It is also most compliant with Article 10 ECHR as it ensures that intermediaries only take down defamatory or other illegal content when they are satisfied that the content provider could not rely on any valid defences.[66]

In the UK, courts need to take account of all circumstances detailed in section 5(6) of Defamation Act 2013 and in Regulation 2 of the Defamation Regulations 2013. In particular, the notice needs to specify why the statement complained of is defamatory of the complainant by setting out first, the meaning which the complainant attributes to the statement, and secondly, the aspects of the statement which the complainant believes to be factually inaccurate, or opinions not supported by fact.[67] Where faced with conflicting claims by the parties in dispute, an intermediary should not be expected to adjudicate, but would need to be exonerated from liability if choosing not to intervene.[68] Higher standards as to the ability to recognize the illegality from the facts supplied might be expected of a large intermediary with access to professional legal advice.[69]

The notice and takedown system creates a certain incentive for intermediaries to take down content whether it is defamatory or not.[70] In the UK, the operation of the section 5 defence has been criticized as cumbersome.[71] The advice to media organizations is therefore simply to remove content immediately once they are notified of a problem instead of having to go through the hoops of the section 5 defence.[72] The internet giants may have the resources to resist takedown requests and defend their position in court.[73] This does not necessarily apply to cash-strapped newspapers. What is more, once a news provider readily complies with a removal request, it will also be obliged to prevent re-posting of the same or substantially the same material in future, thus foreclosing access to potentially legitimate content in perpetuum.[74]

In *Glawischnig-Piesczek* the CJEU held that, in the interest of effective protection of the rights involved, host providers need to remove or block access to content which essentially conveys the same message compared with the information whose content was

[65] BGH, 25 October 2011, VI ZR 93/10 (*Blogger*).

[66] Oster, 'Communication' (n 30) 367.

[67] Defamation (Operators of Websites) Regulations 2013 (SI 2013/3028), Regulation 2(b), (c)(i)(ii).

[68] *Davison v Habib* [2011] EWHC 3031 (QB), para 68.

[69] J Rowbottom, *Media Law* (Hart Publishing 2018) 353 (hereafter Rowbottom, *Media Law*; see *Republic of Poland v European Parliament and Council of the European Union* [2022] ECLI:EU:C: 2022:297, para 75 (hereafter *Poland v European Parliament and Council*).

[70] J van Hoboken and others, *Hosting Intermediary Services and Illegal Content Online* (European Commission 2018) <https://dare.uva.nl/search?identifier=db3fa078-e225-4336-95ec-5d6f25731799> accessed 6 January 2023, 27.

[71] M Jones, 'The Defamation Act 2013: A Free Speech Retrospective' (2019) 24(3) Communications Law 117, 126.

[72] Advice by solicitor Tony Jaffa of law firm Foot Anstey cited in Additional Material for ch 22 of M Hanna and M Dodd, *McNae's Essential Law for Journalists* (25th edn, OUP 2020) <http://www.mcnaes. com> (hereafter Hanna and Dodd, *McNae's*).

[73] Rowbottom, *Media Law* (n 69) 343.

[74] Defamation Regulations 2013, Reg 9; BGH, 27 March 2012, VI ZR 144/11 (*RSS-Feeds*), para 24.

declared to be illegal, even if it is worded slightly differently.[75] However, such measures to prevent repeat infringements need to be consistent with the ban on general monitoring or active fact-finding obligations under Article 15(1) ECD.[76] This ban applies to general monitoring and fact-finding obligations, but not to such that concern specific injunctions pertaining to 'a specific case'.[77] To avoid imposing an excessive burden on host providers, the CJEU clarified that any differences in wording should not be such as to require them to carry out an independent assessment of the content in question.[78] The CJEU accepted that the use of 'automated search tools and technologies' would be sufficient.[79] Reliance on such technologies poses, however, risks for users' fundamental rights, especially as regards content whose assessment requires human judgement such as news reports.[80] The ban on general monitoring has also been incorporated in the DSA.[81] However, the wording used in both *Glawischnig* and Article 8 DSA could be interpreted in the sense that the adjective 'general' only applied to monitoring, but not to active fact-finding obligations.[82] It was initially uncertain whether this might have been a drafting error or a conscious deviation from the ECD wording, with the aim of creating a more provider-friendly regime.[83] This uncertainty has been dispelled by the final wording of recital 30, which clarified that Member States cannot impose general active fact-finding obligations.[84]

Finally, the DSA requires all intermediary service providers to ensure that they 'act in a diligent, objective and proportionate manner' when imposing restrictions on users' content to ensure that the fundamental rights of all parties, including their freedom of expression and media freedom, are respected.[85] It offers greater protection from unjustified takedowns by asking hosting providers to justify their decisions and to inform affected users of redress possibilities, whether the user-generated content in question is alleged to breach the law or their own terms and conditions.[86] Online

---

[75] *Eva Glawischnig-Piesczek v Facebook Ireland Limited* [2019] ECLI:EU:C:2019:821, para 38ff; see also *L'Oréal SA v eBay*, para 141.

[76] On the question whether art 15 ECD is 'retained EU law' in the UK post-Brexit, see Department for Digital, Culture, Media & Sport, 'Guidance: The E-Commerce Directive and the UK' (21 January 2021) <https://www.gov.uk/guidance/the-ecommerce-directive-and-the-uk> accessed 6 January 2023; House of Lords Select Committee on Communications, *Regulating in a digital world* (Authority of the House of Lords, 9 May 2019) 50; G Smith, 'Time to speak up for Article 15' (*Cybereagle*, 21 May 2017) <https://www.cyberleagle.com/2017/05/time-to-speak-up-for-article-15.html>: 'Article 15 is probably saved by virtue of Section 4 of the [European Union Withdrawal] Act'; contra Online Safety Bill Explanatory Notes, para 17.

[77] ECD, rec 47; *L'Oréal SA v eBay*, para 141.

[78] *Eva Glawischnig-Piesczek v Facebook Ireland Limited* [2019] ECLI:EU:C:2019:821, para 45; *Poland v European Parliament and Council*, para 90. See on the more far-reaching take-down and stay-down obligations in Germany, Husovec, *Injunctions* (n 29) 171; BGH, 25 October 2011, VI ZR 93/10 (*Blogger*), para 24.

[79] *Eva Glawischnig-Piesczek v Facebook Ireland Limited* [2019] ECLI:EU:C:2019:821, para 46.

[80] D Keller, 'Facebook Filters, Fundamental Rights, and the CJEU's Glawischnig-Piesczek Ruling' (2020) 69(6) GRUR International 616, 621.

[81] DSA, art 8 and rec 30.

[82] Contra M Rössel, 'Digital Services Act. Innovation und Verbesserungsbedarf des ersten Verordnungsentwurfs' (2021) 2 Archiv für Presserecht 93, 97.

[83] See ECD, art 15(1): 'Member States shall not impose a general obligation ... to monitor ... , nor a general obligation actively to seek facts ... '.

[84] DSA, rec 30.

[85] DSA, art 14(4).

[86] DSA, art 17(1), (3f), (4)2, recs 54, 55.

platforms, which not only store information but also disseminate it to the public, are obliged to set up an effective internal complaint-handling system to enable users to challenge platform decisions within a period of six months, and to inform them of other redress mechanisms including out of court dispute settlement.[87] The extent to which the comment sections of online newspapers could constitute 'online platforms' will be discussed in the following section.

7.3 EU and Comparative Perspectives on the Liability of Online News Websites for User Comments

The legal basis for the liability of online news portals for user comments is predominantly determined by the national legal orders of the EU Member States, not by EU law.[88] The CJEU explained in the *Papasavvas* case that the conditions in which judicial remedies for civil liability may be exercised against online service providers come, 'in the absence of any specific provision of EU law … under the sole competence of the Member States, subject to the principles of equivalence and of effectiveness'.[89] In the UK, website operators can incur liability for defamatory user posts under the principles of defamation law by omission to remove them or by acquiescence in their continued publication.[90] In Germany, portals can face claims for damages on the ground of fault-based liability for user comments.[91] Alternatively, they may be liable as 'interferers' ('*Störer*') for injunctive relief and removal when they have breached a duty of care.[92] As in the UK, the abovementioned hosting safe harbour does not apply to such injunctions.[93]

The CJEU has not yet had occasion to adjudicate on news publishers' liability for users' comments. The *Papasavvas* case concerned an action for damages against a daily national Cypriot newspaper, its editor, and a journalist for harm caused as a result of the online publication of allegedly defamatory articles. The request for a preliminary ruling by the District Court of Nikosia sought to establish *inter alia* whether the immunities under Articles 12–14 ECD applied to the website of an online newspaper. It further enquired if the answer to this question depended on whether the publication in question was an e-paper or an online newspaper, and on its funding model, whether it was based on advertising or on subscription. The CJEU, referring to its judgment in *Google France*, explained that the website's remuneration by advertising income or the fact that its content was freely accessible or behind a paywall, did not have an impact on its entitlement to these immunities.[94] However, the exemption from liability

---

[87] DSA, arts 3(i), 20, 21.
[88] DSA, rec 17.
[89] *Papasavvas and Others* [2014] ECLI:EU:C:2014:2209, para 53 (hereafter *Papasavvas and Others*).
[90] *Metropolitan International Schools v Designtechnica* [2009] EWHC 1765 (QB), para 54; *Godfrey v Demon Internet Ltd.* [1999] EWHC 244 (QB), para 20.
[91] Bürgerliches Gesetzbuch (BGB), §823 (hereafter 'BGB').
[92] BGB, §1004. See on the controversy around the doctrine of 'interference liability' ('*Störerhaftung*') and the extent to which immunities from liability are applicable to it P Paal and M Hennemann, '§7 TMG' in H Gersdorf and P Paal (eds), *Informations- und Medienrecht Kommentar* (Beck 2021) paras 54ff; A Kovacs, *Die Haftung der Hostprovider für persönlichkeitsrechtsverletzende Internetäußerungen* (Nomos 2018) 156ff.
[93] BGH, 11 March 2004, I ZR 304/01 (*Internetversteigerung I*).
[94] *Papasavvas and Others*, para 42; *Google France v Louis Vuitton*, para 116.

only applied to cases in which the activity of the information service provider was of a 'merely technical, automatic and passive nature'.[95] Given that the newspaper had knowledge of and editorial control over the contentious articles published on its website, it was not an 'intermediary service provider' in the sense of Articles 12–14 ECD.

The *Papasavvas* case involved a newspaper's liability for its online editorial content, not for users' comments. Whereas there is paucity of CJEU case law on the liability of online news websites for user comments, this question has been broached in the DSA. The Act distinguishes the subcategory of online platforms among that of hosting providers. Online platforms are 'hosting services that not only store information provided by the recipients of the service at their request, but that also disseminate that information to the public at the request of the recipients of the service'.[96] The distinguishing characteristic of online platforms is that they not only store information, but also make it available to the public. However, the Act carves an exception for those online platforms performing activities which are a minor and purely ancillary feature of another service; which for objective and technical reasons cannot be used without that other service; and where the integration of the feature into the other service is not a means to circumvent the applicability of this Regulation.[97] The preamble to the Act mentions the comment section of online newspapers as an example of a service which could fall outside its framework so as not to burden the press with unduly broad obligations.[98]

Comment sections are indeed mostly a purely ancillary feature of online news services' editorial content. Users' comments are generally posted in response to an editorial piece. The close linkage between the two is manifested in the fact that articles attracting greater attention are often updated more frequently and placed in a more prominent position.[99] The responsiveness of newsrooms to audience reactions does not mean that news organizations endorse the views expressed in the community areas of their site. They explicitly clarify in their Terms and Conditions that users' comments do not necessarily reflect or represent the views of the publication.[100] Even though publishers have an interest in maintaining the quality of content on their sites, including that of user-generated content, they are not necessarily responsible for it. Corrections to user-generated content are not commonly published in traditional corrections columns but are often placed underneath the original article.[101] Occasionally, the nexus between editorial content and users' comments is broken, for instance when users veer off topic. Publishers reserve the right to remove comments when they bear no relevance to the original topic so as to keep the conversation on track.[102] Such

---

[95] *Google France v Louis Vuitton*, para 114.

[96] DSA, rec 13(1)2.

[97] DSA, art 3(i).

[98] DSA, rec 13(1)4.

[99] See Chapter 3, p 36; *Kaschke v Gray*, para 79.

[100] See eg The Guardian, 'Terms and conditions' (*The Guardian*, 19 March 2010) <https://www.theguardian.com/help/terms-of-service>; 'Community standards and participation guidelines' (*The Guardian*, 7 May 2009) <https://www.theguardian.com/community-standards> accessed 28 April 2022 (hereafter Guardian, 'Community standards').

[101] IPSO, 12118-20 *Wadeson v oxfordmail.co.uk*, 5 February 2021 <https://www.ipso.co.uk/rulings-and-resolution-statements/ruling/?id=12118-20> (hereafter *Wadeson v oxfordmail*);

[102] Guardian, 'Community standards' (n 102).

post-moderation of community interaction means that the publication in question has assumed editorial control over the comments posted on that article.

In Germany, the Code of the German Press Council (*Pressekodex*) requires editors to 'ensure compliance with journalistic principles if they detect violations through user-generated content or if such violations are pointed out to them by third parties. In the event that editors select or edit individual user-generated content, compliance with journalistic principles must be ensured from the outset'.[103] In a case concerning below the line comments about a minister's proposal to compensate homosexual victims of justice, the German Press Council found that the news magazine's decision to leave one of the comments up while removing the others breached the guideline about user-generated content in tandem with that about discrimination.[104] On the contrary, the German Press Council rejected the alleged breach of the guidelines where a regional newspaper removed upon notification from its Facebook site comments identifying a person accused of rape.[105]

In the UK, most publications do not generally pre-moderate comments, but they may try to subject community interaction to some level of post-moderation on their own initiative depending on the resources available.[106] Once specific comments have been brought to a publication's attention but have not been removed, editorial control is presumed to have been exercised so that they fall within IPSO's regulatory remit.[107] In a recent case adjudicated by IPSO, an anonymous user unfoundedly attributed responsibility for a stabbing to a 'refugee BLM [Black Lives Matter] supporter' in response to an article about gun ownership in the Thames Valley. IPSO held that the publication did not take sufficient care over the accuracy of the comment since it only removed it eight weeks after the initial complaint had been made and five weeks after it had been notified by IPSO.[108] The moderation of user comments on a publication's website does not, however, fall within IPSO's purview if the complaint does not refer to a specific breach of the Editor's Code. IPSO found this to be the case on an occasion where a complainant raised general concerns about discriminatory comments made in relation to an article, without initially specifying that these were located on the newspaper's website.[109] Newspapers are not responsible for comments made by users on social media except if it is the publication's own social media page.[110] Once

---

[103] Code of the German Press Council, Guideline 2.7 <https://www.presserat.de/en.html> accessed 21 October 2022 (hereafter German Press Code).
[104] German Press Council, 0420/16/1 (2016).
[105] German Press Council, 0051/20/2 (2020).
[106] The Guardian, 'Frequently asked questions about community on the Guardian website' (*The Guardian*, 7 May 2009) <https://www.theguardian.com/community-faqs> accessed 28 April 2022; MailOnline, 'Frequently asked questions' <https://www.dailymail.co.uk/home/article-1204078/Frequently-Asked-Questions.html>.
[107] R Douce, 'IPSO Blog: User-generated comments and coronavirus' (*IPSO*, 17 April 2020) <https://www.ipso.co.uk/news-press-releases/covid-info-blogs/ipso-blog-user-generated-comments-and-coronavirus/> accessed 28 April 2022 (hereafter Douce, IPSO Blog). Comments also fall within the remit of the IMPRESS Standards Code and can be the subject of complaints. See IMPRESS, 'Guidance on the IMPRESS Standards Code' <https://www.impress.press/downloads/file/impress-code-guidance-2020.pdf> 4.
[108] *Wadeson v oxfordmail*.
[109] IPSO, 18685-17 *Evans v The Argus (Brighton)*, 21 January 2018 <https://www.ipso.co.uk/rulings-and-resolution-statements/ruling/?id=18685-17>.
[110] Douce, IPSO Blog (n 107).

the complainant subsequently reported a specific comment on the newspaper's web-site, it was promptly removed together with all other comments. IPSO held that the readers' comments did not fall within IPSO's remit before the complainant had specif-ically drawn them to the moderator's attention.

Further, IPSO has provided guidance on online reporting of sexual offences and on court reporting.[111] Enabling user comments to such reports presents a heightened risk of victim identification or of contempt of court. As a result, publishers need to be more proactive, and an 'actual knowledge' standard might be insufficient. In the case of re-porting of sexual offences, IPSO recommends that publishers actively moderate user comments or disable them altogether. In the case of court reporting, IPSO also advises that publishers consider disabling user comments. Overall, the fact that publishers are liable on specific notice, and that IPSO's remit is engaged, suggests that the obligations imposed on online platforms under section 3 of the DSA would be inappropriate in the case of the online press. The exemption for online newspaper comment sections under Article 3(i) DSA provides a welcome clarification to this effect.

Comment sections on newspaper websites are also exempt in the draft UK Online Safety Bill. This exemption is not linked to the protection offered by the Bill to jour-nalistic content or to the exemption of news publishers' content. It is expected 'pri-marily to exempt "below the line" content on media articles and reviews of directly provided goods and services'.[112] The exemption is effectuated by way of the exclusion of 'limited functionality services', that is, user-to-user services which allow users to communicate only by posting or sharing comments or reviews relating to provider content or by undertaking narrowly circumscribed related actions such as 'liking' or 'disliking' such provider or user-generated content.[113] The Bill clarifies that combin-ations of user-generated content are also exempt from the Bill's scope.[114] This clarifi-cation satisfactorily addresses criticism levelled at the previous version of the Bill over the disqualification of comments on comments from the exemption.[115] Nonetheless, the problem remains that the exemption is limited to comments or reviews *relating to* provider content. A publisher who does not pre-moderate comment sections has little control over the content of user comments. Users would technically be able to post comments that are unrelated to the provider's own content. Confining the exemption to content-related comments throws up definitional issues and opens the possibility for news websites to be caught in the Bill's regulatory net. Also, news sites offering further functionalities such as debate forums, message boards, or games risk being classified as regulated services. Moreover, the exemption for limited functionality services is at the Secretary of State's behest to amend on the ground of the risk of harm

[111] IPSO, 'Guidance on reporting of sexual offences' <https://www.ipso.co.uk/what-we-do/member-publishers/guidance-for-journalists-and-editors/guidance-on-reporting-of-sexual-offences/#Publish ingOnlineAndContemptOfCourt> (hereafter IPSO, 'Guidance on reporting of sexual offences'); IPSO, 'Guidance on court reporting' <https://www.ipso.co.uk/media/2168/ipso-court-reporting-guidance.pdf>.

[112] Online Safety Bill: Explanatory Notes (2021, CP 405), para 37 (hereafter Online Safety Bill Explanatory Notes).

[113] Online Safety Bill 151, 22 June 2023, Schedule 1 Part 1 para 4 (1) (hereafter Online Safety Bill).

[114] Ibid Schedule 1 Part 1 para 5 (b); see also s. 49 (6).

[115] G Smith, 'Carved out or carved up? The draft Online Safety Bill and the press' (*Inforrm*, 30 June 2021) <https://inforrm.org/2021/06/30/carved-out-or-carved-up-the-draft-online-safety-bill-and-the-press-gra ham-smith/>.

posed to individuals in the UK by the service in question.[116] It is explained that this is so that the online safety framework remains responsive to technological change.[117] This clause has rightly been criticized for exposing online journalism to the Damocles sword of 'harm', risking being unleashed at the Secretary of State's discretion without the safeguards offered by primary legislation.[118] Presumably in response to such criticism, a safeguard has been inserted to clarify that Secretary of State regulations cannot have the effect of repealing the recognized news publishers' exemption from the scope of the Bill.[119] This is a welcome clarification. Nonetheless, the fact that the scope of the exemption remains at the Secretary of State's discretion poses a risk that the guarantee may be diluted for some news providers in future.

The removal of newspapers' comment sections from the scope of the Online Safety Bill has been criticized on the ground that these sections are akin to social media platforms like Twitter. A tighter regulation of in scope services would force users to flock to news publishers' comment streams to publish hate speech, so the argument goes.[120] As regards the first part of the argument, it is indeed the case that newspapers, by opening up private discussion spaces, have to a certain extent adopted the social media modus operandi.[121] They too provide a user-to-user service by allowing users to generate content which is then encountered by other users of the service.[122] However, differently from social media platforms, the user-generated content is not free-standing, but is intimately linked to a news publication's editorial content. This means that these comment spaces are subject to the regulatory framework outlined above.

Still, critics lament the fact that news publications have on occasion left threatening comments up on their sites for weeks despite presumably having been notified of their existence.[123] They contrast the large readership of traditional media with the limited average number of Facebook friends.[124] This is a skewed comparison as it elides the often-viral spread of hate speech on social media platforms. Even though the prevalence of abusive and other harmful content on these platforms is relatively low, it reaches a significant proportion of the population by way of its easy online dissemination and algorithmic promotion.[125] As far as news sites are concerned, statistics

---

[116] Online Safety Bill, s 196(9).

[117] Online Safety Bill Explanatory Notes, para 37.

[118] News Media Association, 'Written evidence (OSB0107)' <https://committees.parliament.uk/writtene vidence/39265/pdf/> (hereafter News Media Association, 'Written evidence'); see W Perrin, L Woods, and M Walsh, 'Secretary of State's powers and the Draft Online Safety Bill' (*Carnegie UK*, 14 September 2021) <https://www.carnegieuktrust.org.uk/blog-posts/secretary-of-states-powers-and-the-draft-online-safety-bill/>.

[119] Online Safety Bill, s 196(10).

[120] B Cathcart, 'Government's Online Harms legislation will once again protect its friends in the corporate press' (*Byline Times*, 25 February 2021) <Government's Online Harms Legislation Will Once Again Protect Its Friends in the Corporate Press – Byline Times> (hereafter Cathcart, 'Government's Online Harms').

[121] *Delfi AS v Estonia*, App No 64569/09, 16 June 2015 (hereafter *Delfi v Estonia II*), para 96.

[122] Online Safety Bill, s 2(1).

[123] J Petley, 'Online Safety Bill and the press: A thoroughly unsafe Bill, Part 2' (*Inforrm*, 7 July 2021) <https://inforrm.org/2021/07/07/online-safety-and-the-press-a-thoroughly-unsafe-bill-part-2-julian-pet ley/>.

[124] Cathcart, 'Government's Online Harms' (n 120).

[125] B Vidgen, H Margetts, and A Harris, 'How much online abuse is there? A systematic review of evidence for the UK' (*The Alan Turing Institute*, 24 November 2019) <https://www.turing.ac.uk/sites/default/files/2019-11/online_abuse_prevalence_full_24.11.2019_-_formatted_0.pdf> 5 para 7.

on the frequency of harassment and hate are not readily available.[126] The National Union of Journalists, in its submission to the Online Safety Bill, observed that it is often the same perpetrators that use social media platforms and news sites' comment sections to post abusive comments, including towards journalists.[127] It therefore recommended that content, which does not pass the editorial threshold for other published material, should not be publishable as ' "below the line" commentary dressed up as user engagement'.[128]

As already discussed, the exemption of newspaper websites, including their comment sections, from the scope of the Online Safety Bill rests on the premise that they are well regulated, so that there would be no need to duplicate these efforts.[129] This premise means that, so long as the press is seen to provide a level of protection from abusive user comments, there is no need for a further layer of external oversight. On the contrary, if the press fails in its duty to deal with hate speech in comment sections, the Online Safety Bill foreshadows the alternative of some form of external oversight, while giving residual powers to the Secretary of State to make the call. In Germany, by comparison, the NetzDG does not envisage the possibility of including journalistic websites within its remit.[130] However, the backstop powers reserved for state media authorities indicated earlier also raise the spectre of external press regulation in the face of challenges posed by the proliferation of communication online.[131]

In the following, we will consider the case law of the ECtHR on the liability of online news portals for third-party comments. This will enable us to better appreciate the ways in which the Court balances the competing rights of freedom of expression and reputation, and the parameters under which online news publishers may attract liability for the harm caused by user comments.

7.4 The Case Law of the European Court of Human Rights

The ECtHR has developed an extensive, but not necessarily consistent body of case law on the liability of online news portals for offensive user comments. It had occasion to consider this question for the first time in the well-known case of *Delfi v Estonia*.[132] Delfi, one of the largest internet news portals in Estonia, published an article in which it described the destruction of ice roads between the mainland and some islands as a result of a ferry company's (SLK's) decision to change its ferry routes. The article attracted a larger than average number of comments, about twenty of which contained personal threats and insults directed at SLK's majority shareholder L under the guise of anonymity. While the national courts considered the comments in question to be

[126] ibid 30 para 4.3.5.
[127] National Union of Journalists, 'Written evidence' (September 2021) <https://committees.parliament.uk/writtenevidence/39385/html/> para 9.
[128] ibid para 8.
[129] J Wright, 'Letter to Ian Murray' (DCMS, 10 April 2019) <https://assets.publishing.service.gov.uk/government/uploads/system/uploads/attachment_data/file/794520/20190410_DCMS_SoS_to_Society_of_Editors.pdf>; see Chapter 4, p 100.
[130] Chapter 3, p 71; NetzDG, §1(1)1, 2.
[131] Chapter 3, p 74.
[132] *Delfi AS v Estonia*, App No 64569/09, 10 October 2013, paras 11, 86 (hereafter *Delfi v Estonia I*).

'humiliating and defamatory', the ECtHR characterized them as 'hate speech and incitement to violence'.[133] The curious passion aroused by the delay in the opening of ice roads was due the fact that these roads over the frozen sea offered a more affordable and faster connection between the Estonian mainland and the islands compared to the ferry transport service. The news article itself was balanced and not defamatory, but the portal had a history of attracting vulgar and offensive comments.[134] Delfi had three systems in place by which it dealt with offending posts: an easily accessible automatic notice and takedown system; the occasional removal of offensive posts by the administrators on their own initiative; and a word-based filter.[135] In the present case, none of these mechanisms worked. As a result, the contentious comments stayed up for six weeks by which time L's lawyers notified the applicant company in writing. The comments were expeditiously removed, but L's request for damages was turned down.

The Estonian courts awarded damages, albeit of a considerably smaller amount than originally requested. Crucially, they rejected Delfi's argument that they should be regarded as an intermediary and thus benefit of protection from liability under the E-Commerce Directive. An ECtHR unanimous Chamber judgment held that the domestic courts' rulings did not violate Delfi's right to freedom of expression.[136] The case was referred to the Grand Chamber which upheld the ruling by fifteen votes to two.[137] The ECtHR articulated for the first time, in *Delfi*, the parameters for assessing the proportionality of interferences with the freedom of expression of online intermediaries: the context of the comments; the measures applied by the applicant company in order to prevent or remove defamatory comments; the liability of the actual authors of the comments as an alternative to the intermediary's liability; and the consequences of the domestic proceedings for the applicant company.[138] This template has been resorted to by the ECtHR time and again in its case law on online new portals' liability for third-party comments.

The *Delfi* judgment departs in two important respects from the main tenets of the framework for intermediary liability under EU law and in the domestic jurisdictions under discussion. First, the Estonian courts considered the applicant company to be the publisher of the comments because of its economic interest in their publication. Referring to the Council of Europe Recommendation on a new notion of media, the ECtHR acknowledged that the duties and responsibilities of an online news portal may differ from those of a traditional publisher as regards third-party content.[139] Still, it argued that Delfi, by publishing articles of its own, inviting readers to comment on them, and being solely able to modify or delete them after publication meant that it had gone beyond the role of a passive, purely technical service provider.[140] It emphasized that the scope of its ruling was limited to 'a large professionally managed Internet

---

[133] ibid paras 27, 115.
[134] ibid paras 11, 86.
[135] ibid para 87.
[136] *Delfi v Estonia I*.
[137] *Delfi v Estonia II*.
[138] ibid para 69.
[139] ibid para 113; Council of Europe, 'Recommendation CM/Rec (2011) 7 on a new notion of media' (21 September 2011) <https://edoc.coe.int/en/media/8019-recommendation-cmrec20117-on-a-new-notion-of-media.html>.
[140] *Delfi v Estonia II*, paras 115, 146.

news portal run on a commercial basis', distinguishing it from internet discussion forums, bulletin boards, or social media platforms where third-party content is posted without the discussion being guided by any editorial content.[141] A further important consideration in establishing Delfi's liability was the difficulty of obtaining redress from the authors of the comments, not least due to the lack of mechanisms put in place to that effect by the applicant company.[142]

The Grand Chamber judgment displays a scarcity of reasoning when reviewing the domestic courts' characterization of Delfi as a publisher rather than as an intermediary. The ECtHR was only competent to determine whether the domestic authorities' interpretation was compatible with Article 10 ECHR, not whether it complied with the ECD.[143] Still, given that the ECD 'notice and takedown' framework is the foundational legal framework for intermediary liability in the vast majority of the Council of Europe's Member States, it should have carried greater weight in the assessment of domestic authorities' margin of appreciation.[144] Also, the ECtHR was called to scrutinize the foreseeability of the applicant's liability under the domestic legal framework, into which the Directive had been incorporated. The ECtHR hardly furnished the necessary detail to explain why it should have been clear to Delfi that they could be held liable for the publication of users' comments.[145] This would have been the more pertinent given that the *Delfi* judgment raised novel questions about the liability of an internet news portal for users' comments on which even the domestic courts initially disagreed.[146] The Estonian Supreme Court itself acknowledged the difference between a portal operator and a traditional publisher, whilst it failed to explain why a portal operator should be held strictly liable for comments it had not authored.[147] In the words of the dissenting judges, 'only divine legal counsel could have been sufficiently certain' of the outcome reached by the domestic authorities in this case.[148]

The fact that the publication of user-generated comments was part of Delfi's business model was hardly a reason to deprive it of the ECD safe harbour protections.[149] Comment sections are not only a space for debate and participatory journalism, but also a crucial business tool. They attract users to the site, maximize the time they spend there, and help sell their attention to advertisers.[150] A stricter standard for commercial entities might align with the lower level of protection for commercial expression in the ECtHR's case law.[151] However, the ECtHR's President, Judge Robert Spano, refuted this notion. He explained that such entities do not enjoy lower free speech rights, but that the economic nature of their activities may justify imposing on them more

---

[141] ibid para 116.
[142] ibid para 151.
[143] Oster, 'Communication' (n 30) 360.
[144] See *Delfi v Estonia II* (Judges Sajó and Tsotsoria, dissenting), para 23.
[145] B van der Sloot, 'The Practical and Theoretical Problems with 'Balancing'. *Delfi, Coty* and the Redundancy of the Human Rights Framework' (2016) 23(3) Maastricht Journal of European and Comparative Law 439, 446.
[146] *Delfi v Estonia II*, paras 21ff.
[147] ibid para 31.
[148] *Delfi v Estonia II* (Judges Sajó and Tsotsoria, dissenting), para 36.
[149] ibid para 44.
[150] Manosevitch, 'User-Generated Content' (n 3) 735.
[151] A Sardo, 'Categories, Balancing and Fake News: The Jurisprudence of the European Court of Human Rights' (2020) 33(2) Canadian Journal of Law & Jurisprudence 435, 456.

stringent duties.[152] As mentioned above, an internet service's monetization strategy has no bearing on its exemption from liability.[153] If it was otherwise, these exemptions would only be open to non-profit-making platforms, and thus of very limited use.[154] At the same time, the categorization of service providers as commercial entities can be taken into account when considering 'the measures which are best adapted to the resources and abilities available to them', whilst taking into account 'the other obligations and challenges which they will encounter in the exercise of their activity'.[155] Unquestionably, large commercial entities have greater capacity to monitor the internet than a sole victim of hate speech.[156] However, the fact that they might have the capacity to pre-screen contents, does not necessarily mean that they should be required to do so. The obligations imposed even on large, commercial news portals need to comply with the intermediary liability framework, in particular with Article 8 DSA, and to take heed of the pressures of an increasingly competitive news environment.

The ECtHR further took the fact into account that Delfi was a hybrid platform, combining editorial with user-generated content, so that the discussion below the line was motivated by, and linked to, the news report in question. However, neither the DSA nor the Online Safety Bill consider the nexus between news articles and readers' comments to be a factor heightening online news providers' responsibility, or as a reason to deprive them of the intermediary liability immunities altogether. They even view this connection as a prerequisite for the comment sections' exemption from the safety framework put in place for other digital services. This contrasts with the ECtHR's unspoken view in *Delfi* that news providers need to bear a higher burden of responsibility as regards third-party comments, compared to other online platforms, as their editorial control over the professionally produced content also extends to the comment sections.

The enhanced liability of online news portals puts them at a disadvantage vis-à-vis social media platforms, and is at a remove from their business model and from readers' expectations. Delfi's articles attracted around 10,000 readers' comments daily, a number high enough to render their general pre-moderation or editing prohibitive. Readers do not equate comment sections with the news articles above the line nor do they take them to reflect a news portal's editorial stance.[157] They value the opportunity to debate matters of public interest, often under the cloak of anonymity, framed by news articles' informative content, but not constrained by tight editorial gatekeeping.[158] Still, the ECtHR characterized Delfi as a publisher, and equated this

---

[152] R Spanos, 'Don't kill the messenger—Delfi and its progeny in the case law of the European Court of Human Rights', 8 September 2017, University of Tallinn <Speech_Spano.pdf (ivir.nl)> accessed 28 August 2022.

[153] *L'Oréal SA v eBay*, para 115; *Google France v Louis Vuitton*, para 116; *Papasavvas and Others*, para 42; but see *GS Media BV v Sanoma Media Netherlands BV and Others* [2016] ECLI:EU:C:2016:644, para 51 where stricter obligations were imposed on a for-profit platform to monitor infringing links.

[154] See *Delfi v Estonia II* (Judges Sajó and Tsotsoria, dissenting), para 17.

[155] *Poland v European Parliament and Council*, para 75.

[156] *Delfi v Estonia II*, para 158.

[157] Brunner, 'Liability' (n 4) 171.

[158] See B Reader, 'Free Press vs. Free Speech? The Rhetoric of "Civility" in Regard to Anonymous Online Comments' (2012) 89(3) Journalism & Mass Communication Quarterly 495 (hereafter Reader, 'Free Press vs. Free Speech?').

with the role of an active intermediary, without sufficiently substantiating its conclusion. The fact that the authors of the comments could not modify or delete them after publication is not sufficient to impute liability to the news portal. It might have been otherwise if Delfi had assumed an active editorial role, including through the use of algorithms.[159] However, it is not evident that Delfi modified the contentious comments, ranked them in a particular order, or placed them in a prominent position to attract attention to the story in question.[160]

Second, the ECtHR did not clearly answer the question whether Delfi had knowledge of the existence of the offending comments on its portal or was aware of facts or circumstances from which the illegal activity was apparent. The ECtHR merely observed that, even though the article in issue attracted well above the average number of comments, so that it must have been easily identifiable by the portal, the contested comments were only removed six weeks after they were uploaded on the website.[161] The concurring judges pointedly remarked that Delfi's inactivity for such an extended period of time amounted to 'wilful ignorance'.[162] This is questionable, especially given that the article in question was balanced and neutral. The fact that the article pertained to a controversial matter of public interest should not have sufficed for imposing strict liability, even allowing for Delfi's reputation in attracting degrading comments.[163]

The ECtHR further argued that the illegality of the impugned comments was manifest without the need for linguistic or legal analysis.[164] However, it made little effort to examine these comments closely so as to accurately determine where 'mere vulgar abuse' ended and hate speech began in the context of the online environment.[165] Such a forensic examination would have mattered from a freedom of expression perspective to ensure that lawful comments were not silenced only because they were expressed in an uncivil manner, as unpalatable as such rancorous discourse might have been. At the same time, it should be added that users have as little a right that their comments stay up in a comment section as they have a right that their readers' letters get published.[166]

The Court's argumentation suggests that, even if Delfi did not actively know of the comments in question, it ought to have known of their existence, not least in view of its voluntary monitoring by way of filtering and occasional own-initiative takedowns. This requirement of 'constructive knowledge' departs from the more exacting 'actual knowledge' standard applied in the national jurisdictions examined above. It is also stricter than the standard upheld by the German and UK Press Councils, at least so far as no particularly sensitive topics are involved. It is not evident that Delfi breached its

---

[159] Council of Europe, 'Recommendation CM/Rec (2018)2 of the Committee of Ministers to member states on the role and responsibilities of internet intermediaries', 7 March 2018 <https://rm.coe.int/1680790e14> para 1.3.9.

[160] cf *Kaschke v Gray*, para 81.

[161] *Delfi v Estonia II*, para 152.

[162] ibid, Judges Raimondi, Karakaş, De Gaetano, and Kjølbro concurring, para 15.

[163] cf DSA, rec 20, which sets a high threshold for collusion to undertake illegal activities as an exception from the liability exemptions, whilst clarifying that mere facilitation of anonymous speech does not suffice.

[164] *Delfi v Estonia II*, para 117.

[165] ibid, Judges Sajó and Tsotsoria dissenting, paras 29ff; see *Smith v ADVFN* [2008] EWHC 1797 (QB), para 17.

[166] See German Press Code, Guideline 2.6(2)3 <https://www.presserat.de/en.html>; German Press Council, BK 2-60/09 (2009).

duty to act as a 'diligent economic operator'.[167] It speedily took down the comments when it was made aware of them, thus complying with the ECD requirements for conditional immunity. An obligation to be more proactive might have been justified in a case where the breach of the law in the comment section was foreseeable because of the subject matter of the article generating the comments.[168]

The ECtHR found Delfi liable not for preventing the publication of the comments in the first place, but for allowing them to stay up for so long. It observed that Delfi's mechanisms would have been unobjectionable if they were 'accompanied by effective procedures allowing for rapid response'.[169] However, it did not explain what these procedures might have been, and how the news portal should have better controlled its comment section.[170] By expecting it to take down manifestly illegal comments even without notice, it effectively gave states a carte blanche to require general monitoring in contradiction with their obligations under Article 15(1) ECD (Article 8 DSA). It ostensibly limited the circumstances to which this strict standard of liability would apply to cases of hate speech and direct threats.[171] The nature of comments generated by an article is however difficult to assess without broad filtering and screening of the comment sections.

The ECtHR further observed that imputing liability for readers' comments had not stifled Delfi's growth, or forced it to fundamentally alter its business model.[172] Indeed, in the aftermath of the litigation, Delfi set up a team of five moderators who were tasked with post-moderation and with reviewing all notices of inappropriate comments before removing them if needed.[173] This may not have been an excessive burden for a news portal the size of Delfi, but may have had a detrimental effect on the news coverage of a smaller news outlet struggling to stay afloat. Also, general moderation at risk of strict liability is likely to incentivize precautionary takedowns and have a chilling effect on freedom of expression to a greater extent than if conditional liability applied.

The ECtHR had occasion to reconsider its case law on the liability of online news portals in the case of *Magyar and Index*.[174] While one of the applicants in this case, Index.hu Zrt, was a major Hungarian online news portal, the other, Magyar Tartalomszolgáltatók Egyesülete (MTE), was a self-regulatory association of Hungarian internet content providers. Both published opinion pieces criticizing the misleading business practices of two real estate websites, which attracted vulgar and offensive comments by anonymous users. The company operating the websites brought a civil action before the domestic courts, whereupon the applicants

---

[167] Contra P Valcke, A Kuczerawi, and P-J Ombelet, 'Did the Romans Get It Right? What Delfi, Google, eBay, and UPC TeleKabel Wien Have in Common' in L Floridi and M Taddeo (eds), *The Responsibilities of Online Service Providers* (Springer 2016) 101.

[168] Rowbottom, *Media Law* (n 69) 351.

[169] *Delfi v Estonia II*, para 159.

[170] N Cox, '*Delfi AS v Estonia*: The Liability of Secondary Internet Publishers for Violation of Reputational Rights under the European Convention on Human Rights' (2014) 77(4) Modern Law Review 619, 624.

[171] *Delfi v Estonia II*, para 159.

[172] ibid para 161.

[173] ibid para 32.

[174] *Magyar Tartalomszolgáltatók Egyesülete and Index.Hu ZRT v Hungary*, App No 22947/13, 2 February 2016 (hereafter *Magyar and Index*).

immediately removed the offending comments. The courts found that the comments transgressed the acceptable limits of freedom of expression, and violated the plaintiff's right to reputation. The domestic courts disagreed about the characterization of the comments. While the Regional Court likened them to readers' letters, and held that the applicants were liable for facilitating their publication, the Budapest Court of Appeal distinguished them on the basis that they were unedited.[175] Notwithstanding this difference of opinion, domestic courts agreed that the applicants could not be considered as intermediaries, and concluded that they were objectively liable for the publication of the impugned comments.

The ECtHR distinguished the present case from *Delfi* on several counts. First, it held that the injurious comments did not amount to hate speech or to incitement to violence. Whilst the comments belonged to 'a low register of style', this was not uncommon in online communication.[176] Second, it observed that MTE had no economic interests, being a non-profit association. Third, the ECtHR noted the difference between individual reputation, at stake in *Delfi*, and a company's reputation, at stake in the present case, but gave the benefit of the doubt to domestic courts' identification of valid reputational interests. At the same time, given that there were already ongoing inquiries into the plaintiff's business practices, it was doubtful that the offending comments would have a significant detrimental impact on its reputation anyway. Finally, a further difference consisted in the fact that the plaintiff never asked the applicants to remove the comments, but opted for the avenue of legal recourse instead. The ECtHR concluded that the domestic courts had not struck an appropriate balance between the applicants' right under Article 10 ECHR and the plaintiff company's rights under Article 8 ECHR, nor had they adequately considered the possibility of identifying and holding liable the authors of the comments.[177]

Notably, the ECtHR argued further that the provision of a platform for posting comments was 'a journalistic activity of a particular nature'.[178] Drawing a parallel with *Jersild*, the ECtHR reasoned that especially strong reasons would be needed for finding the applicants liable, much in the same way as a journalist should not easily be punished for disseminating the statements made by another person in an interview.[179] While this analogy may be attractive, it raises the question as to why users' comments should be equated with pronouncements made during an interview rather than with readers' letters. In *Jersild*, the ECtHR placed considerable emphasis on the role of interviews, edited or not, 'as one of the most important means whereby the press is able to play its vital role of "public watchdog"'.[180] While using the interview analogy, the ECtHR in *Magyar and Index* refrained from elevating online news portals' comment sections to quite the same democratic opinion-forming pedestal as interviews.

A more plausible reason for viewing users' comments as akin to assertions made in the course of an interview, rather than to readers' letters, might be the relative lack of control that journalists can exercise over their content. Spotting offensive statements

---

[175] ibid paras 17, 20.
[176] ibid para 77.
[177] ibid paras 78ff.
[178] ibid para 79.
[179] ibid; see *Jersild v Denmark*, App no 15890/89, 23 June 1994, para 35.
[180] *Jersild v Denmark*, App no 15890/89, 23 June 1994, para 35.

amidst the deluge of self-expression in comment sections may be as challenging as halting off-the-cuff remarks in an interview. In both cases, the ECtHR therefore pays attention to the way in which online and traditional media frame the discussion. In *Jersild*, the exoneration of the journalist from liability rested on the framing of the interview in the context of the broadcast as a whole.[181] Similarly, both in *Delfi* and in *Magyar and Index* the ECtHR found the articles generating the comments to be measured and factual.[182] Even so, in the case of live programmes, broadcasters are expected to react quickly and push the 'delay button' to halt defamatory expressions so as to be able to avail themselves of any defences.[183] Differently from *Delfi*, in *Magyar and Index*, the ECtHR took a step back from the imposition of quick takedown duties to cut off offending utterances even without notice, the equivalent of a 'delay button'. It found the measures put in place by the applicants in the form of partial follow-up moderation and a notice and takedown system satisfactory. The Court flatly rejected the domestic courts' assertion that the applicants, by allowing the posting of unfiltered comments, should have anticipated that some of them would be unlawful. It held that this would have amounted to 'requiring excessive and impracticable forethought capable of undermining freedom of the right to impart information on the Internet'.[184] It would have had a chilling effect on the applicants' comment environment, and might have even compelled them to close it altogether.[185]

Nevertheless, the step the Court took back from *Delfi* may be smaller than appears at first sight. Its judgment ended with a stern reminder that the strict liability imposed by *Delfi* in cases of 'clearly unlawful' comments still stands.[186] Even taking the fact-specific nature of the *Magyar and Index* ruling into account, a certain change of heart can hardly be denied. The ECtHR made allowances for the conventions of online communication, and was sensitive to the risk of shutting down online forums in ways it had not been prepared to acknowledge before. The facts on which it distinguished its judgment in *Delfi* hang on a thread. The difference between merely offensive and unlawful comments was glossed over without further elaboration. The fact that Index was a major professional news outlet, and that the comments were unfiltered, no longer seemed to matter.

The ECtHR had further opportunities to fine-tune its case law on news portals' liability for users' comments in the cases of *Pihl v Sweden*, *Høiness v Norway*, and *Jezior v Poland*.[187] In *Pihl v Sweden*, the ECtHR declared inadmissible the complaint by the applicant that his right to privacy and reputation had been breached because the Swedish authorities refused to hold a not-for-profit association responsible for a defamatory comment. Following the publication of a blog post accusing the applicant, Pihl, of being involved in a Nazi party, an anonymous poster alleged that Pihl was

---

[181] ibid para 33; contra *Jersild v Denmark* (Judges Ryssdal, Bernhardt, Spielmann, and Loisou dissenting), para 3 and Judges Gölcüklü, Russo, and Valtikos dissenting.

[182] *Magyar and Index*, para 72.

[183] Hanna and Dodd, *McNae's* (n 72) 327.

[184] *Magyar and Index*, para 82.

[185] ibid para 86.

[186] ibid para 91.

[187] *Rolf Anders Daniel Pihl v Sweden*, App No 74742/14, 7 February 2017 (hereafter *Pihl v Sweden*); *Høiness v Norway*, App No 43624/14, 19 March 2019 (hereafter *Høiness v Norway*); *Jezior v Poland*, App No 31955/11, 4 June 2020 (hereafter *Jezior v Poland*).

a 'real hash-junkie'. Both the post and the comment were removed, once Pihl complained about them, and a new post was published retracting the inaccurate information. Nonetheless, Pihl sued the association for publishing the post and for not having immediately removed the comment. While the national proceedings concerning the blog post were still pending, Pihl submitted a complaint concerning the comment before the ECtHR.

The ECtHR once more distinguished *Delfi* on the facts. The blog was run by a small not-for-profit association, not by a professional media outlet; the post and comment, although defamatory, did not amount to hate speech or incitement to violence; the applicant did not take sufficient measures to identify the author of the comment. The fact that the publisher was a small non-commercial website, unknown to the wider public, meant, in the ECtHR's view, that it was unlikely that the posts would attract a great number of comments or a large audience.[188] The ECtHR thus underplayed the applicant's concern that the defamatory comment had spread, and was searchable. In the event that his concern was well-founded, the ECtHR sought to placate the applicant by pointing to the RTBF/RTE remedy. Its observation that search engines could 'remove any such traces of the comment' is techno-utopian in view of the limitations and uncertainties of this right.[189]

The Court's apprehension about the chilling effect of liability on a non-commercial website is apposite. It does though uphold the spectre of strict liability for bigger, commercial news portals. This stricter standard for commercial entities might create an uneven burden in cases where larger, yet financially weak, online news portals, publishing public interest news and attracting a multitude of users' comments, are required to pre-moderate, while a small non-commercial entity, publishing inaccurate information, that attracts few, easily controlled comments can leave them up until they are challenged. The ruling in *Pihl v Sweden* was especially motivated by the nature of the offending comments.[190] The distinction drawn by the ECtHR between hate speech and defamation was also reflected in the domestic legislation. While defamation is a criminal offence in Sweden, the publication of defamatory third-party content does not constitute a ground on which to hold online platforms liable. This rigid distinction between hate speech and other types of offending comments is problematic. It disregards the missing public interest value of the content generating the comments as well as the grave reputational harm of defamation, if compared with the more abstract, commercial reputational interests involved in *Magyar and Index*.

In the case of *Høiness v* Norway, differently from the cases discussed so far, anonymous offending comments were posted not below the line, but in a forum that featured no editorial content, and where readers could independently initiate debates and submit comments. The forum, which was among the biggest in Norway, had a separate web address but was hosted by and could be accessed via the online news portal Hegnar Online. The news portal had published a series of articles on the relationship of Ms Høiness, a well-known lawyer and former talk show host, with a wealthy, elderly widow from whom she had inherited. The anonymous comments posted in the forum,

---

[188] *Pihl v Sweden*, para 31.
[189] ibid para 33; see Chapter 6, p 172.
[190] *Pihl v Sweden*, para 37.

which were at the heart of the domestic proceedings, bore no direct relation to these articles. Ms Høiness unsuccessfully complained before the national courts about three of these comments, which she claimed amounted to sexual harassment. The ECtHR refrained from examining in depth the nature of the impugned comments, given that they did not reach the *Delfi* threshold of hate speech or incitement to violence.[191] The news portal had systems in place by which it responded to unlawful content in its forum, and which enabled it to speedily take down the comments in question. The ECtHR therefore saw no need to substitute its view for that of the domestic courts.[192] It concluded that the domestic courts did not overstep their margin of appreciation when balancing the applicant's right to reputation with the debate forum's right to freedom of expression.

The judgment in *Høiness v Norway* continues the trend of aligning the ECtHR case law with the exigencies of the EU framework on intermediary liability immunities by setting a high bar for the *Delfi* strict liability regime to kick in. Even though *Hegnar Online* was a large, commercially run news portal, this did not make a difference to the outcome of the case. The judgment in *Høiness v Norway* differed in one more respect from that in *Delfi*. The *Hegnar Online* forum's moderators had not discovered many unlawful comments to remove of their own motion, so that two of the three impugned comments were only taken down upon notice by the applicant's lawyers. Still, the ECtHR, in contrast with *Delfi*, did not find fault with the forum's moderation standards. An exonerating factor, in the ECtHR's view, was that it did not appear that 'the debate forums were particularly integrated in the presentation of news and thus could be taken to be a continuation of the editorial articles'.[193] This argument resonates with the ECtHR's reasoning in *Delfi* where the nexus between news articles and readers' comments was considered to be an incriminating factor. On the contrary, in *Høiness v Norway*, the vulgar comments posted in the forum were not inspired by the articles published in the Hegnar Online news portal. This was a factor in the ECtHR's verdict that the publisher should not be held liable for these comments.

Importantly, the domestic courts had recognized that the reason why the applicant came into the spotlight, and had been targeted by anonymous comments in the debate forum, was the extensive coverage of their inheritance case by the media.[194] Some of this coverage in Hegnar Online's sister publications had even been found to be in breach of journalistic ethics.[195] Admittedly, this may be too remote a causal factor to be factored in the liability chain. However, the ECtHR's reasoning departs once more from the DSA and the Online Safety Bill. Under their regime, the freestanding nature of a debate forum, the fact that the discussion is not framed by editorial content, might mean that it is more akin to social media platforms, and that its hosts would need to comply with heightened, not lessened duties of care. Also, the high threshold of hate speech or incitement to violence in *Høiness v Norway* sits uncomfortably with

[191] *Høiness v Norway*, para 69.
[192] ibid para 74.
[193] ibid para 71.
[194] ibid para 32.
[195] ibid para 15.

a planned amendment to tackle online abuse against women and girls in the Online Safety Bill.[196]

The ECtHR also ruled in favour of freedom of expression in *Jezior v Poland*, a case that played out in the Polish local election context. Jezior, then a candidate for the post of municipal councillor, wrote a blog with news about his town. Users were allowed to comment anonymously but were encouraged to post thoughtful, truthful comments and to disclose their identity. The site was equipped with a content notification system, but notifications were rarely followed up in practice. Occasionally, users' comments were removed if considered offensive to others. Two weeks before the local election, a user posted an anonymous defamatory comment about the then mayor and candidate for re-election (B.K.), accusing him and his family of criminal acts. Jezior immediately removed the comment, and succeeded in doing so each time the comment was reposted. He also activated a system of access control and prior registration of users. However, having been defeated in the local elections, B.K. brought an action against Jezior based on the Polish Law on Local Elections, asking for the comment to be removed, as well as for an apology and damages. B.K. was successful before the domestic courts, which held Jezior responsible for distributing unproven electoral propaganda material. Jezior submitted a complaint before the ECtHR, arguing that his right to freedom of expression had been violated.

The ECtHR observed the usefulness of Jezior's website for the local community and the fact that he did not in any way stir up the publication of the defamatory comments in question. It approved of the quick removal of the impugned comments, and disagreed with the domestic courts' view that Jezior should be held liable because he did not prevent the comments from being posted online in the first place. Recalling its mantra from *Magyar and Index*, the ECtHR held that such an obligation would require 'excessive and impracticable forethought' capable of undermining freedom of expression. The Court further noted that B.K. never attempted to seek redress from the comments' author, and that the comments had been removed by the time he lodged his complaint.[197] It concluded that the cumulative effect of the pecuniary and non-pecuniary sanctions imposed on the applicant would have a chilling effect on his ability to maintain free of charge a website dedicated to local public interest news.

The ruling in *Jezior v Poland* seeks to balance the risk of harm caused by electoral disinformation with the value of publishing local news and facilitating debate on matters of public interest. Given that Jezior had taken adequate measures to detect and remove unlawful content, the Court rightly considered further pre-screening requirements to be excessive. However, it is unfortunate that the Court did not seize the opportunity to elaborate more fully on the proportionality of prior registration requirements during pre-election periods. Jezior did not have such an identification

---

[196] Department of Science, Innovation and Technology, 'Online Safety Bill bolstered to better protect children and empower adults', 30 June 2023 <https://www.gov.uk/government/news/online-safety-bill-bolstered-to-better-protect-children-and-empower-adults>; seventh marshalled list of amendments of 1 February 2023, 22 Clause 36 <https://bills.parliament.uk/publications/51085/documents/3398> accessed 13 June 2023. The proposed Violence Against Women and Girls (VAWG) Code of Practice is a watered-down version of the original plan to adopt secondary legislation against misogynistic abuse on the basis of the Bill. See DCMS, 'Online Safety Bill: factsheet' (19 April 2022).

[197] *Jezior v Poland*, paras 58, 59.

system in place before the contested comment had been placed, and only reluctantly installed it thereafter. In *Delfi*, the ECtHR recognized the importance of anonymity for promoting the free flow of ideas and information online. At the same time, it observed that different degrees of anonymity are conceivable on the internet, and recognized that anonymity, while being an important facilitator of freedom of expression, needs to be balanced against other rights and interests.[198]

The ECtHR had occasion to refine its case law on politicians' liability for users' comments in the case of *Sanchez v France*.[199] As in *Jezior*, this case concerned the liability of an election candidate for comments posted by others on their public social media account. Sanchez, who was standing at the material time as *Front National* parliamentary candidate for the Nimes constituency, published a critical but innocuous post about a political opponent on the public wall of his Facebook account. This attracted comments by two Facebook users criticizing the Muslim community for criminal and unethical behaviour in Nimes. These comments were unrelated to Sanchez's original post. Sanchez argued that he was unaware of the existence of these comments until he was summoned by the police. Nonetheless, the French courts convicted him, as well as the two authors of the offensive comments, for incitement to hatred or violence against a group.

In its Chamber judgment, the ECtHR held that the applicant's criminal conviction did not violate his right to freedom of expression. The Court emphasized the importance of free political debate for a democratic society. At the same time, it pointed out that this freedom is not absolute in nature, but needs to be limited in the case of propagation of hatred based on intolerance.[200] In the ECtHR's view, the comments in question were 'clearly unlawful'.[201] However, Sanchez, as an intermediary, was not convicted for the use of his right to freedom of expression, but for his 'lack of vigilance and reaction' to the comments posted by others.[202] While the comment posted by one of the authors was promptly withdrawn, less than twenty-four hours after its publication, the other author's comments were allowed to stay up for nearly six weeks.[203] The ECtHR agreed with the national courts' assessment that Sanchez had a heightened duty to monitor the posts on the public wall of his Facebook account, which was likely to attract comments of an 'inherently polemical political content'. His status as a political figure meant that he was expected to be more vigilant.[204] The ECtHR further held that the applicant, as the holder of the social media account, 'without any doubt' shared responsibility with the operator of the platform, in reliance on the CJEU's decision in *Unabhängiges Landeszentrum für Datenschutz Schleswig-Holstein*.[205] The parallel

---

[198] *Delfi v Estonia II*, paras 147ff; cf *Delfi v Estonia II* (Judge Zupančič concurring) arguing against online anonymity on internet portals; cf also BVerfG, 19 December 2021 – 1 BvR 1073/20 where the German Constitutional Court held that the ordinary courts had not properly balanced freedom of expression against the protection of personal honour when rejecting the request for the subscriber data of users who had made disparaging statements against a politician on social media.

[199] *Sanchez v France*, App No 45581/15, 2 September 2021 (hereafter *Sanchez v France*).

[200] ibid paras 84, 85.

[201] ibid para 81.

[202] ibid para 90.

[203] ibid para 97.

[204] ibid para 95.

[205] ibid para 98; *Unabhängiges Landeszentrum für Datenschutz Schleswig-Holstein v Wirtschaftsakademie Schleswig-Holstein GmbH* ECLI:EU:C:2018:388, para 42.

drawn by the ECtHR with this CJEU judgment is remarkable. At the very least, further explanation would have been needed. The CJEU decision in question pertained to the joint liability as data controllers for the collection and processing of personal data of visitors to a Facebook page, not to the joint liability for offending comments. Moreover, the page in question in *Unabhängiges Landeszentrum für Datenschutz* was a commercially operated Facebook fan page, not a political candidate's Facebook account.[206]

The *Sanchez* case was referred to the Grand Chamber. The Grand Chamber judgment confirmed much of the reasoning of the Chamber judgment, and reached similar conclusions as regards the alleged breach of the Convention. In particular, the Grand Chamber considered that Sanchez, in view of his status as politician, was more likely to influence voters, and to incite them to adopt unlawful positions.[207] The risk posed by inordinate comments should have been obvious to Sanchez given his professional experience in the digital services field.[208] The ECtHR considered that these findings did not represent a reversal of the well-established principle of a narrow margin of appreciation in the field of political speech, and of the closest scrutiny of an interference with the freedom of expression of a member of the opposition.[209] The opposite is arguably the case. The high degree of vigilance expected of politicians on pain of criminal liability for third-party comments amounts to a clear reversal of its case law, not only on the high status of political speech, but also on the liability of online intermediaries.

At the heart of the *Delfi* judgment was the differentiation between a commercially operated news website and other internet forums where third-party comments can be disseminated. As already discussed, the ECtHR expressly limited the liability for user comments to commercially operated portals.[210] The extension of the *Delfi* standard to members of the public in *Sanchez* poses a risk to the free exchange of ideas as it would compel them to determine without delay whether a certain comment was 'clearly unlawful'.[211] This is a tall order even for a well-heeled intermediary with access to legal advice, let alone for an individual social media user. The latter would undoubtedly feel inclined to err on the side of caution, and remove the relevant comment to avoid liability.[212] The imposition of liability on Sanchez seems the more unwarranted since the comments' authors were identified. Also, differently from *Delfi*, the authors partly exercised control after posting their comments on Facebook, while there was no possibility at the time for the account holder to moderate content in advance. Finally, the ECtHR did not substantiate Sanchez's actual knowledge of the impugned comments, but contended with the *Delfi* constructive knowledge standard. All these factors suggest that the ECtHR's judgment in *Sanchez* represents an ill-motivated extension of the *Delfi* strict liability regime to social media users, and a departure from the robust

[206] Third-party intervention in *Sanchez v France*, 8 April 2022 <https://www.eff.org/files/2022/04/26/20220408_final_sanchez_v_france_md_eff_written_comments_158.pdf> para 11 (hereafter Sanchez third-party intervention).
[207] *Sanchez v France*, App No 45581/15, 15 May 2023, para 187 (hereafter *Sanchez v France II*).
[208] ibid para 193.
[209] ibid para 188.
[210] *Delfi v Estonia II*, para 116.
[211] ibid para 159.
[212] Sanchez third-party intervention, para 17.

protection ordinarily afforded to the right to political expression. This tightening of the liability standard casts considerable doubt on the required foreseeability of the law. The ECtHR's assertion that Sanchez ought to have foreseen the risks posed by inordinate posts in view of his expertise in online political communication is unconvincing.[213] The resort to such 'intellectual acrobatics' to justify an ever further remove from established guarantees of freedom of expression throws into question the Grand Chamber's contribution to securing the unity and coherence of case law and the legitimacy of decisions in cases of particular significance.[214]

7.5 Concluding Remarks

The ECtHR case law on intermediary liability for user comments is marred with uncertainty: from the strict liability regime in *Delfi* to the subsequent closer alignment to the exigencies of limited liability under the E-Commerce Directive and the Digital Services Act to the relapse in *Sanchez*. The balancing between press freedom and personality rights has been highly context-specific, and the parameters for exemption from liability have not been constant. While the commercial character of the online portal has been an aggravating factor in some of the cases, it was immaterial in others. The moderation expectations have also not been clearly thrashed out. The ECtHR considered that the removal of offending comments after six weeks, as in *Delfi* and *Sanchez*, or even after nine days, as in *Pihl*, was belated though it was still a timely enough reaction to exonerate the applicant in the last case.[215] The contours of 'hate speech or incitement to violence' have not been defined with precision. As a result, it remains unclear when the threshold to strict liability is crossed. The existence of this threshold means that online news portals are expected to be circumspect about the comments posted below the line. This pre-screening expectation is at variance from the ban on general monitoring under Article 15(1) ECD (Article 8 DSA) and may be disproportionate for little resourced news providers receiving a plethora of comments.

The ECtHR has so far exercised restraint as regards the scrutiny of the news articles eliciting the comments. It has only commented on their tone as an indication of the way in which they framed the ensuing discussion. Indeed, it cannot be ruled out that the impoliteness found in many online forums is to a certain extent a reflection of a more general 'outrage culture' elevated to a cultural norm by dominant societal forces, including the media.[216] Whilst it is not the ECtHR's role to police civility in media discourse, higher expectations might be placed on the press to regulate its comment sections in cases of offending third-party contributions motivated by polarizing, vitriolic news reports. The ECtHR has, however, hitherto refrained from scrutinizing online news reports' adherence to journalistic norms or their capacity to contribute to a debate of general interest to society as is familiar from other strands of its case

---

[213] See *Sanchez v France II*, Judges Woltyczek and Zünd dissenting, para 243.
[214] See ibid, Judge Ravarani dissenting, para 5; M Bobek, 'What Are Grand Chambers for?' (2021) 23 Cambridge Yearbook of European Legal Studies 1, 5.
[215] See *Jezior v Poland*, para 57.
[216] Reader, 'Free Press vs. Free Speech?' (n 158) 506.

law.[217] This is consistent with the ECtHR's position that it is not its task to question the technique of reporting adopted by journalists.[218] However, it cannot be ruled out that, in cases of flagrant violations of personality rights in user comments, the ECtHR might pay closer attention in future to the public interest contribution of the adjacent news article and to its compliance with journalistic ethics. The different outcome of *Jezior* and *Sanchez* is a case in hand, while it is necessary to make allowance for the fact that only the former concerned a journalistic blog. The ECtHR's disparate levels of sympathy might be partly attributable to the public interest nature of Jezior's blog as opposed to the affinity of Sanchez's social media presence to the far-right ideological spectrum. While this disparate treatment may be symptomatic of the greater protection afforded by the ECtHR to the media compared to private individuals, it is troubling from a freedom of expression perspective.[219]

By inviting third-party comments, partly out of a democratic impetus and partly out of financial necessity, the press has relinquished some of its gatekeeping power and has exposed itself to the prospect of liability. Below the line comment sections and online forums are a far cry from the heavily policed letters to the editor. While readers' letters were as much a reflection of editorial choices as of public opinion, the floodgates have been burst open by giving an unadulterated voice to the public. The freedom of the press to invite users' contributions needs to be robustly protected. The extent to which the press is afforded immunity from intermediary liability will determine its capacity to uphold comment sections, to enable debate and dissent, and to secure a critical aspect of its financial viability. Unquestionably, some of the comments posted below the line are deplorable. However, such comments also serve as a vehicle for the expression of deeper social and cultural currents of thinking. Even if their expression is curbed, this would not necessarily stave off the underlying hostility. At the same time, attendant responsibilities cannot be completely shrugged off, if hateful ideas are not to slip into the mainstream, take root, and become real political talking points.[220] Even though the public needs to bear some of the responsibility for maintaining a constructive environment, the ultimate responsibility remains with the press. The more the press moves into the social media terrain by opening forums for discussion, the more its freedom from external regulation rests on its capacity to effectively self-regulate. For all the tensions between libertarianism and social responsibility, the quest to rein in the 'monsters' that taint the discussion online, threatens to spill over into the domain of the press. Adherence to the cumbersome rituals of exemption from liability provides a lifeline both for freedom of expression and for press freedom online.

---

[217] See Chapter 4, p 80; Chapter 5, p 112.

[218] *Flux v Moldova (No 6)*, App no 22824/04, 29 July 2008, paras 26ff; *Stoll v Switzerland*, App no 69698/01, 10 December 2007, para 146; *Thorgeir Thorgeirson v Iceland*, App no 13778/88, 25 June 1992, para 67; *Oberschlick v Austria (No 2)*, App no 20834/92, 1 July 1997, para 33.

[219] Chapter 4, pp 80, 82.

[220] See F Toepfl and E Piwoni, 'Public Spheres in Interaction: Comment Sections of News Websites as Counterpublic Spaces' (2015) 65 Journal of Communication 465, 484.

8

Regulating Online Newspapers' Video Content

8.1 Introduction

Visuals have been described as 'a defining feature of contemporary news journalism', and videos as 'a central part of news on the web'.[1] Video content is important to illustrate stories, to render them more compelling, and to increase their shareability. Both social media and the newspapers' homepage are exceptionally visual platforms. Given that a lot of traffic comes from them, it is necessary to adapt the content creation process to suit these environments.[2] Adverts, especially programmatic ones, follow the audience. Videos are therefore particularly lucrative in terms of the advertising revenue they attract.[3] Also, legacy publications are increasingly willing to embrace native advertising, including by way of video content, imitating online only publishers, even at a cost to their reputation.[4] Despite the traditional scepticism of the press sector about the journalistic integrity of TV news production and the concomitant threat of tabloidization, online videos posted by print media are likely to focus on 'soft' rather than 'hard' news.[5] Both tabloid and more 'serious' newspapers use audiovisual content to grab the attention of readers and advertisers alike.

It may therefore come as a surprise that, overall, users still prefer to read rather than to watch online news.[6] This preference is less pronounced in the case of younger audiences who are more exposed to online video-sharing platforms (VSPs) such as YouTube, Instagram, and TikTok. There is also geographical variation, with the reading preference being more prevalent in the UK compared to Germany, and even more so when compared to the US.[7] Speed of access to information and an underwhelming video experience due to pre-roll ads are cited as the main reasons why many

---

[1] S Hall, 'The Determinations of News Photographs' in C Greer (ed), *Crime and Media: A Reader* (Routledge 2010) 123; M A Bock, 'Showing versus Telling: Comparing Online Video from Newspaper and Television Websites' (2015) 17(4) Journalism 1 (hereafter Bock, 'Showing versus Telling'); T Harcup, *What's the Point of News? A Study in Ethical Journalism* (Palgrave Macmillan 2020) 26.

[2] X He, 'British digital tabloid in the 21st century and users' motivations in reading digital tabloid news', PhD thesis, University of Sheffield.

[3] N Newman, 'Executive summary and key findings' (Reuters Institute Digital News Report 2014) 13 <https://www.digitalnewsreport.org/survey/2014/executive-summary-and-key-findings-2014/> accessed 21 October 2022; Bock, 'Showing versus Telling' (n 1) 1.

[4] A C Bakshi, 'Why and How to Regulate Native Advertising in Online News Publications' (2015) 4(3/4) Journal of Media Law and Ethics 4.

[5] Bock, 'Showing versus Telling' (n 1) 11.

[6] N Newman, 'Executive summary and key findings' (Reuters Institute Digital News Report 2022) <https://reutersinstitute.politics.ox.ac.uk/digital-news-report/2022/dnr-executive-summary> accessed 24 January 2024, 27.

[7] ibid.

Press Freedom and Regulation in a Digital Era. Irini Katsirea, Oxford University Press. © Irini Katsirea 2024.
DOI: 10.1093/oso/9780198858607.003.0008

users still prefer to read rather than to watch the news.[8] Nonetheless, consumption of online news videos, especially of shorter ones, is on the rise.[9] The distribution of video content on their websites and via VSPs is not the only way by which press publishers seek to capitalize on the increasing audience appetite for audiovisual content. Press publishers seek to engage their audience and to increase their ad revenue also by offering live-streamed events.[10] These pursuits into the terrain originally occupied by broadcasters are being closely watched by regulators across the European Union (EU) and beyond. In the following, we will first consider the EU legal framework for online newspapers' video content before turning to the ways in which such content is regulated in Germany and the UK.

8.2 The EU Legal Framework for Online Newspapers' Video Content: The Audiovisual Media Services Directive (AVMSD)

The AVMSD, the successor to the Television without Frontiers Directive (TwFD), is the most important regulatory instrument for the audiovisual sector in Europe.[11] It was adopted in 2007 and codified in 2010 after a lengthy legislative process with the aim of extending the scope of the TwFD beyond traditional television to the so-called 'on-demand' or 'non-linear' audiovisual media services (AVMS). The latest revision of the AVMSD culminated in the adoption of the Directive's current version in 2018.[12] The delineation of the Directive's scope and the definition of an AVMS have been the subject of intense academic and political debate ever since the adoption of the AVMSD in 2010.[13] A main rationale behind the Directive's adoption was the creation of a level

---

[8] ibid.

[9] M Koliska and others, 'Exploring Audience Perceptions of, and Preferences for, Online News Videos' (2021) 22(9) Journalism Studies 1161, 1162.

[10] See Guardian, 'The Guardian Live' <https://membership.theguardian.com/events?gclid=CjwKCAjwp9qZBhBkEiwAsYFsb9FSc_tQsyxQY0Whs8yZm0HYiCBshtX0NmCt9_kVOQMitWwAbmgnAhoCGUwQAvD_BwE> accessed 30 September 2022.

[11] Council Directive 89/552/EEC of 3 October 1989 on the coordination of certain provisions laid down by law, regulation or administrative action in Member States concerning the pursuit of television broadcasting activities [1989] OJ L298/23; European Parliament and Council Directive 2010/13/EC of 10 March 2010 on the coordination of certain provisions laid down by law, regulation and administrative action in Member States concerning the provision of audiovisual media services [2010] OJ L95/1 (hereafter 'AVMSD 2010'). For further aspects of the TwFD and of the AVMSD see I Katsirea, *Public Broadcasting and European Law. A Comparative Examination of Public Service Obligations in Six Member States* (Kluwer 2008); I Katsirea, 'The Television without Frontiers Directive' in K Donders (ed), *Palgrave Handbook on European Media Policy* (Palgrave Macmillan 2014) 297; T Gibbons and I Katsirea, 'Commercial Influences on Programme Content: The German and UK Approaches to Transposing the EU Rules on Product Placement' (2012) 4(2) Journal of Media Law 159.

[12] European Parliament and Council Directive 2018/1808 of 14 November 2018 on the coordination of certain provisions laid down by law, regulation and administrative action in Member States concerning the provision of audiovisual media services (Audiovisual Media Services Directive) in view of changing market realities [2018] OJ L303/69, rec 4 (hereafter 'AVMSD 2018').

[13] See A Roßnagel, 'Der künftige Anwendungsbereich der Fernsehrichtlinie. Welche Medien können erfasst werden?' in Institute of European Media Law (EMR), *The Future of the 'Television without Frontiers' Directive* (Nomos 2005) 35; W Schulz, *Zum Vorschlag für eine Richtlinie über audiovisuelle Mediendienste*, Arbeitspapiere des Hans-Bredow-Instituts No 17 (Verlag Hans-Bredow-Institut 2006) (hereafter Schulz, *Vorschlag für eine Richtlinie*).

playing field between linear and non-linear services.[14] Nonetheless, the AVMSD only pays lip service to the principle of technological neutrality, while effectively divorcing itself from it by endorsing a system of graduated regulation. On-demand AVMS are subject to a lighter regulatory regime compared to linear services on the ground that they 'are different from television broadcasting with regard to the choice and control the user can exercise, and with regard to the impact they have on society'.[15]

The principle of graduated regulation is not the only aspect of the AVMSD that signifies a departure from the principle of technological neutrality. The exclusion of radio and, initially, of the press from the Directive's scope—due to the resistance of these sectors against European regulation—also signalled a break with this principle. It is the second of these exclusions that is of interest for our purposes. Recital 28 of the AVMSD, as codified in 2010, stated that 'The scope of this Directive should not cover electronic versions of newspapers and magazines'. The exclusion only made its way into a recital, not into the Directive's main text.[16] The question of whether this recital sought to completely exclude audiovisual material made available on the website of a print publication from its remit has been a matter of contention ever since the Directive's enactment. Some argued that this was the case.[17] Others contended that the video sections of online newspapers and magazines should be considered on-demand AVMS if they were sufficiently substantial and self-standing.[18] This would mean that they would be subject to audiovisual-style regulation on, say, protection of minors and advertising, as opposed to only minimal press-style regulation.[19]

Pivotal for the characterization of online newspapers' video content as 'in or out' of scope is the criterion of 'principal purpose'. The 'principal purpose' criterion is one of the seven cumulative criteria that an on-demand AVMS needs to meet in accordance with Article 1(1)(a)(i) AVMSD.[20] First, it must be a service as defined by Articles 56 and 57 of the Treaty on the Functioning of the European Union (TFEU). Second, the service must be provided under the editorial responsibility of a media service provider. Third, the provision of audiovisual content must be the principal purpose of the service. Fourth, the service must consist in the provision of programmes. Fifth, the

---

[14] See AVMSD 2010, recs 10, 80.

[15] ibid rec 58.

[16] On the legislative background to the adoption of rec 28 see I Katsirea, 'Electronic Press: "Press-like" or "Television-like"?' (2015) 23(2) International Journal of Law and Information Technology 134, 137 (hereafter Katsirea, 'Electronic Press').

[17] R Chavannes and O Castendyk, 'Art. 1 AVMSD' in O Castendyk, E Dommering, and A Scheuer (eds), *European Media Law* (Kluwer 2008) para 28 (hereafter Chavannes and Castendyk, 'Art. 1 AVMSD'); see P Valcke and K Lefever, *Media Law* (Kluwer 2012) (hereafter Valcke and Lefever, *Media Law*).

[18] Ofcom Decision, Appeal by NewsGroup Newspapers Limited against a notice of determination by ATVOD that the provider of the service 'Sun Video' that the provider of the service 'Sun Video' has contravened the Communications Act 2003, s 368BA, 21 December 2011 <https://webarchive.nationalarchi ves.gov.uk/ukgwa/20160704204456/http://stakeholders.ofcom.org.uk/broadcasting/on-demand/atvod-archives/scope-appeals/> accessed 16 September 2022, paras 78, 79; Schulz, *Vorschlag für eine Richtlinie* (n 13) 12; D Mac Síthigh, 'Co-regulation, Video-on-demand and the Legal Status of Audio-visual Media' (2011) 2(1) International Journal of Digital Television 51.

[19] See AVMSD 2010, arts 9ff, 12.

[20] See Chavannes and Castendyk, 'Art. 1 AVMSD' (n 17) para 24 et seq. It should be noted that this is not the only method of counting the criteria that an on-demand AVMS should meet. Other methods come up with a different number of criteria by grouping some elements together or also taking some requirements from the recitals into account.

service must be intended to inform, entertain, or educate. Sixth, the service must be addressed to the general public, that is, it must have a mass media character. Seventh, the service must be provided by electronic communication networks. The 'principal purpose' criterion seeks to exclude all services 'where any audiovisual content is merely incidental to the service and not its principal purpose'.[21] The AVMSD 2010 mentioned websites that contained audiovisual elements only in an ancillary manner, such as animated graphical elements, short advertising spots, or information related to a product or non-audiovisual service as well as gambling services, online games, and search engines as examples of such services that should be excluded from its scope.[22]

The requirement that an AVMS must consist in the provision of programmes also has a bearing on the classification of online newspapers.[23] The AVMSD 2010 defined a 'programme' as 'a set of moving images with or without sound constituting an individual item within a schedule or a catalogue established by a media service provider and the form and content of which are comparable to the form and content of television broadcasting'.[24] The attribute of comparability to television broadcasting was further elaborated upon in recital 24. This recital explained that AVMS were television-like when they competed 'for the same audience as television broadcasts, and the nature and the means of access to the service would lead the user reasonably to expect regulatory protection within the scope of this Directive'. The recital went on to clarify, however, that the notion of a 'programme' should not be understood in a static but in a dynamic way, taking into account developments in television broadcasting, so as to 'prevent disparities as regards free movement and competition'. This raised the question of whether the principal purpose and the programme criteria in conjunction with recitals 24 and 28 of the AVMSD 2010 meant that the electronic press fell *in toto* outwith the Directive's ambit.

Further clarity as to the position of online newspapers' video content was provided by the *News Media Online* judgment of the Court of Justice of the European Union (CJEU).[25] This case concerned *Tiroler Tageszeitung*, one of the most important regional dailies in Austria. *Tiroler Tageszeitung* operated a website with a separate video section, which included a catalogue of around 300 videos, between thirty seconds and a few minutes in length. Some of the videos could be accessed via links within articles in other parts of the website, while the majority had no direct connection to the website's text material.[26] The video section had the same design and general navigation system as the remainder of the website. The Austrian Communications Authority (*Kommunikationsbehörde Austria*, KommAustria) held that the newspaper's video section constituted an on-demand audiovisual media service.[27] KommAustria's decision was confirmed by the Federal Communications Senate (*Bundeskommunikationssenat*,

---

[21] AVMSD 2010, rec 22.
[22] ibid.
[23] AVMSD 2010, art 1(1)(a)(i).
[24] AVMSD 2010, art 1(1)(b).
[25] *New Media Online GmbH v Bundeskommunikationssenat* [2015] EU:C:2015:709 (hereafter *New Media Online*).
[26] ibid para 36.
[27] KommAustria, *Tiroler Tageszeitung*, KOA 1.950/12-048, 9 October 2012 <https://www.rtr.at/medien/aktuelles/entscheidungen/KOA_1.950-12-048.pdf> accessed 11 October 2022.

BKS).[28] New Media Online challenged the BKS's decision before Austria's Supreme Administrative Court (*Verwaltungsgerichtshof*). In 2014, the Supreme Administrative Court referred two questions for preliminary ruling to the CJEU concerning the AVMSD concepts of a 'programme' and of the 'principal purpose' of an AVMS.

Advocate General Szpunar began his Opinion by quipping 'We all know what a horse is', meaning that everyone can intuitively identify an audiovisual media service.[29] He argued that neither the website of a daily newspaper containing audiovisual material nor any section thereof constituted an AVMS. The CJEU disagreed. It held that the short form audiovisual content included within the subdomain of the online newspaper was comparable to television broadcasting, and hence met the definition of a programme under the AVMSD 2010.[30] The referring court had expressed doubts in that regard given that television broadcasting does not traditionally offer compilations of short videos. However, the CJEU observed that Article 1(1)(b) AVMSD 2010 defined a programme as 'an individual item within a schedule or a catalogue', not as the entire schedule or catalogue established by a media service provider. The pertinent question to ask, therefore, was whether a single short video within the video section was comparable to television broadcasting. The CJEU answered this question in the affirmative given that the definition of a 'programme' did not stipulate any minimum length, and that television programmes could be short.[31] Also, it held that videos contained in a newspaper website were likely to have an impact on a significant portion of the public, thus fulfilling the requirement in recital 21.[32]

In answering the question as to the principal purpose of a newspaper website, the CJEU considered the meaning of recital 28. It rejected an interpretation of this recital in the sense that video sections are excluded *eo ipso* from the Directive's scope if they are embedded within a website operated by a publishing company. Such a formalistic approach would give AVMS providers *carte blanche* to escape obligations incumbent upon them by integrating them within a multimedia portal.[33] The Court further argued that the decision of whether a certain service is 'in or out' should not be made dependent on the centre of gravity of an operator's activities but should instead focus on the specific service in question. Such an approach would be more conducive to legal certainty in cases where the undertaking's business straddled several fields, increased in scope or changed in nature due to a merger with another undertaking.[34] The CJEU also observed that the compilation of the audiovisual offer in the principal domain or a subdomain of the website could not be a decisive factor lest the website design be tailored in a way so as to circumvent the AVMSD rules.[35]

---

[28] Bundeskommunikationssenat, *Tiroler Tageszeitung*, GZ 611.191/0005-BKS/2012, 13 December 2012 <https://www.ris.bka.gv.at/Dokumente/Bks/BKST_20121213_611191_0005_BKS_2012_00/BKST_20121213_611191_0005_BKS_2012_00.pdf> accessed 11 October 2022.

[29] *New Media Online*, Opinion of AG Szpunar, para 1.

[30] *New Media Online*, paras 19ff; AVMSD 2010, art 1(1)(b).

[31] *New Media Online*, para 20.

[32] AVMSD 2010, rec 21: 'For the purposes of this Directive, the definition of an audiovisual media service should cover only audiovisual media services, … , which … could have a clear impact on, a significant proportion of the general public.'

[33] *New Media Online*, paras 28, 29.

[34] *New Media Online*, paras 30–33.

[35] ibid para 35.

In the CJEU's view, the litmus test for the referring court was whether the service offered in the videos subdomain was independent of the written articles of the online newspaper or indissociably complementary to them.[36] Whilst the CJEU left the final say on this matter to the referring court, it gave clear pointers to guide its decision. The fact that the videos in question were very rarely linked to press articles, and could in most cases be accessed and watched on their own, led the CJEU to conclude that the video section at issue constituted a distinct AVMS that could fall within the Directive's scope.[37] Following the CJEU's judgment, the Austrian Administrative Court upheld the Austrian regulator's assessment of the AVMS quality of the *Tiroler Tageszeitung* videos subdomain.[38]

The judgment in *New Media Online* provided some much-needed clarity on the classification of press video sections as AVMS. The CJEU embraced the BKS's 'independent function' test and explained that the focus needed to be on the principal purpose of the service at issue, regardless of the framework in which it was offered.[39] The CJEU's verdict is remarkable in that it gave short shrift to the AVMSD's tentative exclusion of the press sector from its scope. Despite the exhortation in recital 28 to exempt electronic versions of newspapers and magazines, the CJEU found that the objectives of the creation of a level playing field in the AVMS market and of consumer protection militated against a sector-specific approach.[40]

The *New Media Online* judgment was codified in the course of the latest revision of the AVMSD in 2018. A key objective of the revised Directive was to include within its scope VSPs, thus levelling the playing field with media service providers and ensuring that minors are adequately protected.[41] As regards the video content of online newspapers, the revised AVMSD, in line with the CJEU's verdict in *News Media Online*, no longer recommends the categorical exclusion of the press sector. It clarifies that programmes, including video clips, fall within its scope irrespective of their length.[42] This clarification is linked to the abandonment of the 'TV-like' criterion in the revised AVMSD. The removal of the comparability requirement was meant to take account of 'changes in viewing habits and the convergence of TV and internet services' and means that a greater range of services may now fall within the regulatory ambit.[43] The question whether the requirement of AVMSs' comparability to TV broadcasting had to be retained was a moot point among national regulatory authorities (NRAs) during the revision negotiations. While Ofcom and the French Conseil Supérieur de l'Audiovisuel (CSA) (now Régulateur pour la Communication Audiovisuelle et Numérique (ARCOM)) maintained that this criterion usefully delineated the scope of AVMSD regulation, the German media authorities argued that it had served its

---

[36] ibid para 34.

[37] ibid para 36.

[38] VwGH, 16 December 2015, ZI 2015/03/0004; see J Metzdorf, 'The Revised Audiovisual Media Services Directive 2018 – Has the EU Learnt the Right Lessons from the Past?' (2018) 1 UFITA Archiv für Medienrecht und Medienwissenschaft 260, 279 fn 88.

[39] *New Media Online*, para 33.

[40] ibid paras 32, 33.

[41] AVMSD 2018, rec 4.

[42] ibid art 1(1)(b).

[43] Ofcom, 'London Real', 25 October 2021 <https://www.ofcom.org.uk/__data/assets/pdf_file/0015/227 103/London-Real,-Longstem-Limited.pdf> accessed 2 November 2022 (hereafter Ofcom, 'London Real').

time and that more future-proof solutions were needed.[44] The latter of these views prevailed at EU level. However, in the UK, a post-Brexit comeback of the TV-likeness criterion has been proposed, as will be discussed later.[45]

The revised AVMSD recommends that 'stand-alone parts of online newspapers featuring audiovisual programmes or user-generated videos' should be regulated as AVMS 'where those parts can be considered dissociable from their main activity'.[46] On the contrary, video clips that are embedded in the editorial content of online newspapers or magazines should not fall within scope of the revised AVMSD.[47] An indicator of the embeddedness of the audiovisual offer within the editorial content is the existence of links between the two, which render the former 'merely an indissociable complement' to the latter.[48] Alongside video clips the AVMSD also mentions animated images such as Graphic Interchange Formats (GIFs) as a further example of content that should not be considered to fall in scope.[49] The explicit mention of GIFs departs from the AVMSD's technological neutrality paradigm.[50] Also, the wording of the second sentence of recital 6 raises the question as to whether only video clips need to be embedded in editorial content so as not to be regulatable or whether this also applies to GIFs. Arguably, GIFs would equally need to perform an independent function so as not to be captured by the AVMSD. Ofcom also confirmed that GIFs do not constitute a programme, and do not hence fall within the scope of the AVMSD, unless they are used within a programme.[51] The duration of GIFs varies, and the dividing line between them and short animated cartoon videos is blurred but is in any case immaterial under the revised AVMSD.

The following section will consider the ways in which EU and ex-EU legislators and regulatory authorities have interpreted the AVMSD and have applied the Directive's requirements to hybrid services offered by the press. Before doing so, it is worth noting that the AVMSD is silent as to whether broadcast services need to be licensed

[44] Ofcom, 'Response to consultation on Directive 2010/13/EU on audiovisual media services (AVMSD)' <https://www.ofcom.org.uk/__data/assets/pdf_file/0019/81253/avms_directive_consultation_respons e_ofcom_uk_october_2015.pdf> accessed 5 September 2022, 9; 'Position paper of the Federal Republic of Germany on the Revision of the Audiovisual Media Services Directive (AVMSD)), 3 November 2051 <https://digital-strategy.ec.europa.eu/en/library/contributions-received-public-bodies-avmsd-pub lic-consultation> accessed 25 January 2024; J Weinand, *Implementing the EU Audiovisual Media Services Directive: Selected issues in the regulation of AVMS by national media authorities of France, Germany and the UK* (Nomos 2018) 689 (hereafter Weinand, *Implementing the EU AVMSD*); see A Lange, 'Contribution to the consultation of the European Commission on the Directive on Audiovisual Media Services' <https:// digital-strategy.ec.europa.eu/en/library/contributions-received-individuals-and-research-avmsd-public-consultation> accessed 25 January 2024, 9.

[45] Department for Culture, Media and Sport, 'Up next: The government's vision for the broadcasting sector', April 2022 <https://assets.publishing.service.gov.uk/government/uploads/system/uploads/attachme nt_data/file/1071939/E02740713_CP_671_Broadcasting_White_Paper_Accessible__1_.pdf> accessed 29 September 2022 (hereafter DCMS, 'Up next').

[46] AVMSD 2018, rec 3.

[47] ibid rec 6.

[48] ibid rec 3.

[49] ibid rec 6.

[50] L Woods, 'Video-sharing Platforms in the Revised Audiovisual Media Services Directive' (2018) 23(3) Communications Law 127, 133.

[51] Ofcom, 'On-demand programme services: who needs to notify to Ofcom? Guidance notes', 8 September 2021 <https://www.ofcom.org.uk/__data/assets/pdf_file/0021/224148/odps-scope-guidance.pdf>accessed 21 September 2022 (hereafter Ofcom, 'Guidance') para 3.10 d).

or merely notified. This is presumably because licensing pertains to the regulation of opinion formation and therefore falls within an area of limited EU competence, that of culture.[52]

8.3 Comparative Perspectives on the Regulation of Online Newspapers' Video Content

In view of the uncertainty as to the classification of online newspapers' video content under the AVMSD 2010, several NRAs, including Austria, Denmark, the Flemish Community of Belgium, Slovakia, and Sweden, classified video sections of online newspapers as non-linear AVMS.[53] Other regulators such as the Dutch *Commissariaat voor de Media* faced considerable resistance from the newspaper industry against the classification of their video sites as on-demand services.[54] In the following, the discussion will focus on the regulation of online newspapers' video content in Germany and the UK.

8.3.1   Germany

As already discussed, the online press is regulated in Germany under the label of 'telemedia with journalistic-editorial offerings'.[55] Content-related requirements are laid down in the Media Treaty, while questions of a commercial nature related to jurisdiction and the country of origin principle as well as the providers' information duties and their freedom from licensing and notification are laid down in the Telemedia Law (*Telemediengesetz*, TMG).[56] Journalistic due diligence obligations are also laid down in the Code of the German Press Council and, for print publications,

---

[52] Consolidated Version of the Treaty on the Functioning of the European Union [2016] OJ C202/1 (TFEU), art 167(4), (5); Deutscher Bundestag, 'Rundfunkrechtliches Zulassungserforderniss für Streaming-Kanäle. Vorgaben durch die EU-Richtlinie über Audiovisuelle Mediendienste', WD 10 – 3000 – 031/19 (Deutscher Bundestag 2019) <https://www.bundestag.de/resource/blob/656500/a55ea40c5 71c8cdde91d84c749c4389a/WD-10-031-19-pdf-data.pdf> accessed 25 January 2024 (hereafter 'Deutscher Bundestag, 'Rundfunkrechtliches Zulassungserforderniss') 8.

[53] KommAustria, *Tiroler Tageszeitung*, KOA 1.950/12-048, 9 October 2012 <https://www.rtr.at/medien/ aktuelles/entscheidungen/KOA_1.950-12-048.pdf> accessed 16 September 2022; Council for Broadcasting and Retransmission of the Slovak Republic, Decision No 12-14/43.680, 10 July 2012; The Swedish Press and Broadcasting Authority, Decisions 12/00777-00780 of 29 October 2012; E Machet, 'New Media & Regulation: Towards a Paradigm Shift? New Services and Scope: "What's In, What's out Revisited"', Comparative Background Document, 35th EPRA Meeting, 31 May–1 June 2012, Portorož <http://www. epra.org> accessed 25 January 2024 (hereafter Machet, 'New Media & Regulation) 17; G De Bueger, 'Supervising On-demand Audiovisual Media Services: Best practices and Methodology', Comparative Background Document, 38th EPRA Meeting, 2–4 October 2013, Vilnius <http://www.epra.org> 6 (hereafter De Bueger, 'Best practices'); see also J Weinand, 'The Implementation of the Audiovisual Media Services Directive by National Regulatory Authorities: National Responses to Regulatory Challenges' (2014) 5 Journal of Intellectual Property, Information Technology and E-Commerce Law 88 fn 20ff.

[54] De Bueger, 'Best practices' (n 53) 12.

[55] MStV, §19; see Chapter 3, 72.

[56] Telemediengesetz of 26 February 2007 (BGBl. I S. 179, 251; 2021 I S. 1380), last amended by way of art 3 of Law of 12 August 2021 (BGBl. I S. 3544) (hereafter TMG).

in the press laws of the *Länder*.[57] Compliance with these legal instruments and enforcement of their standards is overseen by the Press Council, in the case of print and online or online only journalistic-editorial telemedia subject to the Council's jurisdiction. Most German publishers' print and online offerings are self-regulated under the Code of the German Press Council.[58] This includes their presence on social media platforms. Journalistic-editorial telemedia offered by TV and radio broadcasters are supervised by the state media authorities (*Landesmedienanstalten*). As already discussed, a controversial feature of the new Media Treaty is the extension of the state media authorities' competence. They are now also responsible for 'other commercial, journalistic-editorial telemedia offers' whose providers have not yet joined the German Press Council or a still to be established recognized self-regulatory body.[59] An important factor differentiating the regime applicable to on-demand services in Germany compared to other EU or ex-EU countries is the absence of a notification requirement.[60] In the UK, on-demand service providers need to submit a formal notification to Ofcom on pain of sanction.[61] In Germany, no such notification is needed.

The dilemma as to the appropriate legal framework for hybrid online press offerings, namely the liberal regime concerning the press or the more restrictive one for on-demand services, has been resolved in Germany in favour of the former as far as the legacy media are concerned. The presumption is that journalistic-editorial telemedia are press-like and are hence subject to the same due diligence obligations as the periodic print media. The understanding of the 'online press' in §19(1)1 MStV is wide, encompassing both text and still images as well as video and audio content.[62] This aligns with the prevailing constitutional view according to which the 'online press' should benefit of press freedom, similarly to its offline counterpart, rather than of broadcasting freedom.[63] At the same time, the line between 'press' and 'broadcasting' is drawn in constitutional terms according to the typical look and feel and the mode of consumption of the medium in question.[64] It is hence necessary to assess whether the service in question primarily consists of moving images or of written content.

In the case of a hybrid service which includes a catalogue of videos, it is necessary to determine if this catalogue is a self-standing service or whether it is merely a supplementary subsection that does not make out the principal purpose of the service. The

---

[57] German Press Code <https://www.presserat.de/en.html> accessed 21 October 2022; eg Landespressegesetz Nordrhein-Westfalen (LPresseG NRW), §6.

[58] S Niggermeier, 'Freiwillige Selbstkontrolle: Deutscher Presserat wirbt mit seiner Zahnlosigkeit' (*Über Medien*, 26 February 2021) <https://uebermedien.de/57673/deutscher-presserat-wirbt-mit-seiner-zahnlosigkeit/>.

[59] MStV, §19(1)2, (3). See Chapter 3, p 75 for the constitutional challenges this raises.

[60] TMG, §4; Weinand, *Implementing the EU AVMSD* (n 44) 391.

[61] Ofcom, 'On-demand programme services: Who needs to notify to Ofcom? Statement', 21 September 2022 <https://www.ofcom.org.uk/__data/assets/pdf_file/0019/224146/odps-scope-statement.pdf> accessed 28 September 2022 (hereafter Ofcom, 'Scope statement') 3ff.

[62] C Fiedler, '§109 MStV' in H Gersdorf and P Paal (eds), *Informations- und Medienrecht Kommentar* (Beck 2021) para 8.

[63] BVerfGE 152, 152 (hereafter BVerfG, *RTBF I*) para 95; BGH, 1 April 2004, I ZR 317/01 (*Schöner Wetten* case); BGH, judgment of 14 October 2010, (2011) *Archiv für Presserecht* 249 (*Any DVD* case); J Kahl, *Elektronische Presse und Bürgerjournalismus: Presserechtliche Rechte und Pflichten von Wortmedien im Internet* (Nomos 2013) 29f, 138.

[64] See Chapter 2, p 95.

decision will need to be made on a case-by-case basis, taking the form and content of the service in question into account.[65] While these criteria mirror those drawn up by the CJEU in *New Media Online* and incorporated in the AVMSD, they differ in one respect. Even though Germany successfully campaigned in favour of dropping the criterion of TV-likeness during the AVMSD negotiations, the German Media Treaty curiously holds on to it as regards the subcategory of TV-like telemedia.[66] It is uncertain whether this requirement will have any implications in practice beyond emphasizing the distinction between on-demand services that consist of moving images and those that primarily include text and still images, as is the case with big parts of the online press.[67]

In Germany, a far thornier question than that of the classification of audiovisual content available on newspaper websites pertains to the regulation of live-streams as on-demand services (telemedia) or rather as linear broadcasts. Telemedia are defined in juxtaposition from telecommunications and broadcasting.[68] Similarly to the UK, broadcasting services require a licence and need to comply with content standards and commercial restrictions,[69] while telemedia do not need to be licensed nor are they subject to quantitative advertising limits.[70] Broadcasting is defined as 'the provision and transmission of journalistic-editorial offers for the general public for simultaneous reception in moving images or sound along a schedule, using telecommunication'.[71] Key characteristic of broadcasting is the existence of a schedule as becomes evident from the definition of a 'broadcasting service' as 'a sequence of contents arranged and timed on the basis of a schedule'. 'Broadcasting schedule' is defined as 'the permanent definition of the content and times on the basis of a schedule of broadcasts, which is determined by the broadcaster and cannot be changed by the user'.[72] The requirement of a schedule has been contentious in academic writing both as regards the needed duration of the overall programme and the minimum number of broadcasts as well as their frequency and regularity.[73]

These questions came to the fore in the case of three live-streams offered online by *Bild*, Germany's highest circulation newspaper. The three live-streams covered current affairs from the areas of politics, sport, and entertainment. Two of them were transmitted weekly on a fixed day and time, while the third one was streamed daily, on an ad hoc basis, linked to specific events. All of them could also be consumed on an on-demand basis. None of them had been licensed as required for broadcasting.[74] The

[65] C Fiedler, '§74 MStV' in H Gersdorf and P Paal (eds), *Informations- und Medienrecht Kommentar* (Beck 2021) paras 18ff (hereafter Fiedler, '§74 MStV').

[66] MStV, §74 MStVff.

[67] ibid para 11.

[68] MStV, §2(1)3: 'Telemedia means all electronic information and communications services, as far as they are not telecommunications services pursuant to Article 3 no. 24 of the Telecommunications Act, which consist entirely in the conveyance of signals across telecommunications networks or telecommunications-supported services pursuant to Article 3 no. 25 of the Telecommunications Act, or broadcasting pursuant to sentences (1) and (2).'

[69] MStV, §§3ff, 52ff, 59ff, 69ff.

[70] MStV, §§17, 74 S. 2.

[71] MStV, §2(1)1.

[72] MStV, §2(2) Nos 1, 2.

[73] F Ferreau, 'Die Zukunft der Rundfunkregulierung. Von der Pandemie-Gegenwart ins Zeitalter des Medienstaatsvertrags' (2020) 3 Archiv für Presserecht 197, 198 (Ferreau, 'Rundfunkregulierung').

[74] RStV, §§20ff (now MStV, §§52ff).

Commission on Licensing and Supervision (*Kommission für Zulassung und Aufsicht, ZAK*) decided that these streams constituted broadcasting as they offered linear programmes for simultaneous viewing in accordance with a programme schedule. The streams often reached a large audience and hence could not qualify for an exemption for broadcasts with less than 500 potential simultaneous viewers.[75] The competent state media authority of Berlin Brandenburg decided that the streamed programmes had to be discontinued unless a licence was applied for. The *Bild* newspaper argued that the programmes were not streamed based on a pre-defined schedule, and that they were, in any case, mainly watched on demand. More importantly, they were only complementary and subsidiary to the publisher's press offerings and should hence enjoy the same rights to press freedom and freedom from licensing. It was further argued that, even if the live-streams were considered as broadcasting, they should equally be exempt from licensing. Online transmission was not characterized by the same spectrum scarcity and high cost as linear broadcasting and should therefore not be subject to the same restrictions.[76]

Bild was successful in obtaining interim measures but was ultimately defeated.[77] The Administrative Court Berlin decided that all three live-streams fulfilled the criteria to be characterized as broadcasting and therefore they required a licence.[78] It observed that the live-streams were designed for simultaneous reception. The fact that they were also available on demand was immaterial. Live transmission was particularly important for the publisher. Had it been otherwise, *Bild* would have discontinued the live-streams. In the Court's view, the fact that Bild is one of the biggest press publishers in Europe underscored its intention to partake in the process of public opinion formation by complementing its print products with live-streams. Live-streaming was especially relevant in this process and therefore needed to be regulated more strictly. The Court held that *Bild*'s success in the press sector in tandem with its multimedia presence increased the intensity (*Wirkungsintensität*) and suggestive power (*Suggestivkraft*) of the streamed programmes, which were also characterized by great immediacy (*Aktualität*) as they pertained to current affairs.[79] The streams were similar to and in competition with public service and private TV broadcasts, especially given that the live-stream format invited direct communication with the public by way of chats, discussions, and user comments.

The Court also made observations concerning the contentious concept of a schedule. It held that no schedule existed in the case of a single transmission if no further broadcasts were in preparation. Where more than one broadcast had been transmitted, as in the case of the *Bild* live-streams, it was immaterial if this had taken place at fixed times or ad hoc, provided there was some regularity in the transmission. Advance programme notifications to users also suggested the existence of a schedule. In the case at hand, users received push notifications on their mobile phones before the start of each stream. All these factors led the Court to conclude that the

---

[75] RStV, §2(3) No 1.
[76] VG Berlin, 26 September 2019, VG 27K 365/18, para 25.
[77] VG Berlin, 19 October 2018, VG 27L 364/18; OVG Berlin, 2 April 2019, 11S 72/18.
[78] VG Berlin, 26 September 2019, VG 27K 365/18.
[79] See Chapter 2, p 15.

Bild live-streams fulfilled the criterion of a schedule. The Court further observed that the unlicensed linear transmission of broadcasts was not allowed as an annex to the company's publishing business. The fact that the undertaking's main line of business was in the press sector was immaterial, and the licensing requirement applied regardless of the lack of spectrum scarcity. *Bild* did not appeal against this judgment, instead applying successfully for a licence for its live-streamed offerings.[80]

Bild's questioning of the need for the continuous application of the licensing requirement in the digital era echoes relevant criticism in academic writing. Licensing was conceived as a means to create an externally pluralistic landscape in conditions of spectrum scarcity. Given that this scarcity is not prevalent online, the need for licensing as a regulatory instrument needs to be justified otherwise and its fundamental rights implications to be weighed in.[81] A possible justification for licensing could reside in the need to protect the process of free opinion formation from the abusive exercise of media power. This justification aligns with the German constitution's understanding of broadcasting freedom.[82] However, it raises the question as to why, in the age of YouTube, linear services pose a greater risk to the process of opinion formation compared to non-linear ones. The immense influence of on-demand services can hardly be ignored.

The state media authorities have consistently argued for a relaxation of the licensing requirement for streaming services and for its replacement by a notification requirement. An impetus for these demands was given by ZAK decisions requiring the licensing of the 2017 men's handball WM live-streams by the Deutsche Kreditbank as well as of the video game live-streams 'PietSmitTV', 'Grongh', and 'GronghTV'.[83] While live-streaming provider Grongh obtained a licence, PietSmit chose to discontinue the live-streams to avoid the bureaucratic burden associated with licensing.[84] A broadcasting licence, beyond its cost implications, comes with increased duties to comply with advertising and protection of minors regulations. In the meantime, the Interstate Media Treaty has taken a deregulatory approach by exempting broadcasting services from the licensing requirement when they are of little significance for individual and public opinion formation or reach, on average, fewer than 20,000 simultaneous users over a period of six months.[85] This so-called *Bagatellrundfunk* (petty broadcasting) exemption should now cover a big part of the game live-streaming services.

---

[80] See Bild, 'Mediathek' <https://www.bild.de/tv/mediathek/livestream/startseite-77204148.bild.html> accessed 26 October 2022.

[81] S Dreyer and W Schulz, 'Schriftliche Stellungnahme zum zweiten Diskussionsentwurf eines Medienstaatsvertrags der Länder vom Juli 2019' (*Hans-Bredow-Institut*, 9 August 2019) <https://www.hans-bredow-institut.de/en/publications/schriftliche-stellungnahme-zum-zweiten-diskussionsentwurf-eines-medienstaatsvertrages-der-laender>accessed 30 May 2020, 7.

[82] F Ferreau, 'Livestreaming in der Corona-Krise—der Anfang vom Ende des linearen Rundfunkbegriffs?' (2020) 5 Kommunikation & Recht 1 (Ferreau, 'Livestreaming').

[83] Deutscher Bundestag, 'Rundfunkrechtliches Zulassungserforderniss' (n 52) 5.

[84] Ö Kajali, 'Gronkh—Letsplayer erhält Rundfunklizenz; strenge Jugendschutzregeln greifen' (*GameStar*, 14 January 2018) <https://www.gamestar.de/artikel/gronkh-letsplayer-beantragt-rundfunklizenz,3324674.html>; 'Keine Rundfunklizenz: PietSmiet schaltet PietSmiet TV ab' (*GamesWirtschaft*, 3 May 2017) <https://www.gameswirtschaft.de/politik/rundfunklizenz-pietsmiet-tv-offline/> accessed 19 October 2022.

[85] MStV, §54(1). cf the previous threshold of at least 500 potential simultaneous users under RStV, §2(3) No 1.

Moreover, the massive surge of live-streaming during the pandemic has paved the way for a simplified notification procedure in the case of cultural, religious, and educational offerings.[86] The state media authorities agreed to provisionally waive the licensing requirement in their case.[87] While this is a temporary measure only, it may pave the way for a more fundamental reconsideration of broadcasting regulation in the digital era. Such a reconsideration would need to take account of the declining TV and rising online news consumption.[88] It has therefore been argued that linear services appear somewhat overregulated and non-linear ones somewhat underregulated from a constitutional point of view.[89] This would militate in favour of a halfway solution. Alternatively, the levelling of the playing field between linear and on-demand services might materialize by way of a rise in regulation for on-demand services. This would, however, be an unlikely outcome. In regulatory terms, levelling of the playing field usually signifies the relaxation of laws applicable to incumbent services while those applicable to newcomers are somewhat relaxed.[90] As already discussed, the AVMSD questionably aligned the level of protection of minors by pitching minimum harmonization halfway between the previous requirements for linear and non-linear providers.[91]

Some argue that the mode of transmission is an unsuitable regulatory benchmark altogether. In their view, regulation should not rest on the technical characteristic of linearity but on the journalistic-editorial influence on public opinion formation.[92] The criterion of impact is indeed relevant in fundamental rights analysis and might yield more equitable results in a convergent media landscape.[93] However, a powerful objection to the use of this criterion as the yardstick for regulation stems from its subjective nature.[94] All media have a potential impact on society, and neither their audience reach nor the value attributed to them are safe yardsticks to measure this impact.[95] Social sciences have not yet yielded clear findings on the effect of the dynamic contemporary news ecosystem on citizen knowledge and democratic decision-making.[96]

---

[86] At the same time, notification for web only radio is not sufficient anymore. A licence is required except for radio programmes that had already been notified prior to the entry into force of the MStV. These are deemed to be licensed programmes under MStV, §54(3).

[87] State Media Authorities, 'Zulassung' <https://www.die-medienanstalten.de/themen/zulassung> accessed 19 October 2022.

[88] See Chapter 2, p 30.

[89] Ferreau, 'Livestreaming' (n 82) 1.

[90] A Savin, 'New Directions in EU Digital Regulation Post-2015: Regulating Disruption' (2020) 11(1) Union University Law School Review (Pravni zapisi) 93, 108.

[91] See Chapter 2, p 25.

[92] C-M Leeb and F Seiter, 'Rundfunklizenzpflicht für Streamingangebote?' (2017) 61(7) Zeitschrift für Urheber- und Medienrecht 573, 575; Ferreau, 'Rundfunkregulierung' (n 73) 201.

[93] See Chapter 2, pp 15, 28; *Animal Defenders International v United Kingdom*, App no 48876/08, 22 April 2013, para 119.

[94] M Cornils and K Liesem, 'Stellungnahme zum Diskussionsentwurf eines Medienstaatsvertrages der Rundfunkkommission der Länder' (*Mainzer Medieninstitut*, NK) <https://www.mainzer-medieninstitut.de/stellungnahme-des-mainzer-medieninstituts-zum-diskussionsentwurf-eines-medienstaatsvertrages/> accessed 29 May 2020 (hereafter Cornils and Liesem, 'Stellungnahme') 3; C Böhler, 'Notwendigkeit einer Rundfunklizenz beim Betrieb von Video-streaming-Portalen' (2017) 33(8) Computer und Recht 541, 545.

[95] Recommendation CM/Rec(2011)7 of the Committee of Ministers to member states on a new notion of media, 21 September 2011, para 13.

[96] Cornils and Liesem, 'Stellungnahme' (n 94) 3.

For now, the formal criterion of linearity, crude though it may be, serves as a proxy for impact that is more conducive to legal certainty.

In the case of the *Bild* live-streams, the Court adhered to the notion that the linear mode of transmission meant enhanced influence on the process of public opinion formation. Interestingly, it argued that this impact was heightened by *Bild*'s dominant multimedia presence. The fact that *Bild* is first and foremost a press publisher did not lead to a loosening of the regulatory grip but to its tightening. This is not least because *Bild* was perceived to be competing in the same turf with broadcasters such as ARD or ZDF, SAT.1, or RTL. So long as a rethinking of broadcasting policy proceeds in baby steps, while convergence advances in leaps and bounds, a spillover to the press sector in an ad hoc manner, by regulatory (over-)reach and jurisprudential fiat, is bound to occur. Such regulatory spillover is likely to take hold the more the press seeks to diversify its revenue beyond readers and advertising to sources such as live-streamed digital only and hybrid events.[97]

8.3.2 United Kingdom

In the UK, the regulation of on-demand AVMS was initially delegated to the Authority for Television on Demand (ATVOD). In March 2010, Ofcom, the UK communications regulator, designated ATVOD, a previously self-regulatory body, as the co-regulator for on-demand programme services (ODPS).[98] In line with the AVMSD 2010, the Communications Act 2003, as originally enacted, stipulated that an on-demand programme service had as its principal purpose 'the provision of programmes the form and content of which are comparable to the form and content of programmes normally included in television programme services'.[99] ATVOD had the power to establish whether a service fell within the ODPS definition, to require the notification of an on-demand service, and to ensure that it complied with statutory obligations, including editorial content rules on material likely to incite hatred, material harmful for minors, and on commercial references.[100] Determinations made by ATVOD could be appealed to Ofcom.[101] Service providers were obliged to pay an annual fee to ATVOD in relation to each notified service. The tariff for regulatory fees was the subject of a yearly public consultation and needed to be approved by Ofcom.[102] These

---

[97] See eg Die Zeit, 'Zeit Veranstaltungen' <https://verlag.zeit.de/veranstaltungen/> accessed 26 October 2022; 'World press trends preview: Publishers upbeat about future business' (*World Association of News Publishers*, 30 November 2021) <https://wan-ifra.org/2021/11/world-press-trends-preview-publishers-upbeat-about-future-business/>.

[98] The term 'on-demand programme service' (ODPS) is used instead of 'on-demand audiovisual media service' in the Communications Act 2003, s 368A.

[99] Communications Act 2003, s 368A(1)(a).

[100] See ATVOD, 'Statutory rules and non-binding guidance for providers of on-demand programme services (ODPS)', 3 May 2012 <https://www.ofcom.org.uk/__data/assets/pdf_file/0023/39173/a2.pdf> accessed 16 September 2022.

[101] See Ofcom, Procedures for the handling of appeals of ATVOD decisions in relation to what constitutes an On-Demand Programme Services [sic], 15 August 2012 <https://www.ofcom.org.uk/__data/assets/pdf_file/0016/33451/appeals-procedures.pdf> accessed 16 September 2022.

[102] ATVOD, 'Regulated services. Regulatory fees' <https://web.archive.org/web/20131122083406/http://www.atvod.co.uk/regulated-services/regulatory-fees> accessed 16 September 2022.

co-regulatory arrangements ended on 31 December 2015. Since 2016, Ofcom is the sole regulator for video on demand.[103]

The regulation of audiovisual material made available on the website of a print publication was the subject of some of the first appeals made to Ofcom against ATVOD scope determinations. In the following, we will concentrate on the *Sun Video* case, but will also draw insights from subsequent Ofcom decisions. *Sun Video* was one of eight determinations made by ATVOD in cases involving audiovisual material on newspaper/magazine websites.[104] ATVOD argued that the video section of the *Sun's* website constituted an ODPS given that the video content was aggregated on a discrete section of the website, which was presented as a consumer destination in its own right, and the programmes could be made sense of without reference to the newspaper offering and were comparable to the form and content of TV programmes. Newsgroup Newspapers appealed ATVOD's determination in *Sun Video* to Ofcom. In December 2011, Ofcom overturned the determination and upheld the appeal.[105] After Ofcom's appeal, ATVOD withdrew the other seven determinations.

Ofcom's decision in *Sun Video* provided a thorough examination of section 368A(1) of the Act given that the case raised 'important and difficult questions under complex new legislation and for which no precedents exist'.[106] Ofcom set aside ATVOD's determination on the ground that it placed too much emphasis on the video section of the *Sun's* website without taking sufficient account of the totality of what was provided on the website. Moreover, Ofcom criticized ATVOD for not sufficiently considering the written content of the *Sun's* website and its relationship to the audiovisual material. On the basis of its own review of the evidence available both at the time of ATVOD's determination and at the time of the appeal, Ofcom reached the conclusion that the video section of the *Sun's* website did not have the principal purpose of providing audiovisual material.

Ofcom considered that an on-demand programme service would be more likely to have its own homepage or to be catalogued and accessed via a separate section of the relevant website; be presented or styled as a television channel; have substantial duration/complete programmes that can be watched independently, rather than 'bite-sized' clips; have no or a limited number of access/content links between the audiovisual material and other content; and have more prominent audiovisual than written material. These characteristics are non-determinative.[107] Therefore, a service having the required principal purpose would not need to display all of them; the presence

[103] Ofcom, 'Ofcom brings regulation of "video-on-demand" in house', 14 October 2015 <https://www. ofcom.org.uk/about-ofcom/latest/media/media-releases/2015/1520333>.

[104] Elle TV; Sunday Times Video Library; News of the World Video; Sun Video; Telegraph TV; Guardian Video; The Guardian YouTube Channel; FT Video; The Independent Video. After the end of ATVOD's <https://webarchive.nationalarchives.gov.uk/ukgwa/20160704204536/http://stakeholders.ofcom.org.uk/ broadcasting/on-demand/atvod-archives/determinations/> accessed 16 September 2022.

[105] Ofcom, Appeal by NewsGroup Newspapers Limited against a notice of determination by ATVOD that the provider of the service 'Sun Video' that the provider of the service 'Sun Video' has contravened section 368BA of the Communications Act 2003, 21 December 2011 <https://webarchive.nationalarchives.gov. uk/ukgwa/20160704204456/http://stakeholders.ofcom.org.uk/broadcasting/on-demand/atvod-archives/ scope-appeals/> accessed 16 September 2022 (hereafter Ofcom, *Sun Video*).

[106] ibid para 4.

[107] ibid para 82.

of some of them could possibly suffice. In Ofcom's view, the video section of the *Sun* website did not meet these criteria given that it did not have its own homepage, it was not presented as a consumer destination in its own right, its audiovisual material lacked independence and was of short duration, there were access and content links between the audiovisual material and other content of the website, and finally, the accompanying written material was more prominent. Given its negative finding on the principal purpose, Ofcom did not need to consider the second requirement of section 368A(1)(a) of the Act at the time, that is, the comparability of the video section to the form and content of television programmes.

Ofcom's decision in *Sun Video* left no doubt that there is some room for the video sections of online newspapers and magazines to be considered on-demand AVMS if they are sufficiently substantial and self-standing.[108] This ambivalence in Ofcom's legal treatment of newspapers' and magazines' video sections was also reflected in ATVOD's 'Guidance on who needs to notify'. This Guidance, also known as 'Scope Guidance', advised on the criteria that are applied by ATVOD when deciding whether a service falls under the definition of an ODPS.[109] The Guidance was subsequently revised so as to better reflect ATVOD's experience since 2010.

The new Scope Guidance contained a non-exhaustive list giving some introductory examples of services that were likely to be considered as ODPS such as catch-up services for broadcast television channels and television programme archive services. It further included two lists of factors to be taken into account so as to decide, first, whether a service was TV-like, and, secondly, whether it had the principal purpose of providing TV-like content.[110] ATVOD explicitly mentioned that the factors in the second of these lists were not determinative, but the same presumably applied also to the first list. These factors were derived from Ofcom Appeal decisions in several cases. The first of these lists is less relevant for our purposes, especially given that the TV-likeness criterion is not included in the current definition of ODPS. Having said that, the DCMS has proposed a revival of this criterion in a bid to align the rules for traditional broadcasters and video on demand services.[111] The aim of this proposal, now taken up in the draft Media Bill, is to ensure that the 'largest, most TV-like' video on demand services are subject the same or similar obligations on standards including harm and offence, accuracy, fairness, and privacy as UK broadcasters.[112] The proposed revamp of ODPS regulation is therefore likely to be aimed at services like Netflix and

---

[108] See ibid paras 78, 79. This view is also taken by Schulz, *Vorschlag für eine Richtlinie* (n 13) 12; D Mac Síthigh, 'Co-Regulation, Video-on-Demand and the Legal Status of Audio-Visual Media' (2011) 2(1) International Journal of Digital Television 51; contra Chavannes and Castendyk, 'Art. 1 AVMSD' (n 17) para 28; see Valcke and Lefever, *Media Law* (n 17).

[109] ATVOD, Guidance on who needs to notify. Application and Scope of the Regulations for Video on Demand (VOD) services, edn 2, 8 April 2010 <https://webarchive.nationalarchives.gov.uk/ukgwa/20100507150933mp_/http://www.ofcom.org.uk/tv/ifi/vod/obligation/Guidance.pdf> accessed 20 September 2022.

[110] ATVOD, Guidance on who needs to notify. Application and Scope of the Regulations for Video on Demand (VOD) services, edn 4.0, 5 February 2014.

[111] DCMS, 'Up next' (n 45) 37; see DCMS, 'Consultation outcome: Audience protection standards on Video-on-Demand services', 31 August 2021 <https://www.gov.uk/government/consultations/audience-protection-standards-on-video-on-demand-services> accessed 29 September 2022.

[112] DCMS, 'Up next' (n 45) 37; Draft Media Bill, Explanatory Notes, para 13 <https://commonslibrary.parliament.uk/research-briefings/cbp-9571/> accessed 17 May 2023.

Amazon Prime, which compete with UK services such as the BBC iPlayer, rather than at online newspapers' video catalogues.

The factors included in the second list relating to the 'principal purpose' criterion emphasized: the existence of a point of entry to a service with its own independent identity; the grouping together of videos in a distinct area; the degree and nature of any linkage between the video on demand content and other content; the question which of these types of content was the primary means of conveying the information sought to be conveyed; and the prominence, quantity and proportion, and relevance to the consumer of the (TV-like) programmes. Representatives of the newspaper industry raised strong concerns that the revised Scope Guidance sought to reopen the debate over regulation of their websites. They expressed their opposition to any statutory regulation of their content and sought clarification that 'newspaper websites do not fall under ATVOD's jurisdiction'.[113] ATVOD clarified that the revision did not intend to change the interpretation of the Regulations so as to bring services within their remit that were previously outside, but only to provide greater clarity.[114] At the same time, ATVOD did not agree that the AVMSD aimed to totally exclude from regulation all online services, which also contained the electronic version of a newspaper or magazine. Nor did it consider that the discussion concerning the classification of electronic press was closed by the Ofcom decision in the *Sun Video* case. Ofcom only held that at the relevant time the video section did not have the required principal purpose. It did not, however, rule out that the service might in future develop in a way that would bring it within the scope of regulation.

Since Ofcom took over as sole regulator of on-demand audiovisual content, it has clarified that such content provided by newspaper publishers would not meet the ODPS definition where it is 'embedded within the journalistic or editorial content of the service'.[115] This might also be the case where there are 'other links between the audiovisual offer and the main activity of providing news in written form', so that the video content would only be an 'indissociable complement' to the written content.[116] Such video content is already regulated under the press codes.[117] At the same time, a standalone section of a newspaper website dedicated to offering audiovisual content could fall within the scope of regulation where the videos are independent of the written press articles available on the site.[118]

Similar assessments need to be made when considering if a standalone section of a newspaper website which is dedicated to hosting user-generated videos on the site could be classified as a VSP. Even though such a section could in theory meet the VSP criteria, Ofcom considers this to be very unlikely in practice given that news providers

---

[113] ATVOD, 'Statement on the adoption of new guidance on the scope of the regulations relating to video on demand services', 5 February 2014, para 3.9 et seq.

[114] ibid para 4.9.

[115] Ofcom, 'Guidance' (n 51) para 3.6 b). The OPDS definition has been updated by the Audiovisual Media Service Regulations 2020, SI 2020/1062 that transposed the AVMSD 2018. The current ODPS definition is laid down in the Communications Act 2003, s 368A.

[116] Ofcom, 'Guidance' (n 51) para 3.18.

[117] See IPSO, 09833-21 *A Man v Mail Online*; IPSO, 07188-18 *Jones v Mail Online* both accessed 30 September 2022.

[118] Ofcom, 'Guidance' (n 51) para 3.18.

commonly exercise editorial control over content on their websites.[119] A video section on a newspaper website would therefore not meet the requirement for the classification as VSP that the provider should have no general control over the videos available on it.[120] Also, if such videos are embedded in the editorial content or if they are interlinked with it in a way that they appear to be only an indissociable complement of the main activity of providing news in written form, they would not meet the VSP definition either.[121] Ofcom acknowledges that the assessment whether a section of a website is dissociable may not always be straightforward and may depend on case-specific factors.[122] The users' perspective needs to be taken into account in this context. Ofcom considers that the following factors may be of relevance: the feel of a service to the users; the purpose, content, and form of the service; and the use, amount, and reach of video content compared with the rest of the service—where such information is available.[123]

The qualitative criterion of users' perception also informed the so-called 'step back' which Ofcom undertook in its *Sun Video* appeal decision. The aim of the 'step-back' was to have more general regard to the AVMSD framework, including by asking whether certain services competed with TV broadcasting. This question would help determine if users considered the audiovisual material on the *Sun*'s website as among their competing options to linear TV programmes.[124] Given that similarity to television has for now been removed from the definition of programmes in the context of the ODPS regime, users' perception concerns the independence of video content from the written text and, more generally, the way in which the service is presented to them.

As regards the purpose, content, and form of the service, Ofcom has identified the following relevant indicators: the way in which the service refers to itself and markets or positions itself against its competitors; the degree and nature of linkage between the programmes and other content; the comprehensiveness of the written articles and their comprehensibility without the aid of the accompanying video content; the prominence of the programmes in terms of the branding and structure of the service; the quantity and proportion of programmes in terms of both absolute numbers and viewing time compared to the written content; and the relevance of the programmes to the consumer.[125] Ofcom's indicators differ from the ones that ATVOD used in the past insofar as the service's architecture or the existence of a distinct point of entry are not decisive criteria. Such technical characteristics are prone to circumvention. Both Advocate General Szpunar and the CJEU advocated against them in *New Media Online*.[126] Having said that, Ofcom's Guidance, in line with the AVMSD scheme, posits that the existence of a distinct area of the website dedicated to the provision of

[119] Ofcom, 'Video-sharing platforms: Who needs to notify to Ofcom? Statement', 10 March 2021 <Ofcom (2021) statement-video-sharing-platforms-who-needs-to-notify.pdf> accessed 4 October 2022 (hereafter Ofcom, 'Video-sharing platforms statement').
[120] Communications Act 2003, s 368S(2)(c)(1).
[121] Ofcom, 'Video-sharing platforms statement' (n 119).
[122] Similar assessments need to be made when determining if a dissociable section of a service constitutes a VSP that may fall to be regulated under AVMSD 2018, arts 28aff.
[123] Ofcom, 'Guidance' (n 51) para 3.19.
[124] Ofcom, *Sun Video* (n 105), para 69.
[125] Ofcom, 'Guidance' (n 51) para 3.12.
[126] *New Media Online*, para 35; Opinion of AG Szpunar, *New Media Online*, para 32.

audiovisual content is still indicative of an AVMS. Indeed, the collation of video content in a standalone catalogue, in tandem with the capacity of programmes to be made sense of independently, must be of relevance as they suggest the offer of a predominantly audiovisual experience.

As for the rest, Ofcom's indicators largely mirror the factors that had been identified by ATVOD in its Scope Guidance. First, in the same way as ATVOD, Ofcom asks whether the programmes need to be viewed to receive the information, education, or entertainment being offered, whether they are the 'primary source of information and education'.[127] In the *London Real* case, Ofcom observed that the accompanying text to the over 1,000 long-format, audiovisual interviews available on the website was of secondary importance only. Other hybrid media offerings may present greater difficulties when attempting to rank different types of content, written and audiovisual, in order of importance.[128] Second, the independent function test, as articulated in the Ofcom Guidance, seeks to ascertain whether video services are independent of the journalistic activities both 'in content and form'.[129] Only then may they be considered a dissociable ODPS. However, the meaning of independence 'in content and form' is not entirely clear. Does the self-standing nature of the video content, as manifested by the absence of links and by its comprehensibility, without recourse to the written texts suffice to bring it in scope? Or does it need to also cover topics that are distinct from those covered in the written press articles? This restrictive interpretation of independence in the sense of a thematic autonomy would mean a further reduction of the scope for audiovisual style regulation of newspapers' video sections and has been partly embraced in academic writing.[130] It is likely that videos serving a purely complementary function to the written stories, in terms of their subject matter, while being visibly interlinked with them, will fall outside the regulatory net.

Third, Ofcom still pays attention to the preponderance of video content in quantitative terms. In the past, this raised the contentious question of whether the yardstick of assessment had to be the totality of a website or rather a specific subdomain. In *Sun Video*, Ofcom rebuked ATVOD for not having taken sufficient account of the totality of what was provided on the *Sun*'s website.[131] By contrast, in *New Media*, the Austrian regulators considered that it would be misguided to examine the entire range of services offered by a service provider.[132] This question has been resolved to a certain extent given that the definition of an AVMS now covers services whose principal purpose or that of 'a dissociable section thereof is devoted to providing programmes'.[133] The

[127] Ofcom, 'London Real' (n 43) 3.

[128] Katsirea, 'Electronic Press' (n 16) 148.

[129] Ofcom, 'Guidance' (n 51) fn 12 referring to DCMS, Consultation outcome: Audiovisual Media Services, Government response to public consultations on the government's implementation proposals, 24 July 2019 <https://www.gov.uk/government/consultations/requirements-for-video-sharing-platforms-in-the-audiovisual-media-services-directive/outcome/audiovisual-media-services-government-response-to-public-consultations-on-the-governments-implementation-proposals>accessed 27 September 2022, para 4.10.

[130] Fiedler, '§74 MStV' (n 65) para 20.

[131] Ofcom, *Sun Video* (n 105), para 5.

[132] See for a more detailed discussion Katsirea, 'Electronic Press' (n 16) 142; I Katsirea, 'Newspaper Websites as Audiovisual Media Services: The *New Media Online Gmbh* Preliminary Ruling' (2017) 1 European Law Review 92, 94.

[133] AVMSD 2018, art 1(1)(a)(i).

choice between a section of a service or a service as a whole no longer needs to be made as either of them can have the principal purpose of providing programmes.

The question of the preponderance of the audiovisual compared to the written content also arises in the context of VSP regulation. The Commission, in its Guidelines on the practical application of the 'essential functionality' criterion, recommends that both qualitative and quantitative indicators be used to assess the amount and relevance of audiovisual content. The quantitative assessment could take the number or the proportion of videos present on the platform as compared to other types of available content into account.[134] Still, comparing the quantity of video to that of written content may prove challenging. Taking the sheer volume of the former into account, one could argue that audiovisual content takes up more space and is therefore more prominent.[135]

Defining the exact amount of written content is not straightforward either, not least due to the hyperlinks present in most websites. In a different context, a US federal district court held that the Child Online Protection Act (COPA)'s requirement that the material 'as a whole' was designed to appeal to the prurient interest, was vague and unconstitutional, in view of the vastness of the internet which defeats an attempt to define 'the whole'. The Court observed that 'even the Web sites for online magazines, without considering the hyperlinks to off-site materials, have greater depth and breadth than their counterpart in print'.[136] Having said that, hyperlinks cannot necessarily be taken into account when assessing the amount of material on a website. *P110 Limited*, a YouTube channel, offered content such as live performances and documentaries, while also including links to other YouTube channels. Ofcom observed that such links were an ancillary element of the service rather than its principal purpose, so that material accessible through them could not be considered to be part of the service.[137] Despite these uncertainties when weighing written against audiovisual content, Ofcom concluded in *Sun Video* without further ado that a sixteen-paragraph article on Amy Winehouse's last recording was more prominent than the two pieces of audiovisual material that were embedded within it, the one three minutes and twenty-one seconds long, the other two minutes and thirteen seconds long.[138]

Finally, in interpreting the 'principal purpose' criterion, Ofcom has regard to the purposes of AVMS to 'serve the interests of individuals and shape public opinion' and to their capacity to have 'a clear impact on a significant proportion of the general public'.[139] At the same time, on-demand AVMS are considered to be 'different from

---

[134] Commission, 'Guidelines on the practical application of the essential functionality criterion of the definition of a "video-sharing platform service" under the Audiovisual Media Services Directive', 7 July 2020 [2020] OJ C223/02, 7.

[135] This is the reason why the quantitative approach has been rejected by other regulators such as the Dutch CvdM and the Belgian CSA. See Machet, 'New Media & Regulation' (n 53) 8; M Betzel, 'Finetuning Classification Criteria for On-Demand Audiovisual Media Services: The Dutch Approach' in IRIS Special, *The Regulation of On-demand Audiovisual Services: Chaos or Coherence?* (European Audiovisual Observatory 2011) 58; P Valcke and J Ausloos, 'Audiovisual Media Services 3.0: (Re)defining the Scope of European Broadcasting Law in a Converging and Connected Media Environment' in K Donders, K Pauwels, and J Loisen (eds), *The Palgrave Handbook of European Media Policy* (Palgrave Macmillan 2014) 319.

[136] *ACLU v Gonzalez*, 478 F. Supp. 2d 775 (2007), para 45.

[137] Ofcom, *P110 Limited*, 5 June 2017 <https://www.ofcom.org.uk/__data/assets/pdf_file/0021/102567/issue-330-broadcast-on-demand-bulletin.pdf> 43, 45.

[138] Ofcom, *Sun Video* (n 105), para 143 et seq.

[139] AVMSD 2018, rec 54; AVMSD 2010, rec 21.

television broadcasting with regard to the choice and control the user can exercise, and with regard to the impact they have on society'.[140] The availability of information on the reach of videos embedded in newspaper websites and on their relevance to consumers could provide greater insights into their impact. In any case, Ofcom's Guidance suggests that such material would only be classified as an ODPS if it was wholly unrelated to the rest of the newspaper's online offering and was housed in a distinct section of its website. One historic example of such a case is the transmission of Channel 5 programmes on the *Express* and *Daily Star* websites in the past. This is a rather exceptional occurrence so far, but such cross-media cooperation is likely to become more frequent in future.[141]

The only example of a newspaper video site that is currently regulated by Ofcom as an ODPS is that of the Mail Plus Briefings.[142] This is a *Daily Mail* website listing videos on thematic areas ranging from royal family gossip and politics to health and fitness, diet, and fashion.[143] There are no links between these videos and the newspaper's journalistic offering on the *Daily Mail* homepage though the videos are often accompanied by some written commentary. This is a more extensive video collection than that operated by other news publishers. For example, *The Telegraph*'s video section consists of a smaller collection of chronologically ordered, less frequently updated videos.[144] Also, Mail Plus Briefings videos have a distinct entry point and are occasionally far longer than those in *The Telegraph*'s video section, which is part of *The Telegraph*'s main website. However, as already mentioned, video length and, to a certain extent, website architecture should not be decisive criteria.

The regulation of UK online newspapers' video content by Ofcom may seem like 'the dog that never barked'.[145] However, another regulatory threat looms on the horizon. News publishers increasingly publish video content on VSPs as a teaser to attract viewers to their websites. Such content falls within IPSO's regulatory remit.[146] News publishers are concerned that it might also be regulated by Ofcom if the qualified 'news publisher exemption' in the AVMSD framework did not extend to such content. They argue that the regulation of their presence on VSPs as ODPS could have a detrimental effect on freedom of the press.[147] In the course of the Online Harms consultation, the government gave an assurance that 'the exemption for news publishers to protect freedom of speech' would apply to all their output including on VSPs.[148] However, Ofcom brushed aside the appeal to press freedom. It wryly explained that its

---

[140] AVMSD 2010, rec 58.

[141] Z Rahvar, *Die Zukunft des deutschen Presserechts im Lichte konvergierender Medien* (Nomos 2011) 108.

[142] Ofcom, 'List of on-demand programme service (ODPS) providers currently regulated by Ofcom' <https://www.ofcom.org.uk/__data/assets/pdf_file/0021/67710/list_of_regulated_video_on_demand_services.pdf> accessed 28 September 2022.

[143] The Mail Plus, 'Videos' <https://www.mailplus.co.uk/tv> accessed 28 September 2022.

[144] The Telegraph, 'Telegraph Video' <https://www.telegraph.co.uk/authors/t/ta-te/telegraph-video/> accessed 28 September 2022.

[145] Charlotte Dewar, IPSO Chief Executive, online meeting with the author on 13 October 2021.

[146] H Fenech, 'IPSO Blog: The Editor's Code of Practice and online video content' (*IPSO*, 11 August 2021) <IPSO Blog: The Editors' Code of Practice and online video content> accessed 30 September 2022.

[147] Ofcom, 'Scope statement' (n 61) para 2.14.

[148] UK Parliament, 'Online Harms consultation', 15 December 2020 <https://hansard.parliament.uk/commons/2020-12-15/debates/1B8FD703-21A5-4E85-B888-FFCC5705D456/OnlineHarmsConsultation> accessed 30 September 2022.

role is 'to interpret the statutory criteria to give effect to the intention of Parliament', and not 'to amend the ODPS scope requirements to create an additional exemption'.[149] This would be for the government and Parliament to decide. This means that if newspapers' video content made available on VSPs was dissociable from the written articles and met the principal purpose test, it would fall to be regulated as ODPS. This signals a warning bell for the press sector given that most large news publishers maintain extensive, self-standing video libraries on YouTube, and increasingly on TikTok.[150] Ofcom qualified the prospect of its regulatory grip extending to newspapers' video sections on VSPs by stating that 'any assessment of these issues is likely to be very finely balanced, particularly where the principal purpose of the service is potentially contentious, and will require careful consideration of the facts of each case.'[151] Such a finely balanced judgement may for example need to be made in order to determine the principal purpose of online newspapers' Instagram presence, which typically consists of compilations of both photos and videos. Having said that, the news video content of Instagram and with it the argument for regulation may be strengthened by the fact that the platform plans to prioritize videos in future, and to turn those under fifteen minutes to TikTok-like reels.[152]

8.4 Concluding Remarks

The increasing appetite for online news video consumption has brought to the fore the porous boundaries between press and broadcasting. While print and broadcast news stem from news organizations with an historically disparate journalistic ethos and regulatory framework, their rapprochement around online news video poses a challenge to these hitherto entrenched divides. The AVMSD framework, as implemented in Germany and the UK, largely shelters news publishers from audiovisual style regulation as regards video content made available on their websites. Nonetheless, the threat of regulation looms large. In Germany, the Damocles sword of regulation by the state media authorities hangs over online only providers' on-demand content following the extension of their competence under the new Media Treaty. Video content live-streamed by press publishers also risks falling under their purview as broadcasting. In the UK, video libraries operated by press publishers on VSPs risk being regulated by Ofcom as ODPS. While press publishers invoke their right to press freedom, regulatory authorities dismiss this claim by arguing that they are bound by the requirements of the law as it currently stands. In the case of online only news media, the impetus for the extension of the German state media authorities' regulatory remit came from the rising concern about dis- and misinformation. In the case of legacy media, the

[149] Ibid para 2.17.
[150] See e.g. Daily Mail <https://www.youtube.com/channel/UCw3fku0sH3qA3c3pZeJwdAw>; The Sun <https://www.youtube.com/c/thesun/videos>; A Kersley, 'Journalism has suddenly taken off on TikTok: What publishers need to know' (*Press Gazette*, 23 June 2022) <https://pressgazette.co.uk/journalism-on-tiktok/> accessed 25 January 2024.
[151] Ofcom, 'Scope statement' (n 61) para 2.19.
[152] C Tobitt, 'Instagram reels: Why news publishers are positive about platform's shift to video' (*Press Gazette*, 3 August 2022) <https://pressgazette.co.uk/publishers-instagram-reels/>.

push for audiovisual style regulation, both in Germany and the UK, is less driven by *content*-related concerns as by *competition*-related concerns, by the desire to level the playing field with on-demand and broadcast news providers. As long as the opinion-forming power of media in a convergent media environment remains uncertain, it is likely that the tug of war between the broadcast sector's calls for fair competition and the press sector's privileged position will continue. In the following chapter, we will turn our attention to the impact of the contested relationship between the press and public service broadcasting (PSB) on the PSB online remit.

9

Regulating Public Service Broadcasting's Press-like Content

9.1 Introduction

Public service broadcasting (PSB) has faced searching questions about its *raison d'être* ever since its inception a century ago. In the UK, the stance of the press towards PSB has been ambivalent at best, hostile at worst. The British Broadcasting Company, as the BBC was called at the time, faced staunch opposition from certain press barons upon its establishment in the 1920s.[1] Fearing competition in the supply of news, they prevented the BBC from broadcasting news and information unless if it had been supplied by specific, authorized news agencies.[2] The only reason some press proprietors welcomed BBC's broadcasting monopoly was because they saw it as the lesser evil when compared to the alternative of commercial broadcasting and the concomitant direct competition for advertising revenues.[3] In Germany, a powerful press lobby has historically also been PSB's most vociferous critic. Already in the late 1950s, press publishers lamented PSB's licence fee-financed, competition-distorting monopoly.[4] Differently from their UK counterparts, major publishers in the German Newspaper Publishers and Digital Publishers Association (*Bundesverband Digitalpublisher und Zeitungsverleger*, BDZV) paradoxically championed the establishment of commercial broadcasting whilst lamenting the presence of advertising on PSB screens.[5]

In recent times, criticism has hardened, accusing PSB of being a relic from the age of spectrum scarcity, a paternalistic curb on viewer sovereignty and consumer choice, an unjustified intervention in an increasingly competitive marketplace. The amount of its funding, its governance, and increasingly the extent of its online remit have come under close scrutiny. In the following, we will first outline the European Union (EU) parameters for the funding of PSB's online services and compare them to the Council of Europe's position. The next section will focus on the German PSB ex ante assessment and on the exclusion of non-programme related press-like services from German PSBs' public service mandate. The emphasis will be on the *Tagesschau-App* case, a protracted dispute about the legality of the popular news app offered by the

---

[1] A Briggs, *The BBC: The First Fifty Years* (OUP 1985) 43, 51ff.

[2] R Coase, 'The Market for Goods and the Market for Ideas' (2022) 19(1) Econ Journal Watch 166, 170 (hereafter Coase, 'The Market for Goods'); D Cryle, 'The Press and Public Service Broadcasting: Neville Petersen's *News not Views* and the Case for Australian Exceptionalism' (2014) 151 Media International Australia 56, 59 (hereafter Cryle, 'The Press and Public Service Broadcasting').

[3] Coase, 'The Market for Goods' (n 2) 170; Cryle, 'The Press and Public Service Broadcasting' (n 2) 58.

[4] B Dernbach, 'Die Debatte um den öffentlich-rechtlichen Rundfunk ist eine mediale Inszenierung. Eine Analyse der Kritik der Zeitungsverleger und den Strategien von ARD und ZDF' (2019) 60 Jahrbuch für Christliche Sozialwissenschaften 195, 205.

[5] ibid.

Press Freedom and Regulation in a Digital Era. Irini Katsirea, Oxford University Press. © Irini Katsirea 2024.
DOI: 10.1093/oso/9780198858607.003.0009

German Association of Public Service Broadcasters (*Abeitsgemeinschaft der öffentlich-rechtlichen Rundfunkanstalten der Bundesrepublik Deutschland*, ARD), which was deemed anticompetitive by newspaper publishers. Over a decade, German courts considered whether the app, as offered on one particular day in 2011, was too text-heavy and hence 'press-like'. This specific dispute was finally resolved, but the feud about the limits of German PSBs' online presence, as manifested in both their websites and apps, is still ongoing. The last section will discuss attempts to limit the BBC's online remit. UK news publishers' grievances also centre on the written content available on the BBC website, but also on the 'soft' nature of some of its offerings, and on its move into the podcast market. The olive branch of peace the BBC proffered to the press by way of the Local Democracy Reporting Service will then be considered. Ultimately, the question will be posed whether formalistic technical criteria for delineating PSB's online remit from that of the press are conducive to creating a democratic media environment.

9.2 The EU and the Council of Europe Approach to PSB's Online Remit

Since the beginning of the nineties public service broadcasters (PSBs) across Europe have been faced with a cascade of appeals at EU level against the allegedly anticompetitive nature of the licence fee and other forms of state support received by them. Initially these attacks were spearheaded by commercial broadcasters claiming that the state financing of PSBs constituted unlawful state aid under Article 107 of the Treaty on the Functioning of the European Union (TFEU).[6] In 1997, the Amsterdam Protocol, which was annexed to the Treaty of Amsterdam, entered into force. Together with the addition of the largely symbolic Article 14 TFEU, it aimed to signal an increased EU awareness of the importance of PSB, and more largely of services of general economic interest (SGEI). However, the 1997 Amsterdam Protocol has not shielded from scrutiny Member States' institutional and regulatory arrangements for organizing and funding PSB.[7] It clarified that it is for the Member States to define the remit but preserved the Commission's competence to assess the effect of national funding mechanisms on trade and competition. Financial and content-related supervision are intertwined.[8] In order to guarantee the proper use of funds, the Commission must know the scope of the public service remit in each individual case. The unresolved conflict in the Amsterdam Protocol between culture and commerce, and the power

---

[6] The post-Lisbon Treaty numbering is used in this chapter except if text predates the entry into force of the Lisbon Treaty.

[7] The Protocol on the System of Public Broadcasting in the Member States, OJ C 340/109, 1997 (Amsterdam Protocol) states that 'The provisions of the Treaty establishing the European Community shall be without prejudice to the competence of Member States to provide for the funding of public service broadcasting insofar as such funding is granted to broadcasting organisations for the fulfilment of the public service remit as conferred, defined and organised by each Member State, and insofar as such funding does not affect trading conditions and competition in the Community to an extent which would be contrary to the common interest, while the realisation of the remit of that public service shall be taken into account.'

[8] C Bron, 'Financing and Supervision of PSB. European Legislation and Current National Developments Concerning Financial and Content-Related Supervision' (2010) 4 IRIS Plus 7 et seq.

struggle between the EU and Member States meant that the embrace of PSB's democratic importance remained half-hearted.[9] Crucially, the Amsterdam Protocol failed to safeguard the right of PSBs to follow their audience to wherever it would access their services.[10] Its attachment to the traditional understanding of PSB as 'broadcasting', meant that it opened up the risk of its subjection to a tight regulatory corset when becoming active online.[11]

The Commission gave more guidance as to the application of the Article 106(2) TFEU derogation and of the proportionality test to PSB in its 2001 Broadcasting Communication.[12] The Communication provided that the financing of PSBs through licence fees usually constitutes state aid. It required a clear and precise definition of PSB, the formal entrustment and independent monitoring of the public service mission, and the limitation of public funding to that necessary for the fulfilment of this mission. It clarified that the Commission's role was limited to checking 'for manifest errors' on a case-by-case basis.[13] Despite these clarifications, the complaints against the financing of PSB continued with increased vigour. In the digital era, the number of market players who contest PSB's online presence has increased. Publishers, keen to capture the attention of their viewers and readers and to protect their advertising revenues, as well as multimedia companies straddling the previously isolated domains of Information and Communications Technologies (ICTs), telecommunications, and audiovisual industries, entered into a headlong battle with PSBs. The battlefield is not so much the traditional television screen as the smartphone, the tablet, and the PC.

The overall attitude of the European Commission towards PSB's online remit has not been unfavourable. Already in its 2001 Broadcasting Communication, the Commission held that the public service remit might even include services that are not programmes in the traditional sense, such as online information services, if they address 'the same democratic, social and cultural needs of the society in question'.[14] In 2009, the Commission revised the 2001 Broadcasting Communication so as to adapt the definition of the public service remit to the exigencies of the new digital media landscape.[15] The 2009 Communication incorporated significant General Court case law as well as the Commission's post-2001 decision-making practice.[16] It clarified that the definition of the public service remit might reflect the diversification of activities in the digital age and include audiovisual services on all distribution platforms.[17]

---

[9] J Harrison and L Woods, *European Broadcasting Law and Policy* (CUP 2007) 295.
[10] C Nissen, *Public Service Media in the Information Society. Report prepared by the Council of Europe's Group of Specialists on PSB in the Information Society (MS-S-PSB)* (Council of Europe 2006) 46 (hereafter Nissen, *Public Service Media*); see J Trappel, 'Online Media within the Public Service Realm? Reasons to Include Online into the Public Service Mission' (2008) 14(3) Convergence 313, 320.
[11] Nissen, *Public Service Media* (n 10) 26.
[12] Communication from the Commission on the application of State aid rules to PSB, OJ C 320/5, 2001.
[13] ibid para 39.
[14] ibid para 34.
[15] Communication from the Commission on the application of State aid rules to PSB, OJ C 257/01, 2009 (hereafter 2009 Communication). For a more detailed discussion of the 2009 Communication and of the Commission's decisions on the PSB digital remit, see I Katsirea, 'Who Is Afraid of Public Service Broadcasting? The Digital Future of an Age-Old Institution under Threat' (2012) 31 Yearbook of European Law 416, 426ff, 432ff (hereafter Katsirea, 'Who Is Afraid of Public Service Broadcasting').
[16] *SIC v Commission* [2008] ECR II-1161; *TV2 Danmark v Commission* [2008] ECR II-2935; *TF1 v Commission* [2009] ECR II-471.
[17] 2009 Communication (n 15) paras 47, 81.

Nonetheless, the support of the European Commission for the online activities of PSBs has not been as unwavering as might seem at first sight. To a certain extent the Commission appreciates the importance of a broad public service remit for the social, democratic, and cultural life of the Union. At the same time, it fears that PSBs' online presence may obstruct the development of commercial operators' new business models.[18] One of the 2009 Communication's most innovative features has been the introduction of an ex ante assessment of significant new media services.[19] Member States have been asked to assess whether 'significant new audiovisual services envisaged by PSBs meet the requirements of the Amsterdam Protocol' by balancing the impact of a new service on the market with its value for society.[20] The Commission clarified that market impact, however substantial, did not necessarily trump public value. State funding for offers with predominantly negative effects on the market might be warranted based on their 'added value in terms of serving the social, democratic and cultural needs of society'.[21] The use of the 'added value' formula did not help to alleviate the concern that PSBs might need to refrain from activities that could be taken care of by commercial operators.[22]

Indeed, the Commission's market-oriented approach means that it is inclined to prioritize the more tangible competition concerns over the more abstract civic and cultural considerations. As a result, it risks being overly susceptible to commercial interests and to contest the need for a strong online PSB presence. The 2009 Communication specifically paid heed to the concerns of print media about the potential negative effects that state aid to PSBs could have on the development of new business models. It acknowledged the contribution of print media to an informed public and to democracy and emphasized the public interest in maintaining 'a plurality of balanced public and private media offer also in the current dynamic media environment'.[23] Fostering the duopoly of public and private media, as a feature of the European audiovisual model, is undoubtedly a laudable aim. Nonetheless, it raises the question of how far PSBs should make concessions to the aggressive demands of commercial media players and accept a restricted role online.

The EU's ambivalent position towards PSB stands in sharp relief against the Council of Europe's solid commitment to it, as evidenced in a series of legal instruments. Recommendation 1878 (2009) of the Parliamentary Assembly of the Council of Europe points out that 'Public service broadcasters should, in accordance with changing user demands, utilise new technologies to increase the accessibility of their services and offer new services including interactive and on-demand media services on all available platforms so as to reach all audiences, and in particular young people'.[24]

---

[18] ibid para 16.
[19] D Grespan, 'A Busy Year for State Aid Control in the Field of PSB' (2010) 1 European State Aid Law Quarterly 79, 86.
[20] 2009 Communication (n 15) para 84.
[21] ibid para 88.
[22] H Moe, 'Governing PSB: "Public Value Tests" in Different National Contexts' (2010) 3 Communication, Culture & Critique 207, 220.
[23] ibid.
[24] Recommendation 1878 (2009) of the Parliamentary Assembly of the Council of Europe of 25 June 2009 on Funding of PSB <https://pace.coe.int/en/files/17763> accessed 5 December 2022; T Mendel, *Public Service Broadcasting: A Comparative Legal Survey* (2nd edn, UNESCO 2011) para 18.

As PSB's digital transformation progresses, the Council of Europe prefers to refer to it by using the term 'public service media'.[25] The Parliamentary Assembly emphasizes the need for strong public service media that are able to counter the information disorder that characterizes the present media environment.[26] It urges Member States to ensure that public service media can make use of the internet, whilst being adequately funded so as to have the means to innovate 'in content, form and technology'. These exhortations take place in full awareness of the fact that it is not only states that pose challenges to public service media but also commercial competitors who allege distortions of the digital news marketplace.[27] The Council of Europe cautions that these challenges may weaken the capacity of public service media to counter disinformation and propaganda. This can be fatal at times of crisis, such as the recent Covid-19 pandemic, which heightens the importance of public service media as both an 'island of trust'[28] and as a force for social cohesion and integration.[29]

The following section will discuss the transposition of the Amsterdam Protocol in Germany as well as the ways in which the German legislator went above and beyond the Protocol's exigencies in a bid to assuage the longstanding tension between the PSBs and the press.

9.3 Reining in Public Service Broadcasters' Online Presence: The Case of Germany

The abovementioned Commission Communications served as the backdrop for a lengthy investigation into PSB funding in Germany. The Commission was concerned, among other issues, that the Interstate Treaty on Broadcasting (*Rundfunkstaatsvertrag*) did not sufficiently specify what kind of online services PSBs were allowed to provide. It merely stated that PSBs could offer print media that would accompany their programmes as well as telemedia services with 'programme related content'. It bemoaned the fact that the required link of telemedia to the programme was not fleshed out in a way that would allow for a clear determination of which online offerings contributed to the same democratic, social, and cultural needs of society as traditional television.[30]

---

[25] Recommendation (2007) 3 of 31 January 2007 of the Committee of Ministers of the Council of Europe on the remit of public service media in the information society <http://www.coe.int>, 2 July 2010; Declaration of the Committee of Ministers of 15 February 2012 on public service media governance <http://www.coe.int>; Recommendation CM/Rec (2012) 1 of 15 February 2012 of the Committee of Ministers of the Council of Europe on public service media governance <http://www.coe.int> accessed 5 December 2022.

[26] Assembly Resolution of 23 January 2019 of the Parliamentary Assembly of the Council of Europe on public service media in the context of disinformation and propaganda http://www.coe.int.

[27] ibid para 5.

[28] EBU Digital Strategy Group, *Media with a Purpose: Public Service Broadcasting in the Digital Age* (EBU 2002) quoted in J Bardoel and G Ferrell Lowe, 'From Public Service Broadcasting to Public Service Media' in J Bardoel and G Ferrell Lowe (eds), *From Public Service Broadcasting to Public Service Media* (Nordicom 2007) 20.

[29] Assembly Resolution 2419 (2022) of 25 January 2022 of the Parliamentary Assembly of the Council of Europe on the role of the media in times of crisis, para 6 <http://www.pace.coe.int> accessed 5 December 2022.

[30] Case E 3/2005, 24 April 2007, *Financing of public broadcasters in Germany*, C (2007) 1761 final, para 234.

The Commission closed this lengthy investigation on 24 April 2007 after Germany gave far-reaching commitments to transform its funding system.[31]

As part of the compromise reached between the European Commission and the German *Länder* (state aid compromise, *Beihilfekompromiß*), Germany introduced a so-called three-step test in the 12th Inter-State Broadcasting Treaty. This test has now been incorporated into the new Media Treaty.[32] The three-step test is modelled after the British public interest test (PIT), to be discussed later in this chapter. An important difference is that the responsibility for the conduct of the three-step test rests on the internal broadcasting councils, not on an external body as in the case of the PIT.[33] It has been questioned whether these internal bodies have the necessary distance from the management of the broadcasting corporations to be able to use their discretion in an independent manner.[34] The entire online arsenal of the ARD and of the ZDF (*Zweites Deutsches Fernsehen*) had to undergo the three-step test by the end of August 2010. The ARD had conducted thirty-five three-step tests by that date. It reportedly deleted over 100,000 individual documents that had been available online. However, all existing online offers were approved in the end, leading critics to describe this 'as a modest result of an almost megalomaniacal bureaucratic procedure'.[35]

Under the three-step test the broadcasting council of the responsible authority, ARD or ZDF, needs to check: first, whether a new or significantly amended digital service satisfies the democratic, social, and cultural needs of society; second, whether it contributes to media competition from a qualitative point of view; and, third, the associated financial cost. A significant amendment is particularly considered to exist where the overall content orientation of the digital service or its intended target audience changes.[36] The first step of the test replicates the wording of the Amsterdam Protocol. It is very general and does not provide specific criteria against which to measure a certain online offer. It requires broadcasting corporations to spell out the communication needs to which their services are responding.[37] However, it is hardly conceivable that there are services in whose defence no democratic, social, or cultural need can be brought forward. Broadcasting councils can plausibly argue that there is either a broad interest in a certain mainstream offering, in which case public broadcasting would act as 'trusted guide', or that there is a niche interest that private media with their profit-making orientation cannot cater for.[38]

---

[31] ibid.

[32] MStV, §32, paras 3–7.

[33] H Gersdorf, '§32 MStV' in H Gersdorf and P Paal (eds), *Informations- und Medienrecht Kommentar* (Beck 2021) para 2 (hereafter Gersdorf, '§32 MStV').

[34] ibid paras 39ff; J Kühling, 'Art. 5 GG' in H Gersdorf and P Paal (eds), *Informations- und Medienrecht Kommentar* (Beck 2021) para 72 (hereafter Kühling, 'Art. 5 GG'); N Wimmer, 'Der Drei-Stufen-Test nach dem 12. Rundfunkänderungsstaatsvertrag. Was ist und wer entscheidet über den Public Value öffentlich-rechtlicher Online-Angebote?' (2009) 25(8/9) Zeitschrift für Urheber- und Medienrecht 601, 608 (hereafter Wimmer, 'Drei-Stufen-Test').

[35] Institute of Media and Communications Policy, 'ARD' (Media Database, 2 December 2022) <https://www.mediadb.eu/en/data-base/international-media-corporations/ard.html> accessed 9 December 2022.

[36] MStV, §32(3)2.

[37] W Schulz, 'The Legal Framework for PSB after the German State Aid Case: Procrustean Bed or Hammock?' (2009) 2 Journal of Media Law 219, 236.

[38] Wimmer, 'Drei-Stufen-Test' (n 34) 606.

The second step is the core of the test. The Treaty indicates criteria to be taken into account so as to decide whether a certain offering is justified: the quantity and quality of already existing, freely available offers, the impact of the planned offering on all relevant markets, and its likely opinion-forming function.[39] This second step indirectly protects the interests of private providers, including those of the press, by examining the contribution of the planned offering to journalistic competition. This protection may, however, be more limited than appears at first sight given that PSB services are unlikely to be qualitatively inferior. A claim of added journalistic value will hence be plausible in most cases.[40] Also, the extent to which the impact on freely available offers will weigh in the overall assessment is uncertain.[41]

The third step consists of an assessment of the financial cost associated with the new or significantly amended offering. It is controversial whether a balancing exercise needs to be carried out between the journalistic added value of the proposed offering and the concomitant additional expenditure. It has been argued that this would be essential to protect licence fee payers' interests.[42] However, the Media Treaty does not require such a cost-benefit analysis. It is worth comparing §32(4) MStV to Article 8(1) (c) of the BBC Agreement.[43] The latter mentions the 'public value of the proposed change', which includes its value for money.[44] Whereas the UK public interest test was inspired by US theories of public sector management that gained increased currency in the 2004 BBC Charter review process against the backdrop of the Hutton enquiry, the German three-step test was introduced following the abovementioned state aid procedure and Commission decision. The calculation of the net-cost of the public service mission within the framework of the state aid procedure serves the aim of avoiding overcompensation, not of ensuring the most cost-effective use of public funds.[45] Consequently, it cannot be the aim of the three-step-test to introduce a new model of financial control beyond the control of overcompensation carried out by the Independent Commission for the Assessment of Financial Requirements of German Public Broadcasting (*Kommission zur Überprüfung und Ermittlung des Finanzbedarfs der Rundfunkanstalten*, KEF), the German PSB auditing commission.

The three-step test, similarly to other ex ante assessments introduced in the aftermath of the 2009 Communication, carried the promise of greater transparency and accountability and a more precise definition of the PSB online remit. PSB critics hoped that it would put an end to what they saw as PSB's boundless online expansion. They expected that it would even create an opportunity for the press and other private

---

[39] MStV, §32(4).

[40] Gersdorf, '§32 MStV' (n 33) para 19.

[41] ibid.

[42] Gersdorf, '§32 MStV' (n 33) paras 20ff.

[43] Agreement dated December 2016 between Her Majesty's Secretary of State for Culture, Media and Sport and the British Broadcasting Corporation. Cm. 9366, art 8 (1)(c).

[44] BBC, 'BBC iPlayer II: Public Interest Test', 19 October 2022 <https://downloads.bbc.co.uk/aboutthe bbc/reports/consultation/bbciplayerpitii/bbc-iplayer-pit-statement.pdf> accessed 9 December 2022, 35, 37ff.

[45] Rundfunkrat des Rundfunk Berlin-Brandenburg, Beschluss zu dem fernsehgebundenen Inhalt ARD Text in der überarbeiteten Fassung des Telemedienkonzepts vom 15. Juni 2010 <http://www.rbb-online. de/rundfunkrat/dst/entscheidungsbegruendung0.file.pdf>, 21 February 2011, 80; V Wiedemann, 'Kein Einfallstor für Marktprimat/Der Dreistufentest darf nicht missbraucht werden' (2009) 68 epd medien 3ff.

competitors to actively shape the PSB online remit, not least by participating in public consultations as part of the market impact assessment.[46] This expectation has been frustrated to a certain extent due to the gaping absence of tangible criteria by which to measure public value. Three-step tests carried out by the ARD and ZDF broadcasting councils have been tainted by subjectivity, exposing them to the accusation of bias and adding arrows to PSB critics' quiver.[47] Instead of overcoming PSB's legitimacy crisis by spelling out its significance, the tests risk becoming empty rituals of verification, thus further exacerbating the tension between the private and the public media sector.

The latest amendment of the Media Treaty with a view to reforming the public service remit and structure, which entered into force on 1 July 2023, allows PSBs greater flexibility to trial new telemedia concepts with restricted audiences for a maximum of six months before initiating the three-step test approval procedure.[48] Crucially, PSBs are also given the flexibility to move some of their channels online. It is uncertain whether they will avail themselves of this opportunity. Even if they do, the success of this experiment is uncertain as BBC Three's failed closure and subsequent revival has demonstrated.[49] Finally, there has been a lively debate in Germany in the context of the PSB reform about the extent to which the PSB remit should encompass entertainment.[50] This debate has been put to rest by a clarification in the amended Treaty to the effect that entertainment is also part of the remit next to culture, education, information, and advice. Importantly, it is underlined that entertainment needs to 'align with a PSB profile'.[51]

Another attempt to manage the tension between the competing PSB and press demands online has been by way of the exclusion of non-programme-related press-like services from the PSBs' own portals and their social media presence.[52] As a result of sustained political pressure from the publishing sector, a provision was inserted into the Interstate Broadcasting Treaty to the effect that PSB telemedia offers may not be press-like.[53] The explanatory memorandum to the Treaty clarified that PSB needed to be distinguishable from commercial offers, not only the commercial broadcasters' ones but also those of other market players active online.[54] This provision, now

---

[46] See Kühling, 'Art. 5 GG' (n 34) para 72.

[47] I Katsirea, 'The Three-Step Test. Three Steps Forwards or Backwards for Public Service Broadcasting in Germany?' in K Donders and H Moe (eds), *Exporting the Public Value Test: Views from Academia and Practitioners* (Nordicom 2011) 59.

[48] Interstate Media Treaty (*Medienstaatsvertrag* (MStV)) of 14./28. April 2020, last modified by the 3d Medienänderungsstaatsvertrag of 1 July 2023 <https://www.die-medienanstalten.de/fileadmin/user_upl oad/Rechtsgrundlagen/Gesetze_Staatsvertraege/Medienstaatsvertrag_MStV.pdf> accessed 20 August 2023 (hereafter 'Dritter MStV') §31(8)3.

[49] See N Thurman, 'When a TV Channel Reinvents Itself Online: Post-Broadcast Consumption and Content Change at BBC Three' (2021) 27(2) Convergence 291.

[50] 'Auftrag des öffentlich-rechtlichen Rundfunks wird reformiert' (*Zeit Online*, 2 June 2022) <Medien: Auftrag des öffentlich-rechtlichen Rundfunks wird reformiert | ZEIT ONLINE> accessed 17 February 2023.

[51] 'Dritter MStV' (n 48) §26(1)8, 9; cf House of Lords Communications and Digital Committee, 'Licence to change: BBC future funding', 1st Report of Session 2022–23, HL Paper 44, 18 July 2022, paras 13–15, 50 (hereafter House of Lords, 'Licence to change').

[52] Begründung zum 22. Rundfunkänderungsstaatsvertrag, 10 <https://www.rlp.de/fileadmin/rlp-stk/ pdf-Dateien/Medienpolitik/22_RAEStV_Begru__ndung.pdf> accessed 18 January 2023.

[53] RStV, §11d(7); now MStV, §30(7).

[54] Begründung zu Artikel 1 – Änderung des Rundfunkstaatsvertrages, §11d <Institut für Urheberrecht und Medienrecht> accessed 17 February 2023.

incorporated in the Media Treaty, stipulates that the design focus of PSB online services needs to be on moving images or sound, while text may not be predominant. It clarifies that the ban on non-programme-related press-like services does not affect TV listings, headlines, broadcast transcripts, information about the relevant broadcaster, and accessibility measures. Nor does it affect telemedia, which present contents from a specific broadcast, including background information, to the extent that they rely on materials and sources used for the respective programme and support, accompany, and update the programme in terms of theme and content. The temporal and content-related reference to a specific programme must be disclosed in the relevant telemedia offer.

The Media Treaty thus draws a distinction between programme-related and non-programme-related services. Whilst the latter may not include text-heavy content, the former are largely unaffected by this requirement. There is only a gentle exhortation that programme-related services also include image or sound as far as this is possible.[55] The criterion of programme alignment speaks to arguments for a tight PSB enclosure on new media platforms. Different views exist as to the role to be fulfilled by public broadcasters online. Some take the view that the chief rationale for PSB, the risks for pluralism ensuing from spectrum scarcity, is not valid as regards internet. They dispute the existence of a pluralism deficit online in view of the inherent diversity of private offers.[56] They even argue that PSBs' online presence might diminish diversity by destroying the business models of the press and of other commercial providers who are also active on the very same pitch. They take the view that the public service remit might only extend to online information services if these constitute a functional equivalent to 'programmes' in the traditional sense.[57] An independent online presence of public broadcasters would be redundant as pluralism is already guaranteed by the variety of services on offer. Moreover, they contend that the delivery of public content across new media is incompatible with the traditional PSB integrative function in view of the internet's fragmented and individualized nature. If PSBs are to counteract this segmentation of interests into ever thinner slices, they need to produce online content that is aligned to their television programming.[58]

Others argue that functional equivalence to traditional programmes would not sufficiently cover the democratic, social, and cultural needs of society given that online offerings act as a special medium in the free formation of public and individual opinion.[59] Commercial online services, so the argument goes, display structural deficits that would need to be made good by public service offerings. These arguments have been most prominently bolstered in recent times by the German Constitutional Court. In its 2018 judgment on the constitutionality of the PSB licence fee, the BVerfG held that 'a broader range of services provided by private broadcasters and a large number of providers does not—in and of itself—already result in quality and diversity

[55] MStV, §30(7)5.
[56] Kühling, 'Art. 5 GG' (n 34) para 85; C R Sunstein, *#Republic. Divided Democracy in the Age of Social Media* (Princeton UP 2017) 27 with regard to niche interests.
[57] C Degenhart, *Der Funktionsauftrag des öffentlich-rechtlichen Rundfunks in der digitalen Welt* (Verlag Recht und Wirtschaft 2001) 65.
[58] ibid 85.
[59] W Hoffmann-Riem, *Regulierung der dualen Rundfunkordnung* (Nomos 2000) 241.

of broadcasting'.[60] The BVerfG substantiated its concerns about the lack of pluralism online with reference to: first, the 'tendencies of concentration and monopolisation in respect of content providers, disseminators and intermediaries'; second, the risks for journalistic quality as a result of commercially funded media; third, the personalization of content, also by means of algorithms, with the aim of maximizing user engagement; and finally, the increase in non-journalistic providers and the associated risks for the quality of information. In the BVerfG's view, all these structural deficits of online communication are responsible for blurring the line between fact and opinion and between editorial content and native advertising. The need for PSB to act as a counterweight by safeguarding diversity and providing guidance amidst the information overflow prevalent online is therefore strengthened rather than diminished in the digital era.[61]

The BVerfG's reasoning has been criticized, for its part, for unquestioningly assuming the continuous need for PSB without engaging in depth with the affordances of digital media, their reception, and consumption patterns. The complexity of the interaction and selection features of online communication with its network effects and shifting frontiers between one-to-one and one-to-many communication would require an analysis that goes beyond a simple reaffirmation of assumptions from the analogue era.[62] Indeed, further empirical research into the factors influencing the formation of public opinion online is much needed.[63] However, the complexity of the online media ecosystem and the uncertainty about its impact on democratic opinion formation does not suffice to question PSB's legitimacy. Existing studies amply demonstrate the challenges for plurality in the digital media landscape.[64]

The dominant role of legacy news providers online means that the risks for pluralism that are prevalent offline also taint the online domain. Risks posed by dwindling journalistic resources and competencies coupled with increased concentration, conditioned by technological shifts, accentuate PSB's importance for forging a well-functioning public sphere. PSBs play such a central role in creating and maintaining democracy, culture, and social cohesion that the wholesale entrustment of their mission to private providers would need to fulfil the most stringent conditions.[65] It would need to be convincingly demonstrated that the private sector is able to fulfil the PSB mission in a comprehensive and sustained manner. Commercial offers would need to serve the entire spectrum of democratic, social, and cultural needs of society by providing a comprehensive range of content accessible to the whole population. These

---

[60] BVerfGE 149, 222 (2018), para 79.

[61] ibid para 80.

[62] E Wagner, 'Die Gegengewichtsfunktionen des öffentlich-rechtlichen Rundfunks' (2022) 5 Archiv für Presserecht 377, 382; E Wagner, 'Unions- und verfassungsrechtliche Spielräume einer Flexibilisierung des Auftrags der öffentlich-rechtlichen Rundfunkanstalten' (2022) 3 Zeitschrift für Urheber- und Medienrecht 165, 169.

[63] M Cornils, 'Vielfaltssicherung bei Telemedien' (2018) 49(5) Archiv für Presserecht 377, 380 (hereafter Cornils, 'Vielfaltssicherung').

[64] ibid 378; C Neuberger and F Lobigs, *Die Bedeutung ders Internets im Rahmen der Vielfaltssicherung. Gutachten im Auftrag der Kommission zur Ermittlung der Konzentration im Medienbereich (KEK)* (VISTAS 2010) 35ff.

[65] D Dörr, B Holznagel, and A Picot, 'Legitimation und Auftrag des öffentlich-rechtlichen Fernsehens in Zeiten der Cloud' (ZDF 2016) <https://tpp.rlp.de/opal/7f41d840e8a2e5744f054a8f9b1fda4b> accessed 25 January 2023, 70.

conditions can hardly be fulfilled in a totally commercial market whose performance, output, and potential for the future is guided by its focus on profit-making. Private providers could contribute to the elimination of punctual deficits but could not overcome the inherent structural deficits of the media market due to their reliance on private sources of funding.[66] For this to happen, commercial providers would need to be subject to a public service mission. This is the case to varying degrees in the UK as regards the commercial public service broadcasters providing Channel 3 services, Channel 4, Channel 5, and S4C. However, the leverage on these commercial providers to comply with public service obligations is significantly weakened as these are not anymore a *quid pro quo* for the lucrative privilege of access to the scarce analogue spectrum. The BBC is hence the cornerstone of the UK PSB system. In the case of the press, its subjection to public service obligations would likely be perceived as antithetical to the libertarian ideal of press freedom.[67]

The requirement of programme alignment in the case of press-like content is currently unproblematic. PSBs' online services usually refer to their radio and television programmes and share with them the same resources, especially as regards news and current affairs.[68] However, the more traditional television functions wander off to the web, the more it will appear legitimate for PSBs to offer original content online.[69] Looking at each online service in isolation would disregard the fact that even services that are not strictly aligned with the television programme are linked with it by means of cross-references and corporate design. Also, the internet presence strengthens PSBs' brand by tying in users.[70]

In a much-discussed case concerning the ARD Tagesschau-App, the oldest and most watched German news programme in app form, German courts concluded that its version of 15 June 2011 constituted a non-programme-related press-like service. The protracted legal dispute began in 2011 when eight newspaper publishers, in tandem with the BDZV, filed a complaint against ARD and Northern German Broadcasting (*Norddeutscher Rundfunk*, NDR) with the competition chamber of the Cologne District Court (Landesgericht Köln, LG Köln). They claimed that the amount of written text on the free app, which was funded by the licence fee, distorted competition. The Cologne District Court upheld the complaint.[71] The fact that the Tagesschau-App concept had been approved by way of the three-step test did not mean, in the Court's view, that the specific version of the app in question was not amenable to

---

[66] On the types of market failure that endemic to media markets, see C E Berg, G F Lowe, and A B Lund, 'A Market Failure Perspective on Value Creation in PSM' in G F Lowe and F Martin (eds), *The Value of Public Service Media* (Nordicom 2014) 105, 112ff.

[67] See C-E Eberle in C Libor and R Schmidkonz, 'Die Aufgabe des öffentlich-rechtlichen Rundfunks in der digitalen Welt. 128. Tagung des Studienkreises für Presserecht und Pressefreiheit e.V. am 20/21.5.2022 in Hamburg' (2022) 5 Archiv für Presserecht 400, 403.

[68] S Heinemann and F Dittrich, 'Die Zukunft des öffentlich-rechtlichen Telemedienauftrags' (2018) 2 Bonner Rechtsjournal 127, 133.

[69] T Held and W Schulz, *Europarechtliche Beurteilung von Online-Angeboten öffentlich-rechtlicher Rundfunkanstalten: Inwieweit beeinflussen die Beihilferegeln die Einbeziehung neuer Dienste in den Funktionsauftrag öffentlich-rechtlichen Rundfunks? Gutachten im Auftrag der Friedrich-Ebert-Stiftung* (Friedrich-Ebert-Stiftung 2004) 59 (hereafter Held and Schulz, *Europarechtliche Beurteilung von Online-Angeboten*).

[70] ibid 17, 59.

[71] LG Köln, judgment of 27 September 2012, 31 O 360/11.

judicial review.[72] The Court argued further that the press-likeness of the app had to be determined by way of an examination of the entirety of the service, not of individual articles. Also, it held that the benchmark against which to compare the Tagesschau-App would need to be the traditional print media, not the publishers' online presence. If this was otherwise, publishers would be at liberty to restrict the PSB remit by expanding their own online offers.[73] The attribute of 'press-likeness' would have to be interpreted as a substitute, even if only partial, for the reading of newspapers and magazines, which would resemble their information density and range.[74]

The Higher Regional Court of Cologne (*Oberlandesgericht Köln*, OLG Köln) disagreed with this position as it considered itself bound by the decision reached in the framework of the three-step test.[75] The legalization effect of this decision covered not only the abstract concept of the app but extended to its actual implementation. On appeal, the BGH dismissed this finding. It ruled that the telemedia concept established guidelines for the design of an offering but could not legitimize specific manifestations ex ante.[76] A further controversial question was whether §11d(7) RStV (now §30(7) MStV) was a market access or a market conduct regulation.[77] The answer to this question turned on the interchangeability of press-like and non-press-like offerings from a user's perspective. The BGH held, somewhat ambivalently, that the provision in question was a not a pure market access, but *also* a market conduct regulation, which aimed to limit PSBs' activities on the telemedia market to protect press publishers.[78] Importantly, the BGH ruled further that press-likeness would need to be assessed based on the entirety of the offering as opposed to just individual contributions. The offering as a whole would need to foreground text and still images and resemble the print edition of newspapers and magazines.[79] Similarly to the LG Köln, the BGH did not consider electronic editions of print media to be a suitable comparator.[80] The BGH made a further concession to PSBs by dismissing the LG Köln's notion that a telemedia offering was 'press-like' simply on account of the density and breadth of the information it offered. The BGH's rather circular reasoning went as follows: PSBs could rely on broadcasting freedom to offer innovative services by way of new technologies; they were therefore not precluded from reporting comprehensively and in depth about all topics covered in the press; to the extent that such reporting might affect press freedom, the interests of press publishers were sufficiently taken into account by means of the ban on non-programme-related press-like services.[81]

The BGH's judgment did not bring the dispute to an end. The case was remitted to OLG Köln, which concluded that the app's version of 15 June 2011 constituted a

---

[72] ibid para 99.
[73] ibid para 105.
[74] ibid para 107.
[75] OLG Köln, judgment of 20 December 2013, 6 U 188/12.
[76] BGH, 30 April 2015, I ZR 13/14, para 54.
[77] In favour of a market conduct regulation B Paal, 'Öffentlich-rechtliche presseähnliche Angebote in Telemedien—Tagesschau-App. Zugleich Anmerkung zu BGH v. 30.4.2015 – I ZR 13/14, AfP 2015, 553' (2005) 6 Archiv für Presserecht 500, 504 (hereafter Paal, 'Tagesschau-App'); contra K-E Hain and T Brings, 'Die Tagesschau-App—Showdown in Karlsruhe (?) Zum Urteil des BGH v. 30.4.2015 – I ZR 13/14, AfP 2015, 553' (2016) 1 Archiv für Presserecht 11, 12 (hereafter Hain and Brings, 'Tagesschau-App').
[78] BGH, 30 April 2015, I ZR 13/14, para 59.
[79] ibid paras 61ff, 65.
[80] ibid paras 64, 65.
[81] ibid para 66.

non-programme-related press-like service.[82] In particular, the OLG Köln held that the existence of interactive elements and hyperlinks to other text-based or audiovisual content did not refute the service's press likeness.[83] Subsequently, the BGH confirmed OLG Köln's decision and held that it could not be the subject of a further appeal.[84] NDR filed a constitutional complaint against OLG Köln's decision on the ground that it had disregarded essential aspects of broadcasting freedom. The BVerfG decided unanimously that the complaint was inadmissible on evidentiary and procedural grounds.[85] However, press publishers' appetite to stave off PSB online competition has not yet been sated. Several publishers, including the local newspapers *Magdeburger Volksstimme* and Bremen's *Weser Kurier*, complain about PSBs' online presence. In the first instance, an arbitration board set up in 2019 by the PSBs and the BDZV, which has been inactive for a long time, will attempt to settle the dispute.[86] Newspaper publishers also argue that the Media Treaty needs to be further concretized to ensure that PSBs will comply with the ban on non-programme-related press-like services.[87] The forthcoming amended Media Treaty contains no change in that regard. However, there continues to be considerable debate about the interpretation of the provision in question.

A key point of contestation in academic writing is whether the emphasis should be placed on the entirety of the telemedia offering or on a specific contribution. Despite the fact that the ban on non-programme-related press-like content is now firmly anchored in the wording of §30(7)1 MStV, some authors contend that PSBs could even publish an online newspaper, so long as the offering's overall centre of gravity was on videos.[88] Others argue that, in line with a constitution-compliant interpretation of §30(7) MStV, PSBs should be allowed to publish *individual* non-programme-related press-like pieces so long as the totality of the offering was predominantly video-based.[89] A certain amount of text is indeed unobjectionable and even required in a hybrid online medium.[90]

The printed press as the reference point for the comparison has also been controversial. Some argue that the comparator should consist of all online offerings that constitute a functional equivalent of a newspaper or a magazine.[91] This broad interpretation of 'press-like' would have rendered a large part of PSBs' online presence unlawful. PSBs, on the other hand, tend to classify their text-based offerings as non-press-like,

---

[82] OLG Köln, judgment of 30 September 2016, 6 U 188/12.

[83] ibid para 56; see also LG Köln, judgment of 27 September 2012, 31 O 360/11, para 103; contra Hain and Brings, 'Tagesschau-App' (n 77) 15.

[84] BGH, 14 December 2017, I ZR 216/16; BGH, 15 February 2018, I ZR 216/16.

[85] BVerfG, 23 February 2022, 1 BvR 717/18.

[86] MStV, §30(7)6; Deutschlandfunk, 'Verlage vs Öffentlich-rechtliche. Der lange Streit um die Presseähnlichkeit' (*Deutschlandfunk*, 21 September 2022) <https://www.deutschlandfunk.de/streit-um-presseaehnlichkeit-100.html> accessed 18 January 2023.

[87] H Hartung, 'Die ARD muss sich an den Medienstaatsvertrag halten' (*Medienpolitik*, 18 April 2023) <https://www.medienpolitik.net/2023/04/die-ard-muss-sich-an-den-medienstaatsvertrag-halten/> accessed 16 June 2023.

[88] §30(7)1 states that '[T]he telemedia offers may not be of a press-type nature'; H Gersdorf, '§30 MStV' in H Gersdorf and P Paal (eds), *Informations- und Medienrecht Kommentar* (Beck 2021) para 42 (hereafter Gersdorf, '§30 MStV'); Paal, 'Tagesschau-App' (n 77) 502.

[89] Hain and Brings, 'Tagesschau-App' (n 77) 15.

[90] C M Davis, '*Die dienende' Rundfunkfreiheit im Zeitalter der sozialen Vernetzung* (Mohr Siebeck 2019) 161, 162.

[91] N Gerhardt, 'Presseähnliche Angebote nach dem 12. Rundfunkänderungsstaatsvertrag. Zur Zulässigkeit von Onlinetextangeboten öffentlich-rechtlicher Rundfunkanstalten' (2010) 1 Archiv für Presserecht 16, 20.

and to subject them to the three-step-test. Proponents of a broad PSB remit go even further. They maintain that only a restrictive interpretation of 'press-likeness' in line with the traditional visual appearance of the press would be constitutionally compliant. In their view, press-likeness consists in the display not only of static text and image combinations, but also of headings and columns. It is submitted that such a restrictive interpretation of 'press-likeness' would render this criterion meaningless given that newspaper-style columns are extremely rare online. 'Press-likeness', as described in the Media Treaty and as interpreted by the BGH, connotes the predominant use of text and still image.[92] The proponents of this narrow interpretation concede that it would likely erode the concept of 'press-likeness' but argue that it is mandated by PSB's constitutional existence and development guarantee (*Bestands- und Entwicklungsgarantie*).[93]

Regrettably, the BGH did not engage with the constitutional dimension of this debate. As a result, the question of whether PSB's mission of ensuring the essential basic provision for all (*Grundversorgung*) as well as its continued existence and development guarantee encompass the offering of non-programme-related text-based content remains contentious. The constitutionality of the exclusion of non-programme-related press-like services from the PSB online remit may seem like an arcane issue at first sight. It does, however, relate to our understanding of mass communication freedoms in the online domain.[94] It goes back to the debate between the 'market failure model' versus the 'cultural model' of PSB. According to the former model, PSB is only there to fill gaps left by the market.[95] Underlying this model is the assumption that commercial services only suffer from certain punctual pluralism deficits that can be remedied by public broadcasters.[96] The implication is that PSBs need to concentrate on these types of offers that are not provided by the commercial sector. This residual role is constantly under threat as private providers expand and diversify their service. Diametrically opposed is the 'cultural model' of PSB.[97] It posits that commercial broadcasting suffers not just from punctual but from structural deficits that can only be filled by a comprehensive public service programme.[98] According to this interpretation, PSBs have an inherent right to follow their audience on all platforms of their choice, to cater for a wider range of interests, and to forge citizenship and solidarity. PSB's expansion

[92] MStV, §30(7)1; BGH, judgment of 30 April 2015, I ZR 13/14, para 65.
[93] H-J Papier and M Schröder, *Verfassungsfragen des Dreistufentests. Inhaltliche und Verfahrensrechtliche Herausforderungen* (Nomos 2011) 93; contra T Vesting, *Die Tagesschau-App und die Notwendigkeit der Schaffung eines 'Intermedienkollisionsrechts'* (KIT 2013) 12 (hereafter Vesting, *Tagesschau-App*); Gersdorf, '§30 MStV' (n 88) paras 48ff.
[94] H Gersdorf, 'Verbot presseähnlicher Angebote des öffentlich-rechtlichen Rundfunks' (2010) 5 Archiv für Presserecht 421, 425.
[95] P Badura, 'Die öffentlich-rechtlichen Rundfunkanstalten bieten Rundfunk und Telemedien an' (2009) 134(2) Archiv des öffentlichen Rechts 240, 247ff; T Prosser, *The Limits of Competition Law: Markets and Public Services* (OUP 2005) 209 (hereafter Prosser, *Limits of Competition Law*); P Booth, 'Introduction' in A Peacock (ed), *PSB Without the BBC?* (Institute of Economic Affairs 2004) 18; P Barwise, 'What Are the Real Threats to PSB?' in D Tambini and J Cowling (eds), *From PSB to Public Service Communications* (Institute for Public Policy Research 2004) 26.
[96] Held and Schulz, *Europarechtliche Beurteilung von Online-Angeboten* (n 69) 60.
[97] Prosser, *Limits of Competition Law* (n 95) 210; R Foster, J Egan, and J Simon, 'Measuring PSB' in D Tambini and J Cowling (eds), *From PSB to Public Service Communication* (Institute for Public Policy Research 2004) 151–52.
[98] Held and Schulz, *Europarechtliche Beurteilung von Online-Angeboten* (n 69) 60.

into a terrain already occupied by its commercial counterparts is not controversial according to this model as market provision is always tainted by these structural deficits, which are linked to their market orientation. The contrast between the 'market failure model' and the 'cultural model' of PSB is paradigmatic of the different philosophies that shaped PSB in the US and Europe.[99] In the US, PSB was introduced at a late stage as a complementary provider who would plug holes in the existing programming. By contrast, in Europe, PSB shaped the media ecosystem. The BBC, the prototypical public service broadcaster, was the sole player for a long time.

The BVerfG has consistently been in favour of the cultural model of PSB.[100] In its earlier case law, it provided certain pointers on how to draw the contested boundary between press and broadcasting freedom. In its *Fourth Television* case, the BVerfG held that the German Constitution (GG) does not bar press undertakings from access to broadcasting, and that a 'journalistic division of powers' is not a constitutional principle.[101] At the same time, it recognized that advertising-funded commercial broadcasting may deprive press undertakings of sources of finance essential to their existence. Such a development would 'affect press freedom, which also guarantees the institution of a "free press", and therefore the existence and functionality of the press'.[102] In the *Fifth Television* case, the BVerfG ruled that the ban on local and regional PSB, with the aim of protecting commercial broadcasters, contravened the core principle of free opinion formation ('*Grundprinzip der freien Meinungsbildung*').[103] It held that market opportunities may be a question of economic freedom, but not of freedom of opinion. Those favoured would be even protected against competitors where these have better and more varied programmes to offer than they do. This sort of prevention of free journalistic competition and intellectual debate is, in the BVerfG's view, not compatible with the Article 5(1) GG guarantee.[104] In the *Sixth Television* case, the BVerfG held that the publication of programme-related printed works, namely of a programme guide, by the West German public broadcaster (*Westdeutscher Rundfunk*, WDR) was protected by broadcasting freedom.[105] Even though demarcation of the spheres of freedom under Article 5(1) GG depends on the chosen means of dissemination, this did not totally exclude the use of another medium. However, if PSBs were to engage in non-programme-related press-like publication, this would no longer enjoy constitutional protection.[106] Notably, the BVerfG clarified that the restriction of PSB to the publication of programme-related printed works also sought to prevent this activity from having an economic goal and thus to risk jeopardizing the economic foundation of the press.[107]

[99] E Zuckerman, 'The case for digital public infrastructure' (Knight First Amendment Institute, 2020) <https://knightcolumbia.org/content/the-case-for-digital-public-infrastructure> accessed 17 January 2023 (hereafter Zuckerman, 'Digital public infrastructure') 19–21.
[100] BVerfGE 73, 118, 155 et seq; BVerfGE 83, 238, 310 et seq.
[101] BVerfGE 73, 118, para 191.
[102] ibid para 202.
[103] BVerfGE 74, 297 ('Baden Württemberg decision').
[104] ibid para 116.
[105] BVerfGE 83, 238, para 445.
[106] ibid para 446.
[107] ibid para 449.

It follows that, on the one hand, the BVerfG posits that broadcasting regulation should not aim at safeguarding the market opportunities of market players, such as the press.[108] On the other hand, it recognizes that the press should not be put at risk by allowing PSB to engage in profit-making activities that encroach on newspapers' sphere of operation.[109] Part of the difficulty arises from the fact that the respective spheres of operation of broadcasting and the press are no longer clear cut. The rigid static image and text versus audiovisual content divide, which was entrenched in the pre-digital world, has been obliviated by the rise of the hybrid medium. Both press and broadcasting lay claim to the affordances of online communication that best enable them to reach their audience. At the same time, it is uncontroversial that media regulation needs to take a holistic approach and to secure the survival of all journalistic media.

The German legislator opted to reach this aim by barring PSBs from using a specific form of communication. Given that form and content are closely intertwined, this intervention impairs PSBs' programme autonomy.[110] Is this legislative device appropriate and necessary to safeguard the sustainability of the press? This is questionable. The criterion of 'press-likeness' is hard to operationalize in the evolving field of online journalism.[111] We have seen that the offering of video content is of existential importance for the press. Are PSBs' online offerings press-like or those of the press TV-like? The criterion of 'press-likeness' is a relic from the analogue era. Attempting to balance out the conflicting interests by way of this elusive criterion is misguided.[112] The provision in question aimed to ease print publishers' entry into the application market. Private publishers' apps, made available on a fee-paying basis, had to compete with the free Tagesschau-App. The ban on PSB text-heavy content was an attempt to justify the press product's added value.[113] However, there is no evidence that the ostensible competition advantage afforded the press vis-à-vis PSB has made a tangible difference to the uptake of its apps. It is not certain that the market gap opened by the ban on PSB non-programme-related press-like services has been filled by subscription apps offered by press publishers rather than by the plethora of free applications made available by other providers seeking to influence public opinion.[114]

In a changing and extremely competitive media landscape, PSBs are eclipsed by tech and content giants such as Amazon, Meta, Netflix, and AT&T. It has been observed against this backdrop that European commercial media groups no longer appear as PSBs' 'historical main competitors but rather as natural partners'.[115] The view

---

[108] BVerfGE 74, 297.

[109] BVerfGE 83, 238.

[110] Hain and Brings, 'Tagesschau-App' (n 77) 15.

[111] Cornils, 'Vielfaltssicherung' (n 63) 384; Vesting, *Tagesschau-App* (n 93) 11.

[112] C Franzius, 'Das Internet und die Grundrechte' (2016) 71 Juristenzeitung 650, 653.

[113] S Ory, 'Rundfunk und Presse im Internet. Die Tagesschau, das iPhone und die tripolare Medienordnung' (2010) 1 Archiv für Presserecht 20, 21.

[114] H Möller, 'Darf man den öffentlich-rechtlichen Rundfunkanstalten die Textberichterstattung im Internet verbieten?' (*Verfassungsblog*, 24 January 2019) <https://verfassungsblog.de/darf-man-den-oeffentlich-rechtlichen-rundfunkanstalten-die-textberichterstattung-im-internet-verbieten/> accessed 29 January 2024.

[115] EBU, 'Public Service Media's competitive environment' (*Media Intelligence Service*, May 2022) 5 <https://www.ebu.ch/files/live/sites/ebu/files/Publications/MIS/login_only/market_insights/EBU-MIS-PSMs_Competitive_Environment_2022-Public.pdf> accessed 17 January 2023.

that the press needs to be guarded from the risk of free PSB offers crowding out its online content seems parochial. PSBs are dwarfed by the overshadowing presence of global behemoths, which put their relevance and reach at risk. Both the press and PSBs suffer setbacks in their core business in a globalized, convergent market. The legislative drafting of §30(7) MStV and the 'Tagesschau-App' saga present a missed opportunity to develop 'collision norms' that would go beyond the requirement for delineation between broadcasting and press freedom.[116]

An example of such a developing 'collision norm' is the prioritization of public interest content on digital intermediary services. As previously discussed, the MStV requires the findability on digital interfaces of PSB content and of private broadcasters' offerings, which especially contribute to diversity of opinion and media pluralism in Germany.[117] A more inclusive definition of public interest content that would not largely equate it with content produced by public and select commercial broadcasters would be desirable.[118] Other media organizations, including segments of the press, also serve the public interest by providing 'the complex of supposed informational, cultural and social benefits to the wider society which go beyond the immediate, particular and individual interests of those who communicate in public communication, whether as senders or receivers'.[119] The prioritization of public interest content in this wider sense, not only on smart TVs and user interfaces, but also on search engines and social media feeds, could support democratic processes. For this to happen, and in view of its freedom of expression implications, prioritization would need to be truly independent so as not to exchange private gatekeeper control with soft censorship.[120] Ideally, it would go hand in hand with the creation of digital public infrastructures that would act as an antipode to the commercially driven, data-thirsty tech giants that dominate the contemporary media ecosystem.[121]

At a time when US scholars are urging the creation of a new national public media system as an alternative to the spent market-based model, media regulation in Europe should also be more ambitious.[122] Instead of focusing on petty disputes and artificial demarcations between print publishers' and public broadcasters' online domains, it should aspire to more forward-looking solutions for a mutually beneficial coexistence in the digital realm. It has been proposed that online intermediaries should be obliged to espouse a two-pillar business model.[123] The first pillar would comprise personalized content in line with platforms' private business interests. The second would be geared to the provision of pluralistic, non-personalized public interest content consisting of a mixture of PSB offers combined with private blogs or vlogs as well as traditional

---

[116] Vesting, *Tagesschau-App* (n 93) 15.

[117] MStV, §84(3), (4); see Chapter 3, pp 58–59.

[118] E M Mazzoli and D Tambini, 'Prioritisation uncovered. The Discoverability of Public Interest Content Online' (*Council of Europe*, November 2020) <https://rm.coe.int/publication-content-prioritisation-report/1680a07a57> accessed 29 January 2024 (hereafter Mazzoli and Tambini, 'Prioritisation uncovered') 14ff.

[119] D McQuail, *Media Performance, Mass Communication and the Public Interest* (Sage 1992) 3.

[120] Mazzoli and Tambini, 'Prioritisation uncovered' (n 118) 42.

[121] See Zuckerman, 'Digital public infrastructure' (n 99).

[122] See W V Pickard, *Democracy Without Journalism?: Confronting the Misinformation Society* (OUP 2020) 164ff.

[123] R Schwartmann, M Hermann, and R L Mühlenbeck, 'Eine Medienordnung für Intermediäre. Das Zwei-Säulen-Modell zur Sicherung der Vielfalt im Netz' (2019) 22(8) Multimedia und Recht 498, 501.

commercial press and TV material. The provision of the second pillar would be a condition for the operation of the first one.[124] This model seeks to overcome the obstacles raised when trying to combine personalized choice with balanced pluralism. This ambitious plan is premised on states' capacity and willingness to co-opt tech giants into a democratic digital public space. These are difficult premises. Ensuring the prominence of public interest content, where this can be found, may be a more workable solution, at least for the time being.

9.4 Reining in Public Service Broadcasters' Online Presence: The Case of the UK

The UK has been at the forefront of developing procedures for measuring the 'value' of public services. The concept of 'public value' was first introduced in 1995 by the Harvard professor Marc Moore with the aim of devising 'a structure of practical reasoning to guide managers of public enterprises'.[125] Before long this concept was exported to the UK and found its way in a 2002 report by the Cabinet's Office Strategy Unit.[126] Subsequently the term was borrowed by the BBC, which used it in the title of a policy document that influenced the 2006 BBC Charter and Agreement.[127] Assessing 'public value' became central to the evaluation of proposed new services and of major changes to existing services by the BBC Trust in the framework of an ex ante procedure, called the 'public value test'.[128] Public value was understood as both consumer benefit, in the sense of an individual user's gain from accessing the proposed service, and as citizen benefit, in the sense of the benefit created for society as a whole.[129] In 2016, with the enactment of the new BBC Charter, the BBC Trust stopped operating as the governing body, its regulatory functions were assigned to Ofcom, and the public value test was terminated.

A public interest test (PIT), conducted by the BBC Board and overseen by Ofcom, has been introduced in its place. A PIT is carried out where the BBC plans to perform a material change to its public services, by launching a new service or by making a change to an existing service that may have an adverse impact on competition.[130] If the BBC views a planned change as not material, but Ofcom disagrees, it has the power to step in and to require the BBC to conduct a PIT.[131] The PIT is met if the BBC Board is satisfied, first, that the proposed change contributes to the fulfilment of the

---

[124] ibid 502.

[125] M Moore, *Creating Public Value: Strategic Management in Government* (Harvard UP 1995) quoted by D Coyle and C Woolard, Public value in practice, Restoring the ethos of public service <http://downlo ads.bbc.co.uk/bbctrust/assets/files/pdf/regulatory_framework/pvt/public_value_practice.pdf>22 March 2012, 5.

[126] G Kelly and others, *Creating Public Value. An Aanalytical Framework for Public Services Reform* (Cabinet Office 2002).

[127] BBC, 'Building Public Value: Renewing the BBC for a Digital World', 2004 <http://downloads.bbc. co.uk/aboutthebbc/policies/pdf/bpv.pdf> accessed 7 February 2023.

[128] Katsirea, 'Who Is Afraid of Public Service Broadcasting' (n 15) 439ff.

[129] BBC Trust, 'Public Value Test (PVT): Guidance on the conduct of the PVT', August 2007 <http:// downloads.bbc.co.uk/bbctrust/assets/files/pdf/about/how_we_govern/pvt/pvt_guidance.pdf> accessed 7 February 2023, 15.

[130] *Agreement Dated December 2016 Between Her Majesty's Secretary of State for Culture, Media and Sport and the British Broadcasting Corporation* (Cm 6872, 2006), s 7(7) (hereafter 'BBC Agreement').

[131] ibid s 9(6)(a).

BBC's Mission and promotes its public purposes; secondly, if the BBC Board has taken steps to eliminate unnecessary adverse impacts on fair and effective competition and; third, if the public value generated by the change justifies any remaining adverse impact on competition.[132] If the PIT is met, and Ofcom agrees that the proposed change is material, it may carry out a BBC competition assessment (BCA) or a shorter assessment focusing on elements of the BCA procedure.[133] Following this assessment, Ofcom will determine if the BBC may carry out the proposed change or if it needs to desist therefrom. Alternatively, the BBC may be able to carry out the proposed change subject to modifications or conditions or it may need to reconsider aspects of the PIT.[134] Ofcom has reviewed plans to launch new services or to amend existing ones on several occasions.[135] It agreed, for example, that proposals to extend the availability on the BBC iPlayer and to increase the BBC local online news offering were not material.[136] In the former case, the BBC had conducted a PIT, while in the latter, Ofcom held that a PIT was not required. These proposals come as part of the BBC Digital First Strategy, which places emphasis on digital while making savings in broadcast news. The draft Media Bill also aims to give the BBC, as well as the other PSBs, greater flexibility in the delivery of their remit, by allowing online content rather than just linear broadcasting to count towards it and towards the fulfilment of their programming quotas.[137] The impctus for BBC's realignment to better suit the digital age comes from altered audience habits, but also from the challenges posed by a two-year licence fee freeze in tandem with the uncertainty over the future of the licence fee.[138]

Meanwhile, a focus of the Mid-Term Charter Review, the review of the governance and regulatory arrangements for the BBC halfway through the BBC's ten-year Royal Charter, is an evaluation of BBC's competition and market impact and of its role in the wider UK media ecology, including the local news sector.[139] In this context, Ofcom launched a consultation to update its guidance on how the BBC's competition impact is assessed.[140] The proposed updates to the Ofcom guidance aim to

---

[132] ibid, s 8(1).

[133] Ofcom, 'Assessing the impact of proposed changes to the BBC's public service activities. Ofcom's procedures and guidance', 29 March 2017 <bbc-public-service-activities-proposed.pdf (ofcom.org.uk)> accessed 8 February 2023.

[134] BBC Agreement, s 11(1).

[135] Ofcom, 'Competition' <https://www.ofcom.org.uk/tv-radio-and-on-demand/information-for-industry/bbc-operating-framework/competition> accessed 10 February 2023.

[136] Ofcom, 'Ofcom review of proposed increased amount of archive content on BBC iPlayer. Conclusion of initial assessment', 30 November 2022 <https://www.ofcom.org.uk/__data/assets/pdf_file/0018/248400/statement-archive-content-BBC-iPlayer.pdf>; Ofcom, 'Review of the BBC's materiality assessment of proposed changes to the provision of local online news in England', 14 December 2022 <https://www.ofcom.org.uk/__data/assets/pdf_file/0032/249476/Local-News-MA-Decision.pdf> accessed 29 January 2024.

[137] Draft Media Bill, cl 1.

[138] Department for Digital, Culture, Media and Sport, 'Up next: The Government's vision for the broadcasting sector', April 2022 <https://www.gov.uk/government/publications/up-next-the-governments-vision-for-the-broadcasting-sector> accessed 10 February 2023.

[139] Department for Digital, Culture, Media and Sport, 'BBC mid-term review: terms of reference', 26 May 2022 <https://www.gov.uk/government/publications/bbc-charter-and-framework-agreement/bbc-mid-term-review-terms-of-reference#:~:text=The%20Mid%2DTerm%20Review%20must,point%20of%20the%20BBC%20Charter> accessed 8 February 2023.

[140] Ofcom, 'How Ofcom regulates the BBC's impact on competition. Proposals for changes to guidance and requirements', 30 November 2022 <Consultation: How Ofcom regulates the BBC's impact on competition> accessed 29 January 2024 (hereafter Ofcom, 'Consultation').

encourage a more productive dialogue between the BBC and its stakeholders, and to increase transparency as regards planned material changes to public services and about Ofcom's role in the materiality assessment. Certain stakeholders, including the Professional Publishers' Association (PPA), requested a formal consultation process as part of the BBC's materiality assessments.[141] Ofcom rightly considered that such a formal consultation process would hamper BBC's efforts to adjust its services to a changing market, but agreed to provide more detailed information on proportionate stakeholder engagement during the materiality process.[142]

At the heart of the PPA's grievances is the perception that the PIT process is fundamentally flawed as it allows the BBC to introduce incremental changes to its services which do not meet the materiality thresholds and thus escape scrutiny.[143] By way of example, the PPA mentions the widening of BBC News Online's scope, not least through the creation of more magazine style content, such as that found in BBC *Stories*, the successor to the BBC *Magazine*.[144] The PPA argues that such content duplicates or even displaces the efforts of independent news publishers and reduces the distinctiveness of the BBC output.[145] It also maintains that the BBC needs to do more to provide links to third-party online material, particularly within news.[146] The News Media Association (NMA) also takes issue with the great amount of written news and feature material produced by the BBC, which falls outside the domain of hard news and is hence 'outside or on the fringes of the BBC's public interest remit'.[147] The tension between the BBC and news publishers in relation to 'soft' content was also discussed in the framework of the Cairncross Review. It was recommended that Ofcom should assess BBC online content and confirm 'appropriate boundaries for [its] future direction'.[148]

In its review of BBC news and current affairs, Ofcom engaged with industry stakeholders' concerns about the alleged expansion of the BBC editorial scope into the remit of newspapers.[149] It took the BBC's argument into account that it had to adapt the tone and agenda of its online and other digital output to engage the harder-to-reach younger audiences. The increased publication of both online video documentaries and in-depth features on cultural and societal issues under the BBC *Stories* brand was part of this effort. Ofcom concluded that, overall, the BBC online news offering broadly reflected its broadcast news agenda, and that it consistently prioritized challenging subjects such as politics and international affairs, business, and

---

[141] ibid para 4.8; Professional Publishers' Association, 'Response to Ofcom Consultation: How Ofcom regulates the BBC', 15 September 2021, 7 <Professional Publishers Association (PPA) (ofcom.org.uk)> accessed 8 February 2023 (hereafter PPA, 'Response to Ofcom Consultation').
[142] Ofcom, 'Consultation' (n 140) para 4.10.
[143] PPA, 'Response to Ofcom Consultation' (n 141) 4.
[144] BBC, 'News' https://www.bbc.co.uk/news/stories accessed 10 March 2023.
[145] ibid 5.
[146] ibid 2.
[147] News Media Association, 'The NMA response to Ofcom's Consultation: How Ofcom regulates the BBC', 9 September 2021 <News Media Association (ofcom.org.uk)> accessed 15 February 2023 (hereafter NMA, 'Response to Ofcom Consultation').
[148] F Cairncross, 'Cairncross Review: A sustainable future for journalism', 12 February 2019 <https://assets.publishing.service.gov.uk/government/uploads/system/uploads/attachment_data/file/779882/021919_DCMS_Cairncross_Review_.pdf> accessed 24 February 2020 (hereafter 'Cairncross Review') 97.
[149] Ofcom, 'Review of BBC news and current affairs', 24 October 2019 <https://www.ofcom.org.uk/__data/assets/pdf_file/0025/173734/bbc-news-review.pdf> accessed 15 February 2023, 19.

economics.[150] However, on the issue of external links, Ofcom agreed that, in line with its Operating Licence and with its first Public Purpose, the BBC needed to provide more links to external content, both to support the wider news industry and to provide users with access to a wider range of information.[151]

News publishers criticize the development by the BBC of material with mass audience appeal, even though it constitutes only a small segment of its news portfolio, by arguing that it is not distinctive enough. The BBC maintains that its focus on distinctive content remains at the core of what it does.[152] Distinctiveness is a factor that is taken into account in the PIT materiality assessment.[153] Yet the notion of 'distinctiveness' is notoriously elusive.[154] If employed as a prescriptive regulatory tool to bluntly measure individual programmes against an ill-defined standard of uniqueness, it risks undermining BBC's remit by making it dependent on whatever 'alleged democracy gap' commercial providers have left for it to plug.[155] This would pose a threat to the BBC's role as a universal broadcaster as it would question its ability to provide its audience with a breadth of quality content across all genres, including popular content. Universality of access and of content are essential PSB characteristics next to its independence and quality of services and output.[156] Universality of access signifies not only geographical availability but also presence on all significant media and platforms in the age of digital convergence. Universality of content means the provision of programming that reflects the interests of all social groups and that includes the entire range of programme genres.[157] Universality is one of the three aims the BBC needs to meet as part of its mission to inform, educate, and entertain the public, the other two being quality and distinctiveness.[158] These policy goals need to be met in tandem, as emphasis on only one of them might undermine the others.[159] As aptly noted, 'a service with no audience—no matter how unique—is as ineffective as output with no public service value'.[160] It is therefore right that Ofcom's test for distinctiveness, differently from that employed by the NMA and the PPA, focuses on the overall BBC news offering rather than on individual online pieces.[161] This ensures that, even if certain BBC online pieces speak to the same audience preferences as those of commercial

---

[150] ibid.

[151] BBC Agreement, Sch 2 (Operating Licence Regulatory Conditions), s 3; BBC Charter, s 6(1).

[152] BBC, BBC's response to Ofcom's consultation 'Modernising the BBC's Operating Licence', 6 October 2022 <https://www.ofcom.org.uk/__data/assets/pdf_file/0030/249348/BBC.pdf> accessed 15 February 2023.

[153] BBC, 'Policy on material changes to the BBC's public service activities and commercial activities' <http://downloads.bbc.co.uk/aboutthebbc/insidethebbc/howwework/policiesandguidelines/pdf/policy_material_changes.pdf> accessed 15 February 2023 (hereafter BBC, 'Policy on material changes') para 2.18.

[154] NMA, 'Response to Ofcom Consultation' (n 147) 2.2.4.

[155] P Goddard, '"Distinctiveness" and the BBC: A New Battleground for Public Service Television' (2017) 39(7) Media, Culture and Society 1089, 1091ff.

[156] Council of Europe, *Report of the Committee on Culture, Science and Education: Public Service Broadcasting* (Council of Europe 2004) para 12.

[157] G Born and T Prosser, 'Culture and Consumerism: Citizenship, Public Service Broadcasting and the BBC's Fair Trading Obligations' (2001) 64 Modern Law Review 657, 676.

[158] BBC, 'A distinctive BBC', April 2016, 3 <https://downloads.bbc.co.uk/aboutthebbc/insidethebbc/reports/pdf/bbc_distinctiveness_april2016.pdf> accessed 15 February 2023.

[159] ibid 4.

[160] ibid 26.

[161] ibid 10.

providers, the range of online news content on offer on every BBC service is clearly distinguishable. Indeed, academic research suggests that the BBC news output across all platforms is distinctive and more informative overall than that provided by market-driven news outlets.[162]

A further bone of contention between news publishers and the BBC pertains to the distribution of existing channels in a different technical format without a materiality assessment. An example is the distribution of the BBC *Newsbeat* material in written online content next to the eponymous teenage radio programme.[163] The BBC considers that distributing an existing channel in a different technical format should not generally be considered a material change.[164] The PPA argues that the availability of BBC *Newsbeat* as part of the BBC News Online website has fundamentally different potential impacts on competition compared to the radio programme and should hence be subjected to a materiality assessment.[165] However, it is doubtful whether this additional distribution avenue actually has such a significant competitive impact. Admittedly, the BBC website is the most used website for news.[166] However, young adults prefer to access news on Instagram, Facebook, BBC One, and Twitter rather than via the BBC website.[167] This is likely because they are more attracted to bitesize and visual content than to long reads.[168] The news publishers' grievance about *Newsbeat* therefore seems somewhat spurious. Along similar lines, the PPA also resents BBC's move into the podcast market, claiming that it impacts its members' ability to develop their strategies, to monetize their products, and to attract talent. They argue that there is cross-genre competition between magazines and podcasts because of the depth of coverage they provide.[169] It is striking that even when they seek to make inroads into audio, a domain originally occupied by broadcasting, news publishers call for ex ante competition regulation to stop PSBs in their tracks and to prevent them from aspiring to be world-leading. The abovementioned dismissal by the BGH of arguments seeking to restrict PSBs' depth of coverage is pertinent in this context.[170]

The tension between news publishers and the BBC has been somewhat eased, but by no means eliminated, by the olive branch offered by the BBC in the shape of the so-called Local Democracy Reporting Service (LDRS). This service was launched in 2017 to support the production of public interest journalism by local newsrooms.[171]

---

[162] S Cushion, 'Are Public Service Media Distinctive from the Market? Interpreting the Political Information Environments of BBC and Commercial News in the United Kingdom' (2022) 37(1) European Journal of Communication 3.

[163] BBC, 'News: newsbeat' <https://www.bbc.co.uk/news/newsbeat> accessed 10 March 2023.

[164] BBC, 'Policy on material changes' (n 153) para 2.3.

[165] PPA, 'Response to Ofcom Consultation' (n 141) 8.

[166] Ofcom, 'News consumption in the UK 2022 report' <https://www.ofcom.org.uk/__data/assets/pdf_f ile/0027/241947/News-Consumption-in-the-UK-2022-report.pdf> Figure 8.2.

[167] ibid Figure 3.2.

[168] See N Newman, 'Overview and key findings of the 2022 Digital News Report' (*Reuters Institute*, 15 June 2022) <https://reutersinstitute.politics.ox.ac.uk/digital-news-report/2022/dnr-executive-summary>; K Eddy, 'The changing news habits and attitudes of younger audiences' (*Reuters Institute*, 15 June 2022) <https://reutersinstitute.politics.ox.ac.uk/digital-news-report/2022/young-audiences-news-media> accessed 29 January 2024.

[169] PPA, 'Response to Ofcom Consultation' (n 141) 7.

[170] BGH, 30 April 2015, I ZR 13/14, para 66.

[171] H Lock, 'Local Democracy Reporting Service: a model for public broadcasters?' (*Public Media Alliance*, 2 November 2021) <Local Democracy Reporting Service: A model for public broadcasters? - Public Media Alliance> accessed 17 February 2023 (hereafter Lock, 'Local Democracy Reporting Service').

The LDRS is one of three schemes that make up the Local News Partnerships between the BBC and the UK regional news industry. The other two are a News Hub service granting partner media outlets access to BBC video material for use online and a Shared Data Unit established to boost the development of data journalism skills across local newsrooms.[172] The LDRS is perhaps the most important of these schemes.[173] It has generated global interest and has occasionally served as a model for initiatives to reinvigorate local journalism further afield, for example in New Zealand.[174] In the UK, there has been a significant number of local newspaper closures since 2005.[175] The resulting reduction in coverage of local institutions and in democratic participation has been vividly described in the Cairncross Review.[176] The decline of local journalism, conditioned by the loss of revenue from classified advertising and by changing news consumption habits as a result of digitization, is by no means confined to the UK. Local news deserts and a concomitant decrease in reporting known as the 'democratic deficit' have also emerged in other countries, most notably in the US.[177]

The LDRS aims to counteract this trend by providing £8 million of licence fee funding annually for the employment of up to 165 Local Democracy Reporters at news organizations across the UK, entrusted with covering single or shared beats.[178] The scheme, which is scheduled to run until the end of the current Royal Charter period in 2027, was initiated and rolled out in tandem with the News Media Association. It has been criticized for allocating most contracts to the 'big three', that is, the three largest local news publishers Newsquest, JPIMedia (formerly Johnston Press), and Reach plc (formerly Trinity Mirror), thus deliberately marginalizing smaller news outlets.[179] Furthermore, it has been argued that the scheme has not been able to offset editorial job losses across the UK local newsrooms, especially given that the LDRS partner organizations have themselves made considerable cuts to their staff numbers.[180] Moreover, the LDRS scheme raises fundamental questions about its alignment with the PSB mission and editorial standards. Should the BBC be involved in the commercial media landscape and be investing its resources to keep local newspapers afloat

---

[172] BBC, 'Local News Partnerships' <https://www.bbc.com/lnp/> accessed 3 March 2023.

[173] D Harte, 'Local Public Service Journalism and the BBC' in R Matthews (ed), *Reappraising Local and Community News in the UK: Media, Practice and Policy* (Taylor & Francis 2021) 1, 5.

[174] Lock, 'Local Democracy Reporting Service' (n 171).

[175] C Tobitt, 'Local newspaper closures: At least 265 titles gone since 2005, but pace of decline has slowed' (*Press Gazette*, 20 August 2020) <UK local newspaper closures: At least 265 titles gone since 2005, but pace of decline has slowed - Press Gazette>.

[176] Cairncross Review (n 148) 21ff.

[177] ibid; P M Abernathy, 'The expanding news desert' (Center for Innovation and Sustainability in Local Media, University of North Carolina 2018) <https://www.cislm.org/wp-content/uploads/2018/10/The-Expanding-News-Desert-10_14-Web.pdf> accessed 3 March 2023.

[178] T Lavender and others, 'Research into recent dynamics of the press sector in the UK and globally' (*Plum Consulting*, May 2020) <https://assets.publishing.service.gov.uk/government/uploads/system/uploads/attachment_data/file/924325/Plum_DCMS_press_sector_dynamics_-_Final_Report_v4.pdf> accessed 29 January 2024, 28.

[179] S Barnett, 'Sustainability of local journalism', Written submission to the DCMS Committee, 31 March 2022 <https://committees.parliament.uk/writtenevidence/107661/pdf/> accessed 3 March 2023.

[180] G N Ramsay, 'Mapping changes in local news 2015-2017. More bad news for democracy?' (*National Union of Journalists*, March 2017) <https://www.mediareform.org.uk/wp-content/uploads/2017/12/mapping-changes-in-local-news-2015-2017-interactive-research-report-march-2017.pdf> 4; S Barnet, 'Cairncross Review: Two cheers and two fears for the future of UK journalism' (*Informm*, 15 February 2019) <https://inforrm.org/2019/02/15/cairncross-review-two-cheers-and-two-fears-for-the-future-of-uk-journalism-steven-barnett/#more-41585> accessed 29 January 2024.

when its own local radio programmes are under threat?[181] And how is it possible to reconcile BBC's due impartiality imperative with the political partisanship that is allowed in the press codes?[182] The LDRS brief states that the scheme's core purpose is to 'provide impartial coverage of the regular business and workings of local authorities in the UK, and other relevant democratic institutions'.[183] It is also stated, somewhat ambivalently, that written content may conform to 'an employer's normal style' while adhering to the highest standards of accuracy and impartiality. Reliance is placed on BBC training to create a 'common standard for media content production'.[184] However, the extent to which this succeeds is uncertain in view of the varied perceptions of the scheme's purpose among partner organizations. There is evidence that certain news publishers direct Local Democracy Reporters (LDRs) to cover certain stories, to generate 'hits' and meet targets.[185] Such level of intervention sits uncomfortably with the requirement of impartiality with which LDRs are meant to comply.

The Cairncross Review recognized that the rules that constrain the BBC as a PSB sometimes give rise to frictions with the local reporters and their host papers.[186] This tension is more problematic given that LDRS stories frequently also feature on the BBC website or even on the BBC flagship TV and radio news programmes.[187] Imposing due impartiality requirements is difficult in the case of news providers who may not be committed to this idea. This even applies to certain Ofcom licensees as was exemplified in the case of RT's challenge of the impartiality norm as an illegitimate interference with freedom of expression.[188] The imposition of an externalized impartiality standard is even more challenging in the current media landscape. The waning policy commitment to PSB means that there is a shortage of skills needed to assess the 'validity, range and weight of countervailing opinions, in ways that the audience will trust'.[189] It is doubtful that this shortage can be overcome by exposing LRDs to BBC training. What is more, as has already been discussed, the due impartiality regime is increasingly perceived as a straitjacket by journalists who have breathed the air of freedom on social media and who are more concerned about building their own persona than about ensuring that 'all viewers, and not just average viewers, have access to the differing viewpoints'.[190]

In recognition of these shortcomings and tensions, Cairncross recommended a robust review of the LDRS and its continuation under the helm of the proposed Institute for Public Interest News, a news industry equivalent to the Arts Council England.[191]

---

[181] See UK Parliament, 'BBC executives questioned on BBC local radio cuts', 10 November 2022 <https://committees.parliament.uk/committee/378/digital-culture-media-and-sport-committee/news/174293/bbc-executives-questioned-on-bbc-local-radio-cuts/> accessed 7 March 2023.

[182] See IPSO Code, Clause 1iv); Chapter 5, pp 117, 120.

[183] BBC, 'Local Democracy Reporting Service' <Local Democracy Reporting Service - Local News Partnerships (bbc.com)> accessed 7 March 2023.

[184] ibid.

[185] National Union of Journalists, 'LDRs call for a say in the future of the local democracy reporting scheme', 3 March 2020 <https://www.nuj.org.uk/resource/ldrs-call-for-a-say-in-the-future-of-the-local-democracy.html> accessed 7 March 2023.

[186] Cairncross Review (n 148) 100.

[187] Lock, 'Local Democracy Reporting Service' (n 171).

[188] *Autonomous Non-Profit Organisation TV-Novosti, R (On the Application Of) v The Office of Communications* [2021] EWCA Civ 1534, paras 23ff.

[189] T Gibbons, 'Impartiality in United Kingdom Broadcasting' (2022) 14(1) Journal of Media Law 11, 17.

[190] Chapter 5, p 127; *Autonomous Non-Profit Organisation TV-Novosti, R (On the Application Of) v The Office of Communications* [2020] EWHC 689 (Admin), para 66.

[191] Cairncross Review (n 148) 100.

This recommendation was not taken forward by the government which expressed unease at the prospect of a state definition of what constitutes 'public interest' news. It argued that 'even an arm's length relationship risks perceptions of inappropriate government interference with the press'.[192] Indeed, as already discussed, governmental scrutiny of the quality of press products sits uncomfortably with press freedom.[193] However, the establishment of the Institute for Public Interest News could align with and even strengthen press freedom as long as regulatory safeguards were put in place to ensure that the funding allocation criteria were fair and transparent and did not aim to suppress speech.[194] Certain value judgements would be inevitable to ascertain that subsidies did not support publications which are already reasonably well-endowed, and which do not necessarily further the public good. Entrusting these decisions to an expert body at arm's length from the government would help to ensure that the subsidies are used to enable the press to discharge its functions, not to distort the market or create a permanent dependence on the state.

Continuous BBC funding cuts coupled with the LDRS's deficiencies is likely to render the continued BBC financing of this scheme unsustainable. The support of local journalism is a laudable aim, but the funnelling of funds from a PSB under attack to profitable commercial news providers may prove counterproductive. A more viable model to counteract the decline in local news reporting needs to be inclusive and to enable all partners to thrive. The LRDS is, however, a valuable blueprint for a development of a more collaborative relationship between the BBC and the press industry, in a way that furthers the public interest rather than being forever tainted by concerns of 'crowding out'. A future BBC funding model and revision of the LRDS has to take the need for adequate and stable BBC resources into account.[195]

Finally, a further measure that would help to ease the tension between the print and PSB sectors is the development of comprehensive regimes to improve users' exposure to diverse public interest content online. In the UK, the prominence of PSB content is ensured in electronic programme guides (EPGs) by way of the EPG Code. The EPG Code, last amended in 2019, applies to linear TV channels only. Ofcom has recommended its extension to on-demand services.[196] This recommendation has been taken up in the draft Media Bill which proposes a privileged position for PSB content on user interfaces beyond the EPG, such as on smart TVs, set-top boxes, and streaming sticks.[197] While a measure of discrimination in favour of PSBs is appropriate in view

---

[192] Department for Culture, Media and Sport, 'Government response to the Cairncross Review: a sustainable future for journalism', 27 January 2020 <https://www.gov.uk/government/publications/the-cairncross-review-a-sustainable-future-for-journalism/government-response-to-the-cairncross-review-a-sustainable-future-for-journalism?> accessed 29 January 2024, para 51.

[193] Chapter 4, p 84.

[194] SeeE Barendt, *Freedom of Speech* (2nd edn, OUP 2007) 112ff; K Bleyer-Simon and I Nenadić, 'News media subsidies in the first wave of the Covid-19 pandemic—A European perspective' (EUI Centre for Media Pluralism and Media Freedom) <https://cmpf.eui.eu/news-media-subsidies-in-the-first-wave-of-the-covid-19-pandemic-a-european-perspective/> accessed 8 March 2023.

[195] See Draft EMFA, art 5, para 3; House of Lords, 'Licence to change' (n 51) para 90.

[196] Ofcom, 'Review of prominence for public service broadcasting. Statement on changes to the EPG Code', 4 July 2019 <https://www.ofcom.org.uk/__data/assets/pdf_file/0028/154459/statement-on-changes-to-the-epg-code.pdf>; Ofcom, 'Review of prominence for public service broadcasting. Recommendations to Government for a new framework to keep PSB TV prominent in an online world', 4 July 2019 <https://www.ofcom.org.uk/__data/assets/pdf_file/0021/154461/recommendations-for-new-legislative-framework-for-psb-prominence.pdf> accessed 14 March 2023.

[197] Draft Media Bill, cl 23.

of their preeminent role in a democratic society, it is necessary to reflect on wider changes that impact our information ecosystem. As discussed earlier, it is necessary to adopt a more holistic view and to develop transparent criteria for the identification and prominence of diverse public interest content online along the lines of the Council of Europe's Recommendation on promoting a favourable environment for quality journalism in the digital age.[198]

9.5 Concluding Remarks

Since the genesis of PSB, debate about its future has been shaped by contrasting viewpoints. At one end of the spectrum, commercial media, most vociferously the press, have been arguing for the dismantling or at least the slimming down of PSB to a complementary role confined to addressing narrowly construed market failures. This view is informed by a neoliberal ideology that puts faith in the market to efficiently allocate resources and provide welfare. At the other end of the spectrum, PSBs, with some support from national governments, have been arguing for a comprehensive public service remit. Being sceptical of the mechanisms of supply and demand in delivering social welfare, they consider that PSB is needed to sustain the public sphere and to protect other critical societal interests. Positions are so entrenched and value-laden that no real debate is possible.[199] This polarized debate has been carried forward to the digital age with little consideration for the profound ways in which the information and communication environment has been altered by technological convergence as much as by political, social, and cultural transformations. Both in Germany and in the UK, the need for state intervention in a market saturated with an apparent plethora of information is as contested as ever. Amidst this uncertainty, the draft Media Bill and the draft amendment to the German Media Treaty both propose to develop and to render more flexible the PSB online remit. At the same time, in both jurisdictions, the attempt is made to draw rigid boundaries between the press and PSB based on arcane requirements related to the form of communication or to PSB's added value. The debate is muddled by petty arguments on whether the criteria of 'press-likeness' or 'distinctiveness' should hinge on PSBs' overall offering or on individual pieces of content. All the while, the networked form of the hybrid medium is blindly resisted. PSB has so far persevered and has succeeded in fending off assaults to its programme autonomy. Nonetheless, the energy it devotes to this fight and to the conduct of ex ante assessments comes at a cost to the fulfilment of its mission. And while these battles are fought, both PSB and the press are undermined by the towering presence of far mightier, global competitors. It is high time the press realizes that PSB is not its competitor but a natural partner and that collision norms are developed that transcend their divides. The attempts at ensuring the findability of public interest content online and supporting local journalism are moves in the right direction. Their development in a more inclusive and equitable manner is the desideratum.

---

[198] Council of Europe Recommendation CM/Rec(2022)4 of the Committee of Ministers on promoting a favourable environment for quality journalism in the digital age', 17 March 2022.
[199] M Burri, *Public Service Broadcasting 3.0. Legal Design for the Digital Present* (Routledge 2015) 46.

10

Conclusion

10.1 Introduction

The processes of convergence and digitalization have altered the technological conditions in which the press operates. They have transformed the press product, which was originally the physical embodiment of ink on paper, but is now disintermediated, caught up in the net's 'cacophony of stimuli', vying to attract and hold our overburdened, short-circuited attention.[1] More than that, they have altered the environment in which the press strives to stake its claim to freedom and to protect its turf from other media players. Historically, most western countries have subjected the press, broadcasting, and the telecommunications sectors to separate regulatory regimes. The advent of electronic media and internet-based services and applications has blurred the technological boundaries between these sectors, and has challenged their regulatory silos.

Convergence has been traditionally committed to neoliberal ideals, aligned with the press's archetypal conception as a free-market medium, hostile to state intervention and subordinate to market forces. In recent times, concern about the online circulation of content that could harm individuals and society at large, has triggered a 'regulatory turn'.[2] National governments have been increasingly striving to develop policies to render online platforms more accountable to the public interest. Some of these policies target platforms' alleged market dominance, while others pertain to the content they distribute. These policies are crafted amidst profound uncertainty about the role of platforms as mere conduits or as media companies. Insofar as they remain wedded to regulatory models from the analogue era, they run the risk of being outdated before the ink is dry.

At the same time, the shift from platform self-regulation to nation-state and supranational regulation has created a new paradigm also for the field of online news media. As has aptly been remarked, ' "regulation" always contains the potential to censor communications'.[3] The prevalent political culture of control driven by fear poses a risk that the totality of the electronic news media might be seen as vectors of the same harms that beset the internet at large. They may hence be gradually transformed from 'technologies of freedom' to technologies firmly placed under the tutelage of the state, or be subjected to 'collateral censorship', with private entities and algorithms suppressing them in the service of the state or of opaque private interests.[4] Journalism's 'boundary struggles' as a result of its lack of professional status exacerbate the risk

---

[1] N Carr, *The Shallows: What the Internet Is Doing to Our Brains* (Norton & Company Ltd 2010) 74.
[2] P Schlesinger, 'After the Post-Public Sphere' (2020) 42(7–8) Media, Culture & Society 1545, 1549ff.
[3] ibid 1558.
[4] See J M Balkin, 'Free Speech Is a Triangle' (2018) 118 Columbia Law Review 2011, 2016.

Press Freedom and Regulation in a Digital Era. Irini Katsirea, Oxford University Press. © Irini Katsirea 2024.
DOI: 10.1093/oso/9780198858607.003.0010

that publications which serve the public interest, the proverbial wheat, get mixed in with the chaff.[5] The formidable obstacles to convincingly distinguishing between recognized news publishers and other journalistic content in the UK Online Safety Bill and in the draft European Media Freedom Act (EMFA)underscore the futility of the attempts to ring-fence journalism.[6] In the best case scenario, they may be well-intentioned yet impracticable, but in the worst, they may open the door for a state-defined press.

The compatibility of incentivized press regulation with press freedom has been fiercely debated in the UK in the context of section 40 of the Crime and Courts Act 2013. The same question has arisen once more, both in the UK and in Germany, in the context of the Online Safety Bill and of the Media Treaty. While Germany has controversially created an incentive for bloggers to join a self-regulatory scheme, the UK has so far resisted the proposal to link the exemption from the Bill to the membership of a press regulator. What has always been a sensitive question, the conditionality of press benefits on membership of a recognized self-regulatory body, is further complicated when the benefit is the recognition of the status as the 'press' itself. This work has sought to trace the search for a new paradigm for the governance of the online press, and to navigate the regulatory ruptures that persist due to the blurred boundaries between broadcast and print media, and between press and non-press actors.

10.2 Press Freedom, Broadcast Regulation, and Non-Press Actors

In his far-sighted work from the early eighties, de Sola Pool warned that the printed press might be subjected to government regulation much like the broadcast media once they came to share the same technologies of transmission. By way of proof, he quoted the Federal Communication Commission (FCC) chairman's question 'whether a newspaper delivered by teletext is an extension of print and thus as free as any other newspaper, or whether it is a broadcast and thus under the control of the government'.[7] These early Cassandra prophecies could be dismissed as fanciful if the delineation between the print and broadcast domains was not currently part of much official thinking about the regulation of the online communication environment. We have seen that, in Germany, the entitlement of online news media to press or to broadcasting freedom has been mired in controversy.[8] This seemingly obscure constitutional controversy had paradoxical real-life implications when the online news portal fragdenstaat.de was forced to publish its blog in print to be able to claim its right to information.[9] The treatment of fragdenstaat.de is typical of the cautious approach towards new media, exemplified by their last resort subjection to state media authorities'

---

[5] See H Sjøvaag, 'Hard News/Soft News: The Hierarchy of Genres and the Boundaries of the Profession' in M Carlsson and S C Lewis, *Boundaries of Journalism: Professionalism, Practices and Participation* (Routledge 2015) 101, 109.

[6] Chapter 3, pp 69–70, 71–72.

[7] >I de Sola Pool, *Technologies of Freedom* (Harvard UP 1983) 1.

[8] Chapter 4, pp 94–95.

[9] ibid.

regulatory purview, whilst continuing with the policy of 'no policy', or depending on one's perspective, a 'policy of freedom' vis-à-vis the traditional press.[10]

The unevenness between benefits and burdens bestowed on legacy media, if compared to the yet indeterminate category of other, online-only journalistic-editorial telemedia, is entrenched in the German Media Treaty. Privileges are extended to the former but not the latter who still need to comply with due diligence obligations. Early indications of the ways in which the state media authorities might police these obligations are not promising.[11] For one thing, their assertion that print media need to avoid one-sided reporting is at odds with the German Press Code, and strikes at the heart of press freedom. Notwithstanding national variations on the theme of objectivity, the right of the press to be partisan is considered sacrosanct. For another, state media authorities' eagerness to contest the accuracy of exaggerated comments posted in a one-person blog bodes ill for the future exercise of their discretion. It is difficult to comprehend why individuals with little reach should be sanctioned for alleged violations of the third-party accuracy standard, while mainstream media regularly commit such transgressions with impunity. We have seen that fact-checking under the banner of transparency is a mixed blessing when it comes to exposing inaccuracies and restoring the public's trust in the news media. It risks producing one-sided, *post hoc* versions of the truth in defiance of core tenets of press freedom such as the distinction between facts and value judgements and the protection of journalistic sources.

The second part of this monograph further explored the porousness of the divide between broadcast and print media in the case of the so far underutilized regulation of print publishers' online video sections both in their websites and in their social media presence.[12] National regulators in the UK and Germany attempt to govern these new services by having recourse to formalistic criteria that have little relation to the reality of online news publishing, such as the self-standing nature of video content or its preponderance compared to the amount of written material. The impetus for audiovisual-style regulation comes more from the desire to level the playing field between print publishers and on-demand service providers than from content-related concerns. The same applies to the regulation of live-streams as broadcasts. In Germany, the imposition of a licensing requirement on broadcasting, but not on on-demand services, has given rise to inequitable solutions in the case of video game streaming services in the past. The exemption of services with limited opinion-forming significance or reach has served to solve these conundrums. At the same time, the subjection of press publishers' live-streams to broadcast regulation erodes existing regulatory divides and throws into stark relief the convergence between historically separate modes of communication.

Convergence is, however, not an inevitable process engendered by technological forces as the techno-determinist perspective would have us believe.[13] Technological evolution does not unfold in a vacuum but is conditioned by socioeconomic and

---

[10] See J Curran and J Seaton, *Power Without Responsibility. Press, Broadcasting and the Internet in Britain* (8th edn, Routledge 2018) 484.
[11] Chapter 5, pp 121, 132.
[12] Chapter 8, pp 225–226.
[13] P Humphreys and S Simpson, *Regulation, Governance and Convergence in the Media* (Edward Elgar 2018) 10.

political imperatives.[14] In both Germany and the UK, press publishers appeal to press freedom to stave off the threat of regulation. In both countries, these clarion calls have been resisted by reference to the AVMSD-inspired regulatory framework or the opinion-forming and competition-distorting potential of the services in question. Both sides are somewhat disingenuous, the press forever masking the economic imperative behind its perennial claim to freedom, policymakers and the judiciary glossing over the ambiguity of the regulatory framework. The evolving policy debates about the organization of the new hybrid media exemplifies the contingent nature of convergence. The integration of previously separate forms of media is not automatic but depends on the weighing up and calibration of the manifold interests and values at stake. Neither the mode of transmission, linear or non-linear, as an imperfect proxy for a service's opinion-forming potential, nor the attractive but inconclusive metaphor of the 'level playing field', can assuredly determine the outcome of these policy debates. In the European jurisdictions under examination, policymakers have seemingly dismissed the provenance of a hybrid service from the press sector's stable as immaterial for its classification. In practice, the regulation of press publishers' video content as an on demand programme service (ODPS) has been very exceptional. Analogies with historic regulatory regimes and thinking hold sway, notwithstanding occasional rhetoric to the opposite. And while the archaic criterion of 'TV-likeness' has been removed from the AVMSD, it has reared its head again in the UK Media Bill's planned broadcast-like regulation of the largest video on demand (VOD) services. At the same time, a mirror-inverted model of regulation has been taking shape in the area of public service broadcasting.

10.3 Press Freedom and the PSB Online Remit

Whilst regulators tentatively extend their reach to online newspapers' financially impactful video content, the press seeks to put a break to the expansion of the online remit of public service broadcasters (PSBs). In this area, the clash between the neo-liberal ideology with its faith in the market, and the theory of social liberalism with its endorsement of state intervention to sustain the public sphere, comes to a head. Press publishers perceive PSBs as their competitors, which deprive them of their ability to successfully monetize their online products. In Germany, they engage in protracted legal battles, while in the UK, they prefer a strategy of constant whining. The German legislator has granted the powerful press lobby a concession by way of the ban on 'non-programme-related press-like services'. Nonetheless, the territorial fights are unceasing. All the while, press publishers stand together with their PSB rivals in the shadow of far mightier foes, the technology-turned-media giants. And the question as to the need for state intervention in a communication environment of plenty is asked with unremitting urgency. Whilst governments have showed some support for the PSB cause in the past, this cannot be taken for granted in future. The failings of the digital information ecosystem underscore, however, the need to ensure the sustainability of

---

[14] W Hulsink, 'Tides in Communication Politics? About Shifting Involvements and Technologies of Freedom and the Relevance of Albert Hirschman and Ithiel de Sola Pool for Today's Communication Studies' (2005) 67(6) Gazette: The International Journal for Communication Studies 569, 571.

public service media, and to enable them to follow their audience wherever it is. PSBs are prime candidates, but they are not the only actors deserving support. Responsible press publishers are equally crucial for a vibrant public sphere. Integrated policies, rather than formalistic, piecemeal solutions, are needed to promote the financial stability of a public-interest-oriented media system. As much as written content is an integral part of PSB's online presence, user comments have become a crucial element for the viability of the online press.

10.4 Press Freedom and Liability for User Comments

A digital media strategy of great financial importance for the digital press is its interaction with the audience by way of comment sections. By opening these fora for discussion, the digital press has moved into the social media terrain with its attendant complications and hazards. Comment sections expose press publishers to the risk of liability if they prove ineffectual in removing offensive comments. The inconsistency in the Strasbourg approach places a question mark over the extent of newspapers' obligations. The balancing between press freedom and personality rights has been context-specific, and the standard of liability has shifted from strict to limited and back again. Higher expectations have been placed on commercial operators in some cases but not in others. Greater legal certainty and an alignment of the European Court of Human Rights (ECtHR) case law with the E-Commerce Directive/ Digital Services Act (ECD/ DSA) framework is imperative if press publishers are to be able to uphold comment sections. These are not only vital for their survival. They also allow them to strengthen the bond with their audience and to further their democratic potential. Having said that, for this democratic potential to be realized, the onus is ultimately on publishers to foster a constructive environment in which all feel welcome to participate. Compliance with the exigencies of the limited liability framework should enable the online press to expand the discursive space without giving hate speech or defamatory comments a floor.

A last topic covered in this monograph, the right to erasure/right to be forgotten (RTE/RTBF), also pertains to the impact of platform logics on the online press.

10.5 Press Freedom and the Right to
Erasure/Right to Be Forgotten

Search engines' comprehensive digital memory has given rise to data protection legislation and to a body of international and national case law on this newly forged right to informational self-determination. Whilst the RTE/RTBF was originally conceived of as a countervailing force against search engines' capacity to never forget, its reasoning has now been transplanted to cases involving online press archives. As a result, a fundamental reconsideration of the balance between press freedom and personality rights has been underway in recent ECtHR and German case law. Neither the fact that online press archives lack search engines' ability to completely profile data subjects nor the profound uncertainty about the technical solutions at hand have halted this swing of the pendulum. Even though courts pay lip service to the risks of anonymization for the integrity of press archives, they are prepared to embrace a time-limited conception of newsworthiness. The absence of consideration for the impact of dereferencing on the completeness of the historical record is also evident in the *NT1 & NT2* judgment. The obligation to anonymize, no-index tag, or even erase information is at odds with the journalistic commitment to accuracy. In line with the social media culture of constant updating, a more innocuous requirement to keep online archived information up-to-date is on the rise. Even this expectation is problematic for under-staffed, underfunded newsrooms. The conflict between personality rights and news value risks stifling critical reporting and creating a memory hole that detrimentally affects journalistic research and the public's right to information.

10.6 In Search of a Regulatory Model for the Digital Press

This monograph has examined the ways in which legislators, policymakers, and the courts vie to thrash out the regulatory framework for the digital press. This exercise is influenced by analogies with concepts that informed analogue regulatory categories, such as the TV-likeness of content or the reproduction of text/image combinations characteristic of print media. Even though these regulatory models are disputed, they continue to have ideological currency in the hybrid media system, and to play into the ways in which real or perceived competitive struggles are fought out. This path-dependent development of the digital press has been partly harmonized by the over-arching European Union (EU) framework as regards audiovisual media services or platform liability. At the same time, national idiosyncratic factors have also influenced the regulation of hybrid services. The treatment of news blogs is a case in point. In the UK non-traditional online journalism is mostly unregulated, while in Germany, the screw has recently been tightened for net native media.

The regulatory landscape is further complicated by the ambivalence as to the role and treatment of online platforms. This uncertainty is exacerbated by the disparity between the more interventionist European and the more permissive US approach. Meanwhile, the risks that are endemic to these platforms have spilled over inexorably into the domain of the online press, exposing it to the risk of liability for violations of personality rights and of a hypertrophic right to reputation. The often-problematized clash between European and US traditions glosses over the differences between European national media systems, which reflect diverse historical experiences and constitutional traditions. There is certainly cross-fertilization between national legal orders in their attempts to grapple with the challenges of platform regulation. At the same time, the solutions they opt for and the sticking points they encounter along the way differ, as evidenced by the NetzDG and the Online Safety Bill, both equally controversial, but each in its own way. The toolkits emerging from this bourgeoning national and EU-level experimentation will hopefully lead to a more integrated, human rights-compliant framework, grounded in reliable empirical research, rather than driven by knee-jerk reactions to 'public shocks'.[15]

---

[15] See T Flew, F Martin, and N Suzor, 'Internet Regulation as Media Policy: Rethinking the Question of Digital Communication Platform Governance' (2019) 10(1) Journal of Digital Media & Policy 33, 35.

The regulatory solutions adopted in the jurisdictions examined in this volume provide, in all their imperfections and contradictions, valuable insights for the much-professed nascent digital constitutionalism as an ordering framework for the algorithmic society.[16] The disparity of these solutions is not necessarily a draw-back. A level of regulatory pluralism and strategic inconsistency can lead to more optimum outcomes in the long run. It is imperative, however, that unintended consequences are monitored along the way to ensure that longstanding guarantees for press freedom do not fall by the wayside. The complementarity between the press and broadcasting models is likely to continue holding sway in the digital ecosystem. For all of de Sola Pool's Orwellian predictions, this asymmetrical regulation might provide a useful blueprint for the emerging shape of internet governance, provided disparate regulatory traditions are not viewed as rigid silos but as sliding doors, allowing cross-penetration in response to democratic needs. Attempting to halt the regulation of online newspapers' video content altogether or to bar PSBs from the provision of press-like services by reference to press freedom ignores the convergent nature of hybrid media. What is required is a more principled discussion that could lead to the development of collision norms conducive to the creation of a democratic online environment. It is necessary to develop a positive regulatory framework, as opposed to only negative measures aimed at tackling competition imbalance or harm. Such a framework would foster a digital environment in which everyone has access to diverse, financially sustainable public interest news media, and is empowered to participate in democracy.[17]

---

[16] O Pollicino and G De Gregorio, 'Constitutional Law in the Algorithmic Society' in H.-W. Micklitz and others, *Constitutional Challenges in the Algorithmic Society* (Cambridge UP 2022) 3, 5; N Suzor, 'Digital Constitutionalism: Using the Rule of Law to Evaluate the Legitimacy of Governance by Platforms' (2018) 4(3) Social Media + Society 1; G Frosio, 'Why Keep a Dog and Bark Yourself?' (2018) 26(1) International Journal of Law and Information Technology 1, 11.

[17] Commission, 'European declaration on digital rights and principles for the digital decade' COM (2022) 28 final; Commission, 'Europe's media in the digital decade: An action plan to support recovery and transformation' COM (2020) 784 final.

Bibliography

Abernathy P M, 'The expanding news desert' (Center for Innovation and Sustainability in Local Media, University of North Carolina 2018) <https://www.cislm.org/wp-content/uploads/2018/10/The-Expanding-News-Desert-10_14-Web.pdf>.

Abrams F, 'The Press Is Different: Reflections on Justice Stewart and the Autonomous Press' (1979) 7 Hofstra Law Review 563.

Adair B, 'Determining if a politician is telling the truth. "Through our 'Truth-O-Meter', we graphically show the relative truth of each claim"' (*Nieman Reports*, 15 June 2008) <https://niemanreports.org/articles/determining-if-a-politician-is-telling-the-truth/>.

Aelst P van and others, 'Political Communication in a High-Choice Media Environment: A Challenge for Democracy?' (2017) 41(1) Annals of the International Communication Association 3.

Alonzo J, 'Note: Restoring the Ideal Marketplace: How Recognizing Bloggers as Journalists Can Save the Press' (2005/6) 9 New York University Journal of Legislation & Public Policy 751.

Ammori M, 'The 'New' New York Times: Free Speech Lawyering in the Age of Google and Twitter' (2014) 127 Harvard Law Review 2259.

Ananny M, *Networked Press Freedom: Creating Infrastructures for a Public Right to Hear* (MIT Press 2018).

Anderson D A, 'Freedom of the Press' (2002) 80 Texas Law Review 429.

Ardia D, 'Free Speech Savior or Shield for Scoundrels: An Empirical Study of Intermediary Immunity under Section 230 of the Communications Decency Act' (2010) 43 Loyola of Los Angeles Law Review 373.

Armstrong M and H Weeds, 'Public Service Broadcasting in the Digital World' in P Seabright and J von Hagen (eds), *The Economic Regulation of Broadcasting Markets. Evolving Technology and Challenges for Policy* (CUP 2007) 110.

Arning M, F Moos, and J Schefzig, 'Vergiss (,) Europa! Ein Kommentar zu EuGH, Urt. v. 13. 5. 2014 – Rs. C-131/12 – Google/Mario Costja Gonzalez, CR 2014, 460' (2014) 7 Computer und Recht 447.

Atamurto T, 'Crowdsourcing as a Knowledge-Search Method in Digital Journalism: Ruptured Ideals and Blended Responsibility' (2016) 4(2) Digital Journalism 280.

Ausloos J, *The Right to Erasure in EU Data Protection Law: From Individual Rights to Effective Protection* (OUP 2020).

Australian Competition and Consumer Commission, *Digital Platform Inquiry. Final Report* (Australian Competition and Consumer Commission 2019).

Badura P, 'Die öffentlich-rechtlichen Rundfunkanstalten bieten Rundfunk und Telemedien an' (2009) 134(2) Archiv des öffentlichen Rechts 240.

Bagdikian H, *The New Media Monopoly* (Beakon Press 2004).

Bagger Tranberg C, 'Proportionality and Data Protection in the Case Law of the European Court of Justice' (2011) 1(4) International Data Privacy Law 239.

Baker C E, *Media, Markets and Democracy* (CUP 2001).

Baker C E, *Media Concentration and Democracy: Why Ownership Matters* (CUP 2007).

Bakshi A C, 'Why and How to Regulate Native Advertising in Online News Publications' (2015) 4(3/4) Journal of Media Law and Ethics 4.

Balkin J M, 'Information Fiduciaries and the First Amendment' (2016) 49 UC Davis Law Review 1183.

Balkin J M, 'Free Speech Is a Triangle' (2018) 118 Columbia Law Review 2011.

Ball J, *Post-Truth: How Bullshit Conquered the World* (Biteback Publishing 2017).

Bardoel J and G Ferrell Lowe, 'From Public Service Broadcasting to Public Service Media' in J Bardoel and G Ferrell Lowe (eds), *From Public Service Broadcasting to Public Service Media* (Nordicom 2007) 20.

Barendt E, *Freedom of Speech* (2nd edn, OUP 2007).

Barendt E, 'Statutory Underpinning: A Threat to Press Freedom?' (2013) 5(2) Journal of Media Law 189.

Barlow J P, 'A declaration of the independence of cyberspace', 8 February 1996 <https://www.eff.org/cyberspace-independence>.

Barnet S, 'Cairncross Review: Two cheers and two fears for the future of UK journalism' (*Inforrm*, 15 February 2019) <https://inforrm.org/2019/02/15/cairncross-review-two-cheers-and-two-fears-for-the-future-of-uk-journalism-steven-barnett/#more-41585>.

Barnett S, 'Sustainability of local journalism', Written submission to the DCMS Committee, 31 March 2022 https://committees.parliament.uk/writtenevidence/107661/pdf/.

Barwise P, 'What Are the Real Threats to Public Service Broadcasting?' in D Tambini and J Cowling (eds), *From PSB to Public Service Communications* (Institute for Public Policy Research 2004) 26.

Battagion M R and A Vaglio, 'Newspapers and Public Grants: A Matter of Quality' (2018) 65(1) Scottish Journal of Political Economy 21.

Bayer J and others, 'The fight against disinformation and the right to freedom of expression' (European Parliament LIBE Committee 2021).

Bekerman M, 'Garry Lineker tweet scandal shows how the BBC has struggled to adapt to the social media age' (*Inforrm*, 18 March 2023) <https://inforrm.org/2023/03/18/gary-lineker-tweet-scandal-shows-how-the-bbc-has-struggled-to-adapt-to-the-social-media-age-marek-bekerman/#more-54207>.

Bell K, 'IPSO Blog: Third party complaints made under Clause 1 (Accuracy)' (*IPSO*, 16 October 2019) <https://www.ipso.co.uk/news-press-releases/blog/ipso-blog-third-party-complaints-made-under-clause-1-accuracy/>.

Berg C E, G F Lowe, and A B Lund, 'A Market Failure Perspective on Value Creation in PSM' in G F Lowe and F Martin (eds), *The Value of Public Service Media* (Nordicom 2014) 105.

Bergström A and M J Belfrage, News in Social Media. Incidental Consumption and the Role of Opinion Leaders' (2018) 6(5) Digital Journalism 583.

Berka W and H Tretter, 'Public service media under Article 10 of the European Convention on Human Rights' (*European Broadcasting Union*, December 2013) <https://www.ebu.ch/files/live/sites/ebu/files/Publications/Art%2010%20Study_finaLpdf>.

Bernard C, *Rundfunk als Rechtsbegriff: Bedeutung, Inhalt und Funktion des Rundfunkbegriffs unter besonderer Berücksichtigung der Multimediadienste* (Springer 2001).

Bernstein D, 'Why the "right to be forgotten" won't make it the United States' (*Michigan Technology Law Review*, NK).

Bertuzzi L, 'Media exemption ruled out in DSA negotiations, but could return' (*Euractiv*, 29 November 2021) <https://www.euractiv.com/section/digital-single-market/news/media-exception-ruled-out-in-dsa-negotiations-but-could-return/>.

Betzel M, 'Finetuning Classification Criteria for On-Demand Audiovisual Media Services: The Dutch Approach' in IRIS Special, *The Regulation of On-demand Audiovisual Services: Chaos or Coherence?* (European Audiovisual Observatory 2011) 58.

Blackman C R, 'Convergence between Telecommunications and Other Media: How Should Regulation Adapt?' (1998) 22(3) Telecommunications Policy 163.

Bleyer-Simon K and I Nenadić, 'News media subsidies in the first wave of the Covid-19 pandemic—A European perspective' (EUI Centre for Media Pluralism and Media Freedom) <https://cmpf.eui.eu/news-media-subsidies-in-the-first-wave-of-the-covid-19-pandemic-a-european-perspective/>.

Blom-Cooper L, 'Press Freedom: Constitutional Right or Cultural Assumption?' [2008] Public Law 260.

Bloom M, 'Subpoenaed Sources and the Internet: A Test for When Bloggers Should Reveal Who Misappropriated a Trade Secret' (2006) 24(2) Yale Law & Policy Review 471.

Borowski M, 'Limiting Clauses: On the Continental European Tradition of Special Limiting Clauses and the General Limiting Clause of Art. 52 (1) Charter of Fundamental Rights of the European Union' (2007) 1(2) Legisprudence 197.

Bobek M, 'What are Grand Chambers for?' (2021) 23 Cambridge Yearbook of European Legal Studies 1.

Bock M A, 'Showing Versus Telling: Comparing Online Video from Newspaper and Television Websites' (2015) 17(4) Journalism 1.

Boczkowski P and L Peer, 'The Choice Gap: The Divergent Online News Preferences of Journalists and Consumers' (2011) 61(5) Journal of Communication 857.

Bodo B, 'Means, not an end (of the world)—The customization of news personalization by European news media' (2018) Amsterdam Law School Legal Studies Research Paper 9/2018, 15 <https://papers.ssrn.com/sol3/papers.cfm?abstract_id=3141810>.

Bodo B, 'Selling News to Audiences—A Qualitative Enquiry into the Emerging Logics of Algorithmic News Personalization in European Quality News Media' (2019) 7(8) Digital Journalism 1054.

Bogart L, 'Reflections on Content Quality in Newspapers' (2004) 25(1) Newspaper Research Journal 40.

Böhler C, 'Notwendigkeit einer Rundfunklizenz beim Betrieb von Video-streaming-Portalen' (2017) 33(8) Computer und Recht 541.

Bollinger L C, 'Freedom of the Press and Public Access: Toward a Theory of Partial Regulation of the Mass Media' (1976) 75(1) Michigan Law Review 1.

Bollinger L C, *Images of a Free Press* (University of Chicago Press 1991).

Bollinger L C, *Uninhibited, Robust, and Wide-Open: A Free Press for a New Century* (OUP 2010).

Bolter L C and R Grusin, *Remediation. Understanding New Media* (MIT Press 2000).

Booth P, 'Introduction' in A Peacock (ed), *PSB without the BBC?* (Institute of Economic Affairs 2004) 18.

Born G and T Prosser, 'Culture and Consumerism: Citizenship, Public Service Broadcasting and the BBC's Fair Trading Obligations' (2001) 64 Modern Law Review 657.

Bossio D and others, 'Australia's News Media Bargaining Code and the Global Turn Towards Platform Regulation' (2022) 14 Policy & Internet 136.

Bracha F Pasquale, 'Federal Search Commission? Access, Fairness and Accountability in the Law of Search' (2008) 93(6) Cornell Law Review 1149.

Brand T, *Rundfunk im Sinne des Artikel 5 Abs. 1 Satz 2 GG* (Duncker & Humblot 2002).

Breitschaft A, 'Evaluating the Linear/Non-Linear Divide—Are There any Better Factors for the Future Regulation of Audiovisual Media Content?' (2009) 20(8) Entertainment Law Review 291.

Briggs A, *The BBC: The First Fifty Years* (OUP 1985).

Bron C, 'Financing and Supervision of PSB. European Legislation and Current National Developments Concerning Financial and Content-Related Supervision' (2010) 4 IRIS Plus 7.

Bronsema F, *Medienspezifischer Grundrechtsschutz der elektronischen Presse. Darstellung des Grundrechtsschutzes in der Europäischen Union und Entwicklung eines Lösungsansatzes für den Grundrechtsschutz aus Art. 5 Abs. 1 GG* (LIT 2010).

Brüggemann M and others, 'Hallin and Mancini Revisited: Four Empirical Types of Western Media Systems' (2014) 64(6) Journal of Communication 1037.

Brunner L, 'The Liability of an Online Intermediary for Third Party Content' (2016) 16(1) Human Rights Law Review 163.

Bruns A, 'Reconciling Community and Commerce?: Collaboration between Produsage Communities and Commercial Operators' (2012) 15(6) Information, Communication & Society 815.

Bruns A, '"Random Acts of Journalism Redux". News and Social Media' in J L Jensen, M Mortensen, and J Ørmen (eds), News across Media. Production, Distribution and Consumption (Routledge 2018) 37.

Bucher T, 'Want to Be on the Top? Algorithmic Power and the Threat of Invisibility on Facebook' (2012) 14(7) New Media & Society 1164.

Bueger G de, 'Supervising On-demand Audiovisual Media Services: Best practices and Methodology', Comparative Background Document, 38th EPRA Meeting, 2–4 October 2013, Vilnius <http://www.epra.org>.

Buiten M C, 'The Digital Services Act: From Intermediary Liability to Platform Regulation' (2022) 12 Journal of Information Technology, Intellectual Property and E-Commerce Law 361.

Bundeskartellamt, 'Improvements for press publishers using Google News Showcase', 21 December 2022 <Bundeskartellamt - Homepage - Improvements for publishers using Google News Showcase>.

Buri I and J van Hoboken, 'The Digital Services Act (DSA) proposal: A critical overview' (IViR Discussion Paper, 28 October 2021) 38.

Burri M, Public Service Broadcasting 3.0. Legal Design for the Digital Present (Routledge 2015).

Cairncross F, 'Cairncross Review: A sustainable future for journalism', 12 February 2019 <https://assets.publishing.service.gov.uk/government/uploads/system/uploads/attachme nt_data/file/779882/021919_DCMS_Cairncross_Review_.pdf>.

Campaign for Press and Broadcasting Freedom, 'Trust in journalism at all-time low' <https://www.cpbf.org.uk/2016/12/12/trust-journalism-time-low/>.

Canadian Association of Journalists, 'The ethics of unpublishing', 27 October 2010 <https://caj.ca/the-ethics-of-unpublishing/#:~:text=Unpublish%20by%20consensus%3A%20No%20one,journalistic%20reasons%20to%20resist%20unpublishing>.

Cappello M (ed), Media Law Enforcement Without Frontiers, IRIS Special (European Audiovisual Observatory 2018).

Carlson M, 'Facebook in the News' (2018) 6(1) Digital Journalism 4.

Carne S and J Jessop, 'Debate: Is self-regulation failing in the UK newspaper industry?' (Institute of Economic Affairs, 18 December 2018) <https://iea.org.uk/debate-is-self-regulation-failing-in-the-uk-newspaper-industry/>.

Carney D, 'Up to Standard? A Critique of IPSO's Editors' Code of Practice and IMPRESS's Standards Code: Part 1' (2017) 22(3) Communications Law 77.

Carr N, The Shallows: What the Internet Is Doing to Our Brains (Norton & Company Ltd 2010).

Cathcart B, 'IPSO: The toothless master rolls over its masters (again)' (Inforrm, 26 October 2018) <https://inforrm.org/2018/10/26/ipso-the-toothless-puppet-rolls-over-for-its-masters-again-brian-cathcart/>.

Cavaliere P, 'From Journalistic Ethics to Fact-Checking Practices: Defining the Standards of Content Governance in the Fight Against Disinformation' (2020) 12(2) Journal of Media Law 133.

Centre for Media Pluralism and Media Freedom, Monitoring media pluralism in the digital era (European University Institute 2022) <https://cadmus.eui.eu/bitstream/handle/1814/74712/MPM2022-EN-N.pdf?sequence=1&isAllowed=y>.

Chandler D and R Munday, *A Dictionary of Media and Communication* (OUP 2016).

Charles A and G Stewart (eds), *The End of Journalism: News in the Twenty-First Century* (Peter Lang 2011).

Chadwick A, *The Hybrid Media System: Politics and Power* (2nd edn, OUP 2017).

Charney J, *The Illusion of the Free Press* (Hart Publishing 2018).

Charney J, 'Free Press: Necessary Illusions' (2019) 15(3) Law, Culture and the Humanities 826.

Chavannes R and O Castendyk, 'Art. 1 AVMSD' in O Castendyk, E Dommering, and A Scheuer (eds), *European Media Law* (Kluwer 2008) 802.

Citron D, *Hate Crimes in Cyberspace* (Harvard UP 2014).

Coase R, 'The Market for Goods and the Market for Ideas' (2022) 19(1) Econ Journal Watch 166.

Coe P, 'Redefining "Media" Using a "Media-as-a-Constitutional-Component-Concept": An Evaluation of the Need for the European Court of Human Rights to Alter Its Understanding of "Media" Within a New Media Landscape' (2017) 37(1) Legal Studies 25.

Coe P, *Media Freedom in the Age of Citizen Journalism* (Edward Elgar Publishing 2021).

Cole M D and C Etteldorf, *Research for CULT Committee—Implementation of the revised Audiovisual Media Services Directive* (European Parliament 2022).

Collins R, 'Internet Governance in the UK' (2006) 28(3) Media, Culture & Society 337.

Collins R, 'Hierarchy to Homeostasis? Hierarchy, Markets and Networks in UK Media and Communications Governance' (2008) 30(3) Media, Culture & Society 295.

Cornia A and others, 'Private sector news, social media distribution, and algorithm change' (*Digital News Project*, September 2018) 15 <https://reutersinstitute.politics.ox.ac.uk/sites/default/files/2018-10/Cornia_Private_Sector_News_FINALpdf>.

Cornils M, 'Vielfaltssicherung bei Telemedien' (2018) 5 Archiv für Presserecht 377.

Cornils M, '§1 LPG Freiheit der Presse' in M Löffler (ed), *Presserecht* (6th edn, Beck 2015).

Cornils M, 'Vielfaltssicherung bei Telemedien' (2018) 49(5) Archiv für Presserecht 377.

Cornils M, 'Die Perspektive der Wissenschaft: AVMD-Richtlinie, der 22. Rundfunkänderungsstaatsvertrag und der "Medienstaatsvertrag"—Angemessene Instrumente für die Regulierungsherausforderungen?' (2019) 63(2) Zeitschrift für Urheber- und Medienrecht 89.

Cornils M, 'Art. 10 EMRK' in H Gersdorf and P Paal (eds), *Informations- und Medienrecht Kommentar* (2nd edn, Beck 2021).

Cornils M, 'Art. 11 EU-GR Charta' in H Gersdorf and P Paal (eds), *Informations- und Medienrecht Kommentar* (2nd edn, Beck 2021).

Cornils M, 'Art. 85 DS-GVO' in H Gersdorf and P Paal (eds), *Informations- und Medienrecht Kommentar* (Beck 2021).

Cornils M and K Liesem, 'Stellungnahme zum Diskussionsentwurf eines Medienstaatsvertrages der Rundfunkkommission der Länder' (*Mainzer Medieninstitut*, NK) <https://www.mainzer-medieninstitut.de/stellungnahme-des-mainzer-medieninstituts-zum-diskussionsentwurf-eines-medienstaatsvertrages/>.

Costello R, 'The Right to Be Forgotten in Cases Involving Criminal Convictions' (2018) 3 European Human Rights Law Review 268.

Cotter K, J Cho, and E Rader, 'Explaining the News Feed algorithm: An analysis of the "News Feed FYI" blog', Proceedings of the 2017 CHI Conference (Association for Computing Machinery 2017) 1557.

Cox N, '*Delfi AS v Estonia*: The Liability of Secondary Internet Publishers for Violation of Reputational Rights under the European Convention on Human Rights' (2014) 77(4) Modern Law Review 619.

Coyle D and C Woolard, 'Public value in practice, Restoring the ethos of public service' <http://downloads.bbc.co.uk/bbctrust/assets/files/pdf/regulatory_framework/pvt/public_value_practice.pdf>, 22 March 2012.

Craft S and C N Davis, *Principles of American Journalism: An Introduction* (2nd edn, Routledge 2016).

Cryle D, 'The Press and Public Service Broadcasting: Neville Petersen's *News Not Views* and the Case for Australian Exceptionalism' (2014) 151 Media International Australia 56.

Cuilenburg J van and D McQuail, 'Media Policy Paradigm Shifts: Towards a New Communications Policy Paradigm' (2003) 18(2) European Journal of Communication 181.

Curran J and J Seaton, *Power Without Responsibility: The Press and Broadcasting in Britain* (7th, edn Routledge 2009).

Cushion S, 'Are Public Service Media Distinctive from the Market? Interpreting the Political Information Environments of BBC and Commercial News in the United Kingdom' (2022) 37(1) European Journal of Communication 3.

Dachwitz I and A Fanta, 'Leistungsschutzrecht: Deutshe Verlage scheitern an Google' (*Netzpolitik*, 29 September 2022) <https://netzpolitik.org/2022/leistungsschutzrecht-deutsche-verlage-scheitern-an-google/>.

Dagoula D, I Katsirea, and J Harrison, 'The Independent Press Standards Organisation and Accuracy: A Comparative Study of Complaints Handling Procedures in Four UK Newspapers' (2023) 1(1) Journal of Applied Journalism & Media Studies 1.

Davies N, *Flat Earth News: An Award-Winning Reporter Exposes Falsehood, Distortion and Propaganda in the Global Media* (Vintage Digital 2011).

Davis C M, *Die "dienende" Rundfunkfreiheit im Zeitalter der sozialen Vernetzung* (Mohr Siebeck 2019).

Deegan M and K Sutherland, *Transferred Illusions: Digital Technology and the Forms of Print* (Routledge 2009).

Degenhart C, *Der Funktionsauftrag des öffentlich-rechtlichen Rundfunks in der digitalen Welt* (Verlag Recht und Wirtschaft 2001).

Department for Culture, Media and Sport, 'Government response to the Leveson Inquiry and its implementation. Section 40 of the Crime and Courts Act 2013 and Part 2 of the Leveson Inquiry', 1 March 2018 <https://assets.publishing.service.gov.uk/government/uploads/system/uploads/attachment_data/file/684678/GOVERNMENT_RESPONSE_TO_THE_CONSULTATION_ON_THE_LEVESON_INQUIRY_AND_ITS_IMPLEMENTATION_.pdf>.

Department for Culture, Media and Sport, 'Government response to the Cairncross Review: a sustainable future for journalism', 27 January 2020 <https://www.gov.uk/government/publications/the-cairncross-review-a-sustainable-future-for-journalism/government-response-to-the-cairncross-review-a-sustainable-future-for-journalism?>.

Department for Digital, Culture, Media & Sport, 'Guidance: The E-Commerce Directive and the UK' (21 January 2021) <https://www.gov.uk/guidance/the-ecommerce-directive-and-the-uk>.

Department for Culture, Media and Sport, 'Online Safety Bill: Communications offences factsheet', 19 April 2022 <https://www.gov.uk/government/publications/online-safety-bill-supporting-documents/online-safety-bill-communications-offences-factsheet>.

Department for Culture, Media and Sport and Department for Science, Innovation & Technology, 'Guidance: Fact sheet on enhanced protections for journalism within the Online Safety Bill', 23 August 2022 <https://www.gov.uk/government/publications/fact-sheet-on-enhanced-protections-for-journalism-within-the-online-safety-bill/fact-sheet-on-enhanced-protections-for-journalism-within-the-online-safety-bill>.

Department for Culture, Media and Sport, 'Up next—The government's vision for the broadcasting sector' (CP 671, 2022) <https://www.gov.uk/government/publications/up-next-the-governments-vision-for-the-broadcasting-sector>.

Department for Digital, Culture, Media and Sport, 'BBC mid-term review: terms of reference', 26 May 2022 https://www.gov.uk/government/publications/bbc-charter-and-framework-agreement/bbc-mid-term-review-terms-of-reference#:~:text=The%20Mid%2DTerm%20Review%20must,point%20of%20the%20BBC%20Charter.

Department for Culture, Media and Sport, 'New laws to help bring great shows to British screens and airwaves', 28 March 2023 <https://www.gov.uk/government/news/new-laws-to-help-bring-more-great-shows-to-british-screens-and-airwaves>.

Dereje L, 'Sorgfaltspflichten auch für Laien im Netz!' (*Verfassungsblog*, 5 June 2019) <https://verfassungsblog.de/sorgfaltspflichten-auch-fuer-laien-im-netz/>.

Dernbach B, 'Die Debatte um den öffentlich-rechtlichen Rundfunk ist eine mediale Inszenierung. Eine Analyse der Kritik der Zeitungsverleger and den Strategien von ARD und ZDF' (2019) 60 Jahrbuch für Christliche Sozialwissenschaften 195.

Desai A C, 'Regulating Social Media in the Free-Speech Ecosystem' (2022) 73(5) Hastings Law Journal 1481, 1506ff.

Desai A C and J A Kroll, 'Trust but Verify: A Guide to Algorithms and the Law' (2017) 31 Harvard Journal of Law and Technology 1.

Deutsche Gesellschaft für Recht und Informatik, 'Stellungnahme in der Vergfassungsbeschwerde des Herrn T. AZ 1 BvR 16/13' 2, 4ff (*DGRI*, 28 April 2014) <https://www.dgri.de/68/pn/2/Stellungnahmen.htm>.

Deutscher Bundestag, 'Presseförderung in den EU-Mitgliedstaaten', 15 April 2009, 10 <https://www.bundestag.de/resource/blob/412690/a9620ecbbccf69b2c7cf017401fdb454/wd-10-019-09-pdf-data.pdf>.

Deutscher Bundestag, 'Rundfunkrechtliches Zulassungserforderniss für Streaming-Kanäle. Vorgaben durch die EU-Richtlinie über Audiovisuelle Mediendienste', WD 10 – 3000 – 031/19 (Deutscher Bundestag 2019) 8 <https://www.bundestag.de/resource/blob/656500/a55ea40c571c8cdde91d84c749c4389a/WD-10-031-19-pdf-data.pdf>.

Deuze M, 'The Web and Its Journalisms: Considering the Consequences of Different Types of Newsmedia Online' (2003) 5(2) New Media and Society 503.

Deuze M, 'What Is Journalism? Professional Identity and Ideology of Journalists Reconsidered' (2005) 6(4) Journalism 442.

Deuze M, 'What Journalism Is (Not)' (2019) 4(1) Social Media + Society 1.

DeVito M, 'From Editors to Algorithms: A Values-Based Approach to Understanding Story Selection in the Facebook News Feed' (2017) 5(6) Digital Journalism 753.

Diakopoulos N and M Koliska, 'Algorithmic Transparency in the News Media' (2017) 5(7) Digital Journalism 809.

Digital, Culture, Media and Sport Committee, *The Draft Online Safety Bill and the Legal but Harmful Debate* (HC 2021–22, 1039).

Digital, Culture, Media and Sport Committee, *The Draft Online Safety Bill and the Legal but Harmful Debate: Government Response to the Committee's Eighth Report* (HC 2021–22, 1221).

Directorate-General for Communications Networks, Content and Technology, *A Multi-Dimensional Approach to Disinformation. Report of the Independent High Level Group on Fake News and Online Disinformation* (European Commission 2018).

DiRoma E, 'Kids Say the Darndest Things: Minors and the Internet' (2018) Cardozo Law Review 43.

Dittmayer M, *Wahrheitspflicht der Presse: Umfang und Gewährleistung* (Nomos 2013).

Douek E, 'Content Moderation as Systems Thinking' (2022) 136(2) Harvard Law Review 526.

Doherty M, 'Should making false statements in a referendum campaign be an electoral offence?', 4 July 2016 <https://ukconstitutionallaw.org/2016/07/04/michael-doherty-should-making-false-statements-in-a-referendum-campaign-be-an-electoral-offence/>.

Döpkens H R, 'Am Scheideweg: Politik für eine freie Presse oder für Google und Facebook?' (*medienpolitik.net*, 27 March 2020) <https://www.medienpolitik.net/2020/03/am-scheide weg-politik-fuer-eine-freie-presse-oder-fuer-google-und-facebook/>.

Dörr D, B Holznagel, and A Picot, 'Legitimation und Auftrag des öffentlich-rechtlichen Fernsehens in Zeiten der Cloud' (*ZDF*, 2016) 70 <https://tpp.rlp.de/opal/7f41d840e8a2e 5744f054a8f9b1fda4b>.

Douce R, 'IPSO Blog: User-generated comments and coronavirus' (*IPSO*, 17 April 2020) <https://www.ipso.co.uk/news-press-releases/covid-info-blogs/ipso-blog-user-generated-comments-and-coronavirus/>.

Douek E, 'Content Moderation as Systems Thinking' (2022) 136(2) Harvard Law Review 526.

Dreyer S and W Schulz, 'Schriftliche Stellungnahme zum zweiten Diskussionsentwurf eines Medienstaatsvertrags der Länder vom Juli 2019' (*Hans-Bredow-Institut*, 9 August 2019) <https://www.hans-bredow-institut.de/en/publications/schriftliche-stellungnahme-zum-zweiten-diskussionsentwurf-eines-medienstaatsvertrages-der-laender>.

Drunen M Z van, N Helberger, and M Bastian, 'Know Your Algorithm: What Media Organizations Need to Explain to Their Users about News Personalization' (2019) 9(4) International Data Privacy Law 1.

Dwyer T, *Legal and Ethical Issues in the Media* (MacMillan 2015).

Dwyer D E and C Painter, 'Erasing the Past: Untangling the Conflicting Journalistic Loyalties and Paradigmatic Pressures of Unpublishing' (2020) 35(4) Journal of Media Ethics 214.

Eberle C E in C Libor and R Schmidkonz, 'Die Aufgabe des öffentlich-rechtlichen Rundfunks in der digitalen Welt. 128. Tagung des Studienkreises für Presserecht und Pressefreiheit e.V. am 20/21.5.2022 in Hamburg' (2022) 5 Archiv für Presserecht 400.

Economic Insight, 'Press sector financial sustainability. A report for the Department of Culture, Media and Sport' (May 2021)<https://assets.publishing.service.gov.uk/government/uploads/sys tem/uploads/attachment_data/file/1073198/DCMS_Economic_Insight_final_report.pdf>.

Edge M, 'Are UK Newspapers Really Dying? A Financial Analysis of Newspaper Publishing Companies' (2019) 16(1) Journal of Media Business Studies 1.

Edwards L and M Veale, 'Slave to the Algorithm? Why a "Right to Explanation" Is Probably Not the Remedy You Are Looking for' (2017) 16 Duke Law & Technology Review 18.

Eecke P van and M Truyens, 'EU Study on the Legal analysis of a Single Market for the Information Society, New rules for a new age?' (*European Commission*, November 2009) <https://op.europa.eu/en/publication-detail/-/publication/a856513e-ddd9-45e2-b3f1-6c9a0ea6c722>.

Eisenstein E, *The Printing Press as an Agent of Change: Communications and Cultural Transformations in Early Modern Europe. Volumes I and II* (CUP 1980).

Eko L, *American Exceptionalism, the French Exception and Digital Media Law* (Lexington Books 2013).

Elixman E, *Datenschutz und Suchmaschinen. Neue Impulse für einen Datenschuz im Internet* (Duncker & Humblot 2012).

Bracha F Pasquale, 'Federal Search Commission? Access, Fairness and Accountability in the Law of Search' (2008) 93(6) Cornell Law Review 1149.

Elvestad E and A Phillips, *Misunderstanding News Audiences: Seven Myths of the Social Media Era* (Routledge 2018).

Emerson T I, *The System of Freedom of Expression* (Vintage Books 1970).

Enis Q van, *La liberté de la presse à l'ère numerique* (Larcier 2015).

Enquete Kommission, 'Dreizehnter Bericht der Enquete Kommission "Internet und digitale Gesellschaft": Kultur, Medien und Öffentlichkeit', BT-Drs 17/12542 (Deutscher Bundestag, 19 March 2013) 12.

Erdos D, 'From the Scylla of Restriction to the Charybdis of Licence? Exploring the Scope of the "Special Purposes" Freedom of Expression Shield in European Data Protection' (2015) 52 Common Market Law Review 119.

Erdos D, *European Data Protection Regulation, Journalism and Traditional Publishers: Balancing on a Tightrope?* (OUP 2020).

Erdos D, 'Special, Personal and Broad Expression: Exploring Freedom of Expression Norms under the General Data Protection Regulation' (2021) Yearbook of European Law 405.

European Broadcasting Union, 'Public Service Media's competitive environment' (*Media Intelligence Service*, May 2022) 5 <https://www.ebu.ch/files/live/sites/ebu/files/Publications/MIS/login_only/market_insights/EBU-MIS-PSMs_Competitive_Environment_2022-Public.pdf>.

Fathaigh R Ó and D Voorhoof, 'The European Court of Human Rights, Media Freedom and Democracy' in M E Price, S Verhulst, and L Morgan (eds), *Routledge Handbook of Media Law* (Routledge 2013) 107.

Fathaigh R Ó, N Helberger, and N Appelman, 'The Perils of Legally Defining Disinformation' (2021) 10(4) Internet Policy Review 2.

FCReporting Watch, 'IPSO: 296 days to correct a factual inaccuracy, effective press regulation?' (*Inforrm*, 23 June 2020) <https://inforrm.org/2020/06/23/ipso-296-days-to-correct-a-factual-inaccuracy-effective-press-regulation-fcreportingwatch/>.

Fechner F, *Medienrecht* (20th edn, Mohr Siebeck 2019).

Fenech H, 'IPSO Blog: The Editor's Code of Practice and online video content' (*IPSO*, 11 August 2021) <IPSO Blog: The Editors' Code of Practice and online video content>.

Fenton N, 'Regulation Is Freedom: Phone Hacking, Press Regulation and the Leveson Inquiry—The Story So Far' (2018) 23(3) Communications Law 118.

Fenwick H and G Philipson, *Media Freedom under the Human Rights Act* (OUP 2006).

Ferreau F, 'Desinformation als Herausforderung für die Medienregulierung' (2021) 3 Archiv für Presserecht 204.

Ferreau F, 'Die Zukunft der Rundfunkregulierung. Von der Pandemie-Gegenwart ins Zeitalter des Medienstaatsvertrags' (2020) 3 Archiv für Presserecht 197.

Ferreau F, 'Livestreaming in der Corona-Krise—der Anfang vom Ende des linearen Rundfunkbegriffs?' (2020) 5 Kommunikation & Recht 1.

Ferreau F, 'Desinformation als Herausforderung für die Medienregulierung' (2021) 3 Archiv für Presserecht 204.

Fiedler C, 'Zunehmende Einschränkungen der Pressefreiheit. Verbraucherschutz, Persönlichkeitsrecht, Datenschutz und Sicherheitsrecht, Datenschutz und unzulängliches Urheberrecht gefährden die Freiheit der Presse' (2010) 54(1) Zeitschrift für Urheber- und Medienrecht 18.

Fiedler C, '§109 MStV' in H Gersdorf and P Paal (eds), *Informations- und Medienrecht Kommentar* (Beck 2021).

Fielden L, *Regulating for Trust in Journalism. Standards Regulation in the Age of Blended Media* (Reuters Institute for the Study of Journalism 2011).

Fielden L, 'Regulating the press. A comparative study of international press councils' (*Reuters Institute for the Study of Journalism* 2012) <https://reutersinstitute.politics.ox.ac.uk/sites/default/files/2017-11/Regulating%20the%20Press.pdf>.

Fielden L, 'A Royal Charter for the Press: Lessons from Overseas' (2013) 5(2) Journal of Media Law 172.

Fielden L, 'UK Press Regulation: Taking Account of Media Convergence' (2016) 22(5) Convergence 472.

Fiss O M, 'Why the State' (1987) 100(4) Harvard Law Review 781.

Fletscher R and R Kleis Nielsen, 'Are People Incidentally Exposed to News on Social Media? A Comparative Analysis' (2018) 20(7) New Media & Society 2450.

Flew T, F Martin, and N Suzor, 'Internet Regulation as Media Policy: Rethinking the Question of Digital Communication Platform Governance' (2019) 10(1) Journal of Digital Media & Policy 33.

Forde S, 'Public Opinion, Markets and Technology: Evaluating the Economic and Political Pressures on the Contemporary News Media' (2005) 19(1) Continuum 141.

Foster R, J Egan, and J Simon, 'Measuring Public Service Broadcasting' in D Tambini and J Cowling (eds), *From Public Service Broadcasting to Public Service Communication* (IPPR 2004) 151.

Franklin B and S Eldridge II, *The Routledge Companion to Digital Journalism Studies* (Routledge 2017).

Franzius C, 'Das Internet und die Grundrechte' (2016) 71 Juristenzeitung 650.

Frosio G, 'Why Keep a Dog and Bark Yourself?' (2018) 26(1) International Journal of Law and Information Technology 1.

Frey D and H Magnus, 'Landesmedienanstalten veröffentlichen Public-Value-Liste. Bild TV ist jetzt "wertvoll"' (*Legal Tribune Online*, 5 October 2022) <Public-Value-Liste im MStV: Bild TV ist nun 'wertvoll' (lto.de)>.

Gaber I, 'Three Cheers for Subjectivity: Or the Crumbling of the Seven Pillars of Traditional Journalistic Wisdom' in A Charles and G Stewart (eds), *The End of Journalism: News in the Twenty-First Century* (Peter Lang 2011) 31.

Garnham N, 'The Broadcasting Market and the Future of the BBC' (1994) 65(1) Political Quarterly 11.

Gaziano C and K McGrath, 'Measuring the Concept of Credibility' (2012) 63(3) Journalism Quarterly 451.

Geller H, 'Where We Are and Where We Should Be Going' in J Lichtenberg (ed), *Democracy and the Mass Media* (CUP 1990) 290.

Gellman R, 'Disintermediation and the Internet' (1996) 13(1) Government Information Quarterly 1.

Gerber O, 'Background document' (50th EPRA meeting, Plenary session 2—Artificial intelligence and machine learning, Athens, 23–25 October 2019) <https://www.epra.org/attachments/athens-plenary-2-artificial-intelligence-machine-learning-background-paper>.

Gerhardt N, Presseähnliche Angebote nach dem 12. Rundfunkänderungsstaatsvertrag. Zur Zulässigkeit von Onlinetextangeboten öffentlich-rechtlicher Rundfunkanstalten' (2010) 1 Archiv für Presserecht 16.

Gersdorf H, 'Verbot presseähnlicher Angebote des öffentlich-rechtlichen Rundfunks' (2010) 5 Archiv für Presserecht 421.

Gersdorf H and P Paal (eds), *Informations- und Medienrecht Kommentar* (2nd edn, Beck 2021).

Gersdorf H, '§32 MStV' in H Gersdorf and P Paal (eds), *Informations- und Medienrecht Kommentar* (2nd edn, Beck 2021).

Gibbons T, 'Freedom of the Press: Ownership and Editorial Values' [1992] Public Law 279.

Gibbons T, *Regulating the Media* (2nd edn, Sweet & Maxwell 1998).

Gibbons T, '"Fair Play to All Sides of the Truth": Controlling Media Distortions' (2009) 62(1) Current Legal Problems 286.

Gibbons T, 'Free Speech, Communication and the State' in M Amos, J Harrison, and L Woods (eds), *Freedom of Expression and the Media* (Martinus Nijhoff 2012) 22.

Gibbons T, 'Building Trust in Press Regulation: Obstacles and Opportunities' (2013) 5(2) Journal of Media Law 212.

Gibbons T, '"Club Government" and Independence in Media Regulation' in M E Price, S G Verhulst, and L Morgan (eds), *Routledge Handbook of Media Law* (Routledge 2013) 47.

Gibbons T, 'Impartiality in United Kingdom Broadcasting' (2022) 14(1) Journal of Media Law 11.

Gibbons T and I Katsirea, 'Commercial Influences on Programme Content: The German and UK Approaches to Transposing the EU Rules on Product Placement' (2012) 4(2) Journal of Media Law 159.

Gibson S and others, 'News Literacy Report: Lessons in building public confidence and trust' (IMPRESS, November 2022) 21 <https://www.impress.press/wp-content/uploads/2023/01/impress-news-literacy-report-2022.pdf>.

Gillespie T, *Custodians of the Internet: Platforms, Content Moderation, and the Hidden Decisions that Shape Social Media* (Yale UP 2018).

Gillespie T, 'Platforms Are Not Intermediaries' (2018) 2(2) Georgetown Law Technology Review 198.

Gilmore D, *We the Media. Grassroots Journalism by the People, for the People* (O'Reilly 2006).

Giomelakis D and A Veglis, 'Investigating Search Engine Optimization Factors in Media Websites. The Case of Greece' (2016) 4(3) Digital Journalism 379.

Globocnik J, 'The Right to Be Forgotten Is Taking Shape: CJEU Judgments in *GC and Others* (C-136/17) and *Google v CNIL* (C-507/17)' (2020) 69(4) GRUR International 380.

Goddard P, '"Distinctiveness" and the BBC: A New Battleground for Public Service Television' (2017) 39(7) Media, Culture and Society 1089.

Goldman E, '"Must Carry" Lawsuit Against Search Engines—Langdon v. Google' (*Tech. & Marketing L Blog*, 8 June 2006) <https://blog.ericgoldman.org/archives/2006/06/must_carry_laws.htm>.

Goldsmith J, 'Regulation of the Internet: Three Persistent Fallacies' (1998) 73(4) Chicago-Kent Law Review 1119.

Goldsmith J and T Wu, *Who Controls the Internet?: Illusions of a Borderless World* (OUP 2006).

Goode L, 'Social News, Citizen Journalism and Democracy' (2009) 11(8) New Media & Society 1287.

Government of Canada, *Canada's Communications Future: Time to Act*, January 2020 <https://publications.gc.ca/collections/collection_2020/isde-ised/Iu37-14-2020-eng.pdf> 158.

Grabenwarter C, 'Begriff der Presse im Sinnes des Art. 5 Abs. 1 S. 2 GG' in T Maunz and G Dürig, *Grundgesetz-Kommentar* (86th supplement, Beck 2019).

Graves L, *Deciding What's True: The Rise of Political Fact-Checking in American Journalism* (Columbia UP 2016).

Graves L and F Cherubini, 'The Rise of Fact-Checking Sites in Europe' (Reuters Institute for the Study of Journalism 2016) <https://reutersinstitute.politics.ox.ac.uk/our-research/rise-fact-checking-sites-europe>.

Greis F, 'Hate-Speech-Gesetz: Regierung kennt keine einzige strafbare Falschnachricht', 19 April 2017 <http://www.golem.de/news/hate-speech-gesetz-regierung-kennt-keine-einzige-strafbare-falschnachricht-1704-127370.html>.

Grespan D, 'A Busy Year for State Aid Control in the Field of PSB' (2010) 1 European State Aid Law Quarterly 79.

Grimmelmann J, 'Speech Engines' (2014) Minnesota Law Review 868.

Grünwald A and C Nüßing, 'Vom NetzDG zum DSA: Wachablösung baim Kampf gegen Hate Speech? Diskussionsstand zu beiden Gesetzesvorhaben und deren Vereinbarkeit' (2021) Multimedia und Recht 283, 286ff.

Guerrini F, 'Storytellers: Content curation as a new form of journalism' (*Reuters Institute*, 2013) <https://reutersinstitute.politics.ox.ac.uk/our-research/newsroom-curators-and-independent-storytellers-content-curation-new-form-journalism>.

Hagen J von and P Seabright, 'Introduction: The Future of Economic Regulation in Broadcasting Markets' in P Seabright and J von Hagen (eds), *The Economic Regulation of Broadcasting Markets. Evolving Technology and Challenges for Policy* (CUP 2007) 3.

Hall S, 'The Determinations of News Photographs' in C Greer (ed), *Crime and Media: A Reader* (Routledge 2010) 123.

Hallin D C and others, *Comparing Media Systems: Three Models of Media and Politics* (CUP 2004).

Hallin D C and P Mancini, *Comparing Media Systems beyond the Western World* (CUP 2012).

Hallin D C and P Mancini, 'Ten Years After Comparing Media Systems: What Have We Learned?' (2017) 34(2) Political Communication 155.

Hampton M, 'The Fourth Estate Ideal in Journalism History' in A Stuart (ed), *The Routledge Companion to News and Journalism* (Routledge 2009) 3.

Hanitzsch T, 'Deconstructing Journalism Culture: Toward a Universal Theory' (2007) 17(4) Communication Theory 367.

Harcu T, *The Ethical Journalist* (Sage 2007).

Harcup T, *What's the Point of News? A Study in Ethical Journalism* (Palgrave Macmillan 2020).

Harrison J and L Woods, *European Broadcasting Law and Policy* (CUP 2007).

Hartmann S, B Holznagel, and J Kalbhenn, 'Stellungnahme zur schriftlichen Anhörung des Ausschusses für Kultur und Medien des Landtags Nordrhein-Westfalen', 12 June 2020, 12 <https://www.landtag.nrw.de/portal/WWW/dokumentenarchiv/Dokument/MMST17-2795.pdf>.

Harvey D, *A Brief History of Neoliberalism* (OUP 2007).

Held T, 'Journalistisch-redaktionell gestaltete Angebote' in R Binder and T Vesting (eds), *Beck'scher Kommentar zum Rundfunkrecht* (4th edn, Beck 2018) §54.

Held T, '§54 Allgemeine Bestimmungen' in R Binder and T Vesting (eds), *Beckscher Kommentar zum Rundfunkrecht* (4th edn, Beck 2018).

Hacked Off, 'Written evidence' (September 2021) <https://committees.parliament.uk/writtene vidence/39134/html/#_ftnref1>.

Hain K-E, 'Ist die Etablierung einer Internetdienstefreiheit sinnvoll?' (2012) 2 Kommunikation & Recht 98.

Hain K-E and T Brings, 'Die Tagesschau-App—Showdown in Karlsruhe (?) Zum Urteil des BGH v. 30.4.2015 – I ZR 13/14, AfP 2015, 553' (2016) 1 Archiv für Presserecht 11.

Hanna M and M Dodd, *McNae's Essential Law for Journalists* (25th edn, OUP 2020).

Harcup T and D O'Neill, 'What Is News? News Values Revisited (Again)' (2017) 18(12) Journalism Studies 1470.

Harcup T, *What's the Point of News? A Study in Ethical Journalism* (Palgrave Macmillan 2020).

Harrison J, *The Civil Power of the News* (Palgrave 2019).

Harte D, 'Local Public Service Journalism and the BBC' in R Matthews (ed), *Reappraising Local and Community News in the UK: Media, Practice and Policy* (Taylor & Francis 2021) 1.

Hartmann B, 'Dienende Freiheit—notwendige Verstärkung oder widerspruchliche Beschränkung subjektiver Rechte?' (2016) 71 Juristenzeitung 18.

Hartung H, 'Die ARD muss sich an den Medienstaatsvertrag halten' (*Medienpolitik*, 18 April 2023) <https://www.medienpolitik.net/2023/04/die-ard-muss-sich-an-den-medienstaatsvert rag-halten/>.

Harvey J D, *Collisions in the Digital Paradigm. Law and Rule Making in the Digital Age* (Hart Publishing 2017).

He X, 'British digital tabloid in the 21st century and users' motivations in reading digital tabloid news', forthcoming PhD thesis, University of Sheffield.

Heims M, 'The Brave New World of Social Media Censorship' (2017) 127 Harvard Law Review Forum 325.

Heinemann S and F Dittrich, 'Die Zukunft des öffentlich-rechtlichen Telemedienauftrags' (2018) 2 Bonner Rechtsjournal 127.

Heins M and S Lefeldt, 'Medianstaatsvertrag: Journalistische Sorgfaltspflichten für Influencer*innen. Macht im Netz VI: Zwischen Selbstregulierung und Aufsicht—Die Regelungen des RStV und MStV' (2021) Multimedia und Recht 126.

Helberger N, 'From Eyeball to Creator—Toying with Audience Empowerment in the Audiovisual Media Services Directive' (2008) 19(6) Entertainment Law Review 128.

Helberger N, P Leersen, and M Van Drunen, 'Germany proposes Europe's first diversity rules for social media platforms' <https://blogs.lse.ac.uk/medialse/2019/05/29/germany-proposes-europes-first-diversity-rules-for-social-media-platforms/> (*Media@LSE*, 29 May 2019).

Helberger N, 'Regulation of news recommenders in the Digital Services Act: empowering David against the very large online Goliath' (2021) *Internet Policy Review* <https://policyrev iew.info/articles/news/regulation-news-recommenders-digital-services-act-empowering-david-against-very-large>.

Held T and W Schulz, *Europarechtliche Beurteilung von Online-Angeboten öffentlich-rechtlicher Rundfunkanstalten: Inwieweit beeinflussen die Beihilferegeln die Einbeziehung neuer Dienste in den Funktionsauftrag öffentlich-rechtlichen Rundfunks? Gutachten im Auftrag der Friedrich-Ebert-Stiftung* (Friedrich-Ebert-Stiftung 2004).

Herman, E. and N. Chomsky, *Manufacturing Consent: The Political Economy of the Mass Media* (Vintage Digital 2010).

Hermida A, 'Twittering the News. The Emergence of Ambient Journalism' (2010) 4(3) Journalism Practice 297.

Hermida A, 'Tweets and Truth: Journalism as a Discipline of Collaborative Verification' (2012) 6(5–6) Journalism Practice 659.

Hermida A, 'Social Media and the News' in T Witschge and others (eds), *The SAGE Handbook of Digital Journalism* (Sage 2016) 81.

Hickman L, 'Exclusive: BBC issues internal guidance on how to report climate change', 7 September 2018 <https://www.carbonbrief.org/exclusive-bbc-issues-internal-guidance-on-how-to-report-climate-change>.

Hindman M, *The Internet Trap. How the Internet Economy Builds Monopolies and Undermines Democracy* (Princeton UP 2018).

Haynes Stuart A, 'Google Search Results: Buried if Not Forgotten' (2013) 35(3) North Carolina Journal of Law and Technology 463.

Hoboken J van, *Search Engine Freedom. On the Implications of the Right to Freedom of Expression for the Legal Governance of Web Search Engines* (Kluwer Law International 2012).

Hoboken J van and others, *Hosting intermediary services and illegal content online* (European Commission 2018) <https://dare.uva.nl/search?identifier=db3fa078-e225-4336-95ec-5d6f2 5731799>.

Hoeren T, 'Das Telemediengesetz' (2007) Neue Juristische Wochenschrift 801.

Hoffmann-Riem W, *Regulating Media: The Licensing and Supervision of Broadcasting in Six Countries* (Guilford 1996).

Hoffmann-Riem W, *Regulierung der dualen Rundfunkordnung* (Nomos 2000).

Hoffmann-Riem W, W Schulz, and T Held, *Konvergenz und Regulierung. Optionen für rechtliche Regelungen und Aufsichtsstrukturen im Bereich Information, Kommunikation und Medien* (Nomos 2000).

Hofmann A, 'BVerwG: Kein presserechtlicher Auskunftsanspruch für ein Wirtschaftsunternehmen mit vornehmlich außerpublizistischem Geschäftszweck' (2019) 17 Neue Zeitschrift für Verwaltungsrecht 1283.

Hölig S and U Hasebrink, 'Germany' (*Reuters Institute Digital News Report 2020*) https://www.digitalnewsreport.org/survey/2020/germany-2020/.

Holznagel B, *Rundfunkrecht in Europa: Auf dem Weg zu einem Gemeinrecht europäischer Rundfunkordnungen*, Jus publicum, vol 18 (J.C.B. Mohr 1996).

Holznagel B, 'Internetdienstefreiheit und Netzneutralität' (2011) 6 Archiv für Presserecht 532.

Holznagel B, 'Internet Freedom, the Public Sphere and Constitutional Guarantees: A European Perspective' in M E Price, S G Verhulst, and L Morgan (eds), *Routledge Handbook of Media Law* (Routledge 2013) 141.

Home Affairs Committee, 'Oral evidence: Hate crime and its violent consequences' HC 20 February 2018, vol 683 Q268.

House of Commons Digital, Culture, Media and Sport Committee, 'Disinformation and "Fake News": Interim Report', 5th Report of Session 2017–19, HC 363, 24 July 2018.

House of Commons Digital, Culture, Media and Sport Committee, 'Disinformation and "Fake News": Final Report', 8th Report of Session 2017–19, HC 1791, 14 February 2019.

House of Commons Public Bill Committee, 'Online Safety Bill', 24 May 2022, Session 2022–23, 1st sitting.

House of Commons Justice Committee, 'Open Justice: Court reporting in the digital age', 5th Report of Session 2022–23, HC 339, 1 November 2022.

House of Lords, 'Media convergence', 2nd Report of Session 2012–13, HL Paper 154, 27 March 2013.

House of Lords Communications and Digital Committee, 'Regulating in a digital world', 2nd Report of Session 2017–19, HL Paper 299, 9 March 2019.

House of Lords Communications and Digital Committee, 'Breaking news? The future of UK journalism', 1st Report of Session 2019–21, HL Paper 176.

House of Lords Communications and Digital Committee, 'Free for all? Freedom of expression in the digital age', 1st Report of Session 2021–22, HL Paper 54, 22 July 2021.

House of Lords Communications and Digital Committee, 'Licence to change: BBC future funding', 1st Report of Session 2022–23, HL Paper 44, 18 July 2022.

House of Lords European Union Committee, *EU Data Protection law: a 'right to be forgotten'?*, 2nd Report of session 2014–15 (TSO 2014) 16 <http://www.publications.parliament.uk/pa/ld201415/ldselect/ldeucom/40/40.pdf>.

House of Lords Select Committee on Communications, 'Press regulation: Where are we now?', 3rd Report of Session 2014–15, HL 135 (Authority of the House of Lords 2015) <https://publications.parliament.uk/pa/ld201415/ldselect/ldcomuni/135/135.pdf>.

Hoven E and H Gersdorf, '§1 NetzDG' in H Gersdorf and P Paal (eds), *Informations- und Medienrecht Kommentar* (Beck 2021).

Hulsink H, 'Tides in Communication Politics? About Shifting Involvements and Technologies of Freedom and the Relevance of Albert Hirschman and Ithiel De Sola Pool for Today's Communication Studies' (2005) 67(6) Gazette: The International Journal for Communication Studies 569.

Humphreys P, *Mass Media and Media Policy in Western Europe* (Manchester UP 1996).

Humphreys P and S Simpson, *Regulation, Governance and Convergence in the Media* (Edward Elgar 2018).

Husovec M, *Injunctions Against Intermediaries in the EU: Accountable but Not Liable?* (CUP 2017).

Hutchins R, *A Free and Responsible Press: Commission on Freedom of the Press* (University of Chicago Press 1947).

Hyung Whan K, 'Media convergence: concept, discourse and influence', unpublished doctoral thesis (City University of London 2019).

Ingold A, 'Digitalisierung demokratischer Öffentlichkeiten' (2017) 56(4) Der Staat 491.

Ingram M, 'Journalists want to recreate Twitter on Mastodon. Mastodon is not into it' (*Columbia Journalism Review*, 15 November 2022) <https://www.cjr.org/analysis/journalists-want-to-recreate-twitter-on-mastodon-mastodon-is-not-into-it.php>.

Jäkel F, 'Internetfreiheit und Grundgesetz—Ist eine Internetfreeiheit wirklich nötig?' (2012) 3 Archiv für Presserecht 224.

Jarass H D, 'Art. 5 GG' in H D Jarass and B Pieroth (eds), *Grundgesetz für die Bundesrepublik Deutschland* (12th edn, Beck 2012).

Jayne W, 'Fairness Doctrine 2.0: The Ever-Expanding Definition of Neutrality under the First Amendment' (2018) 16(3) First Amendment Law Review 466.

Jones C, 'Regulatory Creep: Myths and Misunderstandings' (2004) 8 Risk & Regulation 6 <https://www.lse.ac.uk/accounting/assets/CARR/documents/R-R/2004-Winter.pdf>.

Jones M, 'The Defamation Act 2013: A Free Speech Retrospective' (2019) 24(3) Communications Law 117.

Jouannaud V, 'The Essential-Matters Doctrine (Wesentlichkeitsdoktrin) in Private Law: A Constitutional Limit to Judicial Development of the Law?' in P M Bender (ed), *The Law between Objectivity and Power* (Nomos 2022) 223.

Julian V, 'Reporting on Muslims and Islam' (*IPSO*, 9 November 2020) <https://www.ipso.co.uk/news-press-releases/press-releases/press-regulator-publishes-guidance-on-reporting-of-muslims-and-islam/>.

Kagiaros D, 'Introductory Note to *Bédat v Switzerland (Eur. Ct. H.R.)*' (2016) 25 International Legal Materials 1126.

Kahl J, *Elektronische Presse und Bürgerjournalismus: Presserechtliche Rechte und Pflichten von Wortmedien im Internet* (Nomos 2013).

Kalbhenn J and M Hemmert-Halswick, 'Der Regierungentwurf zur Änderung des NetzDG. Vom Compliance-Ansatz zu Designvorgaben' (2020) Multimedia und Recht 518.

Kalbhenn J and B Holznagel, 'Journalistische Sorgfaltspflichten auf YouTube und Instagram— Neue Vorgaben im Medienstaatsvertrag' in L Specht-Riemenschneider and others (eds), *Festschrift für Jürgen Taeger* (R&W 2020) 589.

Kalogeropoulos A, 'Online News Video Consumption. A Comparison of Six Countries' (2018) 6(5) Digital Journalism 651.

Kalven H, 'Broadcasting, Public Policy and the First Amendment' (1967) 10 Journal of Law and Economics 15.

Katsirea I, *Public Broadcasting and European Law. A Comparative Examination of Public Service Obligations in Six Member States* (Kluwer 2008).

Katsirea I, 'The Three-Step Test. Three Steps Forwards or Backwards for Public Service Broadcasting in Germany?' in K Donders and H Moe (eds), *Exporting the Public Value Test: Views from Academia and Practioners* (Nordicom 2011) 59.

Katsirea I, 'Who Is Afraid of Public Service Broadcasting? The Digital Future of an Age-Old Institution under Threat' (2012) 31 Yearbook of European Law 416.

Katsirea I, 'The Television without Frontiers Directive' in K Donders (ed), *Palgrave Handbook on European Media Policy* (Palgrave Macmillan 2014) 297.

Katsirea I, 'Electronic Press: "Press-like" or "Television-like"?' (2015) 23(2) International Journal of Law and Information Technology 134.

Katsirea I, Newspaper Websites as Audiovisual Media Services: The *New Media Online GmbH* Preliminary Ruling' (2017) 1 European Law Review 92.

Katsirea I, 'Search Engines and Press Archives between Memory and Oblivion' (2018) 1 European Public Law 125.

Katsirea I, '"Fake News": Reconsidering the Value of Untruthful Expression in the Face of Regulatory Uncertainty' (2019) 11(1) Journal of Media Law 159.

Katsirea I, 'Covid-19, fake news and the future of platform regulation. Part 2' (*Sheffield Political Economy Research Institute*, 10 February 2021) <http://speri.dept.shef.ac.uk/authors/irini-katsirea/>.

Keller D, 'Facebook Filters, Fundamental Rights, and the CJEU's Glawischnig-Piesczek Ruling' (2020) 69(6) GRUR International 616.

Kelly G and others, *Creating Public Value. An Analytical Framework for Public Services Reform* (Cabinet Office 2002).

Kenyon A, 'The State of Affairs of Freedom: Implications of German Broadcasting Freedom' in A T Kenyon and A Scott (eds), *Positive Free Speech. Rationales, Methods and Implications* (Hart Publishing 2021) 83.

Kerrsenbrock F G, *Die Legitimation der Medien nach dem Grundgesetz. Zur verfassungsrechtlichen Stellung von Rundfunk und Presse im Zeitalter von Social Media* (Peter Lang 2015).

Kieran M, 'Objectivity, Impartiality and Good Journalism' in M Kieran (ed), *Media Ethics* (Routledge 1998) 24.

Klein I, 'Enemy of the People: The Ghost of the F.C.C. Fairness Doctrine in the Age of Alternative Facts' (2020) 42(1) Hastings Communications and Entertainment Law Journal 45.

Klonick K, 'The New Governors: The People, Rules, and Processes Governing Online Speech' (2018) 131(6) Harvard Law Review 1598.

Klonick K, 'The Facebook Oversight Board: Creating an Independent Institution to Adjudicate Online Free Expression' (2020) 129(8) Yale Law Journal 2418.

Kluth W and W Schulz, *Konvergenz und regulatorische Folgen: Gutachten im Rahmen der Rundfunkkommission der Länder* (Hans-Bredow 2014).

Knoke L and H Krüger, '§2 NetzDG' in H Gersdorf and P Paal (eds), *Informations- und Medienrecht Kommentar* (2nd edn, Beck 2021).

Koliska M and K Chadha, 'Transparency in German Newsrooms. Diffusion of a New Journalistic Norm?' (2018) 19(16) Journalism Studies 2400.

Koliska M and others, 'Exploring Audience Perceptions of, and Preferences for, Online News Videos' (2021) 22(9) Journalism Studies 1161.

Kompa M, 'Staatliche Sperrvervügung gegen Blogger. Landesmedienanstalten praktizieren eine weite Auslegung von §§19, 109 MStV' (2022) Multimedia und Recht 273.

Koreng A, *Zensur im Internet. Der verfassungsrechtliche Schutz der digitalen Massenkommunikation* (Beck 2010).

Koreng A, 'Das "Recht auf Vergessen" und die Haftung von Online-Archiven. Schlussfolgerungen für Pressearchive aus der EuGH-Entscheidung "Google Spain"' (2015) 46(6) Archiv für Presserecht 514.

Korenhof P and others, 'Timing the Right to Be Forgotten: A Study into "Time" as a Factor in Deciding about Retention or Erasure of Data' in S Gutwirth, R Leenes, and P de Hert (eds), *Reforming European Data Protection Law* (Springer 2015) 171.

Kormelink T G and I C Meijer, 'A User Perspective on Time Spent: Temporal Experiences of Everyday News Use' (2020) 21(2) Journalism Studies 271.

Korte S, 'Die dienende Funktion der Rundfunkfreiheit in Zeiten medialer Konvergenz' (2014) 139(3) Archiv für Öffentliches Recht 384.

Kosseff J, *The Twenty-Six Words that Created the Internet* (Cornell UP 2019).

Krattenmaker T and L A Powe, 'Converging First Amendment Principles for Converging Communications Media' (1994–95) 104 Yale Law Journal 171.

Kuczerawy A, 'Intermediary Liability and Freedom of Expression: Recent Developments in the EU Notice & Action Initiative' (2015) 31 Computer Law & Security Review 46.

Kuczerawy A, 'Fighting Online Disinformation: Did the EU Code of Practice Forget about Freedom of Expression?' in G Terzis and others (eds), *Disinformation and Digital Media as a Challenge for Democracy* (Intersentia 2020) 291.

Kühling J, 'Art 5 GG' in H Gersdorf and P Paal (eds), *Informations- und Medienrecht Kommentar* (Beck 2014).

Kühling J, 'Art. 5 GG' in H Gersdorf and P Paal (eds), *Informations- und Medienrecht Kommentar* (2nd edn, Beck 2021).

Kuiken J and others, 'Effective Headlines of Newspaper Articles in a Digital Environment' (2017) 5(10) Digital Journalism 1300.

Kuklis L, 'AVMSD and video-sharing platforms regulation: toward a user-oriented solution?' (*LSE Blog*, 28 May 2019) <https://blogs.lse.ac.uk/medialse/2019/05/28/avmsd-and-video-sharing-platforms-regulation-toward-a-user-oriented-solution/>.

Kuklis L, 'Video-sharing Platforms in AVMSD—A New Kind of Content Regulation' in P L Parcu and E Brogi (eds), *Research Handbook on EU Media Law and Policy* (Elgar 2021) 303.

Kulk S and F Borgesius, 'Google Spain v. Gonzalez: Did the Court Forget about Freedom of Expression?' (2014) 5(3) European Journal of Risk Regulation 389.

Kümpel A S, 'The Issue Takes It All? Incidental News Exposure and News Engagement on Facebook' (2019) 7(2) Digital Journalism 165.

Küng L, N Newman, and R G Picard, 'Online News' in J Bauer and M Latzer (eds), *Handbook on the Economics of the Internet* (Edward Elgar 2016) 445.

Ladeur, K H and T Gostomzyk, 'Gutachten zur Verfassungsmäßigkeit des Entwurfs eines Gesetzes zur Verbesserung der Rechtsdurchsetzung in sozialen Netzwerken (Netzwerkdurchsetzungsgesetz – NetzDG) i.d.F. vom 16. Mai 2017 – BT-Drs. 18/12356. Erstattet auf Ansuchen des Bitkom', May 2017 <https://www.cr-online.de/NetzDG-Gutachten-Gostomzyk-Ladeur.pdf>.

Lamer W, *Press Freedom as an International Human Right* (Palgrave Macmillan 2018).

Lange A, 'Contribution to the Consultation of the European Commission on the Directive on Audiovisual Media Services' 9 <https://digital-strategy.ec.europa.eu/en/library/contributions-received-individuals-and-research-avmsd-public-consultation>.

Lavender T and others, 'Research into recent dynamics of the press sector in the UK and globally' (*Plum Consulting*, May 2020) <https://assets.publishing.service.gov.uk/government/uploads/system/uploads/attachment_data/file/924325/Plum_DCMS_press_sector_dynamics_-_Final_Report_v4.pdf>.

Law Commission, 'Harmful Online Communications: The criminal offences. A consultation paper', 11 September 2020 <https://s3-eu-west-2.amazonaws.com/lawcom-prod-storage-11jsxou24uy7q/uploads/2020/09/Online-Communications-Consultation-Paper-FINAL-with-cover.pdf>.

Lee K and S Molitorisz, 'The Australian News Media Bargaining Code: Lessons for the UK, EU and Beyond' (2021) 13(1) Journal of Media Law 36.

Leeb C-M and F Seiter, 'Rundfunklizenzpflicht für Streamingangebote?' (2017) 61(7) Zeitschrift für Urheber- und Medienrecht 573.

Lehman-Wilzig S and N Cohen-Avigdor, 'The Natural Life Cycle of New Media Evolution: Inter-Media Struggle for Survival in the Internet Age' (2004) 6 New Media & Society 707.

Lent W, 'Paradigmenwechsel bei den publizistischen Sorgfaltspflichten im Online-Journalismus—Zur Neuregelung des §19 Medienstaatsvertrag' (2020) 64(8/9) Zeitschrift für Urheber- und Medienrecht 593.

Lent W, '§17 MStV' in H Gersdorf and P Paal (eds), *Informations- und Medienrecht Kommentar* (2nd edn, Beck 2021).

Lent W, '§19 MStV' in H Gersdorf and P Paal (eds), *Informations- und Medienrecht Kommentar* (2nd edn, Beck 2021).

Lessig L, 'The Zones of Cyber-space' (1996) 48 Stanford Law Review 1403.

Leveson Lord Justice, *An Inquiry into the Culture, Practices and Ethics of the Press* (House of Commons 780, 2012).

Lewis A, 'The Right to Scrutinize Government: Toward a First Amendment Theory of Accountability' (1980) 34 University of Miami Law Review 793.

Lichtenberg J, 'Foundations and Limits of Freedom of the Press' in J Lichtenberg (ed), *Democracy and the Mass Media* (CUP 1990) 102.

Liesching M and others, *Das NetzDG in der praktischen Anwendung. Eine Teilevaluation des Netzwerkdurchsetzungsgesetzes* (Carl Grossman Verlag 2021).

Lock H, 'Local Democracy Reporting Service: a model for public broadcasters?' (*Public Media Alliance*, 2 November 2021) <Local Democracy Reporting Service: A model for public broadcasters? - Public Media Alliance>.

Logan C W, 'Getting Beyond Scarcity: A New Paradigm for Assessing the Constitutionality of Broadcast Regulation' (1997) 85(6) California Law Review 1687.

Lowrey W, 'The Emergence and Development of News Fact-Checking Sites. Institutional Logics and Population Ecology' (2017) 18(3) Journalism Studies 376.

Machet E, 'New Media & Regulation: Towards a Paradigm Shift? New Services and Scope: "What's In, What's out Revisited"', Comparative Background Document, 35th EPRA Meeting, 31 May – 1 June 2012, Portorož <http://www.epra.org>.

Magarian G, 'Forward into the Past: Speech Intermediaries in the Television and Internet Ages' (2018) 71(1) Oklahoma Law Review 237.

Magrath P, 'Press regulation: Why we are unimpressed by IPSO' (*Transparency Project*, 17 October 2016) <https://www.transparencyproject.org.uk/press-regulation-why-we-are-unimpressed-by-ipso/>.

Manosevitch I and O Tenenboim, 'The Multi-Faceted Role of User-Generated Content in News Websites. An Analytical Framework' (2017) 5(6) Digital Journalism 731.

Mantzarlis A, 'There's been an explosion of international fact-checkers, but they face big challenges' (*Poynter*, 7 June 2016) <https://www.poynter.org/fact-checking/2016/theres-been-an-explosion-of-international-fact-checkers-but-they-face-big-challenges/>.

Marietta M, D Barker, and T Bowser, 'Fact-Checking Polarized Politics: Does the Fact-Check Industry Provide Consistent Guidance on Disputed Realities?' (2015) 13(4) The Forum 577.

Markham A, S Stavrova, and M Schlüter, 'Netflix, Imagined Affordances and the Illusion of Control' in A Buck and T Plothe (eds), *Netflix and the Nexus: Content, Practice, and Production in the Age of Streaming Television* (P. Lang 2019) 29.

Mars S de and P O' Callaghan, 'Privacy and Search Engines: Forgetting or Contextualising?' (2016) 43(2) Journal of Law & Society 257.

Marsh K, 'Kevin Marsh, ex-Executive Director, BBC College of Journalism on Issues of Impartiality in News and Current Affairs' (2012) 1(1) Journal of Applied Journalism and Media Studies 69.

Mast T, 'Die Rolle der Massenmedien in Zeiten der Krise' (2020) 3 Archiv für Presserecht 191.

Matthieu D and T Pavlíčková, 'Cross-media *within* the Facebook Newsfeed: The Role of the Reader in Cross-media Uses' (2017) 23(4) Convergence 425.

Mazzoli E M and D Tambini, 'Prioritisation uncovered. The Discoverability of Public Interest Content Online' (Council of Europe, November 2020) <https://rm.coe.int/publication-content-prioritisation-report/1680a07a57>.

McChesney R, *Digital Disconnect. How Capitalism Is Turning the Internet Against Democracy* (The New Press 2013).

McChesney W R, *Rich Media, Poor Democracy: Communication Politics in Dubious Times* (The New Press 2015).

McDonald B P, 'The First Amendment and the Free Flow of Information' (2004) 65 Ohio State Law Journal 249.

McEvedy V, 'Defamation and Intermediaries: ISP Defences' (2013) 19(4) Computer and Telecommunications Law Review 108.

McGonagle T, 'User-generated content and audiovisual news: The ups and downs of an uncertain relationship' in European Audiovisual Observatory, *Open Journalism*, 2 IRIS plus (European Audiovisual Observatory 2013) 7.

McGonagle T, '"Fake News": False Fears or Real Concerns?' (2017) 35(4) Netherlands Quarterly of Human Rights 203.

McLuhan E and F Zingrone, *Essential McLuhan* (Routledge 1997).

McNealy J E and L B Alexander, 'A Framework for Unpublishing Decisions' (2018) 6(3) Digital Journalism 389.

McQuail D, *Media Performance: Mass Communication and the Public Interest* (Sage 1992).

McQuail D, *McQuail's Mass Communication Theory* (6th edn Sage 2011).

Mchangama J and J Fiss, *The Digital Berlin Wall: How Germany (Accidentally) Created a Prototype for Global Online Censorship* (Justitia 2019).

Mecklenburg W, 'Internetfreiheit' (1997) 41(7) Zeitschrift für Urheber- und Medienrecht 525.

Media Insight Project, 'A new way of looking at trust in media: Do Americans share journalism's core values?' (*American Press Institute*, 14 April 2021).

Media Standards Trust, 'The Independent Press Standards Organisation (IPSO)—Five years on. A reassessment' (*Media Standards Trust*, October 2019) <http://mediastandardstrust.org/wp-content/uploads/2019/10/MST-IPSO-2019-Final-Version.pdf>.

Meraz S and Z Papacharissi, 'Networked Framing and Gatekeeping' in T Witschge and others (eds), *The SAGE Handbook of Digital Journalism* (Sage 2016) 95.

Metzdorf J, 'The Revised Audiovisual Media Services Directive 2018—Has the EU Learnt the Right Lessons from the Past?' (2018) 1 UFITA Archiv für Medienrecht und Medienwissenschaft 260.

Michael Davis C, *'Die dienende' Rundfunkfreiheit im Zeitalter der sozialen Vernetzung* (Mohr Siebeck 2019).

Migliore M, 'The Times and The Sunday Times, The UK: James, Your digital butler' in European Broadcasting Union, 'News Report 2019—The next newsroom: Unlocking the power of AI for public service journalism' 15 <https://www.ebu.ch/publications/strategic/login_only/report/news-report-2019>.

Milstein A and M Lippold, 'Suchmaschinenergebnisse im Lichte der Meinungsfreiheit der nationalen und europäischen Grund- und Menschenrechte (2013) 4 Neue Zeitschrift für Verwaltungsrecht 182.

Mitchell P, 'The Nature of Responsible Journalism' (2011) 3 Journal of Media Law 19.

Moe H, 'Governing PSB: "Public Value Tests" in Different National Contexts' (2010) 3 Communication, Culture & Critique 207.

Möller H, 'Darf man den öffentlich-rechtlichen Rundfunkanstalten die Textberichterstattung im Internet verbieten?' (*Verfassungsblog*, 24 January 2019) <https://verfassungsblog.de/darf-man-den-oeffentlich-rechtlichen-rundfunkanstalten-die-textberichterstattung-im-internet-verbieten/>.

Monsees L, 'Information Disorder, Fake News and the Future of Democracy' (2021) 20(1) Globalizations 1.

Müller L F, 'Grundrechtsschutz durch Verfahren im Social Media Recht—Maßgaben für die Moderation nicht-justiziabler Inhalte in sozialen Netzwerken' (2022) 2 Archiv für Presserecht 104.

Napoli P, *Audience Evolution. New Technologies and the Transformation of Media Audiences* (Columbia UP 2010).

Napoli P and R Caplan, 'Why Media Companies Insist They're Not Media Companies, Why They're Wrong and Why It Matters' (2017) 22(5) First Monday <https://journals.uic.edu/ojs/index.php/fm/article/view/7051/6124#2a>.

Napoli P, *Social Media and the Public Interest: Media Regulation in the Disinformation Age* (Columbia UP 2019).

National Union of Journalists, 'LDRs call for a say in the future of the local democracy reporting scheme', 3 March 2020 <https://www.nuj.org.uk/resource/ldrs-call-for-a-say-in-the-future-of-the-local-democracy.html> accessed 7 March 2023.

Negroponte N, *Being Digital* (Hodder and Stoughton 1995).

Nelson M, T Kziazek, and N Springer, 'Killing the Comments: Why Do News Organizations Remove User Commentary Functions?' (2021) 2(4) Journalism and Media 572.

Neuberger C and F Lobigs, *Die Bedeutung ders Internets im Rahmen der Vielfaltssicherung. Gutachten im Auftrag der Kommission zur Ermittlung der Konzentration im Medienbereich (KEK)* (VISTAS 2010).

Neuberger C, 'The Journalistic Quality of Internet Formats and Services: Results of a User Survey' (2014) 2(3) Digital Journalism 419.

Neunhoeffer F, *Das Presseprivileg im Datenschutzrecht. Eine rechtsvergeleichende Betrachtung des deutschen und des englischen Rechts* (Mohr Siebeck 2005).

Newman N, 'Executive summary and key findings' (*Reuters Institute Digital News Report 2014*) 13 <https://www.digitalnewsreport.org/survey/2014/executive-summary-and-key-findings-2014/>.

Newman N, 'Executive summary and key findings' (*Reuters Institute Digital News Report 2015*) 14 <https://reutersinstitute.politics.ox.ac.uk/our-research/digital-news-report-2015-0>.

Newman N, 'Overview and findings of the 2017 Report' (*Reuters Institute Digital News Report 2017*) <http://www.digitalnewsreport.org/survey/2017/overview-key-findings-2017/>.

Newman N, 'Executive summary and key findings' (*Reuters Institute Digital News Report 2018*) <https://reutersinstitute.politics.ox.ac.uk/sites/default/files/digital-news-report-2018.pdf>.

Newman N, 'Executive summary and key findings' (*Reuters Institute Digital News Report 2019*) <https://reutersinstitute.politics.ox.ac.uk/sites/default/files/inline-files/DNR_2019_F INALpdf>.

Newman N, 'Executive summary and key findings' (*Reuters Institute Digital News Report 2022*) <https://reutersinstitute.politics.ox.ac.uk/digital-news-report/2022/dnr-executive-summary>.

Newman N, 'United Kingdom' (*Reuters Institute Digital News Report 2022*) https://reutersinstitute.politics.ox.ac.uk/digital-news-report/2022/united-kingdom.

Nielsen R K and L Graves, '"News you don't believe": Audience perspectives on fake news' (Oxford University, Reuters Institute for the Study of Journalism, Factsheet October 2017) <https://reutersinstitute.politics.ox.ac.uk/sites/default/files/2017-10/Nielsen%26Graves_factsheet_1710v3_FINAL_download.pdf>.

Nieminen S and V Sankari, 'Checking PolitiFact's Fact-checks' (2021) 22(3) Journalism Studies 358.

Niggermeier S, 'Freiwillige Selbstkontrolle: Deutscher Presserat wirbt mit seiner Zahnlosigkeit' (*Über Medien*, 26 February 2021) <https://uebermedien.de/57673/deutscher-presserat-wirbt-mit-seiner-zahnlosigkeit/>.

Nikoltchev S, *Mapping of National Rules Applicable to Video-Sharing Platforms: Illegal and Harmful Content Online* (European Audiovisual Observatory 2021).

Nimmer M B, 'Introduction: Is Freedom of the Press a Redundancy: What Does It Add to Freedom of Speech?' (1975) 26(3) Hastings Law Journal 639.

Nissen C, *Public Service Media in the Information Society. Report prepared by the Council of Europe's Group of Specialists on PSB in the Information Society (MS-S-PSB)* (Council of Europe 2006).

Nolte G, 'Hate-Speech, Fake News, das 'Netzwerkdurchsetzungsgesetz' und Vielfaltsicherung durch Suchmaschinen' (2017) 61(7) Zeitschrift für Urheber-und Medienrecht 552.

Ofcom, 'Addressing harmful online content. A perspective from broadcasting and on-demand standards regulation', 18 September 2018 <https://www.ofcom.org.uk/__data/assets/pdf_file/0022/120991/Addressing-harmful-online-content.pdf>.

Ofcom, 'Various programmes: RT, 17 March to 4 May 2018', Issue 369 (*Broadcast and On Demand Bulletin*, 20 December 2018) 21.

Ofcom, 'Review of prominence for public service broadcasting. Recommendations to government for a new framework to keep PSB TV prominent in an online world', 4 July 2019

<https://www.ofcom.org.uk/__data/assets/pdf_file/0021/154461/recommendations-for-new-legislative-framework-for-psb-prominence.pdf>.

Ofcom, 'News consumption in the UK 2022 report' <https://www.ofcom.org.uk/__data/assets/pdf_file/0027/241947/News-Consumption-in-the-UK-2022-report.pdf>.

Ogbebor B, *British Media Coverage of the Press Reform Debate. Journalists Reporting Journalism* (Palgrave Macmillan 2020).

Ohly A, 'Zwei gordische Knoten beim Anspruch gegen Suchmaschinenbetreiber auf Auslistung. Zugleich Bespreschung von EuGH "TU and RE/Google"' (2023) 125(3) Gewerblicher Rechtschutz und Urheberrecht 147.

Oliver P, 'The Protection of Privacy in the Economic Sphere before the European Court of Justice' (2009) 46 Common Market Law Review 1443.

Ory S, 'Rundfunk und Presse im Internet. Die Tagesschau, das iPhone und die tripolare Medienordnung' (2010) 1 Archiv für Presserecht 20.

Oster J, 'Theory and Doctrine of "Media Freedom" as a Legal Concept' (2013) 5(1) Journal of Media Law 57.

Oster J, *Media Freedom as a Fundamental Right* (CUP 2015).

Oster J, 'Communication, Defamation and Liability of Intermediaries' (2015) 35(2) Legal Studies 348.

Oster J, *Kommunikationsdeliktsrecht: Eine transnationale Untersuchung am Beispiel des Ehrschutzes* (Mohr Siebeck 2019).

Paal B, 'Öffentlich-rechtliche presseähnliche Angebote in Telemedien—Tagesschau-App. Zugleich Anmerkung zu BGH v. 30.4.2015 – I ZR 13/14, AfP 2015, 553' (2005) 6 Archiv für Presserecht 500.

Paal B and M Hennemann, '§10 TMG' in H Gersdorf and P Paal (eds), *Informations- und Medienrecht Kommentar* (2nd edn, Beck 2021).

Papakyriakopoulos O, J S M Serrano, and S Hegelich, 'The Spread of Covid-19 Conspiracy Theories on Social Media and the Effect of Content Moderation' (2020) 1 Harvard Kennedy School Misinformation Review 1.

Papier J-H and M Schroeder, '"Gebiet des Rundfunks". Gutachten von H.-J. Papier und M. Schroeder zu presseähnlichen Angeboten' (2010) 60 epd medien 16.

Papier J-H and M Schröder, *Verfassungsfragen des Dreistufentests. Inhaltliche und Verfahrensrechtliche Herausforderungen* (Nomos 2011).

Pariser E, *The Filter Bubble: What the Internet Is Hiding from You* (Penguin Press 2012).

Park M, 'Separating Fact from Fiction: The First Amendment Case for Addressing "Fake News" On Social Media' (2018) 46(1) Hastings Constitutional Law Quarterly 1.

Parmar S, 'Freedom of Expression Narratives after the Charlie Hebdo Attacks' (2018) 18 Human Rights Law Review 267.

Pasquale F, 'Platform Neutrality: Enhancing Freedom of Expression in Spheres of Private Power' (2016) 17 Theoretical Inquiries in Law 487.

Peacock A, *Report of the committee on the financing of the BBC* (HMSO 1986).

Peifer K N, 'Presserecht im Internet—Drei Thesen und eine Frage zur Einordnung, Privilegierung und Haftung der elektronischen Presse' in J Gundel and others (eds), *Konvergenz der Medien—Konvergenz des Rechts?* (Jenaer Wissenschaftliche Verlagsgesellschaft 2009) 54.

Peifer K N, 'Datenschutz und Medienrecht nach den BVerfG-Entscheidungen zum Recht auf Vergessenwerden' (2020) 6 Archiv für Presserecht 462.

Petley J, 'Lessons for Leveson' (2011) 40(4) Dispatches: Index on Censorship 14.

Petley J, 'Online Safety Bill and the press: A thoroughly unsafe Bill, Part 2' (*Inforrm*, 7 July 2021) <https://inforrm.org/2021/07/07/online-safety-and-the-press-a-thoroughly-unsafe-bill-part-2-julian-petley/>.

Pew Research Centre, 'New Media, Old Media. How Blogs and Social Media Agendas Relate and Differ from Traditional Press', 23 May 2010 <https://www.journalism.org/2010/05/23/new-media-old-media/>.

Phillipson G, *Media Freedom under the Human Rights Act* (OUP 2006).

Phillipson G, 'Leveson, the Public Interest and Press Freedom' (2013) 5(2) Journal of Media Law 220.

Pickard W V, *Democracy without Journalism?: Confronting the Misinformation Society* (OUP 2020).

Pollicino O and G De Gregorio, 'Constitutional Law in the Algorithmic Society' in H-W Micklitz and others, *Constitutional Challenges in the Algorithmic Society* (CUP 2022) 3.

Porcedda M G, 'Sentencing Data-Driven Cybercrime. How Cybercrime with Cascading Effects Is Tackled by UK Courts' (2023) 48 Computer Law & Security Review 1.

Porlezza C, 'Accuracy in Journalism' in *Oxford Research Encyclopedia of Communication* (City Research Online 2019) <https://openaccess.city.ac.uk/id/eprint/22556/>.

Posetti J and K Bontcheva, 'Disinfodemic: Deciphering Covid-19 disinformation' (Unesco 2020) <https://en.unesco.org/sites/default/files/disinfodemic_deciphering_covid19_disinformation.pdf>.

Post D G and D R Johnson, 'Law and Borders—The Rise of Law in Cyberspace' (1996) 48 Stanford Law Review 1367.

Price J and F McMahon, *Blackstone's Guide to the Defamation Act 2013* (OUP 2013).

Prosser T, *The Limits of Competition Law: Markets and Public Services* (OUP 2005).

Puppis M, 'Media Governance: A New Concept for the Analysis of Media Policy and Regulation' (2010) 3(2) Communication, Culture & Critique 134.

Quintais P Q, N Appelman, and R Ó Fathaigh, 'Using Terms and Conditions To Apply Fundamental Rights to Content Moderation' (2023) 24 German Law Journal 881.

Rahvar Z, *Die Zukunft des deutschen Presserechts im Lichte konvergierender Medien* (Nomos 2011).

Ramsay G N, 'Mapping changes in local news 2015–2017. More bad news for democracy?' (National Union of Journalists, March 2017) 4 <https://www.mediareform.org.uk/wp-content/uploads/2017/12/mapping-changes-in-local-news-2015-2017-interactive-research-report-march-2017.pdf>.

Read D, *The Power of News: The History of Reuters* (OUP 1999).

Reader B, 'Free Press vs. Free Speech? The Rhetoric of "Civility" in Regard to Anonymous Online Comments' (2012) 89(3) Journalism & Mass Communication Quarterly 495.

Reed L, *Internet Law: Text and Materials* (2nd edn, CUP 2004) 1–2, 218.

Reporters Without Borders, 'World Press Freedom Index' <https://rsf.org/en/index>.

Ricker R and J Weberling, *Handbuch des Presserechts* (Beck 2012).

Riordan K, 'Accuracy, independence and impartiality: How legacy media and digital natives approach standards in the digital age' (*Reuters Institute for the Study of journalism* 2014) <https://reutersinstitute.politics.ox.ac.uk/our-research/accuracy-independence-and-impartiality-how-legacy-media-and-digital-natives-approach>.

Rössel M, 'Digital Services Act. Innovation und Verbesserungsbedarf des ersten Verordnungsentwurfs' (2021) 2 Archiv für Presserecht 93.

Rössel M, 'Digital Services Act. Eingehende Analyse und Überprüfung der regulatorischen Neuerungen aus dem Trilog und potentieller Lücken' (2023) 2 Archiv für Presserecht 93.

Rosen J, 'The Purposes of Privacy: A Response' (2000–2001) 89 Georgetown Law Journal 2117.

Rosen J, 'Response: The Right to Be Forgotten' (2012) 64 Stanford Law Review <https://www.stanfordlawreview.org/online/privacy-paradox-the-right-to-be-forgotten/>.

Rossen-Stadtfeld H, *Audiovisuelle Bewegtbildangebote von Presseunternehmen im Internet: Presse oder Rundfunk?* (Nomos 2009).

Roßnagel A, 'Der künftige Anwendungsbereich der Fernsehrichtlinie. Welche Medien können erfasst werden?' in Institute of European Media Law (EMR), *The Future of the 'Television without Frontiers' Directive* (Nomos 2005) 35.

Rowbottom J, 'Media Freedom and Political Debate in the Digital Era' (2006) 69 Modern Law Review 489.

Rowbottom J, 'In the Shadow of the Big Media: Freedom of Expression, Participation and the Production of Knowledge Online' [2014] Public Law 491.

Rowbottom J, *Media Law* (Hart Publishing 2018).

Rusbridger A, *Breaking News. The Remaking of Journalism and Why It Matters Now* (Canongate 2019).

Rumyantsev A, 'Journalistisch-redaktionelle Gestaltung: Eine verfassungswidrige Forderung? "Wiedergeburt" des wertbezogenen Medienbegriffes' (2008) 24(1) Zeitschrift für Urheber- und Medienrecht 33.

Sabeel Rahman K, 'Regulating Informational Infrastructure: Internet Platforms as the New Public Utilities' (2018) 2 Georgetown Law Technology Review 234.

Sack R D, 'Reflections on the Wrong Question: Special Constitutional Privilege for the Institutional Press' (1979) 7(3) Hofstra Law Review 629.

Sambrook R, 'Delivering trust: Impartiality and objectivity in the digital age', July 2012, <https://reutersinstitute.politics.ox.ac.uk/our-research/delivering-trust-impartiality-and-objectivity-digital-age>.

Santana A D, 'Mobile Devices Offer Little In-Depth News: Sensational, Breaking and Entertainment News Dominate Mobile News Sites' (2019) 13(9) Journalism Practice 1106.

Sardo A, 'Categories, Balancing and Fake News: The Jurisprudence of the European Court of Human Rights' (2020) 33(2) Canadian Journal of Law & Jurisprudence 435.

Savin A, 'New Directions in EU Digital Regulation Post-2015: Regulating Disruption' (2020) 11(1) Union University Law School Review (Pravni zapisi) 93.

Scanlon T M, 'Content Regulation Reconsidered' in J Lichtenberg (ed), *Democracy and the Mass Media* (CUP 1990) 331.

Schauer F, *Free Speech: A Philosophical Enquiry* (CUP 1982).

Schauer F, 'Towards an Institutional First Amendment' (2005) 80 Minnesota Law Review 1256.

Schlesinger P, 'After the Post-Public Sphere' (2020) 42(7–8) Media, Culture & Society 1545.

Schoch F, 'Konvergenz der Medien—Sollte das Recht der Medien harmonisiert werden?' (2002) 17 Juristenzeitung 798.

Schroeder J, *The Press Clause and Digital Technology's Fourth Wave. Media Law and the Symbiotic Web* (Routledge 2018).

Schulz W, *Zum Vorschlag für eine Richtlinie über audiovisuelle Mediendienste*, Arbeitspapiere des Hans-Bredow-Instituts Nr. 17 (Verlag Hans-Bredow-Institut 2006).

Schulz W, 'The Legal Framework for PSB after the German State Aid Case: Procrustean Bed or Hammock?' (2009) 2 Journal of Media Law 219.

Schwartmann R, M Hermann, and R L Mühlenbeck, 'Eine Medienordnung für Intermediäre. Das Zwei-Säulen-Modell zur Sicherung der Vielfalt im Netz' (2019) 22(8) Multimedia und Recht 498.

Schweda S, 'Hamburg Court of Appeal Obliges Press Archive Operator to Prevent Name Search in Archived Articles' (2015) 4 European Data Protection Law 299.

Scientific Council for Government Policy, *Media Policy for the Digital Age* (Amsterdam UP 2005) 71.

Scolari C A, 'Media Evolution: Emergence, Dominance, Survival and Extinction in the New Media Ecology' (2013) 7 International Journal of Communication 1418.

Seitz A, 'It's a Series of Tubes: Network Neutrality in the United States and How the Current Economic Environment Presents Unique Opportunity to Invest in the Future of the Internet' (2009) 29(2) Journal of the National Association of Administrative Law Judiciary 683.

Seitz W, 'Teil 8 Zivilrechtlicher Persönlichkeitsschutz gegenüber Äußerungen im Internet' in T Hoeren, U Sieber, and B Holznagel (eds), *Multimediarecht* (53th supplement, Beck 2020).

Shahbaz A, 'US initiatives to counter harmful speech and disinformation on social media' (*Transantlantic Working Group*, 11 June 2019) <https://www.ivir.nl/twg/research-brief-u-s-initiatives-to-counter-harmful-speech-and-disinformation-on-social-media/>.

Shirky C, *Here Comes Everybody: The Power of Organising Without Organisations* (Penguin 2008).

Shirky C, 'Newspapers and thinking the unthinkable' (*Edge*, 30 May 2023) <https://www.edge.org/conversation/clay_shirky-newspapers-and-thinking-the-unthinkable>.

Shivek R S and S Bloyd-Peshkin, 'Where Do Facts Matter? The Digital Paradox in Magazines' Fact-Checking Processes' (2019) 13(8) Journalism Practice 998.

Shoemaker P J, T P Vos, and S D Reese, 'Journalists as Gatekeepers' in K Wahl-Jorgensen and T Hanizsch (eds), *Handbook of Journalism Studies* (Routledge 2008) 73.

Shoemaker P J and T P Vos, *Gatekeeping Theory* (Routledge 2009).

Siapera E and A Veglis, 'Introduction: The Evolution of Online Journalism' in E Siapera and A Veglis (eds), *The Handbook of Global Online Journalism* (John Wiley 2012) 1.

Siegel J, 'Oberlandesgericht Hamburg: Ein Urteil gegen Online-Archive' (*iRights info*, 31 August 2015) <https://irights.info/artikel/oberlandesgericht-hamburg-ein-urteil-gegen-online-arch ive/25984>.

Silverman C, 'Verification and Fact Checking' <https://datajournalism.com/read/handbook/verification-1/additional-materials/verification-and-fact-checking>.

Singer J, 'User-Generated Visibility: Secondary Gatekeeping in a Shared Media Space' (2014) 16(1) New Media & Society 1461.

Sjøvaag H, 'Hard News/Soft News: The Hierarchy of Genres and the Boundaries of the Profession' in M Carlsson and S C Lewis (eds), *Boundaries of Journalism: Professionalism, Practices and Participation* (Routledge 2015) 101.

Sloot B van der, 'The Practical and Theoretical Problems with 'Balancing'. *Delfi, Coty* and the Redundancy of the Human Rights Framework' (2016) 23(3) Maastricht Journal of European and Comparative Law 439.

Smith G, 'Time to Speak up for Article 15' (*Cybereagle*, 21 May 2017) <https://www.cyberleagle.com/2017/05/time-to-speak-up-for-article-15.html>.

Smith G, 'Carved out or carved up? The draft Online Safety Bill and the press' (*Inforrm*, 30 June 2021) <https://inforrm.org/2021/06/30/carved-out-or-carved-up-the-draft-online-safety-bill-and-the-press-graham-smith/>.

Smolla R A, 'Information as Contraband: The First Amendment and Liability for Trafficking in Speech' (2002) 96(3) Northwestern University Law Review 1099.

Sola Pool I de, *Technologies of Freedom* (Harvard UP 1983).

Spanos R, 'Don't kill the messenger—Delfi and its progeny in the case law of the European Court of Human Rights', 8 September 2017, University of Tallinn <Speech_Spano.pdf (ivir. nl)> accessed 28 August 2022.

State Media Authorities, 'Programme Supervision' <https://www.die-medienanstalten.de/en/areas-of-interest/programme-supervision>.

State Media Authorities, 'Zulassung' <https://www.die-medienanstalten.de/themen/zulassung>.

State Media Authorities, 'Stellungnahme der Medienanstalten zum überarbeiteten Diskussionsentwurf der Rundfunkkommision der Länder für einen Medienstaatsvertrag' (9 August 2019) <https://www.die-medienanstalten.de/fileadmin/user_upload/die_medienanstal ten/Ueber_uns/Positionen/2019_08_09_Stellungnahme_der_Medienanstalten_zum_Medi enstaatsvertrag.pdf>.

Steinvorth T, 'Durchsetzung des Leistungsschutzrechts für Presseverleger gegenüber marktbeherrschenden Plattformen' (2021) 1 Archiv für Presserecht 10.

Stewart P, 'Or of the Press' (1999) 50(4) Hastings Law Journal 705.

Sunstein C, *Democracy and the Problem of Free Speech* (The Free Press 1995).

Sunstein C, *Republic.com 2.0* (Princeton UP 2007).

Sunstein C, *#Republic. Divided Democracy in the Age of Social Media* (Princeton UP 2017).

Suzor N, 'Digital Constitutionalism: Using the Rule of Law to Evaluate the Legitimacy of Governance by Platforms' (2018) 4(3) Social Media + Society 1.

Tambini D, *Media Freedom* (Polity Press 2021).

Tandoc E, 'Journalism is Twerking? How Web Analytics Is Changing the Process of Gatekeeping' (2014) 16(4) New Media & Society 559.

Tandoc E and J Maitra, 'News Organizations' Use of Native Videos on Facebook: Tweaking the Journalistic Field One Algorithmic Change at a Time' (2018) 20(5) New Media & Society 1679.

Taubman A, 'Introduction: International Governance and the Internet' in L Edwards and C Waelde (eds), *Law and the Internet* (3rd edn, Hart Publishing 2009).

Thieme W, 'Über die Wahrheitspflicht der Presse' (1980) 33 Die Öffentliche Verwaltung 149.

Thomas R J and T Finneman, 'Who Watches the Watchdogs?' (2014) 15(2) Journalism Studies 172.

Thurman N and S Schifferes, 'The Future of Personalization at News Websites. Lessons from a Longitudinal Study' (2012) 13(5) Journalism Studies 775.

Thurman N and R Fletcher, 'Has Digital Distribution Rejuvenated Readership? Revisiting the Age Demographics of Newspaper Consumption' (2019) 20(4) Journalism Studies 542.

Thurman N, 'When a TV Channel Reinvents Itself Online: Post-broadcast Consumption and Content Change at BBC Three' (2021) 27(2) Convergence 291.

Toepfl F and E Piwoni, 'Public Spheres in Interaction: Comment Sections of News Websites as Counterpublic Spaces' (2015) 65 Journal of Communication 465.

Tong J, *Journalism, Economic Uncertainty and Political Irregularity in the Digital and Data Era* (Emerald Publishing 2023).

Trappel J, 'Online Media within the Public Service Realm? Reasons to Include Online into the Public Service Mission' (2008) 14(3) Convergence 313.

Trilling D, P Tolochko, and B Burscher, 'From Newsworthiness to Shareworthiness: How to Predict News Sharing Based on Article Characteristics' (2017) 94(1) Journalism & Mass Communication Quarterly 38.

Tsfati Y, O Meyers, and Y Peri, 'What Is Good Journalism? Comparing Israeli Public and Journalists' Perspectives' (2006) 7(2) Journalism 152.

Tuchman G, 'Objectivity as Strategic Ritual: An Examination of Newsmen's Notions of Objectivity' (1972) 77(4) American Journal of Sociology 660.

Tufekci Z, 'Algorithm Harms Beyond Facebook and Google: Emergent Challenges of Computational Agency' (2015) 13(2) Colorado Technology Law Journal 203.

Ugland E and J Henderson, 'Who Is a Journalist and Why Does It Matter? Disentangling the Legal and Ethical Arguments' (2007) 22(4) Journal of Mass Media Ethics 241.

Uscinski J and R Butler, 'The Epistemology of Fact-checking' (2013) 25(2) Critical Review 162.

Valcke P and K Lefever, *Media Law in the European Union* (Kluwer 2012).

Valcke P, A Kuczerawi, and P-J Ombelet, 'Did the Romans Get It Right? What Delfi, Google, eBay, and UPC TeleKabel Wien Have in Common' in L Floridi and M Taddeo (eds), *The Responsibilities of Online Service Providers* (Springer 2016) 101.

Valcke P and J Ausloos, 'Audiovisual Media Services 3.0: (Re)defining the Scope of European Broadcasting Law in a Converging and Connected Media Environment' in K Donders, K Pauwels, and J Loisen (eds), *The Palgrave Handbook of European Media Policy* (Palgrave Macmillan 2014) 319.

Vandenbergh M P, 'Social Checks and Balances: Private Fairness Doctrine' (2020) 73(3) Vanderbilt Law Review 811.

Vázquez-Herrero J, M Negreira-Rey, and X López-García, 'Let's Dance the News! How the News Media Are Adapting to the Logic of TikTok' (2022) 23(8) Journalism 1717.

Verband Deutscher Zeitschriftenverleger, 'VDZ und BDZV zum neuen Medienstaatsvertrag' (*VDZ*, 5 December 2019) <https://www.vdz.de/nachricht/artikel/vdz-und-bdzv-zum-neuen-medienstaatsvertrag/>.

Vesting T, *Die Tagesschau-App und die Notwendigkeit der Schaffung eines 'Intermedienkollisions rechts'* (KIT 2013).

Vick D W, 'Regulatory Convergence?' (2006) 26(1) Legal Studies 26.

Vidgen B, H Margetts, and A Harris, 'How much online abuse is there? A systematic review of evidence for the UK' (*The Alan Turing Institute*, 24 November 2019) <https://www.turing.ac.uk/sites/default/files/2019-11/online_abuse_prevalence_full_24.11.2019_-_formatted_0.pdf>.

Volokh E, 'Cheap Speech and What It Will Do' (1995) 104 Yale Law Journal 1805.

Volokh E and D Falk, 'Google First Amendment Protection for Search Engine Search Results' (2012) 8(4) Journal of Law, Economics and Policy 883.

Volokh E, 'Freedom of the Press as an Industry or for the Press as a Technology? From the Framing to Today' (2012) University of Pennsylvania Law Review 459.

Voorhoof D, 'Freedom of Journalistic News-Gathering, Access to Information and Protection of Whistle-Blowers under Article 10 ECHR and the Standards of the Council of Europe' in O Andreotti and others (eds), *Journalism at Risk: Threats, Challenges and Perspectives* (Council of Europe 2015) 105.

Vorhoof and others, *Freedom of Expression, the Media and Journalists* (6th edn, European Audiovisual Observatory 2021) <https://rm.coe.int/iris-themes-vol-iii-2020-edition-en-28-april-2021-/1680a24eee>.

Vu H T and M Saldaña, 'Chillin' Effects of Fake News: Changes in Practices Related to Accountability and Transparency in American Newsrooms under the Influence of Misinformation and Accusations against the News Media' (2021) 98(3) Journalism & Mass Communication Quarterly 769.

Wagner E, 'Die Gegengewichtsfunktionen des öffentlich-rechtlichen Rundfunks' (2022) 5 Archiv für Presserecht 377.

Wagner E, 'Unions- und verfassungsrechtliche Spielräume einer Flexibilisierung des Auftrags der öffentlich-rechtlichen Rundfunkanstalten' (2022) 66(3) Zeitschrift für Urheber- und Medienrecht 165.

Waisbord S, 'Truth Is What Happens to News. On Journalism, Fake News, and Post-Truth' (2018) 19(13) Journalism Studies 1866.

Wardle C and H Derakhshan, 'Information disorder: Toward an interdisciplinary framework for research and policymaking', DGI (2017) 09 (*Council of Europe*, 27 September 2017) <https://rm.coe.int/information-disorder-toward-an-interdisciplinary-framework-for-researc/168076277c>.

Warner N, 'Life after Leveson. The challenge to strengthen Britain's diverse and vibrant media' (IPPR 2012) <https://www.ippr.org/files/images/media/files/publication/2012/11/life-after-leveson_Nov2012_9944.pdf>.

Weinand J, *Implementing the EU Audiovisual Media Services Directive: Selected Issues in the Regulation of AVMS by National Media Authorities of France, Germany and the UK* (Nomos 2018).

Weinand J, 'The Revised Audiovisual Media Services Directive 2018—Has the EU Learnt the Right Lessons from the Past?' (2018) 1 UFITA: Archiv für Urheber- und Medienrecht 260.

Wentworth N N, 'Hot off the Press: An Argument for a Federal Shield Law Affording a Qualified Evidentiary Privilege to Journalists in Light of Renewed Concerns about Freedom of the Press and National Security' (2020) 53(3) Loyola of Los Angeles Law Review 745.

Werdermann D, 'Dieser Blogbeitrag ist nicht von der Pressefreiheit geschützt: Zur Reichweite presserechtlicher Auskunftsansprüche von Online-Medien' (*Verfassungsblog*, 21 July 2022) <https://verfassungsblog.de/dieser-blogbeitrag-ist-nicht-von-der-pressefreiheit-geschutzt/>.

West S R, 'Concurring in Part & (and) Concurring in the Confusion' (2006) 104(8) Michigan Law Review 1951.

West S R, 'Awakening the Press Clause' (2011) 58 UCLA Law Review 1025.

West S R, 'Press Exceptionalism' (2014) 127 Harvard Law Review 2434.

Wiedemann V, 'Kein Einfallstor für Marktprimat/Der Dreistufentest darf nicht missbraucht werden' (2009) 68 epd medien 3.

Wimmer N, 'Der Drei-Stufen-Test nach dem 12. Rundfunkänderungsstaatsvertrag. Was ist und wer entscheidet über den Public Value öffentlich-rechtlicher Online-Angebote?' (2009) 25(8/9) Zeitschrift für Urheber- und Medienrecht 601.

Wimmers J, 'Der Intermediär als Ermittler, Moderator und Entscheider in äußerungsgerichtlichen Auseinandersetzungen?' (2015) 3 Archiv für Presserecht 203.

Wimmers J and B Heymann, 'Zum Referentenentwurf eines Netzwerkdurchsetzungsgesetzes (NetzDG)—Eine kritische Stellungnahme' (2017) 2 Archiv für Presserecht 93.

Wissenschaftliche Dienste des Deutschen Bundestages, 'Entwurf eines Netzwerkdurchsetzungsgesetzes. Vereinbarkeit mit der Meinungsfreiheit', WD 10-3000-037/17, 12 June 2017 <https://www.bundestag.de/resource/blob/510514/eefb7cf92dee88ec7 4ce8e796e9bc25c/wd-10-037-17-pdf-data.pdf>.

Witteman C, 'Constitutionalizing Communications: The German Constitutional Court's Jurisprudence of Communications Freedom' (2010) 33(1) Hastings International and Comparative Law Review 95.

Wong B, 'The Journalism Exception in UK Data Protection Law' (2020) 12(2) Journal of Media Law 216.

Woods L, 'Video-Sharing Platforms in the Revised Audiovisual Media Services Directive' (2018) 23(3) Communications Law 127.

Woods L, 'The Duty of Care in the Online Harms White Paper' (2019) 11(1) Journal of Media Law 6.

World Health Organisation, 'Managing the Covid-19 infodemic: Promoting healthy behaviours and mitigating the harm from misinformation and disinformation', 23 September 2020 <https://www.who.int/news/item/23-09-2020-managing-the-covid-19-infodemic-promot ing-healthy-behaviours-and-mitigating-the-harm-from-misinformation-and-disinfo rmation>.

Wragg P, 'The Legitimacy of Press Regulation' [2015] Public Law 290.

Wragg P, *A Free and Regulated Press: Defending Coercive Independent Press Regulation* (Hart Publishing 2020).

Wright J, 'Letter to Ian Murray' (DCMS, 10 April 2019) <https://assets.publishing.service.gov. uk/government/uploads/system/uploads/attachment_data/file/794520/20190410_DCMS_ SoS_to_Society_of_Editors.pdf>.

Xhue F and L Zhu, 'Social Information in Facebook News Feed Ads: Effects of Personal Relevance and Brand Familiarity' (2018) 25(4) Journal of Promotion Management 570.

Yaish H, 'Forget Me, Forget Me Not: Elements of Erasure to Determine The Sufficiency of a GDPR Article 17 Request' (2019) 10(1) Journal of Law, Technology and the Internet 1.

Zuckerman E, 'The case for digital public infrastructure' (*Knight First Amendment Institute*, 2020) 19–21 <https://knightcolumbia.org/content/the-case-for-digital-public-infrast ructure>.

Zurth P, 'The German NetzDG as Role Model or Cautionary Tale? Implications for the Debate on Social Media Liability' (2019) 31(4) Fordham Intellectual Property, Media and Entertainment Law Journal 1084.

Media websites and blogs cited in this book

American Press Institute
Augsburger Allgemeine
BBC
Bloomberg
Buzzfeed
CNBC
Cybereagle
Deutscher Journalisten-Verband Blog
Deutschlandfunk
DigiDay
Frankfurter Allgemeine Zeitung
Full Fact
Gawker
Gizmodo
Golem
Inforrm
IPSO Blog
Journalism Trust Initiative
medienpolitik.net
Netzpolitik
Politifact
Poynter
Press Gazette
Süddeutsche Zeitung
The Economist
The Guardian
The Observer
The Verge
Journalism.co.uk
Media@LSE
Medium
Pew Research Center
Politico
Reuters
SiliconANGLE
Smart Politics
SPERI
Spiegel International
The New Yorker
Transparency Project
Über Medien
UK Constitutional Law Association blog
Vaunet
Verfassungsblog
VG Media
Wired
Zeit Online

Index

For the benefit of digital users, indexed terms that span two pages (e.g., 52–53) may, on occasion, appear on only one of those pages.